THIRD EDITION

# SPURR'S
# GUIDE

## to Upgrading Your
## CRUISING
## SAILBOAT

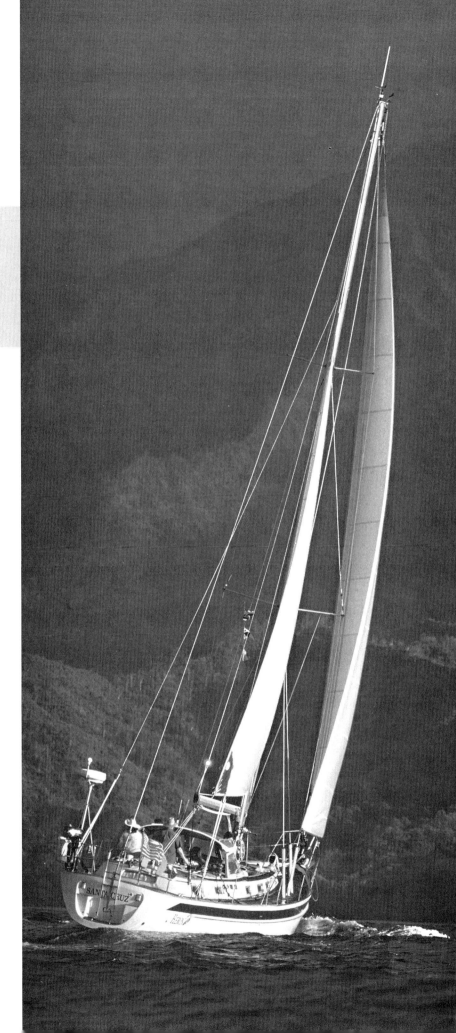

INTERNATIONAL MARINE
/ McGRAW-HILL
Camden, Maine
New York
Chicago
San Francisco
Lisbon
London
Madrid
Mexico City
Milan
New Delhi
San Juan
Seoul
Singapore
Sydney
Toronto

THIRD EDITION

# SPURR'S GUIDE

## to Upgrading Your

# CRUISING SAILBOAT

## DANIEL SPURR

Illustrations by **BRUCE BINGHAM**

*The McGraw·Hill Companies*

1 2 3 4 5 6 7 8 9 QPD QPD 0 9 8 7 6
© 1983, 1991, 1993, 2006 by Daniel O. Spurr
Illustrations © 1983, 1991, 1993, 2006 by Bruce Bingham

*Library of Congress Cataloging-in-Publication Data*
Spurr, Daniel, 1947–
  [Boatbook]
  Spurr's guide to upgrading your cruising sailboat /
   Daniel Spurr ; illustrations by Bruce Bingham.—3rd ed.
      p.    cm.
   Rev. ed. of: Spurr's boatbook. 2nd ed. Camden, Me. :
   Seven Seas Press, 1991.
   Includes bibliographical references and index.
   ISBN 0-07-145536-1 (hardcover : alk. paper)
   1.  Sailboats—Maintenance and repair.   2.  Fiberglass
boats—Maintenance and repair.   I.  Title.
VM351.S63 2006
623.822'3—dc22                          2005037575

Questions regarding the content of this book should be addressed to
International Marine
P.O. Box 220
Camden, ME 04848
www.internationalmarine.com

Questions regarding the ordering of this book should be addressed to
The McGraw-Hill Companies
Customer Service Department
P.O. Box 547
Blacklick, OH 43004
Retail customers: 1-800-262-4729
Bookstores: 1-800-722-4726

Photographs by Daniel Spurr unless otherwise noted.
Photographs on pages 31, 87, 236, and 263 by Bruce Bingham.
Photograph on page 64 courtesy Pearson Yachts.
Illustrations by Bruce Bingham unless otherwise noted.

# CONTENTS

# Introduction
## to the Third Edition

A good life takes sudden turns, and mine swerved crazily in late 1979 when I was offered the job of associate editor at *Cruising World* magazine. After 11 years as an administrator at a Midwestern hospital, I moved to the "city by the sea," Newport, Rhode Island. My colleagues were special: founders Murray and Barbara Davis, editor Dale Nouse, and the staff: George Day, Betsy Hitz, Herb McCormick, Bernadette Brennan, Danny Greene, Lynda Morris, art director Bill Roche, and many more. We had a great time. And with their help, I learned a new trade.

I also began to learn a lot more about boats, meeting cruising legends like Eric and Susan Hiscock, Lin and Larry Pardey, Hal and Margaret Roth, Tom Colvin, Robin Knox-Johnston . . . the list is long. And assignments sent me sailing to the corners of the globe.

But nothing taught me more than moving full-time aboard my Pearson Triton. Summers were spent on a mooring in Newport Harbor, winters at one of the boarded-up resort docks. Every boat project raised questions: How to remove deck core when installing a new piece of gear? How to install wheel steering? How to take apart a corroded windlass? There were a lot of knuckle-busters and many mistakes. But it was fascinating stuff if you're a guy with a yen for adventure and a willingness to pick up a new tool. Books held some of the answers, but not all. So I

wrote *Spurr's Boatbook: Upgrading the Cruising Sailboat*, to answer many of the questions I'd asked of myself. The first edition was published in 1983. Since then I've bought a number of old boats, each requiring rehab; after the Triton came a 1967 Pearson Vanguard, a 1975 C&C 33, and a 1975 Tartan 44. Maybe some day I'll be able to afford a brand-new boat, but I doubt it.

In 1987 I left *Cruising World* to cruise my own boat. After two years I returned to Newport and became editor of *Practical Sailor* magazine, the only nautical publication that attempts to test and evaluate boats and gear without bias. That's because it accepts no advertising. The efforts of many other boating magazines in this area are shameful. But eleven years was enough, and today I am editor-at-large for *Professional BoatBuilder* magazine, and a contributing editor to several others. Plus I'm taking the Westlawn Institute of Marine Technology's course in yacht design. That's one of the great things about boats—there's always something more to learn. Most of the ideas in this book are not original to me, but shared by many others more knowledgeable than I am. Like illustrator Bruce Bingham, with whom I'm honored to share these pages.

If you find here one or two ideas that save an afternoon's work, or your neck some nasty day, you'll have recovered the cost of your investment, and then some. In that event, we'll both be happy.

# ONE

# THE ANATOMY OF
# A CRUISING SAILBOAT

Murray Davis, founder of *Cruising World* magazine, had a saying that there is no such thing as a bad boat, just one marketed deceptively—namely, a coastal cruiser billed as a blue-water voyager. A slightly skeptical Nick Nicholson, when he was editor of *Practical Sailor*, added his two cents by saying, "Yes, and there is no such thing as a *perfect* boat."

Me? I think there are indeed bad boats (Murray, like all publishers, had to worry about advertisers). And a portion of this book is devoted to telling you how to avoid them. I do agree with Nick; there's no perfect anything, unless maybe it's a Ferrari Testarossa.

My first boat was a Snipe, a 15-foot (4.6 m) daysailer. She was a great boat to knock about Michigan's small inland lakes, and on several occasions I packed her with a tent, sleeping bags, and camping gear and cruised across the frigid waters of northern Lake Michigan to Beaver Island and the Manitous. Maybe not too smart, but, hey, you go with what you've got. The Snipe, one of the most popular one-design classes of all times, was not intended for open-water sailing, nor was the 13½-foot (4.1 m) *Tinkerbelle* that Robert Manry sailed across the Atlantic in 1965. Not all stunts end up so happily; others, like Bill Dunlop and his shoebox of a boat, have disappeared at sea. More so in small boats than in big ones, safe passages require a well-fit boat, good seamanship, an eye to the weather, and two shots of good luck.

Because successful ocean passages are made in such a variety of boats, it follows that there is no such thing as the "ideal cruiser." But, just as ancient Greek philosophers sought the perfect form of beauty, we are inclined to believe that somewhere there exists a perfect boat, one that sails well, gives us all the room we require, and pleases our senses as we look over our shoulders rowing toward her in the dinghy.

In reality, every boat is a compromise, not just in design but in personal preferences. What satis-

fies one man or woman appalls the next. I remember once standing on the docks of the Newport Boat Show watching Steve Dashew sail one of his new Sundeer 64s into the harbor. It had a long pilothouse and a low-aspect ratio ketch rig with big-roach, fully battened sails. I thought to myself, "How practical, and in its own modern way, how handsome." The guy standing next to me suddenly blurted out, "God, I've never seen such an ugly boat."

Take multihulls, for instance. Either love 'em or hate 'em. But catamarans and trimarans successfully cruise around the world. No, they don't have the classic beauty of a monohull with long overhangs and a sweeping sheer line, but they're fast, spacious, and nearly level. You also can find motorsailers tied stern-to in Papeete that have made seamanlike passages from Southern California. Fin-keel, spade-rudder racers have passed beneath the five great capes, making circumnavigations at breakneck speeds. And floating gypsy voyagers have lumbered among the islands in heavy-displacement tubs, finding pleasure and security in their turtle pace, even though their vessels may be hard pressed to claw away from a lee shore.

Some of us set off in a radical or otherwise unsuitable boat with a naïveté that later we find alarming.

But most of us survive, emerging, we hope, as Coleridge's "older, wiser man," a mariner not too ancient. Others engage in a diligent apprenticeship, owning progressively larger boats, methodically building upon a rudimentary knowledge until one day they realize that they do, indeed, know something about boats and seamanship.

During the learning process, I suppose most of us have taken inordinate risks. I sailed the Snipe across Lake Michigan when I was 22. Back then it was the only boat available to me, and I would rather have risked the drowning than denied myself the adventure. Today, I am older and more conservative. Since the Snipe, I've bought and upgraded many boats, including a 19-foot (5.8 m) Alacrity and a 17-foot (5.2 m) Silhouette (both British twin-keelers), a Catalina 22 (6.7 m), a Pearson Triton and a Vanguard, a C&C 33 (10 m), and a Tartan 44 (13.4 m). On these I've cruised the Great Lakes, U.S. East Coast, and Bahamas. Most were tough little cruisers, carefully fitted out and maintained as best I could. I tried to make them as comfortable as possible, installing cockpit dodgers, new engines, easy sail-handling devices, hot-water showers, and wheel steering. Remembering the simplicity of the Snipe, I sometimes still yearn for the thrill of putting to sea in a minimal boat, which would enable me to confront nature on a more elemental level.

But when I pause to reflect, I don't want to subject myself or my crew to any unnecessary dangers. Comfort—my favorite music on the stereo, a library of good books, a dry bunk, a glass of wine with my mate after a passage—has become more important. This is not to say I *need* these things to cruise, just that I prefer them that way.

This aging process has repeated itself in the souls and minds of sailors for centuries, and there is an accumulated wisdom there, a body of knowledge if you will, that is available to the men and women who wish today to learn what they can before they themselves set out. While most of this book concerns hands-on projects to upgrade a boat to satisfy this "body of knowledge," it also is sensible to begin with a firm foundation; that is, a boat with a reasonably good chance of doing the things we ask of it. Whether we choose to gunkhole down the Intracoastal Waterway, nose around the Caribbean Islands, or make long bluewater passages to the South Pacific, there are certain design parameters, which if embodied in the boat, will make our cruising more successful. And by successful I mean safer, faster, and more comfortable.

# THE CRUISING IMPERATIVES

At the risk of sounding like my way is the only way, and with all due respect to the excellent texts on designing cruising sailboats, let's put forward a few cruising imperatives, recognizing, of course, that the designer has wide latitude in deciding how best to satisfy them.

## Ability to Take the Ground Without Fear

Everybody runs aground. It's a simple fact of cruising. The more time spent cruising unfamiliar coastal waters, the more frequently you'll run aground. To avoid grounding would mean to avoid going anyplace new. If you live in constant fear of holing the boat or being unable to kedge off, you begin to place restrictions on the places you go and your pleasure is correspondingly diminished. This is not to say that every boat must be able to withstand pounding on a coral reef. But it should be able to hit sand and even small rocks without causing disabling damage. I'm not suggesting you should take inordinate risks, but things happen.

Full-length keels give better protection to rudders than fin keels. But the latter allow the boat to pivot easier if it's necessary to turn the boat around before kedging off. Keels with vertical leading edges won't allow lines or floating debris, such as logs, to easily pass underneath. Conventional wisdom has recommended external lead ballast, because its softness absorbs some of the impact of collision. But regardless of keel type, heavy ground tackle and a windlass for kedging off are essential cruising gear.

## Ability to Survive a Knockdown

No one relishes the prospect of putting the mast in the water. And while circumnavigations have been made without knockdowns, it is a possibility (if not a probability) for which you should be prepared.

Gear commonly damaged by knockdowns are rigs and sails (Chapter 10), portlights (Chapter 9), and just about anything inside the boat (Chapter 3) that is struck by flying pots, batteries, or persons. Gear stored on deck, such as dinghies, jerricans, and ground tackle, must be securely lashed to keep them from being swept overboard or doing damage to pulpits, rigging, and crew.

## Ability to Balance Boat for Self-Steering

Shorthanded crews on cruising boats will have more fun underway and enter port far more rested if the boat can self-steer most of the time. With just a couple aboard, self-steering is essential. Mechanical wind vanes and electronic autopilots (Chapter 7) can be fitted to just about any type of boat, but they will perform better if the design of the boat enables a fairly balanced helm. Ketches are admired for their ability to balance well, as are some yawls and schooners. Sloops and cutters are trickier because the distance between opposing— and therefore balancing—forces on the sails is not as far as the distance between the centers of effort of a jib and a mizzen sail. A boat that doesn't balance well fights the self-steerer every inch of the way and promotes the likelihood of running off course and breaking gear.

## Ability to Beat Off a Lee Shore

Even the best navigators and weather forecasters sooner or later find themselves caught near a lee shore with winds and seas increasing. In this situation a boat that sails sideways is in peril of striking bottom. While a good cruising boat need not be able to point as high as a racer, it should be able to make distance to windward in all but the worst conditions.

The ability to beat to windward is a function of design, which entails the shape of the hull, the ends of the boat, the shape and size of the keel, and the rig. A boat that sails well on all points isn't arrived at by chance on the architect's drafting board, but rather is the product of much skill and experience in bringing together many diverse factors, such as wetted surface area, distribution of weight and volume, shape of waterline plane, location of center of buoyancy and center of gravity, location of center of effort of the sail plan, and so forth.

## Ability to Carry Sufficient Stores

Regardless of boat size and crew, a good cruising boat should be able to carry enough water, fuel, food, medical supplies, line, spare parts, and other necessary gear to meet all the crew's needs for the duration of a passage, plus a safety margin.

Planning for extended cruises outside your home country should take into account the prices for supplies and services and the likelihood that many goods may not be available. You learn to eat and drink what the locals do, stocking up when you can. What, the space beneath the cabin sole is smaller than the cutlery drawer? How about under the bunks? Oh, you planned to store tools there! Maybe the lazarette. Full of life jackets, lines, and fenders? Well, life is full of compromises, isn't it?!

## Ability to Ride Comfortably at Anchor

Most cruising boats spend more time at anchor than underway. A well-known cruising family once told me that during their years of cruising, the highest ratio of sailing to anchoring was about 50-50, and usually much less. Even if you're just cruising for several weeks, you'll rest easier in a boat that has the ability to stay put.

A boat with high freeboard at the bow will tend to blow off and "sail" more at anchor than a boat with more moderate freeboard. Underwater, the distribution of lateral plane determines the resistance to this tendency; a boat with a deep forefoot and long keel will ride more comfortably at anchor.

## Protected Propeller

Sadly, the oceans are no longer as clean as they used to be. Blue-water voyagers today report seeing half-submerged oil drums, logs, containers, nets, and just about every type of conceivable floating garbage. Coastal waters are worse. Discounting junk, there are legitimate hazards such as fish traps, lobster pots, and research buoys that often are poorly marked.

Fouling the propeller with a line or bending the blades by striking a solid object has all the makings of a nightmare, pure and simple. With luck, the weather will be fair, the seas calm, and the water warm. You can secure the boat, lower yourself over the side wearing a face mask, and attempt to cut away the line with a sharp knife. I've done it several times. But these conditions cannot be guaranteed.

The best precaution is preventive planning. A boat without a prop aperture poses a significantly greater risk. On boats with separated keels and rudders, a strut of bronze pipe or length of wire extending between the keel and rudder skeg helps lines and other objects pass safely astern. On boats with unprotected props, a pair of line cutters, such as Spurs (www.spursmarine.com), mounted on the shaft can sever most ropes, but not chain.

A wind vane rudder or servo paddle does a great job of snagging lines. It happened to me while sailing off Newport, Rhode Island, when the wind vane rudder snared a fish float. Try as I might to push the float and line under the rudder with my feet, it eventually required a cold swim to extricate ourselves.

## Comfortable Accommodations

When I first met author, boatbuilder, and cruising sailor Tom Colvin during a cruising seminar at which we were both speaking, he emphasized the importance of bringing the comforts of home aboard the cruising boat. "I like a big, sumptuous aft cabin," he said. "When you reduce cruising to tenement living, I don't want any part of it."

Well, not everyone likes aft cabins or may own a boat large enough to have one. But the point is well taken. The 28-foot (8.5 m) Triton and 32-foot (9.8 m) Vanguard, as examples of smaller, older, low-priced used boats suitable for offshore sailing, can be made very comfortable for two persons for extended periods. But substantial interior modifications may be necessary. In my case, cushions were recovered, bookshelves built, a stereo installed, large lounge pillows purchased, comfortably angled backrests added, and a 5-inch-thick (127 mm) foam mattress cut for the double berth in the forward cabin. I could sleep as well there as in any bed. And in the main cabin I could read a book, watch television, or listen to music as comfortably as in any cushy wingback chair.

## DESIGN AND CONSTRUCTION CONSIDERATIONS

Designing a successful cruising boat is such a complex process, with so many variables to marry, that it is virtually impossible to make dogmatic statements about displacement, underwater shape, and type of rig or hull material without knowing something about the other variables.

Some persons aren't happy unless they're making 12 knots on a light-displacement monohull like the J/105 or F/27 trailerable trimaran; others don't feel secure unless they're sitting deep inside a heavy-displacement, full-keel Colin Archer–type monohull. Despite the impassioned claims of each type's proponents, who's to say one is *better* than the other?

A good percentage of us, however, are less apt to go wrong if we observe the old maxim, "all things in moderation." At least for starters. After mastering a conventional boat, you'll be better prepared to move into more extreme designs, if that is your pleasure. Here we'll describe a "moderate" cruising boat, which is certainly easier than attempting to define the "ideal" cruising boat.

### Underbody Profiles

If we can imagine the various types of sailboat underbodies as a continuum (Figure 1-1), ranging

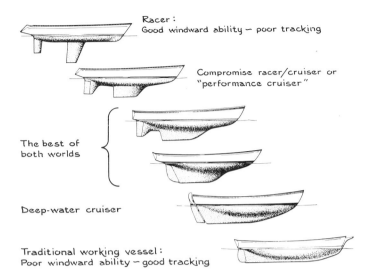

**FIGURE 1-1.** A continuum of underbody profiles ranging from the fin-keel, spade-rudder, lightweight racer to the full-keel, attached-rudder, heavy-displacement cruiser.

from a small fin keel with a spade rudder at one end to a full keel extending from bow to stern at the other end, and if we understand that many configurations in between will probably be effective if the designer has done his or her job well, then we begin to get a picture of what constitutes a moderate underbody profile.

Advocates of full keels cite, sometimes erroneously, characteristics such as greater tracking ability, greater stability, and better ability to absorb a grounding. In fact, a full keel guarantees nothing if the boat is poorly designed. This is not to discredit full keels at all. A full keel with a long straight run and attached rudder takes the ground better and with less chance of damage than a fin keel with spade rudder, which may be bent in a collision or severe grounding (Figure 1-2). Regardless of type, the keel should also allow the boat to *track* well, meaning the boat should hold its course without applying constant correction to the tiller or wheel.

When people think of full-keel boats, many think of the Westsail 32, in which the keel extends from the stem to the transom. While providing good tracking, or directional stability, such keels do make for a wide turning radius. The fact is that most so-called full-keel boats, including those designed under the old CCA (Cruising Club of America) rule, which was popular in the 1960s, have large cutaway forefoots and terminate well forward of the transom, so they extend perhaps

**FIGURE 1-2.** Spade rudders are particularly vulnerable during groundings. Note the crack at the waterline where this rudder split. (*Practical Sailor* photo)

just a third of the total waterline length. The rudder is usually attached to the trailing edge. This configuration provides sufficient lateral surface area for good directional stability (tracking), has less wetted surface, and provides better maneuverability than the Westsail-type keel. The Cape Dory sailboats, designed by Carl Alberg and built by Andy Vavolotis in Massachusetts during the 1970s and '80s, are good examples.

Fin keels vary a great deal, as the top two in Figure 1-1 illustrate. Fin keels generally have less wetted surface area than full keels, so there is less resistance, which in turn makes the boat faster. If you consider that the keel on a sailboat has to do the same thing as a wing on an airplane—namely, provide lift—then it's easy to see that a deep, fairly narrow, high-aspect ratio keel will be more efficient than a long, shallow, fat keel. (The aspect ratio is a comparison of the keel's depth or span in square feet to the keel's area in square feet: aspect ratio = area/depth$^2$.) Increased lift translates into pointing higher, and this is a real advantage in any boat.

With the canoe-sterned Valiant 40, introduced in 1974, Seattle naval architect Robert Perry was credited with popularizing the performance cruiser. A performance cruiser was characterized in part by a generous fin keel with a flat run on the bottom (called the tip chord) and a skeg-mounted rudder mounted well aft. This type has sufficient lateral plane for good tracking ability, and the skeg strengthens and

protects the rudder (*if* the skeg is well made—not all are!). It is a good compromise between the full keel and the fin keel. The Valiant 40's keel, which most closely resembles the keel second from top in Figure 1-1, can be called a cruising fin. It's probably the most common cruising keel today. On boats longer than about 50 feet (15.2 m), however, the rudder usually must be a spade so it can be balanced; that is, locating the leading edge just forward of the stock, which takes pressure off the helm.

In making a choice, you might begin with draft, which dictates where you can take your boat. Novelist and sailor John Barth lives on a river near the Chesapeake Bay. If a boat he admires draws more than about 3 feet (0.9 m), it won't make it to his dock. On the other hand, boats with shoal keels are generally more tender than boats with ballast located low in a fin keel, maybe even in a bulb. Fortunately, Barth is content as a bay cruiser. And never undervalue science: a keel with a NACA-tested (National Advisory Committee for Aeronautics, now NASA) foil shape will give more lift than random shapes created by uninformed builders. As for material, a lead keel is better than an iron keel because lead is denser and much less prone to corrosion.

## Rudder Types

Considering that the rudder steers the boat, and without it the boat is left to the vagaries of weather and the skipper's ingenuity to carry on, utmost attention should be given to its type and method of construction (see Chapter 2).

Full keels (Figure 1-3) allow attaching the rudder to its trailing edge, either inboard (stock emerging through hull) or outboard (stock at the transom). Loads on the full-keel rudder are well distributed, and the keel, especially if it is an inch or so deeper than the rudder, will take the brunt of a grounding. Sometimes when aground, my Vanguard was heeled over almost to the point that the turn of the bilge touched bottom. However, because its rudder is attached to the trailing edge of the keel and a large bronze heel fitting protects the stock, the steering system was never damaged.

When the keel and rudder are separated, I think it is best for coastal cruising to have the rudder fixed to a full- or three-quarter-length skeg (Figures 1-4 and 1-5). The idea behind the latter is that the bottom tip of the rudder can be carried

**FIGURE 1-3.** The Westsail 32 has a full-length keel with an attached outboard rudder. Note the sturdy wood cheeks that strengthen the rudder as it narrows out of the water.

**FIGURE 1-5.** A three-quarter-length skeg provides some support for the rudder, and there should be enough rudder left even if the bottom third is torn away. Rather than a strut, the prop shaft runs through its own skeg.

away, leaving enough rudder aft of the skeg to still steer the boat. If well built (and again not all are), the skeg protects the rudder, provides for a second bearing for the rudder stock outside the hull, and raises the stall angle of the rudder. Steve Dashew also believes that the balanced spade rudder gives the best control of the boat in bad weather. But again, he's a big-boat guy.

But here's the rub: spade rudders, while often the most responsive, are often also the weakest. Not only can a bent stock disable steering (because there's very little clearance between the top of the rudder and bottom of the hull), but striking an underwater object can push the stock up into the hull, breaking the interior supports. And, as

the aspect ratio of the rudder is increased (like the keel, to improve efficiency), the angle at which it will stall decreases. If you've ever been hit by a gust of wind that causes the boat to round up uncontrollably, despite having the helm hard over, you know how scary it can be to have a stalled rudder. Okay, so you end up in irons, fall off, reduce sail, and continue on, but even after you conquer the fear, there remains the frustration of not being in control of your boat.

## The Displacement/Length Ratio

The comparative heaviness of a yacht is determined by its displacement/length ratio. The formula is:

$$\text{D/L ratio} = \frac{\text{Displacement in long tons}}{(0.01 \text{ DWL})^3}$$

or displacement-to-length ratio equals displacement in long tons divided by one hundredth the designed waterline length to the third power. (A long ton equals 2,240 pounds/1,016 kg.) The D/L ratio is useful because it allows you to compare the relative heaviness of boats of different lengths.

Here are a few popular boats, old and new, and their D/L ratios:

| | |
|---|---|
| Olson 40 | 91 |
| Santa Cruz 40 | 102 |
| J/46 | 164 |
| Beneteau 393 | 177 |
| Hunter 456 | 186 |

**FIGURE 1-4.** On this Pacific Seacraft, the propeller is in an aperture in the skeg. This slightly unusual arrangement directs prop wash directly onto the rudder, improving handling under power. Note the cruising fin keel, which is long and not too deep.

| | |
|---|---|
| Tartan 4100 | 186 |
| Catalina 42 mkII | 196 |
| Freedom 40 | 208 |
| Pearson 530 | 211 |
| Sabre 362 | 218 |
| Caliber 35 LRC | 219 |
| C&C 39 | 228 |
| Nor'Sea 27 | 257 |
| Valiant 40 | 264 |
| Nauticat 44 | 266 |
| Valiant 42 | 267 |
| Pearson 323 | 275 |
| Mason 63 | 285 |
| Island Packet 380 | 286 |
| Bristol Channel Cutter | 341 |
| CT 37 | 343 |
| Pearson 35 | 371 |
| Cabo Rico 38 | 375 |
| Southern Cross 31 | 388 |
| Allied Seawind II | 396 |
| Westsail 32 | 435 |

For the purposes of general discussion, we can consider any D/L ratio under 200 as light, between 200 and 300 as moderate, between 300 and 400 as moderately heavy, and any number above 400 as super heavy.

When the Valiant 40 was first touted as an offshore cruiser back in 1975, some critics said its D/L ratio of 264 was too low. Now, thirty years later, after numerous offshore passages and circumnavigations, the boat is considered by some performance-minded sailors as being almost too heavy—certainly for long-distance ocean racing. "Performance," Perry says, "is a moving target." So, apparently, is seaworthiness.

An important consideration for cruisers is the load-carrying ability of a boat. It is not uncommon to carry a ton or more of tools, food, and related gear. A boat with a high D/L ratio means slacker bilges, which translates to more stowage space as well as the ability to take on additional weight without performance suffering—at least not as much as a boat with a low D/L ratio.

The section shape of a hull also has a great deal to do with the boat's motion underway. A boat with firm bilges (low D/L ratio) must be sailed more on the level, and it pounds more eas-

ily. In addition, the motion may be jerky (Figure 1-6). A boat with extremely slack bilges, however, may roll sickeningly. Yacht designer Ted Brewer addresses this issue in his book, *Ted Brewer Explains Sailboat Design*; for the best compromise between comfort and performance, he favors boats with moderate to heavy D/L ratios and moderate beam/waterline ratios (Figures 1-7 and 1-8). The range of D/L ratios illustrated in Figure 1-9 suggests moderation and is consistent with the thinking of many other designers who believe that a D/L ratio of about 300 is close to ideal for a liveaboard, ocean-cruising boat.

You will note that the previous list of D/L ratios for popular boats does not include the Pearson Triton, Alberg 30 and 37, Cape Dory 36, or other CCA-type boats. They have been purposely omitted because their short waterlines result in deceivingly high D/L ratios. This is because the CCA rule penalized long waterlines, and designers "cheated" the rule by drawing long

FIGURE 1-6. This is not the bottom of a cruising boat, but the extreme flatness of this racer's hull form illustrates what a low displacement/length ratio looks like. This boat will actually be able to surf in some conditions, but likely will pound upwind.

**FIGURE 1-7.** This Pearson has a displacement/length ratio in the low 200s, typical of large-volume, series-produced racer-cruisers. While excellent for all-around sailing, this hull form lacks the volume to carry generous amounts of fuel, water, and other stores.

**FIGURE 1-8.** Here is *Viva*'s underbody. The displacement/length ratio of this Tartan 41/44 is about 235. Compared to the boat in Figure 1-7, the turn from the hull into the keel is more radiused and therefore more sea-kindly.

overhangs, which became immersed as the boat heeled, increasing the effective sailing length and hence speed underway. For example, the Pearson Vanguard displaces a modest 10,300 pounds (4,666 kg) and has a waterline length of just 22 feet 3 inches (6.8 m) on a 32-foot 9-inch (10 m) hull; the D/L ratio is 413. If, however, you calculated the D/L ratio on its usual sailing waterline of, say, 26 feet (7.9 m), the D/L ratio drops dramatically to 262. This is true of all boats, but more so of those with short waterlines and long overhangs. What it means is that it's difficult to compare the D/L ratios of boats with distinctly different proportions.

Nevertheless, the trend in recent years certainly has been toward lighter-displacement boats. Speed is attractive, and the easiest way to gain speed is to shed weight and to add waterline length. So while the typical cruising boat today is lighter, it also is longer, which helps make up for stowage space lost to the shallower fairbody (hull without appendages).

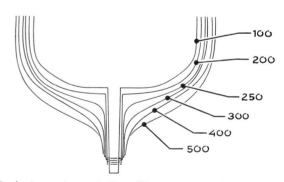

100: Strictly racing, thrill sailing and overnighting
200: Racing, weekending and light cruising
250: All-around good sailing, motoring, long and short cruising with moderate liveability
300: Fair sailing for long cruises but excellent motoring with good liveability
400: Poor sailing but excellent motoring, seakindliness and liveability
500: Terrible sailing but superb liveability. Motoring is good with high power.

**FIGURE 1-9.** The displacement/length ratio is calculated by dividing the boat's displacement in long tons (2,240 pounds) by 0.01 times the designed waterline to the third power. An appropriate D/L ratio depends in part upon the intended use of the boat.

## Bow and Stern

In the past decade or so there has been a trend toward widening and flattening the stern of the boat to give, among other things, more cockpit space and seat locker stowage. This practice has followed on the heels of wider beams to give greater living space below, as well as more power off the wind. These are all pluses certainly and, because a boat derives a good deal of its stability from its beam, it would seem that wide beam and a wide stern would make a very good cruising boat. However, to give the boat a bite on the water and an ability to point high, the bows on these boats are often quite hollow and narrow. The result is a bow and stern out of proportion to one another, and especially when coupled with a relatively flat, shallow bottom and a waterline plane that distorts when heeled, there is often a tendency for such a boat to display excessive weather helm when heeled over.

A decided trend in bows has been to draw them virtually plumb, with very little overhang. This lengthens the waterline, which as noted earlier, increases max speed potential. For a displacement boat, hull speed is 1.34 times the square of the waterline in feet. But boats like the Open Class 60s that compete in round-the-world, single-handed races such as the Vendée Globe are so beamy and shallow that they can actually plane off the wind. Upwind in any kind of sea, they bang like heck. There are other consequences still.

On a reach, a wide stern can give the boat greater power by moving the stern wave farther aft. On a run with following seas, however, a wide stern can cause the boat to slew off. Looking still closer, full ends do provide reserve buoyancy enabling the boat to rise with the waves and not plunge. Tony Lush's *Lady Pepperell*, a 54-foot (16 m) entrant in the BOC Challenge, was severely rolled in the Southern Ocean and ultimately lost. One theory suggested that the bow was too fine, with insufficient buoyancy to keep it from nose-diving into a trough as she slid down a steep wave. Again, a safe conclusion is that moderate beam and light ends, to reduce the tendency to hobbyhorse, contribute to a good cruising boat.

Double-enders have enjoyed something of a renaissance among production builders since the introduction of the Westsail 32 (Figure 1-10) in the early 1970s. Of course, there is really nothing new about this design, adapted as it was from North Sea rescue boats of the previous century.

The pointed stern is favored by some for its reputed ability to part following seas (Robert Perry calls it the "Moses theory"), thus avoiding the yawing motion of boats with wide, flat transoms. While this may be true to an extent, some speed is sacrificed. And if the stern is too narrow, reserve buoyancy also may be dangerously diminished.

Perry gave the Valiant 40 a so-called canoe stern, which is much more rounded than a double-ender's. He says he did it more for the looks than any practical reason (and because his client asked him to make it look like a photo of Aage Nielsen's *Holger Danske* that he'd seen). The Pacific Seacraft line of cruisers also have canoe sterns. A drawback you wouldn't think of until spending time on one is that the narrow side decks and afterdeck are cluttered with stanchions and cleats, making it difficult to step on board and off.

For classic good looks, the traditional counter stern coupled with a spoon bow as seen on, say, the Hinckley Bermuda 40, is hard to beat (Figure 1-11). If a few feet of afterdeck are included as part of the package, so much the better. My Tartan 44 had a nicely made deck box on the afterdeck to house the propane tanks; in good weather, the box was the best seat in the house.

A worthwhile by-product for cruisers from advances in racing boat design is the reverse transom. The paring away of the afterdeck was first intended to reduce weight in the end of the boat to reduce hobbyhorsing. It caught on in family-style boats more as a function of style than anything else. Then some clever fellow recessed the transom, creating the so-called sugar scoop effect in which the topsides continue past the transom, from a few inches to a foot or more. Boarding steps were molded into the transom, and the bottom lip of the scoop was flattened for easy access from a dinghy or a swim.

There is a frightening story about a couple who dropped sails on a windless day in midocean and hopped over the side for a refreshing dip. No, the boat didn't sail away from them. When they tried to climb back aboard, they realized they'd forgotten to drop a ladder or line over the side, and the freeboard was too high for either to grab the rail!

The reverse transom, fitted with handholds and a ladder or steps, seems to be a real advancement in safety (Figure 1-12) over a flat or counter transom. With the latter, if a crew member should go over the side, even wearing a safety harness,

10

**FIGURE 1-10.** The Westsail 32 (left), designed by William Crealock, was based on several generations of Colin Archer–type cutters used in the North Sea. The Tahiti Ketch was another famous offshoot of these boats. The Westsail 32 in many ways started the current popular interest in cruising. It was offered with both ketch and cutter rigs. The Pacific Seacraft 34 (right) has a so-called canoe stern, which is fuller than that of a double-ender, like the Westsail 32. (Pacific Seacraft photo)

**FIGURE 1-11.** Bow shapes vary widely, and while they can affect performance, aesthetics also play a big role. The near boat has a traditional spoon bow. The middle boat's bow has a slight curve. The far boat has a straight, well-raked bow, and more overhang than the others, even though it is, perhaps, more modern. Missing from the photo is a near-plumb bow, popular in the 1990s and early 2000s.

**FIGURE 1-12.** This scoop, or reverse, transom serves many functions: fold-up swim ladder, lockers, and foundation for a radar pole. The stern pulpit holds a stainless steel barbecue and outboard motor. All this makes for a lot of weight in the stern, but that's the way it is on cruising boats these days. (Bruce Bingham photo)

chances are he will be swept to the stern where his only chance of saving himself is negated by a broad flat or counter transom that provides no means of gaining the deck.

## Draft

In considering beam, we should not forget draft. Maxi ocean racers have deep fin keels with double-digit draft. This contributes to their stiffness and hence tremendous windward ability. But 10- and 15-foot (3 m and 4.6 m) drafts are impractical for the cruiser who wants to sail around reefs and islands. In the Bahamas and Florida Keys, any draft greater than 5 feet (1.5 m) will severely limit where a boat can sail without hitting bottom. What shoal keels give away in windward performance is regained by their ability to cruise many beautiful places off limits to deeper-draft boats. In the 1950s, Carleton Mitchell's *Finnisterre* dispelled the myth that centerboard boats were not practical for ocean sailing, though they are seldom seen nowadays on any major ocean-racing circuit. The possibility of jamming the board up or down is just one more potential headache that many cruising sailors can do without. A few years ago, I helped a friend, Patrick Childress, a circumnavigator and professional skipper, deliver a Hinckley 50 centerboard ketch from Virgin Gorda to Maine. He so distrusted centerboards that he kept it raised in the trunk the entire passage. He worried that a loose board might damage the trunk, or that if the pivot pin failed, we'd be towing the heavy board by its pendant.

## Shoal Keel Alternatives

Other than a few trailer sailers with swing keels (which are really just heavily weighted centerboards), designers have looked elsewhere for shoal-draft alternatives. The cheap and easy solution is simply a long, shallow keel (Figure 1-13). Designers of some small boats like the Com-Pac 23 and 25 have opted for this configuration rather than deal with the complications of a centerboard and trunk. But to maintain trailerability, they can't be deeper than about 2 feet 6 inches (0.7 m), which means they won't point well.

Unfortunately, this also is the type of keel most frequently seen on cruising catamarans. The feeling of designers like South Africa's Alex Simonis is that the people who sail these boats, often on charter, aren't very focused on performance anyway, so why bother with centerboards or dag-

**FIGURE 1-13.** The Morgan Out Island 41 has a long, shallow keel, which is ideal for cruising shoal waters but not the best choice for ocean passages. That said, Earl Hinz and his wife successfully cruised the Pacific Ocean for many years on an OI 41. (Bruce Bingham photo)

gerboards that just add to cost and complication? It should be noted that most cruising catamarans are not designed for performance, but more for comfort; freeboard is high and the rigs are small. Other multihull designers, like Chris White and Dick Newick, believe you can have performance *and* comfort, so they usually plan for some type of board that will improve windward performance. Interestingly, the Gemini cruising catamaran is an exception to the above bunch, having a board in each hull.

A more sophisticated solution for monohulls is the wing keel, developed first on the America's Cup Twelve Meter *Australia II*, the boat that wrenched the Auld Mug from the tight grasp of the New York Yacht Club in 1983. Credited to designer Ben Lexcen, with help from Dr. van Oossanen at the University of Delft in the Netherlands, the wing keel is basically a bulb at the bottom of a fin keel, with short wings protruding from each side (Figure 1-14). The wings provide some of the lift lost by shortening the fin keel from, say, 6 feet to 3 feet 6 inches (1.8 m to 1.1 m).

## Twin Keels

It might be pertinent to mention here that twin keels have much to recommend themselves for shoal-water cruising. Long popular in England, even on such well-known production boats as the Westerly line, twin keels have the advantage of keeping the boat upright on the flats when the tide goes out. While they have more wetted surface

**FIGURE 1-14.** The wing keel is a shoal-draft alternative to the traditional keel-centerboard. Advantages are no moving parts and modest lift generated by the wings. (Bruce Bingham photo)

**FIGURE 1-15.** Shelly and Jane DeRidder built their 40-foot *Magic Dragon* with bilge keels and have sailed it thousands of miles across the Pacific. Following a flood, where it was moored in New Zealand's Kerikeri River, they brought it to Opua in the Bay of Islands to inspect the damage.

area than single keels and won't point as high, they do give a damping motion off the wind that is quite pleasing. And, because the keels are generally angled outward from the bilges, a twin-keel boat draws more heeled than when perfectly upright—a twin-keel boat drawing, say, 3 feet (0.9 m), might actually draw 3 feet 6 inches when heeled 25°. This has the advantage of making it easier to kedge off when aground, because draft is automatically reduced as the boat stops and comes upright.

Some years ago, during a cruise in New Zealand's Bay of Islands, I met Shelly and Jane DeRidder, who lived aboard *Magic Dragon* (Figure 1-15), a 40-foot (12.2 m) twin-keel cutter. Shelly was a very innovative, if seat-of-the-pants, designer of cruising boats and gear, including a self-steering wind vane. His *Magic Dragon* was the largest twin-keel cruising boat I have seen, and while Shelly was not unaware of the sacrifices he made to have this particular keel configuration, he and Jane were more than pleased with the boat.

## Inverse Stability

Tragedies in the yachting world always raise questions, and rightly so, about design, construction, and seamanship. The trend toward beamy, flat-bottom boats discussed above, especially those with insufficiently ballasted keels, has not been without penalty. For example, the late English naval architect Angus Primrose ironically appears possibly to have been the victim of design problems with one of his own boats.

Following the 1980 U.S. Sailboat Show in Annapolis, Maryland, Angus and one crew member were caught in a gale a few hundred miles offshore. According to the crew member, who survived by hanging onto a life raft for several days, the boat was knocked down and then rolled over. The crew member stated that the boat did not right itself for about 5 minutes, during which time water entered the cabin through hatches. When a wave finally rolled the boat upright, it was too full of water to save, and it was abandoned.

The boat had the following specifications:

| | |
|---|---|
| LOA | 33' (10 m) |
| LWL | 28' 5" (8.7 m) |
| Beam | 11' 5" (3.7 m) |
| Draft | 4' 5" (1.3 m) |
| Ballast | 3,815 lbs. (1,730 kg) |
| Displacement | 10,525 lbs. (4,772 kg) |

Beam resists the righting moment of the keel, which is also competing with the weight and resistance of the rig underwater. Expanding on this in the 1975 *Cruising World* annual, naval architect John Letcher wrote:

> *It is worth noting on this question of self-righting ability, that typically beamy modern hulls have a limited range of stability, and a stable equilibrium position upside down [Figure 1-16]. Even if it is unlikely that the hull would remain in this relatively narrow stable range for more than the time of one sea passing, this property undoubtedly gives a tendency to hesitate in the 180° position, allowing more time for water to come in through available openings.*
>
> *Once a substantial amount of water is inside, the resulting free surface greatly reduces the stability in the inverted position (especially with a flush deck), so righting follows quickly. At the design stage, a small reduction in beam from modern standards can greatly improve righting ability from angles near 180°.*

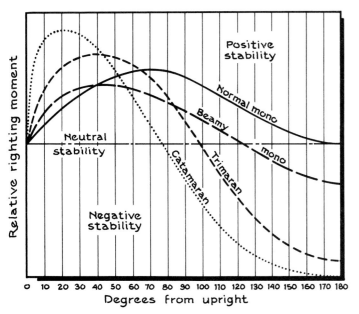

**FIGURE 1-16.** These curves illustrate the limits of positive stability for monohulls and multihulls. It is possible for a monohull to achieve stability upside down, especially a beamy one with shallow draft. If it has not taken on too much water, it will presumably right itself eventually. Multihulls have greater initial stability, but achieve inverse stability sooner, with virtually no chance of righting themselves.

Primrose's boat did right itself with water inside, but was dangerously low in the water and could not be handled to negotiate the waves. Primrose and his crew member believed their boat was sinking and that the best course of action was to take to the life raft. Primrose was swept away.

The 1979 Fastnet Race disaster, which claimed the lives of 15 sailors, prompted a thorough investigation of yacht design, equipment, and crew experience. In summing up the RYA-RORC report, Dale Nouse, *Cruising World*'s editor, wrote, "The report observed that in cases of severe knockdowns (past horizontal and even 360° rolls) the design characteristics which appeared to increase the likelihood of a knockdown include lack of initial stability, wide beam and wide, shallow hull form. There was little indication of any tie between knockdowns and either ballast ratios or length/displacement ratios."

Because wide beam can mean more space below, and because space is so important to liveaboards, it is difficult to dissuade anyone from purchasing a wide-beamed boat. By coupling deep garboards, firm bilges, and deeper draft, however, the chances of achieving inverse stability are lessened.

If one were to follow Letcher's advice and reduce beam from "modern standards," it might appear that interior volume would be correspondingly less. But if freeboard is high and the garboards deep, the narrow boat can have as much interior volume as the beamier, more shallow boat, though the area of the cabin sole diminishes with beam. Figures 1-17 and 1-18 offer some sug-

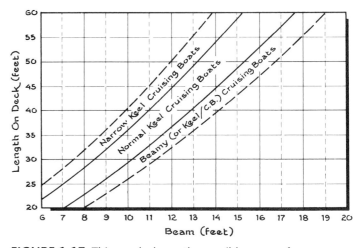

**FIGURE 1-17.** This graph shows the possible range of beams for boats of varying lengths on deck.

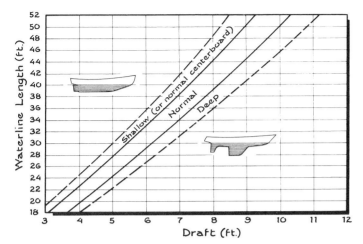

**FIGURE 1-18.** This graph illustrates the possible range of drafts for boats of varying waterline lengths.

gested beam and draft relationships according to waterline length and length on deck.

Of course the other way to recoup volume is by simply buying a longer boat. In addition to extra interior space, you also gain extra speed.

## Limit of Positive Stability

The *limit of positive stability* (LPS) mentioned on the previous page is a complicated procedure most easily accomplished by getting an IMS (International Measurement System) racing certificate from US Sailing. Though you can't easily calculate the LPS yourself, you also can ask the builder or designer for this number.

The LPS number is the angle of heel, in degrees, from which the boat should recover to an upright position after being knocked down. If the number is 120°, the target number suggested in the book *Desirable and Undesirable Characteristics of Offshore Yachts*, and the boat rolls beyond that angle, it will capsize (turn upside down or turtle). This doesn't mean the boat won't come back upright from a capsize, but it does predict its chance of capsize in severe conditions. A boat with an LPS of 100° is more likely to capsize than a boat with an LPS of 120° or 130°.

Look at the curves in Figure 1-16; they tell you something about a boat's stability and hull shape. A steep beginning curve at the left indicates high initial stability, usually characterized by firm bilges and a relatively flat, shallow bottom; that is, a boat with a low D/L ratio. Accompanied by

adequate ballast, such fast hull shapes are said to be *stiff*, resisting the tendency to heel. They like to be sailed relatively flat, with little heel; once heeled to, say, 30°, they may be difficult to handle. Once capsized, they are generally slower to recover than boats with LPS curves that slope upward more gradually. Such a gentle curve indicates a boat with slacker bilges and a higher D/L ratio. It may even be said to be "tender," but it should remain under control even when well heeled. Such boats also have smaller areas of negative stability, and hence they are less likely to remain stable in the inverted position.

Some designers, such as Rod Johnstone, have criticized the 120° figure as being arbitrary and inconsistent with real-world situations. They point out that boats with lower LPS numbers have made many successful offshore passages. While the number is undoubtedly somewhat arbitrary, it was arrived at by a number of experts who studied the capsizes that occurred in the tragic 1979 Fastnet Race and other events. The number represents the considered opinion of experts like Karl Kirkman and Richard McCurdy, and it must be considered a valuable guide, even though we all know that a boat at sea is in a dynamic and often unpredictable set of conditions. There are no guarantees.

There are several other mathematical methods for estimated stability. In Europe, something called STIX is used, also impossible for the average boatowner to calculate himself. It is based on the calculated LPS (called AVS in Europe, or angle of vanishing stability), mass, a displacement-to-length ratio, beam-displacement factor, and others. A simpler formula was promulgated following the Fastnet disaster, called the capsize screening formula. It basically divided maximum beam in feet by displacement divided by (0.9 × 64) to the one-third power. I even included it in the last edition of this book. But the capsize screening formula was aggressively criticized as being too simplistic, and so it has fallen from favor.

In the end, what we want for a good cruising boat is a series of necessary compromises—something between a tender boat and a stiff boat, one that is not too slow but one that has an adequate limit of positive stability. (Few boats meet these criteria as well as the Swans.) And we should never forget that there is no substitute for good seamanship on the part of skipper and crew.

## Sample Stability Ratings

The limit of positive stability (LPS), also called the angle of vanishing stability (AVS), is a mathematical calculation based on the boat's specifications (length, hull shape, displacement, etc.). The following numbers may be found on the Royal Yachting Association's website (www.rya.org).

| | |
|---|---|
| Beneteau First 42.7 | 119 |
| Beneteau First 47.7 | 123 |
| Etap 37 | 122 |
| Dufour 40 | 122 |
| Contessa 32 | 155 |
| Beneteau 50 | 109 |
| Bavaria 44 | 121 |
| X 99 | 111 |
| X 73 | 121 |
| Swan 48 CR | 135 |
| Jeanneau Sun Odyssey 35 | 123 |
| Beneteau Oceanis 411 | 114 |

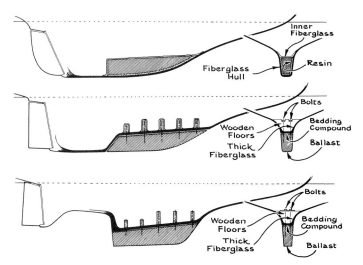

**FIGURE 1-19.** In externally ballasted boats, large keel bolts are sunk into the metal to fasten the ballast to the hull. Internally ballasted boats built in fiberglass have hollow molded integral keels into which the ballast is lowered. Resin or foam is poured in around the keel to fill voids, then the area is glassed over to seal it off.

## Internal or External Ballast?

In wood boat construction, it is common practice to pour molten iron or lead into a female mold and let it cool. The keel is then fitted onto a stub keel and fastened by large J-bolts that were sunk into the ballast at the time it was cast. The bolts protrude through heavy floor timbers and are held in place by washers and nuts. This is the same method used to attach ballast in fin-keel fiberglass boats. Full-keel fiberglass boats incorporate a hollow keel as part of the hull mold, and ballast is cast and lowered inside the cavity before the interior is constructed. There are advantages and disadvantages to each method (Figure 1-19).

The main argument for external ballast is that, with lead at least, the keel often is sufficiently soft to absorb the blow caused by the boat striking a rock or other obstacle. Lead keels may be severely dented in such instances, but the hull remains intact and no water enters—unless the keel bolts are wrenched, and water finds its way through a fissure between the ballast and keel or hull, and then into the bilge. This can and does happen, though much depends on the methods used to fasten the ballast and the way in which the keel bolt loads are distributed inside the boat. It is possible to glass over the lead keel and fair the

laminations into the hull for extra strength, though it's seldom done.

With internally ballasted boats, keel bolts cease to become causes of concern because there aren't any. The fiberglass hull totally supports the weight of the ballast. When an underwater object is struck, the fiberglass around the ballast may be fractured, and water could enter the (hopefully small) open areas between the ballast and the fiberglass keel. However, the ballast cavity is glassed over inside the boat, so theoretically no water should enter the cabin. A more serious problem is encountered if the builder has filled the voids between the ballast and the fiberglass keel with a water-absorbent material. My Vanguard had sheets of end-grain balsa wedged in these spaces, and when I punched a hole in the leading edge of the keel, it took weeks before the area was dry enough to begin repairs.

Discounting the possibilities of running aground, internally ballasted keels give less cause for concern and are basically maintenance free, whereas externally ballasted keels must be watched to make sure the keel bolts are tight and that no water is leaking in. It is also more difficult to keep paint and fairing compound intact on raw lead.

All in all, either method of fixing ballast to the hull is entirely satisfactory for any type of sailing. It is much more a question of how well

# Is Your Boat Worth Upgrading?

This is the $64,000 question, and it is seldom easily answered. Some pundit long ago said that owning a boat is like standing in a cold shower tearing up $50 bills, and he was probably talking about a new boat, never mind a ten- or twenty-year-old boat! At what point do you stop the bleeding, sell, and look for a different boat?

Well, having upgraded a lot of older boats, I've given this question some serious thought. While maintaining and upgrading the C&C 33 and Tartan 44 we used as test boats at *Practical Sailor* magazine, detailed records were kept of costs and man-hours. The short answer, I think, is that a boat is not worth upgrading when the cost to get it sea-ready exceeds resale value. Why throw good money after bad? But there are other considerations. Many of the old, classic designs are no longer made. Take the Vanguard, designed by Phil Rhodes and built by Pearson Yachts during the 1960s. You won't find its beautiful sheer on any modern boat. Say you can buy a 1966 model for $18,000; you could easily spend $25,000 repowering, rerigging, and installing new electronics and safety gear. Now you've got $43,000 invested. You cruise it for five years and then sell it for—what? Maybe your original $18,000, if you're lucky? So the boat cost you $5,000 for each year of operation—but if it made you happy, who cares?!

As a counter example, let's take a 1985 Cape Dory 33 that you bought for $50,000. Suppose it needed only half the new gear of the Vanguard—$12,000 worth. You've invested $62,000. You sail it for five years, then sell it for something less than the original purchase price (because you didn't replace the engine or rigging, and they are now five years older and ready to go), say, $45,000; you've lost $17,000, or $3,400 each year.

Okay, so the Cape Dory 33 was a better financial investment and required less of your time (owner man-hours invested are not included in these examples), but the total costs to operate each are not that far apart—unless you're on a very tight budget, and every dollar counts. In this case, the newer boat usually is the better choice.

Now let's examine the condition of the boat. All boats deteriorate over time, just like your automobile. So over time you'll expect to replace the bilge pump, VHF radio, and cushion covers. It's the big ticket items, like the engine and rigging, that will get you. Cost, of course, depends on the size of your boat. Potentially less obvious are structural problems. Problems common to older boats include wet deck and hull core with delamination of the skins, wet or rotten wood stringers and floors, cracked or failed bulkhead tabbing, and wet rudder core and rusting of metal webbing.

To my mind, there is enough work just fixing even a structurally sound boat that it makes little sense to begin with a boat requiring major repairs that, if left unfixed, represent a safety hazard. Your best assurance of a boat's quality is to retain an accredited surveyor. No matter how much experience you have, don't trust yourself to make these critical judgments because, as we all know, love is blind.

---

the builder has done the job than the method he and the designer have chosen.

## MULTIHULLS

Proponents of multihulls have had a hard row to hoe in winning converts from the staid, conservative ranks of the monohullers. Multihull proponents point to the Polynesian explorers who roamed the Pacific in huge double canoes and catamarans; to Nathanael Herreshoff, who blew past his 1876 Centennial regatta competition in the 24-foot (7.3 m) catamaran *Amaryllis*; and to the safety record of modern pioneer designers, such as Arthur Piver, Norm Cross, James Wharram, Rudy Choy, and Dick Newick.

Indeed, Captain James Cook, on visiting Tahiti in 1777, was impressed by the speed and agility of the native multihulls, which sailed circles around his *Endeavour*. Captain Nat, the most revered name in American yacht design, saw virtue in the multihull, and undoubtedly would

# Upgrading *Viva*

The following table lists the costs incurred for upgrading a 1975 Tartan 44 over a six-year period. The initial purchase price was quite low ($35,000), but that was because *Viva* was a real "project" boat, as evidenced by the $40,000 and hundreds of man-hours I had to invest to make her ready for offshore cruising.

| Job | Cost | Man-Hours |
|---|---|---|
| **Year One** | | |
| Replace portlights and surrounding teak | $400 | 43 |
| Install anchor well drain | $30 | 5 |
| Schaefer 3000 furling | $2,100 | 7 |
| Performance vang | $1,000 | 2 |
| DC electrical panel and wiring | $1,200 | 42 |
| AC electrical panel and wiring | $320 | 20 |
| Link 2000R and Powerline alternator | $950 | 60 |
| Freedom 10 inverter | $895 | 6 |
| Lifesaver 50 solar panel | $550 | 1 |
| Four 6-volt batteries and cable | $220 | 5 |
| Two deck hatches | $1,000 | 4 |
| Two steering compasses | $200 | 4 |
| Swim ladder | $510 | 1 |
| Nicro Dorade vents | $96 | 1 |
| Cold Machine refrigeration | $500 | 5 |
| LPG deck box | $10 | 2 |
| Replace Plexiglas deck lids | $45 | 4 |
| Repair cockpit scupper | $8 | 1 |
| Repair teak transom trim | $1 | 1 |
| Replace bent stanchions | $90 | 1 |
| Replace rudder stops (wire rope) | $30 | 3 |
| Recut genoa, repair mainsail | $1,424 | * |
| Lifelines and gates | $388 | * |
| **Subtotal** | **$11,967** | **218** |
| **Year Two** | | |
| Paint topsides | $500 | 59.5 |
| Install new toilet | $500 | 35 |
| Replace rudder bearings | $245 | 28.75 |
| Winches, used self-tailers | $1,515 | 18.75 |
| Windlass and bow roller | $2,400 | 34 |
| Install new stove | $900 | 3.75 |

| Job | Cost | Man-Hours |
|---|---|---|
| Make V-berth insert | $100 | 5 |
| Replace autopilot drive | $1,200 | 19.5 |
| Replace steering cable and sheaves | $700 | 10 |
| Adjustable genoa lead cars | $950 | 6* |
| Dutchman sail flaking system | $550 | * |
| **Subtotal** | **$9,560** | **214.25** |
| **Years Three and Four** | | |
| Replace standing rigging | $2,700 | 35 |
| Replace running rigging | $500 | 10 |
| Mast electrical wires and lights | $500 | 8 |
| Replace cabin sole | $500 | 20 |
| Other | $700 | 8 |
| **Subtotal** | **$4,900** | **88** |
| **Years Five and Six** | | |
| Repair cabin sole | $100 | 47 |
| Mainsheet leads | $25 | 6 |
| Replumb scuppers | $30 | 2 |
| Replace stanchion bases | $160 | 18 |
| Autopilot | $3,000 | 15 |
| Inner forestay deck fitting | $1,000 | 8 |
| Radar and pole | $2,300 | * |
| Rebuild rudder | $1,000 | 44 |
| **Subtotal** | **$9,615** | **143** |
| Other safety equipment, etc. | $3,878 | — |
| **GRAND TOTAL** | **$39,920** | **663.25** |

* work performed by others

*Notes:*

1. *Costs are from the years 1994–2000 and should be adjusted upward to account for inflation.*

2. *When purchased, the boat had already been repowered with a new Yanmar, and I already owned another expensive piece of gear, an Avon four-person life raft.*

have continued his studies had not the type been prohibited from further competition. The safety of a multihull, as with monohulls, is largely a function of design, construction, and seamanship; multihull accidents are not due to some gross conceptual flaw.

Modern recreational fiberglass multihulls first found a following in Great Britain in the 1960s. Names like Catalac, Prout, and Symons crossed the Atlantic to American shores, but were a tough sell. It didn't help that some were incredibly homely looking. These, as well as the small monohulls of the day, like the twin-keel Westerly line, were built before the advent of core materials, like end-grain balsa and PVC foam. Hulls and decks were solid, single-skin fiberglass, and to keep them light, they weren't very thick. Panels deflected (often called *oilcanning*), and even if they were not likely to fracture, the movement in the hull or deck under foot wasn't very confidence inspiring.

Multihulls waged a long and difficult battle trying to win converts, and eventually won through in the early 1990s. The boats became better looking, and the buying public, always a sucker for big interiors with lots of berths, finally saw the advantages of two hulls (trimarans, with smaller accommodations than monohulls, and usually in just one hull, are favored only by those interested in high performance). Not only is there a lot of volume in a cruising catamaran, but they heel only about 5°. Today, fiberglass multihulls are well accepted.

Let's look at the principal considerations in owning and cruising a multihull.

The hardest hump for monohullers to overcome is the fear of turning turtle. If a multihull flips over, it stays upside down unless there is some fancy righting system (although to date, no righting system has proved itself reliable in nasty conditions). But the multihull doesn't sink! If a monohull rolls over, it should come back to an upright position, providing a lot of water hasn't entered the interior. If it doesn't come back, it sinks. Seems like a toss-up to me.

The purchase cost of all new boats has increased considerably in recent years, and since multihulls are invariably more expensive than monohulls, their cost is prohibitive for many people. Worse, there aren't many good, low-priced, used production multihulls on the market. The fact is that multihulls cost more to build, mostly because of the added surface area, which means more raw materials, more molds, and more man-hours.

Speed is surely a major appeal of multihulls. The first big multihull I sailed was Meade Gougeon's 35-foot *Adagio* (Figure 1-20). It was the first boat built with WEST System brand epoxy, and it is fast. Zipping effortlessly across the placid waters of Saginaw Bay, I was astounded to be sailing faster than the speed of the wind. Later experiences on some of Dick Newick's graceful trimarans, Chris White's powerful Atlantic 50 cat, and even Tony Smith's Gemini 30 have only added to my interest. During a week's cruise of the Chesapeake aboard the Gemini, I figured it was about 50% faster on nearly all points of sail than the 33-foot Vanguard. Instead of making 5 knots, we were doing 8 knots, which doesn't sound like a big difference on the pages of this book, but on the water, it was huge.

Speed is great when you want it, but there are times when the weather turns dangerous, and it is best to slow down the boat. The single-hander or shorthanded crew can become dangerously overtired if speed is such that hand steering is mandatory. Before purchase, it would be prudent to check the ability of any boat, especially a multihull, to heave-to and decelerate. It's hard to forget the terrible story of ocean racer Rob James, who drowned after falling from his trimaran. His crew, however agitated or inexperienced they might have been, were unable to slow the boat sufficiently to pick him up, even though

**FIGURE 1-20.** *Adagio* is a 35-foot (10.7 m) trimaran built by the Gougeon Brothers. It was the first boat they built using the company's WEST System brand epoxy products. Meade Gougeon uses it for family cruising and occasional racing on the Great Lakes. Home port is Bay City, Michigan. (Gougeon Brothers photo)

one crew member was able to actually get a hand on James.

Foremost in my mind, the multihull represents a huge, stable platform that facilitates movement on deck much better than a monohull (Figure 1-21). Not only is the square footage greater, but cats heel only about 5° and tris about 15°. As Tristan Jones observed on launching his trimaran *Outward Leg*, you can put down a cup of coffee, and 15 minutes later it's still standing in the same spot. Without a drop spilled! People afraid of heeling will love the multihull's flat ride.

A problem in smaller multihulls, under about 40 feet (12.2 m), is the creation of a sensible accommodation plan with standing headroom. The small cruising cat must use the space in the bridge for a dinette, berths, or both, and this can raise the cabin top so high that it increases windage, elevates the center of gravity, and mars its looks. Without the bridge as cabin space, however, you are left with just the floats (or *amas*) for accommodations, and most people will find them a bit tight for all-around living comfort.

All but the very largest cruising tris confine accommodations to the main hull since placing excessive weight in the floats is unsafe. Consequently, berths are often placed outboard of the main cabin in the connecting wings (or *akas*). This arrangement is seldom more generous or comfortable than a good monohull of similar length.

Critics say multihulls' wide beams make them difficult and expensive to berth in marina slips,

and there is some truth to this. But since we are discussing cruising boats, it is fair to assume that you won't be spending a lot of nights in marinas, and the multihull's shoal draft permits anchoring in the shallow parts of a bay where keel boats simply cannot go.

Making the switch from monohull to multihull is for many a change of faith. Yet there is a growing body of experience and literature upon which the interested buyer can draw. There is little doubt that good, safe cruising multihulls are available to anyone interested in exploring their inherent advantages.

# HULL MATERIAL

For centuries, wood was just about the only material used for small boats. The Dutch began using steel in the 19th century for boats as small as 9 feet (2.7 m). Only since the 1950s has fiberglass become dominant, and while its virtues are many, it is not the only viable boatbuilding material. Figure 1-22 compares the basic physical properties of the most commonly used materials.

## Fiberglass

The first production fiberglass auxiliary sailboat in the United States was the Philip Rhodes–designed Bounty II in 1956. Later, builder Fred Coleman sold the molds to Pearson, a Rhode Island company that, in the mid-fifties, built small daysailers and runabouts. Its Carl Alberg–designed Pearson Triton (Figure 1-23) was introduced at the 1959 New York Boat Show by cousins Clint and Everett Pearson and was an

**FIGURE 1-21.** Cruising multihulls such as this Lagoon 380 have grown in popularity due to the vast accommodations possible. Many are in service in the charter trade, and to keep neophytes out of trouble, these boats tend to be under-rigged. (Jeanneau)

| Material | Weight lb./cu. ft. | Tensile Strength (psi) | Compressive Strength (psi) | Modulus of Elasticity (psi) |
|---|---|---|---|---|
| GRP mat | 94 | 10,000 | 15,000 | 900,000 |
| GRP W/R | 106 | 35,000 | 25,000 | 2,000,000 |
| Douglas fir (12% moisture) | 34 | 2,150 | 2,000 | 1,600,000 |
| Aluminum | 166 | 42,000 | 32,000 | 10,000,000 |
| Steel | 490 | 60,000 | 60,000 | 28,900,000 |
| Ferro-cement | 168 | 1,600 | 10,000 | 1,300,000 |

**FIGURE 1-22.** Properties of Common Boatbuilding Materials

comparison, the hull of the Tatoosh 42, a good cruising boat designed by Robert Perry and built in Taiwan by Ta Yang during the 1980s, is about 0.36 inch (9 mm) thick at the sheer, 0.47 inch (12 mm) at the turn of the bilge, and 0.59 inch (15 mm) at the keel. The Tatoosh aside, most new boats are of cored construction, making further comparisons difficult.

When buying a boat, it's always a good idea to research the lamination schedule, because the type and weight of fabrics, use of cores, internal reinforcements, and ratio of glass fiber to resin are also important. Some builders refuse to give this information, saying the layup is "thick enough." Thick enough for what? To withstand a bump from a floating log? To withstand a collision with another boat? Here's the lamination schedule for the Corbin 39, a stout cruising boat built in Canada by Corbin Les Bateaux during the 1980s. Note that more than one layer of each material may be used in every step, depending on the part of the boat being laminated.

| Gelcoat (22 mm) | 1-ounce mat |
|---|---|
| 1-ounce mat | ¾-inch Airex core |
| 1½-ounce mat | 1½-ounce mat |
| 24-ounce woven roving | 24-ounce woven roving |
| 1½-ounce mat | 1½-ounce mat |
| 24-ounce woven roving | 24-ounce woven roving |
| 1-ounce mat | |

Twenty-five layers were used in the center of the Corbin 39, and thirty-five layers were used at the keel—exceptionally strong!

While mat and woven roving are still in frequent use, the more sophisticated boats have "engineered" laminates. Where the engineering of simpler laminates is restricted pretty much to making boat bottoms thicker than the topsides (because the bottom has to carry the weight of the interior and mechanical systems), today you'll often find specialty reinforcements specified for specific locations. For example, computer analysis of stresses and pressures on a hull can show engineers where extra reinforcement is required. One such area is where the keel attaches to the hull. Glass fibers oriented in the direction of the loads, radiating out from the keel-hull joint, are stronger than fibers oriented randomly or at right angles to the load lines. Consequently, the engineer might specify a unidirectional fabric be used around the keel-hull joint.

**FIGURE 1-23.** The 28-foot 6-inch (8.7 m) Pearson Triton was the first successful production sailboat built in fiberglass in the United States. More than 700 were completed before production ceased in 1967. Though not as beamy as more modern 28-footers, the Triton was heavily glassed and performed well. In the late 1980s, Jim Baldwin circumnavigated in a Triton named *Atom*.

immediate success. Other good boats, like the Invicta (1960), Bounty II (1961), Vanguard (1962), and Countess 44 (1965), soon followed to round out the Pearson line.

It is common to hear the owners of these boats say that the early Pearsons were built "before they knew fiberglass," meaning that the fiberglass hull thicknesses were based on the engineering knowledge for appropriate thicknesses for wood. "My hull is this thick!" a Triton or Vanguard owner will say, spacing his thumb and finger an inch apart. These guesstimates are about as accurate as fish stories, but there is a little bit of truth to the notion.

The hull thickness of the Triton is something less than ½ inch (12 mm) at the sheer, increasing slightly at the turn of the bilge then to about ⅞ inch (22 mm) at places in the keel. This certainly is a heavier layup than many new boats. In

Here's a list of different specialty reinforcement architectures offered by Vectorply, a maker of fiberglass, carbon fiber, and Kevlar products.

0° and 90° longitudinal and transverse

± 45° double bias

0° longitudinal unidirectional

90° transverse unidirectional

0°, 45°, 45° warp triaxial

45°, 90°, 45° weft triaxial

0°, 45°, 90°, 45° quadraxial

Figures 1-24 and 1-25 give suggested hull thicknesses, according to displacement, for solid skin hulls and those with cores. Today, core materials such as Airex and Contourkore end-grain balsa (Figure 1-26) are commonly used to stiffen hulls and reduce weight. The actual thickness of fiberglass will not be as great as in a solid fiberglass hull, but the stiffening, weight-reducing, and insulating properties of cores make them worthwhile. Also, core materials are less expensive than resin. Core materials were first used in hulls during the early 1970s, and today they are the norm.

The thicker the core, the thinner the inner and outer skins can be—up to a point. For example, racing boats may have very thin skins, such as the all-carbon skins on the 120-foot (36.6 m) maxi catamaran *Orange II* that are only 0.03 inch (0.8 mm) each! However, while stiffness is one thing, both the racer and the cruiser must consider

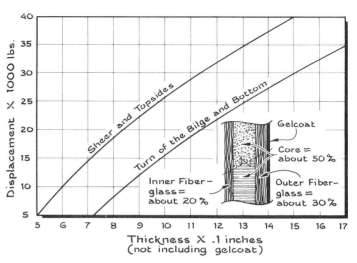

FIGURE 1-25. This graph suggests a lamination schedule and hull thickness for cored fiberglass hulls by displacement.

puncture resistance; there is an increasing amount of floating junk in the ocean, from logs to containers to all manner of debris, and they are potentially deadly. Further, the cruising sailboat must have a sufficiently thick outer skin to withstand the abrasion of sand and rocks should the boat come ashore.

To further stiffen the hull, and to carry and distribute keel loads, many boats incorporate molded fiberglass floor grids. Studying Figure 1-27 gives some clues as to how one might consider strengthening a hull (it wouldn't be easy) that is too thin and/or has insufficient transverse or longitudinal stiffeners. If this describes your hull, you

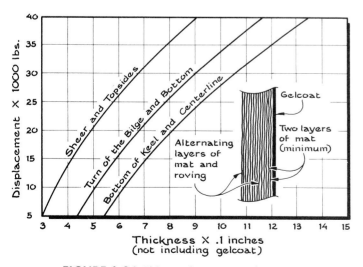

FIGURE 1-24. This graph suggests a lamination schedule and hull thickness for solid skin fiberglass boats by displacement.

FIGURE 1-26. Baltek Corporation manufactures an end-grain balsa product called Contourkore that is commonly used nowadays as a hull core material. The boat being laid up here is a J/24. (Baltek)

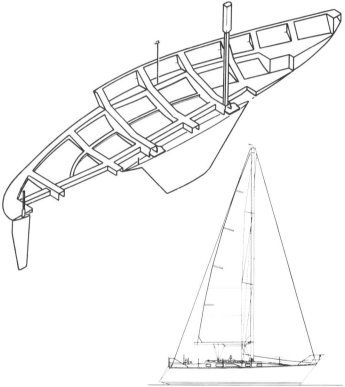

FIGURE 1-27. In order to keep hull thicknesses at a minimum (to reduce weight and cost, yet maintain rigidity), many builders now install a molded floor grid in the hull that is carefully engineered to provide necessary structural supports. The grid pictured here was designed for the Hunter 34. (George Day photo)

might already be aware of the problem by having observed the following:

- Doors don't close
- Bulkheads are cracked or delaminated where they are glassed to the hull
- Standing rigging is perpetually loose

- Hull panel deflects when struck with force (push on it with the palm of your hand)

Osmotic blistering is a condition that during the 1980s and early '90s appeared to affect about 25% of all fiberglass boats. Incidence varied according to geographical region, boat use, type of resins and fibers used in layup, and treatment of the bottom (i.e., sanding before bottom painting). It took considerable research to figure out the reasons, which are several. Briefly, gelcoats are water permeable, and as moisture enters the laminate, certain chemical reactions occur between the water and the hull materials, especially the sizing used to hold the fibers together. Letting the gelcoat cure too hard before laying in the first laminate is another major cause. Seeking escape, the moisture pushes out dime-size areas of gelcoat.

The severity of blistering ranges from cosmetic to structural. In most cases, a blistered boat can be repaired, but unfortunately many boatyards lack the information and expertise to make the best possible repairs. Vinylester and epoxy resins are superior to polyester in providing a barrier against the ingress of moisture. Today it is common practice to use vinylester resin for the skin or first coat inside the gelcoat; in all but higher-end boats, the remainder of the laminate is polyester. This practice has dramatically reduced the incidence of blistering. But it still can occur, especially on older boats. On repaired boats, vinylester and epoxy barrier coats are applied in the hope of preventing future recurrence of blisters.

## Wood

While there are still a few custom boatbuilding shops, mostly in Maine and Washington, that build in wood with traditional plank-on-frame construction, they are not an economic force. A few of the big wooden boatbuilders of the first half of the 20th century, like Dickerson, Hinckley, and Chris-Craft, continued building in wood into the 1960s, but even they eventually had to make the switch to fiberglass. As with any boat purchase, retain the services of a competent marine surveyor to check the boat before purchase. Wood is a wonderful building material—just make certain you aren't buying a hull riddled with rot or weakened by broken ribs. And be realistic in assessing the hours required for repair and annual maintenance.

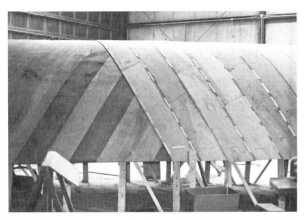

FIGURE 1-28. A typical cold-molded hull is comprised of thin veneers stapled at cross angles over a wooden plug. Coatings of epoxy resin seal each lamination against moisture and, on curing, result in a rigid monocoque structure that is quite stiff. (Gougeon Brothers)

Cold-molded wooden boats saturated with epoxy resin are lightweight, rigid, and more resistant to abrasion than bare planking (Figure 1-28). This method is especially ideal for multihulls. Typical construction might call for multiple veneer laminates of ⅛-inch (3.2 mm) Western red cedar with a final skin thickness of ⅝ inch (16 mm).

## Steel

Small steel pleasure boats have never been popular in the United States. But in Holland, a country lacking abundant timber, steel has been the preferred material for more than 100 years.

The concerns about steel are twofold: rust and poor resale value. Corrosion is certainly a possibility with any metal in the marine environment, but modern zinc primers and polyurethane coating systems do an excellent job of protecting the steel hull. If a steel hull should rust, it has an advantage over aluminum in its telltale streaking, which occurs long before problems become structural. Aluminum corrosion can be virtually invisible, detected only by insidious piles of white powder.

For some reason, people expect to pay less for a steel boat, despite the fact that the hull of a boat generally amounts to no more than 10 to 15% of the total cost. During the past few decades, a number of production steel boat builders have tried and failed to develop profitable businesses. The Amazon line of contemporary Grahame Shannon designs in British Columbia, and some Ted Brewer–designed sloops by Huromic Metal Indus-

tries in Ontario, were notable exceptions. Radiused chines make the Amazons look almost like round-bilge boats, which in steel are more expensive to build than hard-chine hulls; shaping the chines is a cost-effective compromise between the two. Unfortunately, they too are out of business. Below the border, pickings are slim. The long-time metal boat builder Topper Hermanson has retired. There isn't much to choose from on the used boat market either, though occasionally good deals are possible.

The real appeal of steel is its resistance to holing. When naval architect Danny Greene's fiberglass cutter *Frolic* was sunk by a semi-submerged container in Rhode Island Sound, he watched from his dinghy as she settled beneath the waves and vowed to build his next boat in metal. His 34-foot (10.4 m) *Brazen* is the result (Figure 1-29).

Another graphic testimony was delivered to the sailing public when famous French singlehander Bernard Moitessier's *Joshua* was wrecked during a fierce storm at Mexico's Cabo San Lucas. Many of the fiberglass boats in the anchorage were reduced to patches of shredded fiber, while *Joshua* tumbled in through the surf to the beach, scraped and pockmarked, but structurally intact. He sold her on the spot only because she was full of sand, and he had no practical means of refloating her on that coast.

The fact remains, however, that the dominant boatbuilding material today is fiberglass. Actually, the preferred term today is *composites*, because

FIGURE 1-29. Danny Greene's 34-foot *Brazen* is a hard-chine steel cruiser with a wooden deck and distinctive dodger over the companionway. It may look odd but is very functional. Interestingly, *Brazen*'s auxiliary power is a 15 hp, 4-stroke Yamaha outboard, which saves cost and opens up the interior tremendously.

hulls are constructed of a variety of materials—fiberglass, certainly, but also wood or foam cores, further bolstered by judicious use of carbon fiber and Kevlar. Even the builders of superyachts up to 200 feet (61 m), which once were necessarily built of steel with aluminum superstructures, are now switching to composites, and so too are the makers of airplanes, bridges, and utility poles.

### Aluminum and Other Metals

Aluminum is an excellent material for boatbuilding, and contrary to some persons' thinking, can be suitable for homebuilding. For aluminum to have the same strength as steel, its plate thickness must be about 50% thicker. And a good marine-grade aluminum doesn't rust the way steel does, so there is less concern for exposing the metal to the elements, as well as no need to sandblast prior to painting. In fact, the French, who have a predilection for aluminum "escape machines," often don't paint their hulls at all above the waterline.

The Meta Company of Tarare, France, has had favorable results building aluminum cruising boats with triple the usual 4 mm to 5 mm ($^5/_{32}$ inch to $^{13}/_{64}$ inch) thicknesses of most other conventionally plated aluminum boats. The patented Strongall process is viewed by the developers as an answer to the problems of weldment fracture, plate distortion, and electrolysis. Designer Michel Joubert could not have tripled the thicknesses of similarly sized steel hulls because of the excessive weight. But because of the low specific gravity of aluminum, he could design a 39-footer (12 m) displacing 25,000 pounds (11,335 kg).

A few cruising boats have been built of Monel, a metal long used for fuel tanks and sometimes for propeller shafts. It is more corrosion-resistant than steel and quite strong. Copper-nickel alloy (90/10) has been used in the construction of several commercial vessels in Third World countries. While it is about eight to ten times more expensive than mild steel, it is supposedly antifouling, and costs are recouped by never having to haul the boat or spend money on bottom paint.

### Ferro-Cement

Although a few yards dabbled in ferro-cement during the 1970s, most boats built of this difficult material were homebuilt, many according to plans offered by Samson Marine Designs in Canada. A professionally plastered hull can be sufficiently strong for ocean sailing, although abrasion resistance is not as great as steel or fiberglass. But it's not an easy job, mainly because the wire mesh, which is laid over frames to form the shape of the hull, has so many tiny corners it is hard to get all the bubbles out of the plaster when it is applied. Expansion and contraction due to temperature changes eventually cause cracks to appear in the hull. Runnels of rust indicate that moisture has found its way through the cracks to the metal mesh.

If you are considering buying a ferro-cement hull, determine whether professional plasterers were used. And absolutely retain a marine surveyor to check it for you. Regardless, my advice is don't do it, not only because the material is problematic, but resale value is virtually nil.

## RIGS

Cruising sailors argue the various merits of different rigs to no end. I suppose this is only to be expected, because just as there is no ideal cruiser, there is no ideal rig, either. A few observations:

Proponents of two-stick rigs (yawl, ketch, and schooner) make a good point when they say that if one spar is lost, there's always one left to jury-rig. For this reason, the triatic stay, which connects the two mastheads, should be avoided if at all possible, even if it means using running backstays and split or double backstays on the main and jumper struts on the mizzen.

On the other hand, two-stick rigs are usually not as weatherly as sloops and cutters. And they cost more because of the number of spars, extra fittings, rope, and wire. Their best point of sail is reaching, when they can put up more canvas. The fore-and-aft distribution of sail area makes them balance well. In heavy weather, dropping the mainsail and carrying on with just "jib and jigger" is a splendid, easily handled combination.

Garry Hoyt's Freedom 40 popularized the unstayed rig in the 1970s. It wasn't a new idea, but certainly the Freedom line is an appropriate and intelligent resurrection of that concept. (See Appendix C.) Interestingly, by the late 1980s, the company had abandoned the ketch rig in favor of a cat sloop rig, with a large, fully battened mainsail and vestigial jib or "blade" to improve windward performance. I've sailed with Garry and his son on several Freedoms, and believe he has simplified sail-handling chores immensely. I'm impressed with the patented Hoyt Gun Mount, which enables you to raise, trim, and lower a

**FIGURE 1-30.** Multihull designer Chris White's first big project was for himself. *Juniper* is a 55-foot (16.8 m) trimaran that is very fast and very graceful. He chose an unstayed cat ketch rig, which is self-tending and very powerful.

spinnaker without leaving the cockpit. Despite all the lines and clutter on deck, it is amazingly simple and virtually idiot-proof. Doing 360° doughnuts in Newport Harbor, without any possibility of wrapping the chute, sold me.

There are pros and cons to the unstayed rig (Figure 1-30). First, eliminating stays means you no longer have to worry about losing the rig if even just one of several dozen terminals or tangs breaks (corrosion is often the culprit, and difficult to detect, even if the terminal fitting is at the deck). Freestanding spars are being built of aluminum, steel, and carbon fiber and resin. Of these, the latter is the preferred material due to its combination of strength and light weight. Carbon fiber spars are expensive, but price is mitigated to an extent by the fact that standing rigging is eliminated. They also are quite strong, as evidenced by the fact that when Tony Lush's *Lady Pepperell* rolled over in the Southern Ocean, the spars survived intact. This doesn't mean they won't break, however. When gusts hit, bendy carbon masts tend to spill wind, damping the effect. On the other hand, it is difficult to protect them from damage caused by lightning strikes.

Sloops and cutters generally demonstrate superior windward performance, but for them to handle winds ranging from light to gale force, their sail inventories should include a range of sails from drifters to trysails and storm jibs. An advantage of the cutter is that the foretriangle is

divided among two sails instead of just one, which decreases the size of sails that must be handled. So instead of changing sails in heavy weather, you just start reefing or taking them down. Clubfooted staysails, however, must be viewed with suspicion, as they are capable of rapping you on the skull or knocking you overboard if the sail backwinds unexpectedly. A safer arrangement is to eliminate the club and lead the sheet from a block at the clew to a block on the traveler (Chapter 10). Garry Hoyt's patented Jib Boom, found on the Alerion Express that he markets and the Island Packet line, is an improvement on the traditional club in that it is self-vanging, though it still clutters and complicates the foredeck.

Fractional rigs (Figure 1-31) have become popular once again, primarily on racing boats because the spar can be bent backward to optimize sail shape. Yet veteran sailors, such as the late Tristan Jones who claimed more single-handed miles at sea than any other man, have said that the simple masthead rig is hard to beat for cruis-

**FIGURE 1-31.** The Sea Sprite 34, which sports a tall seven-eighths fractional rig, was designed by A. E. Luders and is based on another of his designs, the Luders 33—the second boat sailed by Robin Lee Graham in his solo circumnavigation.

26

**FIGURE 1-32.** The patented Aerorig was developed in England as a way to improve sail efficiency and simplify trimming. (Forespar)

ing. They tend to be slightly shorter than fractional rigs for the same size boat and, consequently, offer less weight and wind resistance high up. The top of the mast also is more rigidly stayed, thereby being less subject to whipping when slamming into head seas. Jumper struts are not required, either.

There are a few other oddball rigs that may merit your consideration. Foremost is probably the Aerorig, marketed for a time in the United States by Forespar (Figure 1-32). Here, a single, long boom extends both forward of the mast and aft of it, so that both the jib and mainsail are set in the same plane and are trimmed simultaneously.

## CHOOSING A BOAT

So what to buy? Let's work through some of the considerations.

### New or Used?

As with most products, newer is better, if only because there is less wear and tear on the various parts. Let's suppose, given reasonable care and no catastrophic events, that a hull is good for thirty-five years, a balsa-cored deck for twenty-five

years, standing rigging for fifteen years, sails for five to ten years, and the engine for fifteen years or 500 hours (or longer, with good maintenance), whichever comes first. Just as a car starts depreciating as soon as you drive it off the lot, so does a sailboat begin deducting time from its probable life span. You may find that its resale value actually increases the first year or two, but this is usually because of the high cost of outfitting it with ground tackle, electronics, safety equipment, and lots of other stuff.

After a few years, age overpowers the equipment list and value begins to fall. Because most of the gear is still fairly new, this is a good time to buy—between about three and seven years.

Older boats cost less, but will require more upgrades. If you can do at least some of the work yourself, however, you can own a larger boat for less. Hey, that's what this book is all about!

### Solid Fiberglass Hull versus Cored

Back in the 1960s and '70s, there were quite a few single-skin hulls built. But the trend has been almost universally toward cores because they add stiffness and reduce weight and cost. As discussed earlier, there's nothing wrong with a cored hull, but there are several things to be aware of. First, delamination or separation of the skins and core is a potentially serious problem. A surveyor can use his hammer to sound for delamination, most often found in the area of impact and around through-hull fittings. Do not underestimate the cost and hassle of repair. Because there are so many good used boats on the market, I'd give any boat with significant hull delamination a miss. Foam cores such as Airex and Divinycell won't turn punky like balsa, but still can delaminate. Airex linear foam is more resilient than balsa and some other foams, and so is used in specific applications, such as the crossbeam-hull connections in high-performance multihulls where fractures of too-stiff materials are a problem.

Some composites experts believe that balsa-cored hulls are time bombs waiting—not to explode, but to turn to mush. For a cruising boat, where weight isn't as much of a concern as with a racer, I like Tom Morris's 1990s-era approach: single-skin hulls stiffened by a foam-cored grid. To compensate for the additional weight, he tried to get as much weight out of other areas of the boat as possible, such as by installing cored bulkheads. But few of us can afford a boat from Morris

Yachts! So I'll just say that for cruising the far corners of the world, a solid, single-skin hull makes more sense to me. If you just can't find one you like, make darn sure the sandwich hasn't delaminated and the outer skin is sufficiently thick to provide some measure of protection against abrasion, and if you install any new through-hulls, use the method shown in Figure 4-8 (Chapter 4), in which you remove the core and replace it with epoxy putty. A compromise position of some builders is to core the topsides, but not below the waterline.

Nearly all decks are cored, most with balsa. Some early fiberglass boats, like the British-made Alacrity twin-keel I owned in the early 1970s, had wood deck beams glassed in rather than coring in the deck laminate itself. This didn't stop the deck from oilcanning when walked on. Balsa is by far the most common choice for deck material, partly because it makes a very stiff panel, and partly because comparable-performing foams may weaken when heated. Most foam-cored decks must be white or very nearly so. Some builders, who aren't too concerned about weight, use materials other than balsa. Island Packet, for example, uses a glass microsphere and resin mix that is somewhat heavier than balsa, but bonds well to the skins and won't rot. Many older boats have localized areas of delamination in the decks. Again, a surveyor can identify these. If the core hasn't been removed around deck fittings, such as cleats and chainplates, water may easily migrate into the core, eventually causing delamination of the skins. Small areas of delamination aren't much of a worry, but if large areas, such as the foredeck, come unglued, pass up the boat and look for another. Drilling holes and injecting resin rarely cures a badly delaminated deck because the core is still wet. The correct procedure is to remove either the outer or inner skin, remove the core, replace the core, and relaminate the missing skin. This is a costly, messy job no one wants to do. A repair yard will charge you a fortune. In my estimation, this is one of the most common problems afflicting older boats, and one of the first reasons why an otherwise serviceable boat may be ready for the landfill.

## Hull-Deck Joint

Screwed-together hull-deck joints are not acceptable, in my opinion. They are favored by economy builders because only one worker is needed to drive the fasteners. Through-bolts with washers and nuts on the inside are much preferable. The future, however, is in chemistry. In the 1990s, structural adhesives, such as Plexus, were developed that form incredibly strong chemical bonds. TPI began using such a product on the hull-deck joint of the Lagoon catamarans it built for Jeanneau.

When I was editor of *Practical Sailor*, contributor Tom Gannon reviewed one of the first Lagoons with a hull-deck joint held together mostly by a structural adhesive (stanchions and some other hardware required fasteners through the joint). The crew delivering one of the first boats into Long Island Sound from Narragansett Bay reported water pouring in through an opening in the hull-deck joint forward by the bow. When Tom asked a TPI engineer what had failed, he was told that a worker apparently had failed to gun in the adhesive over several feet of the joint. So the problem was caused by a careless worker, not a failure of this tough methacrylate adhesive.

You'll see structural adhesives used more and more, replacing old stalwarts like 3M 5200 polyurethane. Most times, the material surrounding the glue joint will fail before the joint. Screws, or no fasteners at all, are acceptable where good structural adhesives are used. Just remember that the joint may not ever come apart again!

## Keel-Hull Joint

Most modern boats have externally ballasted lead keels (iron is a much poorer choice). The key to a good installation is how well the weight of the keel is supported by the hull bottom, and how well the loads are distributed by internal structures. This usually is accomplished by a series of longitudinal and athwartship stiffeners. Wood used to be common, but because it is heavy and subject to rot, many builders began making these stiffeners out of foam and fiberglass. Some builders lay them in individually, others make a mold so that all the supports belong to the same single piece. This is called a *grid* or *grillage*. It may be tabbed to the hull with strips of fiberglass mat or bonded with a structural adhesive. The keel should be bolted through part of this grillage, and the grillage should extend well across the bottom of the boat as well as fore and aft.

## Mast

Both boats with deck-stepped masts and those with keel-stepped masts have made successful, safe ocean passages. However most experienced offshore sailors prefer a keel-stepped mast. Loads from either one must be transmitted to the keel; with deck-stepped masts, a compression post or bulkhead is used to transfer the load belowdecks. This is unnecessary with a keel-stepped mast. More important, a keel-stepped mast is better supported because, even with the loss of a stay, the deck provides a measure of security. And if you should break the mast, a keel-stepped one generally leaves a stub from which you can fashion a jury rig.

## Rig

The masthead sloop is the simplest, least costly, and most efficient rig of all the major rig types. Above 40 feet (12.2 m) or so, one may have a preference for a two-stick rig. And while there's no right or wrong choice, it seems to me that the yawl has more advantages than the ketch. Here's why. The yawl has a larger mainsail and foretriangle, so it will be better to windward than the ketch. And in a blow, the small mizzen of the yawl is all the sail aft you really need to balance a small jib; the mizzen of a ketch might have to be reefed in the same situation. On very large yachts of, say, 75 feet (22.9 m) and more, the ketch may well be preferable if only to keep the height of the mainmast low enough to pass under bridges, and the size of the mainsail more manageable by what is probably a paid crew.

## Quality

It is difficult for many people to assess quality in a boat. What is the difference between a Catalina and a Sabre? A Hunter and a Tartan? Too often people think quality is marked only by joinerwork—"a nice teak interior." In fact, the quality that makes a difference at sea is more subtle: tinned electrical wire running in conduits suspended by hangers every 18 inches (457 mm), per ABYC E-11; quality plumbing hose protected by ferrules where it passes through bulkheads; positive-action, bronze, ball-valve seacocks, not brass residential home–style valves; thick-walled stanchions, preferably secured both vertically and horizontally by through-bolts; sturdy portlight frames and lenses; handholds in all the right places; and so on. By reading, learning from friends, and looking at as many boats as possible (look behind backrests and under floorboards), you'll slowly begin to recognize the difference between poor quality and good quality. Although there are exceptions and acceptable compromises,

in general, quality costs more. Aside from the semi-custom builders like Hinckley Yachts, Morris Yachts, and Alden, among U.S.-series-produced boats I like Sabre, Valiant, and Tartan. Next I'd list Cabo Rico and Caliber. This list is hardly definitive, but it gives you some idea as to where my prejudices lie. Overseas builders I admire include Nautor's Swan, Ta Shing, and Hallberg-Rassy. (See Appendix C for more boats and thoughts about good, used production boats.)

## FURTHER READING

*Best Boats to Build or Buy.* Ferenc Máté. West Vancouver, British Columbia: Albatross, 1982.

*Boatbuilding with Aluminum.* Stephen F. Pollard. Camden, Maine: International Marine, 1993.

*Choice Yacht Designs.* Richard Henderson. Camden, Maine: International Marine, 1979.

*Desirable and Undesirable Characteristics of Offshore Yachts.* Technical Committee of the Cruising Club of America, edited by John Rousmaniere. New York: Norton, 1987.

*Fiberglass Boat Survey Manual.* Arthur Edmunds. Enola, Pennsylvania: Bristol Fashion Publications, 1998.

*The Ocean Sailing Yacht.* Vols. 1 and 2. Donald Street. New York: Norton, 1973–1978.

*Offshore Sailing: 200 Essential Passagemaking Tips.* Bill Seifert with Daniel Spurr. Camden, Maine: International Marine, 2002.

*The Sailing Yacht: How It Developed, How It Works.* Juan Baader. Translated from the German by James and Ingeborg Moore. New York: Norton, 1965.

*Seaworthiness: The Forgotten Factor.* Rev. ed. C. A. Marchaj. London: Adlard Coles, 1996; St. Michaels, Maryland: Tiller, 1996.

*Skene's Elements of Yacht Design.* 8th ed. completely revised and updated by Francis S. Kinney. Norman L. Skene. New York: Dodd, Mead, 1973.

*Steel Away: A Guidebook to the World of Steel Sailboats.* LeCain W. Smith and Sheila Moir. Port Townsend, Washington: Windrose Productions, 1986.

*Ted Brewer Explains Sailboat Design.* Ted Brewer. Camden, Maine: International Marine, 1985.

*Understanding the New Sailing Technology: A Basic Guide for Sailors.* Sven Donaldson. New York: Putnam's, 1990.

*The World's Best Sailboats.* Vol. 1. Ferenc Máté. West Vancouver, British Columbia: Albatross, 2001.

*The World's Best Sailboats.* Vol. 2. Ferenc Máté. New York: Norton, 2003.

*Yacht Design Explained: A Sailor's Guide to the Principles and Practice of Design.* Steve Killing and Douglas Hunter. New York: Norton, 1998.

Some of the books listed here and at the ends of subsequent chapters may be out of print. Consider a library, a used-book store, or the Internet.

# STRENGTHENING MAJOR STRUCTURAL COMPONENTS

*O*ndine, a well-known maxi ocean racer of the 1980s, was built in aluminum of plating that wasn't thick enough to withstand the slamming loads induced by the seas. Before long, the plating buckled inward between the frames. Filler compound was used several times to fair the hull, but ultimately it was necessary to replate major portions of the hull. The yard bill, of course, was astronomical, suggesting that even good designers are not infallible. (And perhaps it wasn't even the designer's fault, but the person who did the engineering, and today they often are not one and the same.) More recently, an all-aluminum Open Class 60 built for the BOC Challenge (now the Around Alone) also suffered buckled plating and structural damage. In the quest for speed or a good rating, shortcuts are calculated risks willingly undertaken. An easy way to increase speed is to reduce weight, but often at the expense of strength. But the cruising sailor, whose only interest is safety, wants only the strongest boat his or her means allow.

## IDENTIFYING WEAK AREAS

The most certain way to determine whether a hull or deck is weak is simple observation. Eric Goetz, a boatbuilder in Bristol, Rhode Island, and a protégé of the Gougeon Brothers, first specialized in cold-molded wood boats and now composites. He's built a lot of exotic boats, including several IACC (International America's Cup Class) boats. Goetz once told me that he tests the decks of his boats by having his heaviest employee jump on the deck. If it deflects (oilcans), he adds deck beams until it stops.

Naval architect Roger Marshall says that a boat built in this manner will be overbuilt, because a deck that deflects may indeed be strong enough to withstand the normal loads imposed by sailing. Repeated oilcanning, however, may eventually lead to failure of the fiberglass laminate or

other construction material due to fatigue. Framing to eliminate all deflection means the boat will be strong enough to withstand the slam-loading of dropping off a wave, as well as be unlikely to develop stress fractures from fatigue. And it also will give the crew that subtle confidence of knowing that the surface beneath their feet is as firm and rigid as the Earth they walk on.

Observing the deflection of hull panels is trickier. Pounding on the side of the hull with your fist is a bit like kicking the tires of a used car. A panel that deflects with the push of a hand *may* in fact be quite strong. But for my boat, I like to know that everything will stay in place as much as possible. A boat that works excessively at some point will begin to show the effects of fatigue: cracked gelcoat, separation of the bulkheads from the tabbing that bonds them to the hull, loose fittings, and doors that won't close.

Of course, a daysail in light winds won't show the problems as readily as a hard beat into heavy seas. But if you've sailed your boat in rough conditions and haven't experienced problems, then perhaps it is strong enough. Compare your boat's scantlings with those recommended by established authorities such as Lloyds of London. Figures 1-24 and 1-25 give an idea of what minimum hull thicknesses to expect for a given size fiberglass boat. Consult Herreshoff's and Nevins' rules for wood boat scantlings. *Skene's Elements of Yacht Design* (see Further Reading at the end of Chapter 1) includes these, plus Wyland's aluminum scantlings. Finally a marine surveyor can help you be more certain of your hull's integrity.

In light of the information available today regarding osmotic blistering, delamination, and the breakdown of the interface between resin and fibers, it is probably unwise for the amateur to consider fiberglass as a suitable material for home building. Early in the history of fiberglass construction, before such failures were observed and documented, this wasn't the case at all; indeed, various home construction products and manuals touted the advantages of fiberglass. Now we know that if a fiberglass hull is to have a long life span, it must be constructed in a humidity-controlled environment; the resin must be carefully metered to prevent a "resin rich" or "resin poor" laminate; the amount of catalyst must be carefully metered, too; and the curing rates of each laminate must be closely observed to ensure good adhesion.

Nevertheless, the amateur can work successfully with fiberglass, both in making repairs and reinforcing the existing structure. First, such work isn't, in most cases, structurally critical, and second, interior and on-deck work isn't subject to constant immersion in water as is the hull exterior.

## A Cost-Benefit Decision

The strength of a hull-deck structure is derived from several factors: the strength (tensile, impact, compressive, etc.) of the skin; building material; hull shape; size; and the reinforcing network of transverse and longitudinal stringers, bulkheads, and attached furniture. With fiberglass boats, it is generally easier to add a bulkhead, knee, hull stiffener, or deck beam than to add fiberglass laminations to a hull that is too thin or improperly laid up. I am tempted to say that if a hull is inadequately built, you might be better off buying a different boat than attempting any major strengthening. But often circumstances won't allow purchasing a different boat, or the boat meets all the owner's requirements save this one problem.

## GLASS FIBERS

Before launching into identifying structural weaknesses and their remedies, you should have a basic familiarity with the different types of fiberglass fabrics and resins used in boatbuilding. You should have some experience performing minor fiberglass repairs—such as patching a hole in the dinghy—before attempting the larger jobs suggested in this chapter. Also take a look at the books listed at the end of this chapter, especially Allan Vaitses' *The Fiberglass Boat Repair Manual* and Ken Hankinson's *Fiberglass Boatbuilding for Amateurs*. They are excellent primers on working with fiberglass.

There are three basic types of glass fibers commonly used by boatbuilders (Figure 2-1). Each has unique properties that make it better for some jobs, worse for others. Other more complex fabrics, such as biaxial and triaxial products, in which several layers of fibers are combined, running in different directions, are commonly used today by builders to better absorb known loads on a given part of the hull or deck. If you're interested, it wouldn't hurt to research such fabrics, but for our purposes, most jobs can be done with the basic three, mostly mat.

## Cloth

Fiberglass cloth is a closely woven fabric available in weights ranging from 2 to 30-plus ounces a square yard (68 to 1,017 $g/m^2$). Ten-ounce cloth (339 $g/m^2$) is one of the most frequently used weights in boatbuilding and is the one most often recommended for the various projects described in this book.

Compared to the other fabrics—woven roving and mat—cloth possesses the greatest strength, yet is the thinnest. It requires less resin to wet out, so is not as stiff as the others, nor as watertight. The ratio of glass fiber to resin is about 50-50. Cloth is frequently used as a sheathing or finishing layer in a laminate because it gives a fairly smooth surface after the resin has cured. However, it is seldom used in hull laminates or in major structural members. It is available in widths from about 38 to 60 inches (0.97 m to 1.5 m) or in rolls of tape in widths from about 1 to 12 inches (25 mm to 270 mm). The tape comes with selvaged edges to prevent unraveling, which is a good thing because cloth is the most expensive of the three kinds of fabric.

## Woven Roving

Woven roving is a thick, loosely woven fabric available in weights ranging from about 14 to 36 ounces a yard (475 to 1,220 $g/m^2$), though 24-ounce (814 $g/m^2$) woven roving is the weight most commonly used in the industry. Because of its higher fiber content, woven roving has more tensile strength than mat, but less than cloth. Because of its loose weave, it does not leave a very smooth finished surface. It is usually sandwiched between layers of mat in building up a laminate. The ratio of glass fiber to resin is about 45:55.

## Mat

Mat consists of chopped strands of glass fiber about ¾ to 1½ inches (19 mm to 38 mm) long. These are laid down in a random pattern that

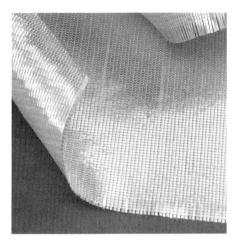

biaxial—fibers are perpendicular to one another

double bias—fibers are 45° in each direction from vertical

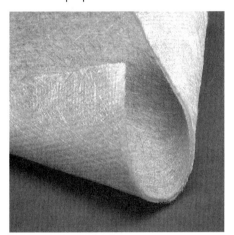

molding mat—nonwoven fabric with a synthetic core
stitch-bonded to chopped strand mat

quadaxial—fibers are oriented 0°, 45°, 90°, 45°

unidirectional woven—fibers run either 0° or 90°

woven roving—heavy, woven fabric that quickly adds
bulk to laminate

**FIGURE 2-1.** In the early days of fiberglass boatbuilding, the most commonly used types of fabric were chopped strand mat, cloth, and woven roving. For simple repairs, you'll still find these in chandleries and hardware stores. However, there have been many advances made in the weaving of new fabrics. Some orient fibers in specific directions to better carry the loads on that part of the hull, deck, or other structure. Others combine two different types, say mat and directional fibers. The fabrics shown here are the mainstays of modern boatbuilding. (Owens Corning)

gives omnidirectional strength. Typical weights range from ¾ to 3 ounces a square foot (229 to 915 $g/m^2$). One and a half and 2-ounce (457 to 610 $g/m^2$) weights are commonly used in the industry. Mat is the least expensive of the three fabrics and takes the most resin to wet out, thereby also making it the most waterproof. The ratio of glass fiber to resin is about 30:70. This means that mat is a weaker laminate than cloth or woven roving—though it does have good bonding characteristics. In a laminate, mat builds up thickness quickly, thereby reducing the number of layers of other fabric required—and labor costs.

### High-Tech Fibers

Conventionally built boats are still constructed of low-cost E-glass (electrical glass) mat and woven rovings. But the trend toward higher performance and lower weight has spurred the development of many new fiber materials that are also stronger, and of course, more expensive.

S glass (structural glass) is extruded in finer strands and is about 30% stronger. Kevlar and carbon fiber weaves are stronger still in some respects. Kevlar doesn't have good compressive strength, and it can have an adhesion problem with some types of resins. Carbon fiber is an acrylic that is stronger and stiffer than S glass, but it doesn't withstand impact well. It's used commonly now for spars—masts, booms, and spinnaker poles—and some builders are also using it for rudderstocks, where, like spars, it can be wound on a mandrel and cooked in an oven to cure the resin. Others are finding selective applications for carbon fiber in the reinforcing of stringers and other components where the loads are easily defined. Spectra, a trade name for Allied Chemical's blue-colored fiber, is actually a cross-linked polyethylene used mostly in sailmaking. It is quite strong, but like Kevlar there are problems yet to be worked out to make it adhere well with conventional resins.

Many of the above fibers are now available in unidirectional rovings, in which the fibers are laid down parallel and held in place by glue or stitching. They are particularly useful when the loads on a given panel are known to run in one particular direction. Biaxial and triaxial fabrics are simply two or three plies of unidirectional fibers laid on top of one another at calculated angles.

The key word in modern boatbuilding is "composite." Engineers are attempting to understand the dynamic that loads impose on a panel (as in the hull or deck or other structure) and to develop strong, lightweight combinations of fibers that maximize the advantage of each type of composite, in terms of tensile strength, point loading, and abrasion resistance. Today custom builders of multihulls and racing monohulls, and some high-tech production builders, are making increasing use of these materials. The heavy-displacement cruising boat is not the most sensible application for the new composite technology, but if you cruise a multihull or high-performance boat, this is the way of the future.

### Thicknesses of Glass Fiber Laminates

Figures 2-2 and 2-3 will help determine how many layers of a certain fabric it will take to achieve a certain thickness. Expect variations of up to 10% as a laminate is built up due to changes in the ratio of glass to resin and the differences in individual laminating techniques.

## RESINS

There are many different types of plastic thermosetting resins formulated for a wide variety of uses in industries today. While boatbuilders use only a few of these, it is important to know how they differ and to use the right resin for the job.

### Polyester

Most sailboat hulls are laid up with polyester resin, though a few companies, like Tartan Yachts, are switching to epoxy, partly for water resistance and better secondary bonding characteristics, and partly to meet stringent air quality standards. (Polyester resin gives off styrene fumes, a regulated, volatile organic compound with specific health effects. See the Health section later in this chapter.) An accelerator is usually already added during manufacturing, so all that you need to do is add a catalyst to start the chemical reaction that causes the individual molecules to start linking together in chains. This process is called polymerization and, incidentally, is the same principle behind the new generation of copolymer (two-part) topside paints, antifouling bottom paints, and even some varnishes.

A difference exists between laminating polyester resin and finishing resin. The former is air-inhibited, meaning it does not completely cure

| Laminate | Plies | Type of Construction Material | Thickness (in.) | % Glass Content | Tens. (psi) | Flex. Str. (psi) | Mod. × 10⁶ (psi) | Wgt. Lam./ sq. ft. |
|---|---|---|---|---|---|---|---|---|
| 1 | 2 | 2 oz. mat | 0.11 | 28.2 | 14,050 | 23,400 | 0.92 | 14.2 oz. |
| 2 | 1 | 10 oz. cloth | 0.100 | 28.4 | 10,500 | 18,550 | 0.89 | 10.9 oz. |
|  | 1 | 2 oz. mat |  |  |  |  |  |  |
| 3 | 1 | 10 oz. cloth | 0.110 | 32.0 | 13,850 | 22,100 | 1.10 | 12.8 oz. |
|  | 2 | 1.5 oz. mat |  |  |  |  |  |  |
| 4 | 1 | 10 oz. cloth | 0.130 | 30.1 | 14,950 | 21,400 | 0.95 | 16.9 oz. |
|  | 2 | 2 oz. mat |  |  |  |  |  |  |
| 5 | 1 | 10 oz. cloth | 0.180 | 32.0 | 13,200 | 18,750 | 0.92 | 22.2 oz. |
|  | 3 | 2 oz. mat |  |  |  |  |  |  |
| 6 | 1 | 10 oz. cloth | 0.120 | 24.9 | 9,090 | 37,600 | 1.47 | 14.9 oz. |
|  | 1 | 1.5 oz. mat |  |  |  |  |  |  |
|  | 1 | 10 oz. cloth |  |  |  |  |  |  |
| 7 | 1 | 10 oz. cloth | 0.180 | 22.6 | 10,500 | 28,400 | 1.20 | 23.0 oz. |
|  | 2 | 1.5 oz. mat |  |  |  |  |  |  |
|  | 1 | 10 oz. cloth |  |  |  |  |  |  |
| 8 | 1 | 1½ oz. mat | 0.254 | 39.2 | 30,300 | 42,800 | 1.59 | 36.0 oz. |
|  | 3 | 2415 Fabmat |  |  |  |  |  |  |
| 9 | 1 | 10 oz. cloth | 0.092 | 42.5 | 18,500 | 28,500 | 0.78 | 11.7 oz. |
|  | 1 | 24 oz. WR |  |  |  |  |  |  |
|  | 1 | 10 oz. cloth |  |  |  |  |  |  |
| 10 | 1 | 10 oz. cloth | 0.125 | 38.3 | 17,050 | 22,850 | 1.25 | 14.0 oz. |
|  | 1 | 1.5 oz. mat |  |  |  |  |  |  |
|  | 1 | 24 oz. WR |  |  |  |  |  |  |
| 11 | 2 | 24 oz. WR | 0.080 | 52.7 | 38,950 | 44,900 | 1.85 | 9.5 oz. |
| 12 | 1 | 24 oz. WR | 0.100 | 53.2 | 29,000 | 45,900 | 2.20 | 13.2 oz. |
|  | 1 | 1.5 oz. mat |  |  |  |  |  |  |
|  | 1 | 24 oz. WR |  |  |  |  |  |  |
| 13 | 1 | 2 oz. mat | 0.125 | 36.0 | 11,500 | 23,000 | 0.73 | 16.4 oz. |
|  | 1 | 24 oz. WR |  |  |  |  |  |  |
|  | 1 | 10 oz. cloth |  |  |  |  |  |  |
| 14 | 1 | 1.5 oz. mat | 0.1294 | 47.0 | 22,200 | 41,800 | 1.90 | 16.6 oz. |
|  | 2 | 24 oz. WR |  |  |  |  |  |  |
| 15 | 1 | 1.5 oz. mat | 0.100 | 47.9 | 24,900 | 31,400 | 1.11 | 14.3 oz. |
|  | 1 | 24 oz. WR |  |  |  |  |  |  |
|  | 1 | 1.5 oz. mat |  |  |  |  |  |  |
|  | 1 | 10 oz. cloth |  |  |  |  |  |  |

*Courtesy Owens Corning*

**FIGURE 2-2.** Laminate Thicknesses

| Laminate Area | Solid Glass/Polyester | Foam Sandwich/Polyester | Foam Sandwich/Epoxy |
|---|---|---|---|
| Layer | Layer of | Layer of | Layer of |
| 1 | 1.5 oz. mat | 1.0 oz. mat | 11 oz. Kevlar-glass hybrid |
| 2 | 10 oz. glass cloth | 10 oz. cloth | CD 180 |
| 3 | DBM 1708 | CDM 1808 | DB 170 |
| 4 | CDM 2408 | DBM 1708 | Core |
| 5 | CDM 2408 | Core | DB 170 |
| 6 | CDM 2408 | DBM 1708 | CD 180 |
| 7 | CDM 2408 | CDM 1808 | |
| Total thickness | 0.416" | 1.288" | 1.141" |
| Weight | 3.057 lb./ft.$^2$ | 2.61 lb./ft.$^2$ | 1.703 lb./ft.$^2$ |

Notes:

1. Fabrics indicated are by Knytex/Hexcell and may be replaced with equivalent.
2. CD 180 designates a 0° and 90° knitted E-glass.
3. CDM 2408 designates 0° and 90° knitted E-glass with 8 oz./yd.$^2$ mat.
4. DB 170 designates a ±45° knitted E-glass.
5. DBM 2408 designates 45° and 45° knitted E-glass with 8 oz./yd.$^2$ mat.
6. Layers progress from 1 outboard to 7 inboard.

Prepared by Ben Souquet at Robert Perry Yacht Designs

**FIGURE 2-3.** Typical Topside Laminate Comparison for 52-Foot Cruising Sailboat

when in contact with air. These resins tend to remain tacky, thus forming better bonds when additional layers of glass fibers are added to the laminate. Finishing resin is non-air-inhibited, meaning it does cure in air. This is achieved by adding a wax to the resin, which rises to the surface and seals the resin from the air. The wax must be removed before attempting any additional bonding or painting. Boatbuilders use laminating resin for all but the last layer, which is laid on with finishing resin. There are, however, resins that have been specially formulated to perform both functions.

Most polyester resins are formulated to cure between 70° and 80°F (21° to 27°C) with the specified amount of catalyst (methyl ethyl ketone peroxide—MEKP) added. It is possible to work at temperatures as low as 60°F (16°C) and as high as 100°F (38°C) by using more or less catalyst. Never work in direct sunlight as this causes the resin to cure too rapidly. Practice is necessary to correctly gauge the right amount of catalyst to be added to the resin. It is best to keep the resin spread out in a shallow tray since the thicker it is, the more heat generated and the greater the danger of it going off too quickly. Also, *never* mix the accelerator (if your resin hasn't already had it added) with MEKP—*the combination is explosive!*

Acetone is the chemical solvent generally used for cleaning brushes and tools, but it can't dissolve resin that's hardened. If you need to thin the resin, use styrene, not acetone, as the latter inhibits curing. Acetone is highly flammable, so don't smoke or introduce open flames in its vicinity.

## Epoxy

Like polyester resin, epoxy requires an outside agent to produce the exothermic reaction necessary to produce a cure. Instead of a catalyst, however, a hardener is used; the mixing ratios are very different from those used for polyester and its catalyst. The Gougeon Brothers' WEST System brand epoxy and System Three epoxy resin are two of the best known of this type in the aftermarket marine industry and are used for both laminating and finishing.

Epoxy resin is considerably more expensive than polyester. It is used most often for repair jobs or when bonding glass fibers to wood and metal because of its better bonding properties. It is compatible with polyester resin and can be laminated on top of existing polyester surfaces. Polyester can be laminated over epoxy as well, but the two never should be used when both are wet. Some epoxies, however, leave amine acids on the surface after curing, so wipe the surface with soap and water before applying paint or polyester resin. It is probably best to stick with epoxy if that's what you started with. Catalyzed epoxy resin eventually will go off in a wide range of temperatures; 70°F is close to ideal. It is best to purchase the solvent marketed by the company formulating the resin.

### Vinylester

Research into the causes of osmotic blistering has revealed that all resins are to some small extent water permeable. Vinylester is superior to polyester in creating a barrier against the ingress of moisture. A growing number of builders are using vinylester for at least the first hull lamination or more after the gelcoat. Because of its higher cost, few builders lay up the entire hull skin with vinylester. Except for underwater hull repairs, the average boatowner has little use for vinylester resin.

## CORE MATERIALS

Most boatbuilders today are using core materials in their hulls to reduce weight, cut down on the high cost of solid fiberglass and to improve panel stiffness. Airex and Klegecell polyvinyl chloride (PVC) foams and Contourkore end-grain balsa are commonly used materials (Figure 2-4). In addition to the above-mentioned properties, they also provide thermal and acoustical insulation. Plywood is still seen in deck sandwiches. It has better compressive strength than most other cores, an important characteristic when through-bolting

FIGURE 2-4. Typical core materials are—from top to bottom—Airex, Contourkore end-grain balsa, and Klegecell.

cleats, fairleads and other fittings. However, if water finds its way into the core it will quickly migrate through plywood, resulting in a rotten mess. This is why only the end-grain of balsa is used. Core materials are sometimes used in subassemblies, such as the sea hood described in Chapter 9.

## MOLD RELEASE AGENTS

Anytime a mold is used to fabricate a hull or subassembly, it is necessary to apply a coating to the mold that prevents the resin from sticking. Wax, petroleum jelly, and specially formulated parting agents all do the job. But purchasing a product specifically intended for this use gives the best results. Most suppliers of fiberglass fabrics and resins also sell a parting agent. The parting agent must be removed from the finished hull before painting or the application of other coatings.

## DISTRIBUTING STRESS

As you read through the projects in this book, it is suggested that you vary the width and length of the individual layers of cloth and mat. There are several reasons for this. By beginning with small pieces, each subsequent layer is placed in direct contact with the bonding surface, ensuring a better bond (Figure 2-5). This technique also prevents

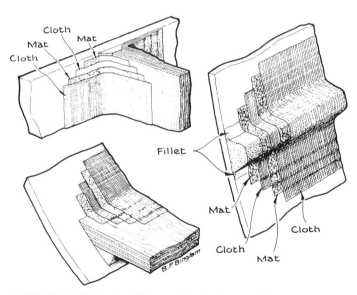

FIGURE 2-5. When building up a laminate over a beam, the first layer should be mat, and it should overlap the surface on each side by about 4 inches, if possible. Succeeding layers of cloth, alternated with mat, should be about ¾ to 1 inch (19 mm to 25 mm) wider than the last.

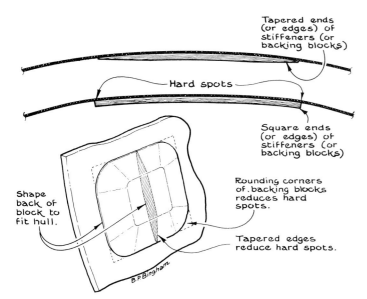

**FIGURE 2-6.** Hard spots in the hull or other panel, which can cause stress cracking, can be avoided by tapering the ends of hull stiffening beams and rounding the corner of backing blocks.

stress at the edge of the laminate. Some repairers, however, recommend applying the largest layer first, and then adding successively smaller layers. This is generally done for cosmetic reasons. It would be interesting to prepare two test panels using each of these methods, then load to destruction to see where the fabrics and substrate fail. However, what is probably more important than choosing between these two methods is prepping the bonding surfaces for the best possible adhesion.

Similarly, when bonding a structural member or piece of furniture to a fiberglass surface, distribute the loads on that member over as much surface area as possible. Tapering the ends of hull stiffeners and rounding the corners of backing blocks will distribute stress loadings better than squared ends that create hard spots or stress risers (Figure 2-6).

## HEALTH

The chemicals used in resins, hardeners, and catalysts can be dangerous. They never should be swallowed or allowed to touch the eyes. Some persons develop skin irritations from contact with epoxy resins, so rubber surgical gloves are advisable.

During the chemical resin-curing reaction, fumes are given off that are dangerous to breathe. Working outdoors is generally safe. But if you're

working in the basement or inside the boat, wear a respirator and use exhaust fans to remove as much of the fumes as possible, and don't hesitate to leave the work area if you begin to experience headache, nausea, fatigue, discomfort of the eyes, or other unpleasant sensations. Be sure to read product labels and abide by all precautions and directions. Styrene fumes given off by polyester resin can cause brain damage and can even kill. The same is true of linear polyurethane paints.

If proper safety precautions are observed, however, there is no reason why the amateur builder or handyman cannot work successfully with fiberglass. It is messy, but it does possess some truly remarkable properties that make it quite suitable for modern boatbuilding and repair.

## DECK REINFORCEMENTS

I once owned a 19-foot (5.8 m) English twin-keel sloop that I sailed all over the Great Lakes. She was over-rigged (large-diameter twin backstays, upper and double lower shrouds), had a bridge deck (unusual on a small boat), and had a beautiful and massive outboard rudder fashioned out of solid mahogany. The hull was perhaps a ¼-inch (6 mm) thick, and the round shape made it rigid enough. But there was no deck or cockpit sole core to provide stiffening. The result was a disconcerting "sproing!" whenever someone stood on them. Instead of using a core, the builders had laminated layers of fiberglass mat over ½ inch (12 mm) wood moldings under the deck. This turned out to be insufficient, as one step on the foredeck quickly demonstrated. Regardless of how strong the deck actually is, if it doesn't *feel* strong, then corrective measures are in order. Crowned decks are stronger than flat decks because there is better distribution of loads. This is an important principle to remember in building any large, load-bearing surface (Figure 2-7). There are several ways to stiffen an oilcanning fiberglass deck. The most effective method would be to glass in a core material to the underside of the deck. The trick is to hold everything in place overhead until it cures. One person I know used wax-coated pieces of thin plywood held up against the overhead with spring-loaded curtain tension rods. An easier way, despite my criticisms of the twin-keeler above, is to glass in one or more athwartship deck beams (Figure 2-8). Beams may be of wood sawn to shape and length and then covered with fiberglass mat. A stronger beam would be to laminate thin

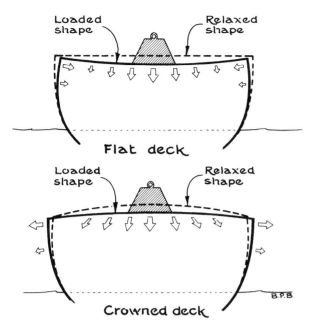

**FIGURE 2-7.** A boat with crowned deck and cabin is stronger, all other factors being equal, than one with flat decks, because it distributes loads over a greater area.

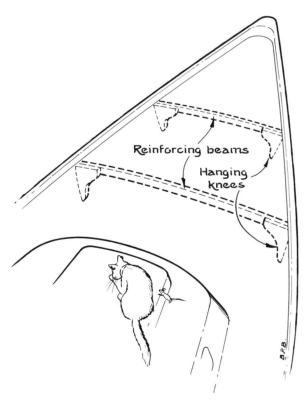

**FIGURE 2-8.** An internal deck beam can be glassed in under the foredeck area and fastened at each end to knees that are also glassed to the hull. Furniture, such as these V-berths, can be integral structural members, especially if they are glassed to the hull.

wood veneers over a form. Fiberglass "beams" or hat sections can be laminated with mat, woven roving, or cloth laid up over wedge-shaped foam; the foam isn't structural, but functions purely as a form.

## Rotten to the Core

A common problem with old fiberglass boats is rotten and delaminated deck coring. End-grain balsa, the most common wooden core material, does a fairly good job of preventing the migration of moisture beyond the immediate area of entry. Small saturated areas are not structurally dangerous, but even small amounts of moisture can cause the fiberglass skin on either side to separate from the coring, thus potentially destroying the I-beam stiffening characteristic of the sandwich.

Sharp point loads, such as dropping a heavy weight on the deck, may also cause delamination. Baltek's AL-600 sealed end-grain balsa (www.baltek.com) is probably superior to conventional Contourkore in preventing delamination.

Small problem areas are typically repaired by drilling holes through the top skin and injecting epoxy resin into the area. When large sections of the deck coring are rotten or delaminating, the only long-lasting solution is to grind away one skin, remove and replace the core material, then laminate a new skin on top. Allan Vaitses gives a good discussion of the difficulties of this process in his book, *The Fiberglass Boat Repair Manual*. On reading it, you will probably come away thinking (1) I should strip my deck of all hardware and rebed everything! and (2) if ever I am faced with replacing an entire deck, I will either sell the boat or shoot myself!

## Making a Deck Beam

To begin, find the location of greatest flex in the deck; it probably will be in the center of the largest unsupported area. The foredeck is a likely place, because often it is built without coring or reinforcing bulkheads.

Fashion a pair of hardwood knees (if you'd like to leave part of the beam exposed) or plywood knees (if you intend to cover them entirely) about 3/4 to 1 inch (19 mm to 25 mm) thick. Cut the shape with a band saw or, if it is thin enough, with a heavy-duty saber saw. Sand to an attractive finish. Locate them opposite one another at the hull-deck joint and sand the hull surface where it will be bonded. Be sure to remove all paint and dirt. A final wipe with acetone will get the surface really clean.

Mix some epoxy putty or, better yet, epoxy resin mixed with ¼-inch (6 mm) chopped strand (cut up small pieces of mat to make your own chopped strand). This is popularly called *mush*. Use a putty knife to spread it between the knee and hull and deck to form a primary bond and to seal the wood from moisture.

With the knee held in place, apply more mush where the hull and wood meet. Chandleries sell yellow plastic spreaders, some with rounded corners, for making nicely radiused fillets. Or, cut a piece of furring strip or a sail batten and round one end. Pull the stick across the mush to form the fillet (Figure 2-9). You can also use a soda bottle bottom. Use your wet finger to smooth small ridges you can't get flat with the stick. Epoxy is hard to sand, so the smoother you get it now, the easier it will be to finish later.

The Gougeon Brothers (www.westsystem.com) suggest making fillets by mixing WEST System 105 resin and WEST System 406 Colloidal Silica for a high-density, high-strength bond. But when the strength of the fillet vastly exceeds the strength of the wood fiber, a combination of 406 Colloidal Silica and 409 Microspheres is suggested for a lower-density fillet. In either case, the fibers thicken the resin and prevent sagging. You can switch to polyester resin for wetting out the fiberglass or stay with the epoxy; I favor the latter for its better adhesion to old polyester. Despite its higher price, you won't be using that much.

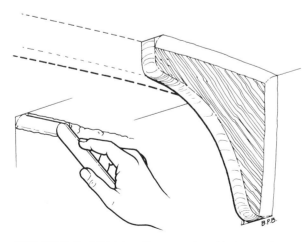

FIGURE 2-9. A fillet functions as a bond between two surfaces. When radiused, it permits fiberglass mat and cloth to conform easier to the bend. A bottle, or batten rounded at one end, or a tongue depressor, forms a nice curve.

A fillet not only provides a basic bond between the knee and hull but also forms a gentle curve to which the fiberglass fabric can conform more easily. This reduces stress cracking. Without a fillet, fiberglass tends to pop out of right-angle corners, thereby reducing strength and producing air pockets.

Once the epoxy fillet has cured, cut short "tabs" of mat, about 3 inches by 5 inches (76 mm by 127 mm). Be sure that both surfaces have been sanded and wiped with a cleaner compatible with your resin. Coat the hull with resin where the tabs go, then lay the tabs in place and dab on more resin until you're satisfied it is thoroughly wetted out. Wetting out means dabbing the mat with catalyzed resin until all whiteness has disappeared from the fibers. The resin will run, so be careful not to put on more than the mat can hold.

Once the resin has cured or "kicked," and the knee is securely in place, you're ready to apply a layer of mat over the entire joint.

Cut alternate strips of 1½-ounce (457 g/m²) mat and 24-ounce (814 g/m²) woven roving (or 10-ounce/339 g/m² cloth) to the length of the joint and in varied widths. Where possible, overlap the knee and hull about 4 inches (102 mm). The first layer should be the narrowest, with each subsequent layer about ¾ to 1 inch (19 mm to 25 mm) wider (Figure 2-5 again). Don't stack layers of the same width on top of each other.

If the curve of the hull makes the strip bunch up, cut slits or darts (triangle shapes) halfway into the mat (Figure 2-10) as close together as is necessary to allow the mat to lie flat on both surfaces.

Wet out the strips of mat on a piece of Formica or other nonabsorbent material (you can use cardboard but will have more wastage; Figure 2-11). Brush a coating of resin on the hull, too, before laying on the mat. This will help ensure a good bond and minimize the amount of resin needed to wet out the mat. Once the mat is wetted out in place, stop. Excessive brushing will only bunch up the fibers and create uneven thicknesses.

Add a wider, second layer of woven roving while the first layer of mat is still wet. Continue alternating mat and woven roving or cloth until you achieve a thickness equal to about half the thickness of the hull. Figure 2-2 will help you determine how many layers are necessary.

When the resin cures, the knee will be a strong structural member. The fiberglass laminate may not look like much, but resin and fiber together

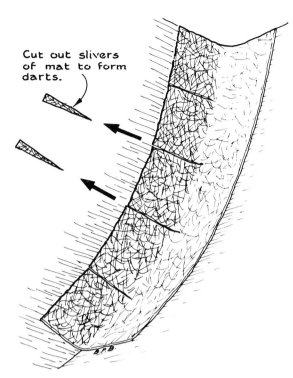

**FIGURE 2-10.** When applying mat or cloth to a curved surface, it usually is necessary to cut small slits or darts every few inches so the material won't buckle.

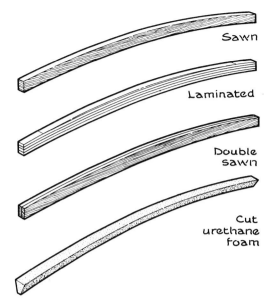

**FIGURE 2-12.** The deck beam can be (from top to bottom) cut from solid hardwood, laminated from thin veneers of wood, made from sawn planks glued together, or fashioned out of shaped blocks of foam.

are incredibly strong—after all, it's the same stuff as your hull.

Next, cut a piece of wood to form a beam between the two knees (refer back to Figure 2-8). You can use an attractive hardwood finished without a fiberglass covering, but it won't be as strong as a beam glassed to the deck. And, if it's covered with glass, the beam might as well be made of cheaper softwood. There are several ways to make the beam (Figure 2-12):

**A.** Cutting from a single piece of wood.
**B.** Laminating and bending thin veneers of wood over a form.
**C.** Gluing sawn planks together.
**D.** Cutting strips of urethane foam.

A laminated beam is stronger than a solid one, but *if* the beam is to be glassed over, the fiberglass cloth and resin will do most of the work. See Figure 2-13 for final beam thickness according to the size of boat.

### Sawn Beams

To draw the cutline for a single sawn piece, hold the beam up as high as you can, flat against the knees on either side. Using a compass with a pencil in one end, put the metal end against the deck. Put the pencil against the beam. Pull the compass

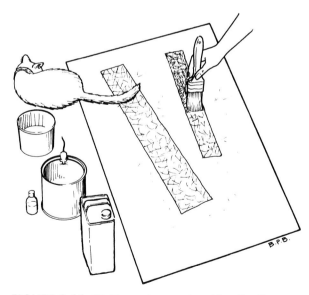

**FIGURE 2-11.** *Wetting out* means brushing the fiberglass with catalyzed resin until all the fibers are saturated and no longer white. Brush out bubbles, but avoid excessive brushing, which causes the fiberglass to come apart.

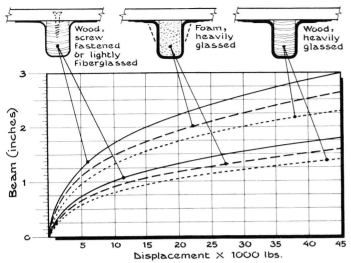

**FIGURE 2-13.** Beam thicknesses increase with the size of boat, as this graph illustrates. Use it as a guide. The upper line gives beam height; the lower, width.

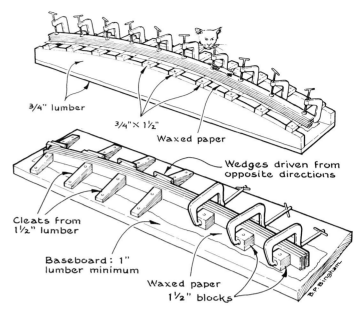

**FIGURE 2-14.** Use C-clamps to bend thin stock over a form or jig and a strong glue or epoxy resin to laminate the pieces together.

across the deck, keeping the compass angle uniform so that the pencil scribes a line on the wood as you go. See Figure 9-28 for a clearer understanding of this technique.

### Glued Beams

If laminating the beam by gluing several 1-inch (25 mm) planks together, use the first plank as a pattern to cut several more.

Glue all the pieces together with epoxy glue or resin or a good waterproof glue such as resorcinol. Clamp with C-clamps, inserting small pieces of wood in between the clamp and beam to help distribute the pressure of the clamp over a greater surface area. When the glue has cured, sand off the glue that has oozed from between the planks. Coating the entire beam with a finishing resin will prevent moisture from rotting or expanding the wood. Also, knock off the sharp edges and corners of the beam with a rasp or router so the fiberglass mat will conform better.

### Laminated Beams

To laminate a beam from thin (⅛-inch/3 mm) veneers, make a mold from several pieces of cheap fir, cut to the shape of the deck (use a compass as described earlier), then nail Masonite or Formica over the tops for a fair curve (Figure 2-14). Or, if

the topside deck directly above where you want to install the beam has a fair curve and is unobstructed by deck gear, you can use it as a laminating form. Cover the deck with a thin sheet of plastic or Mylar so resin doesn't stick to it.

Any wood laminated over a form will experience some springback when released. The amount of springback is difficult to calculate accurately, but the greater the bend, the greater the springback. With experience, a builder can compensate by slightly overbending the laminate, so that the springback will return the member to the desired shape. Alternatively, the member can be planed to shape after the resin is well cured, and all springback finished. For this reason, and because of the difficulty in accurately lofting the lines, it is easier to laminate in situ (in place) than over a form.

### Fastening Beam to Knees

Now, glue the beam to the knees with epoxy; a few nails or screws will hold it in place until the glue cures. You can also use bronze or stainless steel bolts, but they won't really add much strength if you plan to glass over the beam.

### Glassing in the Beam

Form fillets between the beam and deck with mush as described previously. When they've cured, glass over the entire beam. Alternate layers of the same weight mat and woven roving used for the knees, and to the same thickness. To prevent sagging, you may need to add one layer at a time. A layer of cloth will give a nicer finished appearance than mat or woven roving. After it has cured for a few days, sand and paint.

When you consider the surface area of the fiberglass bond, you'll understand why it is stronger than a beam merely bolted to knees and screwed to the deck.

### Foam Beams

Long strips of urethane foam cut in long wedge shapes make for very adequate forms over which you can lay alternate layers of mat and woven roving. The wedge shape gives a better bonding angle for the mat and woven roving to conform to. The foam almost can be considered sacrificial as the covering laminate will carry nearly all the loads. Airex conforms easily to almost any shape; stiffer foam may have to be cut with kerfs to make it lie flush against the deck. The foam can be held in place with a quick-setting glue, but test the compatibility of the glue on a small piece of foam first—some glues will dissolve the foam. The same lamination schedule used for wood beams can be used for foam, too.

### Wood Decks

Wood decks generally are made of planks, plywood covered with canvas, or plywood covered with a single or double layer of fiberglass cloth.

If a wood deck flexes when walked on, it is less likely to be a problem with the original construction than it is with rotting deck beams or loose fastenings. In either case, it is necessary to examine the existing deck beams closely and determine whether they should be left in place and new beams added, or if they should be removed altogether, and new beams installed in their place. Needless to say, if a beam shows any sign of rot, it should be removed. And if one beam is rotten, suspect all others.

In most types of construction, the beams will be supported on either side by shelves. It may be necessary to remove several deck planks to gain access to where the deck beam and shelf join (Figure 2-15). Already you can see you've got a big job on your hands. If deck planking must be removed, the glass or canvas covering the deck

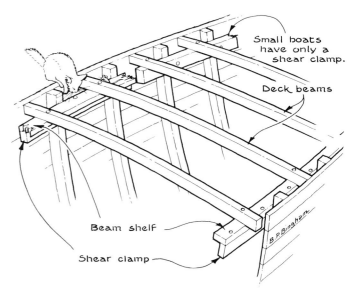

**FIGURE 2-15.** Deck beams are attached at the ends to shelves running beneath the decks. Depending on the configuration, it may be necessary to remove the outer deck plank to remove a rotted beam.

first be torn away to expose the fastenings. Hopefully, only one or two planks at the sides of the deck must be removed.

The old deck beam is most easily removed by sawing it in half. To avoid cutting into the deck, try springing the beam loose from the deck with a wedge. Then insert a thin material, such as Formica, against which the saw can cut without damaging the deck. If the beam has been screwed to the deck along its entire length, first remove the deck covering and take out those fastenings.

The new deck beam can be cut from well-seasoned oak or laminated from smaller thicknesses as described for fiberglass decks.

Unless the deck problem is an isolated one, which can be repaired in this manner, you may find it wise to remove all deck planking and install new beams everywhere. At the same time, you may decide to strengthen the hull-deck joint with hand-sawn knees or welded metal hanging knees (Figures 2-24, 25, 26 on pages 51 and 52).

Ripping out wood is often like opening Pandora's box—it exposes new problems such as rot more extensive than previously thought. You begin rationalizing additional repairs that are facilitated by preparations for the first job. What you end up with is a major restoration project, a season or more out of the water, and many hours of labor.

The alternative is a deteriorating boat of dubious strength.

### Steel and Aluminum Decks

An insufficiently stiffened metal deck is more easily repaired than wood or fiberglass. Unless corrosion is the culprit, the problem is either deck plating that is too thin, or beams spaced too far apart. Assuming you are a handy welder (which you ought to be if you own a metal boat), cutting new beams and welding them in place is largely a matter of copying the method of installation used during original construction. Leave the old beams unless they are corroded.

# HULL FLEX

Flexing of the hull, which is probably most common in the forward topside area, can be corrected in much the same manner as oilcanning decks, but without using knees or shelves. In fiberglass boats, this problem can be eliminated without wood altogether, if one chooses.

### Fiberglass Hulls

The four ways to strengthen fiberglass hulls are adding extra laminations (with or without coring), glassing in longitudinal stringers or ribs, adding partial bulkheads, and glassing in bilge floors. The correct remedy depends on the location and severity of hull flex.

### Extra Laminations

If you can clear a fairly large area of the hull of furniture and other impediments, it is possible to add extra laminations of fiberglass mat, cloth, and woven roving to the hull. This is an extreme measure to bolster a lightly built hull or one that simply wasn't intended to be sailed hard.

The techniques of sandwich construction can be applied here. Add a layer of a core material between any new laminations (Figure 2-16). Airex, Divinycell, and Klegecell foams, and Contourkore end-grain balsa core are all materials regularly used by boatbuilders in the layup of hulls. They decrease weight and increase stiffness. (And, because they are less expensive than fiberglass cloths and polyester resins, they help keep the original construction costs down.)

To reinforce a hull or deck in this manner, it is important that whatever you do to one side of

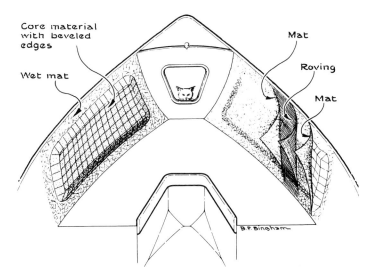

**FIGURE 2-16.** A core material such as Airex can be laminated to inside hull surfaces to increase stiffness. It should be bonded to both sides of the hull to prevent uneven loading.

the hull, you replicate on the opposite side. This is to prevent the unequal distribution of loads on the hull.

Inner liners will make it virtually impossible to add layers of matted cloth or employ core materials as stiffeners. Liners inhibit access to the hull, except in small areas such as through the locker lids underneath berths.

First, remove carpeting, vinyl, paint, or any other hull lining material. Once you're down to bare fiberglass, sand the hull with a coarse-grit paper, no more than #80, and then wash with acetone. Depending on how vertical the hull is, you may decide to apply only one or two laminations at a time, as they tend to sag. With or without a core, extend the reinforcement over as much of the panel as possible to avoid creating a hinge point (due to unequal skin thicknesses) that could cause cracking under load. Extending the laminate from the deck to the bilge is safer than reinforcing just part of the area.

When including core materials, lightly coat one side of the sheet (say ½-inch/12 mm Contourkore) with resin before sticking it against one or two still-wet layers of 1½-ounce (457 g/m²) mat already laid on the hull. (The mat will ensure a strong bond between the core and hull and make the core more watertight.) You may find it necessary to contrive some means to hold the foam or balsa in place until the resin kicks. When it has, finish the job with the last alternate layers of mat and cloth—perhaps one at a time to prevent sag.

See Chapter 9, under making a sea hood, for further details on working with core materials.

## Longitudinal Stiffeners and Ribs

Ribbed stiffeners running vertically tend to duplicate the job of bulkheads and floors. And because more of the loads on a sailboat tend to be longitudinal or diagonal anyway, longitudinal stiffeners generally give better results. Also, longitudinally placed stiffeners are less obtrusive and might be worked into some sort of cleat (brace) for shelving.

There are several ways to form this type of stiffener (Figure 2-17):

**A.** Garden hose

**B.** Plastic or metal pipe

**C.** Cardboard tube cut in half

**D.** Half-round softwood stock

**E.** Top hat sections made from wood or foam

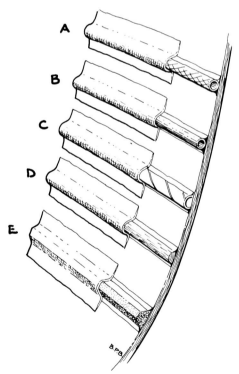

**FIGURE 2-17.** Longitudinal hull stiffeners can be fashioned from: garden hose (A), plastic or metal pipe (B), cardboard tube cut in half (C), half-round softwood stock (D), and top hat sections made with wood or foam (E). These function as forms, over which fiberglass mat and woven roving or cloth are laid.

You can preform top hat stiffeners outside the boat or make them in place using urethane foam or wood. They need not be continuous unless they are load bearing; then a 12:1 scarf is advisable (this will only be done with heavy wood stringers). Also, pad the wood with a thin strip of foam for this same reason. The American Bureau of Shipping recommends that the height of the stiffener be thirty times its skin thickness (a 7½-inch/191 mm tall stiffener should have a ¼-inch/6 mm skin thickness). Wedge shapes widen the base proportionate to the top and form better bonding angles. Fillets still may be necessary. Remove paint or any other covering, clean and abrade the surface with sandpaper, and wipe with acetone.

Secure the wood or foam in place using a compatible quick-setting epoxy glue until the layers of mat and woven roving are laid on. Covering the stringer with four alternating layers of 1½-ounce (457 g/m²) mat and 18-ounce (610 g/m²) woven roving should do the trick, though achieving a thickness equal to half the thickness of the hull remains a good rule of thumb.

Where possible, carry longitudinal stiffeners forward to the stem and join together. Often, however, bulkheads get in the way. Avoid abrupt ends in favor of tapering the stiffener at each end to prevent hard spots.

## Circle and Half-Circle Sections

Create forms for circle and half-circle sections using hose, tubing, pipe, or cardboard tubes cut in half and held in place with glue or duct tape. The bond is not critical, as once it has been glassed over the laminate will do the stiffening, not the form material. Again, sand the surface clean before work commences.

Coat the hull with resin on either side of the form, and coat the form itself. Then lay on precut strips of 1½-ounce (457 g/m²) mat and 18-ounce (610 g/m²) woven roving, overlapping the hull a minimum of 4 inches (102 mm). Increase the width of each successive layer by ¾ to 1 inch (19 mm to 25 mm). Consider using 10-ounce (339 g/m²) cloth for the final layer for a neater, smoother appearance. Sand lightly and paint to finish.

## Partial Bulkheads

If adding a bulkhead seems to be the answer (it couldn't hurt on a boat with an open interior), you get the added benefit of a new place to mount

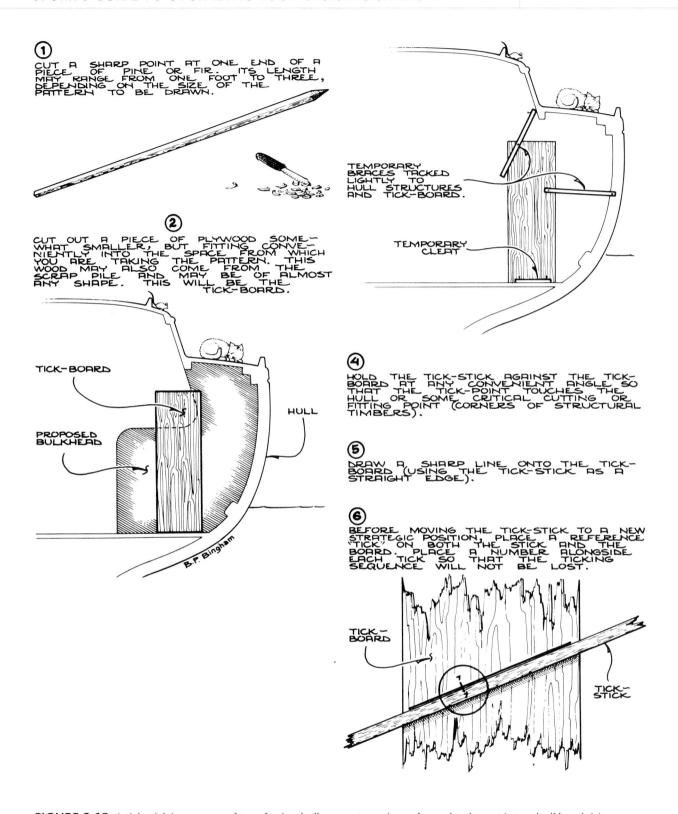

**①** CUT A SHARP POINT AT ONE END OF A PIECE OF PINE OR FIR. ITS LENGTH MAY RANGE FROM ONE FOOT TO THREE, DEPENDING ON THE SIZE OF THE PATTERN TO BE DRAWN.

**②** CUT OUT A PIECE OF PLYWOOD SOMEWHAT SMALLER, BUT FITTING CONVENIENTLY INTO THE SPACE FROM WHICH YOU ARE TAKING THE PATTERN. THIS WOOD MAY ALSO COME FROM THE SCRAP PILE AND MAY BE OF ALMOST ANY SHAPE. THIS WILL BE THE TICK-BOARD.

TICK-BOARD

PROPOSED BULKHEAD

HULL

B.F. Bingham

TEMPORARY BRACES TACKED LIGHTLY TO HULL STRUCTURES AND TICK-BOARD.

TEMPORARY CLEAT

**④** HOLD THE TICK-STICK AGAINST THE TICK-BOARD AT ANY CONVENIENT ANGLE SO THAT THE TICK-POINT TOUCHES THE HULL OR SOME CRITICAL CUTTING OR FITTING POINT (CORNERS OF STRUCTURAL TIMBERS).

**⑤** DRAW A SHARP LINE ONTO THE TICK-BOARD (USING THE TICK-STICK AS A STRAIGHT EDGE).

**⑥** BEFORE MOVING THE TICK-STICK TO A NEW STRATEGIC POSITION, PLACE A REFERENCE "TICK" ON BOTH THE STICK AND THE BOARD. PLACE A NUMBER ALONGSIDE EACH TICK SO THAT THE TICKING SEQUENCE WILL NOT BE LOST.

TICK-BOARD

TICK-STICK

**FIGURE 2-18.** A tick stick is one way of transferring hull curves to a piece of wood to be cut into a bulkhead. Move the point of the stick a few inches down the hull, and trace the end of the stick onto a piece of wood (not necessarily the bulkhead). Remove the wood and stick to the workshop, and lay the bulkhead wood next to the wood with the tracings on it. Place the stick over the tracings, and mark where the tip ends on the bulkhead. Connect all the dots, and you've re-created the hull line.

⑦ MOVE THE POINT OF THE STICK TO THE NEXT CRITICAL CUTTING POINT. DRAW A NEW LINE ON THE TICK-BOARD AND NUMBER THE STICK AND BOARD AGAIN.

⑧ CONTINUE MOVING THE STICK TO NEW POSITIONS, LINING AND TICKING AS YOU GO, UNTIL YOU HAVE TICKED OFF THE ENTIRE PERIMETER OF THE SHAPE TO BE TRANSFERRED.

# DRAWING THE PATTERN

⑨ IT'S BEST TO LAY OFF THE PATTERN ON MEAT WRAPPING PAPER SO THAT YOU CAN ADJUST ITS POSITION ATOP THE LUMBER LATER TO MINIMIZE WASTE.

LAY THE TICK-BOARD, FACE UP, ON TOP OF THE PAPER.

⑩ PLACE THE TICK-STICK ONTO THE TICK-BOARD SO THAT THE STICK ALIGNS WITH ITS ORIGINAL #1 POSITION (AS DICTATED BY THE LINE AND TICK DRAWN ON THE BOARD).

⑪ PLACE A DOT ONTO THE PAPER DIRECTLY BELOW THE POINT OF THE TICK-STICK.

⑫ MOVE THE TICK-STICK TO SUCCESSIVE POSITIONS ON THE BOARD, MAKING DOTS ON THE PAPER AT THE POINT OF THE STICK AS YOU GO, UNTIL ALL OF THE TICK REFERENCES HAVE BEEN USED.

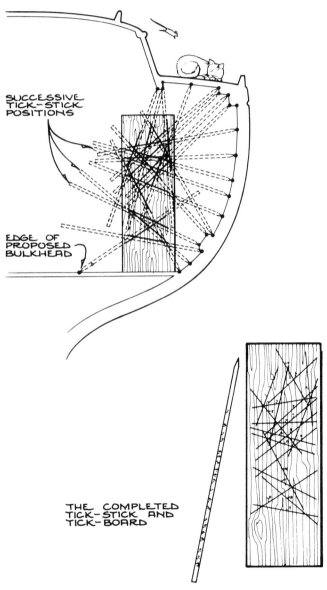

SUCCESSIVE TICK-STICK POSITIONS

EDGE OF PROPOSED BULKHEAD

THE COMPLETED TICK-STICK AND TICK-BOARD

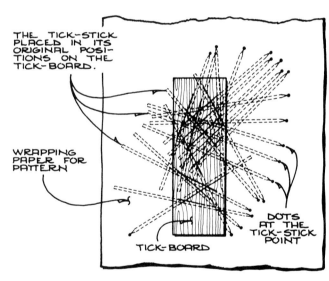

THE TICK-STICK PLACED IN ITS ORIGINAL POSITIONS ON THE TICK-BOARD.

WRAPPING PAPER FOR PATTERN

TICK-BOARD

DOTS AT THE TICK-STICK POINT

⑬ REMOVE THE BOARD FROM THE PAPER. NOW CONNECT THE DOTS USING A FLEXIBLE WOODEN OR PLASTIC BATTEN (OR STRAIGHT EDGE AS CIRCUMSTANCES DICTATE).

THE TICK-BOARD WILL BECOME CRISS-CROSSED WITH STRAIGHT LINES BEARING THE MEMORY OF THE ORIGINAL TICK-STICK POSITIONS. THE MORE TICKS YOU'VE MARKED, THE MORE ACCURATE THE PATTERN WILL BE.

**FIGURE 2-18.** (cont.)

⑭ REFERRING TO YOUR CONSTRUCTION DRAWING OR SKETCHES, DRAW ALL REMAINING DETAILS REQUIRED FOR CUTTING THE FINISHED PIECE ACCURATELY.

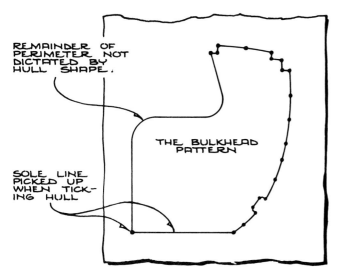

REMAINDER OF PERIMETER NOT DICTATED BY HULL SHAPE.

THE BULKHEAD PATTERN

SOLE LINE PICKED UP WHEN TICKING HULL

⑮ POSITION AND TRANSFER THE COMPLETED PATTERN ONTO YOUR LUMBER USING A TAILOR'S WHEEL. MEASURE AND NOTE ALL NECESSARY BEVELS, THEN START CUTTING.

**FIGURE 2-18.** (cont.)

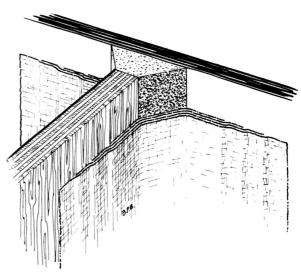

**FIGURE 2-19.** A strip of urethane foam can be cut the width of the bulkhead and used as a cushion between the bulkhead and the hull so as not to make a hard spot. Increasingly wider layers of mat are used to bond the hull. Cut the foam at a 45° angle to save the step of making a fillet.

lighting, instruments, or bookshelves. Adding a bulkhead rather than a hull or deck stiffening beam also has the advantage of tying together the hull, deck, and cabin floors.

A tick stick is the tool used to make a bulkhead pattern. Figure 2-18 (pages 46–48) shows how to use one to transfer hull lines to the piece of wood. (This accomplishes the same thing as the compass shown in Figure 9-28, and also described earlier in this chapter. However, because of hull/ cabin shapes and the size of full or even half bulkheads, it would be difficult to use a compass to transfer lines.)

A third method is to cut a piece of stiff cardboard by trial and error until the correct lines are obtained. Lay the cardboard on the piece of wood that is to become the bulkhead. Trace the line with a pencil and cut with a saber saw.

Because bulkheads form major structural supports for the hull and deck, considerable loads can be exerted upon them, particularly where the hull meets the bulkhead. This is another possible location for a hard spot. In this instance, water exerting force on the outside of the hull causes the unsupported areas to flex, however minutely. The

thin edge of the bulkhead supports the hull in a very small area only. The hull here will not flex like the panel sections to either side. Consequently, some hull cracking or delamination can occur at this spot—unless the bulkhead is installed without creating a hard spot. This is best accomplished by cutting a thin strip of urethane foam the width of the bulkhead (¾-inch bulkheads are standard in the industry for 30- to 40-foot [9.1 m to 12.2 m] boats; where light weight is critical, as on multihulls and high-performance monohulls, bulkheads are often made of a veneer-foam-veneer sandwich). Resting the bulkhead on the foam will provide a cushion between the wood bulkhead and fiberglass hull (Figure 2-19). Cutting the foam at a 45° angle might obviate the need for fillets.

After securely clamping the bulkhead in place, at right angles to the centerline of the boat in both axes, bond the bulkhead to the hull and deck, overlapping the hull a minimum of 4 inches. Increase the width of each succeeding layer of 1½-ounce mat and 18-ounce woven roving.

### Strengthening the Bilge Area

If there is hull flexing in the bilge areas, the cabin sole can be removed and a series of fiberglassed plywood floors added (Figure 2-20). The greater distance they extend up the hull, and the more surface area bonded, the stronger the reinforcement.

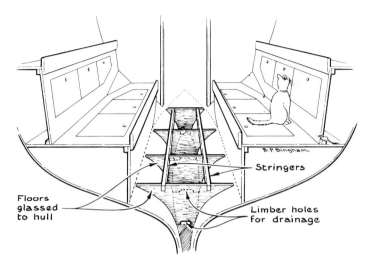

**FIGURE 2-20.** Plywood floors glassed to the hull help stiffen the critical bilge area. Longitudinal stringers can be glassed to the hull and floors at right angles to form a structural grid.

Refer back to the Hunter 34 grid in Figure 1-27. This shows a network of transverse and longitudinally molded beams used to provide stiffness. In adapting these principles to your job at hand, longitudinal stiffeners can be glassed in and interconnected to the transverse members. This would greatly stiffen the hull, though again, if these steps were necessary to create a strong hull, I think I'd buy another boat that didn't require such a massive effort.

### Check Bond of Furniture to Hull

In the forecabin, V-berths glassed to the hull give rigidity to the forward hull area. The same is true of cabinets and furniture in other cabins. If the fiberglass bond between the wood and hull has been broken, you should reglass the joint using four to six alternating layers of 1½-ounce (457 g/m²) mat and 10-ounce (339 g/m²) cloth (for a thinner laminate than woven roving).

### Wood Hulls

Hull flex normally occurs in wood hulls when one or more of the ribs or frames are cracked. This is not uncommon in old wood boats, especially those with steam-bent frames. Sawn and grown frames are stronger, but rarely seen these days.

The easiest method of strengthening a hull plagued by broken frames is to laminate sister frames in situ beside the old ones (Figure 2-21). Bob Vaughn, proprietor of the Seal Cove Boatyard

in Brooksville, Maine, used this method to repair *Desperate Lark*, a 49-foot (15 m) Herreshoff-designed and -built yawl. She was constructed in 1903 with long-leaf pine planking on oak frames. Because she once belonged to a friend's grandfather, I dropped in at the yard during a visit to Maine.

As Bob and I watched two carpenters installing the new frames, he said to me, "If Herreshoff had had epoxy, he'd have used it."

Two-inch by ⅜-inch (51 mm by 10 mm) strips of white oak (red oak doesn't bond as well because of a higher acid content) were cut and worked into place under the bilge and shear clamps, and beside the frame each was replacing. Strips of cardboard were placed between the old frame and new to prevent resin from forming a bond between the two. Resin was not used to bond the new frame to the hull as this would not allow the planks to expand evenly when swelling. Holes were drilled through the entire laminate and temporary 2½-inch (64 mm) #8 screws run into the hull skin to hold the new frames in place until the Cold Cure Epoxy used between the layers had cured. Shims were wedged in between the bilge and shear clamps to help hold the new frames flush to the hull while the holes for the temporary fasteners were being drilled. Bob said that a good deal of "cussedness" helped, too.

When the resin cured, the screws were removed, the holes extended through the hull, larger holes drilled, and 2¼-inch (57 mm) #12 silicon bronze wood screws used from the outside to fasten the planking permanently to the new frames. They were ¼ inch (6 mm) shorter than the temporary screws because they were countersunk and plugged. The holes on the inside were then filled with the epoxy. The eventual thickness of the new frames was slightly less than the old ones, 1¾ inches by 2 inches (44 mm by 51 mm), as compared to 1½ to 2½ inches by 1⅞ inches (38 mm to 64 mm by 48 mm).

In the bilge area, new floor timbers were sawn from 4-inch-thick (102 mm) pieces of oak, and bronze bolts were used to fasten each to the wood keel. This was necessary because the keel bolts had corroded and needed replacement, requiring removal of the old floors. Beneath the mast step, 4-inch laminated oak floors were lofted on the shop floor and made up. In the boat, they extended up three planks on either side.

*Desperate Lark* has one bronze floor timber aft to keep the cabin sole low for headroom. For

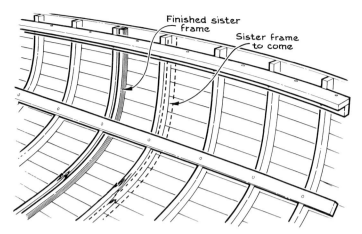

**FIGURE 2-21.** Cracked or broken frames are repaired by installing sister frames in situ. These may be solid wood or laminated, and they are held in place with epoxy, screws, or both.

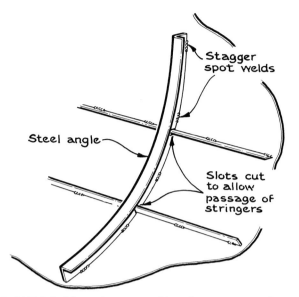

**FIGURE 2-22.** Replacing or adding frames to a steel hull isn't easy. One method is to bend angle bar to the proper shape and spot weld.

this same reason, Lin and Larry Pardey cast their own bronze floor timbers for their 30-foot (9.1 m) *Taleisin.*

As an aside, Bob Vaughn also cautioned against refastening hulls by simply removing the old fasteners and screwing in larger-diameter fasteners. He said there is always some damage to the wood caused by electrolytic action between the wood and the old fastener (the worst are iron and steel), and that a stronger repair results from drilling new holes into new wood, and just plugging the old holes.

*Desperate Lark* was well built and had bronze diagonals throughout the hull, running between the hull and frames. This is an excellent method of further strengthening the hull structure.

### Steel Hulls

Frames on steel boats are made of either angle bar (T-bar) or flat bar, the latter being specified on all Bruce Roberts designs (Bruce Roberts-Goodson is the world's largest purveyor of metal boat plans for amateur construction). Frames are placed on centers ranging from about 15 to 24 inches (381 mm to 610 mm). Adding frames will do little to strengthen the hull, though they will help prevent the plates from pushing inward.

Adding frames isn't an easy task, primarily because of the difficulty in bending the flat bar to the hull curvature. (Panels between frames ultimately do tend to cave in. This is a common phenomenon and doesn't weaken the skin. If a fair hull is desired, fillers can be used, though it can be a hellish

job. It's not necessary to add dozens of frames halving the distance between centers.) A professional welder will do a better job, and unless you're willing to develop your skills through a welding course offered at a local community college or vocational school, don't attempt critical repairs yourself.

Rather than trying to bend the stock, it often is easier to buy or have cut 2-inch (51 mm) strips of steel from a large plate. Weld one piece on edge, perpendicular to the hull in the desired location, then weld the second strip on top of the first at right angles (Figure 2-22). Never weld a long continuous bead all at once as this may distort the plates. Instead, make several randomly placed short beads, let them cool, and then complete the weld in between.

## HULL-DECK JOINTS
### Fiberglass Boats

Hulls and decks are typically joined in several ways. Figure 2-23 shows some of them. Rivets and screws are definitely inferior to stainless steel through-bolts with washers or backing plates to spread the fastener load. It's probably worth the effort to replace them if there is any cracking or excessive leaking at the joint.

Polyurethane and polysulfide compounds are frequently used by builders to seal the joint before the fastenings are drilled. Before applying a com-

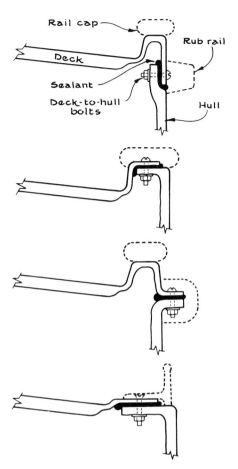

FIGURE 2-23. There are several conventional methods of attaching the hull to the deck. Regardless of the type of joint on your boat, a layer of glass over the inside of the joint strengthens the area and helps prevent leaks.

pound, be certain the area is bone dry. Use fans and lamps, if necessary. Wiping alcohol over the crack will assist in evaporating any remaining moisture. If the joint hasn't been glassed over, and the seam leaks, fill in the cracks with a sealant or glass over with a strong laminate. Note that polyurethane sealants such as 3M 5200 are considered permanent; they're also used for bonding external lead keels to the fiberglass hull.

By removing the toe rail or rub rail (depending on the type of hull-deck joint), you can gain access to the outside of the hull-deck joint. You might consider sealing the joint with polysulfide. A functional and attractive rub rail can be through-bolted over some types of joints. This would protect the joint to a degree, and at the same time, keep the topsides from getting scuffed up at the dock.

A trend in boatbuilding is the use of structural adhesives such as Plexus in place of mechanical fasteners. One of the first builders to use adhesive in the hull-deck joint was TPI, when it built some of the first Lagoon catamarans in the early 1990s. Methacrylate adhesives are so strong that in destruction tests the surrounding panels fail before the joint.

## Wood Boats

As mentioned earlier, the hull-deck joint on wood boats is an area particularly subject to distortion by waves. Traditionally, grown oak knees were cut and fitted horizontally between deck beams and shelves, and vertically between the beams and frames. If the hull-deck area seems to be working, the simplest solution is to replace the knees (Figure 2-24).

Because grown knees are difficult to come by (they are sawn out of the trunks of trees where they lead into the root system), it is far easier to laminate new ones. Carefully measure the angles between the beams and shelves and between beams and frames; make a jig, and lay up new knees that equal the dimensions of the old ones (Figure 2-25).

Another solution is to weld up braces from steel, then bolt them to the beams, frames, and shelves (Figure 2-26). An advantage of welded knees is that there is less likelihood of creating dead air spaces where rot can grow.

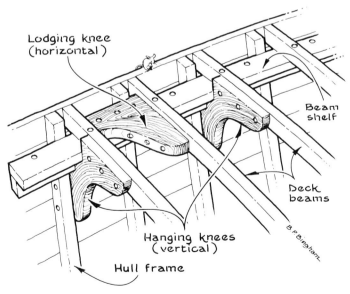

FIGURE 2-24. Hanging knees and lodging knees are used to strengthen planking, frames, deck beams, and shelves. This area is particularly subject to distortion in old boats.

51

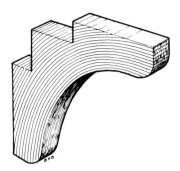

**FIGURE 2-25.** Grown knees are difficult to find. An easier alternative is to laminate them on a jig or form that duplicates the angle of the corner to which they will fit.

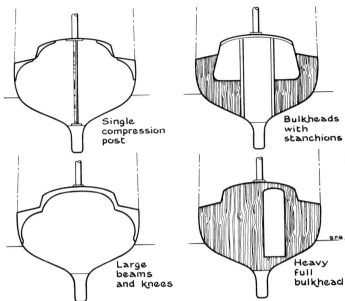

**FIGURE 2-27.** Compression posts transfer the load from the mast to the keel. Sometimes the post runs through the cabin sole directly to the keel; other times, a reinforced cabin sole is used to support the post. Narrow-beam boats may rely on the bulkheads and an internal deck beam to carry the load.

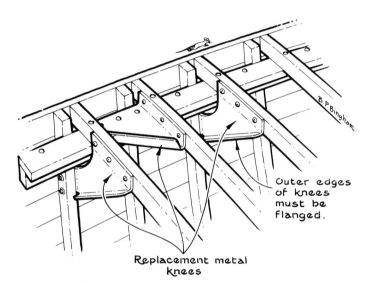

**FIGURE 2-26.** Hanging knees and lodging knees can be fabricated from metal plate.

## COMPRESSION OF THE DECK AT THE MAST STEP

Most forces of the rigging on deck-stepped masts are directed straight down the spar and are transferred to the deck. Not only must the deck be as strong as possible here, the load must be distributed over as wide an area as possible. Boats with beams wider than about 9 feet (2.7 m) can have the cabin walkway offset to one side of the hull so that a compression post may be inserted between the deck and keel. Of course, masts stepped on the keel won't cause problems with the deck, other than occasional stress around the collar if the fit is tight and the rigging loose. Figure 2-27 shows several ways in which the loads from the mast can be transferred to something more sub-

stantial than the deck. The compression post is preferred, followed by a combination of beam and bulkhead. If only a beam can be fitted underneath the mast, it must be very strong and well-secured to handle the loads; this is a problem area in many older boats, including the Pearson Triton.

The deck of my 19-foot (5.8 m) twin-keeler deflected from the mast compression loads so that several cabinet doors wouldn't open unless I jammed in a compression post between the cabin sole and deck. But then I couldn't get into the forward bunk, so a deck beam seemed to be the right solution. The same techniques can be used for adding this beam as were described for the foredeck reinforcing beam project (Figure 2-8). If there are bulkheads to either side in the appropriate place, these could be used to through-bolt the beam in lieu of knees. In the Triton, the beam is supported by four posts, fastened flush to the bulkheads, and run all the way down to the hull. This gives better support to the beam than just knees or bulkheads.

Another possible solution is to install a pad beneath the base of the mast (Figure 2-28). This can be metal—stainless steel or aluminum plate through-bolted to the deck—or plywood glassed

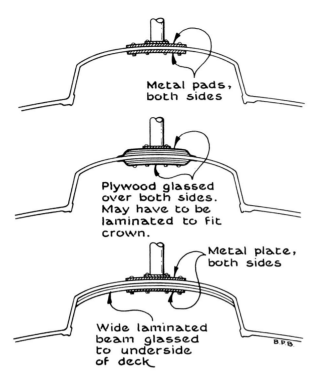

**FIGURE 2-28.** A mast pad of metal or plywood helps distribute the load of the mast over a larger area.

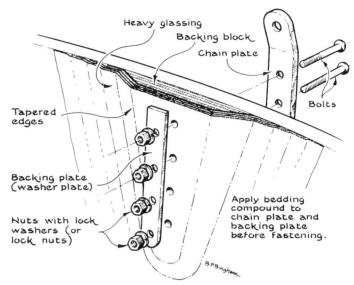

**FIGURE 2-29.** If chainplates appear to be working loose, reinforce them with a backup plate of plywood glassed to the bulkhead or hull. In this drawing, the chainplates are through-bolted to the outside of the hull.

to the deck. The greater the thickness, the stronger it will be. And the larger it is, the better it will distribute loads over the deck. Of course, whatever thickness is added beneath the mast will add to the height of the mast, and toggles will have to be added to the chainplates, or longer tangs installed on the mast if the turnbuckles can't be let out enough to reach the chainplates.

## CHAINPLATES

When chainplates, which link the rigging turnbuckles to the bulkheads or knees, are leaking or working, you may decide to do some work on them. The loads on chainplates and structural members are significant—a ¼-inch (6 mm) $1 \times 19$ shroud has an 8,200-pound (3,718 kg) breaking strength. Even if there is a 4:1 safety factor, loads approaching or exceeding a ton can be exerted on the chainplates and structural members. The more inboard the shrouds, the more this load is increased (see Chapter 10). On racing boats, moving the shrouds inboard enables the headsails to be sheeted in closer, thereby pointing higher. However, on a cruising boat, strength of the rig is more important than narrow sheeting angles.

That is why some boats, such as the Westsail 32 and Morgan Out Island series, have their chainplates attached to the hull sides with through-bolts. This is the widest staying base possible, unless channels are fitted to the hull to move the tops of the chainplates outboard of the hull.

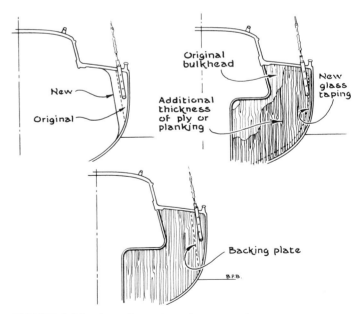

**FIGURE 2-30.** These illustrations show several ways to beef up the chainplate installations. They include enlarging the knee, doubling the thickness of the bulkhead, and adding a backing plate.

Wood backing plates glassed to the inside of the hull will reinforce this critical area (Figure 2-29).

If a chainplate is working, one remedy is to increase its size (see Chapter 10) and that of the structural member to which it's fastened—knee or bulkhead. If the structural member is a bulkhead, probably ¾-inch (19 mm) plywood, either replace with a thicker bulkhead (messy); or reinforce by adding shiplap planking or another piece of plywood to one side, or by using wood or metal backing plates where the chainplates are fastened. Figure 2-30 illustrates these possible solutions.

## EXTERNAL REINFORCEMENTS

The internal reinforcements we have discussed so far are probably the most effective means of making the hull and deck more rigid. However, there

---

# Rotten Chainplate Attachment

A too-common problem on older boats is bulkhead rot where the chainplates attach. Here's how it happens. Most chainplates, especially for shrouds, protrude through the deck. Underway, wave loads tend to twist the hull, and rigging loads tend to pull the hull inward. Though movement of the chainplate isn't even visible, it surely is occurring. The chainplate-deck joint is made waterproof with caulk, but over time the caulk dries and turns brittle, allowing water to enter through tiny cracks. This water travels down the chainplate, through the deck, and to the bolts that secure it through the plywood bulkhead. In the absence of air, the plywood begins to rot (Figure 2-31). And as the rig works, the bolts begin to enlarge the holes, making the shrouds or other stays slack. So you tighten the rigging and exert more pressure on the bulkheads around the bolt holes. Finally there is no more take-up left in the turnbuckles. Shortening the stays does not address the real problem. If you'd thought to remove the chainplates and bolts, you might have observed the cause of the limp rigging.

The cure is to reinforce the bolt holes. If the amount of rot is small, you might elect to dig out the punky wood fibers and inject an epoxy such as Git Rot (www.boatlife.com). This is very viscous resin and will run out unless dammed in place with tape or plastic. If the rot is more extensive, you'll have to pursue one of the fixes shown in Figure 2-30. Because replacing the entire bulkhead is a major—but perhaps necessary—repair, an easier approach would be to sandwich the deteriorating bulkhead with large wood cheeks on either side. These must be anchored to stable areas of the bulkhead with through-bolts.

All this hassle, effort, and money expended can be avoided by keeping a careful eye on the chainplate-deck joint. Remove old caulk, clean, and shoot new caulk into the joint.

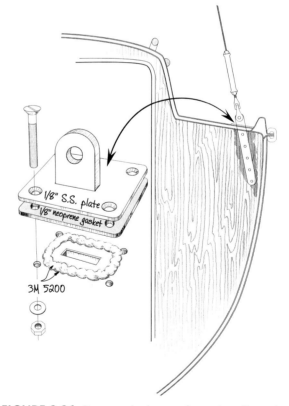

**FIGURE 2-31.** Because rigging works, water often migrates down chainplates and the bulkhead or other plywood structural member. Periodically remove the chainplate to inspect for rot. (Fritz Seegers illustration)

are several options for attacking the problems of flexing from the outside.

## Handholds

One simple trick is to through-bolt a longitudinal stiffener to the deck or cabin roof that doubles as a handhold or toe rail. These can be solid hardwood, such as teak or mahogany, or they can be laminated from thinner pieces. Using a table saw, rip a larger plank into strips from about ⅛ to ¼ inch (3 mm to 6 mm) thick and between 1 and 2 inches (25 mm to 51 mm) wide. Laminate in place by drilling bolt holes and bolting the stiffeners to the deck at the same time you glue the individual pieces together (Figure 2-32). However, it will be more difficult to finish the stiffener after it's installed. The utility of an external deck stiffener is enhanced if you can place it where it also functions as a foothold for working around the mast or at the bow. Be certain to properly bed all through-bolts.

## Teak Decks

A dubious and far more expensive and time-consuming solution is to cover the decks with teak planks (Figure 2-33). They must be bedded in polysulfide and screwed to the deck if it has a core (which it probably doesn't if you're installing teak decks to correct oilcanning), or bonded to the deck with epoxy resin mixed with talc or microfibers to thicken it. Temporary fasteners can be pulled (and the holes filled) after the resin cures. Use a grooved

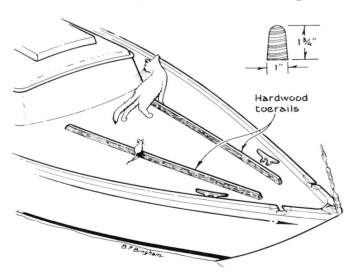

**FIGURE 2-32.** An external deck beam laminated from thin pieces of hardwood then both through-bolted and screwed to the deck helps stiffen areas that oilcan.

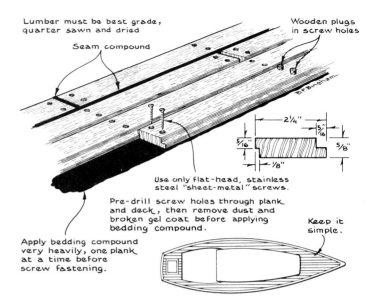

**FIGURE 2-33.** Teak planks help stiffen uncored decks. They may be epoxied and/or screwed to the existing deck. An epoxy-graphite mix to fill the seams has the look of Thiokol or polysulfide without the mess.

cement trowel to achieve a uniform coating and reduce waste. In his book *From a Bare Hull*, Ferenc Máté recommends using polysulfide to fill the grooves on top. But some builders of cold-molded boats, like the Gougeon Brothers, use epoxy resin mixed with graphite (to make it black and protect the resin from ultraviolet attack). But after you've read about what Máté calls "200 hours of screamingly frustrated labor," and after considering the difficulty of doing a good job, it's probably wisest to save teak decks for your next boat.

An alternative is one of the new synthetic teak products such as PlasTEAK (www.plasteak.com) and Tek-Dek (www.tek-dek-international.com).

## WHY I HATE INNER LINERS

If strengthening the hull is just the beginning of your upgrading efforts, it certainly would make sense to do these jobs before remodeling furniture or anything else because you may have to rip out bunks and cabinets to get at the areas of the hull or deck requiring reinforcement.

There are two types of inner liners and both make working on the boat much more difficult; unfortunately, they are the general standard nowadays. The deck liner is a molding of fiberglass that fits the underside of the deck and cabin top. Its purpose is to replace the rough inside of the bare fiberglass hull with a glossy white gelcoated surface. One of the several problems caused by this installation is that it is no longer possible to bond the bulkheads to the deck with fiberglass tape (called *tabbing*). Instead, builders try screwing through the bulkheads into molded ridges in the liner or gluing the bulkheads into the channels. But neither of these methods is as structurally sound as fiberglassing the bulkheads to the deck, and then hiding the deck with some type of removable panel.

As the overhead liner idea took hold, some builders got really crafty and started molding pans with all the bunks, galley, and cabinets figured in. This pan was dropped into the hull before the deck was put on and then bonded to the hull in several places, usually with polyester putty. All the workmen had to do then was trim the pan with pieces of teak and the interior was done. This saves the builder money, and, in all fairness, cannot rot.

It may sound like a good idea, but these pans can seriously interfere with access to the hull. A friend of mine in Newport, who owns a Pearson 32, ran the externally ballasted keel into a rock during a cruise to Woods Hole. The keel and keel bolts twisted, necessitating replacing and reinforcing the structural floors that supported the keel via the keel bolts. The boat has a fiberglass pan, and workers had to cut large sections of it away to get at the hull. Then, once they'd fixed the keel, they had to fix the holes they had cut in the liner—without the benefit of a mold. Such repairs seldom look like new.

In another incident, a boat in Bermuda went up on the beach with sufficient force to dislodge the pan from the hull. The only way to repair such damage would be to remove the deck—the surveyor wrote off the boat as a total loss.

What all this boils down to is that a plywood interior is easier to remove or modify. Plus it is warmer and quieter. Except for major bulkheads, berths and shelving, most other pieces of interior wood can simply be screwed together so that when you really have to get at something, you aren't sawing up your boat. And, if you care at all about how your boat looks inside, remember that it was these pans that led to L. Francis Herreshoff's unflattering epithet about fiberglass boats looking like frozen snot. Kinder critics have likened them to Clorox bottles and the insides of refrigerators.

There is what I consider a good compromise between an all-wood interior and one made up of

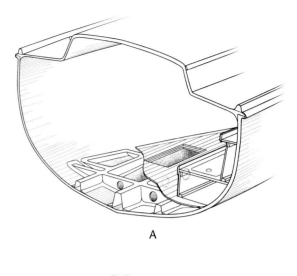

A

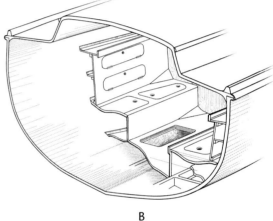

B

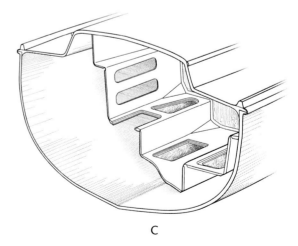

C

**FIGURE 2-34.** Fiberglass pans and structural grids are appropriate in the bilge (A), and even the sole and possibly the berth flats (B), but I don't like to see them extend higher than the berth flats, as they do in C. (Fritz Seegers illustrations)

numerous fiberglass moldings. And it is this: use fiberglass moldings where their wood counterparts are likely to get wet and possibly rot, namely, below the waterline and in the head. Foam-filled stringers make more sense than fiberglass-sheathed plywood stringers and transverse members. A fiberglass sole isn't a bad idea either, though I'd cover it with teak and holly or carpet. The sole would extend to the hull, of course, where it would be tabbed with fiberglass, but I wouldn't extend it upward to form berth foundations (Figure 2-34).

## REINFORCING RUDDERS

Tremendous forces are constantly at work against your rudder, not only underway, but even at anchor or at the dock. Sooner or later in the life of many boats, the rudder will need reinforcing or replacing. Unfortunately, you often can't go out and buy a new rudder the way you buy a new starter or water pump for your car. If the company that built your boat is still in business, it may be persuaded to make a new one for you. Some builders outsource their rudders to companies specializing in building just rudders. For example, Hunter Marine purchased a lot of rudders from Foss Foam Products (www.newrudders.com), which retains the patterns and molds to make replacements. But, unless you're convinced that the original rudder was well engineered, you may decide to beef up the old rudder yourself.

### Reinforcing Wood Rudders

Your plan will depend on what type of rudder you have—wood or fiberglass, attached, spade, or outboard (refer back to Figure 1-1). Pearson's early rudders were made of ³⁄₄-inch (19 mm) mahogany planks held together by pins or drifts inside, much the way an orthopedic surgeon pins a broken leg. The gudgeon straps also help hold the planks together. Hauling out the boat in the winter and exposing this wood to the dry, cold air causes some shrinking and cracking. But unless the planks are working loose, it won't hurt to let the small cracks go as they'll disappear when put back in the water and the planks swell again. Glassing over or screwing in metal straps should strengthen a failing wood rudder satisfactorily (Figure 2-35). If glassing over metal straps, use epoxy resin, as it bonds much better to metal than polyester resin. Use 1½-ounce mat (457 g/m²) and 10- or 14-ounce (339 to 475 g/m²) cloth.

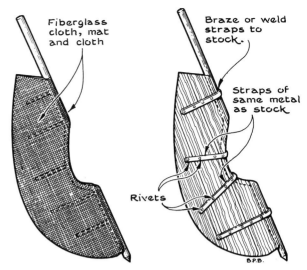

**FIGURE 2-35.** A wood rudder, made up from several boards, may use drift pins run through the rudder's width to hold it together. If the boards begin to work, glassing the entire rudder and adding metal straps will strengthen the rudder.

### Fiberglass Rudders

Making a new fiberglass rudder is another matter. Steel rods commonly are welded to the stock, and a foam core is often laid in and around the rods before covering the whole network with fiberglass.

The reason for using foam is that rudders should be as near to neutrally buoyant as possible. A solid fiberglass rudder would be too heavy and could cause a lee helm. Likewise, an overly buoyant rudder could cause weather helm. While a new all-wood rudder may be positively buoyant, the additional weight of fittings and the water it absorbs over the years eventually make it nearly neutrally buoyant.

As noted, most fiberglass rudders incorporate metal plates or rods welded to the stock. But if these welds break inside, the fiberglass bond to the rudderstock will break in short order and leave you without any control. An offshore cruising skipper must be able to rely on his rudder—*always*.

A fiberglass rudder can be made from male or female molds, though the former is easier for the amateur. To make a male mold, fashion two pieces of plywood to the size and shape desired, and smaller than the final product by the thickness of the laminate that will cover it. Use 1½- or 2-ounce mat (457 or 610 g/m²) and 24-ounce (814 g/m²) woven roving or 10-ounce cloth (cloth is preferred on the outside layer) to cover the

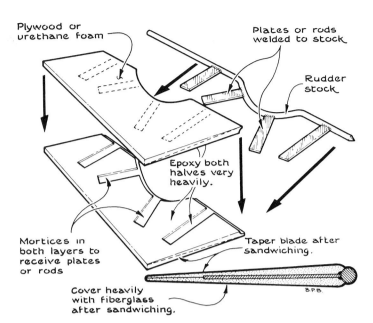

FIGURE 2-36. One way to make a rudder is to cut two pieces of plywood and shape them as desired to form a male mold. Mortise the rudder and welded rods between them. Next, glass over with mat and cloth.

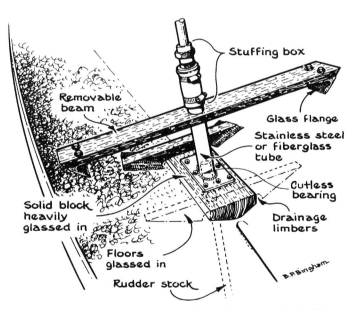

FIGURE 2-37. Wherever the rudder enters the hull, it should be reinforced by glassing in a block of wood with a hole cut for the shaft. Additional strengthening of this critical area can be achieved by glassing in short beams around the block.

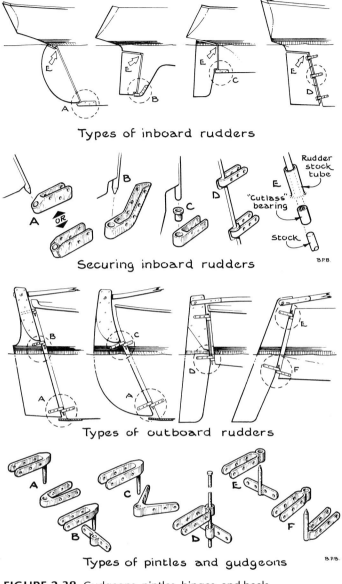

FIGURE 2-38. Gudgeons, pintles, hinges, and heels should be through-bolted where possible. The heel fittings shown are through-bolted to the skeg and help distribute the load of the rudder over a wide area.

board (Figure 2-36). Of course, the rudderstock and welded rods must be incorporated into the design. Notch the wood so that the two pieces can enclose the hardware and lie flush. One possible method is shown.

## Rudder Supports

Vertical rudderstocks should enter the hull either through a glass or stainless steel tube bolted through a substantial block of wood (Figure 2-37). A stuffing box is fitted to the hull or tube to center

**FIGURE 2-39.** The telltale signs of rust streaming down the sides of this C&C 33 rudder prompted me to drop the rudder for closer inspection; this requires unbolting the steering quadrant, removing any fittings at the top, and possibly digging a hole under the rudder. Note the drops of water weeping from the joint where the stock meets the fiberglass shell.

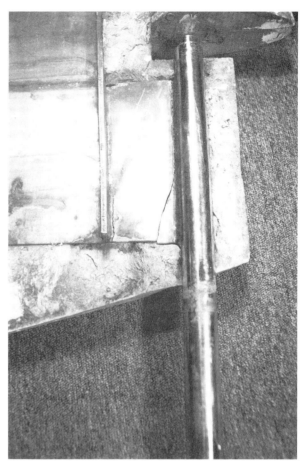

**FIGURE 2-40.** The rudder on this Pearson 34 failed when the weldment attaching the internal plate or webbing to the rudderstock failed. Note that even a piece of the plate itself cracked. (*Practical Sailor* photo)

**FIGURE 2-41.** A larger view of the Pearson 34's rudder shows the size of the webbing. Like most modern rudders, it is a thin fiberglass shell filled with high-density foam, encapsulating the webbing and a portion of the rudderstock. (*Practical Sailor* photo)

the stock and make the opening watertight. If you detect any movement of the rudderstock or in other parts of the steering system when underway, it wouldn't hurt to strengthen the hull here, either by glassing in a heavier piece of plywood against the hull, adding extra layers of mat and woven roving in the area, or glassing in a few beams, between which the backing block can be glassed. (You'll need to remove any existing block to do these repairs.)

Additionally, the stock should be supported higher up, where it passes into the cockpit or wherever else it emerges above deck. There should be a strong collar to support the stock and a bearing plate firmly supported by structural members glassed to the hull.

# Rebuilding *Viva's* Rudder

Walk through any yard where there are a lot of sailboats hauled, and you'll probably see at least a few with lines of rust stain running down the rudder. When I saw it on *Viva*, a 1975 Tartan 44 we cruised back in the 1990s, I wasn't happy. I learned from my friend Bill Seifert, who used to work for Tartan, that the rudder had mild steel webbing. He and I agreed that short of X-rays, the only sure way to determine the condition of the webbing was to open the rudder. The accompanying photos show how this was done and a repair made (Figures 2-42 through 2-52). Actually, I had a new rudderstock machined, and stainless steel webbing welded to it. By saving the old shell, much time and effort was saved. You must be careful when pouring in the new foam that adequate relief holes are available for the excess foam to exit through; if not, you can easily split the fiberglass shell.

**FIGURE 2-42.** *Viva's* skeg-hung rudder was sanded prior to removing from the boat; why sand bottom paint inside the shop? The strong bronze hinge bearing is normally covered by putty on the skeg side. Stainless steel machine screws secure it to the skeg.

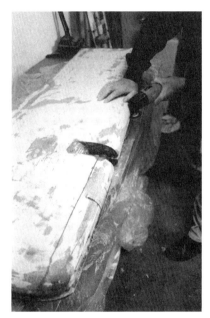

**FIGURE 2-43.** To cut the shell in half, a Fein finish/corner sander was fitted with the optional cutting wheel (developed for cutting casts off people). It was slow going but the cut was clean and did no further damage to the relatively delicate shell.

**FIGURE 2-44.** Once the shell was cut in half, the next job was to chisel away all the 8-pound (3.6 kg) high-density foam inside.

# Rebuilding *Viva's* Rudder (cont.)

FIGURE 2-45. The webbing was glassed with several layers of woven roving to one side of the shell. Many builders simply position the webs in the middle and pour foam all around it.

FIGURE 2-46. The new rudderstock and webs were glassed to the cleaned-out shell, this time using biaxial cloth instead of woven roving.

FIGURE 2-47. Before closing the two halves of the shell, an epoxy mush using ⅛-inch (3 mm) milled fiberglass as filler was smeared around the edges.

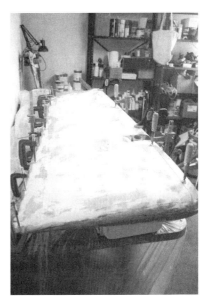

FIGURE 2-48. The two halves were then joined and clamped. Once the mush had cured, the seam was covered with a 3-inch (76 mm) fiberglass tape. The radius of the trailing edge, however, was too tight for the fiberglass, but since there is little load on the trailing edge, this wasn't considered a big problem.

# Rebuilding *Viva's* Rudder (cont.)

**FIGURE 2-49.** The hollow rudder was filled with 8-pound (3.6 kg) foam poured through a funnel. Heat building up inside caused the expanding foam to cure right in the funnel. Because we didn't have the original rudder mold to support the sides during this operation, pieces of plywood were lashed on both sides.

**FIGURE 2-50.** With just 6 inches (152 mm) of space inside the rudder left, the trailer edge blew out. Some builders recommend drilling ventilating holes in the shell sides to prevent this, but they'll require fixing later, of course. We removed the offending foam, filled the gap with epoxy, and clamped together.

**FIGURE 2-51.** After reinstalling, the exterior of the rudder was faired and painted. Knowing its guts are structurally sound gives great piece of mind when crashing along hard on the wind doing 7½ knots.

**FIGURE 2-52.** On finishing this difficult job, advisor Bill Seifert stopped by with this photo of a solid rudder with external stock and webbing, plus zinc anodes to prevent corrosion. Bill said, "Now that you've rebuilt *Viva*'s rudder, this arrangement makes a lot more sense, doesn't it?!" (Bill Seifert photo)

This reinforcement will protect the hull against normal loads and, in the sad event of a grounding, will even help prevent the rudder from being shoved up through the hull. Losing the rudder is one thing, losing the whole boat a catastrophe!

This is why planning for an emergency rudder is so important. It might be as simple as lashing a dinghy oar to a floorboard, but you should figure it out before heading offshore. Chapter 6 provides some further ideas on the subject.

Whether gudgeons and pintles are used to hang the rudder, or gudgeon straps, they should be through-bolted to the rudder and hull or keel. Backing blocks should be glassed in as well, if the skin is thin. Skeg-mounted rudders and rudders attached to full keels should have a heel bearing (usually bronze) that supports the weight of the rudder and also acts as a rudder-to-keel attachment (Figure 2-38, page 58). The heel bearing should extend along the base of the keel or skeg, to which it is through-bolted to help distribute the loads imposed by the rudder on it.

### Common Causes of Rudder Failure

Most modern rudders are thin fiberglass shells filled with high-density foam inside. The stainless steel rudderstock has long, flat pieces of steel (called *webbing*) welded to it that carry the turning loads. Because fiberglass, stainless steel, and foam all have different coefficients of expansion, heating, and cooling cycles, the joint where the rudderstock enters the fiberglass shell can open up, admitting small amounts of water (Figure 2-39, page 59). Fresh or salt water will cause corrosion of the metal inside the rudder, with fresh water on stainless being the best scenario and salt water on mild carbon steel the worst. Even stainless steel can rust, however, especially when there is no oxygen present (which is why you shouldn't cover lifelines or standing rigging with tight-fitting vinyl covers). And not all metal inside rudders is stainless (see the Rebuilding *Viva*'s Rudder sidebar).

Figures 2-40 and 2-41 on page 59 show how the rudder of a 1984 Pearson 34 failed. The owner was entering harbor when suddenly he lost steering. Fortunately he and his crew were able to get the boat secured to a dock before any serious damage occurred. He brought the rudder into the offices of *Practical Sailor* when I was editor. One of the staff, Dale Nouse, cut it open. A large stainless plate was welded to the rudderstock but only over a 7-inch (178 mm) length. All of the rudder loads were transferred to this short weldment, and eventually it broke. Pearson reengineered the rudder on future boats, and no further problems were encountered.

## FURTHER READING

*Complete Guide to Metal Boats: Building, Maintenance, and Repair.* 3rd ed. Bruce Roberts-Goodson. Camden, Maine: International Marine, 2006.

*Fiberglass Boatbuilding for Amateurs.* Ken Hankinson. Bellflower, California: Glen-L Marine Designs, 1982.

*Fiberglass Boat Repair Manual.* Allan H. Vaitses. Camden, Maine: International Marine, 1988.

*Fiberglass Boats.* 3rd ed. Hugo du Plessis. Camden, Maine: International Marine, 1996.

*The Fiberglass Repair and Construction Handbook.* 2nd ed. Jack Wiley. New York: McGraw-Hill, 1988.

*From a Bare Hull: How to Build a Sailboat.* Rev. ed. Ferenc Máté. New York: Norton, 2000.

*The Gougeon Brothers on Boat Construction: Wood and West System Materials.* 5th ed. Meade Gougeon. Bay City, Michigan: Gougeon Brothers, Inc., 2005.

*McLean's Marine: A Manual for the Repair of Fiberglass Boats Suffering from Osmotic Blistering.* 2nd ed. Richard McLean. Piedmont, California: A is A Publishing, 1988.

*The New Cold-Molded Boatbuilding: From Lofting to Launching.* Reuel B. Parker. Camden, Maine: International Marine, 1990.

*Osmosis & Glassfibre Yacht Construction.* 2nd ed. Tony Staton-Bevan. Dobbs Ferry, New York: Sheridan House, 1995.

*Own a Steel Boat.* Mike Pratt. Camden, Maine: International Marine, 1979; London: Hollis and Carter, 1979.

*Sailboat Hull & Deck Repair.* Don Casey. Camden, Maine: International Marine, 1996.

*Wooden Boat Repair Manual,* by John Scarlett; International Marine Publishing Company, Camden, Maine 04843.

*Wooden Boat Renovation: New Life for Old Boats Using Modern Methods.* Jim Trefethen. Camden, Maine: International Marine, 1993.

# THREE

# A SEAGOING INTERIOR LAYOUT

In considering the seaworthiness of a cruising boat, discussion usually centers on the integrity of the hull and strength of the rig. A close third is the nature of the interior accommodations. After all, in bad weather one or all of the crew may be inside. In survival conditions, the helm is lashed, and all hands are ordered below where they should be strapped to their bunks.

Though no statistics are available, it is entirely possible that more injuries occur belowdecks than above. In fact, during a recent Volvo round-the-world race a sailor had to be airlifted off his boat because he broke his knee after being slammed across the cabin while sleeping—belowdecks. Being thrown against a cabinet corner, having a heavy pot land on your head, or getting scalded by a tipped pan of hot water are just a few of the ways that someone can be injured. The interior plan of your boat should be designed with a vision of the worst that can happen.

## TYPICAL PRODUCTION BOAT LAYOUTS

The dinette and standard layouts of most production boats have evolved in part from what works, and in part from what the public has demanded, however ill-informed it may be.

For example, shag carpeting looks cozy, but provides poor footing and once damp is difficult to dry. Dinette tables mounted on flimsy pedestals are nice for coffee hour in the mooring, but are in the way at sea and frequently break when crashed into by a stumbling body. V-berths forward seem practical enough, but in any kind of sea are sickeningly uncomfortable. And as boats have become more beamy, the distance you can be thrown athwartships has become greater and therefore more dangerous, especially as it is sometimes difficult to put handholds and body-bracing points in strategic locations. These kinds of features may work for weekend sails, but not for offshore cruising.

## MY IDEAL LAYOUT

There is certainly room for considerable freedom and personal preference in designing your ideal interior layout, especially on larger boats. And, of course, there are innumerable restrictions: the shape of the hull, length of the hull, positioning of bulkheads, location of chainplates, type of deck (flush or coachroof), headroom, etc. But as long as we're dreaming, giving thought to an ideal layout is at the least instructive, and at most a goal to attempt achieving in your own boat.

Figure 3-1 illustrates many of the points I consider important as well as possible in a boat of about 35 to 40 feet (10.7 m to 12.2 m) LOA (length overall). Beginning at the bow, there is a large forepeak for stowage of seldom-used items that aren't too heavy—sea anchors, cockpit awning, anchor buoys, etc. The forward cabin, usually used for V-berths, has a fold-up pipe berth to port with an oak-topped workbench underneath. To starboard is another folding pipe berth, with storage bins for tools, paint, sails, sewing machine, and other odds and ends. In hot weather, it would be nice to rig up some sort of double berth underneath the forward hatch.

The bulkhead between the forepeak and head compartment could be classified as a collision bulkhead if it is bonded to the hull all around, and the door is gasketed with a positive locking or compression mechanism as in a submarine. Such a bulkhead should be at least 10% of the waterline length aft so that in the event of a hole in the bow area, water will not enter the main living space.

In the main cabin there is a settee and navigation station to port. If the settee isn't long enough to sleep on, because of a footwell for the navigation station, a drop-leaf board with cushion could be fashioned to extend the foot of the berth be-

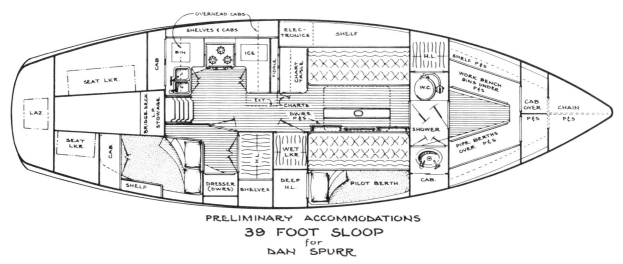

**FIGURE 3-1.** In a 35- to 40-foot (10.7 m to 12.2 m) hull, this layout comes close to my ideal arrangement plan. It is best suited to cooler climates, as the after stateroom will be difficult to ventilate well enough for life in the tropics. V-berths, useless at sea, are the coolest.

neath the chart table. To starboard there is a narrow settee and pilot berth up underneath the deck that makes an excellent sea berth on port tack. The only problem with pilot berths is they are convenient catchalls for various junk when not in use.

Moving aft there is a U-shaped galley to port with deep double sinks, a gimballed stove/oven mounted facing athwartship, and large counter surfaces for food preparation. Opposite the galley is a private quarter cabin with double berth and bureau for neat storage of clothes.

A bridge deck in the smallish cockpit gives additional seating space, has the added benefit of opening up more space in the quarter cabin, and allows the galley to extend a few extra feet underneath the cockpit. There might also be room here for a wet locker to hang dripping foul weather gear. Sharp corners are rounded, handholds are everywhere, the cabin sole is not so wide that one can't always find a surface to brace a hip against, and all sea berths are fitted with lee boards or heavy canvas lee cloths.

Obviously, I haven't thought of everything, and almost infinite acceptable variations are possible. But this layout does meet these major requirements:

- Safety for sleeping and sitting crew
- Adequate storage space
- A safe galley area
- Usable navigation station
- A strong and unobtrusive dining table

Let's now take a look at the major considerations in redesigning an interior, and then study the changes I made to a 28-foot (8.5 m) Pearson Triton as a case history.

## BERTHS

Most production boats are designed for weekend cruising by crews in multiples of two. One couple sleeps in the forward cabin V-berth, the other on a folded-down dinette. Extra kids can be stuffed in pilot berths (Figures 3-2 and 3-3) or quarter berths and, in desperation, still others could put their sleeping bags in the cockpit. It works, but for the cruising single or couple, too much space is wasted by all these berths. It makes good sense to plan your new interior around the number of people who'll actually be living aboard, then make some provision for visits by two more persons. If the setup for guests isn't ideal, remember that they'll probably be sailing with you for only a week or two at a time and that your comfort comes first.

If you have a dinette model and decide to keep the arrangement, then the problem of where to put your brother and his girlfriend is solved. However, it can be a nuisance to have to clear the table every time the berth is made—some things you just learn to live with.

Most dinette tables are notoriously flimsy. A number of very strong stainless steel or aluminum table pedestals are on the market (Figure 3-4), and

**FIGURE 3-2.** While not technically a pilot berth, this single on *Moondrift* will be a good sea berth with the lee cloth tied in place. Note the many drawers underneath and the privacy curtain at left.

one of these would be a worthwhile investment if your existing pedestal has excessive wobble. The base should be through-bolted to the cabin sole with large stainless steel bolts. If the sole looks too thin, a backing plate of epoxy-coated plywood, aluminum, or stainless steel should be fitted, or the pedestal might be taken through the sole and

**FIGURE 3-3.** The pilot berth on the 41-foot (12.2 m) steel *Iron Mistress* isn't much higher than the settee and so there isn't much of a backrest.

**FIGURE 3-4.** Dinette table pedestals should be through-bolted to the floor and must provide plenty of support. This one, made by the Dutch firm of Zwaardvis, is hydraulically operated. Pushing the table down compresses the gas spring, which effortlessly returns the table to the up position when ready. (Zwaardvis)

anchored in a structural member below. Stainless steel is tough to drill with household tools. Since you'll encounter other metalworking jobs you probably won't be able to handle alone, search out a local metalworker/welder and establish a friendly relationship. With his tools, it'll take just seconds to do what would frustrate you for hours.

Two-inch (51 mm) fiddles help keep plates and glasses from sliding off the dinette table at dinner or cocktail hour, but they're tough to sleep on. Fashion removable fiddles (Figure 3-5) by fitting 1/4-inch (6 mm) wood pegs or brass rods into the bottom of the fiddles and then drilling appropriately spaced holes into the table. Experiment with sizes to get a snug fit. At bedtime, pull off the fiddles and stow them on a shelf. If the inboard fiddle also functions as a handhold, a stronger method is to sink threaded rod stock in place of the pegs. Use wing nuts under the table to keep the fiddles tight.

The forward V-berths offer many possibilities for customizing. If you plan to sleep nightly in the main cabin, consider converting the forward cabin to a sail stowage and rope locker by removing the tops of the bunks. Alternatively, one bunk could be converted to a workbench with drawers and bins for tools underneath. Eric Hiscock, when I visited him in Opua, New Zealand, in the early

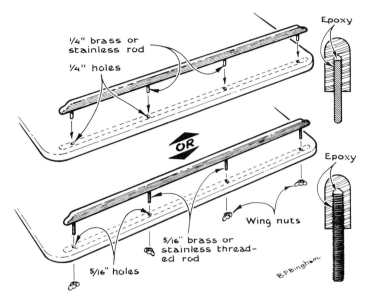

1/4" brass or stainless rod

1/4" holes

Epoxy

OR

Epoxy

Wing nuts

5/16" brass or stainless threaded rod

5/16" holes

B.P.Bingham

**FIGURE 3-5.** Removable fiddles on a dinette make berth cushions fit better when the table is lowered for sleeping, to say nothing about the comfort of your back.

1980s, was proud to show me how he could convert the forward cabin to a darkroom to develop black and white photographs.

Boatbuilders frequently offer V-berth inserts to convert the entire forward cabin into an enormous double berth. This arrangement has its obvious merits, but unless the couple has the shoulders of linebackers, much space on both sides is wasted. On a small cruiser, you just can't afford not to put that space to good use. In the 28-foot (8.5 m) Triton, with a beam of just 8 feet 4 inches (2.5 m), there is sufficient room to build an offset double berth with the foot aft and head forward, if desired. There is still room to walk into the cabin, sit on the edge of the bunk and rest your dogs on the floor while undressing. To starboard there is about 6 square feet (0.56 m²) of bunk space on which to build clothes bins.

In the Vanguard, C&C 33, and Tartan 44, I changed my mind about the offset double as it meant the person outboard had to climb over the other to get out—a habit of skippers nervous about the holding power of their ground tackle. On these three boats, I filled in the V-berth insert, and on the Vanguard I built bookshelves port and starboard, filling the angle between the bulkhead and hull sides. This gave each person a place to keep books, cards, flashlights, letters, and other personal effects—all that "stuff" had to land somewhere! This arrangement allowed both persons to get out without disturbing the other—the

drawback was having to climb headfirst into the cabin and drop out feetfirst. Some days you just wish you owned a larger boat.

Pilot berths tucked like stair steps under the side decks outboard of the settees are nifty for kids because they give a sense of security much like hiding in a tree fort. They are up and out of the way under deck, so adults still awake or moving about aren't stumbling over the errant little legs and arms. And when not in use, pilot berths can be stuffed with bedding, pillows, and other gear. A lee board or heavy lee cloth (see Figure 3-19 on page 74) fitted across the insides of the berth keep these items from tumbling out. A possible disadvantage of pilot berths on boats without great beam is that they force the settees inboard, thereby reducing the width of the cabin sole, and perhaps the width of the settees themselves. If this is the case, an extension berth may be the best solution, enabling the settee to pull out from under the pilot berth at night.

Quarter berths are excellent sea berths, and you would be wise to pause and consider their value before converting this space to some other use. Dropping yourself into one is sometimes like crawling feetfirst into a coffin, but they are snug. If only the head of the berth protrudes into the cabin, lee cloths or bunk boards may not be necessary. Quarter berths occupy little space and can accommodate all sorts of bedding and gear during the day, or at night, depending on the watch hours of its occupant.

The Pearson Vanguard I lived aboard and cruised for six years had the dinette arrangement amidships. The production version had two quarter berths aft, but a previous owner had removed the port-side bunk, added a bulkhead between the under-cockpit area and cabin, and installed a large navigation station (Figure 3-6). Under the bridge, next to the engine box, was a Tiny Tot solid fuel stove. Coal storage was constructed under the port cockpit seat with a special hatch (see Figures 14-8, 14-9, and 14-10). Inside, beneath the chart table, a small door opened to dump out just enough coal to fill the stove and keep the cabin warm on cool and clammy nights.

Beneath the starboard quarter berth were dozens of small drawers for spare parts and tools, all organized for instant identification. Drawers are sometimes more practical than top-loading hatches and bins. It isn't necessary to pull up the cushion to get at things (all the more irritating if someone is on the bunk), and large finger or hand

**FIGURE 3-6.** The port quarter berth of this Pearson Vanguard has been converted to a navigation station. Also, a wood/coal stove has been fitted under the bridge deck.

holes drilled in the drawers minimize the growth of mildew.

These and other customizations were the major reasons I bought the boat. Oddly, within two years I tore out the chart table and replaced the original quarter berth, tore out the backrest and bookshelf on the outboard side of the dinette/settee for greater room, and repowered the aging Westerbeke with a new Yanmar diesel. It was certainly proof that you don't really know what you want in a boat—or what's wrong with it—until you live with it awhile. On reflection, I could have bought a cheaper Vanguard, without all of the custom "improvements," and probably saved some labor as well.

Large aft cabins, usually found in center-cockpit boats but sometimes found under the cockpit in large boats, often feature centerline double berths. These allow both occupants to easily exit on his or her own side. But lee cloths are required to keep them snug underway. I've been on a number of deliveries where I had to share the double with another crew of the same sex. Regardless, a third lee cloth down the centerline is essential, and that probably means replacing the double mattress with two singles. Big centerline doubles are great in port, but lousy at sea.

## STOWAGE

You can't have too much storage space on a small boat. Building drawers and bins out of wood is very labor intensive and only the higher-priced production boats even approach having adequate built-in stowage space. However, this is one area in which you can use your creative genius to great effect, and at little risk of botching up the boat. Areas under the deck and outboard of bunks are almost always the best places to build bookshelves, instrument boxes, can storage, etc. Drawers can be fitted under bunks; hanging lockers and forepeaks can be improved by adding shelves with tall fiddles or facings; nets can be strung underneath the decks (Figure 3-7); and unused bunks can be turned into navigation stations, bureaus, or extra galley space.

Drawers and cabinets are better stowage areas than the bins under bunks, which are usually unpartitioned and poorly ventilated. These spaces can be converted to drawer storage by cutting openings in the facing of the bunk sides and constructing runners and drawers (Figure 3-8).

Only when you've moved aboard for a period of time do you begin to realize the amount of stowage space necessary for comfortable, organized living. It's a nuisance to continually have to dig through layers of clothes or gear to find the

**FIGURE 3-7.** Net hammocks and hanging baskets are great catchalls, even for food, plus they're gimballed.

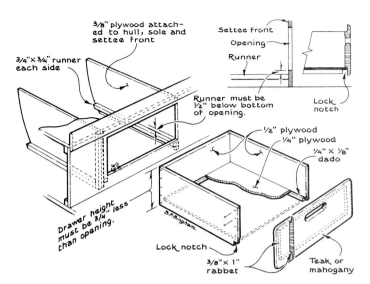

**FIGURE 3-8.** Drawers fitted beneath berths are much more useful and handy than the hatches that require lifting the cushions to gain access.

**FIGURE 3-9.** Space under the companionway stairs of *Altair* is not wasted. The ventilator above circulates air to help prevent mildew. (Sandy Brown photo)

item you want, or to have things sitting out on bunks for lack of places to stow them. Consider your needs carefully, study the space available, and make sketches of alternatives (Figures 3-9 and 3-10). Think through each step carefully before cutting up old furniture or buying materials and tools. Try to picture each piece, how you will measure it, how it will be supported. For example, will there be enough room to use a screwdriver between it and an adjacent surface? If possible, consult with a friend; he may give you time-saving ideas that never would have occurred to you. If you can plan several projects before buying materials, you can save time and money by doing all your shopping at once. And don't hesitate to purchase new tools when necessary; any job is easier with the right tool, the finished product is more attractive, and you'll have the tool for future use.

The galley should have room for pots and pans and tableware, and bins or cabinets that are dry and ventilated for food. Don't forget drawers for the dozens of necessary small cooking utensils.

Counter surfaces of sufficient size for laying out cans and cabbages, cutting vegetables, and making soups are essential (Figure 3-11). The dinette table can be used for this purpose, but this means occupying the space your crew may be using for writing letters, reading, or in the case of kids, drawing and playing games.

Heavy pots must remain secure when the boat is bucking around. Thin veneer facings and shock

**FIGURE 3-10.** A nice touch, plus a practical one, is a dedicated liquor and wine cabinet.

**FIGURE 3-11.** In the small-boat galley, finding sufficient counter space to prepare meals is difficult. Using the ice-box lid doesn't work unless you've really got everything you need out of the box. On this Morris 36, the nav table opposite could be used in a pinch.

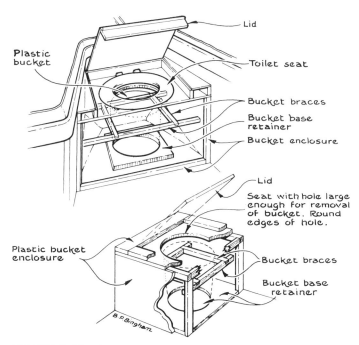

**FIGURE 3-12.** The traditional cedar bucket, though illegal in coastal waters, is a head of the utmost simplicity. Actually, a plastic bucket is much more sensible.

cord will not stop a 10-pound (4.5 kg) iron skillet from launching itself to the other side of the cabin. Nor will an icebox lid without a lock keep the contents inside during a rollover. Visit as many ocean-cruising boats as possible and study how best to solve these problems on your own boat. Also, read the practical sections of sailing magazines and technical boating books; there are dozens of useful tips to be found there.

On small boats, it may be impossible to always have every item safely stowed. Aboard his 34-foot (10.4 m) steel ketch, Danny Greene, a former *Cruising World* editor, keeps his cutlery in a wood holder near the galley. His pots and pans are kept in a bin under the stove. When it gets really nasty, he throws everything into a box and stows it under the cockpit where, at least, the knives won't stab the skipper, and the pots won't brain the mate.

## HEAD

On a cruising boat, the simpler the toilet the better. Even the simplest systems that pump through the hull can become jammed with human waste, toilet paper, sanitary napkins/tampons, and cigarette butts. And no task on board is more onerous than cleaning out discharge lines. Add macerators, chemical rinses, and the other devices used for legalizing heads, and the potential for problems mounts astronomically. That's why some wise old sailors keep espousing the virtues of the ordinary bucket (Figure 3-12). If you need the feel

of a real toilet seat under your bottom, mount one on a board with the bucket underneath—it's no different than using the portable johns at concerts and carnivals. (Yeah, I know, they stink!) If you don't plan to empty it after every use, pour in some of the deodorizing chemicals used for portable toilets. Be advised, however, that at least in the United States, holding tanks are required inside the 3-mile limit.

Offshore, use of a holding tank is neither practical nor required by law. For use in harbor, a small holding tank can be installed beneath a berth or wherever else space is available and connected to the head with a Y-valve that permits either direct overboard dumping or depositing into the holding tank. Pumpout stations are not found everywhere in the world, let alone in the United States. So the system should be designed so the tank can be emptied with a manual pump or carried ashore for discharge. You can install a small flexible holding tank, thus meeting the letter of the law and providing a place to hold wastes when anchored in a crowded harbor (Figure 3-13).

A small washbasin in the head lets crew wash up in some place other than the galley sink, which might be occupied by the cook (Figure 3-14).

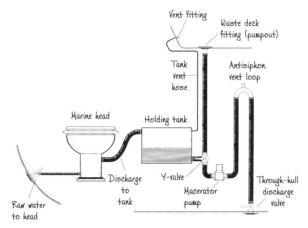

**FIGURE 3-13.** My preferred toilet installation, and West Marine's, directs all waste into a holding tank. From there, it can be pumped out through a deck fitting, or when outside the 3-mile U.S. limit, pumped overboard. (Fritz Seegers illustration)

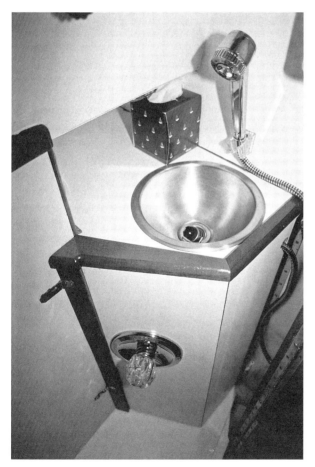

**FIGURE 3-14.** Even a small sink in the head allows you to wash up before leaving.

# FOR COMFORT AND SAFETY . . .

## A Wood Ceiling

The inside of the hull on many older boats is simply spray-painted or covered with glued-on vinyl or short-nap carpet. With age, these coverings often start to peel and mildew. Replacing them with new stain-resistant coverings will make a huge difference to the interior, and the cost is reasonable. For a more traditional treatment, a wood ceiling (that's the nautical term, even though the wood is applied to the hull sides) can turn a shabby hull interior into a classy den. Mahogany, cypress, birch, maple, etc., all may be used.

To install a ceiling, strips of wood or hose must be glassed to the hull with fiberglass mat and epoxy resin, which bonds better than polyester. Use an adhesive putty or quick-setting glue to hold them in place while you glass over with a few layers of mat (see Chapter 2). Another handy method of holding them in place until the resin kicks is to use spring-loaded curtain rods that can be pushed against the wood, then propped against a bunk edge or the other side of the hull (see Figure 3-33, page 82). It may be necessary to cut kerfs on the wood strips (saw cuts across the back) if they won't easily conform to the hull. Sand away all paint from the hull and clean with acetone. If using any toxic chemicals, put an exhaust fan on the hatch to pull out dangerous fumes—styrene fumes from polyester resin can cause serious lung and brain damage and have been known to cause blackouts, heart attacks, and even death. In addition to ensuring good ventilation, buy a quality respirator and wear it. Replace cartridges as directed.

This is a good time to consider gluing in foam insulation between the vertical strips. The cabin will retain warmth and coolness better, and condensation will be reduced. See Chapter 14 for more details.

The horizontal wood paneling could be $5/16$ to $3/8$ inch (8 mm to 9.5 mm) thick and about $1\frac{1}{2}$ inches (38 mm) wide, and screwed to the vertical strips of wood, leaving a small amount of space between each for ventilation. (If you're screwing into wood, use wood screws; if screwing into hose and fiberglass, use #6 sheet metal screws.) The space between the ceiling strips doesn't need to be that wide, but it is important to let the hull breathe, and because hulls do twist under stress, the space will keep the boards from buckling.

# The Metamorphosis of *Adriana*: A Case History

I lived with my Pearson Triton sloop *Adriana* for five years before making major changes to her interior. Most of that time I daysailed her on weekends and spent one- and two-week vacations around the Great Lakes or along the East Coast. I did a few things to her, such as installing a pipe berth for a fifth person (Figure 3-15). But all the other alterations I had planned were never affected until the spring I decided to move aboard.

I allotted six weeks to complete the modifications I had planned. My tentative list looked like this:

- Convert V-berths to one double berth
- Install sink and mirror in place of hanging locker
- Install through-hull head in place of Porta Potti
- Rip out old side-loading icebox and install new top-loading icebox
- Install a table that won't block access throughout the cabin
- Replace companionway stairs to create more galley space
- Build in bookshelves and storage space for food and miscellaneous gear
- Recover all cushions
- Replace curtains and rods
- Locate stoves for easier cooking at anchor and underway

At the end of the six weeks, all these jobs had been completed, including new bottom paint and topside paint, a wind vane, and a few smaller jobs on the rig. I worked on weekends and after work on weekdays. Figure 3-16 shows the before and after arrangements of *Adriana*'s interior.

## CONVERTING V-BERTHS TO A DOUBLE BERTH

The simplest way to make a double berth forward is to make an insert to fill the spaces between the V-berth singles. Lower the fiddles that hold the cushions in place, cut a piece of plywood to fit the opening, screw a fiddle to the aft end of the insert board

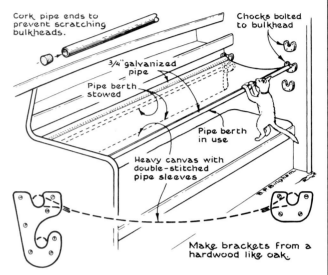

**FIGURE 3-15.** A pipe berth set up over a settee in the main cabin provides a comfortable berth for an extra guest and is quickly stowed out of the way in the morning.

to hold the cushion in place, cut a piece of 4- or 5-inch (102 mm to 127 mm) foam to fit over the board, cover, and you've got a king-size playpen (Figure 3-17).

The only problem with this double berth is that you have to dive in headfirst and often there's no floor space to walk or turn around, nor any place to sit down while undressing. Also, the berth is so wide at the after end that much of the space goes unused.

An alternative, discussed earlier, is an offset berth, either to port or starboard. Remove both V-berth cushions, cut a piece of plywood to angle across the opening, then cut a new piece of foam to fit. Again, a fiddle will hold it in place. Planned correctly, there will still be room to walk into the forward cabin, sit on the edge of the bunk or the after end of the unused berth, and contemplate the hedonistic joy of sleeping in a large, comfy berth (Figure 3-18). The only drawback is the person outboard having to climb over his or her sleeping mate. Everything is indeed a compromise, and this berth configuration is no exception.

# The Metamorphosis of *Adriana*: A Case History (cont.)

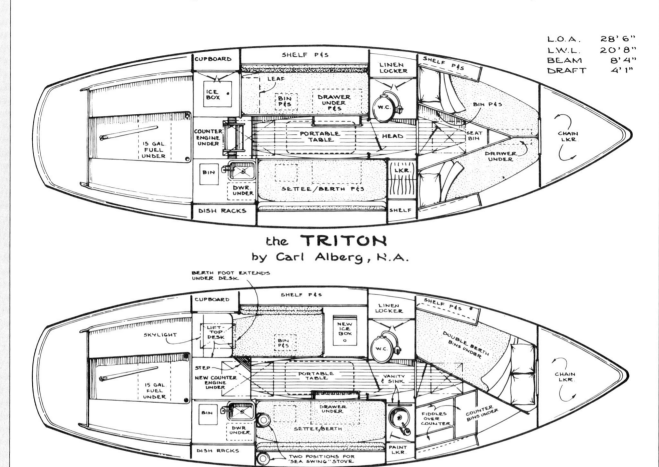

L.O.A. 28'6"
L.W.L. 20'8"
BEAM 8'4"
DRAFT 4'1"

the **TRITON**
by Carl Alberg, N.A.

**MODIFICATIONS to ADRIANA**

**FIGURE 3-16.** These two drawings show *Adriana*'s interior before and after the changes were made, including relocation of the icebox, an offset double berth forward, removal of the companionway stairs, and conversion of the hanging locker to a sink and vanity. The removable table over the starboard berth is not shown.

I wanted to be able to reconvert the berth back to two singles when my children visited in the summer, so I decided to keep things simple. I merely removed the foam double and plywood underneath and replaced them with the original two V-berth cushions. To keep the kids from rolling out or invading each other's space, lee cloths fitted to the inboard edge of each bunk did the trick (Figure 3-19). These same types of cloths or lee boards should also be fitted to those berths in the main cabin that will be used for sea berths. Lee boards can be padded on one side and used as backrests during the day. Install one set of mounts (such as U-shaped blocks of wood

screwed into bulkheads or furniture) at the inboard head and foot of the berth, and another set at the outboard edge. For sleeping, remove the board from its backrest mount, flip it over so the padded side faces the berth, and insert it in the lee board mounting position.

## INSTALLING A SINK AND MIRROR IN A HANGING LOCKER

On a small cruiser, it is almost axiomatic that all clothes will be wrinkled—even if there is a hanging locker to hang dress shirts and jackets. The hanging

73

# The Metamorphosis of *Adriana*: A Case History (cont.)

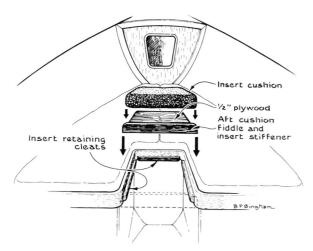

**FIGURE 3-17.** The easiest way to convert forward V-berths to a double is by cutting an insert board and cushion to fit between the two.

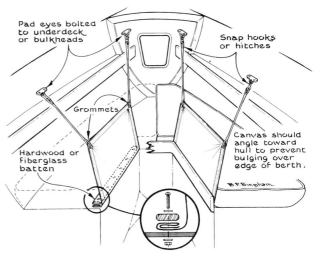

**FIGURE 3-19.** Canvas lee cloths or lee boards should be installed on any sea berth. V-berths can't really be considered sea berths, but I installed lee cloths for my kids, who were 4 and 8 years old at the time. In any case, the illustration shows how they are made.

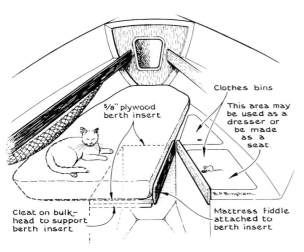

**FIGURE 3-18.** On the Triton, I chose to install an offset double berth on the port side. This left the starboard side for a seat and clothes bins.

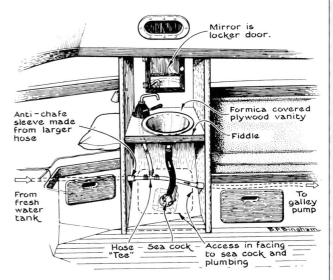

**FIGURE 3-20.** Acknowledging that clothes are always wrinkled on small boats anyway, the Triton's hanging locker was converted to a sink and vanity.

locker on *Adriana* was opposite the head, but it was narrow and difficult to use. It took me about 3 seconds to decide that the space would better be used as a sink for washing up, shaving, combing hair, and brushing teeth.

Adding a sink, however, is not a simple or inexpensive job. Materials required include the sink, sea-

# The Metamorphosis of *Adriana*: A Case History (cont.)

cock, hose to connect them, a pump, hose and T-fitting to connect the pump to the water tank, and a board to mount them on (Figure 3-20). The cost of these items easily could approach $300 or $400. If possible, route the sink drain to an existing seacock in the head or galley. This will save expenses and eliminate an additional through-hull.

Begin by screwing in cleats (¾ inch by 2 inch/ 19 mm by 51 mm lengths of wood) to the sides of the hanging locker. When positioning them, make sure the sink is at a comfortable height, and allow for the thickness of the plywood top and Formica or other laminate such as Wilson Art. Cut the plywood vanity top to size. Paint, varnish, or otherwise seal the edges to prevent moisture from creeping in and causing delamination. Use a fine-toothed (e.g., 32-point) saber saw to cut a piece of Formica to the approximate size, but slightly larger; later, when you're done, you'll trim off the excess with a router. A hacksaw with a blindcut handle also works well; it's slow but accurate. Cut with the Formica upside down to minimize chipping, and keep your blade close to the edge of the workbench or other supporting surface.

With a brush, spread contact cement on both the wood and the underside of the plastic. Two coatings are necessary as there is some absorption. Let it dry for a few minutes. If the pieces are small, you can probably eyeball the placement of the plastic onto the wood; this is important because once the two touch it's nearly impossible to separate them. If the pieces are larger than about 2 square feet (0.19 m²), lay two dowels on top of the wood and lay the Formica on top of them. Look straight down onto the Formica and when it is positioned correctly, just slide out the dowels. Seal the two firmly by placing a block of wood on top and hitting it with a hammer. Start in the center and work out toward the edges. Let it dry before filing the edges smooth and flush with the wood. Exposed edges that can't be covered with wood trim look best with a bevel (Figure 3-21).

Now draw a cutline for the sink and pump holes. Drill a hole inside the circle large enough to accept your saber saw blade. Using a coarse-cut blade or pushing the saw too rapidly causes the thin surface

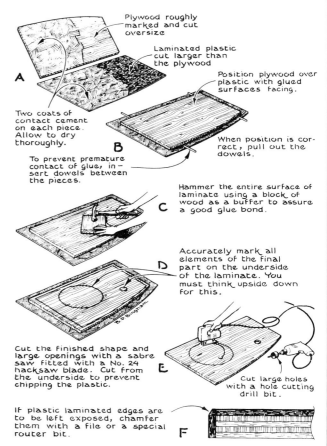

Plywood roughly marked and cut oversize

Laminated plastic cut larger than the plywood

Position plywood over plastic with glued surfaces facing.

Two coats of contact cement on each piece. Allow to dry thoroughly.

When position is correct, pull out the dowels.

To prevent premature contact of glue, insert dowels between the pieces.

Hammer the entire surface of laminate using a block of wood as a buffer to assure a good glue bond.

Accurately mark all elements of the final part on the underside of the laminate. You must think upside down for this.

Cut the finished shape and large openings with a sabre saw fitted with a No. 24 hacksaw blade. Cut from the underside to prevent chipping the plastic.

Cut large holes with a hole cutting drill bit.

If plastic laminated edges are to be left exposed, chamfer them with a file or a special router bit.

**FIGURE 3-21.** Wilson Art laminated plastic (similar to Formica brand) was glued to a piece of plywood. Dowels were used to keep them separated until aligned perfectly. A saber saw was used to cut the holes for the sink and pump.

of the plastic to chip off, so be patient. You'll soon learn to appreciate any cut edge that is covered by a fixture. In this instance, both the sink and pump overlapped the cut edges of the holes and obscured the tiny chips in the Formica.

With that portion of the project completed, I hung the mirror behind the sink to permit access to the paint locker and cut a space in the vanity front below the sink to give access to the seacock (Figure 3-22). It was also a well-ventilated storage bin for carrying bags, ice nets, and foul weather gear. The hanging locker was never missed.

75

# The Metamorphosis of *Adriana*: A Case History (cont.)

**FIGURE 3-22.** Although the area below the sink was crammed with foul-weather gear, it enabled quick access to the seacock if trouble developed.

## INSTALLING A THROUGH-HULL TOILET

For years, my solution to the head problem was a Thetford Porta Potti, which is a self-contained unit containing a 5-gallon (19 L) water compartment and separate waste receptacle. It was inexpensive, easy to operate, and satisfied the letter of the law in the United States.

During a trip from Lake Michigan to Newport, Rhode Island, we traversed the Trent-Severn Waterway through Ontario, and learned that Canada had outlawed portable heads in the Great Lakes. Apparently they doubted that sailors would empty them ashore. They were right; it was a nuisance to lug the apparatus through the cabin, into the dinghy, and then search out a public facility that wouldn't object to our flushing the waste in their toilets.

I traded my Porta Potti to a friend for a leaky through-hull toilet. The biggest chore involved in

making the conversion was installing the two seacocks—one for overboard discharge, the other for seawater flush. (How to do this is described in detail in Chapter 4.) If possible, mount the toilet on a platform above the waterline; moving it outboard may also help elevate it. If you can't, the bowl may overflow from water entering the intake flush; of course you should remember to close the valve after each use, but looping the hose high above the waterline helps. You can't put an antisiphon device in it because the pump would suck air. Screw the toilet to the floor with large square-head lag bolts, or, if you can reach underneath it, use bolts, nuts, and washers. Cut the reinforced hose to the proper length and smear an appropriate sealant over the fitting opening and on the inside of the hose to prevent leaking and make later removal easier.

Fasten each hose with stainless steel hose clamps. The schematic of my preferred system is shown in Figure 3-13.

If the toilet sits below water level and its discharge is submerged (which it should be!), install a vented loop in the discharge hose to prevent water from siphoning in (Figure 3-23). This requires elevating the lines above water level and placing the antisiphon device at the apex of the line. Be sure to screw it to a sturdy surface. Use sealant and hose clamps in all hose connections. I also have one of these on the seawater cooling hose for my diesel engine (see Chapter 8).

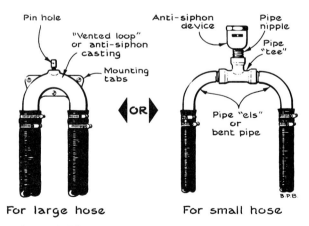

**FIGURE 3-23.** This drawing shows a vented loop, which should be installed above the water level in the head compartment.

# The Metamorphosis of *Adriana*: A Case History (cont.)

## INSTALLING A TOP-LOADING ICEBOX

The Pearson Triton was built with a seemingly ingenious side-loading icebox under the bridge deck on the port side. Ice was loaded through a deck hatch in the cockpit. This compartment was above the food storage area. The food storage area was accessible from the cabin and the two were connected by a small opening in the upper compartment, the idea being that the cold air would fall into the food area below. It was a nice idea, but it didn't work very well, for several reasons. First, the ice melted quickly in the hot cockpit (the lid to the ice compartment was only 1-inch/ 25 mm foam encapsulated with fiberglass). One-inch foam was also used around the entire icebox below, only one quarter of the minimum thickness required for decent insulation. Further, the side-loading door, while handsome and reminiscent of grandfather's icebox eighty years ago, was grossly inefficient. Because cold air sinks to the lowest possible level, every time the door was opened all the cold air fell out.

Partly because I was short on counter space, and partly because putting the new top-loading icebox under the bridge wouldn't have allowed enough room to take off the lid, I resolved to relocate the icebox forward on the port side, next to the bulkhead separating the main cabin from the head.

The first thing I had to do was rip out the old icebox, a task that I approached with not a little trepidation. Peeling off the fake teak veneer on the front revealed wood screws that kept the whole thing together. Prying deeper into the mysteries of the icebox required a crowbar to separate the wood frame from the fiberglass liner. The entire box had been built in situ. The foam was so paltry and half-disintegrated that it was no wonder ice lasted so short a time. The icebox was tacked to the hull in a few places with one layer of glass cloth, and this was easily broken with a hammer and cold chisel. The entire unit was too bulky to remove from the cabin through the main hatch, so it was necessary to smash it into pieces. As it turned out, the box was already in pieces by the time it emerged from its berth beneath the bridge.

Figure 3-24 illustrates the main points of constructing a new icebox without benefit of a premolded liner. Use 2-inch (51 mm) foam all around,

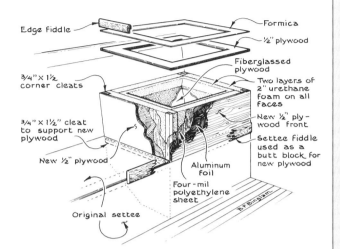

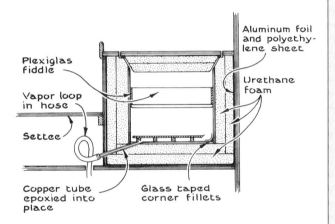

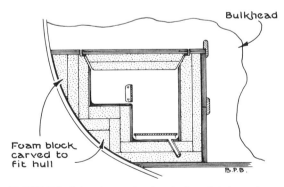

**FIGURE 3-24.** Schematic of an icebox fabricated from plywood, fir framing, and 4 inches (102 mm) of urethane foam.

# The Metamorphosis of *Adriana*: A Case History (cont.)

doubled for a total thickness of 4 inches (102 mm). The more the better. Avoid butt joints, using glued staggered joints instead to help retain water vapors (Figure 3-25). Both a vapor-proof and heat-reflective barrier should be incorporated. Use polyester resin to stick the Mylar and tinfoil to the insides of the plywood housing box. (Bruce Bingham says that polyethylene sheeting is more workable than Mylar.) A space blanket functions as both.

Glue the seams, caulk with contact cement and polysulfide, and tape them with a metal-type tape. Cut plywood to form all surfaces of the box, fit in place, fillet, and glass over with 1½-ounce (457 g/m²) mat. Coat the cured surfaces with pigmented gelcoat or epoxy.

The drain deserves some consideration. This one emptied into the bilge, and some folks complained that this made the bilge smell. A better long-term arrangement would be to pump the water overboard or into a container. You can fit a small pump outside the icebox to drain water. But this does require your attention at periodic intervals. If you go ashore for a day, the ice melts and then sits in its own water until pumped. Few things, besides poor insulation, make ice melt faster than sitting in water. Bruce says his studies show that ice melts about 15% faster if standing in water. On the other hand, it does avoid

the possibility of leaks and algae forming in the drain hose's water trap (a U-shaped loop in the hose that traps water and keeps the cold air from flowing out).

Some persons tap the icebox drain for freshwater drinking, though it seems to me that the water used for making ice is not of the purest quality. Worse, the meltwater usually is contaminated by spilled milk, rotting vegetables, and other decaying matter (Figure 3-26). One solution is to build a sump into the drain that can be pumped dry when it becomes full.

I used Formica to cover the plywood shell of the icebox and fitted mahogany fiddles along the edges of the icebox, so low, flat objects could be left on top of the icebox while underway. Also, this minimized the number of Formica edges that had to be cut without error. You can usually find fiddle material at a well-stocked chandlery or make it from regular stock with a router.

You can make your own lid in a few hours (Figure 3-27). Cut the lid from a piece of mahogany or teak-faced plywood (or any other wood you like). Glass at least 2 inches (51 mm) of foam to the underside, using one layer of 6- or 10-ounce (203 to 339 g/m²) cloth. Leave space around the edges for the lid to rest on the top of the icebox; if you want it

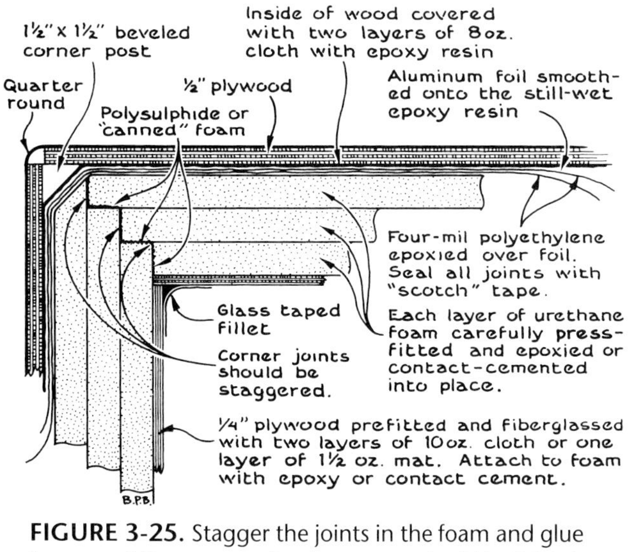

**FIGURE 3-25.** Stagger the joints in the foam and glue to prevent the escape of water vapors. Avoid butt joints.

1½" x 1½" beveled corner post

Inside of wood covered with two layers of 8oz. cloth with epoxy resin

Quarter round

½" plywood

Aluminum foil smoothed onto the still-wet epoxy resin

Polysulphide or "canned" foam

Four-mil polyethylene epoxied over foil. Seal all joints with "scotch" tape.

Glass taped fillet

Each layer of urethane foam carefully press-fitted and epoxied or contact-cemented into place.

Corner joints should be staggered.

¼" plywood prefitted and fiberglassed with two layers of 10oz. cloth or one layer of 1½ oz. mat. Attach to foam with epoxy or contact cement.

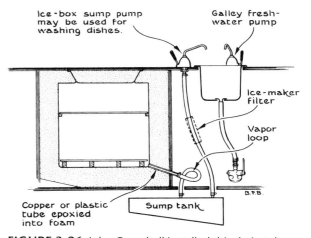

Ice-box sump pump may be used for washing dishes.

Galley freshwater pump

Ice-maker filter

Vapor loop

Copper or plastic tube epoxied into foam

Sump tank

**FIGURE 3-26.** John Campbell installed this drain tube arrangement aboard his 35-foot (10.7 m) junk-rigged schooner so he could hand pump the water into the sink. In my experience, however, this water is seldom pure enough to drink.

# The Metamorphosis of *Adriana*: A Case History (cont.)

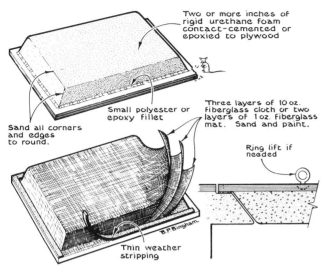

**FIGURE 3-27.** To make an icebox lid, use ½-inch (12 mm) mahogany plywood and 2 inches (51 mm) of urethane foam. A rubber gasket helps seal off the icebox compartment.

**FIGURE 3-28.** The Murray Snap-Apart Hinge works like a clevis pin and is an ideal fitting for anything you want to be securely mounted, yet removable. (South Pacific Associates)

flush, screw in strips of wood to the underside of the plywood icebox top, or make two tops—the first ½ inch (12 mm) narrower all around than the second, which is just a hair larger than the lid.

The upshot of all this is that 15 pounds (6.8 kg) of ice now lasted for four days and longer, depending on how many times the lid was opened. This was a melt rate of just under 4 pounds (1.8 kg) a day. Acceptable performance is about 6 pounds (2.7 kg) a day, 4 to 5 pounds is good, and under 4 is superior. Later, I purchased a foam thermal blanket to cover the ice and food; this functioned as extra insulation (the lid is still the weak link, being only 2 inches/ 51 mm thick) and reduced the size of the compartment being cooled.

## INSTALLING A REMOVABLE TABLE

The Triton is a narrow boat at 8 feet 4 inches (2.5 m). The usual table arrangement is a removable affair that in position hooks onto either side of the door to the head and is supported by a leg to the cabin sole. The only way to get forward is to remove the table.

Murray Snap-Apart hinges have spring-loaded pins enabling the two halves to separate (Figure 3-28).

These ingenious devices can be used in a multitude of places on a boat—sea lockers, engine compartment boards, companionway ladders, and removable dinette tables—on anything you want to hinge and remove. They were just what I needed to mount my dinette table to the backrest of my starboard berth (Figure 3-29). The removable support leg was cut short so it rested on the inboard edge of the berth, just inside the board that holds the cushion in place. The through-bolted hinges supported all the weight one could possibly place on it.

**FIGURE 3-29.** The Snap-Apart hinges were fitted to the Triton's dinette table so it could be removed when the settee was used for sleeping or lounging.

# The Metamorphosis of *Adriana*: A Case History (cont.)

When the bunk was needed for sleeping, the table could be taken off by simply popping the hinge pins; the table was then stowed under the bunk along with the removable support leg.

Had any of the bulkheads been large enough, or better situated, I might have permanently fastened a fold-down table with piano hinges to function as extra surface area for food preparation, navigation, or just odds and ends. Fastening a chain to either corner of the table and to the bulkhead would have been one way to hold it up. A less obstructed method would have been a pivoting brace—the kind used for extra leaves on dining room tables—that folds up flush to the bulkhead when not in use.

## ADDING BOOKSHELVES AND EXTRA STORAGE SPACE

Nothing makes a boat look more homey than a good selection of books. Navigation books and nautical almanacs are, of course, a necessity. On most boats, little book space is provided. A rack for ten volumes above the navigation station is insufficient.

Like many production boats, the Triton had shelves running the length of the main cabin beneath the side decks. These had short fiddles to retain things, but when heeled over, everything tumbled out. The spaces behind the bunk backrests were also wide open, and while they were handy for storing frying pans and aluminum foil, it was always a chore to pull out everything on top to get at something you wanted at the bottom.

My solution was to put a teak veneer facing on the shelves with 4- by 6-inch (102 mm by 152 mm) cutouts for access (Figure 3-30). I nailed cleats to the inboard edge of the original shelf and glued them to the underside of the deck with epoxy, then screwed the facing into the cleats. Below these I built another set of shelves at the same height as the backrests. This closed off the space behind the bunks, but again, access was obtained by cutting out rectangular holes.

To do this, drill a pilot hole and then insert a saber saw to make the cut. If you decide to save the cutout pieces for doors, use a drill the same width as

**FIGURE 3-30.** The shelves behind the berths were enclosed with teak veneer, and the area immediately behind the berths was cut out so that shelving could be installed on top for books.

the saber saw blade and drill them continuously for ½ inch (12 mm) or the width of the saber saw blade. Use a sharp, thin pocket knife to clean out the thin wall between holes. Measure carefully and, before making the cut, use a pencil to scribe the cut line.

Finally I strung shock cord across the shelves that kept books and other items in place. A more conventional method is to simply cut a removable wood bar as shown in Figure 3-31.

**FIGURE 3-31.** A relatively easy way to retain books on a shelf is to make a removable wood bar that sits in U-shaped wood pieces on each side.

# The Metamorphosis of *Adriana*: A Case History (cont.)

## RECOVERING ALL CUSHIONS

*Adriana*'s stock cushions were a burnt-orange vinyl, easy to clean and waterproof, but sticky in hot weather and cold and clammy in the winter. The easiest solution was to make slipcovers. There are lots of fabrics and colors, but to keep costs low, I used red corduroy. A local seamstress whipped them up at a very reasonable price. Velcro was used to seal the backsides so they could be removed and washed periodically. Zippers, especially metal ones, invariably get sticky and, when tugged hard, begin ripping away from the fabric. Perhaps no other improvement made so much difference in the looks of the boat, making it warmer and more modern as well.

## REPLACING CURTAINS AND RODS

The original curtain rods were plastic-coated metal and so tight that the curtain slides always hung up, eventually pulling away from the curtain. After years of resewing, I took off the old rods and replaced them. The pop rivets into the inner liner were easily drilled out with a hand drill and new tracks screwed into the deck liner with ⅜-inch (9.5 mm) screws. Most chandleries sell curtain track and slides that work well, so there's really no need to fabricate your own.

For a time, I considered just using dowels fitted to wood blocks glued to the cabin sides, but these would have been bulky and probably weaker than tracks screwed flush to the cabin. Keep your old curtains for a pattern to make the new ones.

## RELOCATING STOVES

With the small amount of counter space on the Triton, finding a place to put the cookstove was always a hassle, and it's a common problem on most small boats. Usually, the portable two-burner alcohol stove was kept under the bridge with a piece of shock

**FIGURE 3-32.** A Sea Swing stove, fitted with a kerosene burner, was used for cooking underway. The alcohol stove underneath the bridge deck was pulled out for cooking at anchor.

cord. Later I had a welder make a pivoting arm that could be screwed to the side of the galley. A swinging arm, with gimbals on top, permitted using the stove underway. When not in use, the arm and stove could be swung outboard and more or less out of the way.

A better solution for this boat turned out to be installing a Sea Swing stove with a kerosene burner for use underway (Figure 3-32). Two mounting bases let me stow the stove in an out-of-the-way place when not in use. The two-burner alcohol stove was back under the bridge where it could easily be pulled out on the new galley counter top for cooking at anchor. It would have been nice to have a kerosene or gas stove/oven, but on the Triton this would have necessitated shortening one of the bunks and reducing seating space. With pressure cookers and stovetop ovens, stove burners can do most of the things of a conventional oven.

Another important job I undertook inside the hull was replacing gate valves with seacocks. This is described in Chapter 4.

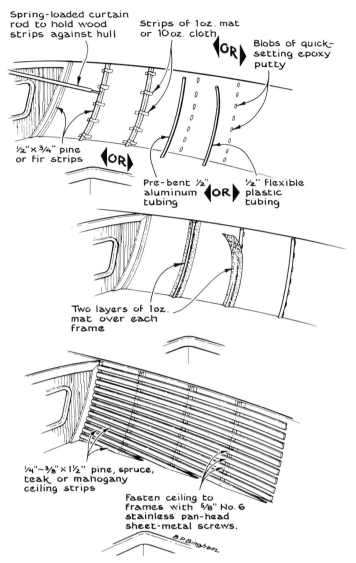

Spring-loaded curtain rod to hold wood strips against hull

Strips of 1oz. mat or 10oz. cloth

**⟨OR⟩**

Blobs of quick-setting epoxy putty

½" × ¾" pine or fir strips

**⟨OR⟩**

Pre-bent ½" aluminum tubing

**⟨OR⟩**

½" flexible plastic tubing

Two layers of 1oz. mat over each frame

¼"–⅜" × 1½" pine, spruce, teak or mahogany ceiling strips

Fasten ceiling to frames with ⅝" No. 6 stainless pan-head sheet-metal screws.

B.R.Bingham

**FIGURE 3-33.** A cedar ceiling attractively covers the sides of bare fiberglass hulls. Consider adding foam insulation behind the wood strips to prevent condensation. Note the spring-loaded curtain rods, which keep the fir strips against the hull until the resin kicks.

Covering the insides of a hull to make it look better presents a dilemma for the offshore sailor. If the hull cracks or is holed, it is vital to be able to get to that spot in order to effect some sort of repair—stuffing in towels, screwing plywood over the hole, draping a collision mat over it, using underwater epoxy, or whatever. The French monohull *Faram Seranissima* was lost in the North Atlantic in 1981 when she struck an object, and the crew couldn't locate the hole. Fiberglass interior liners, commonly used on production sailboats to simplify the building of bunks and lockers, make it almost impossible to reach every inch of the hull. Often the only access is through hatches under berth cushions. Fiberglass is tough to cut or smash away with an ax. A plywood interior can be unscrewed if there is time, or knocked out with an ax in desperation. Also, when those inevitable leaks occur where deck hardware is through-bolted through the deck, liners make it very hard to get at them. Nowadays, many builders are installing removable vinyl panels that can be popped off to provide access to the underside of the deck, especially where hardware is mounted. A wood ceiling does inhibit the speediness and ease of gaining access to the hull, but if it is screwed in, it can be removed without much difficulty, although slowly. In an emergency, destroy it!

## Plywood versus Fiberglass Furniture

As noted above, as well as in the last chapter, most boats built since the 1970s have fiberglass pans or inner liners that incorporate the major pieces of furniture—berth foundations, galley, and so forth. French builder Henri Amel and Catalina's Frank Butler both claim credit for this innovation. These pans often incorporate structural grids that stiffen the hull bottom; better to have fiberglass in the bilge than wood. Because a plywood interior, built up piece by piece, is the most expensive part of such a boat, considerable savings are possible by molding a one-piece pan that eliminates dozens of hand-cut parts.

I've already outlined disadvantages—poor thermal and acoustic insulation, and the inability to access all parts of the hull behind the pans. Plus, they make it much more difficult to modify the interior. In fact, I'm inclined to say that if you want to alter the accommodation plan, you shouldn't buy a boat whose furniture is based on a fiberglass pan; cutting out large pieces of fiberglass may compromise structural integrity and will almost certainly lower resale value. The latter is important, and for that reason I am very careful about any changes I make to the original boat. I, and other buyers, especially hate to see boats in which previous owners have installed various pieces of equipment and then removed them, leaving poorly repaired holes everywhere, from bulkheads to berth faces to the deck.

Nowadays, the only boats with all-wood or mostly wood interiors are custom and semi-custom yachts, though a few, like Tartan Yachts and Sabre Yachts, still incorporate a lot of wood. Small fiberglass modules are ideally suited to the head, shower, and engine bed. Most other brands, however, will present you with a large fiberglass pan that probably includes at least the cabin sole and may extend all the way up to the hull-deck joint. Examine these pans closely before purchase, as you probably should consider them cast in stone, or maybe I should say, cast in glass.

## Ventilation

A last thought on interior modifications is ventilation. Dorades, mushroom vents, and other types of on-deck ventilation will be discussed later. But for the moment, consider the problem of moving air about the cabin—through drawers, between cabins, and into lockers and cabinets to minimize the growth of mildew.

Plastic building vents, used in building construction to let eaves breathe, can be mounted on the sides of galley cabinets, berths, bins, and anywhere else that air has a hard time circulating (Figure 3-34). A hole saw on a hand drill cuts the hole, and the vent pops in.

Bulkheads prevent the free flow of air between cabins, and many liveaboards combat this by cutting large holes in them. When I visited Eric and Susan Hiscock at their anchorage in New Zealand's Bay of Islands, their *Wanderer IV* had a 1-square-foot (0.093 m²) hole cut in the bulkhead between the head and aft cabin. If you're worried about privacy, a small curtain can be hung on one side to close it off when the head

FIGURE 3-35. The advantage of caning in cabinet doors is that they allow air to pass through, thus reducing mildew. But if heavy objects are stowed inside, they could break through the caning during a knockdown.

is in use. You'll be surprised what a difference it makes.

Lastly, drawer fronts without finger holes let the air inside stagnate and allow mildew to accumulate. Even with finger holes, drawers stuffed with clothing trap air. I once found my black dress shoes encrusted with a yellow mustard–like powder after stowing them in a drawer. Consider enlarging the hole, installing a building vent or two in the facing of the drawer, or replacing solid cabinet doors with louvered or cane faces. Caning (Figure 3-35), however, should be avoided on the door of any large locker full of heavy objects, as a can of tomatoes would have little difficulty busting through en route to your forehead.

## Round Corners

An important consideration to keep in mind as you develop your plans is to avoid injury-causing pointed corners. Take a look at some new production boats; most boatbuilders are beginning to do wonderful things with curved laminated surfaces that are not only attractive, but safe.

Rounding pointed corners will require a bit more work on your part, but with a little thought, you'll need no special tools, and you'll be much more pleased with the result. Precut moldings are commercially available in a variety of shapes and sizes. Figure 3-36 will give you some ideas.

## Locking Hatches

Outside companionway locks are found on just about every boat. The standard padlock and hasp

FIGURE 3-34. Small soffit vents, used on houses to ventilate eaves, can be installed in cabinetry to prevent mildew. This boat is a Kells 28.

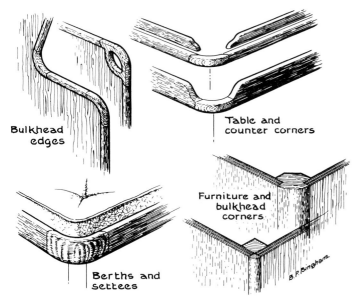

Bulkhead edges

Table and counter corners

Berths and settees

Furniture and bulkhead corners

B.P.Bingham

**FIGURE 3-36.** All sharp or pointed corners inside the boat should be rounded to prevent injury.

arrangement usually suffices to keep intruders out when you're gone. But what about the time when you're *in* the boat, and someone comes aboard?

We've all heard horror stories about people being terrorized by burglars, rapists, and the like. Suppose you see several men with machetes or guns climbing over the rail. Unless you're armed and prepared to blow them away, the safest course is to dart back inside and lock all the hatches. Then, assuming you have a VHF radio, call for help. If your hatches are well constructed and securely locked, it'll take a lot of ax or firepower to roust you out.

Chapter 9 contains directions on how to reinforce your main companionway hatch. Here are a few suggestions on how to lock it from inside and out (Figure 3-37). They also emphasize watertightness, an important characteristic of any hatch, for safety as well as a dry cabin.

The simplest method to secure the hatch from inside is to use a dowel or board that can be wedged between the aft facing edge of the deck and the forward facing surface of the hatch. This does the same thing as dropping a stick on the track of a sliding glass patio door. It's simple and as strong as any lock, and unlike a hasp and lock, there isn't any slop to rattle around in the hopes of working screws loose.

Another method is to use deadbolts that are screwed into the hatch, with small aligning holes drilled into the side of the deck to secure the hatch.

The exact configuration will depend on how your hatch is constructed.

And, of course, you can also use hasps and padlocks for this purpose. Through-bolting the hasps and deadbolts is stronger than screwing them in because in most cases the wood and fiberglass aren't thick enough to provide superior holding power.

## Floorboards

Offshore race rules require that all floorboards be positively secured so that in the event of a capsize they don't fall out and cause damage. If there are no heavy stores below the board, shock cord rove through pad eyes may be sufficient. But because many floorboards are heavy, and on cruising boats the bilge is used for stowage, a better solution is a positive-action, flush-mounted latch or handle. ABI makes a nice mechanism with a removable handle or key (Figure 3-38).

Similar locking mechanisms can be installed on berth top access lids and cubby covers behind settee cushions—in fact, anywhere that stowed objects pose a threat. And just because some lid or cabinet door has hinges, doesn't mean they're strong; if in doubt, replace screws with through-bolts.

## Imagine the Worst

Living aboard for a time will surely point out any shortcomings in the layout of your interior, and odds are you'll make more changes as time goes by. You can't possibly think of everything at once, especially before you've moved aboard or taken an extended cruise. Experience is the best teacher.

Before you shove off, however, have a seat in the cabin and look around. Imagine the boat knocked down with the spreaders in the water, or worse, turning over. What can come loose? Will the frying pan be launched across the cabin? Is the icebox lid hinged? (Those sharp corners could easily penetrate a skull.) Will all the books end up in the bilge? Is there a strainer on the bilge pump hose to prevent it from clogging up?

How about the crew? Can they be secured in their bunks where they won't be hurt? Are tools and emergency gear easy to reach? Can you lock the hatch from the inside if there are intruders on deck or waves breaking over the boat? Don't set sail until you've considered every aspect of safety for yourself and your crew.

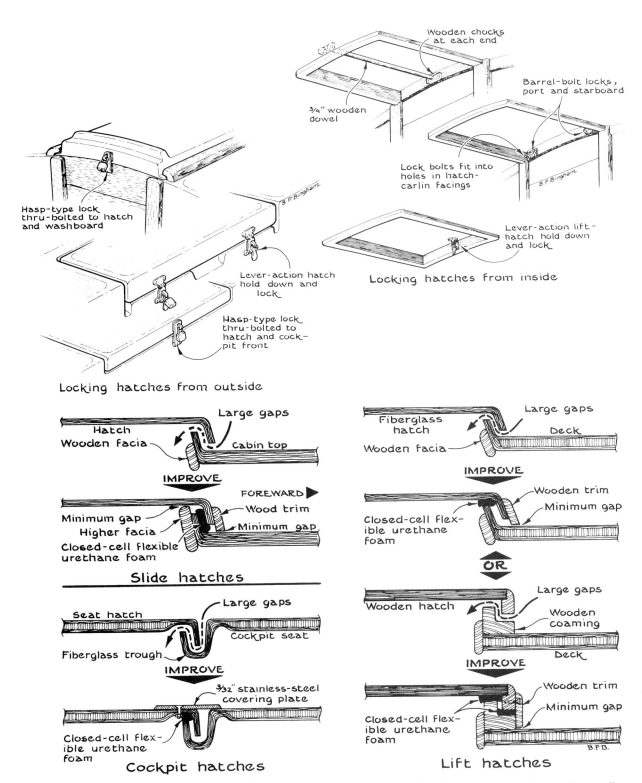

Wooden chocks at each end

¾" wooden dowel

Barrel-bolt locks, port and starboard

Lock bolts fit into holes in hatch-carlin facings

B.P. Bingham

Hasp-type lock thru-bolted to hatch and washboard

Lever-action lift-hatch hold down and lock

Lever-action hatch hold down and lock

**Locking hatches from inside**

Hasp-type lock thru-bolted to hatch and cockpit front

**Locking hatches from outside**

Hatch
Wooden facia
Large gaps
Cabin top

**IMPROVE**

FOREWARD ▶

Minimum gap
Higher facia
Closed-cell flexible urethane foam
Wood trim
Minimum gap

**Slide hatches**

Seat hatch
Large gaps
Cockpit seat
Fiberglass trough

**IMPROVE**

³⁄₃₂" stainless-steel covering plate
Closed-cell flexible urethane foam

**Cockpit hatches**

Fiberglass hatch
Large gaps
Deck
Wooden facia

**IMPROVE**

Closed-cell flexible urethane foam
Wooden trim
Minimum gap

**OR**

Wooden hatch
Large gaps
Wooden coaming
Deck

**IMPROVE**

Closed-cell flexible urethane foam
Wooden trim
Minimum gap

B.P.B.

**Lift hatches**

**FIGURE 3-37.** A good security system on a boat includes some means of locking the hatches from the inside as well as outside. Also, weatherproofing adds to safety and comfort below.

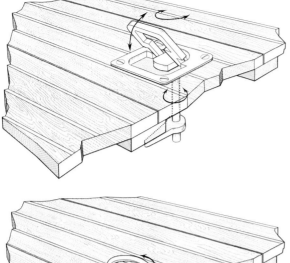

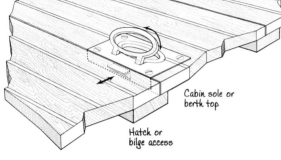

Cabin sole or berth top

Hatch or bilge access

**FIGURE 3-38.** Floorboards must be secured so that they won't go flying in a capsize. This ABI handle/key and flush-mounted mechanism positively locks the board in place. (Fritz Seegers illustrations)

## DISASTER CHECKLIST

▓ Strap batteries to hull or structural wood members with heavy canvas or polypropylene straps and large galvanized eyebolts or other strong fasteners.

▓ Devise a method of securing hatch boards in the cabin sole with locks, deadbolts, or any other method that will keep them in place with the boat upside down.

▓ Do the same for berth lids underneath settees.

▓ Make heavy canvas lee cloths with boltropes on all four sides, or build sturdy bunk boards with secure mounts. Pad eyes to receive the wire cables or nylon rope that tightens them should be through-bolted to bulkheads or the deck or hull.

▓ Make lockers for pots, pans, and canned goods extra strong. Through-bolt door hinges rather than screwing them in, and notch drawers so they don't fly open.

▓ Bilge pump intake hoses must have strainers, and if the bilge is deep and the hose hard to reach, attach strings to them so they can easily be fetched and cleared. At least one bilge pump should be operable from below.

▓ All hatches must be lockable from below with positive-action mechanisms.

▓ Provide safe storage for gimballed lamps in heavy weather; the glass chimneys break easily and are potentially dangerous, not to mention the hazards of spilled fuel.

▓ Securely bolt or glass engine beds to the floors. Be sure the engine is securely tightened to large-diameter mounts.

▓ Ensure all shelves have high fiddles, covering boards, or retaining lines to keep books and other items in place.

▓ Secure all instruments to bulkheads or other strong structural members.

▓ Permanently fix loose ballast to the keel before going to sea.

## FURTHER READING

*Boat Joinery & Cabinetmaking Simplified.* Fred P. Bingham. Camden, Maine: International Marine, 1993.

*The Boat Owner's Fitting Out Manual.* Jeff Toghill. New York: Van Nostrand Reinhold, 1980.

*The Finely Fitted Yacht.* Vols. 1 and 2. Ferenc Máté. New York: Norton, 1979.

*Modern Wooden Yacht Construction: Cold-Molding, Joinery, Fitting Out.* John Guzzwell. Camden, Maine: International Marine, 1979.

*Offshore Sailing: 200 Essential Passagemaking Tips.* Bill Seifert with Daniel Spurr. Camden, Maine: International Marine, 2002.

*The Seaworthy Offshore Sailboat: A Guide to Essential Features, Gear, and Handling.* John Vigor. Camden, Maine: International Marine, 1999.

# INSTALLING AND MAINTAINING SEACOCKS

Seacocks are metal or plastic valves that are attached to through-hull fittings wherever water enters or leaves the hull as part of the plumbing system. Sink drains, toilet discharge, engine seawater intake, and bilge pump discharge are just a few of the through-hull fittings on a cruising boat. On some boats, gate valves are substituted for the more expensive seacock, and in some cases, there is no valve at all. Before going to sea, all through-hulls should be fitted with positive-action seacocks.

Like many boats, the Triton had no seacocks when I bought her. The cockpit scupper hoses were connected to 8-inch-long (203 mm) molded fiberglass tubes bonded to the bottom of the hull. Hose clamps kept the hoses fastened. But rubber does deteriorate over time, and if a hose ever burst, there'd be a real panic on board trying to pull apart the engine compartment boards to reach the tube and plug it with a softwood plug. Softwood plugs should be kept handy no matter what sort of valve is fitted to the through-hull, but a good quality seacock is your best hedge against this calamity. (My friend Bill Seifert does not recommend tying softwood plugs to the seacocks because such areas are typically wet and the wood will swell; he suggests keeping them in an airtight plastic bag in an easily accessible place, like the nav station.)

If the tubes had extended well above the waterline, I would have left them intact, but that was not the case. I cut them off and installed ball-valve seacocks made of Marelon (Figure 4-1). They worked perfectly, required hardly any maintenance, and were incredibly strong. Note that the seacocks were for 1½-inch (38 mm) hose; in my experience, small Marelon seacocks (www .forespar.com) have a tendency to break. What happens is that the ball valves are slightly hygroscopic (porous), causing swelling over time. As the ball sticks in its socket, turning the handle places undue stress on the connecting arm, occasionally resulting in it breaking.

Gate valves (Figure 4-2) look like garden faucets, and are not approved by the American Boat and Yacht Council (ABYC) for this application. Replace them with bronze or Marelon seacocks. In the head, a large bronze Wilcox-Crittenden (www.wilcoxcrittenden.com) plug-type seacock (Figure 4-3) was the standard for many years, but modern ball valves are superior in several ways.

## TYPES OF SEA VALVES

There are three major types of sea valves available today: traditional bronze tapered-plug seacocks; bronze, stainless steel, and synthetic ball-valve seacocks (Figure 4-4); and threaded gate valves.

The plug and ball-valve-type seacocks most often are cast in bronze and may have some parts chromed. Whereas brass is an alloy of copper and zinc, bronze is an alloy of copper and tin, and it obtains significant resistance to corrosion from the tin. Small amounts of aluminum, zinc, and silicon usually are added to increase strength and improve casting properties. Bronze is a good material for seacocks; brass should *never* be used.

Stainless steel ball-valve seacocks can be found with a bit of diligent searching. Steel boat builders may use industrial stainless steel valves, but these typically do not have flanged bases. Whether these are satisfactory depends on the through-hull material (a strong steel pipe welded to the hull may sufficiently resist bending to make a flanged seacock base unnecessary), as well as the type of valve and its base diameter.

ABYC standards used to call for flanged bases, but this was changed some years ago, probably because so many boatbuilders were installing residential-type ball valves. The most common were Apollo valves (made by Conbraco, www .conbraco.com), with the yellow vinyl-covered handles. The 1997 standard now says a valve must be able to withstand a 500-pound (227 kg)

FIGURE 4-1. Marelon seacocks are distributed in the United States by Forespar, which also sells the Marelon Integrated Plumbing System, a modular plumbing system that unfortunately is now sold just to OEMs (original equipment manufacturers, i.e., boatbuilders).

FIGURE 4-2. Bronze gate valves are found on many new and used boats. Here the gate is partially open. They are inferior to seacocks because debris can keep the gate from completely closing without the operator's knowledge, and excessive force can twist off the handle.

FIGURE 4-3. A few decades ago, the most common type of seacock was the tapered plug type. This one is made of bronze by Wilcox-Crittenden.

static side load—imagine a battery coming loose and sliding into a nearby seacock. I'm not aware of anyone who has tested whether unflanged valves pass the test, but certainly a flanged valve is stronger, and there are several manufacturers of them, including Conbraco.

Technological advancements in the fabrication of synthetics have resulted in materials of far greater strength than those of just a few years ago. Plastic through-hulls and seacocks now are available in most chandleries. However, "plastic" is something of a misnomer, as most of these products are strong polymers such as DuPont's Marelon, which is glass-reinforced nylon. Installation of plastic through-hull fittings above the waterline is a common and acceptable practice, although UV exposure is a consideration.

When Marelon fittings were first introduced, many sailors were skeptical about their strength

FIGURE 4-4. Today, the best and most maintenance-free seacock is the chrome-plated ball valve turning in a Teflon seat. Those made by Conbraco are good value. (Bruce Bingham photo)

**FIGURE 4-5.** The ball valve of this Marelon seacock only requires occasional lubrication with petroleum jelly to keep it operating smoothly. Unlike the tapered-plug type, ball valves do not require lubrication to maintain watertightness.

and reliability. Yet Marelon products have a tensile strength of 30,000 pounds per square inch (207 N/mm$^2$). You can prove this to yourself by smashing a Marelon cleat or seacock with a hammer—it hardly scratches! A little Vaseline applied to the ball every season keeps them turning freely (Figure 4-5). For the owner of a steel boat concerned about corrosion caused by galvanic action between dissimilar metals, or anyone wanting to save weight and money, Marelon through-hulls and seacocks are a logical choice. The rare sinking of a steel boat has been reported, however, when a cabin fire melted them. Of course it is probably academic whether anyone will care if the charred shell still floats.

## THE TROUBLE WITH GATE VALVES

There are several shortcomings commonly attributed to gate valves. First, they often are made of brass, which is not sufficiently corrosion resistant for use in a marine environment. Second, they are not positive action; that is, rather than using a lever that is clearly on or off, they employ threaded handles that must be turned several times before fully opening or closing the valve. It sometimes is difficult to know if the valve is closed all the way, or if it has stopped short of sealing due to the presence of a foreign object in the chamber. Third, gate valves typically do not have flanged bodies, which reduces their strength.

## INSTALLING SEACOCKS

The ABYC small-craft standards, Section H-27, specify proper installation materials and procedures. In addition to using flange-bodied seacocks that can be through-fastened to the hull (again, flanges are no longer mandated, but if the seacock has a flange, it must be "securely mounted to the hull"), each seacock should be mounted with a backing block to distribute stress across a greater area of the hull (Figure 4-6). On wood or fiberglass hulls, wood or stainless steel make good backing blocks, though the latter can be difficult to work with. On steel or aluminum hulls, or in any installation where the seacock and hull materials are galvanically incompatible, the ABYC suggests an insulating block of Micarta or similar durable insulating material (Figure 4-7).

While you should, of course, follow the manufacturer's instructions when installing a seacock, the following steps generally will apply.

1. Select a seacock with the appropriate diameter opening for the application at hand. Check that the tailpiece makes a snug fit with the hose. When installing seacocks for cockpit scuppers, use the largest size possible. In fact, it would be very smart to have at least 1½-inch

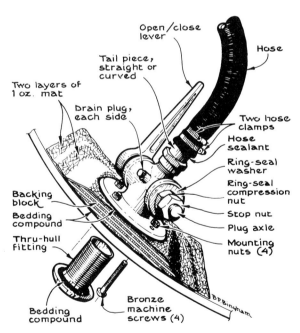

**FIGURE 4-6.** Flanged seacocks should be through-bolted to the hull with a block of wood or other material between the hull and valve to distribute loads.

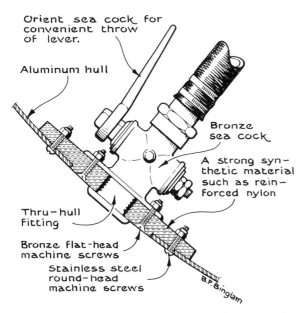

FIGURE 4-7. Bronze seacocks should not be mounted in direct contact with steel- and aluminum-hulled vessels, because the two metals are galvanically incompatible and corrosion will result. This drawing shows a layer of nylon inserted between the valve and hull to insulate them. Marelon seacocks avoid the problem of corrosion altogether because they are synthetic.

(38 mm) scuppers, hoses, and seacocks. They are expensive, but it's important that the cockpit drain quickly when it's filled with water, as might occur from a breaking wave. Carrying hundreds of pounds of water in the cockpit makes the boat handle sluggishly, perhaps making handling so bad as to cause a broach.

2. Locate the spot for your through-hull in a readily accessible place inside. If you cannot reach the seacock in an emergency, it is of little value. Orient seacocks with drain plugs so that the drain plug can be reached for winterizing. And be certain there is enough space to conveniently throw the handle. Plastic seacocks don't have drains, but the unobstructed throw of the handle is still a consideration.

3. Use a backing block of sufficient strength (strong enough so that the area occupied by the through-hull will be as strong as any other area of the hull). Shape the block to fit the curvature of the hull. Note that backing blocks are not mandated by ABYC, but they are strongly recommended.

4. Cut the size hole stipulated by the manufacturer of the through-hull using a hole-saw attachment on your power drill. Start from inside the hull until the pilot drill bit pushes through. Then go outside and finish drilling the hole. On hulls that are cored, you must remove the core material several inches around the hole for the through-hull (use a screwdriver or knife to remove the core), and pour in polyester or epoxy resin to fill the void (Figure 4-8). The reason for this measure is that the compressive strength of core materials is comparatively less than solid fiberglass. Also, it is important to keep water away from the core material. Today, most builders plan all through-hulls before the hulls are laid up; core material is removed from all through-hull locations and solid fiberglass substituted.

5. Drill the same size hole in the backing block, then mock up the assembly by inserting the through-hull from the outside and mounting the seacock on top of it on the inside. Mark on the backing block where you want to drill the bolt holes. (Some seacocks do not have holes predrilled in the flange and will have to

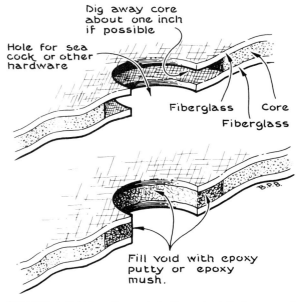

FIGURE 4-8. When through-hulls are installed on cored hulls, the core material must be cut away between the layers of fiberglass and the void filled with epoxy to provide greater hull compression strength when the through-hull is tightened down.

be drilled before this step can be completed.) Drill holes in the backing block and through the hull. You may cause less chipping of the gelcoat outside if you use a smaller bit for the first hole drilled from inside. Then put in the correct size bit and ream out the hole.

6. Apply bedding compound (such as polysulfide) to the underside of the through-hull flange, the seacock mounting flange, the bolt holes, and between the backing block and hull. Use liberal amounts of compound so that it oozes out all around.

7. Insert the bolts and tighten in the manner prescribed by the manufacturer's instructions.

8. If countersinking flat-head bolts, fill in over the bolt heads with epoxy putty compound to achieve a smooth exterior surface.

## ELECTRICAL BONDING

Bonding, electrically connecting metal objects inside the boat to prevent electrolytic corrosion, is done for three reasons: to ground the electrical system, for lightning protection, and for corrosion protection. In this chapter we're concerned only with the last—corrosion. (For more on bonding, see Chapter 13.)

Basically, bonding results in all underwater metal having the same electrical potential, and since it is the difference in electrical potential, between, say, a bronze fitting and an aluminum one, that causes corrosion, theoretically the bonded vessel should be immune from it. But as Charlie Wing writes in his book, *Boatowner's Illustrated Electrical Handbook*, "In general, bonding of immersed metal components *prevents* corrosion due to stray currents from *inside* the hull, but it *causes* corrosion due to stray currents from *outside* the hull."

According to the ABYC small-craft standards, electrically isolated through-hull fittings do not need to be bonded. However, you would be wise, especially if you have a metal hull, to consult these standards and other expert advice in determining whether or not to bond your seacocks and through-hull fittings to other metal and electrical devices on board.

Most valve manufacturers will neither endorse nor criticize the practice of bonding seacocks. To an extent, every boat is different, based on variances in its electrical and mechanical systems. You can measure the electrical potential of each piece of underwater metal, leading to a more informed decision about the benefits of bonding and number and location of sacrificial zinc anodes, which protect more noble metals (like a stainless steel propeller shaft) to which they're attached from galvanic corrosion.

## MAINTENANCE AND OPERATION

Winterize seacocks at haulout and inspect and grease them before launching in the spring. Though they look benign enough sitting there beside the head, and may be operated with reassuring ease, testing is the only way to be certain they aren't corroded or leaking. They won't leak until the boat is launched, and then it's too late to repack the plug. Some skippers drill and tap the housing and insert a zerc fitting so that grease can be periodically pumped into the cavity and plug. This is an especially good idea if you spend six months or longer between haulouts. If your seacocks have drain plugs, you may be able to find zerc grease fittings with matching threads at an auto parts store and simply screw them in.

In-the-water tests are as important as out-of-water inspections. Donald Street tells the story of a misbehaving seacock on *Iolaire*. In order to check for blockage in his sink drain, he closed the seacock and removed the hose. Surprise! Water rushed in. Thinking that he must have turned the handle to its open position by mistake, he threw the handle the other way—and water still gushed in. It turned out that the plug had become wasp-waisted through corrosion and admitted water when either open or closed.

Removing the hose from the seacock tailpiece while in the water is the litmus test. But consider this: a 1½-inch (38 mm) through-hull that is 2 feet (610 mm) below the waterline will admit 71 gallons (269 L) of water per minute! A much safer way of checking is to wait until you're in the sling on launch day and test each seacock by closing it and pulling off the hose. You'll then be able to see if water is leaking in without risking sinking.

Once out of the water, on haulout day, remove the drain plugs in the body of the seacock

91

and allow all water to drain. Frozen water could crack the casting. To be on the safe side, squirt antifreeze into each drain plug hole.

Before launching, include seacocks on your checklist of things to do.

Some ball-valve types come apart, but generally it's not necessary to disassemble them because they are essentially maintenance free. While lubrication isn't specified by many manufacturers, it can't hurt to occasionally squirt some Teflon grease or vegetable oil onto the ball. This requires removing the hose, so schedule this chore before launching. More important, perhaps, is to regularly turn the handle to keep the ball free.

If you have one of the older-style barrel valve seacocks, such as those made by Wilcox-Crittenden, follow this procedure:

1. For tapered-plug types, follow the manufacturer's instructions and remove nut and washer from the side of the seacock. Two wrenches may be necessary. Using a wood mallet, tap out the tapered plug. The various parts are shown in Figure 4-9.

2. Inspect the plug for roughness or scratches. If scratches are light, smooth with an emery cloth. If scratches are deep, apply a valve grinding compound to the plug and cavity, and relap until the plug fits snugly inside the body (Figure 4-10).

3. Cover both the plug and internal wall of the cavity with a waterproof grease, such as Teflon lubricant. Apply liberally as the grease is an important factor in preventing leaks and in facilitating ease of operation. (I forgot to grease a plug-type

FIGURE 4-10. If sand finds its way between the plug and housing, gouges may be found in the two surfaces. These should be smoothed using a valve grinding compound and lap cloth.

seacock one spring and leaks plagued me all that year.)

4. Reinsert the plug and reassemble. Tighten nuts sufficiently to prevent loosening due to vibration. To be certain of the efficacy of your repair, you might again perform a test during launching.

Annual maintenance, as described above, will lengthen the life of your seacocks considerably.

## Softwood Plugs

An additional precaution associated with seacocks is buying tapered softwood plugs that can be pounded into the tailpiece of the seacock in the event of failure (Figure 4-11). Damage from lightning striking the mast and returning to ground through a seacock and corrosion are possible causes of seacock failure, even if rare. Find a matching size plug for each seacock. Conventional wisdom is to tie or tape the plug to the sea-

FIGURE 4-9. The various parts of a Wilcox-Crittenden barrel-type seacock disassembled. The tapered plug is just to the left of the housing; it must be periodically greased to remain watertight and to operate smoothly.

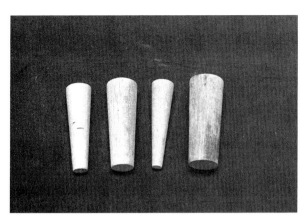

**FIGURE 4-11.** Tapered softwood plugs should be kept on hand to insert into the tailpiece of a seacock in the event a hose deteriorates and/or the seacock fails to close.

cock, but as noted earlier, bilge water and contaminants can swell and foul the plug before it's put in place, thereby making a watertight seal more difficult. Some people think it's smarter to keep the plugs in a plastic bag, each marked for a specific seacock, and store them in an easily reached location. A good compromise might be to store the plug in a watertight/airtight plastic bag taped to the seacock.

An alternative to a softwood plug is a wax ring like those used to seal the base of a toilet. Bill Seifert, with whom I co-wrote *Offshore Sailing: 200 Essential Passagemaking Tips*, says they are easily molded and pressed into place.

## Opening and Closing Seacocks

The general rule about opening and closing seacocks is to leave them closed unless in use. The obvious exception to this would be those attached to cockpit scuppers, which must be left open in order to drain any water, such as rain, from the cockpit. When the boat is left untended for any length of time, close all other seacocks. With respect to those seacocks attached to the toilet, some folks open and close them each time the head is used. Others simply leave them open (assuming there is a separate valve in the toilet), working the handle every once in a while to make sure the seacock is still operating properly. Opening the cooling-water seacock is, of course, a part of your engine start-up procedure.

Maintaining seacocks is a task every cruising sailor should learn how to do. Know the location of every seacock, how to get to it quickly, and how to maintain it.

## FURTHER READING

*Boatowner's Illustrated Electrical Handbook.* 2nd ed. Charlie Wing. Camden, Maine: International Marine, 2006.

*Lightning and Boats: A Manual of Safety and Prevention.* Michael V. Huck, Jr. Brookfield, Wisconsin: Seaworthy Publications, 1995.

*Understanding Boat Corrosion, Lightning Protection, and Interference.* John C. Payne. Dobbs Ferry, New York: Sheridan House, 2005.

# FIVE

# BASIC PLUMBING

Fresh water is essential to our health and survival. In the Great Lakes you are never in danger of dying from thirst. The consumption of salt water, however, is damaging to the kidneys in amounts of more than a pint or so. The technology of watermaking has taken tremendous strides in recent years. High-capacity desalinators are viable for yachts large enough (above about 45 feet/13.7 m or so) to carry auxiliary AC gensets. For smaller boats, breakthrough technology in 12-volt DC units now makes it possible for just about any cruising boat to make its own water. In fact, many cruisers now rely on their watermakers rather than their tanks, though I don't like the idea of relying on electrical and mechanical equipment for survival. At the least, you need an emergency rain catchment system. The conservative approach is to carry adequate water in tanks for the entire crew for the duration of a passage, plus a safety margin. In either case, the boat must be fitted with fixed tanks, a system of pumps, pipes, and a through-hull discharge.

## TANKS

Water tanks are installed at the time of construction because they are generally located in the bilges and under cockpits and berths. Removing a tank is almost always a radical step, requiring dismantling floors and furniture. You are indeed lucky if your builder was clever enough—and sufficiently conscientious—to plan for their periodic removal. Installing a new tank is the reverse of removing one, and almost always a major job.

Before throwing up your arms in despair, let's take a look at your requirements. One of the longest frequently made passages is from Southern California to the Marquesas, a distance of about 3,000 miles (4,830 km) that takes most yachts three to four weeks. A crew will consume, according to some estimates, between 2 and 5 gallons (7.6 to 19 L) per person per day while cruis-

ing. Four persons on a 30-day cruise will need between 240 and 600 gallons (908 to 2,271 L) of fresh water!

On the other hand, I know frugal cruisers who have restricted freshwater usage to a ½ gallon per person per day—a pretty stringent ration compared to the numbers above. This means one wash per person a week, and saltwater cleaning of clothes followed by a quick freshwater rinse. At this rate of consumption, a crew of four on a 30-day passage would need a minimum of 60 gallons (227 L). Cooking and washing requirements also need to be considered.

Roger Marshall, a Rhode Island naval architect, says he thinks a cruising boat's water supply should equal 4 to 5% of its total displacement. A 15,000-pound (6,804 kg) boat, therefore, would carry 600 to 750 pounds (272 to 340 kg) of water, or 75 to 93 gallons (284 to 352 L).

If you purchase a 35-foot (10.7 m) boat with a 75-gallon (284 L) water capacity, consider yourself lucky. Now, suppose you want to double that capacity to 150 gallons (568 L). Short of ripping out berth tops and installing a metal, wood, or fiberglass tank, the simplest solution is to purchase a flexible nylon tank or a watermaker. We'll examine both alternatives.

### Tank Location

Because fresh water weighs 8 pounds (3.6 kg) per gallon (62.5 pounds per cubic foot or 1,001 kg/m$^3$; salt water is 64 pounds per cubic foot or 1,025 kg/m$^3$), it's not difficult to see that a large tank will be holding several hundred pounds of water and that its placement in the boat can be critical to trim.

Racers try to locate fuel and water tanks low and as close as possible to the boat's center of gravity to prevent hobbyhorsing. Tanks mounted in extreme bow and stern sections out of the water may also place stress on the hull.

94

Unfortunately, on most small cruising boats there is not a great deal of choice regarding tank location. With the trend toward lighter displacement boats, there often isn't enough room under the cabin sole to install tanks—water or fuel. Thus they are relegated to the area under midship berths or settees (Figure 5-1). That space then is lost to the storage of anything else, like canned foods. Beyond the comfort factor, this is another reason why boats of moderate to heavy displacement make better cruisers—increased storage space. Anytime tanks must be located to either side of the centerline, such as beneath settees, two tanks are necessary to counter one another, unless you can compensate for excess trim in some other way. And remember that as a tank empties with use, the boat's trim is affected; alternating between port and starboard tanks solves the problem.

## Types of Tank Materials

Traditionally, water tanks were made of metal—aluminum, galvanized steel, or less frequently, Monel or stainless steel. Because of corrosion worries, their installation must be done correctly to prevent salt water from coming in contact with the tank. Advances in plastics technologies have blessed us with many new materials that are completely corrosion free and strong enough to do the job of metal. Today, polyethylene tanks are the norm. They are relatively inexpensive and available in many shapes and sizes. For retrofitting, polyethylene is the way to go. But not all are made equal. In pressure tests I've done, thin-wall tanks may bulge excessively, even potentially

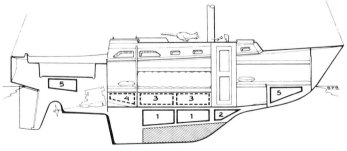

Tank numbers indicate preference of location for the sake of the vessel's performance and motion. Infringement on storage space has been discounted in this drawing.

**FIGURE 5-1.** Possible water tank locations. The nearer the boat's center of gravity, the better, which means avoid installing the tank in the ends of the boat if at all possible as it causes hobbyhorsing, which slows the boat and is annoying.

cracking hose fittings, which are welded in place during the manufacturing process. It's worth paying a little more for thicker-wall brands. Ask and compare.

## Building a Tank

The Gougeon Brothers of Bay City, Michigan, formulators of WEST System brand epoxy (www .westsystem.com) and builders of cold-molded sailboats, have had much experience building wood water and fuel tanks. Meade, the oldest brother, says that ¼-inch (6 mm) plywood is a sufficient thickness for a 40-gallon (151 L) tank; ⅜-inch (9.5 mm) plywood gives an added margin of safety. Two baffles should be installed to keep water from gaining momentum as it sloshes around.

If you plan to locate the new tank underneath a settee or a berth (a good location amidships), obviously you must remove the top of the berth to fit in the new tank. You might find that a commercial tank of the right shape can just as easily be installed in this space. Be certain that the tank—whether store bought or made in your shop—will fit through the main hatch.

Some fiberglass production yards build integral tanks using the hull as one side. But as mentioned in Chapter 2, all hulls flex to a degree, and this occasionally places enough stress on the tank joints to crack them. In fact, a friend of mine once was terribly disappointed when his long-awaited delivery of a C&C Landfall 43 from Newport, Rhode Island, to St. Thomas fell through because the integral tanks started leaking when the boat was launched.

The Gougeon Brothers strongly suggest that water tanks be built separate from the hull so they can be removed to repair the hull, should that ever become necessary.

A counter argument holds that should the hull be punctured in the side of an integral tank, salt water will not enter the cabin—except, of course, when running the sink pump! There is some logic to this stance, but it seems that the likelihood of taking a blow at that fortuitous spot is a crap shoot at best. The salt water will, of course, foul the freshwater supply.

The shape of the tank will be dictated by the shape of the space available. If you want to maximize space utilization, bend thin sheets of plywood or veneer over a jig and laminate in several thicknesses (Figure 5-2). Epoxy resin is a good bonding agent for this job. Of course, you can

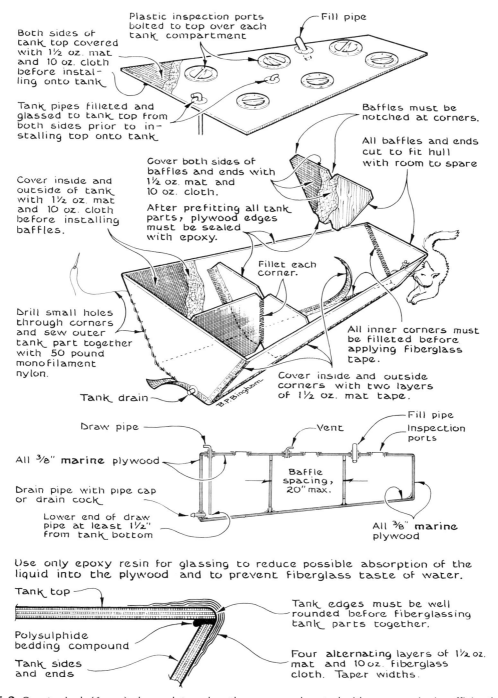

Both sides of tank top covered with 1½ oz. mat and 10 oz. cloth before installing onto tank

Plastic inspection ports bolted to top over each tank compartment

Fill pipe

Tank pipes filleted and glassed to tank top from both sides prior to installing top onto tank

Cover both sides of baffles and ends with 1½ oz. mat and 10 oz. cloth.

After prefitting all tank parts, plywood edges must be sealed with epoxy.

Baffles must be notched at corners.

All baffles and ends cut to fit hull with room to spare

Cover inside and outside of tank with 1½ oz. mat and 10 oz. cloth before installing baffles.

Fillet each corner.

Drill small holes through corners and sew outer tank part together with 50 pound monofilament nylon.

Tank drain

All inner corners must be filleted before applying fiberglass tape.

Cover inside and outside corners with two layers of 1½ oz. mat tape.

B.P.Bingham

Draw pipe

Vent

Fill pipe

Inspection ports

All ³⁄₈" marine plywood

Baffle spacing, 20" max.

Drain pipe with pipe cap or drain cock

Lower end of draw pipe at least 1½" from tank bottom

All ³⁄₈" marine plywood

Use only epoxy resin for glassing to reduce possible absorption of the liquid into the plywood and to prevent fiberglass taste of water.

Tank top

Tank edges must be well rounded before fiberglassing tank parts together.

Polysulphide bedding compound

Tank sides and ends

Four alternating layers of 1½ oz. mat and 10 oz. fiberglass cloth. Taper widths.

**FIGURE 5-2.** Quarter-inch (6 mm) plywood, taped on the seams and coated with epoxy resin, is sufficiently thick for a water tank up to about 40 gallons (151 L). Baffles and limber holes should also be figured in the construction.

also build the tank from flat pieces of plywood, angling the joints to fit the hull.

Fillet the joints (refer back to Figure 2-9) with some sort of resin or putty, with a radius large enough so that the fiberglass mat or cloth will conform closely to the curve. Once you have taped all the seams and the resin has kicked, you can either glass a layer of fiberglass cloth to all the interior and exterior sides or just finish with several coatings of epoxy. Warm resin will penetrate the grain and allow air to escape better than cold, thick resin, so in cold temperatures it is advisable to preheat the resin before applying it. Also, best results are obtained when the boards are horizontal.

## Securing Tanks

All tanks must be securely fastened to the hull and insides of furniture to keep them from moving around and possibly cracking open (Figure 5-3). Two methods are to glass strips of wood to the hull, or alternatively, to glass or bolt blocks of wood to the insides of furniture. You also can run flat steel straps around the tank to hold it in place, using turnbuckles to tension the strap. Be sure to install a hand-size plastic deck plate in the top as an inspection port.

When fiberglassing inside the boat using polyester resin, be sure to mount an exhaust fan on one of the hatches to suck out dangerous styrene fumes, and don't spend more time than necessary breathing the fumes. Wear a respirator, and leave the boat while the resin cures—not only is the smell unpleasant and unhealthy, you could jiggle the bonding surfaces by walking around. Epoxy resin bonds better than polyester, and does not give off styrene, though it is more expensive.

## Flexible Tanks

With today's highly advanced synthetic materials, I'm much in favor of using flexible tanks when the boat's existing tank capacity is insufficient. They

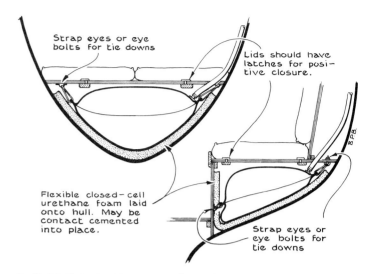

**FIGURE 5-4.** Flexible water tanks can be stowed in hard-to-get-at areas, such as beneath bunks. The manufacturer of the Nauta flexible water tank recommends making a "berth" for your tank so it doesn't roll about.

can be purchased for water, gasoline, and diesel fuel, and also used as waste holding tanks.

The French company Pennel et Flipo makes a high-quality line of flexible tanks that are marketed under the name Nauta (distributed in the U.S. by Imtra, www.imtra.com). So does the Dutch company Vetus (www.vetus.com). They are not inexpensive, but the 840-denier nylon coated with a nitrile compound is very rugged and should last a long time. Unlike inflatable dinghies, which deteriorate largely because of the ultraviolet rays of the sun, storage tanks are well protected inside the boat. And, if measures have been taken to prevent the abrasion of the tank against the hull and furniture, there's not a great deal to worry about.

The Nauta line includes all the piping, deck fills, and valves necessary for a complete installation. One word of caution: these tanks may be supplied to you without the fill, drain, and vent fittings installed. The thought is that your particular installation may require custom location of these fittings. Instructions show you how to cut the tank, insert the fitting, and seal it with an adhesive. If not done correctly, a leak may result. So go slowly. Figure 5-4 shows a flexible tank fitted beneath a berth, with a hose running to a deck fill. Again, consider the effect on trim before choosing a final site.

It is recommended that even flexible tanks be fitted to "berths" to prevent their movement

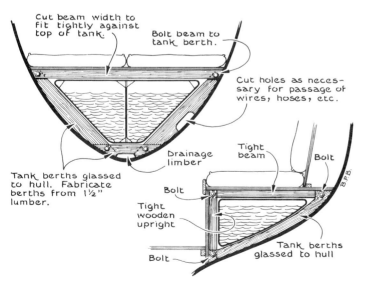

**FIGURE 5-3.** Water tanks should be glassed to the hull with tabbing or held in place by strong boards bolted to furniture or bulkheads.

underway. Bruce Bingham suggests a 1-inch (25 mm) urethane foam liner glued to the compartment. Straps should hold the tank in place, but remember to adjust these to the full position. When the tank is deflated, the tie-downs should fit loosely. Elastic tie-downs can be used to hold the tank in place in any state of fullness.

## PIPING

To move water to and from tanks, pipes are necessary. Copper and brass are occasionally seen on older boats, but today the only real choices are vinyl hose and rigid PVC snap-together systems (Figure 5-5). The easier of the two to route is flexible, nontoxic, clear vinyl hose, readily available in chandleries and hardware stores. The hose should be reinforced with nylon or wire to prevent collapse or explosion under pressure. Hoses for head waste and bilge pumps should be PVC.

Reinforced vinyl hose is easy to work with and can be routed just about anywhere. To pass a hose through a bulkhead or piece of cabinetry, use a brace and bit or hole saw to drill a hole larger than the hose. When the pilot bit pokes through, go to the other side and finish the hole. Conceivably there could be some chafing if the hose rubs against a sharp piece of wood. To prevent this, cut a 6-inch (152 mm) length of larger-diameter hose, slit one side, and slide it over the hose. In neat installations, all hoses are restrained with clamps screwed to the undersides of furniture.

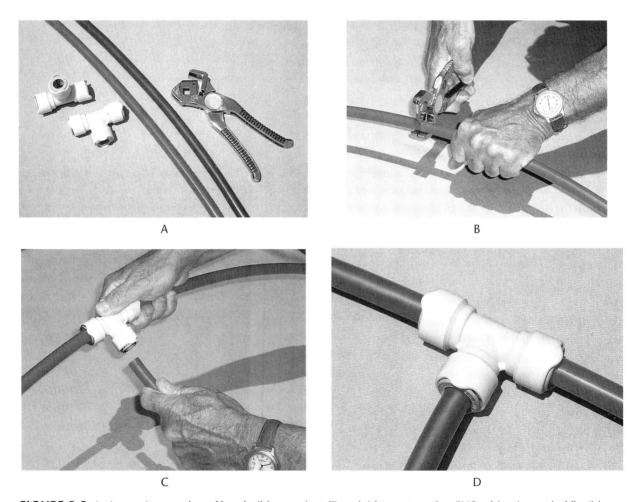

A

B

C

D

**FIGURE 5-5.** An increasing number of boatbuilders are installing rigid snap-together PVC tubing instead of flexible hose. The system by Whale is typical, with numerous fittings, including T-fittings (A). The rigid tubing is cut with a special tool (B). Tubing snaps into place without other fasteners (C). O-rings ensure leak-free connections (D). (Bruce Bingham photos)

## Multiple-Tank Plumbing

Water stored for long periods can grow foul, so it is important not to connect two tanks together to eliminate several feet of hose and a few fittings. Each tank should have its own outlet hose leading to the various pumps it services, but fitted to a Y-valve or T-valve to join with the other tank before it reaches the pump (Figure 5-6). In this way, when one tank is empty, the valve can be switched and the second tank used. Actually, it makes good sense to alternate tanks to minimize the amount of time water will stand in any one tank and to keep the weight in each approximately equal.

## Vents

Each water tank must have its own vent in order for water to be drawn from the outlet hose. Flexible water tanks may have low-profile vents inserted in the nylon skin. Some boats have vent pipes exiting on deck or on the side of the hull, but this is an invitation to salt-spoiled water. If the vent must be on deck, be sure to bend a large U in the pipe and face it aft to make saltwater entry more difficult (Figure 5-7).

Because there is plenty of air in the cabin, there is no reason why vents can't terminate in

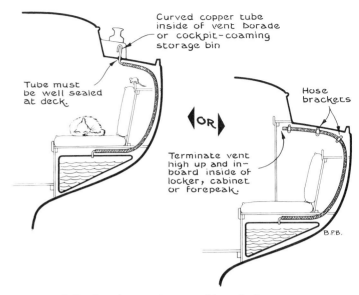

**FIGURE 5-7.** All tanks must be vented in order for water to flow. On-deck vents should be bent to prevent salt water from fouling the tank. Venting inside the boat is safest and simplest.

some obscure location, such as at the back of a cabinet.

## Deck Fills

Deck fills simplify filling tanks and avoid the problem of water dribbling from the hose inside the cabin. Deck fills usually are located on the side decks, which are frequently washed with salt water, dirt, and other debris. Though I have seldom heard anyone complain about water fouled in this manner, many ocean-cruising veterans maintain that tanks should be filled directly through the inspection ports in the tops of the tanks or through special tank-fill hardware. Deck fills can be hard to open if they aren't opened periodically and a light grease applied to the threads.

One advantage of deck fills is that a rainwater catchment system can be routed directly through them into the tank (see Chapter 9). Filling buckets adds an extra step. Whenever filling a tank through a deck fill, it should be your routine practice to wash down the deck around the deck fill before opening the cap. When filling the tanks with rainwater, allow the rain to clean off the awnings or decks for a few minutes before routing the water into the tanks.

The rain itself is usually none too clean, either. Dust, soot, salt, bacteria, and other invisible contaminants can be found in collected rainwater. For

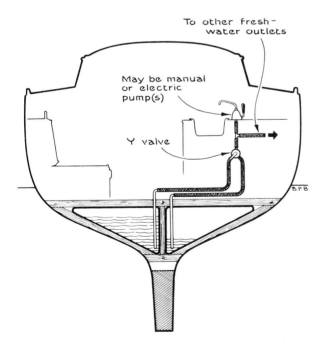

**FIGURE 5-6.** Tanks shouldn't be directly connected to one another to prevent a foul tank from tainting the clean water in its neighbor. A diverter valve permits switching from one tank to the other.

this reason, a catchment system should incorporate a filter between the deck fill and tank. As a further precaution, add a few drops of Clorox bleach or purifying tablets to the tank with each fill. For more on rain catchment, see Figures 9-25 and 9-26.

For all the reasons cited above, apply duct tape over every deck fill before heading offshore. This prevents contamination of the freshwater drinking supply and your fuel. You can easily remove the tape if you want to fill the tanks with rainwater under mild sailing conditions, and you'll want to remove them on arrival in port, if only to minimize the amount of adhesive residue left on deck.

## Gauges

One of the advantages of large water tank inspection ports is that they enable you to estimate how full the tanks are. A more accurate method is to install a clear vinyl hose or sight glass on the exterior of the tank between the outlet and vent; mark it at quarter-full, half-full, and three-quarters full—or by the gallon if you want to be more precise. You can install T-fittings in the lines to make the job easy, unless you have trouble getting a tight fit at the connections (Figure 5-8).

The French-built Amel line of fiberglass ketches, perhaps the most innovative, well-conceived, and well-executed production cruising

sailboats built anywhere, feature a graduated sight glass above the galley sink so that tank levels can be monitored as you cook and wash.

## Through-Hulls

When water is pumped out of a tank for use in a sink or shower, it ultimately must be disposed of somewhere. Rather than toss it overboard, the obvious solution is to route it through a through-hull fitting in the bottom of the boat. They should be securely fastened to the hull and fitted with seacocks to prevent water entering the boat in the event the hoses crack or come off the fitting.

This is such an important point that I devoted Chapter 4 solely to the subject of installing and maintaining through-hull fittings and seacocks. If you have decided to add a shower or second sink, route it to an existing through-hull by putting a Y- or T-fitting in the existing line. Often this is preferable to drilling another hole in the boat and then investing in the expense of a through-hull fitting and seacock. Head sinks can discharge directly into the toilet bowl via a hose pushed under the backside of the seat. The sea chest shown in Figure 5-33 on page 114 also can be used for discharge as well as intake.

## Cockpit Scuppers

An exception to the above statement about combining discharge hoses is cockpit scuppers, which have the important function of draining the cockpit of rain and seawater. It is advisable not to tap into these fittings to drain the water system, especially if seacocks aren't fitted. Salt water could back up through the scupper into the drain hose and find its way into the cabin. Scuppers should be as large as possible; 2 inches (51 mm) or larger would be nice, although on many boats, they are dangerously smaller. Of course, their size is a function of cockpit and footwell volume, but here, bigger is always better. Seacocks for 1½-inch (38 mm) and 2-inch (50.8 mm) through-hulls are expensive, but a worthwhile investment.

An alternative configuration is seen on many racing boats nowadays. The cockpit scuppers empty into hoses that are led aft at a slight downward angle to the transom or under the counter, where they discharge above the waterline (Figure 5-9). If you're worried that water might come back up through the scuppers, reverse scoops or flappers can be fitted to the hull over the discharge hole. The floor of the cockpit must be higher than

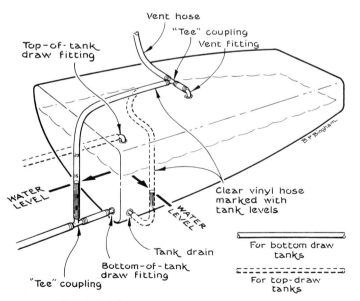

**FIGURE 5-8.** Fashion a simple water level gauge from two T-fittings and a length of clear vinyl hose. As you fill the tank, measure in graduated increments how much you put in the tank and mark the hose accordingly.

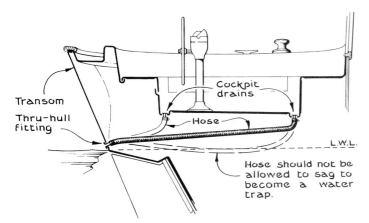

**FIGURE 5-9.** This scupper arrangement obviates seacocks by discharging above the waterline at the transom. However, they won't drain as fast as vertical hoses.

the waterline in order to angle the hoses downward and still exit above the waterline without the safety of seacocks. The advantage is that you can eliminate two through-hulls below the waterline; the disadvantage is that water in the cockpit might not drain as fast as through vertical scupper hoses.

If you're still worried about water backing through the hoses into the cockpit, then you're probably better off with the conventional scupper system that routes the water straight down to through-hulls.

Some of the more radically designed racing boats avoid the problem altogether by opening up the after end of the cockpit well to the transom so that water merely washes itself aft and overboard—simplicity at its finest!

# PUMPS

A new or used sailboat probably has only some of the pumps you will want on board. Engine pumps, such as for raw-water cooling and oil and fuel, come as part of the engine assembly. The average skipper only occasionally will have to familiarize himself with their location, replacement, and maintenance. The head, sink, and icebox may have pumps incorporated in their plumbing systems as well. But what about all those other pumps you may decide to add for safety and for additional comfort while living aboard? What's essential and what's a luxury? Manual or electric? Where to install? What maintenance is required? Let's fit out a typical cruiser with a sensible array of pumps.

## Measuring Pump Capacity

There are several ways of measuring the capacity or amount of water that can be moved by any manual pump. Some are described as pumping so many gallons per minute. But this is not as accurate as measuring the number of strokes per gallon. When comparing the performance of two different pumps with different type ratings, convert one so that you're not comparing "apples and oranges."

For example, if one pump lists 12 gallons (45 L) per minute, and another three strokes per gallon (3.8 L), convert the 12 gallons per minute into strokes per gallon. Guesswork is necessary, but you can come close. If you figure 3 seconds to raise the handle of a navy piston pump, and 2 seconds to depress it, you'll be achieving one stroke every 5 seconds—fast work. But let's assume you can keep up this pace for a short while anyway. One stroke every 5 seconds equates to 12 strokes per minute. The pump's rated capacity is 12 gallons per minute, so dividing 12 by 12 we find that this pump will move 1 gallon (3.8 L) of water per stroke. (Such performance is achieved only by a few hand pumps, namely the big and expensive aluminum Edson.) Obviously, a stronger person will achieve better performance than a weaker one. The second pump moves a gallon every three strokes or ⅓ (0.33) of a gallon per stroke. The first pump has three times the capacity of the second.

Some stores display their pumps fitted to large basins of water. The most accurate way to measure is to pump water into a measured container—how much water comes out with one stroke?

Remember, though, that pumping is hard work. In a matter of minutes, the person will tire and the amount of water being discharged will fall considerably below the pump's rated capacity.

Pumps seldom are asked to move water from one location to another at the same level. Usually water must be lifted first, as from the bilge to the topsides, or from the freshwater tank to the sink faucet. This is called *head*, and is measured by the number of vertical feet the water must be lifted. Head significantly reduces the pump's rated capacity, or at least its advertised capacity.

## The Manual Bilge Pump

The bilge pump is considered by some to be among the most important pieces of gear on the boat. Others contend that bilge pumps rarely are able to save a holed boat, and that their primary function is to clear small amounts of water from the bilge or sump. With the possible exception of a large crash pump driven by the ship's engine, it is true that most pumps simply won't be able to keep up with the amount of water flowing in through a crack or hole. If you recall from the previous chapter that a 1½-inch (38 mm) hole 2 feet (610 mm) below the waterline admits 71 gallons (269 L) of water per minute, it's terrifying to imagine the amount of water that would enter a hole caused by striking a log, rock, or another boat. To save a severely holed boat, it will be necessary to stem the flow with collision mats, mattresses, and underwater epoxy, bailing as you go with sturdy buckets.

I was told this story by a physician who was caught in a gale sailing from Bermuda to Long Island. A wave smashed the main hatch weather boards and partially filled the boat. The bilge pump couldn't empty water fast enough, and the plastic bucket handles kept coming off. What saved the boat were two canvas buckets with wood bottoms. As the saying goes, the best bilge pump is a scared man with a bucket in his hands.

Most manufacturers install a bilge pump as standard or optional equipment. While they will no doubt choose a pump they think is appropriate for your vessel, their choice does not have to be yours.

Next to the proverbial bucket, the simplest type of bilge pump is the navy or piston pump. If, as a child, one of your chores was to pump out the family dinghy or daysailer, you probably used a navy bilge pump (Figure 5-10). This is basically a portable pump for moving small amounts of water, though some larger boats will have one permanently installed in the bilge as a backup to a manual diaphragm pump. The larger navy pumps can actually move a great deal of water—a gallon every two or three strokes. But when you have to pump many hours in order to save the boat, fatigue becomes a crucial factor. The difficulty with navy pumps is that the throw or pull of the piston is quite long, often 24 inches (600 m) or more, and it is accomplished without mechanical advantage. Pulling a lever with vertical throw is more tiring than pushing a lever with horizontal throw.

By far the most common manual pump used on cruising sailboats is the diaphragm pump. In fact, you should install two—one that can be operated by the helmsman, and another that can be operated by someone down below. A diaphragm pump has a large open chamber whose space is in-

**FIGURE 5-10.** The navy or piston-type bilge pump is tried and true, but its capacity is too small, and it is too tiring to operate to qualify as the boat's main pump. (ITT/Jabsco)

creased or decreased by a lever-controlled rubber diaphragm. Rubber valves at either side of the chamber, where the intake and outlet hoses attach, alternately open and close as water is pumped through.

One of the largest diaphragm pumps is made by Edson (www.edsonmarine.com) and is rated at a gallon (3.8 L) per stroke (Figure 5-11). Some are sold mounted on portable boards, others are installed beneath the cockpit or in the bilge. The standard model is aluminum and should be disassembled periodically for signs of corrosion caused by stainless steel screws inside. For smaller yachts, Whale (www.whalepumps.com), Plastimo (www.plastimo.com), and Guzzler (www.thebosworthco.com) all make diaphragm pumps that can handle about a gallon (3.8 L) every three strokes, or 20 gallons (76 L) per minute.

A good diaphragm pump will not easily clog and will be able to pass small bits of wood or other debris. Most diaphragm pumps jam when a foreign object sticks in the valve, keeping it open and preventing a watertight seal in the chamber. When this happens, either the hoses must be re-

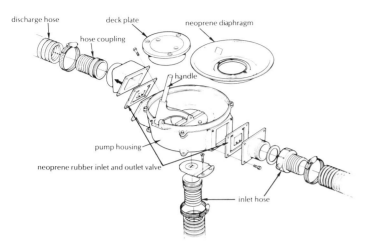

**FIGURE 5-11.** Edson's diaphragm pump is capable of pushing 1 gallon (3.8 L) per stroke, which is about the most you'll get from any diaphragm pump. The company also sells special quick-lock fittings, so owners can pump out their own waste-holding tanks through the deck plate; this should only be done offshore. (Edson International)

**FIGURE 5-12.** Strum or strainer boxes can be fitted to the hose ends to prevent clogging. If located deep in the bilge, attach a string to the hose so you can easily retrieve the end and clear it.

moved or the chamber opened—such as by removing the diaphragm and using a finger to clear away the debris. Jamming isn't supposed to occur in the diaphragm chamber unless a long, narrow object, such as a stick, manages to pass through the valve and become wedged when the diaphragm is depressed. But I've found that dirt and sand lodged around the edges of the valves also can prevent them from sealing properly.

To assist in preventing clogging, the end of the hose in the bilge should be fitted with a strum box or strainer (Figure 5-12). Many types are available. But be wary that even strainers can be sealed by a flat object such as a piece of paper or plastic sucked up against the holes. In fact, I've had more clogging troubles *with* strainers than without them. With centrifugal pumps, strainers are probably important, but diaphragm pumps can pass some debris. Another option is to bend a heavy piece of wire or rod over the opening to prevent an object from pressing up flat against the opening (Figure 5-13).

It sometimes is difficult to know when a pump is clogged as there still can be pressure felt when moving the lever. An easy way to make sure is to check for water coming out of the through-hull discharge. But this can be done only if discharge is above the waterline. This will be a major factor in determining the best location of the pump and its through-hull fitting.

## Bilge Pump Location

There is no best place to discharge a bilge pump. But there are numerous options (Figure 5-14): a separate through-hull with seacock below the waterline; tapped into the cockpit scupper hose below the cockpit floor; through the transom; onto the cockpit floor; through the topsides; or through the coaming onto the deck. The main advantage of mounting it above the waterline is the reassurance of being able to see water pour out. However, locations that may be above water at the dock may disappear below the surface when heeled over

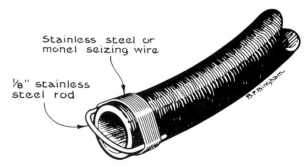

**FIGURE 5-13.** Because diaphragm pumps can pass small debris without clogging, a solution I prefer to the strum box is fastening a piece of bent rod over the end of the hose and lashing it with thin stainless steel or Monel wire.

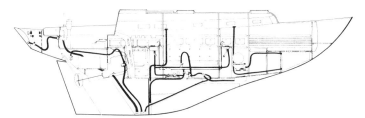

FIGURE 5-14. A well-fit 35-foot (10.7 m) cruising boat often has as many as ten pumps. This boat has three bilge pumps, discharging in various locations. Two are manual, one engine-driven. (Bill Stanard drawing)

underway. And, as bilge water often is oily, it's the last thing you want in the cockpit or on deck, when sure footing is of great importance. I favor a through-hull just under the stern or in the side of the hull several feet above the waterline.

Locating the pump is also a critical decision. A shorthanded crew at sea will want one pump easily operated by the helmsman. This means locating the pump either under the cockpit floor or under or beside cockpit seats. Before cutting any holes, pretend you're sitting at the wheel or tiller, braced for green seas. See where the lever handle would be most convenient. Take into account the amount of throw in the lever also, as you won't want to have to move too far from the helm. Another pump, mounted in or near the bilge and operated by a person sitting on a bunk or on the cabin sole, is good insurance.

## Routing the Discharge Hose

Several factors should be considered in routing the hose. As water passes through a hose or pipe, the interior surface causes friction and retards the flow. To minimize friction, choose hose with a smooth interior wall (even though the exterior appears corrugated by spiral reinforcing wire to prevent collapse); keep the length as short as possible. Avoid sharp bends. Also, the higher the distance the water has to be lifted, the less efficient the pump. Hose routed to through-hulls above the waterline that are not fitted with seacocks should be routed as high as possible to prevent water from running back into the boat in the event the through-hull becomes submerged. Some people advocate looping the hose to prevent siphoning water back into the boat, but this creates additional friction. A better solution is to install a seacock, check valve, or a positive-action, in-line valve that can be opened and closed.

## Electric Bilge Pumps

Electrically powered diaphragm pumps (Figure 5-15) are an alternative. But they are more expensive than their equivalently rated manual counterparts. So-called wobble plate pumps (Figure 5-16), such as those made by Jabsco (www.jabsco.com), Shurflo (www.shurflo.com), and Flojet (www.flojet.com), are superior to older-style centrifugal pumps. They can be run dry without damage and are self-priming. Centrifugal pumps fitted with bronze impellers may be able to run dry for a period of time but they are not self-priming. This means that if the inlet hose is empty, the pump can't draw water from a source below. Pumps with flexible impellers that lap the inside wall of the chamber are self-priming and can lift water as much as 20 feet (6.1 m), but they cannot be run dry.

Pumps with bronze impeller blades will not permit even small debris to pass through and thus can clog easily if not used with a fine-mesh strainer box. Flexible impellers can pass small debris. All these pumps have their place aboard. But I, for one, don't want to depend solely on electrically operated bilge pumps during a disaster at sea—you have to assume that electricity and the

FIGURE 5-15. ITT/Jabsco manufactures a complete line of electric diaphragm pumps, suitable for many uses including deck washes and pressurized water systems. Capacity ranges from 3 to 4 gallons (11 L to 15 L) per minute. (ITT/Jabsco)

**FIGURE 5-16.** The Flojet (left) is one of the new wobble plate pumps. The right photo shows the Flojet and two other brands (Shurflo and Par-Mate) that have three and four small diaphragms. These diaphragms open and close by means of a plate that wobbles on an off-center ball bearing. (*Practical Sailor* photos)

ability to generate it will not always be available. A submersible pump (Figure 5-17) should be installed at the bottom of the bilge. A nonsubmersible electric centrifugal or diaphragm pump can be mounted under a settee, in the galley, in the engine room, or in any other location where its hose can be conveniently run into the bilge.

## Engine-Driven Pumps

For getting rid of large volumes of water, it's hard to beat engine or generator-driven pumps. ITT/Jabsco makes a line of these pumps that will remove 26 to 83 gallons (98 L to 314 L) of water per minute at 1,750 rpm (Figure 5-18). They are belt-driven and may be ordered with either manual or electromagnetic clutches. As long as the engine is running, these pumps will remove the most water with the least effort.

**FIGURE 5-17.** The disassembled view of a Magnum bilge pump shows how it works; note the impeller at upper left, attached to the drive of a small electric motor. Best performance from this type is about 30 gallons (114 L) per minute. (*Practical Sailor* photo)

**FIGURE 5-18.** Engine-driven bilge pumps are belt-driven and can be ordered with manual or electromagnetic clutches. They push from 26 to 83 gallons (98 L to 314 L) per minute. (ITT/Jabsco)

**FIGURE 5-19.** Emergency crash pumps like this Ericson Safety Pump are turned by the engine's prop shaft and can discharge huge amounts of water. The smallest model gets rid of 10,500 gallons (3,974 L) of water an hour at 1,500 rpm.

In real emergencies, you'll be happy to have installed a high-volume crash pump. The Ericson Safety Pump (Figure 5-19) and the Fast Flow Pump are similar in design, both mounting on the engine's prop shaft. The latter can deliver more than 24,000 gallons (90,840 L) an hour at 2,000 rpm. And there's no worry about fatigue or drawing down the batteries, only running out of fuel. It's generally conceded that these types of pumps are the only ones that can save a severely holed boat until help arrives or the hole can be plugged.

### Using the Engine as a Bilge Pump

As a last-ditch effort, the engine's raw-water intake hose can be removed from the through-hull (after closing the seacock) and rerouted into the bilge. When the engine is started, it draws water out of the bilge and runs it through the engine, discharging through the exhaust in the usual manner. This trick is not recommended except in desperation, because bilge water is likely to be oily and full of debris and could clog the engine's water pump or damage other engine parts. Without the engine, you've lost your second means of propulsion, and perhaps more important, your battery charger. Which is why it's nice to have a solar panel or wind generator as a backup—see Chapter 12.

## FRESHWATER SYSTEMS

Cruising in a cockleshell, you can pour water out of jerricans or plastic milk containers. But it's obviously simpler to employ a pump for moving water from the tanks to the galley sink. Many pumps are available, manual or electric, with or without pressure tanks.

### Manual Sink Pumps

The simplest galley pumps are those integral to the faucet and operated by a lever with vertical or horizontal throw. For small sinks, a pump such as the Whale Flipper is compact and easy to use (Figure 5-20).

Manual, foot-operated galley pumps are preferred by some cooks and dishwashers who want to keep both hands free while pumping. Whale makes two types of foot pumps, one operated by depressing a lever with the toe and another that is inset into the cabin floor and depressed by standing on it (Figure 5-21). On a moving boat, it's not always easy to brace yourself comfortably to elevate one foot to operate the pump, but foot pumps do free your hands and are neat, out-of-the-way systems that have become quite popular.

### Pressure Water Systems

An easy way to electrify an existing manual pump is to install a small in-line electric pump. A switch on the faucet fixture is all that's necessary to bring water from the tank flowing out the faucet. Whale makes one that measures about 2 inches by 6 inches (51mm by 152mm) and draws 2 amps (Figure 5-22). To supply running water to more than one location, a larger-capacity pump that

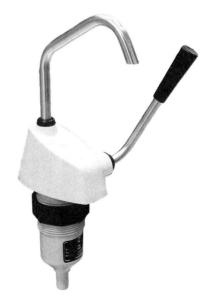

**FIGURE 5-20.** The Whale Flipper is a popular, inexpensive manual galley pump; it is easier to use than up-and-down, piston-type pumps. (Whale)

**FIGURE 5-21.** Whale makes two types of foot-operated galley pumps, the lever-type on the left, and the "tip-toe" type on the right. (Whale)

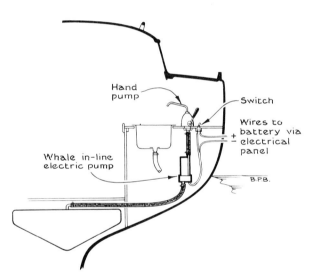

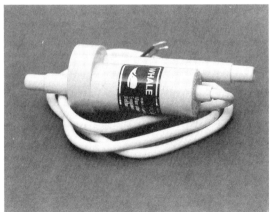

**FIGURE 5-22.** The least complicated way to electrify a water supply is to install an in-line pump with foot or hand switch. (Whale)

can handle about 3 gallons (11 L) per minute is suitable. A pressure switch activates the pump whenever pressure drops below a designated level, usually when the faucet is opened. This is called a demand system.

Pressure water systems are viable options on most cruising boats; the space requirements of a pump and accumulator tank are minimal. There is some debate as to the wastefulness of pressurized water systems. Some claim it encourages needless running of the tap, say when doing dishes. Others suggest that regulating the water supply to a trickle conserves water and frees both hands, which isn't possible when operating a manual pump.

In any case, it's hard to deny the hedonistic pleasure of a shower. And if you're going to install a pressure system, why not go the next step and fit a water heater as well—after all, you don't need anything more than a pail if a cold shower is all you're after.

ITT/Jabsco, Raritan (www.raritaneng.com), and Galley Maid (www.galleymaid.com) make pressure water systems that can deliver up to 12 gallons (45 L) of fresh water per minute. Systems like these provide the accumulator tank, pump, motor, and pressure gauge all in one assembly (Figure 5-23). However, if this unit is too bulky for existing installation sites, components can be purchased separately and tucked away in different locations (Figure 5-24).

The accumulator tank isn't really necessary, if space is a consideration, but it is desirable and inexpensive. When pressure in the accumulator tank drops below a certain amount, a pressure switch in the pump activates the pump and turns it on. All the accumulator tank does is store a small amount of water under pressure so that the pump doesn't

**FIGURE 5-23.** Galley Maid's pressure water system combines all the components in one unit, and it can deliver up to 12 gallons (45 L) of fresh water per minute. (Galley Maid)

come on every time a faucet is opened. But with continuous use, like washing dishes, you get used to the sound of the pump cycling. An accumulator tank also helps minimize pulsations in the lines, more frequently caused by diaphragm than centrifugal pumps. In any event, pulsations aren't really harmful.

Both electric centrifugal and diaphragm pumps can be used on pressure water systems. An automatic cycle or pressure switch will control the amount of pressure; Galley Maid's cuts in at 21 psi ($0.14 \text{ N/mm}^2$), cuts out at 2 psi ($0.06 \text{ N/mm}^2$), and also at 10 psi ($0.06 \text{ N/mm}^2$) if the main water tank runs dry. Running a pressure water system without water can result in damage to the equipment.

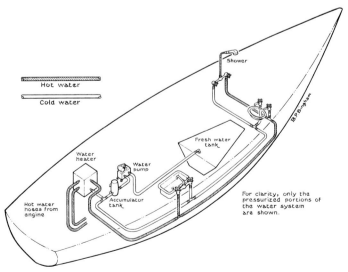

**FIGURE 5-24.** A typical freshwater system with the components split up.

As noted above, the comparatively new wobble plate (or ball bearing drive) pumps are preferable to centrifugal types. These pumps have two to four chambers and valves that are opened and closed by a direct-drive plate (turned by an electric motor) that wobbles on an off-center ball bearing; the plate pushes the individual diaphragms up and down. They are very fast and efficient. A typical Flojet model, for example, has a nominal flow of 3.3 gallons (12.5 L) per minute, drawing an average of 2.9 amps. It is sometimes referred to as a quad chamber pump. A nice feature of the Flojet is the interchangeable barb and screw-on hose fittings that plug into the side of the pump; different sizes are included to match your hose size.

Everyone's experience with pressure water systems seems a little different. Some say water consumption increases by 50% to 100%. Others claim it is virtually the same as a manual pump, though that is hard to believe. I like to confine pressurized water to the shower and use a foot pump for the sink. In fact, after years of living aboard, whenever I'm trying to operate a land faucet in somebody's house, I find myself raising my foot, searching for the pedal in a spastic, idiosyncratic movement, looking, I'm sure, like a dog being scratched in that magic spot!

## Showers

One of the first questions many ask themselves when they contemplate the cruising life is, "How often will I be able to take showers?" Good question!

The answer depends on whether you have space aboard for a shower, and how much water you can carry in the ship's tanks. After all, if you only have 20 gallons (76 L) of water, you can't very well afford to let the crew take 5-gallon (19 L) showers every day. Most newer boats now come with showers, but if yours doesn't, you can add one.

A shower requires just a small space, but does have a few basic requirements: cabin sole space, such as in the head, that can be fitted with a pan and drain for waste water; a deep bilge or clearance under the sole for a waste discharge pump; a pump to supply water to the shower head; and enough room for you and your shower head to get to know one another (Figure 5-25). Standing headroom helps, too, though not essential. And if you want a *hot* shower, obviously some sort of heater also is necessary.

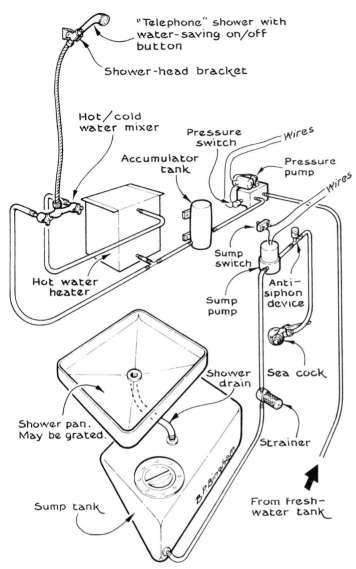

"Telephone" shower with water-saving on/off button

Shower-head bracket

Hot/cold water mixer

Pressure switch

Wires

Accumulator tank

Pressure pump

Wires

Hot water heater

Sump switch

Sump pump

Anti-siphon device

Shower drain

Sea cock

Shower pan. May be grated.

Strainer

B. P. Bingham

Sump tank

From fresh-water tank

**FIGURE 5-25.** Adding a shower is not a simple job. The pan should be molded from fiberglass or laminated from thin veneers in a concave shape and coated with epoxy resin. The sump tank collects runoff, and a pump moves it over the side when the float or manual switch is activated.

Study the shower arrangements on other boats to help you decide how to install yours. The drain is usually a fiberglass pan sunk into the sole, covered with a teak grating (unless the pan is broad and flat enough so someone walking through the head won't trip). It is fairly simple to make a pan by building a plywood box to the dimensions desired, coating it with a mold release agent (see the Making a Sea Hood section in Chapter 9 for more details on making molds and laying in fiberglass), then laying in alternate layers of 1½-ounce (per square foot) mat (457 g/m²) and

10-ounce (per square yard) (339 g/m²) cloth. If you intend to cover the pan with a teak grate, the fiberglass laminate won't need to be as thick as if you intend to stand directly on it. A laminate thickness of ⅛ inch (3 mm) should be sufficient. If it will be walked on, consider using a core material to stiffen it. Use the sea hood lamination schedule in Chapter 9. Don't forget to make a flange on the pan so it can be screwed or bolted to the cabin sole.

Plastic drains can be purchased at chandleries or well-stocked hardware and building supply stores. Stuff a bit of an S.O.S. Tuffy scouring pad in the drain to catch hair and other debris, and prevent them from clogging the pump. Route the drain hose into the bilge or to a sump pump with a float switch that activates the pump when underwater. The pump should discharge through the hull above the waterline. While a seacock isn't always necessary in such installations, it should be used if the through-hull is below the waterline when heeled. At the very least you should have an inline check valve so that water won't siphon back in.

The shower pump can be located just about any place convenient to the freshwater supply tank and head compartment. You can tap into an existing tank hose with a T-fitting to feed the pump and shower. On those sections supplying hot water, use heater hose instead of clear vinyl, as the vinyl will distort. A detachable, handheld spray nozzle that clips to the bulkhead doesn't take up much space. Wired with a pressure switch, the pump will turn on and off as you turn the handle at the mixer or push the shower head button. The pump should be wired to a circuit in the electrical distribution panel in which all member appliances or electronics are compatible. Don't overload the circuit (see Chapter 13).

## Water Heaters

There are two basic types of marine water heaters:

1. Storage tank types with two-way operation—110-volt heating elements for dockside use, and heat exchangers that circulate hot engine water through the tank to heat fresh water from the boat's tanks.

2. Instantaneous demand- or flash-type gas heaters that heat the water as it circulates through a series of copper coils around a gas flame and combustion chamber.

The best type for you depends on how you use your boat and your comfort level with LPG or CNG (generally, both fuels will work with instantaneous gas heaters but you'll have to change the orifice). If you spend a lot of time dockside at marinas, the storage type is probably more efficient, due to the relatively low cost of electricity. It also will meet most of your hot-water needs if you spend a lot of time motoring. During a cruise of the East Coast from Canada to Key West, I found that we motored about half the time—either because there wasn't enough wind to get us to the next night's anchorage, or because we were in the Intracoastal Waterway. A storage heater would have served us well. Allcraft (www.allcraft.net) makes one of the finest, with a 316 stainless steel tank and jacket, and all parts—electric heating element, heat exchanger, thermostat, pressure relief valve, and high-limit switch—are replaceable (Figure 5-26).

For a variety of reasons, on our Vanguard, I installed a Paloma instantaneous gas heater on a bulkhead in the head compartment. There wasn't enough room in the engine room for a storage tank heater; LPG was already aboard servicing the stove and refrigerator; and I didn't want to have to run the engine to take a shower—no

**FIGURE 5-26.** The Allcraft Corporation makes this rugged storage-type water heater with a stainless steel tank and jacket. It has two-way operation: a 110-volt heating element for use with shore power, and a copper heat exchanger that diverts water from the engine's exhaust.

problem at the end of a day motoring, but what about after waking in some anchorage where you've been lounging for a few days and have no need to run the engine?

My gas heater was intended for one purpose only—hot showers! In fact, I never even ran a hose to the galley sink; for dish washing I always put a kettle on the stove after the dinner was cooked, which assured that we never used more than a few cups of fresh water to rinse the saltwater-scrubbed plates and silverware.

Also, the shower was served by its own water tank—a 40-gallon (151 L) flexible Vetus tank mounted under the port quarter berth. This conveniently placed it directly below the low point in the deck, so I could dam the toe-rail drains, open the deck fill plate, and fill the shower tank with free rainwater. Seldom was it necessary to get water from the shore, except in winter months in the northern states.

The Japanese-built Paloma is a fine heater and has been around for years. People in Asia and Europe often install such heaters in their homes to spare the expense of keeping water hot in a large tank all day. Unfortunately, Paloma has no interest in the marine market and will not honor its warranty for those units installed on boats. There are, however, other brands available, like the Bosch AquaStar (www.controlledenergy.com or www.boschusa.com; Figure 5-27) and Rinnai (www.rinnai.us), but you probably won't find them in marine catalogs.

The temperature of the water coming out of gas heaters is regulated by increasing and decreasing the flow rate through the heat exchanger. Thus, to get hotter water you also get less of it. Small units have a temperature rise of about 55°F (13°C) at a flow rate of 1 gallon (3.6 L) per minute. This means that if the water in your tank is 60°F (16°C), you can get 115°F (46°C) water at 1 gpm. Water for showering should be about 105°F (41°C). In colder regions, you might have to retard the flow for adequately heated water. Still, after a cold day sailing, even a dribble of hot water over your head is soothing. The best service is had by installing a hot- and cold-water mixer after the heater for more accurate temperature regulation.

Gas heaters used in closed cabins must have an overhead flue since their high Btu output (38,000 Btu and more) eats up a lot of oxygen. This means cutting a hole in the deck for the flue pipe and cap, so give careful thought to location of the heater before you go to work.

**FIGURE 5-27.** The Bosch W125K instantaneous LPG water heater has a Piezo ignition and is approved by the American Gas Association. Temperature rise is about 69°F (21°C) at 1 gallon (3.8 L) per minute. Its chief drawback is its size: 24 inches high by 7½ inches deep by 10 ⅝ inches wide (610 mm by 191 mm by 270 mm).

## WATERMAKERS

There's a saying that the air is free. Water used to be, too, but in most of the world that is no longer true. Okay, it's so cheap in your house that you hardly think about it, especially if the cost is not billed separately by your local utility. But at many docks outside the United States, you must pay, sometimes handsomely. This makes rain catchment and watermaking systems all the more attractive. Not only do these systems reduce cost, but they also offer a higher-quality product.

Reverse osmosis watermakers are being manufactured in increasingly smaller units, so today just about any boat above about 35 feet (10.7 m) can realistically carry one while cruising. Water is pushed through a semipermeable membrane under pressure, and the salt ions, because they are larger than pure water molecules, are screened out. The osmotic pressure of salt water is 400 psi (2.8 N/mm²), so most watermakers need to operate at double that—800 psi (5.5 N/mm²). At those

kinds of pressures, it's difficult to keep the unit leak free. For this reason and others, watermakers are maintenance intensive. Ignoring them almost guarantees problems.

Pressure is created by a pump, and there are several ways to power it: belt-driven off the engine, 115-volt AC, and 12-volt DC. If there is room in the engine compartment to mount the pump, this is the most efficient option. If you're running the engine an hour or two a day to recharge batteries and the refrigeration system's holding plates, you might as well make water at the same time! But finding space between high-output alternators and compressors may be difficult. Using 115-volt AC will require a genset. Chances are you will never operate a watermaker using shore power as the water dockside is not sufficiently clean; even a drop of oil can destroy the fragile membrane. And watermakers require too much power for most inverters, which aren't terribly efficient anyway (about 15% of the DC energy going in is lost in the conversion to AC). If neither of the first two options work for you, then you're a candidate for 12-volt DC, and there are plenty of choices. There's no free lunch though, as you'll have to come up with the power somehow.

Some larger boats may be able to carry a dedicated engine for a watermaker, such as the Balmar PC-100 Aqua-Pac Watermaker (www.balmar.net; Figure 5-28). Measuring 24 by 16 by 18 inches (610 mm by 381 mm by 457 mm) and

**FIGURE 5-28.** The Balmar Aqua-Pac uses a small Yanmar diesel to drive both a watermaker and battery charger. Steve Pettengill and Georgs Kolesnikovs used one on the trimaran *American Dream* when they set a record for the run from New York to San Francisco. Saving the weight of large water tanks was a priority. (Balmar)

weighing 100 pounds (45 kg), the Aqua-Pac uses a 4.2 hp air-cooled Yanmar diesel engine to drive a 20 gph (76 L) reverse osmosis watermaker and a battery charger rated at 100 amps at 14 volts DC. Fuel consumption is 4 to 5 hours per gallon.

HRO Systems (www.hrosystems.com) and Sea Recovery (www.searecovery.com) are two of the better known manufacturers of engine-driven and 115-volt/230-volt watermakers. Among 12-volt units to check out are those made by SK Engineering (www.skwatermakers.com), Great Water (www.great-water.com), Spectra (www.spectrawatermakers.com), and Village Marine Tec (www.villagemarine.com; Figure 5-29). Current consumption ranges from about 9 amps up to around 40 amps, but the hungrier models also tend to make more water in the same amount of time, so you must balance energy going in against water coming out. For many owners, it will be advisable to run the engine to charge batteries while the watermaker is operating. For this you'll get about 6 to 10 gallons (28 L to 38 L) per hour of very clean water with no aftertaste.

Some watermakers are modular, meaning the major components—pressure vessel, pump, and controls—can be mounted separately, which is attractive if there isn't space for a self-contained unit in which everything is mounted on the same base. Modular systems offer a bit more flexibility in terms of installation but represent a bit more work as well. If you have the space, a self-contained unit is probably better, though you may decide to mount the controls separately in a more convenient location.

Of most interest to the serious offshore sailor on a more modest boat is the ability to make potable water from salt water in an emergency—drought, ruptured tanks, or an abandoned ship

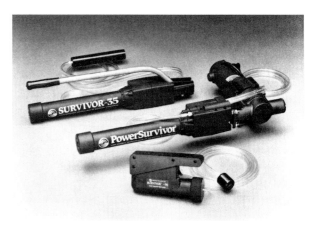

FIGURE 5-30. Katadyn makes several desalinator models, primarily for emergency use. The PowerSurvivors incorporate a 12-volt motor to use every day, if needed. (Katadyn)

scenario. Enter the Survivor-35 and PowerSurvivors, portable watermakers developed for military use in life rafts (www.katadyn.com; Figure 5-30). The Survivor-35 is primarily an emergency, manually operated device for life rafts. In fact, when William and Simonne Butler's boat was sunk by killer whales in the Pacific Ocean, they survived 66 days in a life raft with the Survivor-35 as their sole source of water. The PowerSurvivors are similar units, but incorporate a small 12-volt motor that can produce 1.5 gallons (5.7 L) per hour (in the 40E model) using the ship's batteries to generate power instead of your arm. This device could supplement the freshwater tank supply, but because its output is small compared with larger desalinators, it probably is not a substitute for catching free rainwater or paying attention to tank levels.

## SEAWATER SYSTEMS

For real luxury, a high-lift pump can be installed to provide deck wash, galley rinse, anchor wash, and other useful functions. Without an accumulator tank, the system (Figure 5-31) will provide water only when the pump is running. If you plan to purchase an accumulator tank for saltwater use, be sure to check that it's constructed of corrosion-resistant materials; most are plastic. These systems help keep the yacht clean and also help conserve fresh water by making it possible to rinse dishes in seawater first. For that matter, if the seawater is clean, freshwater rinsing is simply a waste of a limited resource. A filter in the seawa-

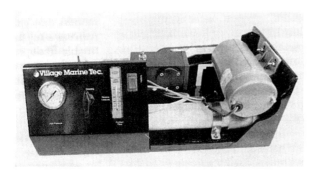

FIGURE 5-29. Self-contained 12-volt watermakers like this one by Village Marine Tec can produce from 6 to 10 gallons (23 L to 38 L) of fresh water an hour, consuming between about 9 and 40 amps. (Village Marine Tec)

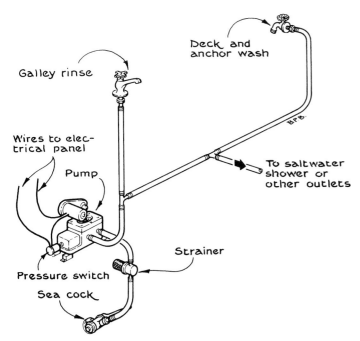

**FIGURE 5-31.** A typical seawater system such as this is ideal for rinsing dishes and washing down the deck.

ter intake before the pump will remove some salt and other junk you don't want in your sink or clogging the pump.

If you cruise with an all-chain anchor rode, washing off the mud caked in the links using buckets dropped over the side can be a back-breaking job. A seawater deck wash with hose and adjustable-spray nozzle that can be operated on the foredeck is a boon in cleaning chain as it comes over the bow roller. Dried mud in the chain locker below can get real smelly!

## ODDS AND ENDS

Besides the basic use of pumps already mentioned, there's an almost limitless number of miscellaneous applications for small and sometimes odd special-purpose pumps.

For transferring fuel, water, or other liquids from one tank to another, use Beckson's Siphon-Mate (www.beckson.com). It is a 11½-inch (292 mm) navy-type pump fitted with a special valve that also enables it to be used as a siphon; as long as the source is higher in elevation than the receptacle, one can stroke it one time to initiate the flow, then stand back and drink a beer while the pump finishes the job. Depressing the handle cuts off the flow.

For toilets that use macerator action to grind wastes into small particles, ITT/Jabsco manufactures small, combination macerator/pump units that can be mounted permanently or kept portable; a unit will empty a 30-gallon (114 L) holding tank in less than 5 minutes. Even toilets without macerators require pumps to push wastes through the hull or into the holding tank.

The easiest way to retrofit a holding tank is by installing a flexible tank. Nauta and Vetus tanks are available in sizes ranging from 14 to 400 gallons (53 L to 1,514 L). They fit neatly under bunks and should be mounted in "berths" in the same way mentioned for flexible water tanks earlier in this chapter. A manual diaphragm pump for over-the-side discharge will be necessary (don't forget the seacock) as well as a deck plate with hose to the tank for shoreside pumpout. (Owing to the nature of the tanks' contents, however, I prefer a rigid polyurethane tank for this job.)

When it's time to change engine oil, getting the old oil out can be a slow, dirty, and tedious operation, especially if your engine doesn't have a built-in sump pump. There are small, manual navy-type pumps made specially for changing oil. One can be mounted permanently in the engine compartment with brackets, so that one hand is free to hold the container. Small plastic bags fastened with rubber bands over the ends will catch the drips. Stick one hose end into the dipstick tube and the other hose end into a disposable container and start pumping. I've tried just about every type of oil retrieval pump ever made—from navy pumps to the dinky things you stick in the end of your electric drill to vacuum systems—and my preference is for one of the more expensive electric pumps like the Reverso (www.reversopumps.com).

## INSTALLING PUMPS

In most instances, installing pumps aboard a yacht is a reasonably simple operation, and one that will give a feeling of satisfaction when done correctly. There's nothing quite so nice as upgrading a boat with a new piece of gear.

Pumps should be fastened securely, either screwed, or in the case of large or manual pumps, through-bolted to a bulkhead or other strong surface, such as a plywood shelf glassed to the hull (Figure 5-32). In some instances it is necessary to reinforce the bulkhead or shelf for receiving diaphragm bilge pumps—long hours of hard pumping can weaken the mounting surface.

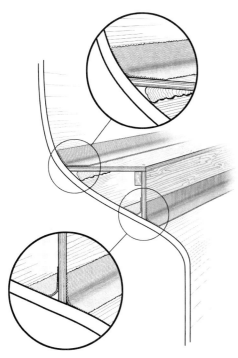

**FIGURE 5-32.** Pumps and other equipment often are most conveniently mounted on sturdy plywood shelves glassed to the hull. (Fritz Seegers illustration)

## Cutting Holes

The most intimidating task involved in pump installations is cutting a hole in the hull for discharge, unless the discharge is routed to another hose and through-hull with a Y- or T-fitting. It is critical to think the procedure through carefully, but it needn't be intimidating. Besides, these are the sorts of things that make a person a more complete skipper, with the knowledge and confidence to make necessary repairs.

Select a through-hull of a size compatible with your hose and, referring to manufacturer's instructions, use the appropriate size hole saw to cut through the hull (see Figure 13-4). Bed the through-hull inside and out with a generous amount of flexible bedding compound and tighten with a wrench. If installing a seacock as well, be sure to through-bolt it to the hull (see Chapter 4). Use two stainless steel hose clamps wherever a hose meets a fitting and periodically check for watertightness.

## Sea Chest

Discharge hoses from several sources, such as a shower drain and sink, can be routed to a stainless steel box called a sea chest. Sometimes three

and four discharge hoses are led to it, but never the bilge pump, as it would restrict water discharge too much for this application. Sea chests also can be used to service multiple seawater pumps from one through-hull fitting (Figure 5-33). Most makers of rigid plumbing systems, like Whale and John Guest (www.johnguest.com), offer manifolds that can perform the function of a sea chest.

## Hoses

When buying a hose, be sure to buy the correct size. Vinyl hose should fit snugly, but it doesn't like being stretched too much. Sometimes the diameter of the discharge hose will be larger than the intake; in fact, a pump with a discharge opening 25% larger than its intake will be more efficient.

I think all marine hose should be reinforced, as unreinforced vinyl hose tends to kink and collapse. Certainly hose for heads and pressure water systems exceeding about 20 psi (0.14 N/mm²) must have reinforcing wires wound spirally into the wall. Clear nylon tubing isn't as thick-walled as nylon hose, and it shouldn't be used on water systems unless for air vents or some other function that doesn't stress it very much. In fact, I can't think of a good application for clear, unreinforced vinyl hose anywhere.

Independent lab tests I commissioned at *Practical Sailor* showed rigid PVC pipe absolutely prevents odors from permeating through its

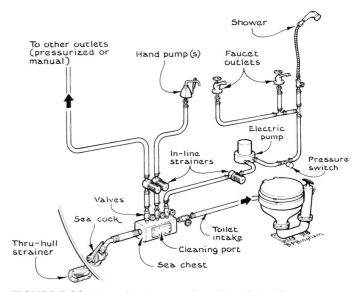

**FIGURE 5-33.** A sea chest is an enclosed box that either supplies several faucets from one intake source or drains several sources through one through-hull.

114

walls. Among PVC hose, which is more easily routed through a boat's interior than rigid pipe, OdorSafe from Dometic Sanitation Systems (www.dometicsanitation.com) was ten times more resistant to odor permeation than other brands. But it's also somewhat more difficult to bend.

All hose should be nontoxic, and while this is the type generally sold by marine chandleries, if you buy elsewhere, be sure to ask. Garden hose changes the taste of water, so leave it home for the garden.

When connecting hose to connectors (seacocks, pumps, sink drains, etc.), use a pipe sealant on the connector to ensure a watertight seal.

### Emergency Considerations

Make sure every pump aboard is in an accessible location. If one stops—and the likelihood is that sometime during a pump's life it will—your life could depend upon how fast you can make repairs and resume operation. Diaphragms can tear. Electrical connections corrode, and belts slip. Leave enough space around the pump to accommodate both your hands and necessary tools. Some pumps come apart without screwdrivers or wrenches. One would be wise to check the method of disassembly before purchasing a pump. Inside seat lockers, under galleys, and in the bilge are common and usually convenient locations. And carry spare parts such as diaphragms and impellers.

### Diverter Valves

It's not uncommon to use one pump for two compartments, such as one freshwater pump for two tanks or a bilge pump for two separate parts of the bilge or cabin. A diverter valve allows you to close and open the passage to each compartment (Figure 5-34). Similarly, a Y-fitting enables two pumps to discharge through one outlet, which saves on hose and through-hulls. Head wastes in the holding tank can be diverted to the deck pumpout or, by switching the diverter valve, directed overboard when beyond the 3-mile (4.8 km) limit off the U.S. coastline.

### Float and Pressure Switches

All boats, especially those that have a tendency to leak (and what boat doesn't?!) or those left untended for extended periods of time, should be fitted with an automatic sensing device that will

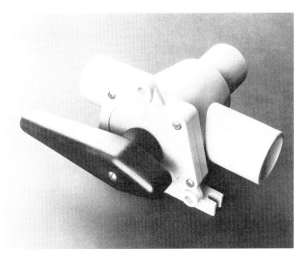

**FIGURE 5-34.** This diverter valve is used in plumbing systems to connect two different water supplies and allow the discharge of two sources through one through-hull. (Whale)

turn on the electric bilge pump when water reaches a certain level. Be sure to buy a model that turns on at a higher water level than it turns off.

Float switches that turn on and off at the same height are constantly turning the pump on and off each time the water laps the sensing device. The next time you step aboard—that is if your boat is still afloat—you could find your battery totally discharged. Float switches also are used for automatic shower sump pumps.

In pressure water systems, pressure switches activate a pump when a faucet is opened. In some instances, check valves in the lines (devices that permit the flow of water in one direction only) prevent electric bilge pumps from accidentally siphoning water back into the boat.

Float switches, because they are immersed in water a good deal of the time, are prone to failure. Recent developments include sonic switches that electronically sense the presence of water, and floats that are designed to keep the electrical connections above water at all times. My tests have favored the Ultimate Pumpswitch (www.ultra safetysystems.com).

## PUMP MAINTENANCE

Most pumps require little or no maintenance. Check manufacturer's instructions to be sure.

The O-ring in navy-type pumps eventually wears and squirts water up the piston. Donald Street, in *The Ocean Sailing Yacht* vol. 2, describes a means of replacing the O-ring on bronze-bodied pumps with a packing nut filled with greased flax and soldered to the top of the pump.

The most likely repair you'll have to make on other types of pumps is replacing the impeller or diaphragm. Again, carry spares, or, if available, the manufacturer's spare parts repair kit.

Munster Simms Engineering (Whale pumps) has some good suggestions on repairing torn or

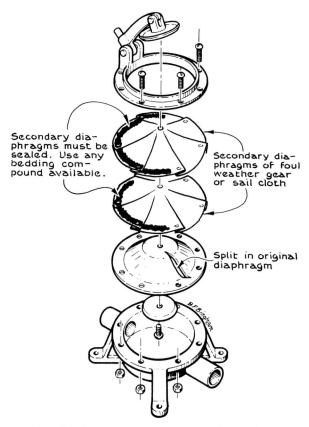

Secondary diaphragms must be sealed. Use any bedding compound available.

Secondary diaphragms of foul weather gear or sail cloth

Split in original diaphragm

**FIGURE 5-35.** A ripped diaphragm can be repaired at sea by inserting a piece of sailcloth or foul-weather gear over the diaphragm.

damaged diaphragms. A piece of sailcloth, foul-weather gear, canvas, plastic food bag, or other type of plastic-coated material that is strong and nonporous can be fitted over the old diaphragm to plug the hole (Figure 5-35). "First inclination," a company spokesman says, "is to dispense with the damaged diaphragm, but as the split is likely to be only a small part of the diaphragm area, it will provide excellent support for the substitute material." Use the makeshift diaphragm in two layers, one on either side of the old diaphragm, creating a sandwich.

A frightened crew member with a bucket still may be the most efficient pump. But in an emergency there are other chores for him or her to tend to, like steering the boat, which will reduce or eliminate his effectiveness as a bailer. Adequately sized and properly installed pumps are essential to any well-found yacht, while freshwater and saltwater conveniences, which don't have to be extravagant, will certainly make life aboard more enjoyable.

# FURTHER READING

*The Complete Live-Aboard Book.* Katy Burke. Newport, Rhode Island: Seven Seas Press, 1982.

*The Gougeon Brothers on Boat Construction: Wood and West System Materials.* 5th ed. Meade Gougeon. Bay City, Michigan: Gougeon Brothers, Inc., 2005.

*The Ocean Sailing Yacht.* Vols. 1 and 2. Donald Street. New York: Norton, 1973–1978.

*66 Days Adrift: A True Story of Disaster and Survival on the Open Sea.* William Butler. Camden, Maine: International Marine, 2005.

# SIX

# STEERING SYSTEMS

There are five basic types of steering systems suitable for cruising sailboats: tiller, cable, hydraulic, worm gear, and rack and pinion. Push-pull (used on outboard motor boats) and pull-pull systems both use a cable run through a length of flexible conduit between the wheel and the rudderstock. Pull-pull steering sometimes is a clever solution to difficult installation problems on small boats, but neither is strong enough to handle the loads of offshore sailing.

Chances are you'll stick with the type already on your boat, but there are advantages and disadvantages to each type, and you could decide to incur the expense of modifying or changing to another system altogether.

## TILLER STEERING

Tiller steering is by far the simplest and easiest system to repair. Make a spare or emergency backup tiller either from solid wood (being careful to cut with the grain), laminate one over a form (Figure 6-1), or fashion one out of pipe. If the main tiller breaks, dig into the lazarette and bolt on the spare. If the tiller head casting breaks, you'll need to jury-rig some method of attaching the tiller to the rudderstock. If you're desperate, a pair of big Vise-Grips or a crescent wrench might be clamped on, with a piece of pipe fitted over the handle to give greater leverage. But squeezing a round shaft with jury-rigged tools is futile in heavy weather; a stock squared at the end offers much surer attachment with an emergency tiller. However, this is a job for the machine shop, and removing the stock is often difficult. It's more sensible to drill a hole through the stock to receive a bolt securing the tiller.

Most reasonably balanced boats up to about 45 feet (13.8 m) can be steered with tillers. Pelle Peterson designed the 1980 tiller-steered Swedish Twelve-Meter, *Sverige*, which was over 60 feet (18.3 m) LOA. The loads on the helm are very much a function of balance and therefore design, though the size of the boat is also a factor. With a self-steering device, less time is spent at the helm, so the added convenience of wheel steering is diminished. Also, vanes that require control lines led to the helm are much easier to connect to a tiller than a wheel. A tiller gives more feedback to the helmsman than any type of wheel steering, a desirable feature on a small boat. However, on a large boat, especially if it has more-than-normal weather helm, tiller steering may be too punishing.

I think it would make sense to design a boat for cable-quadrant wheel steering as its primary system, but with a tiller, say, aft, over the afterdeck, out of the way. The tiller could be used for the self-steering wind vane control lines and be ready should the wheel steering go down. Even some existing boats might be able to set up this "belt-and-suspenders" approach if the emergency tiller can be installed without getting in everyone's way.

## CABLE STEERING

Cable steering is perhaps the most common steering seen on today's larger production boats (Figure 6-2). It is frequently fitted to boats that could just as well be steered by tiller. But it does serve the dubious function of making some skippers feel as though they are steering a bigger boat. On the plus side, wheels do give the helmsman more "feel" and quicker turning than any other system besides the tiller. The difficulty with any cable system is that sooner or later the cable, Nicopress terminals, cable clamps, roller chain, or master link will fail. Like an airplane mechanic, your job, then, is to inspect and service the system before failure occurs.

Edson (www.edsonmarine.com), the largest manufacturer of steering systems in the United States, offers many variations on the cable-quadrant type. These include dual-ratio quadrants

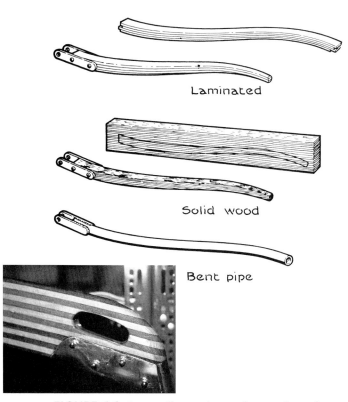

**FIGURE 6-1.** A new tiller can be cut from a piece of hardwood such as oak, laminated from thin pieces of hardwood over a form, or made from a piece of bent pipe. When cutting from a solid piece of wood, be sure to go with the grain as much as possible. When laminating (inset), use a good waterproof glue, such as resorcinol or epoxy resin in liberal amounts.

for greater responsiveness; compact, prefabricated sheave boxes for boats with raked rudderstocks (such as the Vanguard and many other older boats); and radial types that use a flat, round plate fitted over the rudderstock rather than a quadrant. These steering systems, like most others, seem to have been developed not so much for their particular steering characteristics, but to adapt to a particular cockpit construction and its relationship to the rudderstock.

In the event the cable fails, it is essential to be able to fit an emergency tiller until you are able to make repairs with a spare length of 7 × 19 wire, clamps, and master links. If this is not possible on your boat, determine if the rudderstock can be extended above the cockpit sole and squared or drilled to receive a tiller head.

Needless to say, an outboard rudder presents far fewer problems as the rudderhead is more easily adapted to a spare tiller than an inboard rudderstock.

Some wheel steerers are located far aft in the cockpit, just forward of the rudderstock. Often this does not permit fixing an emergency tiller of any sufficient length to allow a helmsman to control the boat off the wind. Consider relocating the wheel farther forward in the cockpit with longer cables or more sheaves as necessary. If this isn't possible, the emergency tiller may have to be formed in an unusual shape to clear the pedestal, perhaps with a large hump in it (see the Emergency Steering Systems section later in this chapter).

Installing cable steering systems is more difficult than, say, rack and pinion, but can be accomplished by the diligent worker. The first task is to determine where to mount the pedestal in the cockpit—are there obstructions underneath the cockpit floor? Can you crank winches comfortably? Is there enough sitting and/or standing room behind the wheel? If the cockpit floor oilcans, glass in a piece of ½- to ¾-inch (12 mm to 19 mm) plywood, depending on how much stiffening is required, under the cockpit.

Drill the mounting holes for the pedestal and a centering hole so you can locate it from underneath. The number and size of holes for the cable may vary with brand and model, so be sure to read the manufacturer's instructions carefully. Gener-

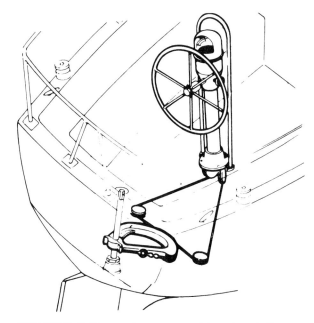

**FIGURE 6-2.** The most common cable system is the pedestal or cable-quadrant type pictured here. The steering wheel drives a chain fixed to a sprocket. The ends of the chain are attached to wire rope, usually 7 × 19, which runs through sheaves to the quadrant attached to the rudder shaft. (Edson International)

118

ally, after everything is centered, one large hole is drilled—through which pass the wire cables, throttle and transmission cables, and electrical wires for the red compass light mounted atop the pedestal.

To machine the rudderstock, it is necessary to remove the rudder from the boat. When I installed wheel steering on the Vanguard, I had to dig a fairly deep hole under the rudder before it would drop out; alternatively you could ask the yard to lift the boat with its Travelift when you're set to go.

Remove the heel bearing, as well as any hinges, straps, gudgeons, or pintles that secure the rudder to the keel. On old boats such as the Vanguard, these are fastened by driving bronze rods (drift pins) through the rudder or keel and peening over the heads. To remove the rudder, you must grind away the overlapping cap, then drive the rod out with a second rod and hammer. To reinstall, use a new rod. Someone must hold a heavy weight, such as an anvil, on the opposite side while you peen over the ends, one at a time. It's tough work. Steve Krous, a drummer in a local band, helped me out; drummers, I learned, have highly developed hand muscles.

On our Tartan 44, the skeg-hung rudder (see Chapter 2) had one large bronze hinge inset into both the skeg and rudder and covered over with polyester putty. To remove it, I had to chip out the brittle putty. Instead of drift pins, the hinge was secured with large machine screws and tapped (threaded) holes in the hinge on the opposite side.

On spade rudders, there may be bearings inside the hull that have to be removed, too. And on any through-hull rudderstock without a tube extending between the hull and underside of the cockpit floor, there will be a stuffing box or other seal to prevent water from pouring in.

If your boat's rudderstock does turn through a fiberglass tube that extends from the hull to the underside of the cockpit floor, it will be necessary to cut a section away above the waterline to install a stuffing box and expose a section of the stock so that the quadrant or drive wheel can be attached (Figure 6-3). The stuffing box should be strongly glassed to the tube with epoxy resin and a laminate of mat and cloth.

There are various ways to attach the quadrant to the rudderstock, including machining the stock with a keyway, through-bolting, or drilling and tapping for stainless steel cap screws (Figure 6-4). The keyway is the standard method and is very strong.

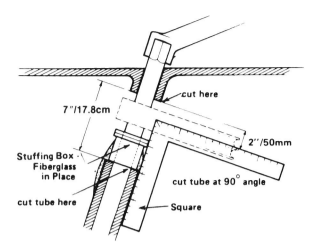

**FIGURE 6-3.** A stuffing box must be fitted to the rudderstock above the waterline, and above it a section of stock must be exposed to fasten the quadrant or drive wheel. (Edson International)

With the pedestal in place and the quadrant mounted on the rudderstock, mount the idlers or sheave box under the cockpit floor. Adjustment of the idler sheaves can wait until the other sheaves are fixed in place. These may be through-bolted to plywood supports glassed to the hull and the outboard side of the cockpit seats (Figure 6-5). Mock up the installation using C-clamps to hold these sheaves in place. Then use a length of shock cord in place of wire to check for alignment. Lead the ends over the pedestal sprocket, through the cockpit floor, then over the idler sheaves and outboard sheaves, and tie them to the quadrant. When you are certain that all sheaves are properly positioned, through-bolt the outboard sheaves, fasten the quadrant to the rudderstock, and tighten the idler sheaves.

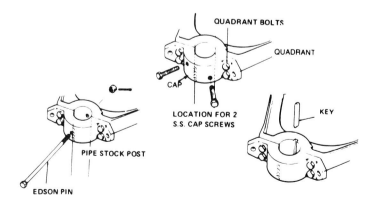

**FIGURE 6-4.** Of the many ways of attaching the quadrant to the stock, this drawing shows three: with a machined keyway, with a through-bolt, and drilled and tapped holes for cap screws. (Edson International)

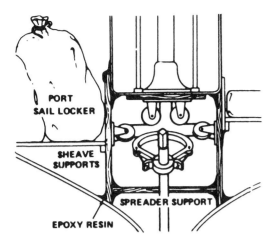

FIGURE 6-5. The outboard sheaves must be securely mounted under the cockpit floor. One method is to glass in plywood supports to the hull and outboard side of the cockpit seats. (Edson International)

Now mount the roller chain and cut two lengths of $7 \times 19$ or $7 \times 37$ wire 1 foot or so longer than required. Use Nicopress terminal fittings and thimbles where the wire attaches to the roller chain. Use cable clamps and thimbles to fasten the wire to the take-up eyes or other mechanism on the quadrant (Figure 6-6). This will enable you to shorten the wire if it stretches later on. When all is in place, turn the wheel hard over to hard over and have someone below check for misalignment, wracking, or other distortion in the system.

Lastly, you must incorporate some method to prevent the quadrant from turning so far that the rudder is damaged. Options include:

- Glass rudder stops to the underside of the cockpit floor and fit an arm to the rudder-stock that will hit the stops before the rudder turns too far to port or starboard.

- Bolt a pin to the quadrant that will hit the stops.

- Glass 2 by 4s to the cockpit and hull with metal plates so that when the quadrant swings from side to side, it hits the metal plates before the rudder hits the hull (Figure 6-7).

Rudder stops are built into the prefabricated sheave boxes, which simplifies the job. Figure 6-8 shows all the major parts for an Edson system using a four-sheave box.

Edson recommends lubricating the needle bearings in the pedestal bowl with Teflon while spinning the wheel, but don't overgrease as it

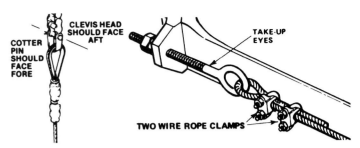

FIGURE 6-6. The roller chain is fastened to the wire with thimbles and Nicopress fittings and the wire to the quadrant with cable clamps. (Edson International)

can run onto the brake pads. Oil the chain with 30-weight motor oil—not grease—to penetrate the links. Wipe the wire with tissue soaked in oil. Broken or hooked strands will snag the tissue. Replace the wire every five years or less regardless of its condition. Check for play in the system by locking the wheel over and trying to move the

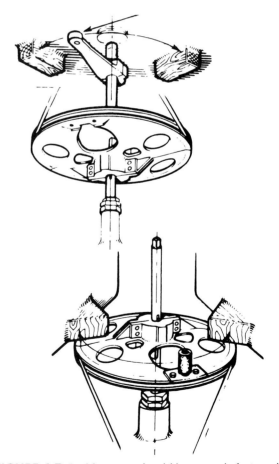

FIGURE 6-7. Rudder stops should be securely fastened to some part of the hull or cockpit, independent of the steering system. This illustration shows two methods. (Edson International)

**FIGURE 6-8.** Before beginning to install the Edson pedestal system on the Vanguard, I arranged all the parts on a dock for inspection. The four-sheave box in the foreground simplified the job, since I didn't have to fiberglass mounts to the underside of the cockpit for independent sheaves.

quadrant; the wire should be tight enough so that it doesn't move, but not overly tight. Wire jumping out of the sheave or quadrant is a common occurrence, most often caused by owners unwilling to crawl into a seat locker or under the cockpit to make an annual inspection of their steering systems.

Periodically check all screws, bolts, and clevis and cotter pins. Under power, put a crew member below where he or she can view the quadrant and cable as you put the helm hard over—look for any sign of bending, creaking, or other indication of potential failure.

## HYDRAULIC STEERING

Hydraulic steering relies on a system of pumps and hoses through which a fluid is pushed under pressure to actuate a piston(s) that pushes a tiller arm

attached to the rudderstock (Figure 6-9). Like a worm-gear steerer, there is little feedback from the rudder to the helmsman, and you cannot center the wheel; that is, mark the wheel when the rudder is aligned on centerline because the wheel doesn't always return to the same spot. But, unlike a worm gear, the wheel reverses itself when you take your hands off. The principal advantage of hydraulic steering (and pull-pull cable) is that the hoses can be run just about anywhere under the cockpit regardless of configuration or obstacles. That's why it's often installed on center-cockpit boats. It also is quite a powerful steering system.

However, it is one of the more failure-prone types of steering systems, especially due to scarred piston walls and dirty seals where the hoses connect to the reservoir tank and piston. A crack in the nipples can cause a pressure loss in the system, which, of course, causes loss of steering. Dirt is a hydraulic system's worst enemy, and strict cleanliness must be observed when working on connectors or when bleeding the system (which involves pouring fluid into the reservoir while drawing off fluid—and air bubbles—from the highest point).

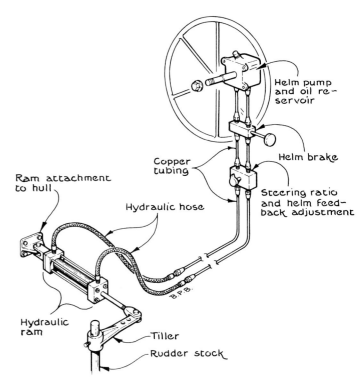

**FIGURE 6-9.** Hydraulic steering uses hoses and fluid much like power steering uses fluid in your car. The weak link in this system is the connecting fittings, which if they leak, can cause a loss of power and attendant loss of steering. Feedback to the helmsman is relatively poor.

Repairs are further complicated by the fact that many of the typical problems can't be seen and are difficult to trace. With cable, at least, you can grab the offending parts with your hand. Working on hydraulics in any kind of sea is not fun. Keep oil-absorbent pads on hand for soaking up spilled hydraulic fluid; you can buy special brands that absorb oil but not water. These "diapers" are also handy to use under leaky engines.

## WORM GEAR

Next to the tiller, the most foolproof steering systems are worm gear (Figure 6-10) and rack and pinion. Worm gear's almost total lack of feedback to the helmsman is disconcerting; however, on large boats it is a tolerable, if not sometimes desirable, quality. With high-quality gear and linkage, there is practically nothing that can break. However, because the rudderstock cannot freewheel with the gear attached, fitting an emergency tiller would take some time, unless there is enough

FIGURE 6-11. Both worm-gear and rack-and-pinion steerers are mounted aft in the cockpit, and a housing is generally fashioned to cover the mechanisms and provide seating for the helmsman. This boat has worm gear.

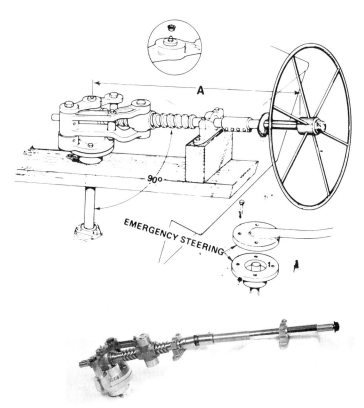

FIGURE 6-10. Worm-gear steering is one of the most foolproof, next to the simple tiller. There is little or no feedback to the helmsman, but the boat will hold course when you take your hands off the wheel. (Edson International)

room to install a long enough tiller to provide enough leverage to turn the stock with the gears attached. The recommended method is to remove the gear, and bolt a specially welded plate and tiller to the stock.

Due to the inherent friction in the system it is possible to take your hands off the helm with worm gear and have the boat hold course. This is why worm gear is called nonreversing. This means, however, that the rudder must be very strong, because the helm won't swing easily when forces are exerted on the rudder—odds are the rudder will break before the worm gear.

The limitation of worm gear and rack and pinion is that the wheel must be located close to the rudderstock, which on a center-cockpit boat is impossible. The worm gear generally is bolted inside a housing at the after end of the cockpit, either forward or aft of the rudderhead (Figure 6-11).

The housing is often constructed to form a helmsman's seat, with the wheel positioned virtually in the helmsman's lap.

Edson's Simplex worm-gear steerers range from 3.25 to 6 turns hard over to hard over in 90°, which is about twice that of cable systems; e.g., for a 35-footer (10.7 m), the difference is about 3.25 versus 1.8 turns. This is one reason why worm gears most often are fitted to heavy, full-keel boats that track well, thereby requiring less attention to the helm. A lighter fin keel boat loses its responsiveness with worm-gear steering.

A previous owner of my Vanguard had installed worm-gear steering, and after spending several seasons trying to get used to its peculiarities, I replaced it with an Edson cable-quadrant system and was much happier. Sailing to windward is the easiest point for the worm gear—very little effort is required, but inexperienced persons on my boat never learned to anticipate the heading-up, falling-off cycle of the boat; because there *is* no feel, you have to wait until the bow moves one way or the other before correcting, and then you usually correct too much. Off the wind it was impossible to keep the boat from yawing, especially with quartering seas. The lack of feedback and 3-plus turns lock to lock, I concluded, was a dangerous combination in bad weather.

## RACK AND PINION

Rack-and-pinion steering is a geared system that incorporates a geared shaft (the pinion) rolling over a geared quadrant (the rack). They are suitable for boats up to about 40 feet (12.2 m) and 30,000 pounds (13,602 kg) displacement. Versions are available for all types of rudders and stern shapes. Mounted aft in the cockpit, similar to the worm-gear steerer, it also has similar wheel placement limitations because the rack must be fitted to the rudderstock. Figure 6-12 shows a typical installation. Simplicity of installation is one of its virtues. The gears must be securely through-bolted to a sturdy surface (e.g., plywood glassed to the cockpit or a box—perhaps doubling as a helmsman's seat—covering the gear). The rack must be mounted 90° to the rudderstock. A short section of the stock should be left to fit an emergency tiller.

Rack and pinion is a simple and robust steering system, and unlike worm steerers, there is complete feedback of the rudder to the helmsman. Lock-to-lock turns of Edson models are about 1.6 in 70° and 1.8 in 80°.

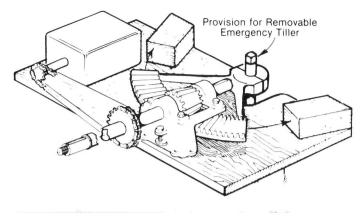

**FIGURE 6-12.** Rack-and-pinion steerers incorporate a geared shaft (pinion) and a flat, geared bar (rack). They are sturdy mechanisms and are located aft in the cockpit. (Edson International)

Maintenance of rack-and-pinion steering is straightforward—use 30-weight motor oil on the shaft bearing and a Teflon grease on the gear teeth. For worm gear, use 30-weight motor oil on the pivot points and water pump grease on the worm itself. If you have installed a universal joint in the wheel shaft to mount the wheel at a more comfortable angle (rack-and-pinion and worm-gear steering must be fitted to the rudderstock at right angles), periodically pack the universal joint with grease, giving attention to its protective rubber boot.

## INSTALLATION

Wheel steering systems can be installed by the enterprising individual, although there is a need to consult closely with the manufacturer to be sure you have selected the right system and model to fit your boat. Shaft lengths may need customizing, but if you have carefully measured the pertinent dimensions of your cockpit, rudder shaft angle,

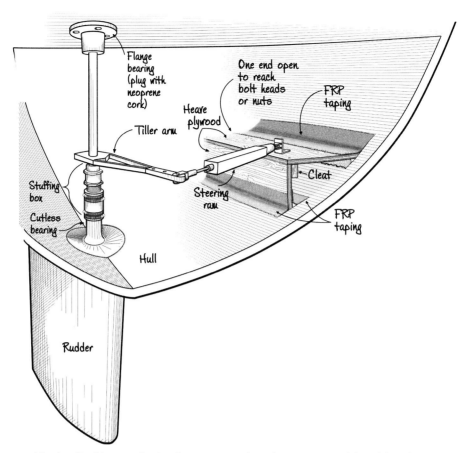

**FIGURE 6-13.** Linear and hydraulic drives are by far the most popular. They are powerful and fast, but consume a fair amount of electrical power, especially when working hard. The foundation for the drive unit must be structural. Edson makes cast-bronze tiller arms. Note the emergency tiller stock extensions. (Fritz Seegers illustration)

etc., most of that can be done by the manufacturer before it's delivered.

Perhaps the most important point in installing any wheel steering system is fastening parts to the hull, cockpit, or housing. Tremendous forces are placed on steering systems, so every part should be through-bolted, not screwed. Other parts, such as mounts for sheaves and idlers, may need glassing or welding to the hull. Follow the guidelines for hull preparation and lamination techniques in Chapter 2. If a cockpit floor seems weak (it flexes when you stand on it), reinforce the floor by glassing at least ½-inch (12 mm) plywood underneath it before mounting a heavy pedestal. See the Cable Steering section above for more details.

## AUTOPILOT ADAPTATIONS

Cable, hydraulic, worm-gear, and rack-and-pinion steering systems all can be fitted with autopilots for self-steering. This is generally accomplished with a hydraulic ram or linear drive (Figure 6-13; see also Figure 7-7) that is attached directly to the rudderstock. An older, slower, and less-powerful type is the servo-drive motor connected to the cable steerer's wire or, in the case of worm gear and rack and pinion, the steerer shaft by a roller chain and sprockets (Figure 6-14). With cable and hydraulic systems, the autopilot may be located on a platform in the lazarette or in a cockpit seat locker, where the cable or hose may be routed near it. It also may be mounted in the steering box or under the cockpit near the rudderstock or steering gear. In any installation, the autopilot must be located somewhere adjacent to the rudderstock, steerer shaft, or, in the case of cable steering, near the cable. Mechanical and electromagnetic clutches can be fitted to engage and disengage the autopilot drive motor.

There are also autopilots that mount in the cockpit and turn the steering wheel by means of a belt and drum (see Chapter 7).

It is best if you choose your steering system and self-steering device at the same time to achieve

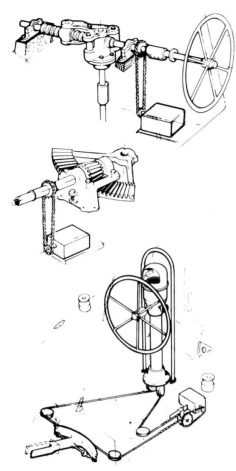

**FIGURE 6-14.** Wheel steering systems can be adapted to under-deck autopilots. A less favored method today is adding a sprocket to the steering shaft and connecting it to a motor by means of a chain. I had to use the type of drive shown at bottom (cable-quadrant) on my Tartan 44 because there wasn't enough room in the stern to mount a hydraulic or linear drive. (Edson International)

the most efficient match. For example, a wind vane is most compatible with tiller steering, especially if it is a servo-pendulum vane with control lines led to the helm; although control lines can be adapted to wheels, vanes work better on tillers. If you have hydraulic steering, a hydraulic ram that operates on the quadrant is the most sensible. On below-deck pilots, the type of drive is equally or more important than the guts of the little black control box with electronic controls mounted in the cockpit. Ram and linear drives that attach directly to the main steering quadrant, or to a tiller arm keyed to the rudderstock, are more positive attachments than rotary drives installed in line with cable steering systems, where there is always some inherent slop.

Bob Verhaeghe, who manufactured a steering vane called Cruising Yacht Systems, used to promote his product with the advice: "Save the money you would have spent on a wheel and invest it in an autopilot or wind vane. Then you won't need the wheel; in fact, you'll probably be glad you don't have it."

# EMERGENCY STEERING SYSTEMS

When wheel steering fails, an emergency tiller that is easily shipped may save the day, though emergency tillers are almost always a lot more work, so the captain and crew will need to take frequent turns. Physical effort aside, there are common difficulties trying to get any emergency tiller concept to function: With pedestal steerers, the pedestal is often too close to the rudderstock; with worm gear, the gear may need to be removed to allow the rudderstock to freewheel. And with worm gear and rack and pinion, access to the rudderstock may be difficult.

Figure 6-15 illustrates several methods of modifying the end of the rudderstock to accept a stout emergency tiller. If you have converted from tiller to wheel steering, it may be possible to leave the tiller head attached to the stock, which will then make it possible to fit a modified tiller to the stock that will clear the wheel (Figure 6-16).

Unlike the raked rudderstocks shown in Figure 6-16, the rudderstocks on most modern boats are vertical, making clearance with the pedestal even more of a problem. One possible solution is

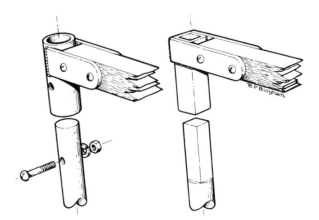

**FIGURE 6-15.** Provisions for emergency steering are a must. If the rudderhead cannot be modified to accept an emergency tiller, the top of the shaft can be squared or drilled for a pin to hold the tiller.

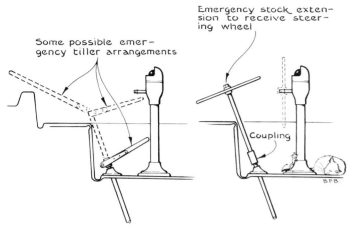

**FIGURE 6-16.** Older boats with raked rudderstocks may make fitting an emergency tiller easier, but clearance distances are critical and vary from boat to boat.

to custom fabricate an emergency tiller with a hump in it to clear the pedestal (Figure 6-17).

As a last resort, with a more or less vertical rudderstock it may be possible to reverse the tillerhead on the stock, and mount the tiller facing aft—what the hell, it's worth a try. George Day, former *Cruising World* editor, tells of the time he was aboard a 50-foot (15.2 m) ketch in the Miami–Montego Bay Race. Speeding along at

1 A.M. on a quartering reach under full sail, the steering cable snapped just as they were passing between Cat Cay and Eleuthera. An emergency tiller could only be fitted facing aft. The crew took 15-minute turns sitting on the afterdeck using both feet to steer. As if this wasn't difficult enough, they had to keep remembering to push when they used to pull and vice versa!

Steering is an important enough function to justify saying this—if an emergency backup system cannot be fitted, buy another boat.

But what happens when the rudder itself fails? On some boats, the gudgeons and pintles aren't sufficiently strong or their fastenings may be undersized. With fiberglass rudders, the rudderstock may break loose from the rudder blade, spinning freely.

There are at least three options: steer with sails alone (pretty impractical); build a makeshift rudder (difficult and probably not very strong unless prefabricated—Figure 6-18); or use the wind vane rudder (comparatively easy if your boat is equipped with a vane that uses an auxiliary rud-

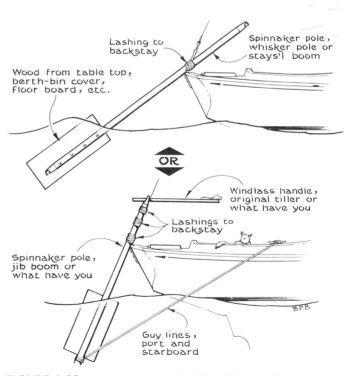

**FIGURE 6-18.** An emergency makeshift rudder can be fashioned from pieces of plywood and 2 by 4s (carried aboard for this and other emergency purposes) or from a spinnaker pole and hatchboards. The best plan, however, is to prefabricate the rudder before you go cruising.

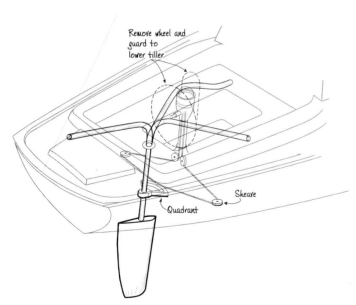

**FIGURE 6-17.** An emergency tiller may be fabricated from aluminum pipe with a hump in it to clear the pedestal. (Fritz Seegers illustration)

der). The most realistic way of preparing for this contingency on a majority of cruising boats is to build an emergency rudder beforehand.

## Making an Emergency Rudder

Figure 2-36 on page 58 shows how to make a fiberglass rudder. Through-bolt gudgeons to the transom and weld pintles to the rudderstock so the emergency rudder can be lifted from a seat locker, or wherever else it's stowed, and mounted without having to screw or bolt anything in some dubious, jury-rigged fashion. The rudderstock should be drilled to receive an emergency tiller, also kept handy.

Ingenious sailors without prefabricated emergency rudders have reported marginal success using spinnaker poles lashed to hatch covers and ropes led from the rudder to port and starboard winches (Figure 6-18 again). But to accomplish this in storm conditions requires more luck than handy workmanship. You'll be well rewarded for planning ahead.

Alternatively, Scanmar International (www.selfsteer.com) makes the SOS emergency rudder out of 316 stainless steel, accompanied by sturdy mounting brackets (Figure 6-19).

## Wind Vane Auxiliary Rudders

The Hydrovane (www.hydrovane.com) is one type of wind vane that uses an auxiliary rudder to steer the boat. Should the main rudder become disabled or fall off, you would have no difficulty steering the boat to port with the vane rudder. And some vanes, like the Auto-Helm (www.selfsteer.com), have trim tabs on the trailing edges that require very little effort to turn the boat. Servo-pendulum-type steering vanes do have paddles in the water, but oscillate sideways to generate power, and are not for steering the boat.

**FIGURE 6-19.** The 35-pound (16 kg) SOS emergency rudder from Scanmar is set up prior to leaving on your cruise. It stows in four pieces belowdecks until needed. (Scanmar International)

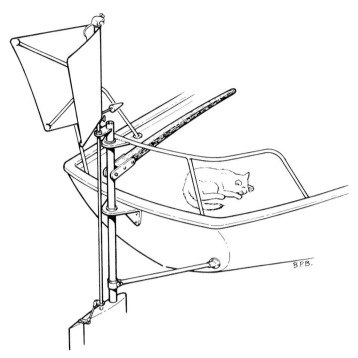

**FIGURE 6-20.** A wind vane self-steering device can be used for emergency steering if it uses an auxiliary rudder. Some models incorporate a trim tab on the auxiliary rudder, which could be used to steer the boat by fastening Vise-Grips to the trim tab shaft, drilling the shaft, or welding a section to the rudderstock to receive an emergency tiller.

If the wind vane rudder can function as a primary rudder, conceive of a method to fit the tiller to its rudderstock. A weldment can be added to the rudderstock to receive a bolt-on tiller during an emergency (Figure 6-20).

## WEAK LINKS IN THE STEERING SYSTEM

Because it is underwater, the rudder is subjected to considerable forces and is often a weak link. Over time, even the best engineered system can show signs of fatigue.

Check for potential problems in several places. An inboard rudder blade should be well secured to the stock. Good fiberglass designs incorporate metal arms welded to the stock that are encased by the rudder (see Chapter 2). Examples of things to look for are cracks in the gelcoat and laminate and play in the blade relative to the stock. Wood rudders may have bronze or stainless steel arms sandwiching the blade, or drift pins driven through the planks. Look for splitting of the planks (not

minor checking), corrosion around welds, and discoloration of the bronze fittings, indicating overstressing.

Stock supports inside the hull are potential problem areas (see Chapter 2), as is the tiller head. Aluminum castings can crack unexpectedly, and there is virtually no way, short of X-rays, to foresee their development. Welded stainless steel or forged bronze is much stronger.

On outboard rudders and keel-hung rudders, gudgeons and pintles or hinges carry the load. Screws are insufficient to attach the hardware to the hull and rudder; through-bolts must be used. If the dimensions of the hardware seem too small for the job, consider replacing them with more massive fittings.

Wood cheeks, or aluminum or stainless steel side plates, are important elements of outboard rudder strength. Often they are used to receive the tiller as well, and they must be strong enough to resist twist. Through-bolting the cheeks or plates to each other through the rudderhead is the only acceptable attachment method (Figure 6-21).

Tillers, especially laminated ones, will break most often where they are bolted to the tiller head. Delamination is one sure sign that trouble is brewing, as is spongy wood around the bolt hole. Periodically remove the tiller from the fitting and inspect the bolt holes for signs of rot or delamination. Don't hesitate to replace the tiller when these signs are present. You know that when it does break, it'll happen when you are hard pressed in heavy weather. You can mortise stainless steel side plates to the tiller to take the strain, or in an emer-

**FIGURE 6-21.** Outboard rudders are in many ways the sturdiest and easiest to repair. Their one weak link is the rudderstock and cheek blocks, which should be sturdy and through-bolted. Gudgeons and pintles should also be heavy duty and through-bolted.

gency, cut off the aft end of the tiller and drill a new hole.

Cable systems fail most often where the wire, Nicopress, or cable clamps come apart. Water may find its way into these parts and begin the diabolical, arcane process of corrosion. Tarnished or frayed wire strands are one sign, but as with the rigging, there's no certain way to determine what is going on inside the terminals. X-rays are the only sure method, but they are not always possible or practical. There are two-part liquid products such as Spotcheck (www.magnaflux.com), available at auto supply stores, that can be applied to a terminal, quadrant, or other casting to help define cracks, sort of like the stuff dentists use to pinpoint cavities (see Chapter 10). It is a good idea to replace the wire cable and connecting fittings every five years or so just to be on the safe side.

Worm-gear and rack-and-pinion steering might well outlast the boat and even yourself. I can envision scuba divers coming upon an old, sunken boat—a disintegrated hull, a skeleton, and all that's left intact are a few heavy, metal fittings, most notably the steering gears. Apply a Teflon grease every season and check the mounting bolts, and you've probably done all that's necessary to protect the system.

Once you know that the steering system of your boat has been constructed as strongly as possible, and that you have an adequate backup system, you've eliminated one of the major sources of worry in offshore cruising.

## FURTHER READING

The Edson catalog: go to www.edsonmarine.com and click on Sailboat Catalog.

*The Ocean Sailing Yacht.* Vols. 1 and 2. Donald Street. New York: Norton, 1973–1978.

# SEVEN

# SELF-STEERING SYSTEMS

Self-steering is not a requirement for good cruising. Many yachts have made their way around the world with the captain and crew steering every league of the way. Joshua Slocum balanced his sails to steer *Spray*, sometimes resorting to sheet-to-tiller arrangements. Robin Knox-Johnston sailed around the world alone in a ketch—with only the helm lashed.

In recent years, sheet-to-tiller steering has become almost forgotten, despite the efforts of people like John Letcher and Lee Woas, who spent years experimenting and writing about various arrangements. The necessary gear consists of a few small blocks, a few lengths of small-diameter line, and a length of surgical tubing. The only installation is screwing in a few pad eyes in the cockpit to attach the blocks, lines, and tubing. (For additional information on this method of self-steering, see the reading list at the end of the chapter.) In my experience, to be successful with sheet-to-tiller steering, you first need a boat that tracks well. Second, it works best on the wind, as do most marginal self-steering devices, and third, it takes a watchful eye and regular fussing. But then, what else is there to do?

The Age of the Microchip, has enormously simplified self-steering, to the point that electronic autopilots are by far the most popular choice of cruisers. A quality cockpit-mounted tiller pilot or wheel pilot for a small boat costs less than $1,000. Pilots with far superior below-deck drives run around $3,000. This is a small price to pay for hours of freedom at sea. Instead of steering and growing tired or bored, the crew can navigate, read books, cook meals, sleep, or work. Hey, so there *are* other things to do besides fuss with the self-steerer!

## AUTOPILOTS VERSUS WIND VANES

Electronic autopilots operate differently than mechanical wind vanes. They use electrical power from the battery, so it is necessary to have some means of keeping the battery charged. Running the engine is one method; using a solar panel, or wind or water generator are others (see Chapter 12).

Autopilots steer magnetic compass courses; whereas mechanical wind vanes steer courses relative to the wind direction. When the wind direction changes, an autopilot continues to steer the same course, even if the sails start slatting. Some companies do offer wind sensors so that the pilot steers a course relative to the wind rather than a compass course, but these haven't been widely accepted, maybe because wind directions are often shifty.

A wind vane continues to steer the same course relative to the wind even though the boat's heading has changed. In both cases, the watch is usually alerted by the new sounds or feel of the boat relative to the wind and water, and adjustments are made. Each has its advantage and disadvantage, and ideally I would own both.

It used to be that weekend sailors investing in self-steering frequently opted for the electronic autopilot, because it was less expensive; steered while motoring; and did not require adding a large, heavy, and possibly ungainly looking support bracket on the transom. In contrast, cruisers planning to stay away from home for months or years usually invested in the wind vane. There is security in not having to rely on electrical power to make the boat steer itself. A good self-steering wind vane system will steer the boat even in gale conditions, when the crew may be exhausted and survival depends on keeping the boat on course a few more hours. However, if the boat becomes flooded, batteries cease working, and corrosion can ruin the electronic circuits of the autopilot. On the other hand, a breaking wave may damage the wind vane. Even on the strongest units, the vane is usually lightweight (by necessity, to pick up wind shifts) and can be carried away by wind or water.

But in the 21st century, the majority of cruisers and other sailors are opting for electronic autopilots, eschewing installation of a big, clunky steering vane on the transom. Which is not to say that vanes are obsolete, only that they are losing favor.

In shorthanded, long-distance ocean races, far fewer boats are equipped with wind vanes; the skippers rely instead on electronic autopilots. The reasons are several. First, the boats are lighter and faster now, and wind vanes have a hard time maintaining control at surfing speeds that often are in the teens and may top 20 knots. This is especially true of multihulls. Even state-of-the-art autopilots are severely tested. Inadequate reaction time and insufficient power on the pilot's part are common causes of broaching, knockdowns, and pitchpoling. Nearly all long-distance ocean racers carry spare autopilots because the harder they work the quicker they fail. The cost-conscious cruiser is well-advised to hand steer in really rough conditions, slow down the boat so it balances well and takes the load off the pilot, or simply heave-to. Second, wind vanes represent unnecessary drag, and if you're in a race, you need all the help you can get.

## ABOVE-DECK AUTOPILOTS

The least expensive autopilots are designed for tillers. These portable units are mounted in the cockpit, often against the coaming, with the drive shaft coupled to a stud installed in the tiller. The location of the stud is important because it determines the quickness of rudder response. Tiller Master (no longer made, but still serviced—see www.electricmarine.com) recommended its unit be fixed to the tiller between 14 and 33 inches (36 cm and 84 cm) from the rudderstock or axis. For example, the stud should be mounted 18 inches (46 cm) from the rudderstock on Catalina 30s, and up to 33 inches (84 cm) on the Westsail 32, which has a large outboard rudder. Drive shaft extensions are available for installations in which the stud must be more than 33 inches from the rudderstock to compensate for the larger swing of the tiller.

To figure how powerful your autopilot must be to safely steer your boat, attach a fisherman's scale either to the tiller at different distances from the tiller head, or to a spoke of the wheel. Trim the boat for maximum weather helm on a windy day and read the number of pounds indicated on the scale. To obtain foot-pounds, multiply the number of pounds by the distance in feet from the tiller head to the point of scale attachment (for example, 35 lbs. × 2 ft. = 70 ft. lbs; or 15.9 kg × 0.61 m = 9.7 kgm or 94.9 Nm). To be on the safe side, double this number (70 × 2 = 140 ft. lbs., or 31.7 kg × 0.61 m = 19.3 kgm or 190 Nm), and compare it to the specifications listed for the autopilot you're interested in. If an autopilot can only apply, say, 100 foot-pounds (13.8 kgm) of force, it probably will have a tough time keeping your boat on course in heavy weather. Of course, it may work fine in better conditions, especially if the boat is well balanced.

And if all this seems a bit complicated, you can simply use the reference table provided by the pilot manufacturer, which usually says something like, "Model X for boats to 25 feet, Model Y for boats from 26 to 35 feet . . ." and so on. You see the same sort of simplistic buyer's guide offered for anchors. The problem is that such tables fail to take into account many characteristics of the boat, such as waterline length, beam, displacement, and in this case, the all important matters of how well the boat tracks and whether it has a lot of weather helm.

Raymarine's Autohelm ST4000 series of tiller-type autopilots (www.raymarine.com) separate the compass and electronic circuit board from the push rod. With the compass mounted below-decks, it and the attendant wiring are better protected. The less expensive ST2000 (Figure 7-1), with all components integral, is advertised as capable of applying tiller loads up to 170 pounds (79 kg), and, on a "typical 30-footer," power consumption averages about 200 milliamps—less than a single navigation light. Gerry Spiess steered his 10-foot *Yankee Girl* across the Pacific with one of these units without ever recharging his batteries. Not that you'll be able to do this on a more substantial boat, but you get the idea: the less the pilot works, the less current it draws from the batteries.

Installation is fairly simple (Figure 7-2). A gudgeon is provided with these units for mounting in the cockpit. The most preferred electrical hookup is a socket mounted out of the weather in the cockpit, perhaps in a seat locker, and wired to a circuit on the distribution panel. A spare circuit is always preferable, especially for a device that requires a lot of current. If you do have to double up with other equipment, avoid radios such as a VHF, which could develop static if the autopilot

FIGURE 7-1. The Autohelm ST2000 tiller pilot can steer a magnetic course or one relative to the wind when using the optional wind vane accessory. (*Practical Sailor* photo)

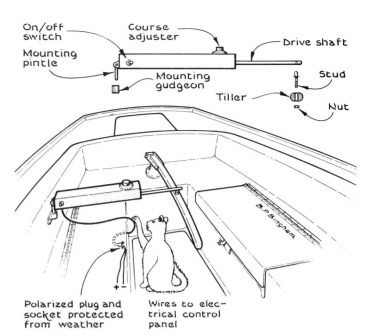

FIGURE 7-2. Installing a tiller-type autopilot is not difficult. The mounting brackets are screwed to the coaming or another part of the cockpit, and two wires are led via a connector to the positive and negative bus bars.

isn't sufficiently noise suppressed. You could wire it to terminals already used for another piece of equipment, such as the VHF or depth sounder. Because it's important to get as much juice as possible to the motor, splicing into undersized wiring is like asking your heart to play basketball while you breathe through a blanket. Most autopilots come with in-line, slow-blow fuses. If loads are excessive or polarity is reversed, the fuse will blow. All wire ends should be tinned with solder when making connections to prevent corrosion, and the ends leading to the circuit should have soldered crimp lug terminal eyes (see Figure 12-24).

Some tiller-mounted autopilots can be adapted to wheel steerers by means of a bracket bolted across the wheel (Figure 7-3). However, the throw of the ram (the distance the rod can be extended) is limited in range and operates in just one plane, so only minor corrections are possible. I don't recommend this setup.

And I'm lukewarm about the many wheel pilots currently on the market. Designed for cable-pedestal steerers, they typically employ a ribbed rubber belt connecting the drive motor (mounted on the cockpit floor or pedestal base) to a drum that bolts to the spokes of the wheel steerer. The belt may slip under heavy load; one solution is to clamp it to the sprocket with Vise-Grips. I figure that if it's slipping, it's not up to the task at hand, and so take over the steering manually. The Auto-

FIGURE 7-3. Tiller-type autopilots, such as this Tiller Master, can be adapted to wheel steerers by means of a bar or sprocket. (*Practical Sailor* photo)

helm ST4000 is geared directly to the sprocket, thus eliminating the belt and its proclivity for slipping, but also preventing any means of tightening the mechanism. It does get rid of the annoying clutch mechanism, which is a really low-tech device.

In my experience, these pilots are neither sufficiently fast nor powerful enough to handle a heavy cruising boat in even moderate conditions. Occasionally I've heard more positive tidings; one was from the delivery skipper of a PDQ 32, who said the wheel pilot worked well. I note, however, that this catamaran has almost neutral helm and tracks well.

A useful accessory to most autopilots is a remote dodger (controller; Figure 7-4). This handheld device, which is connected to the autopilot by a long, flexible insulated wire (soon to go wireless!), enables you to change course to avoid danger by just moving the toggle in your hand. When the toggle is released, the boat returns to its original course.

Most above-deck pilots—tiller and wheel types—are, in my opinion, too light for continuous use in a wide range of conditions, except for small boats where the loads are minimal. They simply don't have the power, reaction time, and "intelligence" required to keep a boat from broaching in difficult conditions. On the Vanguard, I used an Autohelm 3000 wheel pilot only in moderate conditions; when the boat started rounding up despite the pilot's best efforts to counter, and when I couldn't trim the sails any better, I disengaged it and steered by hand. On *Viva*, our Tartan 44 (13.4 m), we had a Benmar rotary drive (because there wasn't enough room around the steering quadrant to mount a hydraulic or linear drive) directed by a Robertson

**FIGURE 7-4.** A remote controller possesses a variety of useful features in addition to remote dodging, including a man-overboard function and waypoint programming. (Raymarine)

**FIGURE 7-5.** The Autohelm ST4000 wheel pilot is mounted on the steering pedestal. The fluxgate compass and "brain" of the pilot are mounted separately. It has a geared drive system, whereas the ST3000 uses a belt drive, which can slip in heavy conditions. (Raymarine)

control. This was much more satisfactory than the wheel pilot.

Wheel pilots are mass produced and sold at low prices through mail-order discount catalogs, so if you do plan to use one of the popular brands such as Raymarine and Robertson (Figure 7-5), it wouldn't hurt to take a spare. But at any price you are better off investing in a heavy-duty, below-deck pilot.

## BELOW-DECK AUTOPILOTS

For larger boats, which require greater power to turn the helm, more sophisticated systems are needed. Raymarine, Benmar (www.benmarmarine .com), and B&G (www.bandgusa.com) are major manufacturers of electronic autopilots adaptable to most steering systems (see Chapter 6 for autopilot installations on various types of steering).

Historically, electronic autopilots generally can be divided into three types: hunting, non-hunting proportional deadband, and non-hunting proportional rate. The hunting-type autopilot was developed in the 1930s and, in comparison with the proportional rate autopilots sold today, is relatively simple. A compass detected the amount the rudder was to port or starboard of the desired heading and, via a control unit, activated a motor drive connected to the rudderstock to make corrections. (These three components are typical of all autopilots.) The system continually searched the correct heading, causing a zigzag course. Power consumption and wornout components were shortcomings of the hunting-type of autopilots.

A decade later, the proportional deadband autopilot was developed to eliminate excessive hunting. In effect, a "deadband" was introduced into the system where the helm was not corrected. When the error exceeded the limits of the deadband, the helm was corrected proportional to the heading error.

Today, many of the more sophisticated autopilots have done away with the deadband, though they still operate on the proportional rate concept. The electronic control unit determines both the rate and amount of correction to be applied. To prevent relays from burning out (electromechanical switches that start the drive motor rotating clockwise or counterclockwise), these autopilots use transistors, which can be enclosed in a separate housing or inside the drive motor enclosure. This type of relay is of particular value to the hydraulic steering system because of this system's inherent slip (slop between the helm and the rudder), which can cause excessive corrections.

A major advantage of below-deck pilots is the ability to mount them directly to the rudderstock or in-line with cable or hydraulic steering systems. Also, they are shielded from the weather.

The basic components are a compass, a control unit, and a drive unit. The compass may be magnetic or fluxgate, which senses the Earth's magnetic field by electrically excited wire coils, or a gyro, which is very expensive but the only reliable type in the extreme northern and southern latitudes where magnetic anomalies render the others next to useless. That said, most consumer-grade pilots today use a fluxgate.

The control unit is a microprocessor that provides feedback and modifications to the programmed deadband and gain, which is the speed of correction. Many modern control units are programmed to "learn" the behavior of the boat in a given sea state, such as the cycle of falling off the wind and heading back up, and making corrections in concert with this natural pattern.

The drive unit is the mechanism that actually operates on the rudderstock. Selecting a drive unit is as important as selecting the control unit. There are three major types: linear, rotary (Figure 7-6), and hydraulic. The first and last connect directly to the rudderstock, while the rotary is inserted into the existing steering system. In a linear unit, the power of a high-speed, low-torque electric motor is reduced by a ball screw actuator to a slow-speed, high-torque output; a pushrod connects to a quadrant or tiller arm keyed to the rudderstock. A rotary unit uses a small electric motor to obtain a low-speed, high-torque output by means of chains, sprockets, sheaves, and idlers. A hydraulic unit incorporates an electric motor and pump that power a hydraulic linear ram. Others include constant-running power packs and hydraulic/linear combinations.

The linear drive (Figure 7-7) is more efficient than the rotary and has less slop than the hydraulic, but it is limited by the length of throw of its pushrod. The rotary drive adapts well to cable steering; it may be placed in line with the existing cable, set up to directly turn the steering shaft, or connected to a second quadrant. It can turn indefinitely in either direction and also works with rack-and-pinion and worm-gear steerers. If the

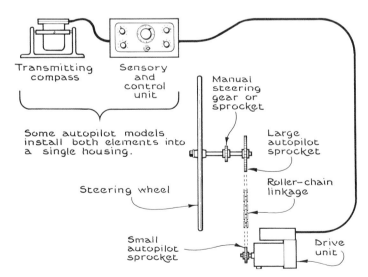

**FIGURE 7-6.** While linear and hydraulic drives are preferable because they operate directly on the rudderstock, rotary drives (such as this one by Benmar, and installed on our Tartan 44) offer more flexible installation.

local dealer/technician for assistance. Based on your cockpit configuration, type of steering, and below-deck space, he will be able to give you valuable guidance in selecting the type of drive unit best suited to your boat.

Both the tiller type and more sophisticated below-deck autopilots can sometimes be fitted with accessory wind vanes so that the boat is electronically kept to a course relative to the wind instead of steering a strict compass course. A number of single-handed race competitors have tried to use the wind vane interface, but none to my knowledge has reported much satisfaction with it. Possibly the vane is too small and skittish; a larger blade dampened by a counterweight might be less influenced by the whimsy of the wind.

Here's a short take on the three types of drives:

- Linear drives turn the boat faster than rotary drives and draw less power than hydraulic drives; therefore, they are often the preferred choice.

- Hydraulic drives are more powerful and faster than linear drives but draw more power. When Dodge Morgan sailed non-stop around the world in *American Dream*, he used a linear pilot for most of the trip but resorted to the hydraulic drive when conditions got nasty—he didn't have enough electric power to run the hydraulic drive all the time.

- Rotary drives are almost obsolete, but sometimes, as in the case of our *Viva*, they solve difficult installation problems.

**FIGURE 7-7.** *Airco Distributor*, a 50-foot (15.2 m) Rodger Martin design in which Mike Plant won his class in the second BOC Challenge, is equipped with several autopilots and drives, including a Robertson linear drive (attached), and behind it an Autohelm linear drive and Robertson hydraulic drive, all mounted and ready to be engaged should the previous one fail.

boat already has hydraulic steering, it makes sense to consider a hydraulic or hydraulic/linear drive, which is very powerful.

Some models may be interfaced with an existing compass on board. Most sales brochures tout the features of the control unit; today microprocessing technology can incorporate remote dodging, sea state or sensitivity adjustment, rudder angle indicator, GPS interface via NMEA ports (an industry standard protocol enabling different instruments to share data), course correction based on a memory of steering characteristics under sail and power, off-course alarm, auto tacking, and wind vane interface. Some of these features are programmable.

Because you can spend $6,000 and more on such an autopilot, consult the manufacturer or a

## WIND VANES

Mechanical wind vanes do not rely on electrical power. This is a distinct advantage for world cruisers, particularly because in midocean it is not so important to always steer a compass course. In fact, steering a course relative to the wind means fewer trips on deck to trim sails. If you've wandered a few miles south of your planned route, so what? You're still hundreds of miles from your destination.

There are several basic types of wind vanes (Figure 7-8):

**A.** Vane to rudder (direct to tiller or wheel)

**B.** Vane to trim tab on rudder

**C.** Vane to auxiliary rudder

**D.** Vane to trim tab on auxiliary rudder

**E.** Vane to servo-pendulum to rudder

**F.** Vane to servo-pendulum to auxiliary rudder

It is difficult to say that one system is far better than another because different boats vary considerably in size, underwater configuration of keel and rudder, and rig type. Small boats less than 25 feet (7.6 m) for example, may successfully use type A, but owners of large boats may find that it often lacks the necessary power.

In many ways, the trim tab attached to the main rudder (B) is excellent—there is no cumbersome and complicated gear mounted on the transom, and there is less water resistance than with the auxiliary rudder type. The problem for owners of old boats is that the trim tab is most easily fitted if it has been designed for the boat from the beginning—i.e., a custom boat. Outboard rudders can accept a trim tab with little difficulty, but inboard rudders present problems. A rudder with a straightline trailing edge can be fitted with a trim

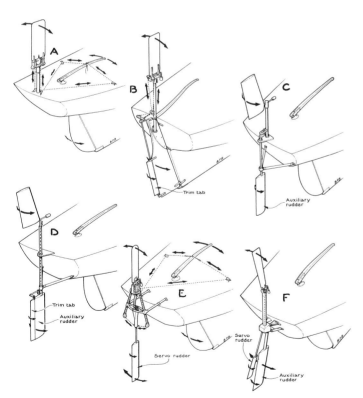

**FIGURE 7-8.** Types of wind vanes: vane to rudder (A), vane to trim tab on rudder (B), vane to auxiliary rudder (C), vane to trim tab on auxiliary rudder (D), vane to servo-pendulum to rudder (E), and vane to servo-pendulum to auxiliary rudder (F).

tab more easily than one with a round shape. Assuming the trim tab can be fitted, the trim tab shaft must be run up through the hull in a tube glassed inside the hull to the deck where it must link with the wind vane. The weight of the rudder and how easily it turns affects the sensitivity of this system; most boats will probably have better luck with a different system.

Vanes with auxiliary rudders (C, D, F) can be used as backup steering systems should the main rudder fail (Chapter 6). Servo-pendulum vanes (E, F) are typically the most powerful, though the mechanisms are more complicated, and they cannot be used for emergency steering. Don't confuse the servo-blade with the auxiliary rudder. Because vanes are somewhat delicate and are perched in a vulnerable position over the transom, it is helpful if the servo-blade or rudder is easily shipped. Preferably it has a simple kickup feature that clears the water when there are fishing nets, lobster pots, or floating debris; also, when hand steering, you don't need an extra appendage fighting you all the time. That, I think, is a problem with the auxiliary rudder types, which must be locked perfectly in line for hand steering; and because of the far aft location of the rudder, the turning radius of the boat is greatly increased.

When shopping for an autopilot or wind vane, it is wise to consult with the various manufacturers, other people with similar size and shape boats (your sister ships would be best), and those who have sailed with the vane you're considering. Because sizing is a critical factor, most vane gear manufacturers now sell directly to customers. Making a purchase is a long-distance project. To get the best advice and service from the vendor, you should send photographs of your boat's stern, shot from the side, stern, and quarter. They also will want dimensions from the top and bottom of the transom to the water, the angle of the transom, height of any stern rail above deck, the displacement and length of the boat, type of keel and sailing rig, and main rudder steering system. Custom metalwork may be required.

Wheel steerers with few lock-to-lock turns can be fitted with large drums for those types of vanes connecting to the helm (Figure 7-9). Popular self-steering vanes include the Aries (Figure 7-10; www.ariesvane.com), Monitor (www.selfsteer.com), Hydrovane (Figure 7-11; www.hydrovane.com), Sailomat (Figure 7-12; www.sailomat.com), the Australian-made Fleming

**FIGURE 7-9.** The Atoms wind vane can be used with wheel steerers by means of a large pulley bolted to the wheel. It will work with wheels having three or less full turns from hard-to-port to hard-to-starboard.

(www.flemingselfsteering.com), and the Canadian Voyager (www.voyagerwindvanes.com).

## Installation

The simplest type of wind vane to install is the vane to rudder (A), which is mounted on the

**FIGURE 7-10.** The Aries wind vane is built in England and is one of the most popular. It is of the servo-pendulum variety with a horizontally pivoted vane. The boat is *Crédit Agricole*, winner of the first BOC Challenge. (Herb McCormick photo)

**FIGURE 7-11.** The Hydrovane uses an auxiliary rudder and a horizontally pivoted vane. (Geraldine La Chance photo)

afterdeck and turns the boat's tiller or wheel by means of lines led through blocks in the cockpit. As with other types, some special brackets may be necessary to securely mount the gear on the deck, which will vary, of course, according to the particular configuration of each boat. The cockpit blocks are straightforward and may be attached to pad eyes through-bolted to the cockpit coaming.

**FIGURE 7-12.** The Sailomat is a Swedish self-steering unit that is unique in that it employs both a servo-pendulum blade and auxiliary rudder. Dame Naomi James used the Sailomat during her single-handed circumnavigation.

If you're installing a trim tab on your boat's main rudder (B), be sure to through-bolt the trim tab gudgeons and pintles or gudgeon hinges, especially if the fiberglass skin of the rudder is too thin to securely receive self-tapping screws.

With auxiliary rudders (C, D, F), the forces are much greater than with the aforementioned types. The auxiliary rudderstock is mounted on the hull by means of a bracket that must be through-bolted to the transom (Figure 7-13), preferably with backing plates (plywood, stainless steel, or aluminum) between each washer/nut and the hull. There is often some sort of deck support as well, and these too should be through-bolted. Bedding compound should be used to seal each bolt hole from moisture. Installation is somewhat simplified since no lines need to be led to the helm in the cockpit.

Servo-pendulum wind vanes (E, F) will mount in essentially the same manner as those with auxiliary rudders, as the servo-blade requires similar support on the transom.

**FIGURE 7-13.** Schematics of the Monitor wind vane. (Scanmar International)

While each manufacturer's installation instructions will vary, they will usually specify that the vane be located as close to the centerline as possible, though distances as much as 6 inches (152 mm) to one side or the other may be tolerable.

Similarly, the vane and auxiliary rudderstock (if there is one) should be as near vertical in the fore-and-aft axis as possible. If the boat is out of the water and sitting level in its cradle, a plumb can be used to determine the proper rudderstock position. If it is not level, the boot stripe can be extended aft past the transom with a string, and measuring 90° from it, vertical can be established. Slight errors are not likely to be critical.

The vane shaft and rudderstock also should be vertical in the athwartship axis. This is easily determined using measurements from either side of the transom to the rudderstock. When the distance is equal on either side, measured at two separate places on the rudderstock—one higher than the other—the rudderstock is vertical.

## Wind Vane Adjustments

While wind vanes differ in design and operation, they have several features in common—a clutch to engage and disengage the vane from the steering and a mechanism for adjustment so that the desired course is achieved. To fine-tune the course heading, some units require adjusting the pilot sheets to the helm (Monitor; Figure 7-14), changing the horizontal axis of the vane (Hydrovane), or turning some sort of wheel that changes the relationship of the vane and rudder (Sailomat).

## Self-Steering Expectations

Years ago, before buying a CYS vane for my Pearson Triton, the now-defunct manufacturer urged me to write down a list of conceptions I had about vanes—how I thought a vane would change my sailing habits. Here's the list I gave him:

- Boat will steer the same with vane disengaged
- Vane will weigh down the stern of the boat
- Drag will reduce speed
- Vane will get in the way when not in use
- Will take a lot of experience to learn how to use
- Must be disengaged when changing headsails

- Will not work when motoring
- Will have to lash helm
- Will have marginal performance down-wind
- Will make even short passages easier

After a few seasons' use, here's what I found about the accuracy of my list. The boat did not turn as easily with the vane disengaged. This was because the vane rudder was farther aft than the boat's rudder, and so a wider turning arc resulted. With the more popular servo-pendulum steerers, the servo blade is easily retracted, removing any effect on the helm.

The vane did not weigh the stern down at all. The rudder had positive buoyancy, and the total weight of the entire unit in the water was less than 10 pounds. Boat speed did not seem to be affected. In fact, you could make the case that the fine trimming of sails required for optimal wind

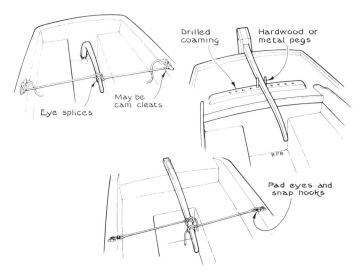

**FIGURE 7-15.** There are dozens of ways to lash the helm, from a single length of line to commercial devices with jam cleats. When used in conjunction with self-steering, a type that permits infinite adjustment (as opposed to, say, thole pins) is more satisfactory as it's often preferable to adjust the helm than the wind vane. For wheel steerers in light conditions, the brake may be sufficient to lock the steering in place; in rougher conditions, lash a line securely to one of the spokes and tie it off somewhere in the cockpit.

vane performance actually resulted in improved speeds.

Though it looked complicated, it did not take long to learn to use it. For changing headsails, vanes can either be disengaged, and the helm given over to a crew or autopilot, or temporarily adjusted to compensate for the change in location of the sail plan's center of effort.

I never found the vane really suitable for motoring and used my autopilot instead.

While the CYS and other auxiliary rudder/trim tab vangs work best when the helm is lashed (Figure 7-15), other types work through the tiller or wheel by a rope led to the helm. Both have the potential for creating obstacles to moving freely in the cockpit.

Our first cruise with the CYS self-steering vane was from Newport to Martha's Vineyard (Figure 7-16). We logged about 100 miles over five days, and despite the fact that much of the sailing was between islands, all told we steered the boat by hand for only about 30 minutes. This left time to play games with the kids in the cockpit, go below for a change of clothes, or raid the icebox.

Near shore, wind directions do change frequently, so attention to course is necessary. But

**FIGURE 7-14.** The servo-pendulum Monitor vane is unique in its all stainless steel construction. It has emerged as one of the most popular vanes in recent years. (*Practical Sailor* photo)

**FIGURE 7-16.** During a week's cruise to Martha's Vineyard, our new vane steered all but about the 30 minutes needed for dropping and hoisting the anchor.

once we got the hang of the adjustment mechanism, it was a cinch to make course corrections. We found ourselves arriving in port far more rested than on earlier cruises when one person was always shackled to the helm. None of the joy of sailing was lost either; in fact, tweaking lines and playing with the vane satisfied the tinkerer in me.

## Buying a Wind Vane

Mechanical wind vanes are not inexpensive, and though more costly than tiller-type autopilots, they may be about the same price as some more sophisticated below-deck autopilots. Therefore, you should carefully evaluate the models available and their suitability to your particular boat.

For moderate- to heavy-displacement boats, or those with considerable weather helm, it is necessary to fit a powerful vane. Servo-pendulum

types are quite powerful and have been highly favored by many long-distance sailors. The servo-blade amplifies the power of the gearing to the sheets connected to the helm. The servo-type has a natural yaw-dampening tendency, which is beneficial. Horizontal-axis vanes are more sensitive and extract more power from the wind than vertical-axis vanes, but cannot weathercock to set the course. Some people may find the network of control lines led to the helm a nuisance. With a little thought, the system should work on center-cockpit designs.

Auxiliary rudder wind vanes operate independently of the boat's steering system and can be used as an emergency backup steering system. Without a trim tab, however, the auxiliary vane rudder may experience difficulty generating the necessary power to turn the boat's larger main rudder.

With a trim tab or servo-type, a small tiller pilot may be connected to it for improved performance downwind. A small autopilot can drive a big boat if it derives its true power from the servo-oar or trim tab.

The unit should be intelligently engineered to withstand forces from any direction—and the sea *can* put a big load on steering gear! Most loads are in the horizontal axis, so sheer strength is more important than compressive strength. Materials should be strong and corrosion resistant. The design, while seemingly complicated on first impression, should be understandable and repairable by the crew at sea. The parts must be strong enough to withstand the loads imposed, yet not so heavy as to place unnecessary weight on the transom. Aluminum and stainless steel are used most often, but beware of corrosion where the two meet. Breaking down the unit annually to check the parts is a good idea. Reset stainless fasteners with something like Loctite or Duralac. The linkage must operate smoothly and freely to ensure maximum sensitivity. Especially when sailing downwind in light air, sensitivity is critical. Bearings are often made of strong plastics such as Delrin and Torlon—check for durability and ease of maintenance and replacement.

Be wary of units with dissimilar metals in direct contact—some corrosion will surely develop.

Other points to consider:

- A removable vane and/or auxiliary rudder is preferable to prevent damage at the dock from other boats. And some models inhibit maneuverability, something you don't want when sailing in harbors.

■ Underwater components should be strong and preferably connected to the bracket with shear pins or protected by some other means.

■ Because different sea states have differing effects on steering, it is desirable to have some method of damping the rate and amount of correction (a crude version of proportional rate correction in autopilots).

■ The vane should disengage quickly so you can manually steer to avoid floating objects and collisions.

## FURTHER READING

*Electrical and Electronic Equipment for Yachts.* John French. New York: Dodd, Mead, 1974.

*Self-Steering for Sailboats.* Gerard Dijkstra. Boston: Sail Books, 1979.

*Self-Steering for Sailing Craft.* John S. Letcher. Camden, Maine: International Marine, 1974.

*Self-Steering Without a Windvane: A Comprehensive Manual of Natural and Sheet-to-Tiller Steering Systems for Sailboats.* Lee Woas. Newport, Rhode Island: Seven Seas Press, 1982.

*Wind-Vane Self-Steering: How to Plan and Make Your Own.* Bill Belcher. Camden, Maine: International Marine, 1982.

*Windvane Self-Steering Handbook.* Bill Morris. Camden, Maine: International Marine, 2004.

# EIGHT

# REPOWERING

The power plant is probably the most blessed and cursed piece of equipment on a small sailboat. Certainly it is one of the most expensive. It is a little strange that there are mechanically oriented persons who love analyzing how best to jury-rig the replacement of a broken gooseneck, but who can't tune an engine to save their lives. There are obvious advantages to being able to perform basic maintenance functions—lower cost, freedom from the incompetencies of the local yard, and safety, if and when your skills are called upon in a critical situation.

Engines are indeed wonderful when they work properly, and absolutely dreadful when they don't. My thinking is that if I'm going to rely on an engine, I'd better be able to *rely* on it. This requires performing routine maintenance and making basic repairs. And it means owning the simplest engine possible. A diesel is the answer. Before describing a typical conversion from gas to diesel, or simply replacing an old wornout diesel with a new one, let's consider the alternatives.

## GASOLINE ENGINES

Until the early 1980s, almost all midsize yachts were fitted with gasoline engines. U.S. Coast Guard regulations required venting the bilge, bilge blowers, spark arrestors, and so forth. The ubiquitous Atomic 4 was a good engine, and tuning it was no more difficult than changing the plugs, points, and condenser, and setting the timing of the family car. A few tools and an hour with a knowledgeable friend were all that was really needed to learn how.

Tales of yachts blowing up have a tendency to scare people into choosing diesel power rather than helping them make a rational choice. There are advantages to gas engines. They are less expensive; they accelerate faster; and it is sometimes easier to find a mechanic who will work on them.

## EMERGENCE OF THE SMALL DIESEL

Today, almost all boatbuilders have switched to diesel. The reasons are twofold: new Coast Guard regulations added to the list of required safety gear and thus to the cost of the gas-powered boat; and the availability of smaller, lightweight, competitively priced diesels suitable for small sailboats.

The advantages of small diesels are many. Diesel fuel will not ignite, even if a match is touched to it. Because diesels do not have spark plugs and points and distributors—compression, not electricity is used to combust the fuel—batteries are not required except for electric starting. Some small diesels may be started by hand. The confidence this gives is considerable. An added bonus is diesels burn fuel at a slower rate than gas engines, so the equivalent tank of fuel will give extra hours of motoring. A curious fact about diesels is they burn 12,000 times more air than fuel—a much higher ratio than gasoline engines. In a poorly ventilated compartment, they can literally asphyxiate themselves, something to consider when switching power plants.

For many years, the UK-built Perkins 4-108 was the standard of the industry; at 50 horsepower, it was also one of the smallest. Today, Perkins is owned by Caterpillar (www.caterpillar.com), and has assigned management of its marine engines to Sabre. These days it's not much of a player in the small marine diesel market. Westerbeke (www.westerbeke.com) made a similar engine to the 4-108, but the company has lost market share in propulsion engines, faring better with auxiliary generators, or gensets as they're often called. The early Yanmars (www.yanmarmarine.com) were noisy and not much appreciated; however, they have long since been reengineered, and because of the company's low pricing and aggressive marketing, Yanmars are now the most com-

**FIGURE 8-1.** Universal, manufacturer of the Atomic 4 gasoline engine, is now owned by Westerbeke, which offers the 25 hp M-25XPB as a replacement. It is freshwater cooled and weighs 295 pounds (134 kg). While not a drop-in replacement, it has similar measurements to simplify shaft alignment and engine bed modifications. (Westerbeke)

**FIGURE 8-2.** I spotted the fellow pictured here while standing on the pier at Opua in New Zealand's Bay of Islands. The wind had died, and he was determined to make the pier before dark. A sculling oar is an alternative to these sweeps.

mon. I've owned several and found them reliable and easily serviced. Universal, which built the Atomic 4 was bought by Westerbeke, and switched to diesel (Figure 8-1). Of its B-series, Westerbeke says "The M-25XPB, M3-20B, and M-35B offer many similar dimensional characteristics to the Atomic 4, making for a much easier installation." It goes on to caution that they're not direct drop-in replacements for the Atomic 4. Expect to make some modifications to your old engine beds. Other diesel brands you may see include Bukh (www.bukh.co.uk), Lugger (www.lugger.com), Isuzu (www.isuzuengines.com), Farymann (www.farymann.com), Volvo Penta (www.volvopenta.com), Nannidiesel (www.nannidiesel.com), and Vetus (www.vetus.com).

The decision to repower with diesel is certainly a significant one—it will cost time and money—but if you have great plans for your boat, you will be glad that you did so.

## GOING ENGINELESS

Engineless boats are not so uncommon as you might think (Figure 8-2). Garry Hoyt built the first Freedom 40 without an engine, and amazed observers in the Caribbean by tacking the cat ketch in and out of moorings under sail—alone—to prove the worthiness of his boat and rig (Figure 8-3).

Lin and Larry Pardey continue to sail the world's oceans—now in their second boat, the 30-foot (9.1 m) *Taleisin*—without an engine. They

use sweeps from the cockpit or scull with a stern oar when there is no wind and when they have to maneuver in tight quarters.

Danny Greene, a former associate editor of *Cruising World*, lived aboard his 26-foot (7.9 m) cutter *Frolic* for many years, making passages to the Caribbean and back to Newport each year without an engine. By eliminating the inboard engine, the amount of additional storage space under the cockpit was considerable, enhanced by cutting out the footwell to avoid being swamped by breaking seas (see Chapter 9). The after end of the boat was like an extra room. On a small boat, there is never enough storage space, especially for Danny, who carried numerous tools, a portable Honda generator, jerricans of water, etc.

On the downside, Danny was often forced to sail nonstop from Newport to some place like St. Martin, because most of the seaports along the East Coast have narrow channels, which he felt were too risky to try entering without auxiliary power. Danny's present boat, a 34-foot (10.4 m)

**FIGURE 8-3.** The original Freedom 40 had no engine but instead a pair of sweeps. Garry Hoyt, who developed the boat, decried the noise and wasted space caused by engines. But he deferred to public opinion, selling most customers a 50 hp diesel to go along with their new boat. (Garry Hoyt photo)

steel ketch, has a 15 hp four-stroke outboard for harbor maneuvering; he chose it because while he wanted the ability to maneuver in tight quarters, he still didn't want the expense, headache, and loss of space associated with an inboard auxiliary. Obviously, his tastes run a bit eccentric, but it's hard to argue with his utilitarian philosophy. The Pardeys fitted an outboard to *Seraffyn* (their first boat) when they transited the Panama Canal, where regulations require that vessels be able to sustain 5 knots.

Another alternative is to equip the boat's tender with an outboard, and, by lashing it alongside, maneuver the boat through channels and crowded moorings. Using a yawl boat in this manner was a common practice among old sailing ships, and occasionally is still used by the windjammer charter fleet.

## REPOWERING

Boat engines don't seem to last as long as those in automobiles, perhaps because the loads are heavier (water is denser than air). As with any internal combustion engine, one of the best things you can do to promote longevity is to regularly change the lubricating oil. So it is not uncommon to find a 25-year-old boat that has been repowered at least once, and sometimes twice. At the least, its engine will have required a rebuild.

I've repowered two boats—a 28-foot (8.5 m) Pearson Triton and a 32-foot (9.8 m) Pearson Vanguard. The first had an Atomic 4 gas engine, the same 30 hp fire-breather that had been fitted to thousands of other sailboats during the 1960s and '70s. It was a trusty piece of machinery. But the day came when the end of its useful life was in sight. One of the new, lightweight, economical diesels was the logical choice for repowering both boats.

European, Japanese, and American engine manufacturers offer complete ranges of diesels, from 5 hp one-lungers to powerful three-, four-, and six-cylinder power plants for large yachts. For the Triton, I installed a 12 hp BMW, which unfortunately is no longer available in the United States, the company having conceded the marine market to Yanmar. Years later I repowered a Pearson Vanguard with a Yanmar 3GM30F; the routine is the same for both boats and engines.

Tools required for installation are surprisingly few, and only the drill, sander, and saber saw are power. Screwdrivers, hammer, crowbar, hacksaw, and others are of the hardware store variety. Most foreign-made engines come with a small set of metric wrenches, but so few are necessary that they wouldn't be expensive to purchase. You'll want a good set for future maintenance, plus a socket set.

Completing the project, from the moment the first old wire is ripped out to the satisfying moment when the new engine turns over for the first time, will probably take a first-timer something on the order of 100 man-hours of labor, plus 10% over and above the cost of the engine and associated parts in miscellaneous expenses such as hoses, screws, paint, and control cables. You'll bruise a few knuckles, but at least have the satisfaction of knowing just how everything fits together. Not to mention saving an enormous amount in labor— $80 average yard labor rate × 100 hours (probably less for experienced mechanics who can do the job faster) = $8,000.

### Pulling the Old Engine

The first step in converting from gas to diesel power is to get rid of the old engine. Unhook each wire that leads to the engine. On a gas engine, you'll have wires to the solenoid, alternator, coil, and so forth that are not needed for diesels and can simply be removed. Retain the battery leads—positive and negative. On most new diesels, a wiring harness plugs into the back of the engine on one end and the back of the ignition panel on the other. This is simplicity itself, and one look at the harness will dispel any fears of having to rig a maze of new wires to make the engine run.

The engine compartment on most smaller boats is cramped. In order to lift the old engine from its bed, you may have to remove the alternator. In the Triton, I also had to yank the Atomic 4's voltage regulator on the adjacent bulkhead. You'll also need to remove all hoses, including the freshwater line to the exhaust, the return line to the thermostat, and the hose to the water pump. The transmission linkage, which on the Triton was an archaic contraption with a formidable shift lever inserted through a deck plate on the cockpit floor, also has to come out. If you have pedestal wheel steering, the new engine controls—throttle and transmission shift—will run up through the pedestal to levers on either side of the compass.

The Triton had an old copper, water-jacketed exhaust pipe that needed to be disconnected from the exhaust manifold at the back of the engine. Though it was one of the best systems available, such a system is seldom seen today. Flexible exhaust hose is the choice. To get it out, I had to use a cold chisel to break it into several pieces. The Vanguard already had a conventional exhaust, from when the Westerbeke had replaced the original Atomic 4, but it was old and greasy, and so we yanked it, too. Water lift mufflers are not very expensive.

Remove the throttle and choke (if gas) cables from the engine as well as the gas line and water temperature and oil pressure gauge lines. Remove the gas line from the tank end first in case there is a gravity feed to the engine; you don't want to fill up the bilge with fuel! Removing existing instruments may leave unsightly holes in the cockpit footwell or wherever else they are mounted. Hopefully, the new instrument panel will cover them, but if not, you may have to cover them in some other clever way.

The last item to be disconnected before the engine can be pulled is the propeller shaft coupling. Because this is often a wet environment (water leaking through the packing gland, etc.), you can expect corrosion of the coupling bolts. As with any seized fastener, resist applying total brute force to your wrench. Instead, spray WD-40 or

another penetrating fluid around the head of each bolt and allow it to go to work. Then put the wrench on each bolt head and tap with a hammer. Keep repeating until the bolt loosens. It may be necessary to apply heat from a small butane blowtorch.

Lifting the engine from the cabin can be done in several ways, depending on the equipment available. If your yard has a crane, the operation is greatly simplified. If you're doing this in your backyard, a chain fall may work. With the Triton, I positioned a 6-inch by 6-inch (152 mm by 152 mm) piece of oak used for making cradles horizontally over the companionway hatch and led a chain fall from the crossbar to the lifting eye on top of the engine (Figure 8-4). I placed old blankets along the sill of the bridge to prevent the chain from chewing up the teak. The area looked as though it were dressed for surgery. And indeed it was. The transplant was about to begin!

Most engines have cast or welded lifting eyes to which the chain fall or other tackle can be secured. With the Triton, we hoisted the engine as high as possible and then swung it aft onto the bridge deck. We then transferred the chain to the yard's front-end loader, which lifted it off the boat. With the Vanguard, the repowering job was done in the water at Oldport Marine's dock. The tackle and boom on their mooring barge was used to hoist the leaky Westerbeke out of the cabin (Figure 8-5).

**FIGURE 8-4.** To lift the old engine out of the boat, we placed a stout piece of oak over the companionway hatch and used a chain fall to lift the 310 pounds of steel and iron high enough to swing into the cockpit. The Atomic 4, like most engines, has a lifting eye to connect the chain.

FIGURE 8-5. To remove the Westerbeke diesel from the Pearson Vanguard, Oldport Marine in Newport, Rhode Island, used the boom and tackle on their mooring barge.

No matter the age or problems with the old engine, you can probably find a buyer for it. First ask the local marine mechanic if he's interested; often these guys can rebuild the engine and turn a nice profit—or at the least, scavenge it for parts.

With the old engine removed, you'll now be staring at years' worth of grease, oil, gunk, and other bilge atrocities ground into the hull in and around the engine compartment. The next task is to clean it up. A good-quality bilge soap with the ability to emulsify oil will greatly help. My friend Bill Seifert, who runs a yacht management company, recommends following a scrub with degreaser with a pressure wash.

With the engine compartment now empty, it is an excellent time to perform other work in this area. If, for example, the raw-water intake for engine cooling has a gate valve or flangeless ball valve, it'll be much easier to replace it now than after the new engine is in place (see Chapter 4).

### Installing the Bed

BMW offered a molded fiberglass engine bed that can be cut to fit almost any hull. This somewhat simplified the job, but in most cases you'll more than likely have to either modify the existing beds or stringers, or remove them and glass in new stout oak beds. This is what I did in the Vanguard.

Once the hull is thoroughly cleaned, lightly grind the hull area to which you'll bond the new

beds (Figure 8-6). Determine the dimension and location of the hardwood stringers by studying the engine schematic provided by the manufacturer and your measurements of the engine area (Figures 8-7 and 8-8). These surfaces are seldom flat or perfectly horizontal, so careful planning is required (see below). Your margin of error in the vertical axis is limited by the range of adjustment in the motor mounts. If, say, their range of travel is 3 inches (76 mm), try to place the stringers so that the engine will be aligned with the propeller shaft with the mounts in the middle; this way, you'll have 1½ inches (38 mm) of adjustment up and down to get alignment just right.

Use mat and a finishing layer of cloth to bond the stringers directly to the hull. Four layers of mat should be sufficient, with generous overlap onto the hull. Don't forget to make fillets where the wood meets the hull (see Chapter 2 for more guidance). Use epoxy resin. On top of the Vanguard's stringers, two thick steel plates (24 inches

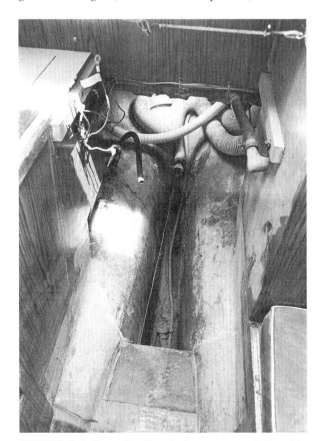

FIGURE 8-6. Once the Atomic 4 was removed, the old fiberglass engine beds were cut off with a saber saw and then ground flush with the hull using a belt sander. The alignment wire used to position the new bed is visible exiting from the stuffing box.

**FIGURE 8-7.** Oldport Marine does a lot of repowering jobs and to speed up the process has a jig for each model. Here the jig for the 3GM30F is positioned over the old beds to help determine where the new beds must be installed.

by 4 inches by ½ inch/635 mm by 102 mm by 12 mm) were drilled to accept the Yanmar's motor mounts. If you can't through-bolt the steel plates to the beds, a couple of long lag bolts run deep into the wood will have to suffice (Figures 8-9 and 8-10).

On the Triton, the Atomic 4 engine beds consisted of two vertical thick pieces of fiberglass glassed to the hull; a flange on top accepted the engine mounting bolts. Most of the two beds were easily cut away with a saber saw, and what was

left was hammered and pried off with a crowbar. This was perhaps the most physically demanding job of the entire project, but as one helper kept saying, "It's not a matter of *if* it will come, just when."

"When" turned out to be later than expected, but after a few hours the last globs of resin were ground off with a belt sander. The belt sander, equipped with aluminum oxide paper, was also the best tool to thoroughly clean up the area on the hull where the new bed would be glassed in. (A good mask and goggles are required safety gear.)

As noted above, the most important part of any power plant conversion is making the new bed line up with the propeller shaft. Heavy rubber motor mounts adjust vertically about 3 or 4 inches (76 mm or 102 mm). The mounts may allow some engine adjustment athwartships, but not much. Therefore, it's critical that the new engine bed be installed within the limits of these adjustments. Fortunately, I was shown a simple method of accomplishing this seemingly impossible task. If you don't have a jig as we did for the Vanguard's new Yanmar diesel, here's how it works:

Remove the propeller shaft. The Triton shaft coupling was virtually amalgamated with the shaft, so it was necessary to remove the propeller first and then pull the shaft out inside the hull. Buy a coil of pliable copper or stainless steel wire and run it through the stuffing box, hull, and Cutless bearing outside to the propeller aperture

**Front view**

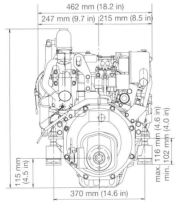

**Right side view**

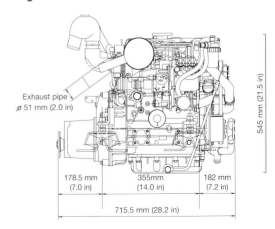

**FIGURE 8-8.** The schematic drawing of your engine is used to determine several important dimensions, especially the distance between the center of the engine-half coupling and the bottom of the motor mounts. A Yanmar 3YM30F is shown here. (Yanmar Marine)

**FIGURE 8-9.** The old Westerbeke beds in the Vanguard had to be modified with wooden blocks (right) and ¼-inch (6 mm) steel plates, drilled and tapped to accept the Yanmar's motor mount bolts. The trial-and-error modification of beds is invariably the hardest part of any repowering job. The tabbing of the stringers to the hull should include at least one layer of glass applied over the top of the wood. Radius the corners so the glass will conform to the shape. Once cured, it's time to lower the engine onto the beds and secure the motor mount bolts.

box in such a manner that it would rest in the hull at the same angle as the wire, and at an elevation that would permit the engine-half coupling to be bolted to the shaft-half coupling. The critical measurement here, obtainable from the manufacturer's schematic, is the distance between the center of the engine-half coupling and the bottom of the rubber engine mount—say 2.44 inches. The top of the bed, then, should be 2.44 inches (62 mm) below the wire. Even without the custom box, this measurement gives you a reference point from which you can determine elevation of the new beds you'll glass to the hull.

In taking my measurements, I planned to keep the bed an inch or so low and achieve a perfect alignment by adjusting the engine mount bolts upward. Since the mount bolts had 4 inches of play, 3 inches of reserve space were left in the event of a measuring error.

**FIGURE 8-10.** The finished beds with the surrounding area painted. This not only facilitates cleaning but makes it easy to spot any fluid leaks.

deadwood or some other fixed object—a jackstand (poppet) if necessary. Wrap the end around a screwdriver, stick, or nail and by eye position the wire so that it is in the center of the Cutless bearing. Then fasten the end of the wire coming inside the boat to some point in the cabin so that the wire is taut and in the center of the stuffing box (Figure 8-11). What you've done, in effect, is to extend the line of the propeller shaft over the engine bed. This becomes your all-important reference for lining up the engine bed.

With the special fiberglass engine bed box provided by BMW, the next step was to cut the

This is an appropriate point to mention constant-velocity drive units (Figure 8-12), which connect the engine to the propeller shaft. Two constant-velocity joints and a thrust bearing permit a misalignment of up to about 8° with some systems. Makers include Aquadrive (www.aquadriveusa.com) and PYI (www.pyiinc.com). Periodic realignment isn't necessary, and much softer (the rubber is more pliable) than normal engine mounts can be used to reduce vibration and engine noise. On the other hand, CV joints are one more moving part that can wear out. Some mechanics have told me that the more misalignment, the shorter the life span of the joint.

One decision you should make early is whether or not to buy a new propeller shaft. Even if you can reuse the old one, its length may have to be shortened. This, of course, is determined by the

**FIGURE 8-12.** Marine flexible drive couplings, such as the Python P140-T from PYI, feature two constant-velocity joints (similar to those used on the front ends of cars with front-wheel drive) and a thrust bearing to provide a flexible coupling between the engine and prop shaft. Vibration and noise are reduced. (PYI)

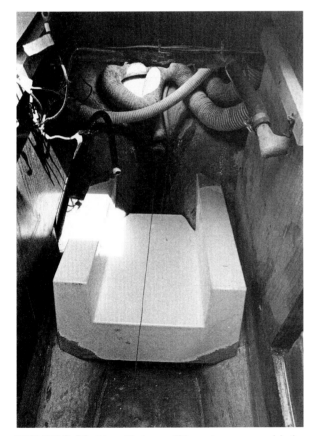

**FIGURE 8-11.** It's unlikely you'll be using a premolded fiberglass engine bed, such as this one provided by BMW (when they were in the marine engine business), but it more clearly shows the wire led through the shaft log and into the cabin as a reference line for vertical and fore-and-aft placement.

final fore-and-aft location of the engine. In both of my repowering jobs, the old shafts were worn around the stuffing box, and so were replaced.

If you elect to replace the shaft, only two measurements are important, rather than three. The bed and holes are positioned with attention to the centerline of the shaft and the vertical elevation of the shaft couplings; fore-and-aft distance is no longer that critical. As a result, on the Triton, we let the new engine protrude a few inches farther into the cabin than the old one. But this meant making changes to the boards covering the engine compartment. (As it turned out, this prompted me to enlarge the counter space around the galley, something I had wanted to do for many years.)

Lower the new engine into place with the same mechanism used to pull the old engine—chain fall, crane, what have you. Have someone above and below to guide it into place and to avoid scraping cabinetry (Figure 8-13).

## Ancillary Hookups

Once you've bolted the engine to its beds, complete the ancillary hookups. However, the final alignment of the engine to the shaft should be done in the water, as all boats, even those constructed of heavy fiberglass, may change shape from the cradle to the water.

The immediate tasks are to install fuel lines, water hoses and exhaust, ignition wiring, and throttle and transmission controls.

**FIGURE 8-13.** The Yanmar 3GM30 was lowered through the companionway hatch the same way the old Westerbeke came out. A chain fall is a good way to gently lower a heavy weight when you get close.

▓ **Ignition and wiring harness:** The new ignition panel can be mounted on a teak plate and placed over the holes left by the old instruments in the cockpit, or mounted elsewhere in the cockpit or cabin convenient to the helm (Figure 8-14). Connecting the wiring harness will probably be no more involved than snapping one end into the back of the engine and the other into the rear side of the ignition and instrument panel, or the latter may be prewired. New battery cables may be necessary if the distance from the engine to the batteries has increased. Solder the terminal fittings to the ends of the cable.

▓ **Throttle and gear shift:** Single-lever throttle and transmission controls can be mounted in the same spot as the old throttle lever or in a new site if it suits you better. Two control cables are fastened to the control plate linkage, led fair to the linkage on the engine, adjusted, and fastened tight. You need only be certain that no sharp bends occur in the cables that might hamper movement of the inner wire in its sheath, and that the nut and barrel on each end be adjusted so that the gears—forward, neutral, and reverse—engage positively, and that full throttle on the lever corresponds with full open position on the engine throttle lever. Boats with pedestal wheel steering will generally have the throttle and transmission cables run to handles mounted on the pedestal (Figure 8-15).

▓ **Cooling system:** The old seawater intake can be used to feed the new engine's cooling system. Even if the new engine is freshwater cooled, you'll still need seawater to cool the fresh water via the heat exchanger. Because they are no doubt aged and grimy, take time to replace the hose from the seacock and through-hull, as well as the hose clamps.

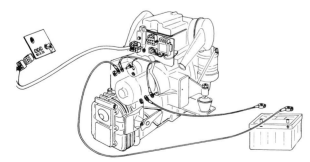

**FIGURE 8-14.** This schematic shows the wiring harness, which snaps into a panel on the backside of the engine, and includes the ignition and engine warning lights; it also shows where the battery cables lead. Very simple!

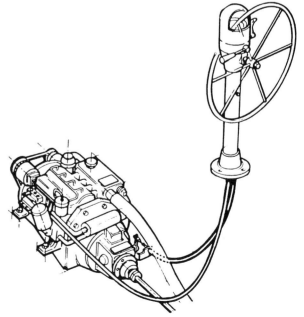

**FIGURE 8-15.** Engine throttle and transmission cables are run under the cockpit and up the pedestal to controls convenient to the helmsman. Locknuts at the engine end of the cables should be adjusted for specified idling speed and positive engagement of the gears.

Run a length of reinforced heater hose from the intake seacock to the suction side of the water pump. Then run a length from the other side of the pump to a vacuum-release valve mounted well above the waterline, perhaps on the backside of a bulkhead, and then to a fitting on the exhaust manifold. This prevents water from siphoning through the line into the engine. On my engines, water was introduced into the exhaust system inside the engine, so no fancy or difficult plumbing was necessary. But some engines introduce the water into the exhaust at a fitting on the exhaust manifold; therefore, extra hose and fittings may be required. Anchor all hoses with cable mounts to either existing bulkheads or tie them off to existing wires or hosing in the engine compartment.

Small diesel exhaust systems (Figure 8-16) may consist of reinforced radiator-type hose run from the exhaust outlet on the engine to a plastic water lift muffler to the exhaust tube in the transom. (My water lift was made by Vetus, but Allcraft (www.allcraft.net) makes a nice water lift in stainless steel.)

The position of the water lift muffler is important. It should be mounted as low as possible to the rear of the engine so that when the engine is turned off, water in the hose extending from the muffler to the exhaust tube on the transom does not exceed the capacity of the muffler and thus enter the engine. Measure their respective capacities to be sure. Loop the hose as high as possible to the underside of the deck before bringing it down and fastening it to the exhaust tube. An additional "silencer" further quiets the exhaust.

**Fuel lines:** Diesels require a return fuel line (Figure 8-17) from the injection pump back to the tank. This line must not enter the tank too close to the feed line, as returning fuel is hot and should not be continually recycled. Also, drilling into an old tank to insert a fitting is dangerous. Even when the tank has been professionally purged, many are loath to risk a spark igniting any residual fumes.

The easy solution is to replace the vent line fitting with a T-fitting, using one end for the return fuel line and the other for the vent. If you can't find one that will fit the threads on your tank, a small radiator repair shop can drill a hole in one side of the old fitting and solder a barbed nipple to it (Figure 8-18).

**Shaft and propeller:** Before launching, install the new shaft and propeller. Measure the distance between the engine-half coupling and the end of the Cutless bearing in the stern tube. Most prop shops use dimensions calculated to the SET, or small end of taper.

Before installing the new shaft, it's prudent to replace the Cutless bearing and flax in the packing nut at the stuffing box. In addition to the conventional stuffing box, which is packed with greasy flax to prevent leaking through the shaft log, there are maintenance-free shaft seals such as the Lasdrop (www.lasdrop.com). These are particularly useful where there isn't space to easily fit a wrench for loosening and tightening the conventional, adjustable types. If you're committed to the conventional packing gland, synthetic flax that doesn't drip is superior to the old stuff.

You might also consider fitting a flexible synthetic spacer between the engine and shaft, such as those made by Soundown (www.soundown.com) or PYI (Figure 8-19). These spacers reduce vibration and noise, and more important, prevent stray electrical currents in the water from causing corrosion in the engine. But if you do this, you can't use the engine for grounding the electrical system— you must use a dedicated ground plate instead. Most new diesels are fitted with sacrificial zincs, but it's nice knowing you have double security. Be sure to account for the width of this spacer when measuring the length of the shaft.

**Launch and alignment:** With one person in the cabin adjusting the mounting bolts, another should position himself under the cockpit where he can see the coupling and call out instructions to raise or lower. By rotating the shaft with your hand, you

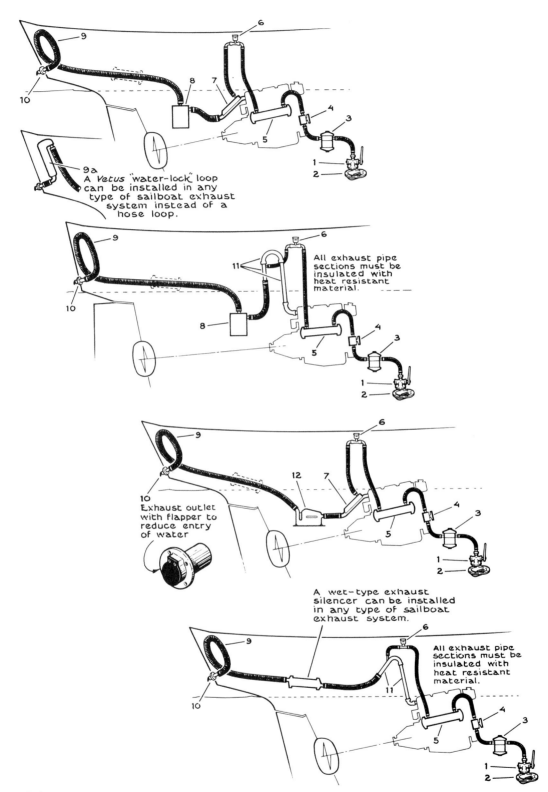

**FIGURE 8-16.** The exhaust system recommended by Vetus includes a water lift muffler (12), a silencer, and a water-lock gooseneck at the transom to prevent water from entering the engine through the exhaust hose. Other systems also are shown for other types of engines. Seacock (1), scoop/strainer (2), in-line "clearable" strainer (3), raw-water pump (4), heat exchanger (5), vented antisiphon loop (6), water injection exhaust elbow (7), water lift muffler (8), high loop in exhaust hose (9), transom exhaust fitting (10), high-dry metal exhaust pipe with insulated water injector on downside (11).

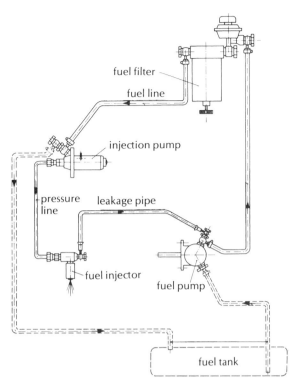

FIGURE 8-17. This is a basic schematic for a small diesel fuel line system. Note that, unlike a gasoline engine, diesels require a return line to the tank for unused fuel.

can see where the two coupling halves begin to kiss one another. You have a near perfect alignment when all four coupling flanges barely touch. Hunker down on the engine mounting bolts so that nothing can vibrate out of place. A few drops of Loctite help prevent the bolts from loosening, and also in removal later. While a feeler gauge is the traditional method, an

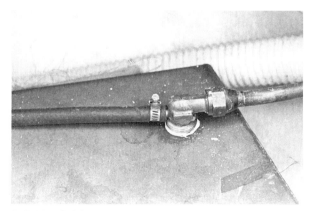

FIGURE 8-18. My old tank vent fitting was modified to accommodate the return fuel line from the engine, which entered from the left.

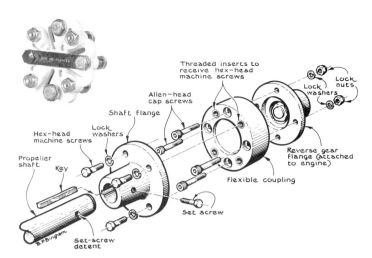

FIGURE 8-19. Synthetic spacers inserted between the shaft and engine coupling prevent stray electrical currents in the water from causing corrosion in the engine. They also smooth out any slight misalignment of the engine and shaft.

easier way is to insert a piece of paper between the two couplings, then study the imprints and grease markings for uniformity (Figure 8-20).

When the engine is started, check hoses for leaks and the engine bed for vibration.

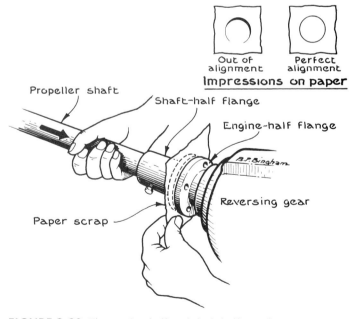

FIGURE 8-20. The engine-half and shaft-half couplings should kiss simultaneously to assure proper alignment between engine and propeller shaft. Rotating the shaft by hand with a piece of paper in between will reveal if any part of the two surfaces are touching.

# HOW MANY HORSES?

Tom Colvin, a yacht designer and builder of metal boats who has a good many blue-water miles beneath his keel, suggests half a horsepower per long ton (2,240 pounds/1,016 kg) for an ocean-cruising sailboat. The thinking here is that such a craft will use the engine primarily for recharging batteries, maneuvering among moorings, and occasionally motoring through doldrums. For a coastwise cruising sailboat, which may find itself powering against foul tides or racing darkness to make port, 1 horsepower per ton of displacement is recommended. Colvin's horsepower recommendations for various boats are given in Figure 8-21. He is well known for his unorthodox views, however, and most cruisers will find his recommended engine sizes small for their purposes, especially if they plan to cruise the canals and waterways of the world.

A contrasting opinion belongs to Ron Holland, a yacht designer most noted for his race boats and luxury superyachts like *Mirabella*, the world's largest sloop. His ideal cruiser has a stronger engine, he said, because "it helps you achieve more because you aren't so reliant on the wind." While hull shape is certainly a factor, it's interesting that many production yards (presumably building coastal cruisers) fit engines with 4 to 5 horsepower per long ton.

Boatbuilders today usually figure horsepower at four to five times displacement tonnage. Thus, a 6-ton boat would require an engine with a continuous horsepower rating of 24 to 30 horsepower.

In the classic text, *Skene's Elements of Yacht Design*, Francis Kinney gave several formulas for determining the horsepower needed to drive a boat at varying speed-length ratios. His 29-foot (8.8 m)

waterline *Santa Maria*, displacing 22,000 pounds, required an engine delivering 26.4 hp. He added one-third more so that the engine wouldn't have to be driven at top rpm to achieve hull speed. Consequently he selected a 35 hp engine. Figured into the equations is propeller efficiency, which varies radically among folding, two-blade, and three-blade types. You can probably get by with a smaller engine if fitted with a variable pitch prop, but what you save in dollars on the engine may be spent on the sophisticated gearing mechanism of the prop.

During a cruise of the U.S. East Coast, sailing both "outside" and motoring "inside" the Intracoastal Waterway, I kept meticulous records of engine running time. I found that we used the engine about 51% of the time, far more than I had anticipated. This is not, I think, unusual for coastal cruising, for even when sailing, good overnight anchorages may be 30 miles (49 km) and farther apart. This means that to make port by nightfall in a dying wind, running the engine is necessary unless you are willing to flop around all night waiting for daybreak before entering. Also, despite the cruiser's best intentions of avoiding schedules, the truth is most of us make plans to meet people at certain waypoints, attend festivals, or beat the cold at our backs, and so make itineraries based on a certain number of miles made each day or week. A good, powerful engine, to my mind, contributes greatly to happy cruising.

# FUEL CAPACITY

Colvin says 40 hours of smooth-water powering is adequate for most boats; 20 hours for ocean-cruising craft. He further suggests purchasing a

| Waterline | Tons | 10 HP | Speed in Knots at 15 HP | 20 HP | Maximum Usable Horsepower | Maximum Speed |
|-----------|------|-------|-------------------------|-------|---------------------------|---------------|
| 30 FT | 5 | 6.70 | 7.30 | — | 16.2 | 7.3 |
| | 10 | 5.60 | 6.15 | 6.60 | 35 | 7.3 |
| | 15 | 5.00 | 5.50 | 5.90 | 58 | 7.3 |
| 35 FT | 10 | 6.05 | 6.70 | 7.10 | 35 | 7.9 |
| | 15 | 5.35 | 5.90 | 6.40 | 58 | 7.9 |
| | 20 | 5.00 | 5.45 | 5.85 | 81 | 7.9 |
| 40 FT | 15 | 5.75 | 6.35 | 6.80 | 58 | 8.45 |
| | 20 | 5.35 | 5.85 | 6.25 | 81 | 8.45 |
| | 25 | 5.05 | 5.55 | 5.85 | 105 | 8.45 |

**FIGURE 8-21.** Tom Colvin's chart from *Cruising as a Way of Life* for maximum usable horsepower according to waterline length and displacement.

slow-revving diesel capable of being hand-started. Such an engine can be fitted with a large prop that will give the necessary push when the weather blows up. Of course, this causes more drag than a small propeller, but as he says, "choose an engine with a few big horses—not one with lots of little ponies."

Naval architect Roger Marshall suggests that fuel tankage hold an amount equal to 3 or 4% of total displacement—450 to 600 pounds (204 to 272 kg) for a 15,000-pound (6,801 kg) boat, or 60 to 80 gallons (227 L to 303 L), which works out to 7.5 gallons per pound (13 L per kg).

Most sailing auxiliaries are equipped with tanks that are on the small side since it saves expense and weight. This explains why cruising people are so often seen with jerricans lashed to the shrouds and pulpits. Adding a fuel tank is not out of the question, assuming there is space below, and it can be located so as not to adversely affect trim. The more fuel you can carry, the less often you have to divert to a marina for fill-ups. I've had to alter course by several hundred miles when there was no promise of wind and fuel was running short.

## PROPELLER SELECTION

Choosing the right propeller for a given boat and engine makes all the difference in performance and fuel efficiency. There are so many variables affecting correct pitch and size that scientific selection is difficult for the average person.

Propeller sizes are given in a pair of numbers, such as $13 \times 9$ or $12 \times 8$. The first number refers to the diameter of the blades in inches. The second refers to the pitch, or angle of the blades, and is the number of inches the prop theoretically should move forward with one revolution (Figure 8-22). The greater the pitch, the bigger the "bite" the prop takes.

Many engines have reduction gears to the propeller shaft. A 2:1 reduction gear means that the engine is always turning twice as fast as the prop shaft. An engine with 2:1 reduction gear would use a larger prop than one with direct drive. The smaller size for direct drive is necessary because, though the prop turns faster, there is less torque to keep it turning under load.

Racing sailboats use folding and feathering props to minimize drag while sailing. Folding props have blades that collapse backward to form a small cone; feathering props have blades that

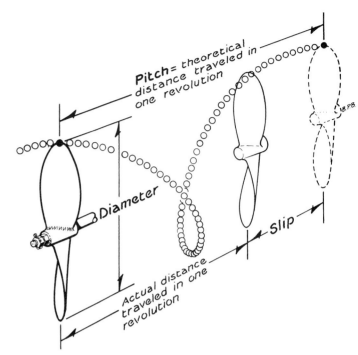

**FIGURE 8-22.** Propellers are referred to by two numbers. The first number indicates the diameter in inches; the second indicates the pitch, which is the theoretical number of inches the prop will move in one revolution through solid matter.

change pitch to a horizontal position so that the least surface possible is exposed to the passing water. Studies by Michigan Wheel Corporation (www.miwheel.com) on drag tests indicate that fixed two-blade props locked in the vertical position offer about 15 to 20% more resistance than feathering two-blade props. Folding props are mostly for racers; they offer little draft under sail, although they sometimes don't open on cue (Figure 8-23).

For the cruising sailor, it is less a decision and more a matter of personal inclination whether to power to windward or accept what Neptune delivers and do your best under sail alone. To effectively motorsail in heavy seas, a large propeller with high pitch coupled with reduction gear is the best combination. But the increased drag exacts a price in sailing performance.

There is a choice to be made between two- and three-bladed props as well. The two-bladed prop will give about 5 to 10% more speed than the three-bladed prop under sail, though the latter is slightly more fuel efficient under power and vibrates less. It also improves control and power when backing down, especially at slow speeds.

FIGURE 8-23. Folding props make for very little drag resistance under sail as they rely on centrifugal force to open. Some brands—like the Gori (inset)—are geared together so that they open at the same time and, presumably, more reliably. (Steel Team A/S)

A good automatic feathering propeller such as the Max-Prop from PYI combines several important advantages: more speed under sail (due to reduced drag); superior performance backing down (because the blades rotate to present the same leading edge and pitch as when in forward); and the end to shaft freewheeling (Figure 8-24). These props are expensive, but considering that dragging a fixed prop through the water costs a great deal of speed, it is certainly worth considering. The downside to the Max-Prop is reduced efficiency in forward due to the flat blade design; this means slightly more rpm are required than with a similar fixed prop.

Variable-pitch propellers (Figure 8-25) have much to recommend them in that the pitch can be adjusted for different speeds and sea conditions, depending on the torque required. This is done manually inside the boat. A brilliant alternative is the Autoprop (www.autoprop.com), which automatically adjusts pitch according to the load on the blades (Figure 8-26).

When repowering with a new engine, it may be that the old prop will work just fine. To find out, unfortunately, the boat must be in the water. Run with the engine in perfect running order, put

FIGURE 8-24. The Max-Prop automatic feathering propeller reduces drag while sailing and, under power, actually improves performance in reverse, owing to the flat blades. The exploded view shows the gears; the inset photos show the blade shape in profile, and how little surface area there is to cause resistance when the blades are feathered. (PYI)

**FIGURE 8-25.** A variable-pitch prop allows adjustment under way for varying sea states.

it at full throttle with all gear on board, and watch the tachometer. At full speed, the tach should reach the engine's rated maximum rpm. If the engine fails to achieve the rated rpm, the prop may be too large or the pitch too great. Conversely, if the engine turns too fast, the prop is too small or the pitch too little. Most prop shops have "loaners" that they'll let you use to find the correct "wheel" for your boat. Their expertise will significantly decrease the time you spend in trial-and-error matchmaking.

**FIGURE 8-26.** The Autoprop (left) is an ingenious design that automatically adjusts pitch (right) according to the load on the blades. Tests at MIT showed it is more efficient than the Max-Prop, but with slightly more drag under sail. (Brunton's Propellers)

# FILTERS

New engines come equipped with secondary fuel filters attached. This is one of the most important pieces of equipment on your diesel because dirty fuel clogs the injectors and is the most common cause of poor performance or engine failure.

The filters are called secondary because it is assumed and recommended that you install another filter between the tank and engine. Fram (www.fram.com) makes excellent marine filters that remove all water and all solid contaminants down to 1 micron in diameter. Racor (www.parker.com/racor) also makes an excellent filter (Figure 8-27), which has a glass bowl enabling visual inspection and a petcock at the base to drain off water and contaminants.

Some clean-fuel fanatics also use funnel filters to strain the diesel fuel as it is pumped into the tank. Westerbeke recommends filtering diesel fuel with a 200-micron mesh screen.

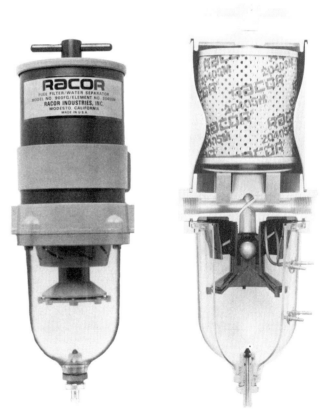

**FIGURE 8-27.** A secondary fuel filter is good insurance against dirty fuel clogging your injectors. This one is made by Racor and features a glass bowl for visual inspection and a petcock to drain off water and other contaminants. The cutaway view shows the location of the filter and passages. (Racor)

# NONELECTRIC STARTERS

Larry Pardey once wrote an article for *Cruising World* in which he praised the hydraulic starters used on working watercraft. His thought was that every diesel should have some alternative means of starting besides electric. Because large engines are difficult to start by hand, he reasoned, why not use these hydraulic starters on cruising sailboats? A Web search will quickly reveal a variety of products marketed not only to the commercial marine industry but to other industries as well, such as mining and oil exploration, generally harsh environments where temperature, gases, or remoteness of location necessitate backup engine starting systems.

As a sampling, the Simms Starter (www.springstarter.com), a spring starter formerly made by Lucas Marine, is wound up by hand in twelve turns and, when released, turns the flywheel just like your regular starter motor (Figure 8-28). It is powerful enough to start a six-cylinder, six-liter diesel engine. Another British manufacturer, IPU (www.ipu.co.uk), offers not only spring starters, but hydraulic, air, and nitrogen starters.

In any event, if your diesel is too large to be started by hand, or isn't fitted with a manual crank, give some thought to installing a backup starting system. A wrench dropped across the terminals of your battery can short it instantaneously and leave you without starting power.

# CUTLESS BEARINGS/ STUFFING BOXES

Two pieces of engine-related gear that are all too often ignored are the Cutless bearing and the stuffing box (Figure 8-29). The Cutless bearing is a bronze tube with a grooved rubber liner that fits inside the fiberglass tube through which the prop shaft exits the hull. (Just to set the record straight, BFGoodrich, the original manufacturer, called its bearing a "Cutless" bearing, meaning it will cut less on the prop shaft; however, the original advertising used a pirate's "cutlass" as a logo, hence the confusion as to proper spelling and pronunciation.)

After a few years, the rubber liner becomes worn and smooth inside, which can cause wobble in the prop shaft. You won't see Cutless bearings in chandlery display cases, but a well-stocked store will have them in the back room.

Next time your boat is hauled, give a tug on the shaft to check for slop in the Cutless bearing. Replacing it would be relatively simple if it (1) wasn't marine, (2) didn't live underwater, and (3) wasn't invented to vex people who think working on boats is fun. With the shaft out, pound out the Cutless bearing with a hammer, using a section of wooden dowel of the right diameter. There should be a few setscrews or Allen screws to keep the bearing from spinning inside the shaft log (the hollow fiberglass tube in the hull through which the shaft passes), covered by fiberglass or putty. These must be removed first before driving out the bearing. Chip away at the deadwood an inch or

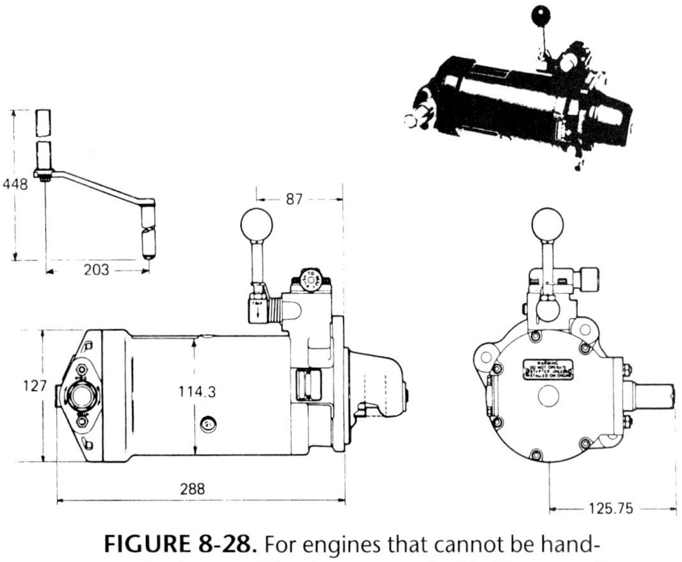

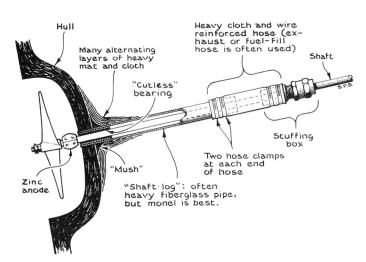

**FIGURE 8-28.** For engines that cannot be hand-cranked, a good backup system is this Simms spring starter. (Kinetco)

**FIGURE 8-29.** The Cutless bearing and stuffing box are critical to holding the shaft in alignment. They should be periodically inspected and serviced as necessary.

FIGURE 8-30. So-called dripless shaft seals like those from Lasdrop and the PSS Shaft Seal from PYI (top) replace the conventional stuffing box; precision-mated surfaces rely on compression to keep water from passing. The bottom photo shows the nitrile O-rings. (PYI)

so in from the end of the bearing until you find the screws. On several occasions, however, I've had to use an open-ended hacksaw to cut the bearing into two halves before they'd come out.

The stuffing box helps hold the shaft in alignment. A length of flax is "stuffed" inside the box between the first parts and is lubricated by seawater. Old petroleum-based flax should be replaced every few years. Now, however, there is dripless packing, which is synthetic and guaranteed to last the life of your boat. Try West Marine and similar outlets. The stuff works.

Tightening the stuffing box or packing gland decreases the amount of water permitted entry to the flax. The general rule with conventional flax is to tighten the box so that water periodically drips from the box. If you find the presence of any water in the bilge disconcerting, try dripless packing or one of the dripless seals such as those from Lasdrop or PYI (Figure 8-30).

## SOUND INSULATION

Lining the engine box with 1 to 2 inches (25 mm or 51 mm) of lead-lined foam (Figure 8-31) significantly cuts down engine noise. Use contact cement to glue it to the box, but be sure the glue

FIGURE 8-31. Lining the engine box with lead-lined foam 1 to 2 inches thick significantly reduces engine noise.

won't dissolve the foam. Seal exposed edges and seams with aluminum or Mylar tape. Enclose as much of the engine under the cockpit as possible by glassing boards to the underside of the cockpit (called curtains) and then gluing foam to them.

## FURTHER READING

*Boatowner's Mechanical and Electrical Manual: How to Maintain, Repair, and Improve Your Boat's Essential Systems.* 3rd ed. Nigel Calder. Camden, Maine: International Marine, 2005.

*The Care and Repair of Small Marine Diesels.* Chris Thompson. Camden, Maine: International Marine, 1982.

*The Care and Repair of Marine Gasoline Engines.* Loris Goring. Camden, Maine: International Marine, 1981.

*Diesel Engine Manual.* Perry O. Black. 4th ed. Rev. by William E. Scahill. Indianapolis: T. Audel, 1983.

*Outboard Engines: Maintenance, Troubleshooting, and Repair.* Edwin R. Sherman. Camden, Maine: International Marine, 1997.

*Propeller Handbook: The Complete Reference for Choosing, Installing, and Understanding Boat Propellers.* Dave Gerr. Camden, Maine: International Marine, 1989.

*Sailboat Auxiliary Engine Maintenance.* Brick Price. Los Angeles: Clymer Publications, 1975.

*Troubleshooting Marine Diesels.* Peter Compton. Camden, Maine: International Marine, 1998.

# AN EFFICIENT DECK LAYOUT

So far we've talked about changes necessary to the interior and enclosed systems of a boat to make it a good, safe cruiser. The deck is no less rife with potential problems. Rig, sails, and canvasmaking will be discussed in later chapters; in this chapter inspection of the boat is confined to the deck area, to weaknesses (many inherent in new boats), and to possible solutions.

As with the boat's interior, the best deck layout is arrived at only after a season or two of sailing. You learn where it's most convenient to put your feet down, the most convenient pathway to the stern (often cluttered with jerricans, solar panels, outboard motor bracket, flag, etc.) to tend the dinghy painter, and the places where people prefer to sit. Eventually you begin to settle on how best to add equipment or make changes to existing features.

You can often identify a true cruising boat by the amount of stuff (I'd like to say junk) on deck. Sometimes it seems there just isn't room belowdeck for everything—barbecue grill, second anchor and rode, dinghy oars, and much more. Many of us feel that this stuff is essential, and that our lives would be more difficult or less pleasant without it. But let me chasten thee: gear on deck weathers quickly; obstructs access around the boat; is in danger of being swept away in a storm, often to the endangerment of crew and other fixtures, such as stanchions and lifelines; and is just plain ugly. There's nothing worse than a rusty bicycle lashed to the stern pulpit. To my mind, if you can't fit it belowdeck in a locker, don't bring it.

Okay. As we've seen in the preceding chapters, most production boats aren't set up for offshore sailing—not that they should be, since the usage of most boats is coastal and infrequent. While some necessary upgrades, like rigging jacklines, aren't permanent modifications, there are other things you might want to do, like installing a sea hood over the companionway hatch or devising a system of rain catchment. Here we go.

## BOWSPRITS, PLATFORMS, AND PULPITS

Starting our deck tour at the bow, let's look at the bow pulpit and think about ground tackle. Your boat probably has bow and stern pulpits, with stanchions and lifelines between. Bow platforms and bowsprits are less commonly fitted as standard equipment, though many of the Taiwanese boats of the 1970s and '80s were built with them. That's huge, because retrofits are tricky and expensive. Traditionally styled bowsprits or platforms on which to neatly fit the anchor roller are typically made of wood; more modern designs, such as the Caliber and Island Packet boats, have reinforced-fiberglass moldings—not as attractive, but still highly functional. If the pulpit is through-bolted to the deck, using large washers or backing plates on the underside, you might as well be satisfied with it. Welded pulpits are preferable to fitted ones (separate pieces held together with joints and setscrews), as the latter can rattle and vibrate loose (Figure 9-1). Perhaps the easiest solution is to through-bolt the stanchion to its base. Use an acorn or Nylok nut.

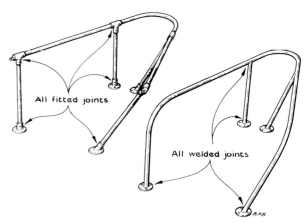

All fitted joints

All welded joints

**FIGURE 9-1.** Welded pulpit joints are stronger than fitted joints. See Figure 9-13 for other securing methods.

## Bow Rollers

A serious cruising boat should be able to set two anchors with the rodes running over their own rollers to a windlass. Most boats are built with chocks just port and starboard of the forestay. This will never do. For one thing, when the anchor is hauled out of the water it will scrape the stem and topsides. The anchor rollers must be set far enough forward of the stem so this doesn't happen.

Anchor rollers not only facilitate setting and hauling the anchor but also permit stowing a plow-type anchor, although in bad weather offshore it should be brought below and secured. Frank Mulville, an English single-hander with numerous ocean crossings and whom I had the pleasure to know, described in his book *Single-handed Cruising and Sailing* a convenient anchoring system in which the rode is led back to the cockpit and tripped to run free when the decision is made to lower away. This, of course, would not be possible without some sort of roller at the bow.

For retrofitting rollers, Windline (www .windline.com) makes a full line of anchor rollers and supporting brackets that can be adapted to almost any type of anchor and boat (Figure 9-2).

If your boat has a toe rail that extends to the bow, you may need to cut a piece out of the toe rail plank to fit the roller flush on deck or add a piece of wood under the roller to elevate it above the toe rail. Be certain the point of the anchor flukes won't hit the hull when pulled in tight on the roller. Teak would be a good choice here, as would a large backing plate of ½-inch (12 mm) fiberglass or ¾-inch (19 mm) hardwood (Figure 9-3). The loads on the roller and bracket, especially when kedging off, are substantial.

## Bow Platforms

Full-on bowsprits and platforms, either made of hardwood or reinforced fiberglass, allow locating

**FIGURE 9-3.** Without a bow platform, care must be taken to protect the topsides. Note the stainless steel protection, the wooden spacer to elevate the custom welded roller, and the retaining lock pin above the anchor shank. (*Practical Sailor* photo)

the rollers farther forward than the stainless steel products from Windline, mentioned above. Often the two rollers are staggered, so that one is at or near the end of the platform and the other set aft—maybe 1 foot (305 mm). The reason is simply to provide room for each anchor underneath the platform. Rollers should be large and sized to the stock of the anchors. Locking pins keep the anchor from jumping off the roller in bumpy seas—but they are not a substitute for securing the chain on deck.

On boats with weather helm, there's a secondary benefit of adding a bow platform or bowsprit, and that is to relocate the headstay farther forward. This moves the center of effort of the sail plan forward and reduces weather helm.

On an outboard sloop or cutter rig, a downhaul on the jib saves going forward onto the sprit (Figure 9-4). A platform and rail on top of the sprit gives additional security (Figure 9-5). If you have decided to add a sprit or platform for a bow roller and are using teak, don't bolt directly through the teak to the deck. Even with a good backing plate, the compression resistance of teak isn't good, and the bolt heads will crush the wood. A better choice is to clamp the inboard end of the sprit or platform to the deck with a metal strap (Figure 9-6).

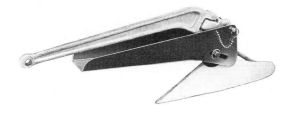

**FIGURE 9-2.** Windline manufactures a complete line of bow rollers for all types of anchors and bow configurations. Note the locking pin to hold this CQR down on the roller. (Windline)

FIGURE 9-4. Suggesting the danger of walking out on a long sprit to change headsails, *Gretel*, a 90-foot, three-masted schooner, has the traditional netting underneath the bowsprit to provide footing. On a modern cruising boat, a platform on top of the sprit, plus pulpit, increases safety.

FIGURE 9-5. Contemporary practice is to construct a flat platform over the bowsprit, or more commonly, leave out the bowsprit altogether. Note how neatly the Danforth and CQR anchors on this Krogen 38 are stowed, and how quickly they can be deployed.

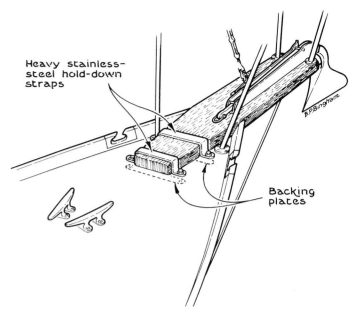

FIGURE 9-6. Because teak's compressive strength is poor, large pieces subject to stress, such as bowsprit platforms, shouldn't be bolted directly to the deck. A metal strap is a better method.

# ANCHOR WELLS, CHAINPIPES, AND WINDLASSES

Some anchors don't stow well flat on deck, and this is one reason why plows mounted on outboard rollers are so popular. For securing lightweight types such as the West Marine (www.westmarine.com), Danforth (www.danforthanchors.com), and aluminum Fortress (www.fortressanchors.com), bolt chocks to the deck; for fisherman-type anchors, unpin and disassemble them, then lash them to a stanchion as well as secure them in chocks.

In practice, however, anything on deck is bound to obstruct traffic, possibly causing someone to trip or stub a toe. It's better to get anchors out of the way. Small boats sometimes suspend a lightweight anchor under the bow pulpit on hangers made by Nautical Engineering (248-349-1034) or Windline, but these are not a good idea offshore.

## *Anchor Wells*

The surest way to get a lightweight anchor out of the way is to stow it belowdecks. A trick in recent years has been to mold anchor wells into the foredeck. A well-designed one has a drain over the side that gets rid of water and lets you wash down the anchor in the well without getting the deck dirty. Also, it should have a locking mechanism to keep the lid from flying open if the boat is knocked down. Provisions should be made to lash the anchor inside the well to prevent it from flailing about or crashing against the lid in severe conditions.

Anchor wells may hold the anchor horizontally or vertically. The one in Figure 9-7 holds the anchor securely in place, though a strong lid with hasp and lock is still necessary. Most anchor wells are custom fiberglass moldings made by the boat's manufacturer, but over the years there have been a few companies making lockers for retrofitting. I imagine it would take a courageous person to cut such a large hole in his deck! If you do undertake the job, be certain to grout out the core material around the hole, and fill it with epoxy resin thickened with wood flour, chopped strand, or microfibers (see Figure 4-8). This provides increased

**FIGURE 9-8.** Though the owner of this boat obviously isn't using an all-chain rode, the below-deck windlass compartment is a nifty idea. As expensive as windlasses are, and as much as they are regular toe-stubbers, this arrangement makes a lot of sense. (*Practical Sailor* photo)

strength for handling the compression loads that occur when bolting hinges and hasps, and to prevent moisture from reaching the core material.

Check the size of built-in anchor wells to make sure they are large enough to hold the size of anchor you want to carry. Chain usually is an afterthought in these below-deck arrangements. Some builders mount a horizontal windlass in the anchor well, which neatly gets it off the deck, but it may make operation and maintenance more difficult, and runs the risk of drowning the motor and gears in seawater (Figure 9-8).

### Making an Anchor Well

If you're really enterprising, you can fabricate an anchor well from plywood and glass it over with mat and polyester resin. Fair the outside edges and fillet the inside corners so the mat doesn't have to conform to sharp angles—it won't. Locate it where it won't interfere with the windlass, chain pipe, and chain locker in the bow. Don't forget an overboard drain and a secure lid, which you can mold out of fiberglass over a male form (see the sea hood project later in this chapter), or make up out of wood.

## Windlasses

A windlass mounted between the bow roller and forward mooring cleat(s) is a useful piece of gear

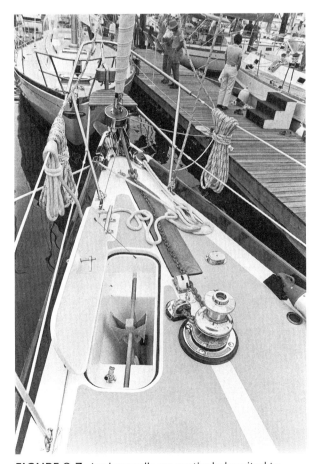

**FIGURE 9-7.** Anchor wells are particularly suited to lightweight anchors, which don't ride well in bow rollers or on bow platforms. Note the sacrificial teak board to protect the deck from the chain. (*Practical Sailor* photo)

on any boat and essential on most boats larger than 30 feet (9.1 m; Figure 9-9). It can take the strain out of shipping anchor in ordinary conditions and is one of the best ways to break out an anchor fouled on the bottom.

One stormy October day on Lake Michigan, Gene Correll—an old sailing friend—and I hauled his boat off a beach after it had broken its mooring pendant. The 33-foot (10 m) Pearson Vanguard lay in about 2½ feet (76 cm) of water; the hull drew 4½ feet (1.4 m). We took one long line off the masthead and attached it to the main halyard. Then after leading it to an anchor several hundred feet abeam, we used a halyard winch to careen the boat as much as possible. We led a second anchor toward deep water with about 300 feet (91 m) of line. With the small SL-200 Simpson Lawrence windlass on the foredeck, we winched his 7-ton boat inch by inch toward deeper water, with only a 35-pound (16 kg) CQR dug into the sand to hold. Every time a knot attaching the two lines jammed in the bow chock, it was necessary to lash a spare line to the rode outside the knot, pull the knot through, then unlash the extra line.

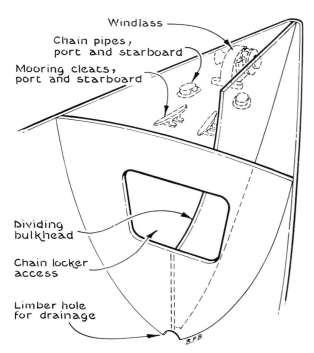

Windlass

Chain pipes, port and starboard

Mooring cleats, port and starboard

Dividing bulkhead

Chain locker access

Limber hole for drainage

**FIGURE 9-9.** A safe and powerful anchoring system includes a large anchor locked to a bow roller, a samson post or large cleat for tying off nylon rode, a windlass, a watertight chain pipe, and a reinforced compartment for chain.

On numerous other occasions, I've used the electric Ideal windlass on our boat to kedge off; it got a real workout on the Intracoastal Waterway.

Larry Pardey points out that windlasses with aluminum-cast bodies should be avoided in favor of bronze or iron bodies. The reason is that an aluminum housing in direct contact with stainless steel bolts will corrode and make disassembly difficult. When the old Simpson Lawrence (www.lewmar.com) on my Vanguard began giving me trouble, I decided it was time to take it apart and lubricate the moving parts. Too late—the cast-aluminum body, encased in vinyl, and the warping drum crumbled in my fingers. Larry Pardey was right, of course.

Not long after, I went to Cliffe Raymond, head of Ideal Windlass Company (www.idealwindlass.com) in East Greenwich, Rhode Island, and told him I wanted a small, manual windlass, just for those times when you can't bring in the anchor by hand. He said to me, "The two things people hate doing most on sailboats are changing headsails and hauling anchors. Today, everyone seems to have headsail furling gear, but you hardly ever see people buying electric windlasses. Manuals," he added, "are too slow and too much work. Besides, if you're cruising you should have an all-chain rode, and if you have an all-chain rode the only way to retrieve it is with an electric windlass." Well, hardcore cruisers certainly know this to be true (Figure 9-10).

I installed an electric bronze capstan on the foredeck, sized for the best ¼-inch (6 mm) chain. It had a manual option, which reassured me, though it was seldom used. Thousands of miles later, I had to admit that it was one of the most useful and important pieces of gear aboard.

No longer was bringing in the anchor an onerous chore (like the joke about the new parents lying in bed listening to the baby scream; one says to the other, "Well, if it's not *your* turn, and it's not *my* turn, whose turn is it?"). In fact, it was so easy, just stepping on the foot switch, we found ourselves falling over each other to be chivalrous: "I'll bring up the anchor." "Oh, no, let me!"

The advantages of an electric windlass are numerous. The electric windlass permits anchoring with an all-chain rode, which increases holding power tremendously; the recommended 7:1 scope is reduced to just 4:1, which is especially helpful in tight quarters. It encourages you to reanchor if your first attempt puts you too close to another boat or the shore. Without it, you're often tempted

# Metals and Wood

Just about everything on deck is made of wood, metal, or some sort of fiber (as in rope). There is often more than one specific material suitable for a given job, and choosing wood for a winch base, rather than metal or a plastic like King Starboard, is often a matter of personal preference. So, too, is the choice of mahogany over teak or stainless steel over bronze.

The manufacturers of good-quality gear have carefully chosen the material they think best for a specific item, but depending on your boat's hull and deck material—or other unique problems—you may wish to seek out gear made from less common materials. For example, if you have teak decks, you may prefer sheet blocks with wood shells rather than urethane synthetics. See Appendices A and B for more information on common woods and metals used in boatbuilding. Included is the galvanic series, which should be referred to whenever mating dissimilar metals.

to "wait and see," which often leads to trouble in the middle of the night. Kedging off sandbars is almost too easy; row out an anchor in the dinghy (rope rode usually, since the chain's catenary weight makes it difficult to get the anchor very far from the boat), then row back to the boat, step on the button, and watch as the boat pulls itself up to the anchor as surely as a dog follows a steak bone.

Lastly, when on those occasions the ground tackle does drag, an electric windlass saves critical time. Once I was anchored in the Exumas when a thunderstorm swept through the roadstead at midnight. Two neighboring islands and several

**FIGURE 9-10.** In Pulpit Harbor, Maine, we unexpectedly ran into some relatives of friends; I first noticed Jim Sheldon in the process of reanchoring his Albin Vega, a handle in one hand and a deck wash hose in the other—it didn't look easy, but at least he wasn't handing buckets!

coral reefs confined our maneuvering area to half the size of a football field—there wasn't much room, or time, to waste bringing up the two anchors. If we'd had to do it by hand, we would have come a lot closer to disaster than by using the electric windlass.

On smaller boats with just several hundred amp-hours in the battery bank, it is necessary to run the engine whenever the windlass is operated. But this shouldn't be a problem since you need to charge the batteries daily anyway, and as long as you have an auxiliary, it seems prudent to at least idle the engine during anchoring maneuvers where other people's boats, if not your own, are at risk.

Installation is fairly easy. Cut the prescribed hole in the foredeck, add mounting bolt holes, and drop in the windlass. Fashion a suitable backing plate and snug it down. Run the electric cables aft to a breaker switch, then to a battery. That's it. The cables are heavy and must be sized to the load and length of run to prevent excessive voltage drop; try to keep it between 3 and 10%. Think battery cables—1/0, 2/0, and maybe even larger.

## Selecting a Windlass

Coastal cruising boats anchor just about every night, and sometimes getting the anchor to set takes several attempts. This means you'll be using the windlass a lot. You need a heavy-duty windlass, not one of the lightweights seen in the discount catalogs at very low prices.

Just as Cliffe Raymond advised me, I advise others to spend the bucks on an electric windlass—for all the reasons given above. Among electric models there are essentially two types: vertical and horizontal. Vertical models have the advantage of locating the motor belowdecks, out of the weather, and are somewhat less obtrusive on the foredeck. Horizontal models may have two wheels, or one chain wheel and a warping drum, but positioning for a fair lead with the rode is often more difficult than with the vertical model. Because the chain only makes a 90° turn with the horizontal windlass, the center of its wheel must be at least as high as the bow roller, which may mean having to block up the windlass to ungainly heights. Rodes generally make a 180° turn around the vertical windlass.

After deciding between vertical and horizontal, you next must figure out whether you want an all-chain rode or chain-rope combination. A common choice is an all-chain rode for the primary anchor, say 250 feet (76 m) on a big plow, and a rope rode with chain leader for the secondary anchor, maybe 40 feet (12 m) of chain (some recommend the length of the boat) and 300 feet (91 m) of nylon rope. A chain-rope combination requires a special splice so that the chain wheel can handle this "bump" in the rode. Simpson Lawrence used to have a patent on such a chain wheel, but that ran out in 1992, and now all the other makers offer the same configuration.

Now determine the windlass size. You can go with the manufacturer's recommendation or do your own calculations. A number of books on anchoring offer tables indicating the load on a rode, given the boat size and wind strength. For example, Robert Smith's classic text, *Anchors: Selection and Use,* says a 36-foot (11 m) boat in 30 knots of wind will have a 276-pound (125 kg) load on the rode. Data once published by the American Boat and Yacht Council was much higher. In any case, once you're settled on a believable number, you'll want to buy a windlass that provides that much power, plus a safety margin.

A simpler rule of thumb is to triple the weight of your entire ground tackle system and purchase a windlass that can lift that much continuously.

As for brands, I tested a number of popular vertical windlasses while at *Practical Sailor.* All use electric motors geared to the chain wheel. The less expensive brands generally had smaller motors turning through more gears, while the more expensive models had big starter-type motors turning through fewer gears. For the test, we mounted each windlass in the loft of an industrial building and made it lift iron weights until its

FIGURE 9-11. On *Viva* we installed an Ideal electric capstan and all-chain rode for the Delta anchor. The stainless steel Windline anchor roller and bracket at left of the stem, for handling the secondary lightweight-type anchor, hadn't been mounted yet.

breaker tripped. Some models never reached their advertised maximum. The Ideal V1Q topped that particular test, lifting 200 pounds at 70 feet per minute, with a maximum pull of 850 pounds (385 kg). (As mentioned above, I bought one and installed it on *Viva,* our Tartan 44; Figure 9-11.)

## A COMPLETE GROUND TACKLE SYSTEM

Figure 9-12 illustrates the various components of a complete ground tackle system as found on most serious cruising boats. These include a substantial bow roller, chain stopper, chain tensioner, and chain pipe. Vertical windlasses usually incorporate the chain pipe into the base casting because the chain stripper in the chain wheel is going to make the chain peel off and drop right next to the windlass. The pipe should come standard with a

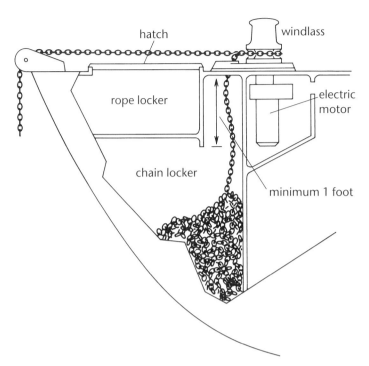

hatch

windlass

rope locker

electric motor

chain locker

minimum 1 foot

**FIGURE 9-12.** Here's another view of a ground tackle system showing the critical elevation of horizontal windlasses and the other hardware required. (Jim Sollers illustration)

with limber holes drilled for drainage and chain fed by a wood trough, will keep this potentially unruly serpent tamed. If the chain isn't self-stowing, someone must go below to flake it, which is a nuisance. Voyager and author Hal Roth says tall, narrow storage is better than wide, flat compartments and, as chain is smelly, wash it down as it comes aboard. Rinsing chain using buckets dropped over the side is backbreaking work; a seawater deck wash (see Figure 5-31) makes this lousy job ridiculously simple (tap the seawater through-hull at the galley sink, mount a pump in the line leading to the underside of the foredeck, and install a hose connector on the top of the deck to fasten a short length of garden-type hose with an adjustable nozzle).

## LIFELINES, STANCHIONS, AND SAFETY LINES

In heavy weather, standard practice is to don a safety harness and fix it to some object on deck that is securely fastened. The fastening location should permit movement to all locations desired, such as the mast base, yet not allow the person to fall so far over the side that he cannot regain the deck. Lifelines, despite their apparent strength, are not the best choice for this purpose. The Fastnet disaster of 1979 and the Whitbread Round the World Race of 1973 recorded deaths due to failed lifelines. Perhaps no other description of death at sea is so chilling as the recollections of the crew of a French Whitbread boat who watched their skipper disappear overboard. He had his safety harness clipped to the lifeline when the boat was knocked down and he was sent flying along the deck. The harness hook snapped off the stanchion tops one by one. When he reached the end of the boat, the lifeline snapped, putting him in the water with no tie to the boat. Quickly, he was swept away, never to be seen again.

cover, usually with a slot for the chain. In bad weather, modeling clay pressed inside the pipe and around the chain keeps out most water.

If you do not have a windlass or must install your own chain pipe, select a sturdy model made of stainless steel or bronze—never plastic. And examine how it is made weathertight. Some have clips on the inside of the lid to fasten the end of the rode; in the anticipation of bad weather, you might want to unshackle it from the anchor, which will be stowed below.

Use strong lashings on the anchor to keep it from flopping around on the foredeck. On more than one occasion, I've seen people sailing with an anchor dangling over the side—dangerous in any conditions.

Generally, it is not considered wise to place too much weight in the ends of the boat because this increases the boat's tendency to hobbyhorse. Keeping the weight amidships gives a steadier motion. For this reason, chain, if possible, should be led aft, perhaps under the forward berths. But don't impede its deployment with a poorly thought out installation; on many boats, chain stowage in the forepeak may be the best you can do. A strong plywood compartment reinforced with fiberglass,

Use the largest-diameter wire possible. The stanchion holes may require enlarging, or you may have to buy wire without a plastic covering to obtain a $5/16$-inch (8 mm) or larger diameter. And though the plastic covering is gentler on hands and almost universally seen, stainless steel corrodes in the absence of oxygen, so don't be surprised when you see bare-wire lifelines on boats belonging to really experienced skippers. Most often, $7 \times 7$ or $7 \times 19$ wire is used for lifelines, but as there's no real need for flexibility, $1 \times 19$ wire is a stronger choice.

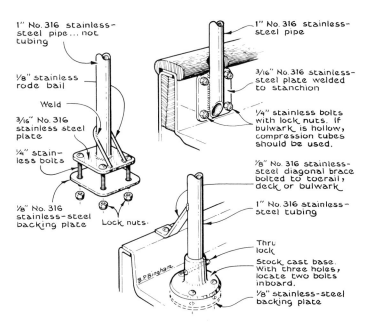

**FIGURE 9-13.** Stanchion bases through-bolted only to the deck are not as strong as those also bolted to a vertical support, such as a bulwark. Stanchions should be welded or through-bolted to their bases, because Allen screws only dimple the metal and are not very secure.

Nevertheless, lifelines serve several important functions: a handhold when going forward, a brace for the legs, and containment for sails dropped on the deck. Most offshore races specify lifeline standards. The Offshore Racing Council (ORC) specifies double lifelines and stanchions of at least 24 inches (610 mm) height (some sailors feel 27 to 30 inches or 686 to 762 mm is better), through-bolted or welded to the deck. They should be spaced no more than 7 feet (2.1 m) apart. Custom-made stanchions of 1-inch (25 mm) 316 stainless steel pipe (which has a thicker wall than tubing) will be stronger than most commercially available types. Weld them to ³⁄₁₆-inch (5 mm) bases with four bolt holes.

Some stanchion mounting methods are superior to others. On most production boats, the stanchion is bolted flush on deck (Figure 9-13).

If the boat has a toe rail of several inches height, or better yet, bulwarks of 6 inches (152 mm) or more, the stanchion also can be bolted in the vertical plane, which is much stronger.

Quality stanchions should be welded to their bases or fastened by bolts or roll pins, not by Allen setscrews, which only dimple the metal and let loose as soon as a strong force is exerted.

## Jacklines Are the Real Lifelines

Veteran single-hander Frank Mulville once showed me the lifeline system he used on his Hillyard cutter, *Iskra*. He ran a length of wire from stem to stern, fastened at each end to pad eyes through-bolted to the deck (Figure 9-14) and seized at the shrouds to keep it at waist level. Today, flat nylon webbing that won't roll underfoot the way wire does is more commonly used. Minimum breaking strength is 5,000 pounds (2,268 kg). Belay port and starboard webbing to cleats forward and aft, though not right at the stern as this would allow a person to be dragged in the water behind the boat in the water by his safety harness. Or, you can make up a single length of jackline that runs port and starboard through a strong ring or block at the bow (Figure 9-15).

A good safety harness such as those made by Lirakis (401-846-5356) should have two attachment lines, one long and one short; which one you use depends on where you're hooked and where you have to go. Also, with two lines you can move past any interruptions (by hooking the free one before unhooking the other) in the jackline without ever being unhooked from the boat. Ideally, jacklines should be rigged so you can reach the forestay, mast base, and all other critical points on deck without being able to go overboard. This, however, is not always easy to accomplish.

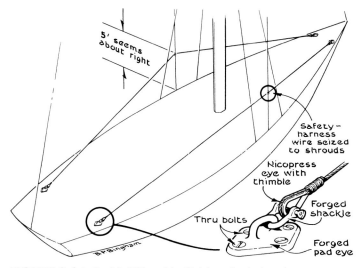

**FIGURE 9-14.** On his Hillyard-built *Iskra*, single-hander Frank Mulville used a single length of large-diameter wire run from stem to stern to attach his safety harness line. It was seized at the shrouds to hold it chest high and required unhooking only once on a trip up or down the deck.

**FIGURE 9-15.** Nylon webbing is more commonly used today for jacklines because it doesn't roll under foot like wire. (Bill Seifert photo)

If sailing alone, or alone on watch with an autopilot steering, it is very important to have some means, such as a tripline, of disengaging the autopilot or vane so that the boat will round up, slow down, and permit a man overboard to gain the deck. An easy means of climbing aboard also is essential. It is hard to do when the boat is moving, especially if you can't grab a firm handhold. A scoop transom, or a series of transom steps, make self-rescue a legitimate possibility, though the stern rises and falls far more than midships, making the maneuver difficult and dangerous.

## REQUIREMENTS OF A SEAWORTHY COMPANIONWAY

There are five basic requirements for a good main hatch: (1) it should be small, not much more than shoulder width; (2) the weather boards should be solid hardwood or plywood, preferably ¾ inch

(19 mm) thick, or Lexan; (3) it should be as watertight as possible; (4) the retaining channels that hold the weather boards must be very strong; and (5) there should be devices to lock the sliding hatch and weather boards inside and outside.

Reinforcing the retaining channels is a good place to start beefing up the main hatch. Protection against vandals and thieves is an added bonus. If your channels aren't up to spec, remove them and follow the cross-sectional plan in Figure 9-16. Use ¾-inch (19 mm) thick hardwood. A strip of ⅛-inch (3 mm) stainless steel through-bolted to the cabin wall and locking mechanisms such as barrel bolts on the weather boards are extra insurance against boarding waves, crowbars, or the forces that sometimes knock weather boards *out* when the boat is dropped hard off a wave. Inside, a piece of thick teak or other hardwood, several inches wide, should be through-bolted to the cabin wall.

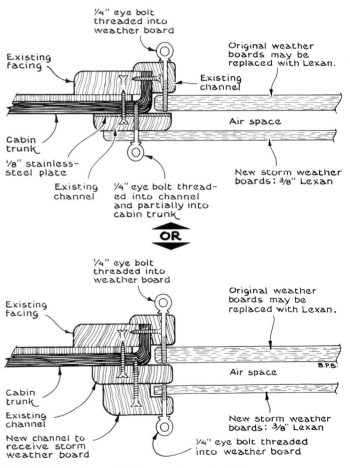

**FIGURE 9-16.** The retaining boards that hold the companionway slide (weather boards) can be beefed up by making provision for a storm shutter.

169

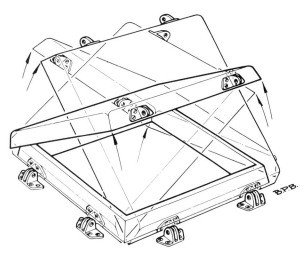

**FIGURE 9-17.** More air and less water gets below when the forward hatch can be opened in any direction. Bruce's clever drawing illustrates how this is possible.

If your boat doesn't have a flange, as pictured, then bolt through both the interior and exterior pieces.

Figure 9-16 also shows a storm shutter of ⅜-inch (10 mm) Lexan that can be quickly screwed to the steel plate in the event of really nasty seas.

Hatches should be able to be locked from both inside and outside, as should the weather boards themselves—even if the hatch is open. Deadbolt slides do the trick well for the weather boards and might work for the hatch. Figure 3-37 suggests other ways to lock hatches.

The forward hatch also should be lockable from inside and out, and it is smart to give some thought to having the hatch open either forward or aft (Figure 9-17). A rubber gasket around the perimeter of the hatch and a lever-action lock increases its watertightness. Additionally, a locking mechanism such as a hasp through-bolted to the deck on the outside gives extra strength against boarding waves.

Hatch frames are made of plastic (no good), extruded aluminum (most common), extruded stainless steel (heavy), and cast aluminum (best). Lenses usually are some sort of shatterproof polycarbonate or acrylic. Of course, they must be strong enough to step on and tolerate a dropped winch handle or spinnaker pole. On many older boats, the hatches are crazed, warped, or leaking and, therefore, candidates for replacement. The trick is to find one that fits the original opening.

And they must fit flush to the deck and be bedded properly with the recommended sealant. Major makers include Lewmar (www.lewmar.com), Atkins & Hoyle (www.atkinshoyle.com), Bomar (www.pompanette.com/bomar), and the French company Goïot (www.plastimousa.com/goiot.htm).

Traditional skylights over the saloon are functional, and they look good on the right kinds of boats. However, they usually leak. If you must have one, construct it strongly enough so the full weight of a man can fall on it without breaking. This means using a shatterproof material such as Lexan and bolting brass rods or wood stringers over it. For more on light and ventilation, see Chapter 14.

## CLEATS

The location of deck hardware is easy to take for granted when you buy a boat, but when adding, say, a cleat, it's surprising how perplexing the many considerations can be. Cleats should be angled about 15 to 25° to the lead of the halyard, sheet, or dockline in order to distribute the load on the bolts holding the cleat to the deck, and to make cleating and uncleating the line easier (Figure 9-18). Most cleats are much too small for the size and number of lines the cruising sailor will want to use them for. Naval architect Ian Nicolson says that cleats on most boats can be enlarged 40%.

Breast cleats mounted on deck amidships are seldom seen on stock boats, but they are of im-

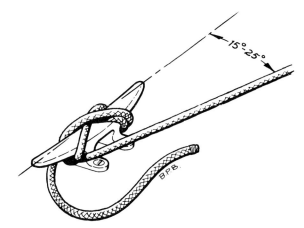

**FIGURE 9-18.** Cleats should be angled at about 15 to 25° from the lead of the line for strength and ease of operation. For every ⅛ inch (3 mm) of line diameter, add 1 inch (25 mm) to the length of the cleat horns.

**FIGURE 9-19.** The breast cleat on this Krogen 38 is too small and is obscured behind the shrouds.

mense help when rafting to another vessel, for furnishing a place to cleat off a fender or spring line at the dock, or for attaching the rode of an anchor used to keep the boat off the dock. Select the largest cleat feasible for the location, and mount it clear of stanchions and shrouds. The cleat in Figure 9-19 is undersized and hidden behind the shrouds. This boat spent a winter next to me in Newport, and when I asked the owner if I could tie a breast line to it, he said no. He'd let someone do that the previous year, and the cleat was nearly pulled from the deck.

In addition to large cleats in the bow for anchoring and mooring, there should be large cleats on each quarter. Four-bolt cleats are stronger than two-bolt cleats. Be sure to buy good quality—you don't ever want to see snapped horns on your own boat (shame!).

This brings to mind again the business of using large through-bolts and backing plates of plywood, aluminum, or ½-inch (12 mm) fiberglass. There is no excuse for having a flimsy piece of deck gear, because no matter how light the use you intend for it, sooner or later someone will inadvertently test it for you.

A note on belaying lines: Many persons seem to overdo it. Perhaps they believe the additional wraps and hitches lessen the chances of the line coming loose. In fact, one wrap around the base, followed by one figure eight, with the last part tucked under, is as secure as it's going to get. Tying a Gordian knot on every cleat only increases the time required to uncleat the line. And nearly every line on a boat should be capable of being removed *instantly*.

## MAST PULPITS

On larger boats, pulpits to port and starboard of the mast provide a sense of safety and sure footing when working at the mast base in rolly seas. They often look a bit weak to me, as the stanchion bases are often more or less in a straight line, and they are tall with no diagonal bracing.

The advantage of mast pulpits is that you can lean against them when working on the leeward side of the boat, and if to windward and the boat rocks the other way, you have a brace to support yourself. But on smaller boats, say under 40 feet (12.2 m), there usually isn't sufficient deck space to justify their expense and labor.

If you do decide to install mast pulpits, place them far enough away from the mast so you can still crouch down inside them. There are times when we all want to get down on our knees because the next wave looks like it's breaking at the spreaders.

An alternative is to through-bolt foot chocks at strategic spots around the mast to give better footing. A wedge-shaped length of teak cut 2 inches (50 mm) high will do the job.

## PROPANE TANKS

Propane is one of several fuels (diesel, kerosene, alcohol, and compressed natural gas are others) you might select for the galley stove/oven, cabin heater, and possibly water heater. Chapter 12 discusses the pros and cons of each fuel. But for the moment, assuming you have propane, you must also determine where on deck to locate the bottles. Because propane is heavier than air and can collect in the bilge if spilled, cylinders must be located in an area isolated from the cabin—on deck or in a vented, vapor-tight locker.

Some newer boats have rather ingenious hiding places for tanks built in and around the cockpit or sunk into the deck. The common characteristic of these installations is that each molded compartment has an overboard drain to rid the area of water and any leaked gas. With a vent on top, the danger of explosion at the bottle is almost nil.

### *Locating the Locker*

On boats without production propane storage, there are several options that permit a vented, drained locker. The first decision is whether the locker can best be mounted above deck or below. If above, a place on deck must be found where the locker will neither obstruct anyone nor foul lines. As Larry Pardey did on *Taleisin*, I built a deck box on my Pearson Vanguard just forward of the cabin, in front of the forward hatch. There is an overboard drain drilled into the side of the box. The propane lines are led through a hole in the deck (you can buy commercial stuffing boxes for this purpose) under the box, which has been caulked well with bedding compound. They are led aft to the galley and supported under the side decks. The box makes a nice spot to sit while motoring in mild weather. But even though it is through-bolted to the deck, it might not hold together under a large boarding wave. Of course, losing the tanks isn't really a matter of survival.

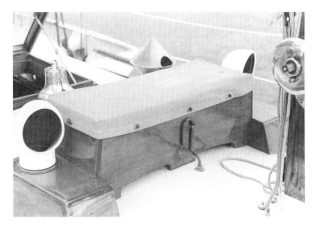

FIGURE 9-21. This handsome deck box has a canvas cover, and in addition to providing stowage for the LPG tank (viewed from the opposite side), it also makes a comfortable seat. (*Practical Sailor* photos)

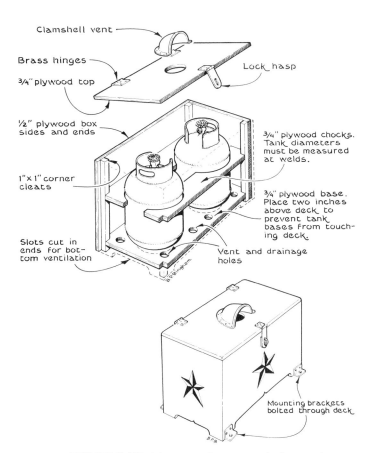

FIGURE 9-20. A homemade propane locker can be built of plywood, with 1-inch-square (25 mm²) cleats and retaining boards cut to the shape of the tanks to hold them in place.

Some things you just live with and hope for the best.

The deck box for the tank should be strong enough to jump on and built of plywood, plywood reinforced with fiberglass at the seams, or hardwood. The tanks should be secured inside the box with U-bolts and straps or wood framing (Figures 9-20 and 9-21). They should never be placed in direct sunlight. Even inside deck boxes, the temperature should be watched because heat causes the gas to expand, possibly enough to blow the relief valve. Install vents.

Some experts question the safety of horizontal tanks, thinking that the liquid gas might slop into the J-shaped pickup tube inside, accumulate at the regulator, and eventually bypass it into the boat. I've sailed many miles with horizontal tanks without a problem. This is not to say I couldn't one day blow up the boat, only that I

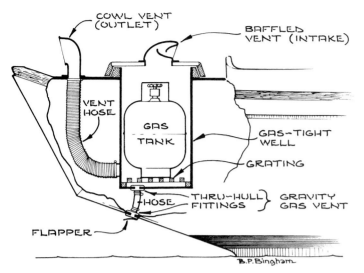

**FIGURE 9-22.** A portion of the lazarette can be glassed off for propane tank storage. No gas should be able to escape into the cabin, and the locker should be fitted with an overboard vent drain.

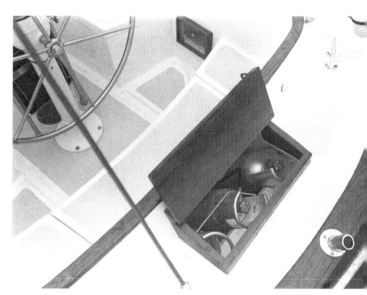

**FIGURE 9-24.** Otherwise wasted space under the afterdeck was accessed for LPG tank stowage and covered with an inconspicuous teak box top. The tanks are sealed from the boat's interior and fitted with an overboard discharge. (*Practical Sailor* photo)

can't imagine testing this type of tank any more stringently.

Another method is to partition off part of a cockpit locker with plywood and fiberglass, mount the tanks inside, and drill a hole overboard above the waterline (Figure 9-22; see also Figure 11-11.)

Seaward Products (www.seawardproducts. com) manufactures tank lockers for #5 and #10 cylinders (Figure 9-23), which are suitable for mounting in, say, a seat locker or lazarette, thereby saving fabrication time in plywood and glass. Despite having lids, they still require overboard drains.

Figure 9-24 shows several LPG tanks stashed in a lazarette very near the stern. CNG tanks do not require overboard discharge but are not very popular for a variety of reasons (discussed in Chapter 11).

**FIGURE 9-23.** Seaward Products makes molded propane tank lockers that can be adapted to many locations. (Seaward Products)

## WATER FILLS AND RAIN CATCHMENTS

There is no little disagreement amongst sailors as to the best location for water fills. On many boats, the cap is situated on a side deck, forward or aft. A deck plate key or two-pronged spanner wrench opens the cap and a tube or hose channels water into the tank. One objection to this practice is the possibility of salt water seeping through the cap and fouling the fresh water in the tank. An easy preventive is pressing duct tape over the fill when heading offshore. Applying Teflon or water pump grease to the cap threads also helps. Some people like to fill tanks directly from below. The topside water-fill advocates object to the inevitable wetting of bunks and the rest of the cabin when a hose is taken below.

If adding a tank, you can easily purchase chromed bronze deck fill fittings from companies like Perko (www.perko.com), from catalogs, and from your local chandler. Most fittings accept 1½-inch (38 mm) hose.

One reason to locate the deck fill at the gunwale is that it can be opened during a rainstorm to top off the tanks. To maximize the benefit, find the lowest point on deck. To calculate the surface

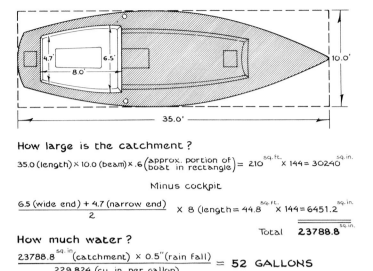

How large is the catchment?

35.0 (length) × 10.0 (beam) × .6 $\left(\substack{\text{approx. portion of}\\\text{boat in rectangle}}\right)$ = 210 sq. ft. × 144 = 30240 sq. in.

Minus cockpit

$\dfrac{6.5 \,(\text{wide end}) + 4.7 \,(\text{narrow end})}{2}$ × 8 (length = 44.8 sq. ft. × 144 = 6451.2 sq. in.

Total  **23788.8** sq. in.

How much water?

$\dfrac{23788.8 \text{ sq. in.} (\text{catchment}) \times 0.5''(\text{rain fall})}{229.824 \text{ (cu. in. per gallon)}}$ = **52 GALLONS**

**FIGURE 9-25.** The deck can be used as a rainwater catchment, emptying directly into a water tank fill pipe. Let the rain wash off dirt before opening the cap.

of the deck area required to yield a given amount of water in the tank, let's assume the deck is crowned along the boat's centerline of the boat. We already know that 231 cubic inches (3,785 cm³) equals 1 gallon (3.8 L) of water.

From the calculations (Figure 9-25), ½ inch (12 mm) of rain will yield 52 gallons (197 L) of water. This can be improved by increasing the surface area of the catchment area. Awnings that funnel water into a pipe and thence to a deck fill are another method (Figure 9-26).

Whenever filling tanks in this manner, wait for the rain to clean off the deck or canvas for a few minutes before opening the deck fill cap. A filter in the line will remove residual dirt and other contaminants.

On the Vanguard, I installed a Vetus (www .vetus.com) flexible water tank under the port quarter berth, and fed it by means of a hose and deck fill located at the low point of the deck. When it began to rain, I plugged the clearing port in the toe rail, made a dam behind the deck fill with a towel, opened the fill plate, and let 'er rip. Though this tank was designated only for the shower, it would have been easy to install a Y-valve in the line from the tank to the shower and fill the main tank, too. Thanks to this rain catchment system, the number of shoreside water fill-ups was significantly reduced, and considering that in many places, the Caribbean included, you have to pay for water, rain catchment is more than a convenience—it saves money, too.

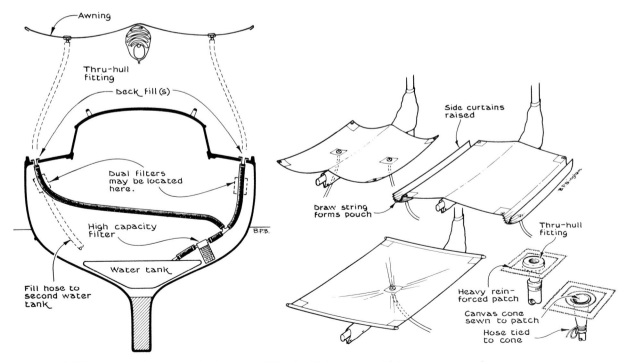

**FIGURE 9-26.** Awnings slung over the boom and fitted with hoses are viable rainwater catchments.

# DECK DRAINS

The ability of a deck to clear itself of water—from rain or sea—is largely a function of its design. Like a lot of boats, the Triton has a dead spot on either side of the deck just forward of the transom, which curves slightly upward. The gelcoat here gets stains from stagnant water, and the only easy remedy is constant sponging and applying rubbing compound or a polish such as Star-Brite. A more difficult remedy would be to build up the area so water runs off to a scupper or deck drain.

Because the Triton has a fiberglass toe rail, it is not possible to drill a hole through it to let the water run off. Were the toe rail teak, it would be a simple matter to make an overboard drain. If the deck is poorly designed; the trim of the boat changes from the designed waterline; or the coamings, toe rails, or other features impede the drainage of water on deck, first see if there is a way to route the water directly overboard. If not, it's fairly easy to install a scupper with hose led to the cockpit scupper hose via a Y-fitting or to any other through-hull fitting in the hull. Granted, this is a lot of work for a minor irritation, but some may find it worthwhile, especially those who can't stand things out of order.

# MAKING A SEA HOOD

For any kind of cruising, a sea hood (also called a storm hood or hatch turtle) mounted over the forward end of the main sliding hatch is essential. When water washes over the deck, as at some time it surely must, the vertical opening between the deck and the hatch allows it to stream inside the cabin. A sea hood provides the forward protection while the tracks of the hatch do their best to protect the flanks. Closing the hatch and inserting weather boards, with the possible addition of a Lexan storm shutter as mentioned earlier in this chapter, protects the top and aft sides. A sea hood also provides a place to snap on a cockpit dodger. Without it, the dodger must be designed with the complication of a sliding hatch in mind (e.g., one solution is to construct a low bridge over the sliding hatch, similar to a traveler bridge, and snap the dodger to it).

A satisfactory sea hood can be fabricated out of solid hardwood or out of plywood with fiberglass and/or a hardwood such as teak covering it. The weakness of this construction is that flat surfaces are not as strong as rounded ones. After all,

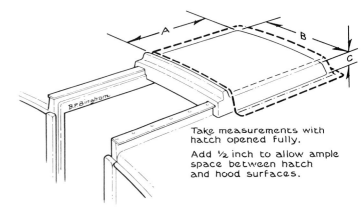

**FIGURE 9-27.** Measure the size of your sea hood carefully, making certain it will be high enough to let the hatch slide underneath and that the flanges won't interfere with other fittings.

you'll want to be able to stand on it to furl the mainsail. Molding a crowned fiberglass sea hood in a female mold makes much sense.

To make your own, take approximate measurements of the area to be covered. Figure 9-27 will help.

Purchase some 1- by 4-inch (25 mm by 102 mm) furring strips, a piece of Masonite, and some screws. To take more precise measurements, mock up a cardboard sea hood over your hatch. Be sure the hatch can be pushed all the way open without hitting the sea hood. Similarly, don't extend the sea hood too far over the hatch opening, which would obstruct access below.

Transfer the curve of the deck by placing a 1- by 6-inch (25 mm by 152 mm) board horizontally on deck, just forward of the hatch. Use a compass (Figure 9-28) to follow the deck and

**FIGURE 9-28.** To transfer the deck to the mold frame, follow the deck line with a compass, scribing a mark on the board as you go.

scribe a line on the board. After this board has been sawn, it becomes the forward end of the mold. The back of the hood will be open to make room for the hatch, but it will be necessary to cut a second board to fit the back of the mold to hold it together during lamination and to keep the Masonite curve fair.

Build in a flange on the forward end and sides of the mold so that you can lay the fiberglass cloth over it (Figure 9-29). Leave the edges ragged and trim them later. This flange will be the place where the sea hood is later through-bolted to the deck. Nail the Masonite over the four-sided frame (Figure 9-30).

After you have tested the mold to be sure it fits the deck, take it into the garage or some sheltered area where you can work with fiberglass. If working inside the boat, be sure it is well ventilated, as polyester resin gives off harmful styrene fumes. More expensive epoxy resins do not.

Because fiberglass cloth and mat do not bend well to sharp corners, you will need to radius the corners with fillets of epoxy putty or resin mixed with microballoons or Cab-O-Sil (www.cabosil .com) (Figure 9-31).

FIGURE 9-30. Lay Masonite over the top of the frame and nail it down. Note the curve in the end pieces and the radiused flanges.

Alcan Baltek Corporation (www.baltek.com) in Northvale, New Jersey, maker of Contourkore end-grain balsa, gave me the following lamination schedule:

20-mil-thick gelcoat
$1\frac{1}{2}$-ounce mat
6- to 7-ounce cloth
$1\frac{1}{2}$-ounce mat
$\frac{1}{2}$-inch Contourkore end-grain balsa
$1\frac{1}{2}$-ounce mat
6- to 7-ounce cloth
$1\frac{1}{2}$-ounce mat
$1\frac{1}{2}$-ounce mat

FIGURE 9-29. The corner of the mold shows the $\frac{1}{4}$-inch (6 mm) furring strip nailed to the mold frame side. The corner has been radiused so that the cloth, which will form the flange, will lie smoothly and not bunch up.

FIGURE 9-31. Fillets must be made with putty where the side pieces meet the Masonite. The gentle curves created by the fillets permit better conformance by the fiberglass cloth.

An optional layer of 6- to 7-ounce cloth on the outside will leave a smoother finished surface than mat. Flange thickness is about ⅜ inch (10 mm), sufficient for bearing loads and for bolting through to the deck. Figures 9-32 through 9-35 show how the precut and darted rolls of mat, cloth, and balsa were glassed in. Ten-ounce cloth was used in place of 6-ounce, and the gelcoat dispensed with in favor of a simple paint job on completion. Or, I could have brushed on the gelcoat after pulling the hood from the mold, rather than brushing it on inside the mold before the mat and cloth were laid in.

Cover the entire inside of the mold with wax paper or a parting agent. Then, with cheap disposable brushes, latex gloves, and acetone solvent standing by, wet out the mold with resin. Then lay in a precut piece of mat and wet it out with the brush. Saturate the strands of fiberglass so that no air bubbles exist. It's not as hard as it sounds. For small projects like a sea hood, a paint brush is suitable. Avoid too much brushing as the mat will begin to fall apart.

Polyester resin, like other two-part systems, requires a catalyst to make the resin cure. The speed with which curing occurs varies with temperature

**FIGURE 9-32.** Wax paper or a standard parting agent must be used to cover the mold before laying in the mat and cloth. This prevents the fiberglass from bonding to the mold.

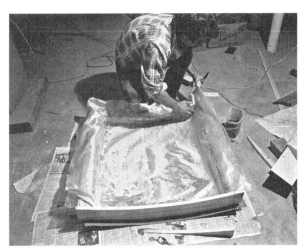

**FIGURE 9-34.** After the mat is wetted out, a layer of 10-ounce cloth is pushed into place and also wetted out.

**FIGURE 9-33.** Here, the first layer of 1½-ounce mat has been precut and laid into the mold. Polyester resin is used to saturate the mat, and a cheap brush used to wet it out. Note the slits and darts in the far end to prevent bunching on the curve.

**FIGURE 9-35.** With three layers of mat and cloth in the mold, ½-inch (12 mm) Contourkore end-grain balsa is cut and placed in the mold.

and with the amount of catalyst used. If you haven't worked with it before, mix up a small amount in a clean container according to the ratios specified on the side of the can and let sit. Observe how long it takes to go off. Poke it with a stick at various stages to see how it is hardening. When applying the resin to the mold, you'll want sufficient time to lay in and wet out mat and cloth before it hardens. The resin shouldn't harden in less than 35 to 40 minutes; if it does, put less catalyst in the next time. There's nothing wrong with a slow cure; in fact, up to a point, the longer the cure, the stronger it will be. Sometimes it takes overnight, and you go to bed worrying that not enough catalyst was used. But by morning, the resin is invariably rock hard.

While the first layer is still wet, lay in a precut piece of cloth and wet that out, too, followed by another piece of mat. You can now fit in the core material. It will probably be necessary to cut some pieces so that the core extends nearly to the edge of the mold, about a ¼ to ½ inch (6 mm to 12 mm).

I discovered after I had pushed the balsa in place that the mat and cloth at the sides were sagging, and that it would have been better if I had designed an outward angle greater than 90°. To hold the layers of mat and cloth flush against the frame mold, I placed some strips of wax paper against it, then a board propped up by bricks (Figure 9-36). This worked satisfactorily.

When the resin kicked, I followed with the last four layers of mat and cloth, and let it cure for several days. Then I pried the sea hood from the mold, cut the rough edges with a saber saw and

FIGURE 9-37. After the sea hood was popped from the mold, surface indentations were filled with a fairing compound, then sanded.

ground them down with a belt sander. A file and sanding block finished it off.

I discovered several voids and depressions in the surface of my sea hood, primarily because the wax paper bunched up in the corners. Had I to do it over, I would use a regular parting agent or try paste wax. To fair out the surfaces, trowel on a fairing compound with a putty knife or plastic spreader; once cured, give it a good sanding (Figure 9-37). For paint, a two-part polyurethane is the most glossy and durable, though the one-part paints are much easier to use. Two coats give a nice luster. See Chapter 15 for help on painting.

Now, place the sea hood in position on deck and drill holes through the sea hood and deck. Drill one at a time, inserting a round head stainless steel bolt in the last hole before drilling the next. This will insure all bolts fitting in the end. Space bolts about 6 inches (150 mm) apart.

If there is a core in the cabin top (coachroof), coat the insides of the holes with epoxy glue or resin (see the Bedding Deck Fittings sidebar, page 189). Mix up a batch, plug the bottom with tape, and pour into the hole. After a minute, remove the tape and catch the excess resin. This coating will seal off the grain of the core and prevent moisture from entering should the bedding compound later come loose and permit deck water to enter the hole. A rotten deck core is almost a complete write-off—very expensive to fix and disturbing to live with.

Use polysulfide or another good bedding compound on the threads of each bolt, under the

FIGURE 9-36. When the mat and cloth began sagging along the sides, I cut strips of wax paper and placed them between the wet resin and a board supported by bricks—it worked.

**FIGURE 9-38.** The sea hood was painted and through-bolted to the Triton's deck. A bedding compound was used to seal it.

washer, and under the head. Run the bolts through and have someone below put on a washer and nut. If you carefully measure the length of bolts needed, hexagonal acorn nuts can be used that will look better than regular nuts. Alternatively, you can sometimes buy plastic or vinyl finishing caps that fit over the nuts to conceal them and reduce the chance of injury if someone hits his or her head on the nut.

It also would be a good idea to bed the entire perimeter of the sea hood before placing it onto the deck for the last time. After all, the whole idea is to keep water out, and it is doubtful that a completely watertight seal can be had from just mating two bare surfaces of fiberglass. Alternatively, you could lay in lengths of weather stripping.

A piece of teak stripping screwed or bolted to the forward edge of the sea hood will lend an attractive look, help conceal the raw edge of fiberglass, and also function as a splash board. If you've done the job right, you should be able to stand on top of the sea hood and jump up and down without causing it to crack (Figure 9-38).

## COCKPITS

Along with the berths, the cockpit is the most-used locale on a sailboat. Here the boat is steered, and in it happens most of the navigation, lounging, and the many other daily activities that make up life on board a cruising boat.

It follows that the cockpit area design is of preeminent importance. What are the requirements of a good cockpit? Let's list some:

- Comfortable seating, level or heeled
- Small volume, to minimize amount of water that could fill it
- Large scuppers
- Good visibility over the cabin
- Surfaces to brace feet when heeled
- Easy to handle sheets and lines
- Convenient access to lockers and/or lazarettes
- Convenient helm
- Bridge deck or high companionway sill
- Long enough to lie down in
- Protection from wind and water

The list could go on ad infinitum. The basic theme, as repeated over and over in this book, is comfort, safety, and utility. The stipulation of comfort is more than hedonism. An exhausted crew is a crew capable of placing the entire vessel in danger; a rested crew is stronger and makes better decisions.

Utility concerns the ability to efficiently carry out the multifarious functions necessary to keeping the boat going each day. The ease with which you can handle lines, find the jerrican in the cockpit locker, toss a life ring to someone overboard, trim the mainsheet, or lie down for a snooze are all factors to consider when selecting a boat. Unfortunately, many of these characteristics are not known until after you've sailed a number of miles. A sea trial helps, but you can't possibly answer all the questions on a short run.

### Seating

Seating comfort depends to an extent on your individual body and how it fits the boat (Figure 9-39). The seats are more than likely molded into the deck, and changing them is a drastic measure. But if you're unusually short or tall, chances are other boats will present the same problem as yacht designers use fairly standard ergonomic data based on averages—15-inch (38 cm) seat width, 18-inch (46 cm) seat height, and so forth.

Backrests can be moved inboard more easily than outboard. False backrests can be fashioned from wood (or plywood covered with fiberglass) to shorten the distance between the back and the boat's centerline. If the distance to the nearest foot brace is too long (Figure 9-40), new backrests might be considered. Of course, the width of the seat also will be shortened, unless the seat is

179

**FIGURE 9-39.** Comfortable seating depends on the match between an individual's body and the distance between backrests and foot supports. Poor seating causes unnecessary fatigue, the enemy of good judgment at sea.

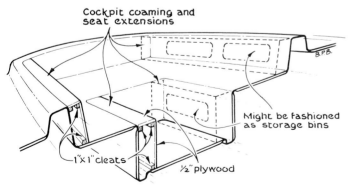

**FIGURE 9-40.** Here's one way to shorten the distance between the backrests and footrests. Screw cleats to the seat and backrest; enclose the area with ½-inch (12 mm) plywood and cover with several layers of fiberglass mat and cloth. Sand and paint. Side cutouts could make storage room for winch handles, line, and the like.

extended over the footwell. Then, space for legs and feet is a consideration. People usually are most comfortable and least tired if their legs can extend straight to the footrest so that leg muscles don't need to be flexed. Sitting for long periods with knees bent and tensioned is very tiring.

The simplest option may be the use of cushions to adjust dimensions, but unless secured to the seat or backrest with something like hook-and-loop tape (Velcro), they tend to fall off when the boat heels, and you stand up.

## Cockpit Size

Dealing with too large a cockpit is more serious a problem than the relative discomfort of an ill-designed cockpit. A boat at sea can and more than likely will be pooped sooner or later. We were pooped on the Triton one summer while sailing in Green Bay. Thirty-knot winds were whipping up steep, breaking 6- to 8-foot (1.8 m to 2.4 m) seas in the shallow bay. As the wind increased, we furled the main on a roller boom up to the numbers. Suddenly, a wave larger than the rest reared up and broke over the cockpit. The next instant we were sitting up to our chests in water. As the boat rolled, half the water rushed overboard. Now the water was only filling the footwell and we were no longer quite so anxious. The scuppers required several minutes to drain the remaining water. (As a footnote, Carl Alberg, designer of the Triton, calculated that a flooded cockpit would lower the stern just 6 inches/152 mm.)

This sort of spine-tingling soaking can happen most anytime when seas are steep. Boats with large footwells, no bridge deck, or a low companionway sill invite disaster. A footwell that measures 5 feet long by 2½ feet wide by 2 feet deep (1.5 m by 0.76 m by 0.6 m) can hold 25 cubic feet (0.7 m³) of water. Since each cubic foot weighs about 60 pounds/27 kg (64 pounds/29 kg for salt water), the footwell can hold 1,500 pounds (680 kg) of water. Add to this the amount of water that could be held between coamings above the seats, and the figures are even more staggering.

The Offshore Racing Council limits cockpit volume to 6% LOA times maximum beam times freeboard aft. For example, a 32-foot (9.8 m) boat with 9½-foot (2.9 m) beam and 3-foot (0.9 m) freeboard aft—32 by 0.06 by 9.5 by 3—is limited by this rule to a 54.72 cubic foot (1.5 m³) cockpit. Also, the cockpit floor under these rules must be 0.02 × LWL above the waterline.

Hal and Margaret Roth, blue-water sailors who have published several books on how to outfit cruising boats, modified their Spencer 35, *Whisper*, by radically extending the cabin several feet aft. Hal did this not to increase living space below, but to minimize cockpit size.

From one point of view, a cockpit can never be too small. Naval architect and boatbuilder Tom Colvin told me once he has built just three boats with cockpits. He said he simply doesn't believe in them for offshore sailing. But comfort is its own dictum. If you're going to spend 50% of your time in the cockpit, it really should have a comfortable length and width—at least enough to lie down in.

Crouching or sitting cross-legged on a flat surface is, however, tiring, so some thought should be given to seating of an adequate height, and a comfortable amount of space for the feet. Deck boxes, coamings, and raised helmsman's seats are a few possibilities.

## Frolic's Shallow Footwell

Aside from having no footwell at all (very safe, but no place to stand up in without hitting your head on the boom), the best arrangement is the shallowest. In the late 1970s Danny Greene fabricated a cockpit that is as safe as any I've seen. After several years sailing his Mystic 10-3 to the Caribbean from Newport each fall, and getting pooped off Bermuda one time, he decided that even a conventionally sized footwell was too large. He cut off the footwell from below and fiberglassed in a new floor only 4 inches (102 mm) below the seats. He used plywood and fiberglass mat with polyester resin. Figures 9-41 to 9-44 illustrate the various permutations of his cockpit arrangement. The floor grating can be mounted flush for sleeping, inverted to provide a foot brace, and elevated for dining—a safe and functional arrangement, though it takes getting used to.

## Shortening the Cockpit

Excessively large footwells can be made smaller in several ways. Depending on the tiller or wheel location, part of the footwell can be boxed off either permanently or temporarily during offshore passages (Figure 9-45). The area could also be used for storage, accessible from the cockpit or down below.

Plywood fiberglassed to the sides of the footwell also can work well. Don't forget to sand

**FIGURE 9-41.** *Frolic*'s cockpit was modified for safety offshore. The footwell was cut off from underneath with a saber saw, and a new floor glassed in just several inches deep. Seat lockers also were glassed shut.

**FIGURE 9-42.** A teak-planked grating was made to fit the footwell. In this configuration, it is flush with the seats—an excellent idea for sleeping outside in the tropics.

**FIGURE 9-43.** With the grating upside down, the longitudinal supports provide footrests when heeling.

181

**FIGURE 9-44.** With a box or some other flat object underneath, the grating elevates for use as a dining table.

the gelcoat off the footwell surfaces and to wash with a solvent like acetone before laying in glass. When new, gelcoat contains mold release agents that will prevent good adhesion unless removed. And old gelcoat, being slightly porous, holds dirt and oil that also prevents adhesion.

On *Iskra*, Frank Mulville shortened the cockpit by dropping in a bottomless wood box that was securely fastened to the footwell sides. A canvas was stretched taut over the rest in bad weather. While this might not have withstood a real blast, it would slow down and perhaps deflect some incoming water over the side.

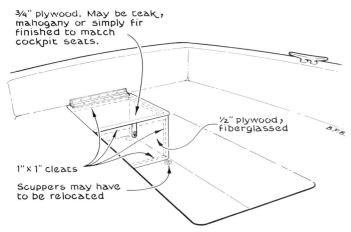

3/4" plywood. May be teak, mahogany or simply fir finished to match cockpit seats.

1/2" plywood, fiberglassed

1" x 1" cleats

Scuppers may have to be relocated

Box may be located at either end of cockpit.

**FIGURE 9-45.** To minimize the volume of the footwell, one end can be closed off with plywoood and fiberglass. A watertight, lockable lid gives access to new storage. Scuppers might need to be relocated.

## Seat Lockers

Seat lockers should have deep, molded gutters to allow water to run off. They should be deep enough so they won't overflow into the locker when a wave breaks. If the gutters aren't deep enough, glue a rubber gasket around the inside perimeter of the lid and install a lever-action lock that compresses the gasket lid tightly. Other solutions are to run scupper hoses from the gutters into the cockpit or screw a thin wood or Plexiglas strip over the crack between the lid and seat (don't screw to both or you won't be able to open it!). Also arrange a method of locking the lid, using locks and hasps or other secure locking mechanism. After once finding himself locked inside a seat locker, Bill Seifert cautions that the hasp should be mounted on the bottom and hinged upward. What happened to Bill was this: While working in the seat locker on some piece of equipment, he inadvertently knocked out the stick propping up the lid. The lid slammed shut and the hasp, mounted on the lid hinged downward, locked itself over the staple. It took him awhile, but Bill managed to extricate himself by using his Leatherman utility tool to unscrew the nuts from the hasp.

A drastic measure is to seal the lid off altogether and gain access to the locker area from below. This means going below to fetch fenders and lines and, admittedly, might be impractical on some boats. But there is security in knowing there are no openings on deck except for the hatches and vents.

Not all lockers have to be deep. You could make one only about 6 inches (152 mm) deep, so even if it did fill with water, there would be no great danger. In it you could store winch handles, bilge pump handles, small bits of line, the ship's horn, sail ties, and all those other odds and ends that are needed on deck, sometimes at a moment's notice.

## Blower Openings

The U.S. Coast Guard requires bilge blowers for gas engines. On my old Triton, the blower was mounted on the footwell wall. If the cockpit filled with water, it ran through this hole into the locker and then into the bilge. With the new diesel installed, the blower was no longer required (because diesel fumes are not explosive); I removed it and sealed the hole—one less weak link to worry about!

The blower hose led to a vent on the afterdeck where air from the bilge was expelled. Next to it was another vent to introduce air into the bilge, also required by the U.S. Coast Guard. Although the blower was no longer required, the vents were retained to remove unpleasant fumes and provide the engine with air. In heavy weather, these cowls should be removed and deck plates screwed in.

### Engine Controls

Engine controls mounted in the footwell wall, if not recessed or protected by a bar, are susceptible to damage from an errant foot or dropped winch handle. I've had the ignition key broken off inside the lock in this way.

Another method of protecting the engine instruments is a Plexiglas cover that is hinged above the panel. To start the engine or kill it, simply lift the plate up, and lower it when done.

### Compass Location

Placing the compass in a convenient location so that it can be read from anyplace in the cockpit shouldn't pose any significant problem. On the centerline is preferable, but sometimes this is too much in the way and makes it vulnerable to breakage. With good, visible lubber lines, the compass can be mounted on the aft side of the cabin, either to port or starboard of the companionway hatch, or one on both sides if need be. With pedestal wheel steerers, of course, the problem is licked by placing the compass on top of the pedestal. On some older wood boats with tiller steering, a binnacle was mounted in the middle of the cockpit just to place the compass on centerline and in an easily viewed location. What's important is that the compass lubberline be parallel to the ship's keel, and free from the magnetic influence of metal objects.

## LIFE RAFTS, MAN-OVERBOARD POLES, AND OTHER SAFETY EQUIPMENT

Life rafts are expensive—thousands of dollars for a good one. Folks who cannot afford them sometimes rely on their hard or inflatable dinghy to serve this hopefully-never-needed function.

Life rafts are difficult to deploy in a gale with steep, breaking waves. If possible, a life raft canister should be mounted somewhere on deck or near the cockpit where it can be opened, inflated, and launched successfully.

An ideal spot is in the cockpit footwell, covered by a fabricated enclosure that not only contains the life raft but reduces the volume of the footwell at the same time.

On deck forward or on the afterdeck are two other possible sites, but here they are as vulnerable as the deck boxes discussed earlier in this chapter. Some new boats are built with cavities molded into the cockpit specifically to house the life raft. This could be accomplished on an older boat, perhaps using a seat locker in the same manner as was described for a propane bottle locker.

Man-overboard poles are generally mounted in a tube fixed to the stern pulpit, sometimes with the tip run through a piece of PVC tube lashed to the backstay. Life rings, the patented Lifesling (www.thesailingfoundation.org/lifesling.htm; Figure 9-46), MOM (www.switlik.com/stg; Figure 9-47), and horseshoes can be easily mounted in the special holders sold by manufacturers, which are clamped to stanchions or the stern pulpit. There is a degree of comfort in storing life jackets somewhere near the cockpit, such as in a seat

**FIGURE 9-46.** The nonprofit Sailing Foundation of Seattle developed and patented the Lifesling overboard rescue system. It provides 20 pounds of flotation, 150 feet of floating line, and a means of assisting the victim back aboard with a halyard and winch. (*Practical Sailor* photo)

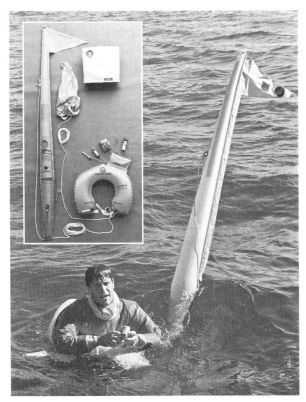

FIGURE 9-47. The MOM (man-overboard module) from Survival Technologies is designed to help the victim draw attention to his position with whistles and lights, and keep him afloat until help arrives. Unlike the Lifesling, it is tossed with the understanding that the boat may take some time to drop sails and return. (*Practical Sailor* photo)

locker, but there's no real reason why they can't be stored just as safely down below in a readily accessible place. Flares should be kept dry and are best stored in airtight pouches in a well-ventilated locker in the cabin. Pelican dry boxes (www.pelican.com) are excellent. Except for the life raft, most safety and emergency equipment can be brought on board with little construction of special housings or holders. Finding the best storage places is more a matter of studying the peculiarities of your boat than unraveling some arcane secret that only ancient mariners know.

## LIGHTS

U.S. Coast Guard requirements specify certain navigational lights for certain size boats. According to the most recent amendments to the International Regulations for Prevention of Collisions at Sea (72 COLREGS), sailing vessels under 20 meters (65 feet) are required to carry red and green sidelights and a white stern light. Under 12 meters

(39 feet), these lights may be combined in a single lantern carried at the top of the mast, popularly known as the masthead tricolor. Under power, even with sails raised, the tricolor is not legal, and the regular sidelights and stern light must be shown along with a white bow (mast) light.

Not only is it important that your boat conform to the Rules, but you also should be able to recognize the various light patterns of ships, so you know what you're dealing with (maybe a tug and tow) and in what direction it's heading. *Chapman* is but one source of required lights.

Almost all cruising sailboats are sold with this lighting system already installed. The ship's 12-volt battery bank is the power source. Oil lamps may be carried as backups. Sidelight lamps can be fastened to boards on the shrouds and the stern lamp carried on the stern rail.

The lamps should be removable from the mounting boards for refilling and bringing below in rough weather. Properly sealed electric lights are easier to deal with and certainly less expensive.

## BOOM GALLOWS

One of the most important, handiest, and sometimes most bothersome additions to the deck are boom gallows. This heavy-duty crutch for the

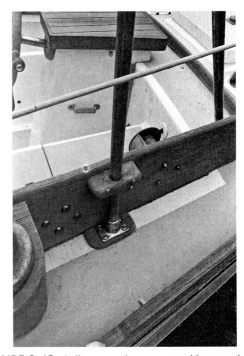

FIGURE 9-48. Gallows can be supported by stanchion pipe, fastened in stanchion bases, and supported by coaming braces.

boom can be used to lash the boom in heavy weather, thus preventing it from swinging even the slightest distance. When all hell breaks loose, you don't want to risk the boom and furled or reefed mainsail banging back and forth—the blocks and boom bails could break, or if the topping lift snaps, the whole mess could come crashing down into the cockpit.

Gallows are seldom offered as standard or even optional equipment on new boats. While custom bronze corner fittings can be purchased to join the vertical supports and gallows pipe or board for about $450, a very serviceable set of gallows can be built with hardware store materials.

Determining where and how to mount the vertical poles to the deck is the most important consideration. Figure 9-48 illustrates one approach, using stainless steel pipe and base. Height should enable someone to stand in the cockpit without hitting his head on the gallows. Of

**FIGURE 9-50.** I spotted *Timshel*, with the unusual boomkin, at the Port Townsend Wooden Boat Festival. The gallows are simple but sturdy—steel pipe supports, solid teak gallows, and three crotches with leather pads.

course, if the gallows are mounted over the cabin, this won't be a problem. The boat looks best in profile with the boom horizontal; that is, parallel with the waterline. But for the boom to swing freely above the gallows, the gooseneck should be on a track that rides up when the mainsail is hoisted. Unfortunately, on many modern boats the gooseneck is fixed—to save the builder the expense of the track I suppose.

The top member can be another length of pipe welded or joined with right-angle pipe connections to the vertical pipes. A more attractive method is to laminate several thin strips of attractive hardwood, bend it over a form, glue with epoxy resin, and clamp it fast until cured (Figure 9-49). If using stainless steel pipe, save your drill bits and have your local metalsmith drill them for you.

Most boom gallows have three stations for resting the boom, one on centerline and one each side of center (Figure 9-50). Cut these from the hardwood and cover with leather tacked in with bronze tacks or boat nails.

Boom gallows are handy places to dry out bathing suits, tie a bunch of bananas, fasten one end of a cockpit awning, or function as a hand-

**FIGURE 9-49.** Anchored in Eleuthera, Bahamas, my daughter Adriana and her namesake struck a pose that shows nicely the laminated mahogany and ash boom gallows I made. Stainless steel pipe was used for the support structure. It was secured by the coaming and stanchion bases on deck.

**FIGURE 9-51.** Arches can be more than superfluous stylish "extras"—they can be functional as well. Guy Bernardin's BOC boat *Biscuits Lu* has a welded steel arch that is home to radar, speaker, lights, and various antennas. Note the wind generators and boarding handhold on the transom. (*Practical Sailor* photo)

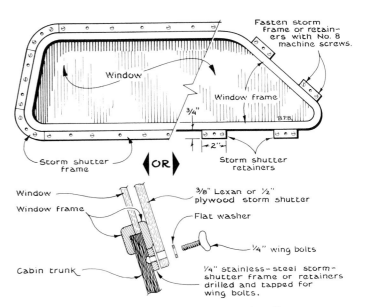

**FIGURE 9-52.** Storm shutters should be fitted to all large ports. Steel plates bolted to the cabin sides with machine screws and wing nuts make the quickest and easiest installation.

hold when leaning over the side to pee. When well made, they also contribute rugged good looks.

## ARCHES

Arches are a development of the gallows, with styling borrowed from the spoilers on race cars. First put on sexy, muscle powerboats by flamboyant Italian designers, arches are useful for mounting radomes, radio and nav instrument antennas, cockpit lights, hangers for strobes and man-overboard poles, and even stereo speakers. Some gallows today are styled as arches, or as naval architect Robert Perry likes to call them, "linguine struts." Though easy to dismiss as faddish, they can be functional additions to the deck (Figure 9-51).

## STORM SHUTTERS

Portlights are one of the most vulnerable parts of a yacht. They are the thinnest material between the inside of the boat and the sea and often the weakest. Large ports are especially dangerous, and all too common on many boats. In his classic analysis of damage to boats in *Heavy Weather Sailing*, Adlard Coles asserted that more ports are broken on the lee side by the cabin slamming against the water than those broken by waves hitting against them on the weather side. In late 1982, the 58-foot *Trashman* sank, with loss of life, primarily because storm shutters were fitted

only to the weather-side ports. In either case, storm shutters should be on hand to protect any port larger than 6 or 8 inches (152 mm to 203 mm) across.

Storm shutters can be made from many materials. Edward S. Brewer writes that ⅜- to ½-inch (10 mm to 12 mm) plywood, ⅛-inch (3 mm) aluminum, and 5/16- to ⅜-inch (8 mm to 10 mm) Lexan are suitable. Because few production boats have provisions for storm shutters, it may be necessary to machine the hardware. The shutters should overlap the port by an inch or more, and be fastened by a wing bolt screwed into a plate through-bolted to the cabin side around the circumference of the port (Figure 9-52). A 1-inch by 2-inch (25 mm by 51 mm) stainless steel plate, drilled and tapped for 5/16-inch (8 mm) machine screws will make putting up the shutters a quick and easy job when heavy weather threatens. Another way is to bolt wood channels to the cabin side and slide in a Lexan shutter held in place with retaining pins.

## BULWARKS

Sure footing at the perimeter of the deck is essential. Low, molded toe rails are better than nothing, but could be supplemented by bolting a length of 1-inch by 2-inch (25 mm by 51 mm) teak on top.

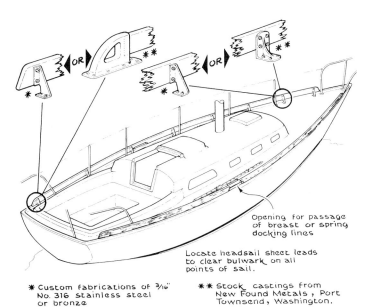

Opening for passage
of breast or spring
docking lines

Locate headsail sheet leads
to clear bulwark on all
points of sail.

\* Custom fabrications of ³⁄₁₆"
No. 316 stainless steel
or bronze

\*\* Stock castings from
New Found Metals, Port
Townsend, Washington.

**FIGURE 9-53.** Bulwarks give more security when working on deck than low toe rails. New Found Metals makes handsome end fittings of bronze for this purpose, as well as gallow corners and other items.

An even better plan is adding 6-inch-high (15 cm) bulwarks (Figure 9-53). New Found Metals of Port Townsend, Washington (www.newfound metals.com), makes handsome cast-bronze fittings for hardwood bulwark ends that accept $3^5/_{16}$-inch (84 mm) boards. Elevating the boards an inch off deck allows water to run off. If you have molded-in toe rails, installation will be complicated, unless there is a flat surface for the hardware. Here custom fabrications may work better. Also plan for hawseholes so you can still use your breast cleats. You can't begin to appreciate the sense of security good bulwarks provide until sitting on the foredeck in a gale, trying to change jibs.

## PROTECTED HELM

The standard cockpit enclosure is the canvas dodger (Figure 9-54), usually fit over a collapsible frame of stainless steel (good choice) or aluminum (not-so-good choice). Compared to a pilothouse or other rigid structure, the dodger has several advantages: it's relatively inexpensive (though you might beg to differ after pricing one); it's collapsible, so that in fine weather you can knock it down and let the breezes blow over your body; it has a minimal affect on the lines of the boat; and

**FIGURE 9-54.** This otherwise standard dodger has zip-open windows in the front and an attached sun awning extending from the aft edge.

it's removable. The disadvantages: the fabric generally requires waterproofing; the fabric fades and eventually must be replaced; and because it's collapsible, the vinyl windows must be fairly thin, making them wavy and sometimes hard to see through.

Among production cruising boats, the glass windshield (Figure 9-55) solves the visibility problem associated with acrylic dodger windows. Swedish builder Hallberg-Rassy makes regular use of this feature, now a trademark. Cruising sailor, designer, and author Steve Dashew favors a structural pilothouse in his Deerfoot and Sundeer boats (Figure 9-56). The helm is aft, outside, but the boat can be controlled by the autopilot from inside the pilothouse. In addition to instruments and 360° visibility, there are two full-length seats with cushions that can seat six or eight crew, or two sleeping. Having delivered a Sundeer 64 to

**FIGURE 9-55.** Like other models in the line, the Hallberg-Rassy 352 has a fixed windshield for superior wind protection and visibility. It also helps tension the canvas dodger more taut.

**FIGURE 9-56.** The Sundeer 64 has what might be called a hard dodger cum pilothouse; it's structural, but there's no helm inside. Two bench seats/berths and full instrumentation allow the watch to navigate and adjust course by autopilot, all out of the weather.

**FIGURE 9-57.** The Wavestopper fiberglass hardtop is an aftermarket alternative to soft dodgers. (Wavestopper)

Bermuda, I can attest that this is a great place to do watch duty.

In recent years, there has been a definite trend toward hardtop dodgers, and even more permanent structures, aided in part, I suspect, by the public's observing of the single-handed, round-the-world race boats, like the Open 60s. These skippers don't want to be out in the weather any more than necessary.

On *Viva*, we installed a fiberglass hardtop called the Wavestopper (www.wavestopper.net), invented by Dan James of Seawind Canvas in Bellingham, Washington (Figure 9-57). It mounts on a stainless steel frame. The structure is sufficiently rigid so that you can have your sailmaker or canvasmaker sew side curtains with thick polycarbonate or acrylic windows that won't wrinkle or get wavy. The Wavestopper can hold the weight of an adult—about 225 pounds (102 kg). A bonus is that you can mount stuff on top of the hardtop; we put two 50-watt solar panels up there, where they're pretty safe—unless you drop the boom on them. For a boat that doesn't come with a pilothouse or fixed windshield, the Wavestopper is, to my mind, one of the most sensible solutions. If you want to build your own, read Thomas Head's *The Hardtop Book*.

Last, if you're sailing the extreme latitudes, think about a bubble (Figure 9-58), through which you can observe your heading, check the sail trim, and look for icebergs.

**FIGURE 9-58.** In extreme latitudes, a bubble enables the crew to keep watch and observe sail trim from below.

# Bedding Deck Fittings

Using backing plates for through-deck fittings is important (Figure 9-59). Cleats, winches, stanchions, and any other item that is subject to strain should be installed with backing plates or, if the stress is more moderate, with large washers. If the holes are close together, washers may do the job just as well. Either way, the idea is to distribute the stress on the bolts over as much area as possible. This point was made abundantly clear to me one spring day when my Triton was hit by a maladroit sailor on another boat and bolts holding the bow pulpit bases to the deck were nearly ripped right through the deck—the washers simply were too small.

Liberal amounts of good-quality bedding compound must be used to prevent leaks and rot in the deck core material. Leaks are one of the easiest ways to ruin a boat, so do it right. Polysulfide compound, such as 3M 101 and Sikaflex 291 LOT, are excellent for this job, although all are adhesives as well and could make future removal difficult. Silicone products are also frequently used, though they're not as durable or adhesive as some other types.

The best bedding job will seal wood cores with epoxy dabbed onto the inside of the hole. Put masking tape over the hole from the inside, pour a small amount of epoxy into the hole from the outside, let it sit a few minutes, then go below again, remove the masking tape, and catch the epoxy in a cup. A boss ensures a tight fit. (A boss is a carved wood or formed metal plate, flat on one side to receive the cleat or winch, and curved on the other to the shape of the deck or mounting surface.) Use bedding compound under the boss, on threads, and under the heads of fasteners.

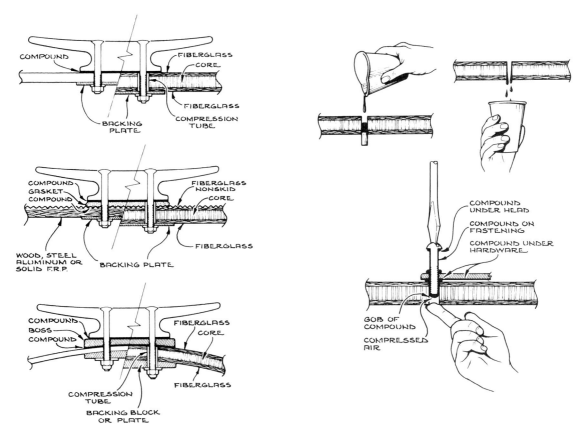

**FIGURE 9-59.** Proper installation of deck fittings includes through-bolting, backing plates, and liberal amounts of bedding compound.

# Full Deck Awning

In the tropics, decks can get real hot, and then life on deck becomes unpleasant. And, of course, heat is transferred through the deck to the cabin. Biminis help shade the cockpit, but without side curtains the sun will still shine through except when it's directly overhead. If you're planning to spend a lot of time in the tropics, especially anchored, have your canvas-maker design a full deck awning. Here's a classic Columbia 50 anchored at Eleuthera, Bahamas, all in shade (Figure 9-60).

**FIGURE 9-60.** A full deck awning.

## FURTHER READING

*Adlard Coles' Heavy Weather Sailing.* 30th anniv. ed. Peter Bruce. Camden, Maine: International Marine; London: Adlard Coles, 1999.

*Anchors: Selection and Use.* 3rd ed. rev. Robert A. Smith. [S.1.]: R.A. Smith, 1996.

*Big Book of Boat Canvas.* Karen Lipe. Camden, Maine: International Marine, 1988.

*Brightwork: The Art of Finishing Wood.* Rebecca J. Wittman. Camden, Maine: International Marine, 1990.

*Chapman Piloting: Seamanship and Small-Boat Handling.* 64th ed. Elbert S. Maloney. New York: Hearst Books, 2003.

*Cruising Under Sail.* 2nd ed. Eric Hiscock. Oxford; New York: Oxford University Press, 1978.

*The Hardtop Book.* Thomas W. Head. Fort Myers Beach, Florida: Head Yachts, 1993.

*Metal Corrosion in Boats.* 2nd ed. Nigel Warren. Dobbs Ferry, New York: Sheridan House, 1998.

*The Ocean Sailing Yacht.* Vols. 1 and 2. Donald Street. New York: Norton, 1973–1978.

*Offshore Sailing: 200 Essential Passagemaking Tips.* Bill Seifert with Daniel Spurr. Camden, Maine: International Marine, 2002.

*The Self-Sufficient Sailor.* Lin and Larry Pardey. New York: Norton, 1982.

*Single-handed Sailing.* 2nd ed. Frank Mulville. Woodbridge, Suffolk, England: Seafarer Books; Dobbs Ferry, New York: Sheridan House, 1990.

# RIGS AND SAILS

The sailboat's rig and sails are its means of propulsion and the features that most distinguish it from other types of watercraft. Like the auxiliary engine, they have many moving parts, all working in concert in their job of making the boat move. The loads on the rig and sails are considerable, and so it is not surprising that torn sails and dismastings do occur.

The weekend sailor can afford to take a few chances—waiting an extra year to replace standing rigging, limiting inspections for corrosion to a walk around the mast, and sailing with torn batten pockets until season's end. Not so the cruiser. Replacement parts and repair services are not so easily obtained away from home port, nor affordable if cruising on a limited budget. In some countries, parts and services may be nonexistent. And if these aren't reasons enough to invest in a good rig and a large sail inventory, the cruiser should remember his boat and his life—and the lives of his crew—may depend upon their functioning.

## TYPES OF RIGS

Determining the best rig for cruising is an argument so seldom resolved that this in itself admits the utility of all different types. However, coastal cruisers generally favor the more weatherly rigs, as a greater percentage of their sailing time is spent beating to windward. Blue-water passage makers are more inclined to choose a good reaching rig, such as the ketch or schooner, because the distances they cover enable them to plan trade wind routes and the more comfortable, off-the-wind points of sail (Figure 10-1).

It seems that everyone has a favorite rig. Certainly there is no lack of widely divergent opinions in the cruising literature, so it is not my purpose here to summarize the pros and cons of each rig. Like everyone else, though, I too have

some opinions and observations on the subject, and these are contained in the following section.

### Sloop, Cutter, Ketch, and Yawl

Determining how to strengthen the rig and obtain well-made sails is partly contingent on the type of rig, and how it will handle both heavy and light weather. A ketch or yawl, with two masts, has a few more options than the single-masted sloop and cutter.

The mizzen on the yawl (Figure 10-2) is only used in light to moderate winds when the course is off the wind; going to windward, it is often furled on the boom. Because the yawl's mizzenmast is shorter than the ketch's, it isn't used as often to fly a mizzen staysail. Yet the yawl's mainmast is taller than the ketch's. In fact, it may be about the same height as a similarly sized sloop, only the boom may be shorter to make room for the mizzen.

Yawl and ketch mizzens are used somewhat similarly to the staysail on the cutter, namely keeping the center of effort near the middle of the boat. When the wind reaches about Force 6, a 35-foot ketch handles nicely with mizzen and jib alone. Because these two sails are located at more or less equidistant ends of the boat, they balance nicely, and the boat will steer itself quite happily.

In the same conditions, the cutter will drop the jib, partly because it is farther forward, often on a bowsprit. The closer you confine sail handling near to the mast, the safer it is. No one wants to go out on a long sprit in a gale and try to bring down even a small jib. Also, keeping the staysail set and dropping or furling the jib has the effect of moving the center of effort aft; reefing the main moves it forward. The two changes cancel each other, and the boat continues to balance well. Without the staysail, a smaller jib would have

**FIGURE 10-1.** Two-stick rigs excel off the wind—reaching and broad reaching—and so are favored for trade-wind passages. Also, the center of effort is kept lower than on a sloop, making the boat heel less.

to be set, and in combination with even a reefed main, the center of effort is often too far forward, possibly causing a neutral or lee helm.

Contrast this to the sloop (Figure 10-3). When the sail area carried in the foretriangle is reduced, it has the effect of moving the center of effort aft. With a full main, weather helm increases. Reefing the main pushes the center of effort forward—sometimes too far. A storm trysail and storm jib should be designed for the sloop to complement one another, achieving a degree of balance that is manageable under every condition. In severe conditions, the boat should be able to lie ahull, run under bare poles, lie to a sea anchor, or fly just a storm trysail to keep the bow to the wind.

The more combinations possible, the better. If this sounds like a condemnation of sloops, it isn't. Sloops are often the fastest of the four rigs. They certainly go to weather best and are the least expensive to buy and maintain. Certainly they are the simplest, and it's hard to beat simple just about anywhere in life, especially at sea.

Tristan Jones preferred the yawl because the mainmast is tall enough to carry lots of sail in light air; the boat can balance under mizzen and jib alone; the mizzen is not so huge as to blanket the main the way a ketch's mizzen does downwind; and in light air, a mizzen staysail is an alter-

**FIGURE 10-2.** The yawl (left) was favored during the heyday of the CCA rule, but that ended in the 1960s. Designers today find little use for it, feeling that the mizzen does little more than add to the boat's cost. It does, however, allow you to sail jig and jigger, with the mainsail down, and that's a very comfortable ride with a balanced helm. You can also set a mizzen staysail in light air. At anchor (right), the mizzen sail of a yawl also makes a good riding sail to prevent the boat from veering to port and starboard.

**FIGURE 10-3.** The sloop is hard to beat for simplicity, efficiency, and overall speed on all points of sail. Here, our old 1967 Pearson Vanguard beats out of Narragansett Bay bound on a year's cruise. (Susan Thorpe Waterman photo)

native to the large head sail—blooper, reacher, gollywobbler, cruising chute, etc.

Eric Hiscock, on the other hand, praised the virtues of the ketch for blue-water sailing, because most time is spent reaching, and the size of each individual sail is smaller.

Figure 10-4 illustrates how similar size sloops, cutters, ketches, and yawls add and shorten sail.

## The Cat Ketch

The cat ketch rig popularized by Garry Hoyt's line of Freedom boats is one of the most radical developments ever to hit the mass-production market (refer back to Figure 8-3). True, there are other oddball rigs such as the Lungstrom (butterfly), Chinese lug, Aerorig (refer back to Figure 1-32) and Gallant, but despite the efforts of their supporters, they really haven't been accepted by the average cruising man as well as the Freedom rig.

One reason is Hoyt's marketing skills, and another is the sheer logic and simplicity of the cat ketch rig.

The rig is not new. In the late 1800s and early 1900s, a number of working and recreational craft were rigged with freestanding spars of equal or near-equal height. The New Haven Sharpie, for example, was a common sight on Long Island Sound and also used by oystermen in the Carolinas. The rig was introduced to Florida waters by R. M. Monroe in the 1870s.

More recently, in 1948, Bill Tritt, head of Glasspar in California, had built for his Dincat daysailer the first unstayed fiberglass spars. And in 1973, Jerry Milgram's cat ketch, the *Cascade*, tore up the Southern Ocean Racing Conference (SORC) prompting rule changes penalizing the rig. What Hoyt did was to bring together several "old" ideas and meld them into a new concept: freestanding spars, sleeved sails, and wishbone booms. Today there are a number of variations on this theme—fully battened sails, rotating wing spars tapering into a trailing edge with a conventional sail track, deck-mounted booms, single-masted freestanding rigs, and so on.

Of most interest to the cruising sailor is the freestanding spar that eliminates literally dozens of wires and fittings, any one of which could give out and threaten the entire rig. With the freestanding spar, there is only one part—the mast itself—and if it is engineered strongly enough, why worry?

Initially, Hoyt and the Freedom builders, Tillotson-Pearson, tried fiberglass spars, but they tended to whip and bend. They found the answer in carbon fiber, a very strong high-tech material that is also very expensive. As mentioned in Chapter 1, when Tony Lush pitchpoled his 54-foot (16.5 m) *Lady Pepperell* in the Southern Ocean, the spars were still standing when the boat righted. Until then, no one had taken a freestanding cat ketch, carbon fiber rig below the great capes and through the Roaring Forties.

## The Cat Sloop

A principal shortcoming of the cat ketch rig is its inherent slowness in winds under 10 to 12 knots, and its inability to point as high as the conventional sloop. After a number of years pushing the cat ketch rig, Freedom began switching to what might be called the cat sloop: a large, fully battened mainsail and vestigial jib, "blade," or "accelerator," set on a minimally tensioned forestay and shaped by a flexible boom/batten patented by David Bierig and called the CamberSpar. It is self-tacking and self-vanging. This configuration worked well enough for Freedom that the cat ketch rig was ultimately dropped entirely, even on boats as large as 45 feet (13.7 m; Figure 10-5).

Designer Robert Perry, an astute observer of the industry, was unimpressed: "So they reinvented the sloop because the cat ketch was slow. What are they going to do next, reinvent the overlapping genoa? And reinvent the winch after that?"

Mark Ellis's Nonsuch line capitalized on the popularity engendered by Freedom. Instead of carbon fiber spars, however, his freestanding rigs were aluminum, and always just simple cats—one spar, one sail. Yves-Marie Tanton, Richard Black, and Eric Sponberg are three other designers who have made a little money with the freestanding rig. This fraternity challenged conventional wisdom regarding rigs, won some acceptance, and garnered a small share of the cruising sailboat market. Yet interest in unstayed rigs seems to have reached a plateau, leaving the masthead Marconi rig still undisputed king of the mountain.

## Double Headsails

As length and displacement increase, there is a temptation to add a staysail to divide up the sloop's foretriangle and give more options in making up sail combinations. The resultant rig is not a cutter but a double-headsail sloop (Figure 10-6). This rig offers a lot of versatility and safety, espe-

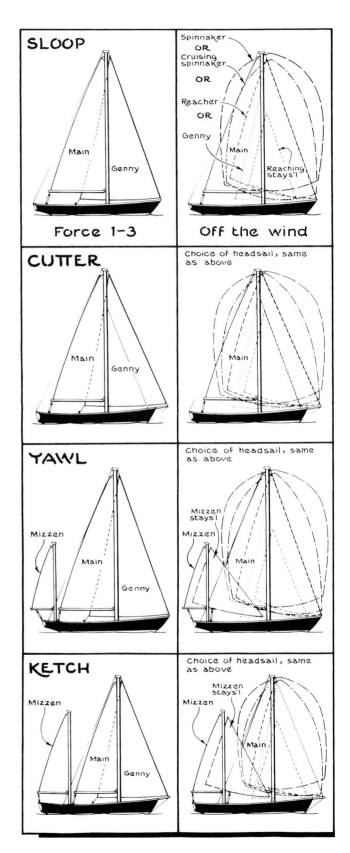

FIGURE 10-4. These drawings illustrate how similarly sized sloops, cutters, ketches, and yawls might add and shorten sail in varying wind conditions. Definitions: **Sloop**—single mast with main and jib; may be fractional rig. **Cutter**—single mast with main, jib, and staysail. Mast is stepped near center of boat, distinguishing it from a double-headsail sloop, which has the mast stepped farther forward. **Yawl**—two masts with main, jib, and mizzen; mizzen is shorter than ketch mizzen and is stepped aft of the rudderstock. May have double headsails. On ketches and yawls with outboard rudders, the size of the mizzen is more telling. **Ketch**—two masts with main, jib, and mizzen; may have double headsails. Mizzenmast is about two-thirds the height of mainmast and is stepped forward of the rudderstock.

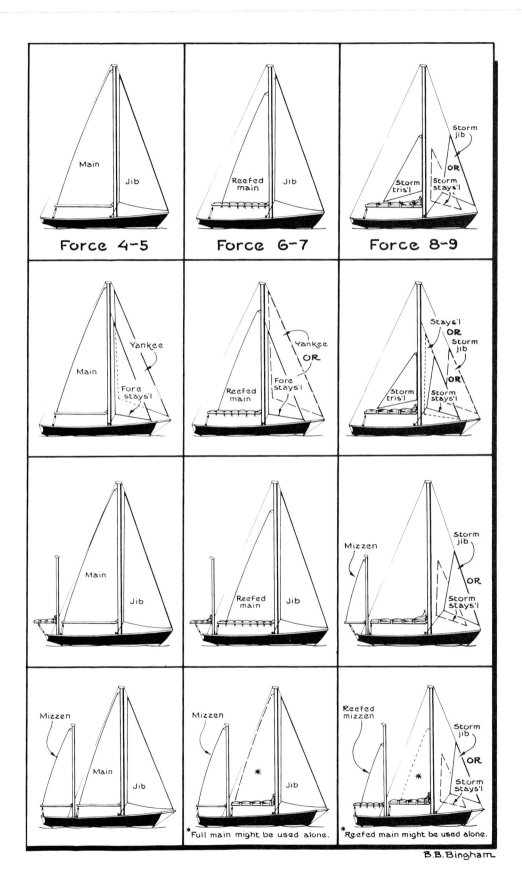

Force 4-5    Force 6-7    Force 8-9

**FIGURE 10-5.** The Freedom 36 features a fully battened mainsail with lazy jacks, plus vestigial jib or "blade" that is tensioned in part by one of Dave Bierig's patented CamberSpars, so that it is self-vanging as well as self-tending. (Freedom Yachts)

cially offshore. To make the change from a conventional sloop, you need to do the following:

1. Install a new stay from the mast to the foredeck—wire, terminals, tang, turnbuckle, deck plate.

2. Install running backstays or lower aft shrouds that attach at the same height as the new inner forestay to equalize the load on the mast.

3. Make or purchase a sail, perhaps with a set of reef points sewn in or with luff tape for furling.

4. Rig the sail with sheets, blocks, fairleads, pad eyes, cleats, traveler, and car.

5. The original jib and genoas can be retained, though an option is to build a Yankee or high-cut lapper à la cutter, if you plan to use both headsail and staysail often. Not really recommended.

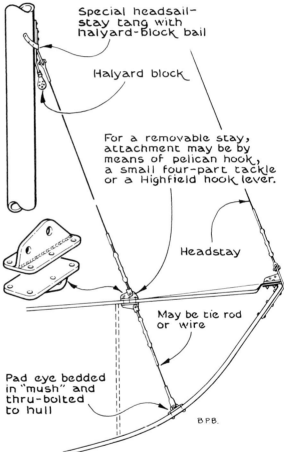

**FIGURE 10-6.** When the wind increases too much to carry the roller furling genoa, it can be rolled up, and a staysail set on the inner forestay, a sail that is also easy to make self-tending for safer maneuvering in close quarters. A removable inner forestay can be added to a sloop to fly a staysail in heavy weather or for ease of single-handed maneuvering. The illustration shows how the inner forestay must be secured to the hull.

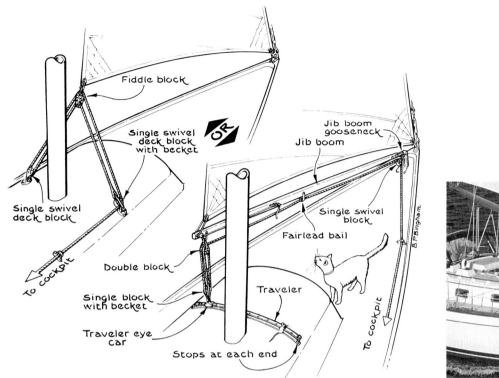

**FIGURE 10-7.** The staysail or working jib can be made self-tending (left), so that it needn't be sheeted in after each tack. Nonoverlapping jibs can be made self-tending in several ways. A jib boom helps to keep the sail flat, but only Garry Hoyt's patented Jib Boom (right) makes the sail self-vanging. Island Packet features this device on all of its boats. (Bruce Bingham photo)

Sloops as small as about 32 feet (9.8 m) can still benefit from the advantages of double headsails even though their masts are several feet farther forward than a cutter of the same size. Adding a bowsprit to smaller boats spreads out the sail plan and leaves more room for a staysail of honest size. It would be wise to consult a yacht designer or sailmaker to determine the effect of any sail plan change on overall balance.

Many summers ago, I was sitting at my mooring in Newport Harbor watching a single-hander on a Pearson 323. Before approaching the harbor entrance, he dropped the jib, set an inner forestay (it had been lashed back at the mast), set a clubless staysail (Figure 10-7), and sailed into the harbor looking for a mooring. Later he rowed by and stopped to chat. Besides using the staysail for stormy weather, he said that it was most useful when single-handing in close quarters because it is self-tending, not so large as to obscure his view, and quick to drop. Though the Pearson 323 wasn't designed for double headsails, adding a staysail gave his sloop greater versatility for handling a variety of conditions. And here was an impor-

tant side benefit: It also provided a backup to the forestay.

The double-headsail configuration described above usually allows enough space between the forestay and inner forestay to tack a jib without having to walk it through the slot. Genoas probably won't fit through the slot, however, and will have to be walked through or at least partially rolled up before tacking. That's the case on many open class 50s and 60s. On the forestay furler is set a large, light-air headsail, while on the inner forestay and furler is set a smaller, heavier headsail that can be carried to Force 6 or 7 (Figure 10-8).

## Conversions

Just as the addition of an inner forestay converts a sloop to a double-headsail sloop, it is possible to convert a sloop to a yawl, or vice versa. A number of maxi ocean racers built in the 1960s and '70s were originally rigged as yawls and ketches, in part because at that time sailcloth and winches were inadequate to handle the larger sail areas required on a 70- to 80-foot (21 m to 24 m) sloop.

**FIGURE 10-8.** With double headstays set close together, the forestay will carry a large light-air sail; the inner forestay will carry a heavier, smaller jib, though not necessarily a staysail. Yet a third, removable, inner forestay may be set up for that function. With this setup, the larger sail must be furled to tack through the narrow slot between stays.

With developments in sails, furlers, and winches, practically all big boats, including the 247-foot (75.2 m) *Mirabella V*, are today sloop rigged.

But just to prove that everything comes full circle, the 1989–90 Whitbread Race was won by *Steinlager II*, a New Zealand ketch. And more recently, the 140-foot (42.7 m) *Mari Cha IV* was given a ketch rig for her ocean-racing record attempts. In 2003 she succeeded in shattering the New York to England record by finishing in six days, 17 hours. She registered speeds in excess of 40 knots!

It is doubtful that the cruising sailor would wish to trade his yawl rig for a sloop; more likely, he would elect to go in the other direction—from sloop to yawl (Figure 10-9).

Before making such a conversion, it would be a good idea to consult a naval architect or at least a very experienced sailmaker. A thorough study of the hull and sail plan are necessary to calculate the position of the new mizzenmast, sail area of the mizzen, and possible shortening of the main boom and mainsail. Generally, the center of effort of the sail plan has to be slightly forward of the center of lateral resistance; this dimension is known as *lead* and affects how the boat balances (lee helm, weather helm, neutral helm).

Chainplates will have to be added to take the stays of the new mizzen. These can be the through-deck type, but chainplates bolted through the sides of the hull are strong and give a wider staying base. There is also less potential for leaking, and ultimately these will be easier to install.

The step for the mizzenmast must be precisely located, probably on the cockpit sole or afterdeck, and support of this area should be given much thought. On fiberglass boats without cored decks, glassing in plywood (better compressive strength than foam or balsa to resist through-bolting loads of the step) underneath is important (see Chapter 2). It may or may not be necessary to insert a compression post between the bottom of the cockpit sole or afterdeck and hull, but if it is, be certain to distribute the loads of the post over as wide an area as possible. Unlike beneath the mainmast, there is no keel under the mizzen to take the load.

Triatic stays connecting the mastheads of the main and mizzen should be avoided, if at all possible. If the mainmast goes over the side, there is no point in sending the mizzen mast with it, as the mizzenmast can be jury-rigged on the mainmast step. Thus the mainmast backstay will have to be either led slight off-center past the mizzenmast or split forward of the mizzenmast, or twin backstays will have to be installed, making sure they don't interfere with the swing of the mizzen boom.

Mizzen shrouds can be led forward—if they don't obstruct the mainmast's boom—and a set of shrouds led aft for support. Forestays are obviously out of the question, as are backstays unless there is a very large boomkin. If upper forward shrouds are not used, jumper struts and stays resist the aft bending moment caused by aft-leading spreaders and shrouds.

In sum, the advantages of a yawl are its ability to use the mizzenmast as a jury-rigged mainmast, set a riding sail for heaving-to or at anchor, set a balancing sail on a reach, and furnish a point from which to set a mizzen staysail on a reach. The mainsail and foretriangle remain large enough for good windward and downwind performance.

## SPARS

Regardless of the rig material chosen, the thickness of its mast, or aspect ratio, the guiding principle for the cruiser must be a rig's ability to stand up to years of hard use. The conventionally stayed rig must be held rigidly enough to survive a knockdown, whereas it is expected that the freestanding mast will deflect under load. Carbon fiber has the best combination of strength and weight. Aluminum remains the standard. Some older boats, including even fiberglass boats from the Far East imported during the 1960s and early 1970s, may still have hollow wood or solid wood spars. Used properly, each material can make a viable spar.

### *Materials*

Extruded aluminum spar sections are by far the most common today. Solid wood spars are satisfactory on short, gaff-rigged boats, but are not as strong as hollow wood spars, such as the Herreshoff box method of construction. An attractive feature of the box section is that a serviceable replacement spar can be made just about anywhere in the world. In his book *One Hand for Yourself, One for the Ship*, Tristan Jones described the

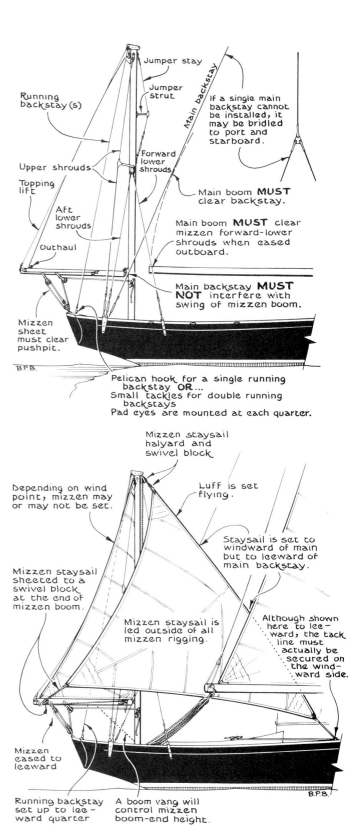

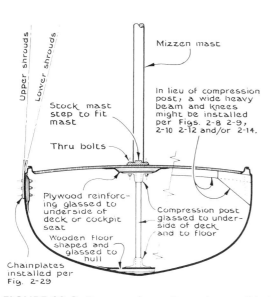

**FIGURE 10-9.** On some sloops, it may be possible to convert to a yawl rig by adding a mizzenmast. The main boom may need shortening.

materials and glues required to do this (a 36-foot/ 11-meter spar can be made from a dozen 14-foot/ 4.3-meter prescarfed, seasoned lengths of spruce, glued with resorcinol or epoxy). He suggests storing them under the deck in the cabin, passing through bulkheads if necessary. Hollow spars are vulnerable to dry rot and require periodic varnishing and inspection. Where the gooseneck, tangs, and spreaders are attached, the hollow wood spar should be filled with blocks of solid wood.

Carbon fiber spars are rapidly increasing in popularity, despite their high cost, and "thems" that can afford them happily pay up. After delivering one of his new 44s from Maine to Rhode Island for the annual Newport boat show, builder Tom Morris told me that he could think of no other upgrade that made more of a performance difference than going to a carbon mast. With less weight aloft, the boat sailed more upright, and therefore was more comfortable and faster. There are half a dozen carbon sparmakers in the United States, including GMT Composites (www.gmtcomposites. com), Forespar (www.forespar.com), Van Dusen Racing Boats (www.vandusenracingboats.com), and Southern Spars (www.southernspars.com).

Before making the jump to carbon, however, do some research on the current methods of providing electrical grounds. A weakness of carbon is its low melting temperature, meaning a lightning strike could bring it down. Running a copper strip down the mast as is done on wooden spars won't work because the electrical charge may yet damage the spar where the strip is fastened. Also, lightning is more likely to strike a spar that provides a path to ground. Stan Honey, the brilliant inventor (he came up with the virtual yellow first-down stripe on televised football games) and navigator (with Steve Fossett in his record round-the-world sail aboard *Cheyenne*), told me that after much thought they decided to leave *Cheyenne*'s mast ungrounded and hope for the best.

I once sailed in the annual Carriacou workboat regatta in the Grenadines aboard a 68-foot (20.7 m) Swedish schooner with tapered steel spars, but for most smaller cruising boats, the weight of steel is prohibitive. It's workboat material, not for yachts.

Determining the dimensions and wall thickness of aluminum spars is best left to an experienced sparmaker, though Figure 10-10 gives rough estimates. Considerations include the height of the spar, fractional or masthead rig, method of staying, boat stability, type of aluminum used, and

| Yacht Size Approx. Waterline Length (feet) | Typical Mast Section (inches) | Wall Thickness (inches) | Approx. Mast Weight (lb./ft.) |
|---|---|---|---|
| 18 | 4.5 × 3 | 0.08 | 1.15 |
| 19 | 4.8 × 3.2 | 0.08 | 1.21 |
| 21 | 5.2 × 3.9 | 0.09 | 1.51 |
| 22 | 5.5 × 3.6 | 0.10 | 1.81 |
| 22 | 6 × 3.6 | 0.10 | 1.97 |
| 24 | 5.5 × 4.25 | 0.13 | 2.3 |
| 26 | 6.3 × 4.8 | 0.13 | 2.47 |
| 28 | 8 × 4.5 | 0.13 | 2.94 |
| 30 | 7.8 × 5.5 | 0.16 | 3.67 |
| 33 | 8 × 6.6 | 0.16 | 4.35 |
| 35 | 9.5 × 6.5 | 0.16 | 4.9 |
| 45 | 10.5 × 7.5 | 0.21 | 6.7 |
| 50 | 12 × 8 | 0.25 | 9.7 |
| 80 | 14 × 10 | 0.25 | 11.5 |

**FIGURE 10-10.** A general guide to sizing aluminum alloy masts. (Proctor Masts)

whether the spar is to be stepped at the keel or on deck. A cruising spar should be as thick as is feasible, with consideration given to weight aloft and the ability of the stays and shrouds to hold it in column with a given staying base.

## Repairs

Once an aluminum spar is buckled or even slightly dimpled, it must be repaired. Aluminum spars can be fitted with a smaller-diameter sleeve that extends a number of feet above and below the break; in fact, the spars of most large boats are sleeved to begin with.

I once owned a 17-foot, 3-inch (5.3 m) Silhouette Mark I that had a solid spruce spar. One day, sailing in a fresh breeze, a shroud swaging cracked, sending the spar over the side. I found a skilled woodworker who was able to scarf in a new section, tapering the V-shaped scarf almost 3 feet (0.9 m). This saved the considerable delay and expense of making a new mast. A hollow wood spar might also be repaired using similar methods.

## Maintenance

Anodizing is an electrolytic process that helps prevent corrosion and yields a harder finish than standard, unfinished aluminum. Because tougher environmental laws regarding hazardous waste make anodizing expensive and onerous, many new boats now are offered with painted spars (two-part linear or aliphatic polyurethanes such as Awlgrip are commonly used—see Chapter 15). Bristol, Rhode Island, sparmaker Eric Hall, however, says that paint is largely for cosmetic purposes and that no significant gain in corrosion resistance is obtained over anodizing or even bare aluminum. Painted spars require touching up and, every so many years, sanding to bare metal followed by recoating. Anodizing, though not as attractive, is a better finish. As noted, environmental regulations, which affect the disposal of chemicals used in anodizing, are making anodizing too costly (the toxic waste dilemma) and will probably spell its demise in the sparmaking business.

The fewer holes drilled in an aluminum extrusion the better. Of course it is necessary to drill holes or weld on plates for mounting bosses, tangs, winches, and cleats, and these should be placed with some knowledge of how holes and welds can weaken a section. Small holes are of no great concern, but larger holes, such as for inspection or internal halyard exits, should be staggered to minimize weakening of the mast (Figure 10-11).

Stainless steel fasteners are not galvanically compatible with aluminum and can cause serious corrosion over a period of time. While it is common practice in New England and elsewhere to leave spars standing during winter haulout (a dubious practice), they should be unstepped every few years and major fittings, such as spreader bases and tangs, removed to inspect for corrosion. Similarly, cracks should be dealt with promptly. A stopgap measure is to drill a hole at each end of the crack to prevent it from spreading. Have the crack welded at the earliest opportunity. Periodically check all weldments for cracking; lubricate all movable parts, such as blocks and sheaves; and look for signs of wear, such as where wire halyards pass over sheaves. File rough edges to prevent chafe.

Deck-stepped spars should have drain holes at the base to allow water inside the spar to drain out. It is quite likely that the base of the mast frequently will be wet, and thus it is important that the mast step or heel plate be of the same material as the mast to prevent corrosion. Drain holes at the base actually may introduce water inside. For this reason, Ross Norgrove, in his book *Cruising Rigs and Rigging*, recommended inserting a ta-

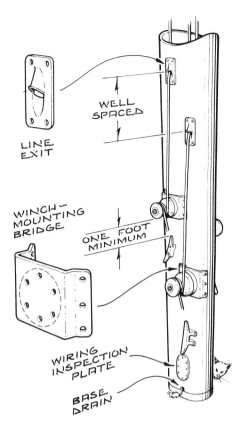

**FIGURE 10-11.** Fittings added to aluminum masts must be spaced above and below each other to prevent weakening.

pered plug bedded with Thiokol just below where the lowest halyard exits (assuming internal halyards, which introduce more water inside the spar than external halyards). This solution makes even more sense on keel-stepped masts, because water draining inside the boat only adds to the condensation, and being in an enclosed area also increases the potential for corrosion and dry rot. Tight-fitting deck collars on keel-stepped spars are a must, too, if water is to be kept outside—where it belongs.

## Deck-Stepped and Keel-Stepped Masts

For the ultimate in strength, the ocean-cruising boat should have a keel-stepped mast, because if a shroud or stay lets go, the deck helps support the mast (acting as a fulcrum), hopefully long enough to bring the boat about on another tack and ease the load. In the same situation, a deck-stepped mast is already gone. Tom Colvin points out that following a dismasting, a keel-stepped mast may well leave a stub long enough to be brought up to deck level and jury-rigged to carry a small sail. On

201

**FIGURE 10-12.** *Cruising World* founder Murray Davis's *Turtle*, an Ushant 40 motorsailer built in England, has large tabernacles for lowering the spars. This is a nice feature if the canals of Europe are on your itinerary.

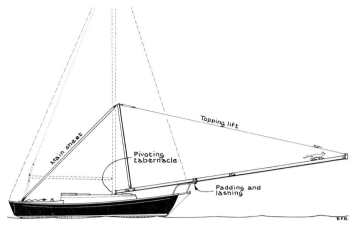

**FIGURE 10-13.** With a large tabernacle and a little brainpower, the spinnaker pole or boom can be used to raise and lower a deck-stepped spar.

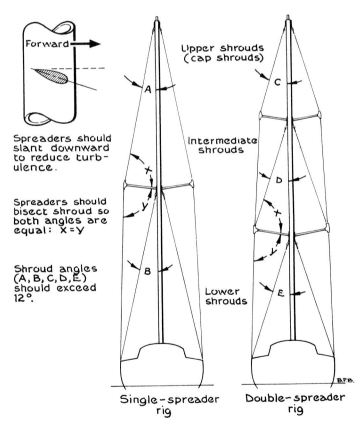

**FIGURE 10-14.** Spreaders must be strongly secured to the mast and bisect the shroud angles.

the other hand, a deck-stepped mast is more likely to come down in one piece (if the cause is broken rigging) and is less likely to damage the deck.

Coastal cruisers, especially those anticipating sailing in canals and under low bridges, must admit the advantages of the deck-stepped mast, especially one mounted on a tabernacle. A tabernacle (Figure 10-12) with a large through-bolt provides a fulcrum to raise and lower the spar by removing just the lower bolt. See Figure 10-13 for a system of raising and lowering the mast.

## Spreaders

Spreader failures, along with wire terminal failures, are probably the most common cause of dismastings, and so must be strong and properly installed. Most rigs have single or double spreaders (Figure 10-14), though occasionally you see a

large boat with three or more. Because the wider the shroud angle the less load exerted on the spar and the shrouds, a cruising boat should have the widest spreaders possible, without extending to the rail of the boat. (Spreaders are notorious for locking with your neighbor's during raft-ups or damaging themselves when the boat is tied to a high pier.) Racers have brought their shrouds more inboard during recent years to narrow the sheeting angle of headsails, giving them better windward ability. But this is of less concern to the cruiser, who is more interested in keeping his rig standing than pointing a few degrees higher. Chainplates installed through the sides of the hull achieve a wider staying base than chainplates located on the side decks or cabin top. It is annoying when walking forward to have to step around shrouds mounted inboard. Outboard chainplate installations can get in the way too, if the lower shrouds are angled too low over the side decks.

For the cruising boat, the shroud angle from the masthead should be no less than about 12° out from the perpendicular line of the mast. The angle can be increased by shortening the spar (not very realistic), widening the spreaders, or adding another set of spreaders, enabling the first set to be moved higher up. The second set also reduces the load on the first set. While double spreaders strengthen any rig (the load on upper shrouds is reduced by about 15%), they are particularly advisable on boats over about 45 feet (13.7 m), where the spar height is such that the shroud angle becomes too narrow.

Fixed and articulating spreaders are both reasonable choices, with the latter having the edge because of its ability to move fore and after under stress, such as when the mainsail is let out on a downwind run. Neither fixed nor articulating spreaders must be allowed to shift position up or down. All spreaders should bisect the shroud angle at the spreader tip (Figure 10-14) so as not to create uneven forces on the spreader and to prevent the spreader from moving up and down.

On aluminum masts, the spreader bases should be welded or through-bolted to the mast with compression tubes over the bolt inside to distribute loads to both sides of the mast. On wood spars, they should be fastened with wood screws into pilot holes whose diameters have been carefully calculated to ensure a tight fit. Coat the screw threads with linseed oil to keep water away from the raw wood. The holes should be proportionately shorter than the length of the screws and narrower in diameter by at least the thickness of the screw threads.

Airfoil section spreaders with tapered leading and trailing edges are commonplace on racing boats now because they offer less wind resistance. They should be angled down on the leading edge

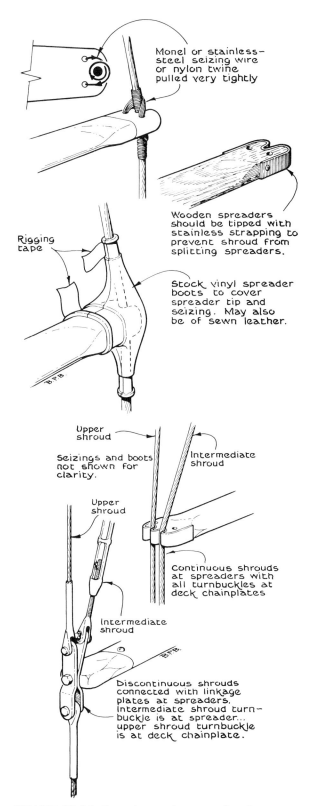

**FIGURE 10-15.** Shrouds must be secured to the spreader tips to prevent them from jumping out. Sail chafe protection, such as rubber boots, should be fixed to the spreader tips.

10 to 15,° so they offer less wind resistance when the boat is heeled (Figure 10-14).

Regardless of spreader tip configuration, they should not allow the shrouds to jump out when sudden loads are exerted on the rig, such as when slamming into head seas or jibing (Figure 10-15). Rubber spreader boots, leather, or other antichafe material should be taped to the spreader tips to prevent chafing overlapping headsails or eased mainsails. But remove them periodically to check for corrosion, especially if stainless steel wire is used against aluminum.

## SPINNAKER HANDLING SYSTEMS

Many cruisers eschew the spinnaker because it is a tricky sail that can be a bear to tame, and once wrapped around the forestay, difficult to untangle. Of greater appeal are the large, lightweight, multipurpose sails that can be set on whisker poles and tacked downwind. Or asymmetrical spinnakers set on a short sprit, often extendable as on the J-Boat model line. You can't run dead downwind with an asymmetrical, but rather take long boards (legs or tacks) broad reaching.

Garry Hoyt, developer of the Freedom line, patented the Hoyt Gun Mount (Figure 10-16) to make conventional spinnaker handling practical for everyone. Though only installed on the earlier Freedoms, the Gun Mount's principles could be the basis for a similar system for many boats. The pole, or yardarm, as Hoyt liked to call it, slides through a pivoting sleeve securely fastened to the bow pulpit. Control lines led aft to the cockpit enable the crew to not only hoist the sail and trim it from tack to tack, but also to furl it. And because both tack and clew are captured by the pole, wraps are impossible. In fact, Garry's son Jeff took me sailing once on a Freedom 21 and impressed me by doing 360s in Newport Harbor, even sailing backward, with nary a fear of wrapping the spinnaker!

An obvious requirement of a homemade system is a strong bow pulpit. Forespar now markets the Gun Mount system for retrofitting to other boats.

Regardless of the type of spinnaker flown, you can take a lot of the stress out of the experience by using a snuffer. The Chutescoop (www.chutescoop.com) and ATN Spinnaker Sleeve (www.atninc.com/sleeve.html) are fabric tubes

**FIGURE 10-16.** The Hoyt Gun Mount is a patented device that allows the spinnaker to be hoisted and lowered from the cockpit with both tack and clew captured by the "yard" to prevent wraps. (Freedom Yachts)

**FIGURE 10-17.** The ATN Spinnaker Sleeve is pulled up to set the sail and pulled down to contain it. Such devices as this and the Chutescoop take much of the risk out of flying traditional spinnakers. (ATN)

hinges in and locks against the mast when not in use. As you climb up you must pull out each step above you, then fold them up behind you as you descend. A similar step is made by ABI (www.abimarine.com).

Another alternative is the Mast Mate (www.mastmate.com), a flexible nylon ladder hoisted on the sail track or slot. Individual nylon loops are sewn onto a long runner. They don't provide the foot support of rigid steps and can't be used when the mainsail is up, but the beauty of the system is that it folds up and stows below when not needed.

The method that seems favored by single-handed racers is derived from mountain climbing gear. The ATN Topclimber (www.atninc.com/topclimber.html) uses leg power to ascend and a one-way rope jammer to control descent (Figure 10-19). Unique to this device is the ability to stand in the stirrups and work above the masthead, and that's important, because that's where

through which the spinnaker is fed. In use, the sleeve contracts at the masthead. When it's time to douse the sail, haul on the control lines to pull the sleeve down over the length of the spinnaker. It's fast and efficient. When not in use, the spinnaker lives in the sleeve rather than a sailbag (Figure 10-17).

## GOING ALOFT

The ability to quickly ascend the mast for repairs, reeving replacement halyards through the masthead sheaves, or gaining a lookout for reefs or other objects of concern, is important to cruisers. The bosun's chair is the traditional device used for this purpose, but this generally requires a second person on deck to winch it up. It is not a very practical substitute for ratlines or a crow's nest as a lookout.

A previous owner of my Pearson Vanguard had installed simple aluminum mast steps from the boom to the masthead, and I used them frequently. They do like to catch halyards and other lines, however, and so a thin wire was run down from the top step to the base of the mast, fastened with wire lashings to the outer tips of each step. This helped prevent fouling lines, but didn't eliminate them altogether.

Mast steps come in a variety of materials and designs. One clever type is the folding MastWalker (Figure 10-18; www.mastwalker.com); each step

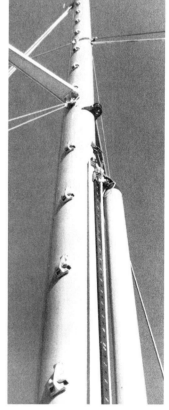

**FIGURE 10-18.** Mast Walkers are aluminum steps that fold against the mast when not in use, thereby reducing windage and vastly minimizing the chance of fouling halyards.

**FIGURE 10-19.** Another ATN product, the Topclimber, uses leg power to hoist you up the mast. A one-way jam cleat controls descent. (ATN)

the action is. Bosun's chairs usually leave you a little short.

## STANDING RIGGING

Standing rigging is the system of wires, terminals, and fittings that hold a stayed spar upright and in column. In determining the size and strength of its various parts, the wire is generally regarded as the necessary weak link, meaning that every other part—bulkhead, chainplate, tang, terminal, turnbuckle pin, etc., should be stronger than the wire. If the terminals are engineered to 110% of the breaking strength of the wire, little is gained by engineering the chainplates or tangs to 150%. In practice, however, most terminals fail at less than breaking strength of the wire and, therefore, deserve the most scrutiny.

### Types of Wire and Rod

Galvanized wire was once the standard standing rigging material, but now stainless steel is found on most boats. Stainless steel $1 \times 19$ wire rope is generally used for standing rigging, and $7 \times 19$ wire rope, because of its greater flexibility, is used for running rigging. There are numerous variations of these two, such as $7 \times 7$ and $6 \times 37$. The first number refers to the number of strands in any given length of rigging, the second to the number of wires in each strand (Figure 10-20). Fiber cores are sometimes added to increase flexibility, which is important for running rigging where wire rope passes through sheaves and blocks under tremendous strain. The fiber core, however, lessens the strength of the wire compared to wire-core rigging.

In preparing a boat for cruising, common-sense advice is to replace all standing rigging with wire rope one size larger—for example, $7/16$-inch (11 mm) diameter for $3/8$-inch (10 mm) diameter, which increases breaking strength by 5,000 pounds (2,268 kg) for $1 \times 19$ wire (Figure 10-21). Larger turnbuckles, clevis pins, chainplates, and tangs will probably need to be fitted so that each part is stronger than the wire. If a fitting has a lower breaking strength than the wire, no advantage is gained. Ross Norgrove's formula is to multiply ballast by 2 to determine the breaking strength of the wire. For example, 7,000 pounds (3,175 kg)

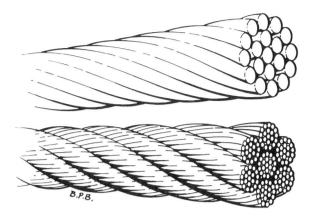

**FIGURE 10-20.** 1 × 19 wire is generally used for standing rigging, and 7 × 19 for running rigging.

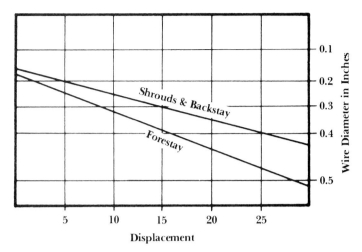

**FIGURE 10-21.** Suggested wire diameters for cruising boats. (*Boat Data Book,* Ian Nicolson)

ballast times 2 equals 14,000 pounds (6,349 kg) breaking strength of the wire. From Figure 10-22, either ⁵⁄₁₆ or ⅜ inch (8 mm or 10 mm) wire should do the job, with the latter giving a substantial safety margin. However, additional weight aloft is never a good thing because it adversely affects stability; so while strength is important, there's also no point in going overboard with wire size.

Rod rigging, originally developed for biplane rigging in World War I, was introduced to the sailing world on several boats of note, including the J-boat *Ranger*, and later when Navtec rigged the 12-Meter *Heritage* for the 1970 America's Cup races. The principal advantage of rod is that it stretches about 35% less than wire, and so forestay sag is less and sail shape more efficient. Further, the elastic limit (the amount a material can be stretched and still return to its former dimension) of wire is about 40% of its breaking strength. For rod it is about 80%. And, because headstays are tensioned to about 50% of breaking strength, this can result in permanent stretch of wire forestays. Another advantage is that because rod is solid, smaller-diameter rod can be manufactured to the same breaking strength as larger-diameter wire (Figure 10-23). This means less windage at about the same weight.

Navtec rod rigging and some brands of wire rope, such as Universal's Super Stainless, are made from Armco Steel's (now part of AK Steel) product, Nitronic 50. It is more corrosion resistant than 302 and 304 stainless, and stronger than 316 stainless. Nitronic 50 is an alloy including carbon, manganese, phosphorus, sulfur, chromium, nickel, molybdenum, nitrogen, columbium, and vanadium; it has many industrial applications in addition to sailboat rigging. Of course, it is much more expensive than 302/304 stainless steel wire rope, but its greater corrosion resistance means longer life (see Appendix B).

While rod rigging has been controversial in cruising circles due to occasional reports of it

## BREAKING STRENGTH OF WIRE (POUNDS)

| Diam. | 1 × 19 Stainless steel | 7 × 7 Stainless steel | 7 × 19 Stainless steel | Dacron | Nylon | Manila |
|---|---|---|---|---|---|---|
| ¹⁄₁₆ | 5,00 | 480 | 500 | | | |
| ³⁄₃₂ | 1,200 | 920 | 1,050 | | | |
| ⅛ | 2,100 | 1,700 | 1,760 | | | |
| ⁵⁄₃₂ | 3,300 | 2,600 | 2,400 | | | |
| ³⁄₁₆ | 4,700 | 3,700 | 3,700 | | | |
| ⁷⁄₃₂ | 6,300 | 4,800 | 5,000 | | | |
| ¼ | 8,200 | 6,100 | 6,400 | 1,650 | 1,650 | 600 |
| ⁹⁄₃₂ | 10,300 | 7,600 | 7,800 | | | |
| ⁵⁄₁₆ | 12,500 | 9,100 | 9,000 | 2,500 | 2,500 | 1,000 |
| ⅜ | 17,500 | 12,600 | 12,000 | 3,700 | 3,700 | 1,350 |
| ⁷⁄₁₆ | 22,500 | 16,500 | 16,300 | 5,000 | 5,000 | 1,750 |
| ½ | 30,000 | 21,300 | 22,800 | 6,400 | 6,400 | 2,650 |
| ⁹⁄₁₆ | 36,200 | 26,600 | 28,500 | | | |
| ⅝ | 47,000 | 32,500 | 35,000 | 10,000 | 10,000 | 4,400 |
| ¾ | 67,500 | 45,500 | 49,600 | 12,500 | 14,000 | 5,400 |
| ⅞ | 91,400 | 60,200 | 66,500 | | | |

**FIGURE 10-22.** Breaking strength and weight of different size and type wires.

| Size | Breaking Strength (lb.) | Diameter (in.) | Stretch[b] | Weight/100 ft. (lb.) | Drag[c] |
|---|---|---|---|---|---|
| −12 Navtec standard | 12,500 | 0.281 | 2.11 | 21.3 | 4.1 |
| 5/16 1 × 19 wire | 12,500 | 0.323 | 3.00 | 21.0 | 6.3 |
| 5/16-diameter rod[a] | 13,000 | 0.312 | 1.75 | 26.2 | 4.7 |
| −12 Navtec HP rod[d] | 11,600 | 0.250 | 2.11 | 18.0 | 3.8 |
| −17 Navtec standard | 17,500 | 0.330 | 2.11 | 29.3 | 4.9 |
| 3/8 1 × 19 wire | 17,500 | 0.385 | 3.00 | 29.4 | 7.5 |
| 3/8-diameter rod[a] | 18,100 | 0.375 | 1.68 | 37.8 | 5.6 |

[a] This rod is same nominal diameter as wire.

[b] Stretch is measured in inches/100 feet at load equal to 25% of breaking strength.

[c] Drag is measured in pounds/100 feet of rigging at 22 knots. Based on Stevens Institute data.

[d] Manufactured from MP35N.

**FIGURE 10-23.** This table compares the properties of Navtec rod rigging with 1 × 19 wire of equivalent breaking strength.

breaking without warning, even at dockside, most failures can be traced to improper installation. This has been most common at the spreader tips, where tubes are bent over the spreader tip to duplicate the angle of the shroud—an error of more than 2 or 3% causes fatigue of the rod. Discontinuous rigging, in which each shroud terminates at a link plate attached to the spreader tip, provides full articulation and reduces problems of fatigue at the spreader tip. However, rod rigging's greatest disadvantage to the world cruiser is the difficulty in carrying spare shrouds and stays—minimum coil size is 200 times rod diameter, or 50 inches for ¼-inch rod (1.3 m for 6 mm). This is an important consideration because a length of wire slightly longer than the longest stay should be carried in reserve, with a means of fastening terminal fittings.

## Adding Shrouds and Stays

The general rule to be observed aboard the cruising boat is that every wire should have a backup in the event of a rigging failure. This does not necessarily mean two parallel wires running from the same chainplate to the same tang on the mast, but simply another wire that can absorb a large share of the load if the primary wire breaks.

Twin forestays enable hanking on twin jibs for downwind sailing (Figure 10-24), but unless they are anchored by separate fittings, the alternate loading on one stay and then the other can cause fatigue of tangs and possibly stemhead fittings. An inner forestay, such as the one shown in Figure 10-7, can be set in heavy weather to help keep the mast in column and, hopefully, keep the spar standing if the forestay goes—at least long enough to ease the load and make repairs.

Single backstays are easily replaced with twins, one to each quarter. This requires fitting chainplates (see Figure 10-9) either on the hull sides or

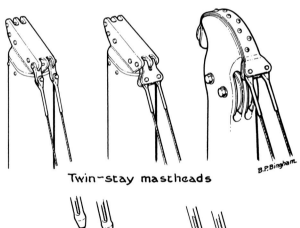

Twin-stay mastheads

B.P.Bingham

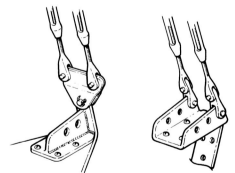

Twin-stay stemheads

**FIGURE 10-24.** Twin forestays not only provide the rig with backup strength, but they enable setting twin jibs for downwind sailing.

to knees glassed inside at the hull-deck joint (refer back to Figures 2-8, 2-29, 2-30, and 2-31). At the masthead, two tangs must be fitted. Alternatively, the single backstay can be left, and running backstays added port and starboard (Figure 10-25). Running backstays are frequently seen on gaff-rigged boats in which the gaff prevents rigging a single backstay on centerline, and on double-headsail boats, in which the running backstays support the mast where the inner forestay attaches. This leads us to another important principle: for every mast support, there should be an equal and opposite support to keep the mast rigidly stayed in column.

Double lower shrouds are better than single lowers because not only do they provide support athwartships, but also slightly fore and aft of the upper shroud. Double-spreader rigs should have intermediate and upper shrouds, either continuously run from masthead to deck or discontinuously run to link plates at each spreader tip.

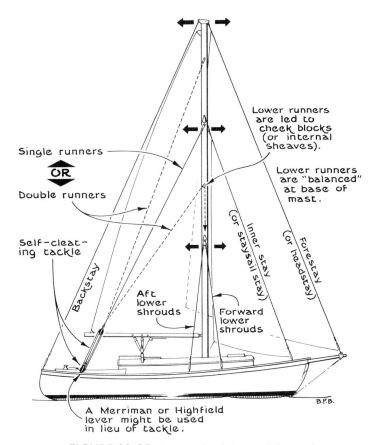

**FIGURE 10-25.** Running backstays, while cumbersome, back up the backstay and oppose the inner forestay's forces to keep the spar in column.

## Terminals

Warm salt water poses the greatest danger to standing rigging, and the point of attack is frequently the terminal fittings connecting the wire to the turnbuckle, tang, or chainplate. Almost every type of terminal encloses the wire and prevents quick evaporation of water, which eventually begins to corrode the wire. Typical terminals are shown in Figure 10-26.

The least expensive method, and one of the strongest, is the hand-spliced splice. Unfortunately, splicing $1 \times 19$ wire is very difficult; $7 \times 7$ wire is generally favored, but then the extra stretch of $7 \times 7$ must be lived with. Toggles can be inserted between the turnbuckle and chainplate if at some point the turnbuckle cannot take up the slack.

Poured sockets are used on elevators and cranes, which should say all that's necessary about their strength. Zinc is heated with a torch and poured into the cone of the socket to form a metallurgical bond. Ross Norgrove gives good step-by-step instructions for making poured sockets in his book *Cruising Rigs and Rigging*.

In contrast to the metallurgical bond of poured sockets, and the friction bond of hand-splicing, most other terminal types rely on mechanical bonds; that is, by squeezing the terminal onto the wire. Properly executed, mechanical bonds are very strong, but there is always the risk of excessively or unevenly distorting the wire. In the case of swaging, there is danger in failing to achieve uniform loading on the wires inside. Here is one area in which rod rigging excels. The end of the wire is flattened by a process called cold heading. The cold-formed head is made by inserting the end of a length of rod in a vise, and the end is smashed with a hydraulic piston. The head then is inserted into a specially machined rod seat at the end of the turnbuckle (Figure 10-27)—the assembly is partially articulated to alleviate stress and is incredibly strong.

The greatest virtue of the Norseman and Sta-Lok terminals is the ease with which an ordinary person can fasten them to wire. Wrenches, pliers, wire cutters, and seizing twine are the only tools and parts necessary. Properly done, they are strong and even reusable, with the exception of the cone, several of which should be carried as spares. Figure 10-28 shows how these terminals are fitted.

Talurit and Nicopress terminals both have the advantage of wrapping the wire around a thimble and a bit of extra strength that is gained by the additional friction of the wire against the thimble. Nicopress fittings can be installed by the skipper with the help of the double-action Nicopress tool, which should be carried aboard. In a real emergency, cable clamps are helpful, but they cannot be strained too much (plus they're ugly).

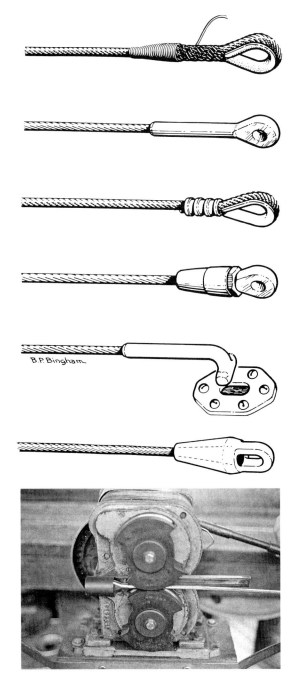

FIGURE 10-26. These terminal fittings are typical of those found on most sailboats today (photo). From top to bottom: hand-spliced eye, roller-swaged terminal, Nicopress terminal, Norseman terminal, hook-in T terminal, and poured socket terminal.

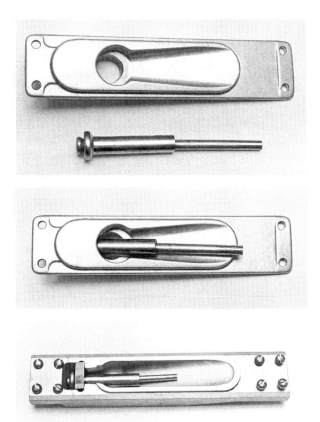

FIGURE 10-27. Navtec's internal stemball tang, showing the cold-formed head at the end of the rod. (*Practical Sailor* photos)

At *Practical Sailor*, we did destruction tests on eight different types of terminals, all on ¼-inch (6 mm) wire. The Sta-Lok and Castlok terminals failed at 8,000 pounds (3,628 kg), Norseman at 7,300 pounds (3,311 kg), a standard swage at 7,700 pounds (3,492 kg), Nicopress at a surprising 8,800 pounds (3,991 kg), and rope clamps at just 4,400 pounds (1,995 kg). Our recommendation was to use swage fittings on the top ends of stays (due to less windage, lighter weight, and lower cost) and Sta-Loks (for ease of replacement without special tools) on the bottom.

## Turnbuckles, Tangs, Thimbles, and Chainplates

Turnbuckles, tangs, and chainplates (Figure 10-29) should be matched in size with the wire and terminal fittings to which they're attached. The breaking strength of any fitting should exceed the breaking strength of the wire—up to two times as much for blocks and sheaves with wires pulling

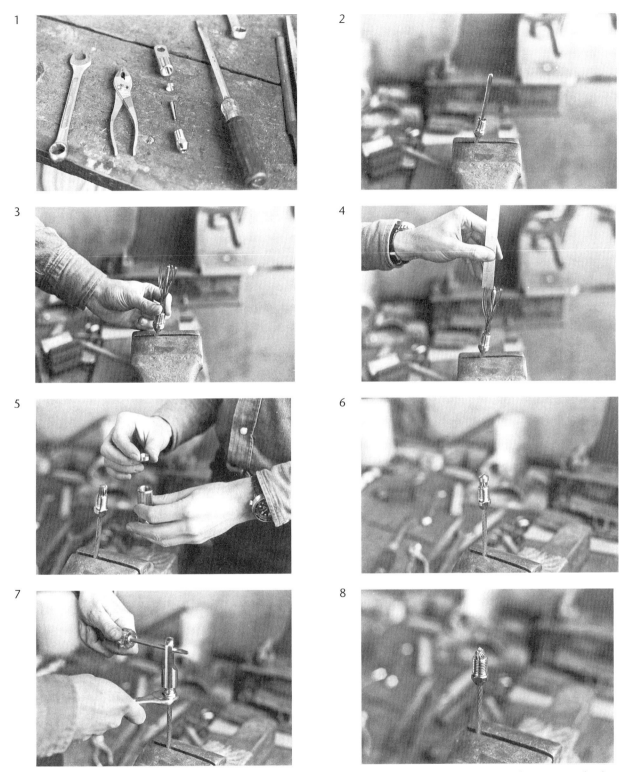

**FIGURE 10-28.** Installation sequence for fitting a Sta-Lok terminal to wire: Parts of a terminal—end, cap, cone, body, and tools required (1); slide body over wire (2); unlay wire by turning with pliers (3); slide on cone—distance from top of core wire should be same as the core diameter, about $3/32$ inch/2.4 mm (4); either drop cap into end fitting (5); or fit on top of all the wire strands (6); screw on end fitting to body (7); take off end fitting and inspect the wires (8)—do they overlap? Is one caught in the slit of the cone? Are they making indentations on the top of the cone? Reassemble with Loctite on threads and silicone caulk on wire ends.

## STAINLESS STEEL CHAINPLATE SIZES

| | A | B | C | D |
|---|---|---|---|---|
| Wire Diam. | Pin Diam. | Radius | Offset | Maximum Thickness |
| 1/8" | 1/4" | 3/8" | 1/16" | 3/16" |
| 5/32" | 5/16" | 7/16" | 1/16" | 1/4" |
| 3/16" | 3/8" | 1/2" | 1/8" | 5/16" |
| 1/4" | 1/2" | 11/16" | 1/8" | 3/8" |
| 9/32" | 1/2" | 11/16" | 1/8" | 3/8" |
| 5/16" | 5/8" | 13/16" | 3/16" | 1/2" |
| 3/8" | 5/8" | 7/8" | 3/16" | 1/2" |
| 7/16" | 3/4" | 1" | 3/16" | 9/16" |
| 1/2" | 7/8" | 13/16" | 1/4" | 11/16" |
| 9/16" | 7/8" | 1 1/4" | 1/4" | 11/16" |
| 5/8" | 1" | 1 3/8" | 1/4" | 3/4" |

**FIGURE 10-29.** Table for determining chainplate size.

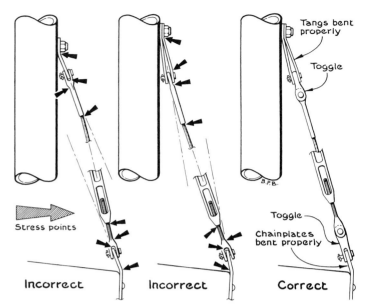

**FIGURE 10-30.** Turnbuckles, terminals, and tangs must lead fair to prevent stress loading. Toggles help the wire articulate and prevent unnecessary stress on the wire and terminals.

parallel to themselves. Check the specifications of any fitting you buy for its working and ultimate tensile strength.

Forestays tend to sag off more than any other stay, and if an unfair load is placed on any fitting, such as the terminal, turnbuckle, or tang (Figure 10-30), consider adding a toggle to provide greater articulation of the wire and terminal and to prevent twisting. This will lengthen the life of the wire.

Turnbuckles and clevis pins will not unscrew or pop out if you insert cotter pins or wire through the barrel and end parts. A few turns of sail-maker's tape over the barrel and sharp ends of wire and cotter pins will protect sheets and sails from chafe, as will turnbuckle boots.

One way to measure the strength of a turn-buckle is by examining the size of the pin at the ends that hold the terminal eye or chainplate. Make sure it is sufficiently large to be of greater breaking strength than the wire.

## Fasteners

Rivets, machine screws, self-tapping machine screws, and self-tapping sheet metal screws (Figure 10-31) are used for fastening fittings to spars—cleats, blocks, bails, and winches. Where possible, secure highly stressed hardware, such as spreader sockets, winches, and tangs, with machine screws bolted through the width of the spar with compression tubes and locknuts. When using dissimilar metal fastenings on an aluminum spar, you can prevent corrosion by inserting a gasket of Micarta, surgical rubber, sheet nylon, or Formica, and wrapping vinyl tape over the threads. Use a thread-lock compound such as Loctite or fit locknuts to prevent them from vibrating loose.

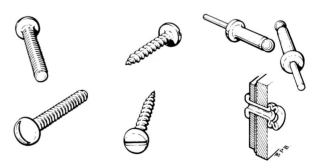

**FIGURE 10-31.** Machine screws, self-tapping screws, and pop rivets are the three fasteners typically used for fastening fittings to aluminum spars.

Elsewhere on the spar, where a fitting is not duplicated on the other side to facilitate bolting through its width—or where access up inside the spar is not possible—self-tapping machine or sheet metal screws are the most practical. Good results can be had with rivets, too, which some riggers prefer over screws. Sail track, small blocks, and other light hardware can be fastened with rivets or screws. Boom bails for vangs should be through-bolted with compression tubes. The critical factor in using self-tapping sheet metal screws is the diameter of the pilot hole: too small, and the screw won't thread all the way snugly; too large, and the threads of the screw won't bite deep enough into the spar wall. A rule of thumb is to drill the pilot hole abut 75% of the diameter of the screw size. For example, for a ¼-inch (6 mm) screw, use a ³⁄₁₆-inch (5 mm) drill bit. A lubricating wax (an auto paste wax will do) smeared over the threads will help it drive in and prevent snapping the head off the screw if it jams. This exercise imparts the scary knowledge of just how little thread engagement there really is in a spar. And this is why you should never use a mast-mounted winch to hoist a person in a bosun's chair.

Blind drive rivets are installed either with a special tool or by hitting the expanding pin with a hammer. Pilot holes should be the same diameter as the rivet for a snug fit. To remove old pop rivets, grind the head down or drill it out with a larger-diameter bit. Then drive any remainder of the rivet through with a punch and hammer.

Self-tapping sheet metal screws and pop rivets can be purchased in stainless steel or aluminum. The former is stronger, but will corrode slightly in contact with aluminum. Using a thread-lock compound such as Loctite Threadlocker Red or Blue, or an antiseize compound, will help minimize galvanic action and make later removal much easier. Loctite Red sometimes requires heat to loosen, which is why the company makes the less tenacious blue variety. Hall Spars recommends a yellowish paste called Duralac.

# INSPECTING RIGGING

Standing rigging doesn't last forever. Boats in the tropics will need stays, terminals, and some associated hardware, such as tangs, replaced more frequently as warm salt water is highly corrosive. It's tempting to give a number, like every ten years, but even wire makers and riggers are loath to venture such guesstimates. The reason is that every boat is different, and no one wants his name on an expensive dismasting.

That said, there are many boats in northern climates with rigging more than fifteen and even twenty years old. Would I cross an ocean with twenty-year-old rigging? No. Time to replace it.

For some peace of mind in the meantime, remove the mast from the boat every, say, three years and go over every piece very carefully. Look for discoloration of the metal, usually brown stains. Remember that stainless steel is not totally stainless—316 grade will look cleaner than 304. Unfortunately, the most common cause of rigging failure is inside terminal fittings, where you can't see. There will probably be some discoloration of the wire where it enters the terminal, but if excessive, this may be the time to replace the stay. Not all stays have to be replaced at the same time. Doing one or two every few years reduces the work and financial impact. If a stay has any meathooks (broken wire strands), replace it immediately.

For a more thorough inspection, use a product such as Spotcheck (www.magnaflux.com) applied to the terminals, tangs, and other fittings. Spotcheck is a two-part penetrating dye that makes very tiny cracks visible to the naked eye. It's cheap insurance.

# RUNNING RIGGING

Running rigging consists of all the fiber and wire ropes used to raise, lower, and trim sails. Breaking a halyard is not usually a catastrophe, though if it happens when hove-to with storm sails, quick action is required to regain control of the boat. Because the breaking strength of running rigging is seldom tested under straight loads, most problems are caused by chafe—unfair leads, rough-edged sheaves, and rubbing against standard rigging.

## Types of Line

Manila rope is seldom seen on boats nowadays, and there is really no reason it should be, considering the very real advantages of modern synthetic ropes such as nylon and polyester (Dacron). These two products, available in three-strand, braid, and plaited versions, can do most of the line jobs required on a modern cruising boat.

Nylon is slightly stronger than polyester and has more stretch—about 17% of its length under load. Because of its elasticity, nylon is most suitable for applications where you want the line to function as a shock absorber—anchor rodes, docklines, and dinghy painters. And that's usually in its three-strand form.

Polyester has about half the stretch of nylon and so is preferred for halyards, sheets, guys, and vangs; prestretched rope has, of course, even less stretch. It's nearly always used in braid form, never three-strand, as the latter stretches more. Single-braid has no cover; double-braid has a braided core and braided cover.

Kevlar-reinforced line has less elasticity than nylon or polyester and a high breaking strength; however, it doesn't like to bend over a tight radius. And because of its added cost, its usefulness to the cruiser is limited. Racers commonly use high-tech fiber cores, such as Vectran, Spectra, and Technora, sometimes without covers, just to reduce weight and windage. While the cruiser can benefit from these virtues as well, there are disadvantages from using line with too small a diameter: they are harder to handle and require more turns on a winch or cleat to hold.

Polypropylene is sometimes used for dinghy painters because it floats and will not foul the mother ship's propeller when the line is slack. However, this line isn't good for tying knots, as it continually wants to spring back. And it won't coil to save your life. It is not as strong as nylon and polyester, which prejudices its use as a painter.

Not many years ago, halyards were commonly made with 7 × 19 wire spliced to polyester rope tails. 7 × 19 wire is used because of its flexibility, which enables it to bend around relatively small-diameter sheaves without distorting the lay of the strands. Today's high-tech, low-stretch fibers make all-rope halyards the smart way to go.

## Blocks and Sheaves

Blocks are used in abundance on any boat, to gain purchase power and to fairly direct the lead of the line. Just a few of their applications are jib sheets, mainsheets, travelers, halyards, boom vangs, and handy billies. The size of the block should be sufficiently large to withstand the loads exerted on it by line under load. An old rule of thumb is that for every ⅛ inch (3 mm) of line diameter, the block diameter should be increased 1 inch (25 mm). Especially when using stronger modern

### SHEAVE SIZES FOR ROPE CORDAGE

| Rope Size, inches | Recommended Sheave Diameter, inches | Minimum Sheave Diameter, inches |
|---|---|---|
| ¹⁄₁₆ & ⅛ | 1 | ⅝ |
| ³⁄₁₆ | 1½ | 1 |
| ¼ | 1¾ | 1 |
| ⁵⁄₁₆ | 2 | 1⅛ |
| ⅜ | 2¼ | 1¼ |
| ⁷⁄₁₆ | 2½ | 1¾ |
| ½ | 2¾ | 2¼ |
| ⁹⁄₁₆ | 3¼ | 2⅝ |
| ⅝ | 3½ | 2⅞ |

Note: *Rope sizes are diameters.*

**FIGURE 10-32.** Table for determining block size. (*Boat Data Book*, Ian Nicolson)

materials, however, adhering to this formula results in overkill. For example, Figure 10-32 says a 2¼-inch sheave is adequate for ⅜-inch line, where the formula suggests 3 inches. Check the manufacturer's specifications for safe working loads, making sure the block is stronger than the line on it.

Sheaves for wire, such as those at the masthead for wire halyards, should have deep grooves to keep the wire from jumping out. The sheave diameter should be about twenty to thirty times the wire diameter. For example, a ³⁄₁₆-inch (5 mm) wire should have a sheave between 3¾ and 5½ inches (95 mm to 140 mm) in diameter, and every block should have some sort of retainer over the top to guarantee the wire stays put (Figure 10-33).

The key thing with blocks is to select ones with an adequate safe working load (SWL) rating. This number is usually about half of its breaking strength. If you overload a block, it may break. There are a number of different types of blocks. Those with ball bearings have less friction but usually lower SWL ratings. Needle bearings can handle more. Highest SWLs often are the simplest sheave systems. In recent years, so-called hollow blocks, in which the spindle has been replaced by a large cross section of stainless steel tubing, have gained in popularity, partly because they are less expensive to manufacture. This design also distributes loads over a wider surface area. Here let

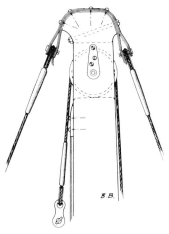

**FIGURE 10-33.** Masthead sheave diameters should be about twenty to thirty times the diameter of the wire. A U-strap should be fitted to the top to prevent the wire from jumping out.

me put in a plug for Garhauer Marine Hardware blocks (www.garhauermarine.com). This Southern California company makes high-quality hardware at a fraction of the price of bigger brands like Lewmar and Harken. A lot of Bill Felgenhauer's stuff is a little heavier, but each carries a ten-year warranty. He even makes blocks with titanium cheeks, again at much lower prices.

## Mainsheet

The closer to the mast the mainsheet is attached to the boom, the more power is required to trim the main. Mainsheets can be attached to the deck anywhere from a traveler over the main companionway hatch to the bridge deck, to a traveler mounted on a beam across the cockpit, to a traveler through-bolted to the afterdeck and attached to a boom bail or a swiveling tang at the end of the boom (Figure 10-34). The more power required

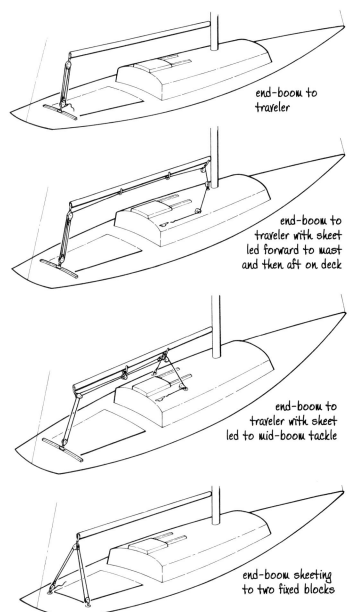

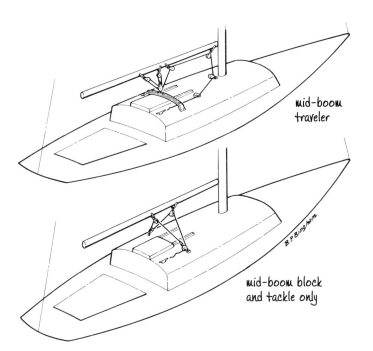

**FIGURE 10-34.** Various mainsheet arrangements.

to trim the mainsail, the more blocks are required to provide the necessary purchase power, and the greater the likelihood of needing a winch for assistance.

Travelers give better control of the mainsail's shape and are standard fare on most modern boats. They usually are located on the cabin top or bridge deck. That's because most boats have mid-boom sheeting (owing to shorter booms). While travelers do seem to add unnecessary complication, and extra rope to organize, they allow finer control of mainsail trim.

On older boats with longer booms, a double block at the boom end, and single blocks through-bolted to the aft end of the cockpit and to either side of the boom, usually provide sufficient purchase power to control the mainsail and boom (if not, increase the purchase ratio). An advantage or disadvantage of this arrangement is that the mainsheet is kept aft of the cockpit and out of everyone's way, accessible to the helmsman. Alternatively, Figure 10-35 shows end-boom sheeting secured at the steering pedestal. On shorthanded boats under sail with one crew forward searching an anchorage or tending the anchor, the helmsman must be able to handle the mainsheet, and that's not easy if it's on the cabin top.

An intriguing boom-end arrangement is to rig two independent mainsheet tackles, one to port and one to starboard (Figure 10-36). Obviously, tacking requires judicious timing in the release of one mainsheet as the other is being trimmed. Yet when close reaching, the leeward mainsheet functions as a boom vang, while the weather mainsheet controls trim. Not only does this system obviate the clutter of a vang at the mast base, which often interferes with dinghy stowage, it also eliminates uncontrolled jibes. There is, however, an abundance of rope aft in the cockpit.

## Halyards

Not many years ago, the standard halyard was either all-wire or wire with a rope tail. Wire reel halyard winches were dangerous devices that depended on a clutch and brake system; if they let go with the handle in place, you could break an arm. I've bought several boats that came with them and replaced them as soon as possible with conventional winches. Of course, this meant switching from wire halyards to all rope. Before the new generation of low-stretch fibers, all-rope

**FIGURE 10-35.** This single-point attachment for the mainsheet obviously doesn't allow as much fine trimming as a traveler, but it certainly is convenient to the helmsman, which is a consideration for the shorthanded crew. (*Practical Sailor* photo)

halyards meant some sag in the luff of the sails. Happily, that's no longer a problem with a polyester or Spectra parallel-core rope. All-rope halyards used in conjunction with blocks shackled to the masthead, or masthead sheaves, and hoisted by self-tailing winches, are the epitome of simplicity. They are the easiest to replace if a halyard breaks.

Internal halyards reduce noise and windage, but they are more difficult to fish through the spar and exit hole should one break and need replacing. With all-rope halyards, a ready-made backup consists of a coil of spare line kept in a locker, cut to length ahead of time, and spliced at one end with an eye for fishing through the masthead block. Carry enough line to replace at least one halyard and a set of sheets.

In recent years there has been a decided trend toward leading halyards aft to the cockpit. This

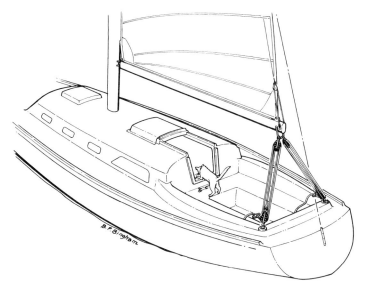

**FIGURE 10-36.** Twin mainsheets is a rather novel arrangement. While more cumbersome during tacking, the leeward tackle can function as a close reaching vang.

practice has the obvious advantage of allowing crew to raise and lower sails from the relative safety of the cockpit. But it's not always that simple. When lowering sails, crew will have to go forward anyway to furl the mainsail or bag a jib/genoa that's not on a roller furler. And the added friction caused by the extra blocks and sheaves sometimes makes hoisting sails real grunt work. Figures 10-37, 10-38, and 10-39 show several setups.

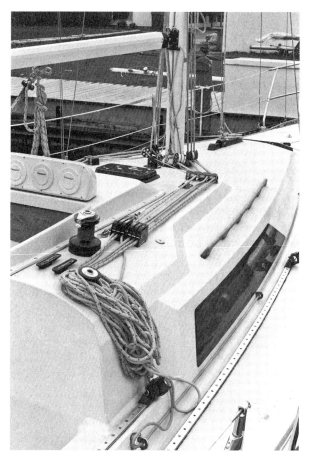

**FIGURE 10-38.** A neater arrangement is to lead lines through cheek blocks and then aft to stoppers. (*Practical Sailor* photo)

**FIGURE 10-37.** Halyards led aft to the cockpit are the current fashion as this arrangement minimizes time spent working on deck at the mast. On this boat, however, the lines drape across the hatch and seem to clutter the deck. (*Practical Sailor* photo)

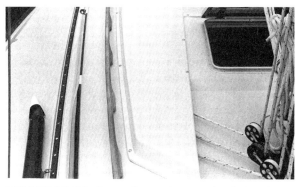

**FIGURE 10-39.** Concealing and protecting halyards and other lines led aft underneath a fiberglass cover adds to costs but eliminates the chance of tripping on them. (*Practical Sailor* photo)

## Jib Sheets

Polyester jib sheets should be sized not so much for strength as for comfort in handling. Figure about ⅜-inch (10 mm) line for a 30-foot (9 m) boat, and ⅞₆-inch (11 mm) line for boats between about 40 and 50 feet (12 m to 15.2 m). Smaller line cuts into the palms. And if each sheet is long enough for a knot about 5 to 6 feet (1.5 m to 1.8 m) from the tail, you won't need to reach out on deck for the tail when preparing to come about.

Snap shackles should not be used to attach the sheets to the clew. When the boat is headed up or in irons, the flapping of the sail makes the shackle a dancing murder weapon. Better to tie bowlines in the sheets; they won't let go (like snap shackles), won't hurt your noggin, and are easily untied.

Some people like to give each sail its own set of sheets, permanently attached. These are sized to the sail in terms of both diameter and length. However, this means that when changing head-sails the old sheets must be gathered and coiled, and the new sheets led through the blocks and fairleads back to the cockpit—a nuisance unless it's really necessary. It may make more sense to have several sets of sheets ready—one for small headsails, another for large genoas, and a third for light-air nylon sails. If you've got two head-sails permanently set on furlers, however, you won't have to worry about changing sheets—until setting the staysail or storm jib.

## Downhauls

"Downhaul" is a word that has almost lost its meaning, thanks to roller furlers. But for those of you who still have hanked-on sails, a downhaul is a thing of beauty.

When it's blowing hard and the boat is tossing about in a seaway, or is about to anchor or dock, being able to drop the jib from the cockpit saves a trip to the bow. With double lifelines and criss-crossed lines or netting between them, the sail will stay on deck long enough to reach smooth water or change point of sail to achieve a steadier motion before moving forward to bag the sail.

Each hanked-on headsail should have its own downhaul.

Splice an eye in the end of a ¼-inch or ⅜-inch line (6 mm to 10 mm) through the top jib hank (not to the head, as this will fall below the top hank once the halyard is slack and may jam; Figure 10-40). Or a shackle can be used if you want

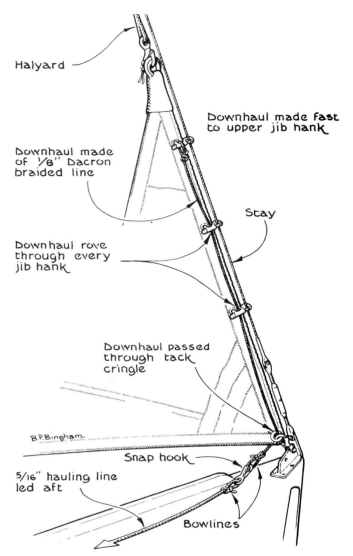

**FIGURE 10-40.** Downhauls should be attached to the top jib hank, either by a snap shackle or bowline. It is then led to a block at the bow and aft to the mast or cockpit.

to unclip it from the sail. The downhaul is then led through a block at the bow and aft. An eye splice at the tack end clips to a permanently rigged line on deck, run through fairleads to the cockpit or mast, depending on where the halyard is cleated off. You can dispense with the splice and shackle if you decide instead to simply tie a bowline to the jib hank. To keep the downhaul from flying about, it can be run up through all the other hanks if there's enough space. At the very least, there should be a cleat to secure the other end of the downhaul back at the mast or cockpit.

Mainsails with the boom gooseneck on a mast track also have downhauls to tension the luff. To

218

hoist the sail, release the downhaul, and when the headboard reaches the masthead, the boom rides up. Belay the halyard and then pull on the downhaul until the luff looks right. This system, as opposed to a fixed gooseneck, allows the boom to ride clear of the gallows.

## Boom Vangs and Preventers

The purpose of a boom vang is to flatten the sail and remove twist. The purpose of a preventer is to prevent jibing. When off the wind, soft vangs (made of rope and blocks) are often led to the rail (Figure 10-41) to act as jibe preventers, but in heavy conditions, a jibe can cause the boom to break at the point of attachment.

In its normal configuration, fastened to the base of the mast, the vang is used judiciously to control sail shape and thereby improve speed. Larger boats usually fit rigid vangs that have multiple purchase inside to make the job easier. Hydraulic vangs also are available. Unfortunately, vangs get in the way of stowing dinghies on deck.

There are a wide variety of methods to attach boom vangs to the boom: with specially designed clips that fit into the sail track, claws that surround the boom (mostly for roller reefing), bails bolted to the boom, or pad eyes welded to the underside of the boom. If you convert to roller reefing, be sure you can unhook the vang so it doesn't

**FIGURE 10-42.** The nonhydraulic boom vang is a powerful and comparatively inexpensive method of controlling mainsail shape and eliminating the need for a topping lift. (*Practical Sailor* photo)

prevent the boom from rotating, and remove any large, sharp objects on the boom, such as cleats or winches, that might rip the sail. These are some of the reasons why slab or jiffy reefing has replaced the rotating boom as a means of reducing mainsail area. Better sail shape is another.

Powerful rigid vangs such as Navtec's hydraulic models (www.navtec.net), and several nonhydraulic types (Figure 10-42), such as Hall Spars' Quik Vang (www.hallspars.com) and Offshore Spars' Offshore Vang (www.offshorespars.com), merit consideration for the cruiser. In addition to extra power for controlling sail shape, they can support the boom with the mainsail furled, thus eliminating the topping lift. Broken topping lifts have been responsible for knocking more than one sailor in the head with a dropped boom, sometimes fatally.

A preventer is not intended to control mainsail shape, but rather to prevent the boom from jibing. A stout line is led from the end of the boom forward to a cleat, pad eye, or block on deck (Figure 10-43). These should be well reinforced with backing blocks to distribute loads. The greater the angle between the boom and preventer, the stronger it will be. Leading the tail of the preventer all the way aft to the cockpit lets you adjust it for changes in mainsail trim without going forward.

Wishbone booms, popular on some unstayed rigs, possess an inherent self-vanging characteristic that tends to obviate the need for formal vanging. A wishbone cat rig, where the mast is located practically at the stem, is virtually impossible to rig with a preventer, because there is so little room

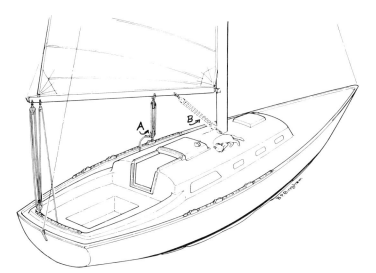

**FIGURE 10-41.** While it is common practice to attach boom vangs to the rail (A) when running downwind to flatten the sail and to prevent jibes, it's also a good way to break the boom in two. In high winds or seas, it's much smarter to use the preventer shown in Figure 10-43. It's best to leave the vang in its intended location (B).

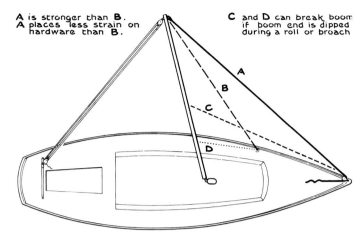

**FIGURE 10-43.** A simple jibe preventer is run from the end of the boom to a point forward on deck. This point—a stanchion base or pad eye—must be reinforced under the deck with a backing block.

forward of the mast to attach the preventer line. Wishbone booms, however, better absorb the shock of a jibe than a conventional boom.

## Lazy Jacks

One of the best ways to control sails being lowered is by way of lazy jacks (Figure 10-44). These are lines led from the boom to a point on the mast; they run on both sides of the sail, so when it is lowered, it naturally flakes on top of the boom and doesn't tumble down over the deck. As you may want to control their tension, they should be led to a single line—perhaps to the topping lift—that runs through a block on the mast and down to a cleat. The other lines can be run under the boom or terminated to strap eyes screwed into the boom. The number of lines depends on the size of the sail.

Patented lazy jack systems have become popular marketing gimmicks of some sailmakers and other entrepreneurs. The Dutchman (www. mvbinfo.com), for example, uses a number of lines laced through a widely spaced, vertical series of cringles; when the sail is dropped it falls on top of the boom, "skewered" as it is by the control lines. These systems seem like a lot of money for what you get—mostly a length of line, some attachments, and an *idea*. With a little ingenuity, you can make your own but you will probably want a sailmaker to cut and sew the cringles in the sail. An advantage of the Dutchman over conventional lazy jacks is they don't interfere with hoisting the mainsail (catching the headboard under a line happens with lazy jacks unless you're truly

head to wind, and the head of the sail is not flapping back and forth). Also, the polypropylene line is very small and light. And if you're worried about what the system will look like on your boat, the lines are practically invisible.

## Whipping Lines

All lines—running rigging, anchor rodes, painters, outhauls, etc.—should have their ends whipped to prevent ugly mare's tails. Not only are they unseamanlike, they snag cleats and eat away good (and expensive) line like a cancer. There are several methods of whipping, and the simplest can be mastered by a young child—so there's no excuse for not learning how to do it properly. Hervey Garrett Smith's *The Marlinspike Sailor* has a good chapter on whippings. If you can't or won't master whipping, at least dunk the ends in that dip-whip stuff! (West Marine sells a 4-ounce can of flexible vinyl Liquid Rope Whipping for about $8.)

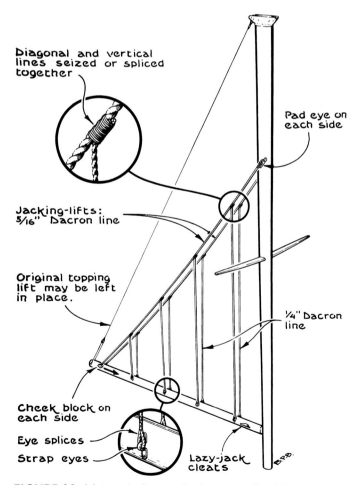

**FIGURE 10-44.** Lazy jacks contain the mainsail as it is lowered.

# SAILS

A good inventory of sails represents a substantial investment. It only makes sense to give serious thought to their type, material, weight, special features, and number. Because even a modestly sized cruising boat will have literally thousands of dollars tied up in sails, they should be cared for with equal thought and attention.

Most of us make lists of things we'd like to add to our boats. Some of these items are bound to cross the line between what's essential and what would "be nice to have." Sails, it often seem, take a second seat to this other gear, especially the latest electronics. But filling a gap in the sail inventory (for instance, buying a 130% genoa to add to the working jib and #1 genoa headsail inventory) can make all the difference between an enjoyable sail and one in which the boat just won't move because the right combination of sails can't be found. Even if you have roller furling and think your one headsail can do it all, that's not really the case when cruising. There will be times when you would like a larger light-air sail, and times when you absolutely must have a smaller heavy-air sail.

## *Types of Sailcloth and Weights*

The day of the cotton sail has long since passed. Nowadays, mainsails and headsails are almost universally made of Dacron or Terylene (a product similar to Dacron made in England). Spinnakers and very light off-the-wind headsails are made of nylon. Race boats have sails made of Kevlar, Mylar, and Spectra. The best are sails molded of film with practically no porosity. Laminated hybrid sails are slowly entering the cruising market. But these cloths are more expensive than the old standbys and require extra care in handling because they can be damaged by improper furling or folding. While sails such as those with load-directional reinforcements have remarkable abilities to hold shape, their frailties make them less attractive to the cruising person. After more developmental work is done, perhaps materials such as these will be viable for the cruising boat. Certainly being able to stow a headsail on a furler minimizes some of the potential harm.

Sailcloth is woven from two sets of threads: those that run the length of the bolt are called the *warp* threads, and those that run at right angles along the width of the bolt are called the *weft*, or filler, threads. If the warp and weft threads are of the same size, strength, and stretch, the cloth is called *balanced*. If one set of threads is stronger than the other, the construction is called *unbalanced*. Because sailcloth is woven from threads passing over and under one another at right angles, a load on the bias (Figure 10-45) elongates the cloth by forcing the individual threads to fill the tiny spaces between them. When there's no space left, stretch stops.

The strain on the edge of a sail is proportionate to its length, especially the unsupported edge from the clew to the head. On a high-aspect mainsail (any sail whose luff is at least 2½ times longer than the foot), for example, the strain is greatest along the leech. The cloth used for this type of sail is woven with weft threads larger than the warp and pulled tighter. Low-aspect mainsails are made from cloth that is more balanced and, therefore, lower in bias stretch.

To inhibit stretch, sails are stabilized by washing and heat-processing the cloth to induce shrinkage—sort of like preshrunk jeans. Then a filler and/or finish is added, often a polymer resin, that minimizes porosity and helps protect the threads from fatigue and ultraviolet deterioration. Special cloths are woven for the charter industry and for leech protection on roller furling headsails that have been treated with additional ultraviolet inhibitors. But this process makes the cloth heavier, quite stiff, and unsuitable for across-the-board application. Sails should *always* be covered or

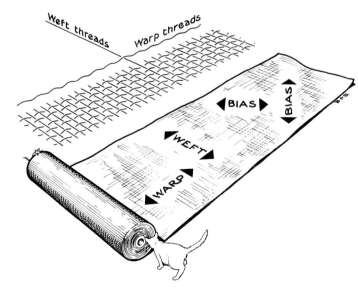

**FIGURE 10-45.** Sailcloth is woven with threads running at right angles. It is most subject to stretch when loads are placed on the bias.

221

bagged when not in use to prevent unnecessary exposure to ultraviolet rays.

Sailcloths are distinguished by their weight in ounces for a given area. In the United States, the American Bureau of Standards stipulates the area as 28½ inches by 36 inches (724 mm by 914 mm). The United Kingdom uses ounce per square yard. Elsewhere in Europe, the metric system weighs cloth in grams per square meter. If ordering sails in another country, it is important to know which system is being used.

There are many factors involved in determining the correct weight cloth for a given sail. These include typical wind force, area, aspect ratio, stiffness of the boat, and displacement. While your sailmaker is the best advisor, a bit of knowledge on your part will help you talk more intelligently with him or her and give you a basis for overruling if you see your needs differently than he or she does.

A sail made from cloth that is too light will stretch out of shape prematurely, and a cloth too heavy for its application won't achieve a very good shape, especially in light air. On the other hand, light cloth achieves a better shape and reduces weight aloft, while heavier cloth, with its necessarily heavier thread, has greater tear strength.

Mainsails and working headsails are often made from the same-weight cloth. Light, intermediate, and heavy genoas are made from progressively heavier cloths below and above the weights of working sails. Racing sailors carry different-weight genoas of the same size for different wind conditions. This enables them to maximize speed at all times. But the cruising sailor may not have the room or cash to indulge in this luxury. Also cloth weights recommended by most sail lofts, in my experience, tend to be the weights used by the majority of their clientele; that is, the weekend racer/cruiser. Cloth weights for cruising may run a bit heavier. But evolving developments make it possible to build lighter, more efficient sails than ten or twenty years ago, thanks to airfoil research and computer-aided designs. Determining the right cloth weight for a given boat must take into account many variables, including the size of the sails, type of rig, displacement, and stiffness of the boat, as well as how the boat is used.

A rough formula suggested by Jeremy Howard-Williams, in his book *Sails*, derives the weight (oz./yd.²) for working sails by dividing the waterline length of the boat by 3 and subtracting 10%. Add 10% for coastal cruising, 20% for oc-

casional offshore passages, and as much as 30% for a stiff, heavy-displacement, offshore cruising boat. As noted above, however, developments in the sailmaking industry now permit the building of lighter sails, so this rule-of-thumb calculation probably runs a bit toward the heavy side. Consult your sailmaker for advice and make it quite clear just what sort of cruising you intend to do.

## Sail Reinforcements

To stand up to the wear and tear of everyday use, good cruising sails need reinforcement. The corners of each sail—tack, clew, and head—should have several layers of cloth heavier than the sail itself sewn on top of each other and extending at least several feet into the sail. To a point, more layers are better. The size of reinforcing patches at the tack and clew of the sail should be about $\frac{1}{12}$ the length of the luff and leech respectively, and $\frac{1}{8}$ the length of the foot. A two-ply leech adds strength to this critical area, as does tabling the raw edges all around. Not only is the leech unsupported for the most part, but the placement of batten pockets is likely to subject it to a certain amount of chafe. Batten pockets should be sewn of several layers with nylon protectors sewn into the inside end to prevent chafe. Triple stitching is a worthwhile additional expense.

Similarly, those panels where reef points are sewn in should at least be reinforced with heavier-weight patches or be sewn with two-ply cloth and patches on top. Follow the rule of thumb above for the size of these patches.

Aaron Jasper, a Newport, Rhode Island, sailmaker, says that he doesn't recommend hand-sewn cringles on large boats because they tend to distort under load. Navy bronze or plastic cringles with stainless steel nails to grip the cloth are now standard in his loft; a hydraulic press is used to secure the two halves together, taking the skill and risk out of making a cringle.

Seams are particularly susceptible to chafe and ultraviolet deterioration because of the exposure of the threads used to sew panels together. Tape can be applied over seams, or, as is more common in many lofts, a liquid plastic such as Seam Kote or Plastiseam (www.sail-making.com) is brushed over the seams, doubling their resistance to chafe and ultraviolet deterioration.

Bolt ropes, headboards, sail slides, jib hanks, and luff tape must be properly sewn to the sail, using the correct-size thread for the job and the correct stitches. Sail slides and jib hanks are probably the items most subject to failure, and the ones you should be able to replace yourself underway.

Battens can be made from wood or fiberglass, though the latter is much more common today, partly because fiberglass ones are easier for the manufacturer to taper, and partly because they bend easier and are stronger. Corners should be well rounded, and a cap or tape applied to the ends to prevent chafing the batten pocket and sail.

## The Battenless, Roachless Mainsail

Some cruising sailors, no doubt distraught over the number of hours spent repairing batten pockets, advocate the use of battenless, roachless mainsails. On the plus side, battens and batten pockets are eliminated, which may be the single largest cause of sail repairs. And, on boats with excessive weather helm, the reduction in sail area can make the boat balance better. In his book *After 50,000 Miles*, Hal Roth makes a case for the battenless, roachless mainsail. And veteran cruisers Jane and Shelly DeRidder feel the lack of aggravation is well worth the slight loss in speed.

On the negative side, a battenless, roachless sail will never achieve the same desirable shape of a conventional sail. The reduction in sail area will cause a loss of speed, and while some justify it by saying sailboats are so slow anyway, what's another ½-knot drop in speed, I'm inclined to think that that ½ knot is all the more important *because* sailboats are so slow. Using a roachless main on a well-balanced boat could cause neutral or slight lee helm, which would not be desirable.

On several of my newer mainsails, my sailmaker has designed a full-length upper batten, which tends to stabilize the leech and reduce wear—at least on the upper portions.

Speaking of new sails, those of you with old sails should be aware that they may be the cause of any unusual weather helm you are experiencing. As a sail loses shape over the years (often caused by using the sail in winds that are too strong), the position of maximum draft is moved aft, which in turn pushes the aft end of the boat sideways and the bow higher. You might be surprised what a difference a new, properly cut sail will do to improve balance, speed, and windward ability.

## The Fully Battened Mainsail

Just as the roachless, battenless mainsail has its proponents, so too does the fully battened mainsail. It's been around a long time, most notably in the form of the Chinese lug rig, which is several thousand years old. "Rediscovery" of the design by sailmakers has caused no little debate. Here are some pros and cons:

- **Greater sail area.** Full-length battens allow larger than normal roaches, which increase sail area and speed off the wind; however, the backstay limits the ultimate size of the roach. Running backstays can be used in place of a backstay, as on the large multihulls, but this is an impractical rig for a cruising boat.

- **Lighter weight.** Full-length battens permit the use of lighter-weight sailcloth, but this savings is more than lost by the weight of the battens. Even with normal weight cloth and battens, the total added weight for a 35-foot (10.7 m) boat might be only 15 pounds (7 kg).

- **Durability.** If short battens are bad because they cause chafe, full-length battens must be worse. Plus, if the cloth weight is less, ultraviolet degradation will be quicker. Better to stick with the normal weight cloth. Proponents say that because flogging is minimized, the life of the sail is extended.

- **Easy handling.** Loads tend to wedge the battens against mast, making the sail more difficult to hoist and lower. This is why you'll want to invest in proprietary sail track and batten cars.

  One of the real advantages of these sails is the neat way in which the battens flake the sail down over the boom, especially if used in combination with lazy jacks.

- **Superior sail shape.** Fully battened sails might provide better shape in light air if the battens are light. But in heavy air, you'll need heavier battens, and it is impractical to change battens every time wind velocity changes.

- **Superior speed.** Off-the-wind boat speed may increase but not enough to make a great deal of difference to the cruiser.

- **Cost.** Fully battened mainsails cost about 25% more.

- **Quietness.** When motoring to windward or coming head to wind for anchoring or

223

mooring, fully battened sails don't make as much noise or flap as hard, a feature appreciated by everyone.

Tom Clark, who was a fine maker of traditional sails in Connecticut, wasn't a fan of fully battened sails. When someone touted them by pointing to the long history behind Chinese lug rigs, he snorted and said, "The Portuguese sailed to China 400 years ago without battens. The Chinese still haven't sailed to Portugal."

## Sail Inventories

The well-found cruising boat should carry sails for all types of weather, ranging from ghosting conditions to full-blown gales. Of course, much of the inventory will apply to those middle and more normal conditions. But shortchanging yourself by skipping storm sails or drifters means endangering the boat and crew at worst and subjecting them to excessive heel or irritating slatting at least.

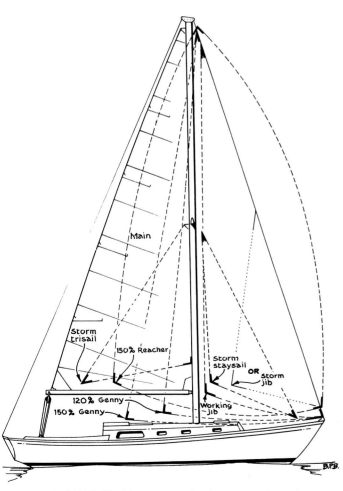

FIGURE 10-46. Suggested sail inventory for a sloop.

Naturally, there is the problem of stowing a large inventory of sails, especially on smaller boats. Too frequently, the interior layout of modern production boats ignores sail stowage space—forepeaks are small and inaccessible, cockpit seat lockers are infringed by large aft quarter cabins, and lazarettes disappear with cockpits pushed all the way to the stern to make more room below. This can be partially overcome if the working sails can be furled and stowed on deck. Club-footed jibs and staysails have the advantage of being easy to furl and stow. Roller furling genoas keep the sail off the deck entirely. Other sails should be stowed below if at all possible; if not, furl them along the deck, protected with specially sewn canvas covers and lashed to the stanchions.

The following are suggested minimum sail inventories for sloops, cutters, ketches, and yawls, including optional sails.

**Sloop with single headsail** (Figure 10-46):

Mainsail
Working jib
No. 1 genoa (150%)
No. 2 genoa (110% to 130%)
Drifter, reacher, or cruising spinnaker
Trysail
Storm jib
Optional:
  No. 2 jib
  Second mainsail

Note: a genoa designated as #1 or #2 does not refer to a specific percentage of foretriangle size (the LP measurement, which is a perpendicular from the luff intersecting the clew, is used in determining 130%, 150%, etc.). Rather, #1 or #2 refers to the largest headsail carried on board, next largest, and so on.

**Cutter and double-headsail sloops** (Figure 10-47):

Mainsail
Yankee jib
Staysail with reef points
Trysail
Storm jib
Drifter, reacher, or cruising spinnaker
Optional:
  No. 1 Yankee jib

No. 3 Yankee jib

Small or storm staysail

**Ketch or Yawl** (Figure 10-48):

Mainsail

Mizzen working jib

No. 1 genoa (150%)

No. 2 genoa (110% to 130%)

Drifter, reacher, or cruising spinnaker

Trysail

Storm jib

Optional:

No. 2 jib

Mizzen staysail

When cruising with a limited sail inventory, the light-air genoa is often not included. The weight of the sail and sheets keep the heavier cloth genoa from filling. A trick to reduce weight is to

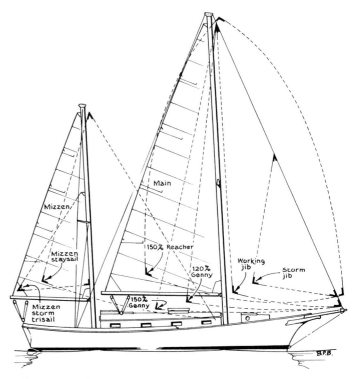

**FIGURE 10-48.** Suggested sail inventory for a ketch or yawl.

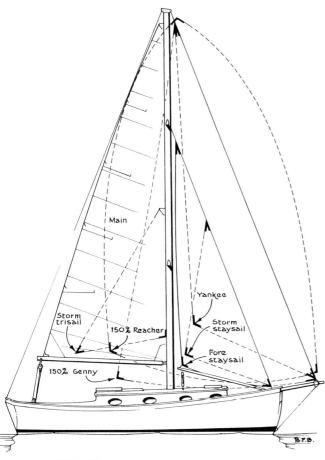

**FIGURE 10-47.** Suggested sail inventory for a cutter and double-headsail sloop.

take off the standard sheets and use a smaller-diameter line. The diameter of most sheets is chosen more for handling, not for strength, and in extreme light airs, moving down a size or two won't hurt.

## Options for Roller Furling Headstays

The foregoing recommendations assume hanked-on headsails, which are fast going the way of the dinosaurs. The recommendations still are helpful, though, in at least showing the range of sail sizes needed. Because a roller furling headsail is only efficient for about two-thirds of its size (meaning when rolled up more than two-thirds, its shape stinks, and the boat won't point or balance well), heavy- and light-air options are required.

Earlier in this chapter, inner forestays were discussed for the express purpose of flying a staysail in heavy air. It can be hanked on (preferable if you want a removable inner forestay) or set on a furler. So when the wind pipes up, you roll up the genoa (not larger than about 130 to 135%) and set the staysail (Figure 10-49).

An alternative to the staysail, especially appealing on small boats where the foretriangle really isn't large enough to subdivide, is the ATN

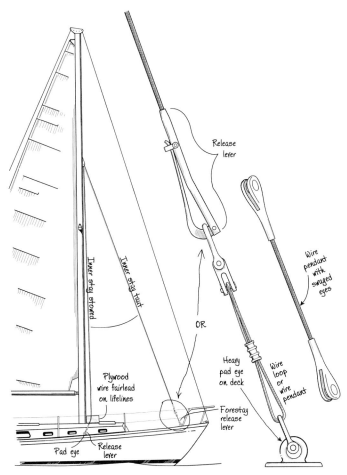

FIGURE 10-49. A removable inner forestay is a popular solution to providing for a heavy-air sail on a boat with a roller furling genoa. The old Highfield lever has been superseded by more modern quick-release levers such as this one by ABI. Because the stay is too long to secure at the base of the mast when not in use, a Nicopressed wire loop or swaged pendant is sometimes added to the stay when setting up and removed when the stay is to be stowed. (Fritz Seegers illustration)

Gale Sail (Figure 10-50; www.atninc/gale/html). It has a reinforced sleeve that rides over the furled headsail. Considered a storm jib, it's available in several preset sizes. A decided advantage is that with a storm jib set on the existing forestay, you don't need an inner forestay and the attendant running backstays—a lot of hardware. On the other hand, once you switch down from the mainsail to a trysail, you want the center of effort of the sail plan nearer the mast, so the boat balances well. The combination of a trysail and storm jib far forward may not balance as well as a trysail and staysail. You'd have to experiment. Another

FIGURE 10-50. An alternative to setting a staysail on its own stay is the ATN Gale Sail, which has a sleeve that fits over the furled-up headsail.

concern I have about the Gale Sail is setting it in bad weather, because you have to feed it over the furled headsail and secure it as you go with hook and loop—all the while braced on the bow, probably getting soaked. Definitely a safety harness and jackline operation.

## Making Your Own Sails

Should you decide to sew your own sails, you will need four things: (1) a heavy-duty sewing machine; (2) a large floor area to lay out cloth; (3) cloth, thread, and other hardware; and (4) some instruction on how to do it. There are a number of good books on how to make sails and you should be read these thoroughly. Considering the cost of sailcoth, building your own sails is a sensible alternative. Sailrite Enterprises (www.sailrite.com) specializes in sail and canvas kits, supporting them with how-to videos and detailed instructions in PDF format. Everyone I know who has dealt with Sailrite has nothing but good things to say. The company offers all the different types and weights of cloth, thread, and hardware, and even the preferred sewing machine. The savings you can achieve by building your own sails is substantial, not to mention the independence it gives you.

Some years ago, my friend Danny Greene finished a passage from Puerto Rico to Haiti with a new suit of sails he made on a hilltop above a friend's house in Puerto Rico. He wrote that the sails performed beautifully, despite the insects, cockroaches, lizards, cats, and dogs that hampered his work. "There are still a few unidentified tails sewn into the seams," he later wrote, but, considering their performance, obviously he got his money's worth from Sailrite.

## Getting the Sails Made

When shopping for new sails, give the same specifications to three or four lofts and compare prices. Discuss your needs frankly with each one. Be aware that many lofts may try to sell you more than you want or sails other than what you prefer. This usually happens because sail lofts often are run by racers who are anxious to stay on the cutting edge of technology. That is fine, but if you're planning to sail across the South Pacific to Australia, you don't need Mylar panels, zippers, and many of the go-fast options. Some options *are* useful, such as windows with trim yarns for helping you get the most out of each sail, leech lines, and perhaps cunninghams to control the luff. But the bottom line is that long-term durability is more important than short-term performance. The more sure you are of what you want when you go in, the better the chances you'll end up with what you want when you come out.

There are a number of discount lofts, including some "offshore" companies doing business in the Far East, whose prices are tempting. While the same quality and weight cloth may be used as the higher-priced lofts, savings are often obtained by using less stitching and smaller patches. Plus, there are optional extras such as spring-loaded batten pockets, sail slides on shackles, triple stitching, and fancy batten pocket enclosures. The point is that prices of sails vary, and they are sometimes negotiable. This is most often true in the fall and winter when sail lofts aren't as busy; they need the work to keep staff earning their salaries over the dark, cold months of winter. Try to negotiate in April the same price you were quoted at the fall boat show, however, and chances are they'll tell you they don't even have the time to make the sail until July.

Most major sail lofts today, including Shore, Hood, Doyle, and North, use computer-aided design (CAD) programs to lay out the panels, and plotters and laser cutting machines to make sails. Some lofts have these at each location, others use a central shop to do all the cutting and mail the individual panels back to the local loft for assembly.

It is not uncommon, especially when taking big orders, for the head sailmaker to go sailing with the client for an hour or so to observe the existing sails and learn more intimately what the client expects. Some offshore lofts count on you to take the measurements of your rig (the P, E, J, I, etc.), or if your boat is a popular "stock" model, like a Catalina 42, they'll use the dimensions given in their files. Most of the time this works out okay, but not always. Regarding the latter, builders often make subtle changes to their boats that are never fully documented. There are occasional differences in rigs and fittings even among different hull numbers of the same model boat. The most certain way to avoid surprises when you bend on new sails for the first time is to have had the sailmaker take his own measurements. That way, any mistakes are his fault, not yours or the builder's.

There is a human element that cannot be entirely controlled. Take confidence in the fact, however, that if unsatisfied, you can always take the sail back and ask for alterations. On large racing boats, alterations are routine. This alone recommends using a local loft.

Rod Stephens said that cruising sailors should sail their boats at 95% efficiency of the racing skipper. Whether or not you agree, the point is that the cruising skipper should know something about the theory of sails, trim, and what will best meet his needs.

## Reefing Systems

Perhaps no other alteration to your sails is as important as the sewing of reef points. Whether you use roller reefing or slab (jiffy) reefing (Figure 10-51), it is important to achieve a flat set on the main. Failure to achieve this can impair your ability to handle the boat. My Triton once was pooped in Green Bay because the roller reefing boom left such a belly in the sail that the boat wouldn't point—a beam reach was about the best it would do. Not even stuffing towels into the foot of the sail or pulling the boom as far to windward as possible made any difference. The next year I

227

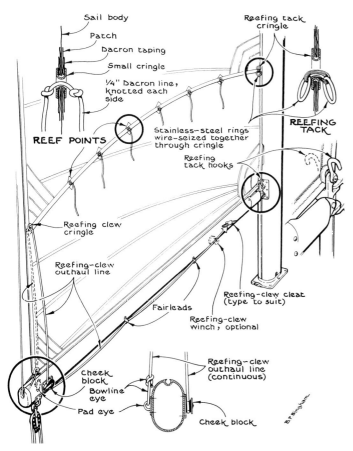

Sail body
Patch
Dacron taping
Small cringle
1/4" Dacron line,
knotted each
side
REEF POINTS
Stainless-steel rings
wire-seized together
through cringle
Reefing tack
cringle
REEFING
TACK
Reefing
tack hooks
Reefing clew
cringle
Reefing-clew
outhaul line
Fairleads
Reefing-clew cleat
(type to suit)
Reefing-clew
winch, optional
Cheek
block
Bowline
eye
Pad eye
Reefing-clew
outhaul line
(continuous)
Cheek block

FIGURE 10-51. Slab reefing is quick and results in a flat set of the mainsail. If you double-end the reefing line (not shown), you can always reef on the windward side of the boat.

installed slab reefing and experienced no more problems.

The ability to reef down in a blow is vital. Heel is reduced, speed is seldom lost (and actually may be increased if the boat excels at lower angles of heel), and the crew will certainly feel safer.

To install slab reefing, the mainsail must have one or more sets of reef points sewn in. These are cringles pressed or sewn over reinforced patches on the sail, and because the sail is not made entirely flat, the line of points will not be straight. Your sailmaker will know where to place them. Two or three sets are desirable if you are to get maximum use from your mainsail in worsening conditions.

Once the reef points are sewn in, take a length of 3/16- to 1/4-inch (5 mm to 6 mm) polyester line and cut it into 3-foot (0.9 m) lengths (longer if your mainsail exceeds about 300 square feet/28 sq. m). Run the line through a cringle and tie knots on either side so that it hangs evenly on either side.

You'll also need a cheek block bolted or screwed to the boom for each set of points and a cleat forward near the gooseneck, so you can pull in the leech after slackening the halyard. A reefing hook should be fixed to the gooseneck to secure the cringle at the luff of the sail. And lastly, a length of line must be led from a pad eye on one side of the boom, up through the cringle at the leech, down through the cheek block, and forward to the cleat. Fairleads keep this line from sagging off the boom.

To use slab reefing: (1) ease the mainsheet; (2) take up the topping lift; (3) slacken the main halyard; (4) fit the luff cringle over the reefing hook at the gooseneck; (5) take up the halyard; (6) pull in on the reefing line until the clew is tight to the boom, then cleat it; (7) ease the topping lift; and (8) sheet in the sail and tie the lines in the reef points under the boom using a reef knot. This whole process takes very little time—a minute or two with practice.

## Headsail Roller Furling

Changing headsails is one of the most strenuous and onerous jobs when sailing. Reluctance to expend the effort to change down in size can lead to being dangerously overcanvased in high winds. Similarly, failing to change to a larger, lighter-weight sail means poor light-air performance, a problem all too often solved by turning on the engine. For many people, roller furling headsails are the answer. Tremendous advances in recent years have created more reliable and efficient gears, but roller furlers still have limitations, and anyone planning to install one for offshore sailing should be well aware of their design, construction, and fallibility.

New furling gears appear like better mousetraps. Some use airfoil-shaped aluminum sections that slip over the existing headstay, others use substantial one-piece extrusions that replace the headstay. Almost all systems require some modification to the headstay. The furling drums may have sealed stainless steel bearings and races or Torlon bearings in open races that require regular rinsing with fresh water. Some drums can be removed quickly for racing, others cannot.

Modern furling gears can be reefed sailing upwind but not all the way down to the proverbial "postage stamp." A *Practical Sailor* survey showed that most users could safely reef down about 22% without padded luffs—which help

228

maintain shape—and about 30% with padded luffs. This means that in the best of conditions, a 150% genoa cannot even be safely reduced to 100%. Consequently, the cruiser needs to be able to hoist smaller sails for strong winds.

Changing headsails using the grooved extrusions is a risky proposition in rough weather. Luff tapes aren't captured as are hanks, and the sail can pull out as fast as you feed it in. A better solution is to rig an inner forestay, perhaps removable, and hoist conventional hank-on sails when the going gets tough (refer back to Figure 10-7). Be sure to secure the furled sail, with lashings if necessary, to prevent it from unfurling and flogging itself to shreds.

Hood Yacht Systems (www.hoodyachtsystems.com) was a pioneer in furling gear development, but it has lost market share to a number of newcomers, especially Harken (www.harken.com), Schaefer (www.schaefermarine.com), and Furlex (www.seldenmast.com; Figure 10-52). French ocean racers have proven the Profurl (www.profurl.com) gear with sealed bearing races (Figure 10-53). The German-made Reckmann (www.reckmann.com), at twice the price of almost all others, is the Rolls-Royce of the lot, but usually it is seen only on large, high-end yachts.

Installing furling gear is about a half-day job that can be accomplished by a reasonably handy person. If you don't feel up to it, a professional rigger is the way to go, but he'd like you to buy it from him, not some discount catalog. Follow instructions closely, especially where the angle of the halyard to the head swivel is critical: a mistake here can result in wrapping the halyard under heavy load.

Single-handed ocean racers such as Phil Weld, who won the 1980 Ostar in the trimaran *Moxie*, and Philippe Jeantot, who won the first two BOC Challenges in *Crédit Agricole*, made believers of many skeptics. If a single man could rely on furling gear to take him safely across an ocean, through every wind condition without failing, then why couldn't the average cruiser trust them? In fact, the aging Weld said he couldn't have won without being able to simply "dial" the amount of sail he wanted. Modern furlers are vastly improved from the first generation of gear. Today, furling gear is essential equipment on single-handed racers and large cruising yachts; coupled with hydraulic power and electric winches, furling gear has changed the design and use of large sailing yachts dramatically. On an 80-footer (24 m),

**FIGURE 10-52.** The Furlex headsail furler is provided as a complete kit, including new headstay. (Seldén Mast photo)

**FIGURE 10-53.** The French-made Profurl headsail furling gear has been the popular choice of single-handed ocean racers. (*Practical Sailor* photo)

it is no longer necessary to have a dozen crew lugging headsails up from the cavernous racks below; instead the captain steps on a padded switch and trims the sail effortlessly.

### Mainsail Furling Gear

Lagging behind headsails, but not forgotten, are the growing number of mainsail furling gears. Many people got their first look at this innovation when they heard the weird howling sound of Hood's Stoway internal mainsail furling system somewhere down the dock (like someone blowing over a giant soda bottle mouth). Hood later developed a canvas flap to cover the slot, but it seemed seldom used. Hood's system required buying a special spar from the company that was very expensive and made it hard to justify for retrofitting existing boats.

For a decade or longer, mainsail furling devices concentrated on in-the-mast and behind-the-mast systems (Figure 10-54). Like jib furling, they have improved. The Furlex Main from Seldén Mast (Figure 10-55) involves an add-on extrusion that is riveted to the aft side of the mast. The worrisome aspect of all these, however, is freeing the sail if it jams above deck level. Plus, you generally have to be more or less head to wind to reef the sail. And there's a fair amount of friction, so a winch is required, often electric on bigger boats.

Hood also pioneered in-boom furling with its Stoboom, but it too has been superseded in the

**FIGURE 10-54.** FaMet Marine's mainsail reefing gear is another behind-the-mast system intended for retrofitting. The slot created between the mast and leading edge of the sail is not terribly efficient, but that's the price you pay for convenience. (*Practical Sailor* photo)

marketplace by Schaefer (Figure 10-56), Profurl, and Leisure Furl (Figure 10-57). In-boom systems are generally cheaper to retrofit, have the advantage of lowering the center of effort of the sail as its size is reduced, and keep all mechanisms at deck level where they can be worked on. Unlike in-the-mast and behind-the-mast systems, in-boom furling sails can have battens to better control shape and minimize leech flutter. On the downside, the boom angle is critical to reefing in-boom sails, so a rigid vang is required; on most of the systems, the boom-to-mast angle has to be around 87°, give or take a degree or two. And no furling mainsail will have the shape of a conventional sail, as furling mainsails have to be cut flatter.

The case for headsail furling doesn't stand up as well for mainsails, since the mainsail is self-tending, and jiffy reefing systems are simple, effective, and cheap by comparison.

Except on the very largest yachts, where money is nothing and the pursuit of relaxation and pleasure everything, mainsail furling gears seem unnecessary on most ordinary cruising boats under 50-something feet.

## WINCHES

Dollar per pound, these finely made mechanisms are among the most expensive gear on any boat. All of the major brands are good. Figure 10-58 recommends winch gear ratio for a given size sail; as with anchors, err on the large side. Winches do require some maintenance each year, principally taking off the top part and greasing the gears. Water pump or Teflon grease is usually recommended.

Self-tailing winches are now standard on most new boats. Marine consignment shops are full of non-self-tailers. The laborsaving convenience of the self-tailer must be experienced to be fully appreciated. On *Viva*, I retrofitted the original two-speed Lewmar #32s with three-speed self-tailers of the same size; suddenly, trimming headsails was a one-person job instead of a two-person job (Figure 10-59).

Bottom-action winches, while rarely seen on racing boats, do make sense for the cruiser. The winch handle needn't be removed every time the sheet is led around the winch, but on the negative side, they are slower than top-action winches. Murray, a New Zealand company, manufactures handsome bottom-action winches in bronze (Fig-

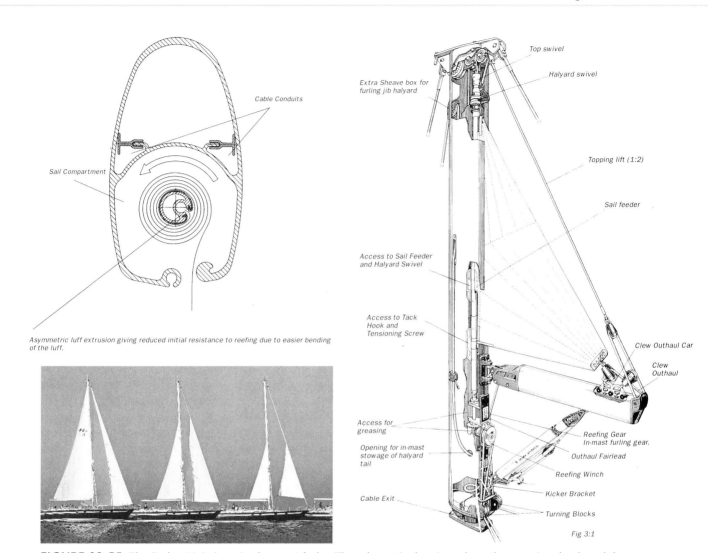

Asymmetric luff extrusion giving reduced initial resistance to reefing due to easier bending of the luff.

**FIGURE 10-55.** The Furlex Main is an in-the-mast furler. The schematic drawings show the parts involved, and the photo shows how nifty it is to reef the main with the touch of a button wired to an electric winch. Of course, the outhaul and halyard must be simultaneously eased. (Seldén Mast photo)

ure 10-60). Eric and Susan Hiscock swore by them; Lin and Larry Pardey swear by them still.

## Single-Winch Sheeting

Because of the high cost of quality winches, there is merit to using one winch for sheeting and another for halyards. A bridge deck makes a good central location for the sheet winch, which, because you've only bought one, can afford to be a bit bigger than required. With a large winch mounted on the bridge deck (Figure 10-61), and both sheets long enough to reach the winch at all times, it is a simple matter to unwrap and wrap the other when tacking. If cockpit coamings obstruct a fair lead from the deck blocks, you can in-

sert a roller into the coaming. Or you may be able to use flared stainless steel tubing through the coaming if the line doesn't turn sharp corners. The best part is that when the boat is heeled far over, no one has to go down on the leeward rail to trim the sails as it's all done from the security of the center-cockpit area.

## Single Halyard Winch

This same arrangement used for sheets can be used for halyard winches, with the use of cleats, turning sheaves and linestoppers (Figure 10-62). Many racing and cruising boats lead lines back to the cockpit, with winches mounted on the cabin top. They should be through-bolted to the

**FIGURE 10-56.** Schaefer Marine is the most recent company to introduce an in-boom furling system. Like the others, it has the advantage of keeping all mechanisms at deck level where they can be more easily worked on. The photo shows the external track; the illustration shows the bearing races at each end. (Schaefer Marine)

**FIGURE 10-57.** The Leisure Furl in-boom system was the first to solve some of the problems encountered with the early Hood Stoboom. While boom angle is still important (about 87° to the mast), as is a rigid vang, it rolls without bunching up. The North American distributor is Forespar. The close-up photos show the through-mast drive with control line. If the line breaks, the sail may be lowered by inserting a winch into the drum. (Forespar)

| | Winch Power Ratios | | | | |
|---|---|---|---|---|---|
| | 10:1 | 20:1 | 30:1 | 40:1 | 50:1 |
| | Maximum Sail Areas | | | | |
| Main/Mizzen/Foresail/Self-Trimming Headsail Sheets (Based on a 4:1 block purchase) | to 200 | to 400 | to 650 | to 1,000 | |
| Genoa/Jib/Working Staysail Sheets | to 100 | to 200 | to 300 | to 400 | to 600 |
| Light Staysail Sheets (Secondary cockpit) | to 150 | to 275 | to 400 | to 600 | to 900 |
| Spinnaker Sheets | to 200 | to 400 | to 900 | to 2,000 | to 4,000 |
| Main/Mizzen/Foresail Halyards | to 200 | to 300 | to 400 | to 600 | to 1,000 |
| Genoa/Jib/Working Staysail Halyards | to 200 | to 275 | to 350 | to 500 | to 800 |
| Spinnaker Halyard | to 300 | to 600 | to 1,500 | to 3,500 | to 5,000 |
| Light Staysail Halyards | to 300 | to 400 | to 500 | to 700 | to 1,000 |

**FIGURE 10-58.** Winch selection chart.

**FIGURE 10-59.** Lewmar three-speed self-tailing winches make a one-person job out of trimming headsails, even on larger boats.

**FIGURE 10-60.** White Star Products (www.whitestarproducts.co.nz) makes the Murray line of bronze bottom-action winches (distributed in the U.S. by Imtra, www.imtra.com). The crank is geared low for extra power in trimming sheets just right.

deck and well bedded. Perhaps I'm old-fashioned, but this arrangement doesn't work as well for me as it obviously does for many others. Somehow it seems to require more grunting than winching from the mast.

## HALYARD LEADS, CLEATS, AND CLUTCHES

The single halyard winch concept requires that halyards be led aft via turning sheaves or fairleads at the base of the mast. Linestoppers or rope clutches (which can bleed line tension gradually) are commonly used to snub them because it wouldn't be possible to cleat the halyard without removing it from the winch. And since the winch must be cleared to make room for the next halyard, some method of securing the halyard in front of the winch is necessary—linestoppers, rope clutches, clam cleats, or cam cleats.

As noted above, I'm not a big fan of linestoppers, cam cleats, and clam cleats. Having sailed on numerous boats with them, it seems to me they are prone to slipping and require considerable effort at times to jam the handle down hard enough to make it hold. But design improvements have been made, especially to rope clutches. I like the Lewmar Superlock models.

The whole logic for leading halyards aft seems a bit suspect anyway. So what if you can raise and lower sails from the cockpit? You still have to go forward to unfurl the main when it's going up and to gather it in when it comes down. Being able to drop sails from the cockpit may give you a few extra seconds of security, but in a blow (which is the only time this security is really necessary), a headsail loose on the foredeck won't stay there for long. Of course, nets on the lifelines and lazy jacks

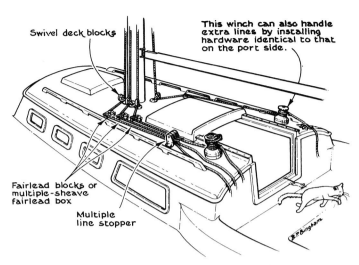

**FIGURE 10-62.** A single winch mounted next to the companionway hatch and a set of linestoppers can do the job of two or more mast-mounted halyard winches. Depending on the number of lines, two winches may be more advantageous.

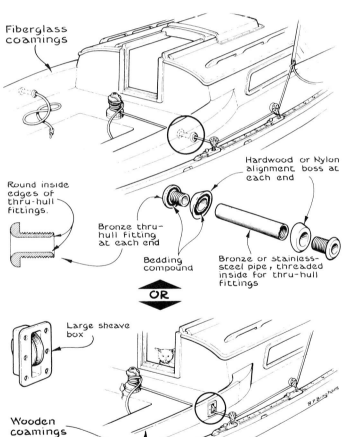

**FIGURE 10-61.** On *Frolic*, a large single winch was used amidships on the bridge deck (photo), instead of two separate winches at the coamings (illustration). The illustration shows how the sheets might be led through coamings.

on the main do assist in keeping these sails under control, but again, it is only a delaying tactic, unless you have roller furling on both headsail and mainsail.

# FURTHER READING

*Advanced Sailboat Cruising.* Colin Mudie, Geoff Hales, and Michael Handford. London: Nautical, 1981.

*The Art & Science of Sails: A Guide to Modern Materials, Construction, Aerodynamics, Upkeep, and Use.* Tom Whidden and Michael Levitt. New York: St. Martin's, 1990.

*Canvaswork & Sail Repair.* Don Casey. Camden, Maine: International Marine, 1996.

*The Care of Alloy Spars and Rigging.* David Potter. New York: Scribner, 1980.

*The Complete Canvasworker's Guide: How to Outfit Your Boat with Fabric.* 2nd ed. Jim Grant. Camden, Maine: International Marine, 1992.

*Cruising Rigs and Rigging.* Ross Norgrove. Camden, Maine: International Marine, 1982.

*Make Your Own Sails.* Rev. ed. R. M. Bowker and S. A. Budd. New York: St. Martin's, 1975.

*The Marlinspike Sailor.* Hervey Garrett Smith. Camden, Maine: International Marine, 1993.

*The Ocean Sailing Yacht.* Vols. 1 and 2. Donald Street. New York: Norton, 1973–1978.

*One Hand for Yourself, One for the Ship: The Essentials of Single-Handed Sailing.* Tristan Jones. Dobbs Ferry, New York: Sheridan House, 1990.

*The Sailmaker's Apprentice: A Guide for the Self-Reliant Sailor.* Emiliano Marino. Camden, Maine: International Marine, 1994.

*Sail Power: The Complete Guide to Sails and Sail Handling.* Rev. and updated ed. Wallace Ross with Carl Chapman. New York: Knopf, 1984.

*Sails.* 5th ed. Jeremy Howard-Williams. Clinton Corners, New York: John de Graff, 1983.

*The Splicing Handbook: Techniques for Modern and Traditional Ropes.* 2nd ed. Barbara Merry. Camden, Maine: International Marine, 2000.

# ELEVEN

# GALLEY SYSTEMS

Eating well at sea, or at the dock, is a pleasure to be regarded as highly as fine weather, a sound boat, and a compatible crew. When everyone is pleased with the food, inclement weather and other annoyances don't seem so serious. But when the food is lousy, it exacerbates every other problem, making more sensitive crew members whine and gripe, and taking the edge off even the most optimistic.

Health and safety are involved in cooking, too. Albeit some single-handed passage-makers live on beans and sardines for weeks at a time, they are by and large a hardy lot who know themselves and what it takes to be comfortable. For some, the prospect of cooking *anything* is more insufferable than a boring diet. Not so for most of us, especially when we aren't moved to stoicism by the competitiveness of a race with other sailors, or we aren't trying to prove something to ourselves.

Choosing a balanced diet for each member of the crew is not within the scope of this book. But providing the space and major equipment to prepare food certainly is. A sailor can survive with a few ounces of water each day for several weeks, longer by adding a few ounces of food. For the person in a life raft, cooking is impossible, unless drying fish fillets in the sun is a form of baking. Under normal circumstances, however, the crew will want tasty meals, and the ease with which these can be prepared will go a long way toward making a cruise happy and memorable.

## REQUIREMENTS OF A GOOD GALLEY

The well-thought-out galley has sufficient storage space for foodstuffs: cans, boxes, jars, and bottles. Cutlery, plates, and pans should be stowed in a secure place where they won't fall out when the boat heels, yet be within arm's reach when the cook wants them.

Under-deck areas are often wasted spaces; near the galley they can be converted to convenient storage for plates and glasses. Quarter-inch (6 mm) plywood can be cut with a saber saw, framed with cleats, glued, and nailed to form holders for these items (Figure 11-1).

Cutlery is best left inside drawers that are notched inside the facing to keep them from spewing their contents when the boat heels (Figure 11-2). Plywood spacers or plastic Rubbermaid cutlery dividers inside drawers maintain a semblance of order. Secure plates by vertical dowels (Figure 11-3), and where ventilation is important to keep foods from rotting, vinyl-coated metal wired baskets are helpful (Figure 11-4).

Pots and pans, especially the heavy cast-iron variety, are best stored low, for better weight distribution and for safety. Underneath the galley or in a padded bin against the hull is all right, but the latter location often requires a long reach. Try to avoid bins that force reaching across the stove, which is dangerous when the burners are lit.

Few boats have proper pot and pan stowage so you'll have to use your ingenuity. If worse comes to worst, dump them all in a box with a secure lid and stow it. You certainly don't want cast-iron skillets flying around in heavy weather.

The galley sink should be deep and, if possible, a double model. With two sink compartments, dishes can be washed in one and rinsed in the other. They should be wide and deep enough, say 10 inches (254 mm), so you can pass a dish beneath the spigot—a high one helps. If your sink is small, try using a plastic basin to wash dishes with salt water and soap (Prell shampoo and Joy detergent make suds well in salt water), then transfer them to the sink for a freshwater rinse. A seawater pump at the galley sink helps conserve fresh water. (For more on pumps, see Chapter 5; to install a seacock at the intake through-hull, see Chapter 4.)

The resulting conservation of fresh water cannot be appreciated until you've carried water to

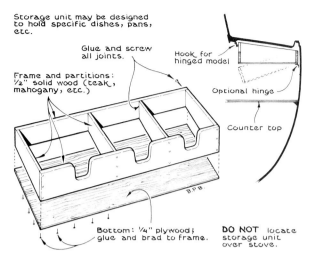

FIGURE 11-1. Plates and glasses can be stored in plywood cabinets you can make yourself. Areas under the deck and adjacent to the galley are convenient choices and don't take up otherwise usable space.

your boat in jerricans or tried to drain off water from awning or deck catchment systems (refer back to Figures 9-25 and 9-26). Living aboard at the dock, with the luxury of unlimited fresh water from a nearby hose and faucet, definitely dulls your appreciation for this precious commodity.

The stove is as important as any other element of the galley, and selection of fuel type no less so. The first decision is whether to have stovetop burners or a stove/oven combination (Figure 11-5). With pressure cookers and hay boxes, turkeys and roasts can be satisfactorily cooked on a stove top, but the end result is a little less certain. Fresh bread, a tough product to come by at sea or in se-

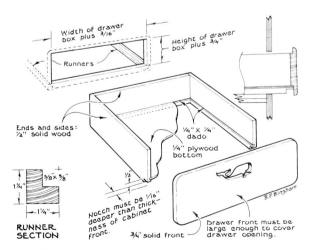

FIGURE 11-2. Cutlery should be placed in divided drawers with notches to prevent it from spilling out when the boat heels. Make finger holes for ventilation.

FIGURE 11-3. Plates can be held in place by vertically installed dowels in a cubby behind the galley counter.

cluded anchorages, is most easily baked in an oven. So, if there's space in your galley, give extra thought to an oven.

A stove/oven, however, must be fitted to one spot permanently by virtue of its size alone. Almost always, it will be mounted to face athwartship

FIGURE 11-4. The life of foods susceptible to rot often can be extended by storing in a well-ventilated area, such as these coated metal wire baskets.

**FIGURE 11-5.** The popular Force 10 stove/oven. Note the adjustable retaining fiddles to hold pots, oven window guards, and the galley safety bar mounted across the front of the stove. (Force 10)

and gimballed so that it swings as the boat rocks, minimizing the chance of dumping a pot full of hot stew over the cook's bare legs. (Burns are extremely serious injuries and must be avoided in every possible way. Always carry a good supply of burn cream like Silvadene to treat burns until professional medical care can be obtained.)

Gimballing is not always necessary when cooking, and always a nuisance when you're not. A deadbolt that locks the stove to the bulkheads on either side is a wise installation.

High stove fiddles—3 to 4 inches (76 mm to 102 mm)—will keep most pots on the burner even if the stove isn't gimballed. Free-thinking Tom Colvin challenges conventional thought by advocating ungimballed stoves mounted to face fore and aft in the galley. The gimbals, he says, only increase the likelihood of scalding the cook, and facing fore or aft means that if the boat is suddenly rocked the pots will fly sideways, athwartship, while the cook will probably fall away from the stove, forward or aft, at the same time he or she goes sideways. In other words, cook and stew won't meet. And the best place for a galley, according to Tom? In the forward cabin! Most motion is athwartships, he reasons, which affects the bow no more than the midships area. And if the boat is beating into seas, yes, the motion forward

is worse, but who wants to cook then, anyway? Tom says he has built three boats for clients with the galley forward, and though each was at first skeptical, after months of cruising, none of them wanted any changes.

As Tom points out, there is an obvious danger of cooking in a seaway, where the cook may be thrown against the stove and burn him or herself on the burner or, more likely, with the contents of the pot or pan. A strong bar through-bolted to the counter, across the front of the stove is a partial preventive measure (Figure 11-6). And recessing the stove 6 or 8 inches (152 mm to 203 mm) from the bar helps equally well.

The reverse of this problem is when the stove is to windward or uphill, and the cook must brace on some surface to leeward to stay near the stove. A canvas belt with a sliding shackle on one end can be used to brace the cook's back, but be careful that it doesn't hold the cook too close to the stove. If a hot pot starts sliding toward the cook, the brace just about eliminates the cook's chances of getting out of the way (Figure 11-7). For this reason, Tom Colvin doesn't approve of galley straps, either, though it's hard to brace yourself near the stove without one. Bill Seifert solves this problem by wearing a heavy apron when he's inside the galley strap.

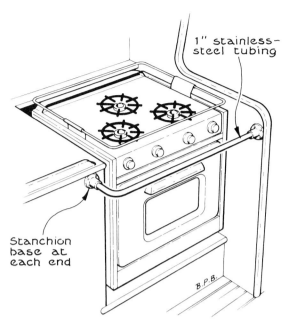

**FIGURE 11-6.** Ideally, the stove should be recessed from the front of the galley counter and a strong stainless steel bar bolted across the opening to prevent the cook from being thrown onto the stove.

1" stainless-steel tubing

Stanchion base at each end

B.P.B.

Base hardware should be bolted to surfaces ... not screwed.

**FIGURE 11-7.** Galley straps give the cook something to brace against when the boat is heeled, but if the boat lurches the other way, the strap could prevent the cook from escaping. Wear a protective apron.

# TYPES OF FUELS

There are at least a half-dozen types of fuels for marine stoves. As you consider which fuel to use aboard, take into account safety, availability, cost, and Btu output.

## Denatured Alcohol ($CH_3CH_2OH$)

For years, most new boats sold in the United States were equipped with alcohol stoves. The reasons were twofold: it is the cheapest type of stove available to the manufacturer, and for years it was about the only fuel people felt was safe. Boating literature, abetted by the U.S. Coast Guard, proclaimed that because alcohol and water mix, a fire could easily be extinguished. Of course, anyone who has experienced a galley fire knows that finding a bucket of water while the curtains go up in flames is not all that simple. And oftentimes, water just displaces the alcohol, which continues to burn.

It is ironic that alcohol, once considered the safest fuel, is now being regarded as one of the most dangerous. Sailing publications have carried a number of stories in recent years describing horrible burns resulting from alcohol stove spills. With a pressurized stove, the most common cause is failing, on first use, to sufficiently heat the burner to the temperature required to vaporize the fuel. While the burner is still hot, someone opens the throttle, sending more alcohol into the cup. However the burner isn't hot enough to vaporize the alcohol and burn safely (a temperature of 689°F or 365°C is required), but it is hot enough to ignite the liquid alcohol, sending flames spewing upward. If the throttle stays open, the entire contents of the tank can fuel the fire. If the stove is gimballed, the burning alcohol can spill over onto someone's legs. The moral of the story is that if the burner isn't hot enough to vaporize the alcohol the first time, WAIT for at least several minutes before trying that burner again.

Other reasons to treat alcohol stoves gingerly are that the flame is very pale and in sunlight is often impossible to see. Dark-colored burners help distinguish the flame. Put a pan over the burner when priming. Not only does this contain the flames somewhat, it also darkens the burner area, making the flames easier to see.

Alcohol vapors are heavier than air and do not blow away as readily as you might think. If alcohol vapor in the air exceeds 3.3%, and a heat source is applied, ignition can result, another reason for caution.

Alcohol's heat output is only 2,500 to 3,000 Btu (British thermal unit—the amount of heat required to raise the temperature of 1 pound/ 0.45 kg of pure water 1°F). This is about half the output of LPG or CNG. Boiling a pot of water takes about 8 to 10 minutes. Nonpressurized alcohol stoves are said to take a bit longer, but the several I have owned seemed to work about as well as the pressurized types. The advantage of a nonpressurized model is that if an accident does occur, fuel will not continue to be pushed through the burners and into the cup, nor is there a danger of flare-ups because no priming is required.

The Dometic (www.dometic.com) Origo nonpressurized alcohol stove does away with the Primus-type burner altogether (Figure 11-8). It works something like a Sterno stove, but much better. The tank, which is essentially the entire inside body of the stove, is packed with an inflammable pulp, which in turn is soaked with alcohol. A wire mesh holds the pulp down in place. A fondue-type plate slides over the opening to extinguish the flame. Kenyon (www.kenyonappliances.com) also makes a nonpressurized alcohol stove, but with smaller tank and less output.

Other reasons not to buy an alcohol stove are the odor of the fuel vapors and cost. Alcohol, costly enough in the United States, is prohibitively expensive in some areas of the world and not even available in other areas.

### Kerosene

Like alcohol, kerosene vapors make some crew members seasick in short order. Unlike alcohol, it burns much hotter (3,500 to 4,000 Btu), boiling a pan of water in about 5 minutes.

Kerosene is almost universally available, and it is comparatively cheap, compared to alcohol. In the 1980s, Tristan Jones wrote that kerosene is the only fuel to consider for global passagemaking— a thoroughly British and probably dated point of view.

On the downside, the priming operation of kerosene stoves can be dangerous, mainly because alcohol is required to preheat the burners. Substitute primers, such as mineral spirits, produce hotter flames and can ruin the burners. Kerosene, derived from diesel oil, does not evaporate like alcohol. It must be watched carefully to prevent it from soaking into insulation, upholstery, or other absorbent materials where it could pose a future danger—let alone a nasty smell. More highly refined grades of kerosene are frequently available through chandleries; they smell better and burn cleaner but are correspondingly more expensive.

Nevertheless, kerosene remains the choice of some traditionalists. (See Chapter 14 for a permanent kerosene tank-and-plumbing system.)

### Diesel

Diesel oil comes with the same admonitions as kerosene, but otherwise is a safe cooking fuel, and if the boat has a diesel auxiliary—which almost every boat does—there is the added advantage of not having to add an extra tank for the stove. A separate fuel line can be run from the fuel tank to the stove.

Diesel burns quite hot and precautions must be taken to install tiles or stainless steel around the stove area to protect the hull and woodwork from overheating.

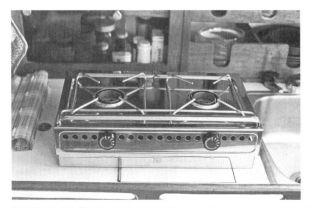

**FIGURE 11-8.** The Origo 3000 alcohol two-burner stove (left) is nonpressurized. Alcohol is poured into the two fiber-filled canisters (right), and a Sterno-type cover is slid over the top to extinguish flames.

**FIGURE 11-9.** A Dickinson diesel stove eliminates carrying a different type of fuel if the auxiliary engine is also diesel. (Dickinson Marine)

In his book, *After 50,000 Miles*, Hal Roth makes a strong case for the diesel stove, which also can be used for heating in cold climates, such as in the Pacific Northwest. Roth writes that he almost always uses it on low setting and claims that at full power it could melt scrap iron. The desirability of such a stove is unquestionable on a sail to Iceland, but for the cruiser in tropical climates, you'd feel you were Alec Guinness roasting in the tin torture chamber at the POW camp in *The Bridge on the River Kwai*.

Diesel stoves must be vented through the coachroof of the boat. This requires some bending of the stovepipe to keep it clear of interior fixtures and deck gear. In cold weather, the fuel needs to be preheated to aid ignition. And, as many of these stoves are quite heavy, installation is often difficult. Dickinson (www.dickinsonmarine.com) makes a fine range of diesel cookers (Figure 11-9) as does Taylors (www.blakes-lavac-taylors.co.uk) in England.

## Liquid Propane Gas (LPG)

Butane ($C_4H_{10}$) and propane ($C_3H_8$) are gases turned to liquid under pressure in special bottles.

When released from the bottle in the stove burner, the liquid returns to its gaseous form. Both are very explosive, burn hot and clean, and because they are heavier than air, can collect in the bilge if a leak occurs.

Propane poses a vexing choice. On one hand, it is dangerous. On the other, it burns hot and clean and is available in most countries. When cruising outside the United States, you'll need to carry metric fittings to fill the tanks ashore. LPG has an output of between 5,000 and 6,000 Btu, about twice that of alcohol. Food and water are heated more quickly.

Two of the major dangers with odorless LPG—asphyxiation and explosion—are now minimized because the law requires that chemicals be added to make the gas easily detected by smell. These chemicals are nontoxic. Also, solenoid switches in the fuel lines at the tank shut off the line when activated by a manual switch in the cabin near the stove. Thermocouples located in the burner flame automatically shut off the line if the flame goes out. Without these, and with the burner still open, fuel would continue to pour into the cabin. Religiously closing fuel lines at the tank via the manual solenoid switch and at the stove after each use also lessen the chances of disaster. (See the Installing an LPG System section later in this chapter for more details.) In fact, the safest practice is to shut off the fuel at the tank while the burner is still lit. When all the fuel in the line has burned, the flame will go out; then the stove burners can be shut off. Ron Barr, a former charter captain, and later a co-founder of the Armchair Sailor Bookstore in Newport, Rhode Island, suggests keeping on hand a short piece of mechanical plumbing with a petcock to bypass the solenoid in the event of electrical failure on board. "When your batteries go flat," he says, "you might want to put on a cup of tea to console yourself!"

Today, LPG is the near universal choice of fuel. That's what builders are putting on boats, and that's what people are using. There's no need to fear propane if you take the simple precautions mentioned above and periodically check for leaks by dripping soapy water on connections. It's clean, cheap, and universally available.

## Compressed Natural Gas (CNG)

Critics of LPG often cite the attributes of CNG, because it is lighter than air and will rise and dissipate into the atmosphere, given some overhead

241

ventilation. Like LPG, it is relatively nontoxic, meaning that breathing the vapors will not cause injury or death. What is potentially dangerous is that a leak in an enclosed cabin displaces the air and can cause suffocation. CNG, of course, is also explosive, but with only a quarter the force of LPG. CNG's ignition temperature is 1100°F (595°C), while LPG's is 800°F (427°C), and the percent of gas in the air by volume required for ignition is about twice as much for CNG (5 to 15%) than for LPG (2 to 9.5%). Nevertheless, you should regard CNG with the same caution as LPG—it is a combustible gas, and it is dangerous. Chemicals are added to CNG to make it easy to detect by smelling.

The American Boat and Yacht Council (ABYC) allows both annealed copper or approved flexible hose for LPG. CNG, however, is incompatible with copper (unless internally tinned), so flexible hose must be used with it. Of course, flexible hose with push-on type connectors makes routing the hose and making connections much simpler.

Trying to gimbal a stove with copper tubing, however, is impossible. So short flexible hoses are used with LPG where it connects with the stove. But it's one more joint to worry about. With CNG or LPG, a flexible fuel line system reduces possible leaks due to vibration of flared copper fittings. Where the hosing passes through bulkheads or any other barrier, use rubber ferrules (short tube or bushing) to prevent abrasion. Alternatively, you can slit open a 6-inch (152 mm) length of clear vinyl hose on one side and slide it over the fuel line where it passes through a bulkhead.

A further attraction of CNG is that because the bottle opening is so small, an accidentally damaged regulator will let so little gas escape there would be no danger of the bottle launching itself into your face. With LPG this is a possibility, though not necessarily a likely one. The amount of pressure in a CNG burner is less than half that of LPG and about $\frac{1}{100}$ that of alcohol or kerosene. And because CNG is the cleanest fuel of all, burner clogging is minimal. However, CNG fuel consumption is greater than propane or kerosene, though less than alcohol.

The major drawbacks with CNG are that it not only burns quickly, but it is only available on the U.S. seaboards—and then, only at certain authorized dealers. The bottles, which by federal law are "purchased" on a permanent lease-back arrangement to ensure periodic inspection, can be mailed to one of several distributors—such as the Corp Brothers (www.corpbrothers.com/marine. htm) in Providence, Rhode Island, by UPS.

CNG, for a time, gained favor with racing sailors, who thought it was safe to stow the tanks in the boat's bilges, thus keeping weight near the center of gravity and out of the boat's ends. CNG fumes nevertheless can collect against the overhead, making this practice extremely unsafe.

The bottom line is: Use LPG.

## Electricity

Large motorsailers and powerboats may have electric ranges that operate just like the ones in your home, but these are vessels with enormous generators to provide sufficient electrical power for cooking and dozens of other functions. On a 25- to 45-foot (7.6 m to 13.7 m) sailboat, electric stoves are hardly worth considering. Not only is it difficult to generate enough juice without shore power—even with wind, water, and solar generators—but because everything in a small boat sooner or later falls prey to salt air, electrical appliances should always be viewed with suspicion.

A word of caution: If you're using a residential-type range or refrigerator aboard your boat, the neutral-to-ground link on the back of the appliance must be separated to avoid risk of electrical shock. Study ABYC E-11 for specific requirements and information on properly grounding both AC and DC electrical systems.

## Sterno

Sterno is the canned fuel used in some camp stoves and fondue sets. A match lights the solid fuel inside, which burns quite harmlessly. Unfortunately, it doesn't burn hot enough to do much good for cooking. I have carried a few cans to use in a Sea Swing stove just in case I couldn't get the kerosene burner to work, a contingency yet to arise.

A better choice is to use a small propane or butane bottle in something like Force 10's Seacook gimballed stove (www.force10.com). Note, however, that this product uses a 16-ounce (3.8 L) bottle, which the ABYC does not recommend for use in the boat's interior. It does allow use of the smaller 8-ounce (1.9 L) canisters used by such ungimballed, camp-style stoves as the Kenyon Express II.

To sum up, the consensus of most cruisers is that LPG is the best all-around fuel. It is efficient, odorless when burning, cheap, and available worldwide. Alcohol, kerosene, and diesel just don't measure up. For those people afraid of explosions, choosing a fuel is difficult. My advice is to familiarize yourself with gas and the safety devices available and, as the old 1960s saying went, "Learn to love the bomb."

# INSTALLING AN LPG SYSTEM

Determining stove and tank locations is the first step in installing your own LPG system. As mentioned in Chapter 9 (Figures 9-20 through 9-24), propane tanks must be stored on deck or in a vapor-proof locker where the gas cannot possibly enter the cabin.

The ABYC requires that the tank housing have a bottom vent of at least ½-inch (12 mm) inside diameter, located at least 20 inches (508 mm) from any hull opening. Standard A-1 has all the details.

Most marine tanks are made of aluminum as they are more corrosion resistant than steel, and range in size from about 5 to 20 pounds (2.3 kg to 9.1 kg) of gas. Steel tanks, which usually come with cheap enamel finishes, should have all the required stickers removed and should be repainted with a tough epoxy paint. Gas fill-up stations can provide you with new stickers to apply afterward. Each cylinder is fitted with a manual shutoff valve and a safety relief valve. Vertically installed cylinders are most common, though there are some that can be mounted horizontally. Never mount a vertical cylinder on its side, because it does not have the special J-shaped tube to prevent liquefied gas from reaching the outlet valve.

It makes sense to join two cylinders with a valve that permits switching from the empty tank to the full one. Not as much extra space is required for the second tank, and there's an obvious advantage in having more fuel and less frequent refillings. Two small tanks are easier to carry than one large tank, and while one is ashore being filled, you still have the other for cooking. Open only one cylinder valve at a time.

Inside the deck box, chock each cylinder well using wood and hold the cylinders in place with straps to prevent any movement, especially when you are using copper tubing for fuel lines.

Use fuel lines appropriate for LPG gas. ABYC permits both hose and annealed copper tubing (Grade K or L), as specified by the American Society of Testing and Materials (ASTM). As mentioned earlier, gas experts familiar with the problems of copper in the marine environment recommend the use of flexible gas hose, thereby removing the risk of corroded or cracked tubing. Also it is much easier to route flexible hoses through the boat. Where it passes through bulkheads, clear plastic hose is slipped over to prevent chafe.

The tubing diameter will vary with the amount of fuel carried, generally between ¼ inch and ⅜ inch (6 mm to 9.5 mm). The latter can service appliances burning up to 75,000 Btu, much more than the typical marine stove. Secure the copper tubing or flexible hose with nonferrous clips that will not bite or crimp the fuel line—plastic electrical clips work well.

An electrically operated solenoid shutoff valve must be installed in the fuel line immediately after the tank and outside the cabin. A light tells whether the switch is activated or not. Locate the solenoid panel where it is easily seen and operated from the galley.

Thermocouple heat sensors installed at every burner and in the oven add another measure of safety by automatically shutting off the system when the flame goes out. Lastly, a gas detector or "sniffer" will sound an alarm if a leak develops. The sniffer will draw some juice, but not much. (Chapter 12 discusses ways of keeping the batteries topped off without an engine.) Your LPG installation should resemble that in Figure 11-10.

In the eventuality of a leak, it is helpful to have an ignition-proof blower installed in the bilge to rid the area of fumes.

After installation is complete, test the system for leaks by pressurizing it to a minimum of 5 pounds per square inch (412 N/mm²); a pressure gauge in the line will give you a reading. Dab each connector with a solution of water and liquid detergent to see if bubbles appear. If they do, you have a leak. Another method is to install an in-line leak detector, available from trailer supply stores. If no leaks appear, close off the appliance valves, open the cylinder valve, and note the pressure. Then close the cylinder shutoff valve and observe the pressure gauge. It should not change for at least 15 minutes. If no change occurs within this time period, the installation is sound, and you can begin using the stove. If the pressure drops, go back and recheck each connection and the burners. Never check for leaks by applying an open flame to the suspected site! Periodically check the system, about once each month.

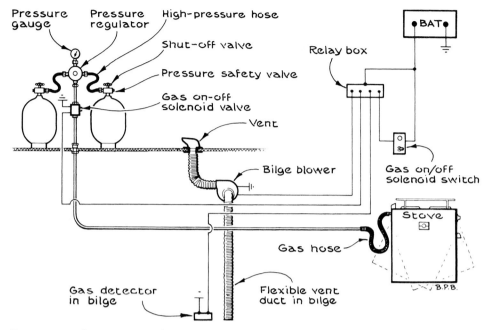

Gas solenoid off and bilge-blower on relays may be activated by the gas detector or by the flame-out thermocouples.

**FIGURE 11-10.** A proper LPG installation features a ventilated bottle locker; vapor-tight ferrules where lines pass through bulkheads; solenoid switches to shut off gas; and bilge blowers and sniffers as safety features.

If you don't have a pressure gauge (in which case you're in violation of ABYC standards), open the gas line to the stove, with the valve at the tank shut off. After 15 minutes, open the valve at the stove burner (keeping the tank valve closed) and strike a match. If the burner lights, the lines are able to retain pressure. If it doesn't light, the gas has leaked out, and you must check all connections for the leak source.

# REFRIGERATION

There is little doubt that most of us are happier with cold beers, frozen steaks, and crisp lettuce than with warm drinks, tinned meats, and wilted greens. Obtaining ice once a week—or even more—is an ordeal we all tire of quickly. After a year or two of this, you may decide either to forget ice altogether and adapt your eating and drinking habits, or to install some sort of mechanical refrigeration.

The icebox is of critical importance to the effectiveness of any refrigeration system. Chapter 3 details the construction features of an effective icebox—4 inches (102 mm) or more of insulation, staggered joints, taped seams, tinfoil reflective barrier, Mylar moisture barrier, gasketed lid, etc.

Here we'll concern ourselves with how to keep the box cold with gas and mechanical refrigeration.

## *Basic Types of Refrigeration*

Many refrigeration units on medium to large sailboats use engine-driven *compressors* to compress gas from an *evaporator*, which becomes hot, and push it into a *condenser*, where it is cooled and condensed to a liquid. An evaporator changes it back to a gas and to a much colder temperature, before sending it on its way through another cycle. HFC-134a is the currently approved, ozone-friendly gas, which is nontoxic and inflammable. Grunert, Glacier Bay, Sea Frost, and Technautics are some of the better-known names in holding-plate systems.

The development of hermetically sealed compressors made possible small, quiet, and maintenance-free portable units. The latest refrigeration systems, such as Waeco's Cold Machine (www.waecousa.com), run off 115-volts AC and 12-volts DC instead of belts driven by the auxiliary engine. A small electric motor drives the compressor, so you only need to run the engine periodically to keep the batteries charged. Still, engine-driven compressors probably require less engine running time.

Both engine- and battery-driven systems have compressors, evaporators, and condensers. They also have some sort of metering device, ranging from a simple capillary tube to an expansion valve, which determines how much gas is reaching the evaporator. A capillary tube is nothing more than a length of tubing with a small pinhole, whose diameter and length has been carefully determined to regulate the amount of gas passing through. An expansion valve is, more accurately, a needle valve that opens and closes in response to pressure and temperature, thereby regulating the refrigerant gas.

There are two ways of cooling the condenser: air and water. In air-cooled types, the refrigerant gas is cooled by passing through coils of tubing inside an array of cooling fins, the same sort of thing you see on motorcycle and lawnmower engine heads. The fins absorb the heat and dissipate it into the outside air with the help of a small electric fan. It is a simple system that requires little maintenance. Its only disadvantage is that the condenser must be located in a well-ventilated spot. The engine room is likely too hot and poorly ventilated; underneath bunks is a possible site, but will require some sort of caning or other vent in the bunk face to let air in and out.

Water-cooled condensers function like heat exchangers. The gas passes through a tube that is surrounded by a water jacket full of circulating cold seawater. The seawater can be obtained by tapping into the engine-cooling system, so that raw water drawn in by the engine's water pump passes through the refrigerator's water jacket before it reaches the engine. The water temperature is not increased much, but because any malfunction jeopardizes the all-important engine, some refrigeration systems use separate pumps and through-hull fittings to obtain their cooling seawater.

### Dometic

While I was preparing my Vanguard for cruising, I decided to rip out the old, poorly insulated icebox and replace it with a Dometic three-way, front-opening refrigerator (www.dometic.com). It was recommended to me by John Kuhn, who cruised a Vanguard for many years in the Caribbean and South Pacific. He said he had paid his way to New Zealand fixing other people's holding-plate systems, while his Dometic required only the occasional cleaning of the gas orifice.

Having built an icebox before, and knowing the amount of labor involved only to be faced with lugging ice again, I decided to take a gamble for $450 on a 2.5-cubic-foot (0.07 m$^3$) unit. Gas refrigerators are marketed mostly for the RV industry (hence the unfortunate front-loading feature), and they are not as well insulated as they should be for boats. But I began to see them installed on multihulls, and I recalled that Eric Hiscock once had extolled his kerosene-fueled refrigerator (same principle, different fuel). Low cost, cheap fuel, and good recommendations persuaded me.

I hacked out the icebox and built a set of gimbals to mount the new fridge. Gas refrigerators don't function very efficiently if permanently out of level, but work fine if they can swing. It's only a problem when underway for long periods and, on reflection, I probably should have mounted it in a fixed position and either run it off the ship's 12-volt system (the third way is 110 AC shore power) or shut it down altogether on passages. A more compact, tidy installation is possible if you don't have to allow for swing room, and makes through-deck venting much easier. Venting is important to move out heat from behind the fridge, which affects the cooling of the box.

Another problem complicating the issue of whether or not to gimbal is having the refrigerator's contents fall out when the door is opened. This happens when the unit is not locked in place, and the weight of the door upsets the balance.

After more than three years of service, the Dometic needed a new thermostat. In hot subtropical weather, it could have benefited from additional insulation glued to the sides of the fridge (recommended to me by other Dometic fans), though it always made ice, which always made me feel a little smug, sitting in the cockpit clinking my micro-cubes!

LPG refrigerators obviously aren't for everyone, especially those predisposed against gas on board. But it worked okay for me, and in the right circumstances, I can see myself using this system again—on a multihull or powerboat. I describe my experience here only because so many people apparently have had the same thought and have asked me about these units.

Now let's take a brief look at both a typical engine-driven system and a popular battery-powered system.

### Sea Frost

Sea Frost makes small, easily installed, engine-driven refrigeration units (www.seafrost.com).

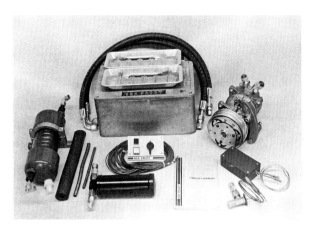

**FIGURE 11-11.** The Sea Frost refrigeration unit is engine driven, requiring about 60-plus minutes of daily engine running time. (Sea Frost)

Total operating weight is about 75 pounds (34 kg), and parts consist of a block, compressor, condenser, and valve/control unit (Figure 11-11). The block is actually a holding or eutectic plate that is full of brine. When frozen, it "holds over" the cold just like a block of ice. The difference between this system and an icebox is that instead of rowing ashore for more ice, you just turn on the engine for as little as 30 to 45—but probably more like 60-plus—minutes a day. Not bad.

I first became acquainted with the Sea Frost during a visit to Arthur Martin in Kittery, Maine. Arthur, who once helped Ray Hunt design the Concordia yawl, became a bug about energy efficiency. He designed a 48-foot (14.6 m) powerboat by tripling the dimensions of his Appledore rowing/sailing pod. We took a ride aboard the Energy 48, and one of the first things Arthur mentioned was the Sea Frost refrigerator. "It does just what they say it will," he said. In a well-insulated box, very little running time is required. Various block and plate sizes are available. The single block mounts high up in the icebox and occupies about the same amount of space as 20 to 25 pounds (9 kg to 11 kg) of ice. The belt-driven compressor mounts on or close to the engine (such as an adjacent bulkhead). An eight-position bracket with a swing arm allows some flexibility in mounting the compressor. The condenser is inserted in the engine's raw-water cooling line, and the valve/control unit is usually mounted outside the icebox somewhere. The parts are connected by copper refrigerant lines and Swagelok double ferrule fittings.

The most difficult task will be mounting the compressor in the engine compartment, especially if there is little clearance around the engine, or if the engine is small and doesn't have an external alternator and pulley. Of course if clearance is the only problem, you usually can make some modification to the engine compartment by moving one side a few inches farther away from the engine.

Two ice cube trays put into a 70°F (21°C) box will freeze after 20 minutes of engine running time—provided the icebox is well insulated. The temperature will drop to about 21°F (–6°C) after an hour of running time. Less than one hour of daily engine running time is required to keep the icebox at 45°F (7°C) or less.

## The Cold Machine

For years, Adler Barbour manufactured Cold Pump engine-driven refrigeration units, which were widely used industrially and on cruising sailboats. With the development of small, DC-powered hermetic compressors, Adler Barbour began producing a small, inexpensive 115-volt and 12-volt unit that cycles (runs intermittently) off shore power or off the ship's batteries. The Cold Machine, now made by Waeco USA (Figure 11-12), will fit any box up to 9½ cubic feet (0.27 m³) and is divided into two basic installation components: the freezer compartment with ice trays that goes inside the icebox (vertical and horizontal models are available), and the compressor/evaporator/condenser package that can be installed in any well-ventilated (it's air cooled) site up to 15 feet (4.6 m) from the icebox. This site can be anywhere temperatures don't exceed 130°F (54°C) and that has at least two separate openings of at least 10 square inches (65 cm²) each.

The compressor draws 5.6 amps and cycles about 20 to 30 minutes each hour, so daily consumption is about 45 to 67 amp-hours. At the

**FIGURE 11-12.** Waeco's Cold Machine uses a compressor run by an electric motor that cycles off the ship's battery. (Waeco USA)

246

dock, there is obviously no difficulty in supplying this amount of power. But at anchor or underway, that's a lot of amps to come up with. No matter how many amp-hours are in your battery bank, if you aren't realistic about the Cold Machine's power needs, you could be disappointed.

You probably will find that if you rely on the engine for charging the batteries, you'll need to run it several hours a day. I think that's too much for the cruising boat. A better solution is to use an alternative energy source (Chapter 12). With a well-insulated icebox, two 50-watt solar panels are capable of keeping the batteries sufficiently charged to power the Cold Machine efficiently. As always, much depends on the ability of the icebox to retain cold, the contents of the icebox, and how often it is opened.

Installing the Cold Machine is very simple, requiring only a hand drill, a screwdriver, and wrenches. You will probably have to fashion a platform for the compressor package—perhaps from plywood—and mount it beneath a berth or in a cockpit seat locker (refer back to Figure 5-32). Lead the wires to the battery directly to the terminals or to the battery selector switch—not to the distribution panel or charger, if there is one.

## CONTEMPLATING CHANGES

The galley is one place worth splurging on. But on small boats, there often isn't room to spend much money, even if you have it. When I lived aboard my Pearson Triton, I often sat on the settee in the main cabin surveying the meager galley, contemplating enlarging it to include a stove/oven and deep double sink. To do this I would have to rob the starboard settee of several feet, which would make it too short to sleep on. I scanned the cabin for solutions. Perhaps the starboard bunk could be extended through a cutout in the bulkhead into the old hanging locker area beneath the sink and vanity. So why didn't I just get out the saber saw and do it? Like every other change I made to the Triton, I needed time to consider the implications.

Eventually I realized that the Triton was simply too small for my purposes. I'd remarried, and needed extra room and amenities to keep my wife

happy. And a good decision it was to buy a bigger boat, since during our cruise of the East Coast and Bahamas, she became pregnant and her dimensions grew!

Then even the much larger Vanguard seemed to shrink—that's the way it is with boats. Naturally, I made many modifications to the new boat as well, all made possible because of the built-up wooden interiors (a fiberglass pan with molded furniture foundations would never have permitted so many changes). It was never ideal, but certainly more than adequate. Some things, such as narrow doorways and limited counter space, you just learn to live with.

The real proof that a change is necessary is when you simply can't live with the present arrangement any longer. When you find yourself clutching a crowbar with white knuckles, don't resist the urge! Do it! Until then, make the best of what you've got. I'd rather have cabin seating space for three friends to enjoy a good bottle of wine and good stories than a full-service galley with microwave and Cuisinart and no place to sit.

## FURTHER READING

*After 50,000 Miles.* Hal Roth. New York: Norton, 1977.

*Marine Refrigeration for the Do It Yourself Sailor.* Rev. ed. Art Smith. Fort Lauderdale, Florida: Art Smith, 1978.

*Marine Refrigeration Guidebook.* 2nd ed. Howard M. Crosby. St. Petersburg, Florida: Crosby Marine, 1983.

*The Ocean Sailing Yacht.* Vols. 1 and 2. Donald Street. New York: Norton, 1973–1978.

*One Hand for Yourself, One for the Ship: The Essentials of Single-Handed Sailing.* Tristan Jones. Dobbs Ferry, New York: Sheridan House, 1990.

*The Perfect Box: 39 Ways to Improve Your Boat's Ice Box.* Edgar Beyn. Annapolis, Maryland: Spa Creek Instruments Co., 1982.

*Refrigeration for Pleasure Boats: Installation, Maintenance, and Repair.* Nigel Calder. Camden, Maine: International Marine, 1991.

# TWELVE

# GENERATING ELECTRICAL POWER

Picture this: A cruising sailboat flies into English Harbor in Antigua after a long day's sail. The couple on board drops sails, readies the ground tackle, and finds a nice spot away from the other yachts. Customs and immigrations can wait for morning; they're too tired now to deal with the paperwork and hassle.

When everything is tidy, they settle back in the cockpit to watch the sun go down. A couple of beers are brought up from the icebox, the tabs are popped—and guess what? They're warm!

Perhaps an Englishman wouldn't mind that the ice melted days ago, but Americans are used to drinking their beers cold—anything else just doesn't make it. What to do?

Independence afloat means different things to different people, and certainly it is a goal of people who cruise—almost a nonnegotiable fact of cruising life.

Whether you equip your boat with a powerful diesel-fueled generator (genset) to run the refrigerator, microwave oven, and hot-water heater, or you choose to simplify your energy needs by using oil running lamps and eating nonperishable foods, the basic fact of cruising is that at sea, the boat must be able to provide all its energy requirements. Self-reliance is further enhanced by minimizing the amount of energy-producing fuels that must be brought on board.

Traditionally, fossil fuels have furnished humans with their chief source of energy—to propel their many vehicles, cook their food, and heat their homes. Yet we have learned we can no longer expect these fuels to last forever—the Earth, our home, is of finite size, and the fuels within it of limited supply. Even while they are still available, the cruising sailor may find it difficult to pay premium prices for these fuels, assuming she can even find them in the remote outposts of the world to which she travels. Because electrical power is the most important type of energy used on boats—with the possible exception, or addition, of liquid fuels for stoves and engines—this chapter focuses on the many ways of generating electricity efficiently and economically.

During the past decade, a heightened energy-consciousness among scientists, businesspeople, and politicians has introduced us to new ways of generating the electrical power necessary to live our lives in the manner to which we have so easily become accustomed. The sun, water, and wind—three of the four fundamental elements thought by ancient Greek philosophers to comprise all matter (the fourth was earth)—are the sources of power for most of the generating devices in use today aboard boats. Because of the high cost of research and development, it is understandable that most research efforts have centered in industrial circles, with practical application spinoffs trickling down to the consumer much later. Such was the case with the microcomputer chip and Teflon. Enough has happened in the business of alternative energy that it is appropriate today to take stock of developments and assess their usefulness to the cruising sailor.

## BATTERIES

Most forms of generating electrical power aboard boats depend on storing that energy in one or more batteries. This marvelous invention enables you to draw upon the battery when you need electricity. Without batteries, you would be able to use the lights and instruments only when the charging device (be it a wind-, water-, or engine-driven generator, or solar panel) was in operation.

Selecting an appropriate battery for this task is an important choice. The deep-cycle, lead-acid storage battery with its heavy plates, as opposed to the standard automotive type, is the best type of battery to run most sailboat accessories. A dedicated heavy-duty or deep-cycle battery should be reserved for the engine, so that running appliances won't wear down your engine-starting battery. A three-way switch isolates each battery for use and charging, and permits using both when they are weak and you need all the power you can get.

Batteries "make" electricity by means of a lead-acid chemical reaction. Read Charlie Wing's *Boatowner's Illustrated Electrical Handbook* for a detailed description of how this works. Suffice it to say here that each time a battery is discharged, crystals build up on the plates. This process is called *sulfation*. Some of the lead flakes off and drops to the bottom of the battery case. Eventually, there is so little lead left in the plates that a small discharge current exhausts them, or so many sulfation flakes build up that they connect negative and positive plates and short-circuit the battery. In either case, the battery must then be rebuilt or replaced. And because sulfation and self-discharge (the chemical reaction goes on even with the battery at rest) are part of the natural life of a battery, a battery's useful life is limited. But you can maximize that span by avoiding deep discharges of more than 50%, maintaining electrolyte levels, and periodically using the equalization phase of the charging regimen to most fully return each cell to its original state of charge. (More on this later.)

Good batteries aren't cheap. But they are a very important investment for the cruising sailor. It is not uncommon nowadays for a 40-foot (12.2 m) cruising boat to carry a battery bank (two or more batteries wired together) of 600 to 800 amp-hours. With this amount of current capacity, one battery can be used strictly for starting the engine, and the others used for running lights, electronics, and other onboard appliances. And, unlike having just one 80-amp-hour car battery, you won't be in constant danger of seriously depleting your electrical supply.

There are three basic battery chemistries available to the boatowner: flooded, gelled electrolyte (gel-cell), and AGM (absorbed glass mat).

The oldest type is the flooded, in which liquid sulfuric acid provides the connection between the positive and negative plates in the battery. The acid, in combination with water, is called electrolyte. During charging, gases are given off that enter the atmosphere around the battery and some water is lost, which must be periodically replaced with distilled water. Electrolyte, too, can be replaced when the batteries age—that's the advantage and disadvantage of flooded batteries: you

can keep them functioning for a long time, but they require attention.

Sealed, maintenance-free batteries like the gel-cell battery have a lot of appeal because there's not much maintenance required other than keeping the terminals clean. During charging, gases put off by the gel—sulfuric acid, phosphoric acid, fumed silica, and water—recombine and reenter the system without venting, as occurs with a conventional flooded battery. Critics (mostly those who sell flooded lead-acid batteries) claim they can be discharged 50% only about 500 times, roughly equivalent to the life expectancy of a Sears Die-Hard. Top-quality flooded batteries are supposed to handle 1,000 to 2,000 cycles (discharge and recharge). For the average owner, comparative performance is tough to measure since so many batteries are murdered by poor electrical systems and ill-informed owners. Gel-cell batteries have some advantages: they have a lower self-discharge rate (about 3% a month compared to 6 to 7% for flooded), have a higher tolerance for vibrations, and are leak proof. Their disadvantage is that they cannot be charged at more than 14.2 volts and so cannot be mixed with flooded batteries.

AGM batteries have glass mats between the positive and negative plates that are saturated with electrolyte. During charging, oxygen passes through pressure valves in the mats to recombine with hydrogen on the negative plates. The result is low internal resistance and a long life. Like gel-cell batteries, AGM batteries require no maintenance, are leak proof, and have low rates of self-discharge. They also can be stored on their sides. Their disadvantages are that they are expensive and heavy, and the electrolyte cannot be replaced if the battery is damaged from overcharging.

Some electrical generating devices often do little more than trickle-charge the battery, even if they are capable of higher charging rates during periods of high wind, fast speed, or direct sunlight. Trickle-charging supplies about 0.1 amp (100 milliamps) and tends to damage battery plates. In a deep-cycle battery, the plates are stronger than in standard marine or automotive batteries, and thus are able to stand up longer to the deleterious effects of trickle-charging. Overcharging also can be a problem and to prevent this a modern multistage regulator, rather than the old-fashioned automotive-type regulator, should be used regulate the output of the engine's alternator.

### 6, 12, or 24 Volts

Most electrical boat equipment operates on 12 volts, although some gear is available in 24 volts, which offers distinct advantages, the main one being that 24 VDC equipment uses half the amps of 12 VDC equipment. (Note that watts divided by volts equals amps. Compare: 100-watt lightbulb/ 12 VDC = 8.3 amps; 100 watts/24 VDC = 4.16 amps.) This also means that the size of the 24 VDC conductor (wire) between the battery and load (bulb, pump, etc.) can be smaller and lighter.

On the Seguin 52, built by Lyman Morse Boatbuilding, there are three electrical systems: 115 VAC (volts alternating current), 24 VDC (volts direct current), and 12 VDC. All cabin lights, pumps, winches, autopilot, fans, and the oil change pump run on 24 VDC. The equipment operating on 12 VDC includes the stereo, fuel and water tank gauges, sailing instruments, the radar and chart plotter, the VHF and SSB radios, DC refrigeration, and the watermaker backflush. One of the two refrigerators is powered by 115 VAC.

You can make 24 VDC either by buying 24 VDC batteries or wiring two 12 VDC batteries in series (Figure 12-1). To do this, connect the positive terminal of one battery to the negative terminal of the second battery. Do the same for the other two terminals. This doubles the voltage: 2 × 12 = 24. Many owners also use two 6 VDC batteries to supply the 12 VDC system. The advantages are twofold: lower cost and less weight per individual battery. When batteries are wired in parallel (positive to positive, negative to negative), total output voltage remains the same but amperes double. This is why you turn the three-position battery switch to "All" when trying to start the engine with low batteries.

## MEASURING ELECTRICITY

Before looking at the various means of generating electrical power, let's review some basic terms (Figure 12-2) and a table for measuring the amount of electricity used on board. This way, you can determine more accurately how much electricity you'll need to run the various electrical gadgets on your boats.

Let's assume you have a 12-volt electrical system and a 12-volt battery.

*Volts* refers to the electrical potential of your battery. Put another way, it is the potential difference between two points in a conducting wire—in this case, your battery.

*Amps* is the amount of electrical current that flows from your battery. Because your battery's voltage is nearly constant, the current drawn by most appliances also will be nearly constant. Current is a rate of flow, and therefore it is incorrect to say "amperes per hour." This is like saying "knots per hour."

*Watts* is a term used to rate some electrical items, such as lightbulbs.

Amps × volts = watts. Watts/volts = amps. So, if you run a 15-watt fluorescent bulb on a 12-volt system, you are drawing 1.25 amps (15 watts/ 12 volts = 1.25 amps). Amps × hours of operation = total ampere-hours. By listing all your electrical appliances, along with their amps and hours of

---

**ELECTRICAL MEASUREMENTS**

| AMPS X VOLTS = WATTS | AMPS X HOURS OF USE = AMPHOURS |
|---|---|
| WATTS ÷ VOLTS = AMPS | MA = 1/1,000 AMPS |
| WATTS ÷ AMPS = VOLTS | |

**DEFINITIONS**

| | |
|---|---|
| AMP | amount of current flowing (like water through a pipe) |
| VOLT | pressure or push of electricity (like amount of water pressure in a pipe) |
| WATT | a measure of electrical power (746 watts = 1 horsepower) |
| GENERATOR | any machine that generates electricity. More specifically, a machine that generates direct current (DC). |
| ALTERNATOR | a machine that generates alternating current (AC). In battery-charging alternators, AC is internally changed to DC before reaching the battery. |
| INVERTER | turns applied signal upside down (reverses its phase). Changes DC to AC. |

**FIGURE 12-2.** A brief glossary of electrical terms and equations

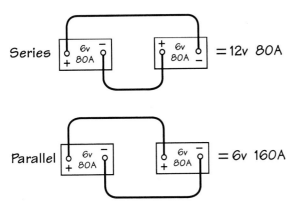

**FIGURE 12-1.** Series versus parallel battery wiring.

## AUXILIARY GENERATOR WORKSHEET

### Current Used

| Load/Appliance | Current/Amps | Hours of Operation | Total Amp-Hours |
|---|---|---|---|
| Stereo | 5 | 3 | 15 |
| Bilge Pump | 4 | 0.5 | 2 |
| Cabin Lights | 10 | 3 | 30 |
| VHF-Receive | 0.5 | 16 | 8 |
| GPS | 1 | 16 | 16 |
| Running Lights | 2 | 4 | 8 |
| Autopilot | 3 | 8 | 24 |
| Refrigerator | 6 | 8 | 48 |
| | | Total | 151[1] |

### Current Generated

| Load/Appliance | Current/Amps | Hours of Operation | Total Amp-Hours |
|---|---|---|---|
| Generator #1, engine | 20 (average amps) x | 5.75* (expected hrs opr) = | 115 |
| Generator #2, solar panel | 3 (average amps) x | 12 (expected hrs opr) = | 36 |
| | | Total | 151[2] |

Note: Resistance affects charge rate.

### Battery Size

Daily amp-hours used (151) × 4 = 604, minimum size battery bank in Ah

* Adjust engine hours charge so (2) exceeds (1)

**FIGURE 12-3.** You can use this worksheet to determine the amount of electricity used on board; I've provided a sample. The formula for determining total battery amp-hours is a minimum; many cruising boats carry a bank of batteries with far greater capacity.

operation, you can estimate your daily usage of electricity (Figure 12-3).

As the worksheet shows, you multiply your total daily amp-hours used by a factor of 4 to get the minimum size of the battery bank in amp-hours. Why 4? So you don't discharge the battery bank more than about 25%, to promote longer battery life. Due to inefficiencies in charging, the actual amount of discharge will be higher, hence the conservative factor of 4 to 6. If your cruising style means you'll be spending days at a time in remote anchorages, running appliances without running the engine, then multiply by 5 or 6 instead.

Remember that a milliamp is one-thousandth of an amp. Thus, 50 milliamps equals 0.05 amp. A solar panel advertised as producing 30 to 35 amp-hours per week is only producing about 600 milliamps (8 hours of sunshine × 7 days = 56 sunlit hours; 56 × 600 milliamps = 33,600 milliamps, or 33.6 amp-hours each week). Also, panels are usually rated at peak efficiency, 90° to a bright sun, and obviously such a condition cannot occur all day, every day. Don't trust claims about so many amp-hours per week; honest specifications are made in watts.

As you compare data on generator output, keep in mind that resistance (level of battery charge) affects generator output. As a battery charges, generator output decreases. Don't expect always to get the same output the manufacturer claims—you may keep your batteries charged higher than the level used during testing, or the manufacturer may have taken statistical liberties that distorted the unit's performance.

The wind, of course, is more fickle than the

## OUTPUT OF DIFFERENT GENERATORS

| Generator | Cost* | Output | Hours of Operation | Total Amp-Hours |
|---|---|---|---|---|
| Water Generator | $1,200 | 5.0 amps @ 6 knots | 12 hours | 60 Ah |
| Solar Panels (two 50-watt) | $1,100 | 2.64 amps avg. skies | 12 hours | 31.75 Ah |
| Wind Generator | $1,100 | 7.0 amps @ 15 mph wind | 12 hours | 72.00 Ah |
| *January 2006 prices. | | | | |

**FIGURE 12-4.** This table is a rough comparison of three different alternative energy generators. Prices are approximate, and the outputs have been taken from manufacturers' literature.

predictable fall of night, but no less so than the possibility of cloud cover. While a wind generator may produce more amps when it's blowing 15 mph, there will be occasions of no wind at all. The amps produced by a water-driven generator can be accurately calculated if you know how much time you'll spend sailing and at what speed. But since speed is predicated on the wind available, water-driven generators, too, offer no guaranteed amount of energy. As for solar panels, the percentage of clear days can help you determine their practicality, and this, of course, varies around the world.

Evaluate your sailing patterns, consider the geographical regions through which you'll be sailing and then assess the different products (Figure 12-4). Different persons may well come up with different answers. In his book *Boatowner's Illustrated Electrical Handbook*, author Charlie Wing has an excellent section on alternative power. He carefully estimated the cost to operate various solar panels and wind generators. He found that solar panels cost about $2 per kilowatt hour, while wind generators are slightly lower at about $1.70 per kilowatt hour.

## ENGINE ALTERNATORS

Assuming your boat has an auxiliary engine, and that your primary means of charging batteries is the engine's alternator, your first step should be to evaluate the alternator's efficiency. Most alternators on 30 to 50 hp engines are only rated at about 50 amps—too small. Worse, the regulators are typically automotive types, which control the rate of charge, and reduce amperage too quickly. A battery's life is extended if it's fully recharged before using again; this means that the electrolyte, as tested by a hydrometer, should be about 1.265 at mid-latitudes, and voltage, as indicated by a digital or analog voltmeter, should be

about 12.6. To do this with minimal running time, you may need to upgrade the standard alternator from 50 amps to 75, 100, or even 165 amps, depending on the number of amp-hours in the battery bank.

So-called high-output alternators are almost mandatory on most modern cruising boats. Buy one rated at about 25 to 40% of your battery capacity (100 to 160 amps for a 400 amp-hour bank). Balmar (www.balmar.net) makes a line of large-frame, high-output alternators with oversized bearings and high-ampere diodes. They also have big fans to keep the alternator cool, as heat quickly reduces output. They do require dual ½-inch (12 mm) belts, which may require changing the pulley on the engine. They don't come cheap—expect to pay more than $1,000.

On *Viva*, the electrical domino effect ended up costing us a bunch of money, but the result was a system suited for cruising. Here's what happened. When we bought the boat, it had an old 12-volt Cold Machine icebox refrigeration system. Unfortunately, the compressor had failed so I replaced it. In talking with the manufacturer, I learned that a minimum of 300 amp-hours battery capacity was recommended. *Viva* had but two Group 27 (90 amp-hour) batteries. So I bought four 6-volt batteries yielding 440 amp-hours capacity. This forced me to replace the 55-amp alternator on the 3GM Yanmar diesel with a 160-amp high-output alternator. And to control its output, I next bought a Link 2000R inverter/charge control, two-bank battery monitor, and alternator regulator. This system implements the recommended four-stage charge curve described in the next section. It also tracks just about everything but your mood—charge efficiency, depth of discharge, amp-hours remaining, and much more. I installed it myself. Routing the many tiny wires that go everywhere was a little tedious, but the payoff was complete knowledge of my batteries' health and status. We could now run the refrigerator and autopilot most of each day without running the engine and without worrying about running the batteries dead. On the other hand, we were several thousand dollars poorer.

## REGULATORS

Besides increasing alternator output, a three- or four-stage regulator (Figure 12-5) that automatically adjusts the amount of amps going into the battery according to its "needs" saves engine running time and lengthens battery life. The idea is to quickly bring the battery up to an 85% charge, slow it down until it reaches 100%, then preserve it at that level, without causing the gassing that boils the electrolyte and damages the battery's plates.

Rick Proctor, founder of Cruising Equipment Company (now part of Xantrex), promotes what he calls the Ideal Charge Curve. It has four phases. In the first *bulk* phase, the charge in amps is 20 to 40% of total battery capacity (20 to 40 amps for a 100-amp battery); for flooded batteries, the voltage is about 14.4 volts; gel-cell batteries must be charged at a lower rate, about 14.1 volts. This phase continues until the battery is about three-quarters charged. In the second *acceptance* phase, the voltage remains the same, but amps are steadily reduced until the battery is nearly fully charged. In the final *float* phase, voltage is reduced to around 13.5 volts (13.7 volts for gel-cell batteries); it's not charging now but performing "maintenance" without the battery losing electrolyte. Four-stage regulators incorporate a fourth phase called *equalization* that runs a high voltage through the battery in an attempt to reverse sulfation and promote longer battery life. It is done only on flooded batteries. Equalization will kill a gel-cell battery.

## MAKING AC WITH INVERTERS AND FUEL-POWERED GENERATORS

Most ship's electrical systems are 12-volt DC, though a growing number of boats over 45 feet (13.7 m) frequently also use 24 and/or 36 VDC systems. AC electrical systems also are fairly standard, though on many boats they are used only at a dock where shore power is available. The typical smaller boat will have a few AC receptacles in the cabin for a coffeemaker, television, or portable air conditioner.

How to get AC away from the dock? There are essentially three choices: (1) carry an auxiliary or portable AC generator that runs on gasoline or diesel fuel, (2) install an inverter to convert AC from your DC house batteries, and (3) install an engine-driven AC alternator. The latter is seldom used, as most engines already are heavily loaded with high-output alternators and refrigeration compressors.

On large vessels, a diesel- or gasoline-fueled generator, such as those manufactured by Onan (Figure 12-6), may be installed in the engine compartment. These generators are best suited to heavy, continuous loads like air-conditioning and refrigeration. Besides providing almost unlimited electrical power, some models also may be rigged

**FIGURE 12-5.** Sophisticated electronic battery monitors and amp-hour meters indicate more accurately the rate of charge and when the battery is fully charged. The Xantrex Link 2000R unit is a package of several instruments, including an alternator controller that automatically adjusts the amount of charging current in four stages. (Xantrex)

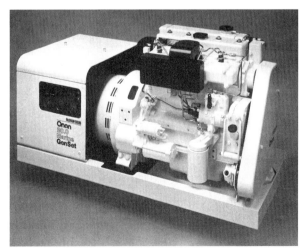

**FIGURE 12-6.** A 20 kW diesel auxiliary generator by Onan has a water-cooled exhaust for quiet operation. (Onan)

with a belt and clutch to the propeller shaft and thereby serve as a backup means of propulsion. Gasoline and diesel models are available.

Cruisers on small boats often carry a portable generator (Figure 12-7) so that tools such as a power drill or jigsaw can be used for fixing or making things. Most run on gasoline, which can be obtained from the dinghy's outboard motor supply.

An inverter, while small compared to a fuel-powered generator, can do some of the same things, but not all. Hooked up to the batteries, it can convert DC voltage to 110-volt AC—the net result is the same as the AC fuel-powered generator—it's simply a different means to the same end. However, an inverter won't recharge your battery, and up to about 15% of the available power is lost between the source and appliance.

Of the many companies making inverters, Xantrex (www.xantrex.com), which bought pioneer Heart Interface (Figure 12-8), and Charles Industries (www.charlesindustries.com) are two of many. Some household tools and appliances are not designed for operation with the square wave generated by some old-fashioned inverters. If buying a cheap square-wave inverter, first check what you're going to run on it to see if it will work. Incandescent lamps, electric shavers, soldering irons, and other devices that present a resistive or small inductive load work well with square-wave inverters. Problems may be experienced with radios, televisions (which may hum or buzz), tape recorders, and electric drills (which may fail to start).

Today, most of the top-quality inverters produce either a modified sine wave or true sine wave

FIGURE 12-8. Xantrex inverters feature modified sine waves for running most appliances on board, including computers. Some units also have built-in battery chargers for use with 110-volt shore power. (Xantrex)

that is suitable for running computers and other sensitive electronics.

The third solution to providing AC power is to install an engine-driven AC generator. This looks much like the DC generator or alternator already on your engine and works the same way; that is, by pulley and belt. They are heavy, however, and because they only work with the engine running, are viewed more as a substitute for a genset when space isn't available. Inverters have captured this market. A drawback to fuel-powered generators and AC generators is that you must listen to the noise of an internal combustion engine in order to reap the benefits. AC generators can recharge batteries if wired to a battery charger or built with integral converters. Inverters won't recharge your battery, unless it has a built-in battery charger, and then only when hooked up to shore power. Cost and peace of mind—yours and your neighbor's—are important considerations.

## WATER-DRIVEN GENERATORS

When assessing the various means of charging, it is important to consider how much time will be spent sailing and how much time will be spent at anchor. While some wind-driven generators will work when the boat is either in motion or at rest, water-driven generators only produce electricity when moving. Tapping the ocean for power is, however, a natural solution.

There are essentially two types of water generators: those with propellers that are trailed be-

FIGURE 12-7. A Honda portable generator.

hind the boat, and those that are turned by a pulley off of the main engine's propeller shaft.

On the face of it, alternators designed to be pulley-driven by the freewheeling propeller sound nearly ideal, because the shaft is there anyway, doing nothing while you sail. Its potential energy might as well be harnessed. Some innovative cruisers, including Steve and Linda Dashew's early Deerfoot boats, incorporate auxiliary propellers and shafts just for this purpose. This saves wear and tear on the engine's transmission, which is a costly piece of equipment. Sailing hundreds or thousands of miles with the prop freewheeling is adding unnecessary hours of wear to your transmission.

A further hindrance is that two props increase drag to a level that some sailors may find unacceptable. Drag, of course, is a consideration with any water generator towed behind the boat. This makes a case for reconsidering use of the engine's propeller. Studies have shown that there is little difference in drag between freewheeling propellers and those locked in place, though if the prop is vertically aligned behind the keel when locked, drag tends to be less.

One of the best known water-driven generators is the Aquair 100 (Figure 12-9) alternator made by Ampair Natural Energy (www.ampair.com). This water turbine is trailed behind the boat on 60 feet (18.3 m) of braided rope, though a variation of it can be bolted to a transom strut. The

**FIGURE 12-9.** An Aquair 100 water generator. (Ampair)

12-volt model generates 3 amps at 5 knots while producing 25 pounds (11 kg) of drag. And because drag squares with velocity, it's not difficult to see that at high speeds it would be advisable to retrieve the generator and stow it below. A 24-volt model also is available, but as we saw above, output in amps will be half. At anchor, the Aquair 100 may be converted to a wind-driven generator by fitting the stern pulpit-mounted generator unit with a 26-inch-diameter (0.66 m) set of wind blades.

Fourwinds (www.fourwinds-ii.com), LVM (www.lvm-ltd.com), and Ferris Power Products (www.hamiltonferris.com) also make water and wind generators. Five amps at 6 knots is "guaranteed" by Ferris for its water-driven generator.

## WIND-DRIVEN GENERATORS

There are a rapidly growing number of wind-driven generators available on today's market—some of which can be used both underway and at anchor, and some—the larger models—only at anchor.

Wind generators have undergone some changes during the past two decades. Earlier in their development for marine use, you had the choice of either a big unit hung in the rigging with 60-inch (1.5 m) blades or small mast-mounted trickle chargers producing only milliamps. In recent years it seems that most manufacturers have settled in the middle ground with permanently mounted units that have somewhat smaller-diameter blades yet produce a respectable output. The rigging-suspended Wind-bugger (www.windbugger.com; Figure 12-10) is rated at 1 amp in 5 knots of wind and 7 amps in 15 knots.

The cousin of the Aquair 100 is the Ampair 100 (Figure 12-11), a permanent-magnet wind generator that has been powered up from the first Ampair 50 introduced in the 1970s. It features a six-blade wind turbine measuring 3 feet (0.9 m) in diameter, the largest the company feels is safe for permanent mounting on yachts. It is still more compact than the Windbugger's 54-inch (1.4 m) blades and, consequently, can be allowed to spin in higher wind velocities. The Ampair delivers up to about 2 amps in 12-knot winds and a little over 4 amps in 20-knot winds.

The smaller the blades, the less the output, but also the less often the turbine will have to be

**FIGURE 12-10.** The Windbugger can be mounted on a pole aft of the cockpit or suspended in the rigging. Both mounts rotate 360° and start producing in winds of about 5 mph. (Gerard Pesty photo)

**FIGURE 12-11.** The permanently mounted Ampair 100 produces about 2 amps in 12-knot winds. (Ampair)

shut down in high winds and the less wind resistance. Permanent mounts are less hassle and may be able to operate while sailing, whereas rigging mounts are used only at anchor. Figure 12-12 compares performance.

Most wind generators use permanent magnet rotors to minimize losses in energizing the magnetic field. AC is converted to DC, usually by means of a rectifier. The unit should be protected by an in-line fuse, and a regulator is strongly recommended. Some manufacturers say that a regulator isn't needed if you're living aboard and drawing the battery down constantly. That's true, but what happens if you go ashore for the day, and the batteries already have been topped off by motoring into the anchorage? Play it safe and install a regulator to protect your batteries from overcharging. The Air X Marine wind generator incorporates three-stage voltage regulation in-

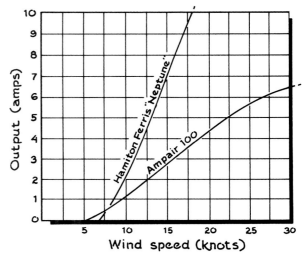

**FIGURE 12-12.** This graph illustrates the dramatic difference in output between portable (Ampair 100) and permanently mounted or in-the-rigging (Neptune) wind-driven generators, especially at higher wind speeds.

**FIGURE 12-13.** The Air X Marine is a popular newer model that features built-in current regulation.

ternally (www.windenergy.com). Its carbon fiber blades are supposed to begin feathering at high wind speeds.

Single-handed ocean racers favor wind generators over water-driven units because there is less drag, though output is roughly equivalent.

Handle all units, especially the portable types, carefully when demounting; a cut on the arm or skull could be dangerous. Turbine blades can be slowed by unhooking the electrical lead wires and crossing them. The simplest way is to turn the unit 90° to the wind by means of the rudder. In any case, some sort of remote brake is strongly recommended.

Common mounts are on the mizzen mast of a ketch or on a pole mounted at the stern of a sloop. I know of at least one case where a person was seriously injured by a pole-mounted wind generator when the tide went out, lowering the wind generator to dock level. Figures 12-13 through 12-15 show several mounting options.

I've tested most of the major brands, including those mentioned here, and developed a healthy fear of the large units. I also don't care for the noise the large models make. On the other hand, the very small generators don't produce enough to

**FIGURE 12-14.** On ketches, the mizzen mast is a logical place to mount a small- to medium-size wind generator.

**FIGURE 12-15.** Gerard Pesty's 54-foot (16.5 m) trimaran *Architeuthis* obtains power from the wind, water, and sun. Note the Aerowatt wind generator at the mizzen masthead and the Motorola Hydroalternator on the transom. Also on board are solar panels and a prop shaft–driven water generator, which are not visible in this photo. (Gerard Pesty photo)

make them seem worthwhile. My preference is for a small- to medium-size generator with a blade diameter of no more than about 42 inches (1.07 m).

## SOLAR

A significant departure from the "active" generator/alternator types is the "passive" solar panel. The heart of the photovoltaic energy concept is the solar cell.

The solar cell is a semiconductor device that converts light energy directly into electrical energy. Silicon solar cells are made by doping silicon crystals with other chemicals. When phosphorus is added during the growth of the crystal, the silicon develops negatively charged electrons; when boron is added, positively charged carriers appear. The crystals—polycrystalline silicon or monocrystalline silicon—are then sliced into wafers. Incoming light particles called photons are absorbed by the electrons within the silicon wafer and create both positive and negative charges. A photocurrent flows, voltage develops, and electricity is produced. All silicon solar cells produce about the same amount of voltage—about 0.5 volt—so many of them are used in series to produce voltage sufficient to be of use in charging batteries. The more solar cells, the bigger the panel, the more output obtained. Wiring two or more panels in a parallel circuit increases the output of amps.

Several years ago Arco Solar (bought by Siemens, which is now part of Shell Solar) introduced its new "thin film" technology, in which a semiconductive gallium arsenide coating is mated between the two layers of glass instead of the conventional cells one is accustomed to seeing. I installed two of the Genesis 5-watt panels (about $100 each) on the Pearson Vanguard, and they worked fine for several years before water worked its way inside the laminate and corrosion took its toll. Obviously, such small panels aren't going to produce much (a couple of amp-hours on a sunny day), but they did make a difference, especially in preventing the self-discharge of batteries for those periods when we weren't aboard for several days at a time.

A few of the companies making panels for marine application are BP Solar (www.bpsolar.com), Shell Solar (www.shellsolar.com), Kyocera (www.kyocerasolar.com), and Uni-Solar Systems (www.unisolar.com). The latter makes flexible panels that take more abuse—such as footsteps and dropped winch handles—than glass-covered panels. They also feature triple-junction technology that minimizes losses due to shading; where conventional series-wired panels lose more output due to shading than the amount of surface area covered, Uni-Solar panels' loss is roughly proportional to the area covered. The downside is that these panels aren't as efficient as conventional polycrystalline panels. Nevertheless, Uni-Solar panels are susceptible to the same problems as the others—corrosion of the wire leads and water entering the delicate circuitry through failure of the transparent face. Neither are they particularly abrasion-resistant. A 45-watt Uni-Solar panel sells at discount for about $225.

Tempered glass covers allow the most light through but are easier to crack than plastic covers. In place of glass, Tedlar and Tefzel plastic coatings by DuPont have light transmission factors of about 94 to 95%.

Panel temperature affects output of solar panels, both extreme heat and cold. Providing ventilation space behind a panel to keep it cool in hot weather is a good idea (Figure 12-16). Mounting the panels so they can be adjusted to face the sun directly will increase output, though this is not always feasible, especially on a narrow monohull. Most panels have blocking diodes that prevent discharge of the battery at night.

John Campbell, a British journalist who spent some years cruising the Caribbean, says, however, that his tests showed the amount of current lost by the diode when charging exceeded the amount lost at night when the diode was removed. The

**FIGURE 12-16.** Aboard the *Architeuthis*, Gerard Pesty locates his solar panels wherever they give the most output. Tilting the angle toward the sun and leaving an air space behind the panels maximizes output. (Gerard Pesty photo)

## EFFECT OF TILTING PANELS ON OUTPUT

| Local Time | Sky Condition | Sun Elevation Above Horizon | Lying on Deck | Tilted* |
|---|---|---|---|---|
| 8:15 AM | Veiled | 10° | 0.15 | 0.25 |
| 8:45 | Slightly Veiled | 15° | 0.25 | 0.60 |
| 9:10 | Clear | 21' | 0.60 | 1.60 |
| 9:30 | Clear | 25° | 0.75 | 1.75 |
| 10:00 | Veiled to Overcast | 30° | 0.60 | 0.90 |
| 10:30 | Clear | 35° | 1.30 | 1.80 |
| 12:15 PM | Veiled (Bright) | 55° | 1.70 | 2.30 |
| 3:00 | Clear | 45° | 1.60 | 2.00 |
| 5:00 | Clear | 39° | 1.50 | 1.90 |
| 7:00 | Slightly Veiled | 16° | 0.25 | 0.40 |
| 7:30 | Veiled to Overcast (Gray) | — | 0.07 | 0.10 |
| 8:00 | Veiled to Overcast (Gray) | — | 0.03 | 0.03 |

*\* Perpendicular to Sun's Rays*

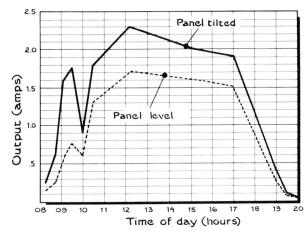

Flat panel output = 13.5 amp hours
Tilted panel output = 18.25 amp hours
DIFFERENCE: 4.75 amp hours

**FIGURE 12-17.** To determine the difference in output between a flat, fixed solar panel and one continually tilted toward the sun, Gerard Pesty and Jean-Philippe Malice conducted an experiment aboard *La Malicieuse*. The table and graph show the results: about 35% more power from the tilted solar panel.

French filmmaker Gerard Pesty has experimented with many types of alternative energy devices, including solar panels, aboard his 54-foot (16.5 m) trimaran, *Architeuthis*. On a friend's boat he conducted tests measuring the output of two 40-watt solar panels, one mounted horizontally and the other rotated to track the sun. Figure 12-17 shows the results. Figures 12-18 through 12-23 show a variety of possible mounts.

Common causes of solar panel failure are breaking or crazing of the glass cover and corro-

main reason diodes are used to prevent current flowing out at night is to save the skipper the trouble of switching off the circuit. So, if you are willing to wire in a switch and merely flip it off at dusk, the diode can be eliminated altogether with no trade-off in current losses.

That said, a regulator is highly recommended, and obviates the need for a diode or switch, as the regulator will disconnect the panel at night when no current is flowing. Some panels are labeled "self-regulating," suggesting that you don't need to spend $75 on a regulator; what it really means is that the panel's current output at battery charging current is less than about 1% of the battery's capacity in amp-hours (e.g., less than 4 amps for a 400-amp-hour battery bank).

**FIGURE 12-18.** A small panel mounted on the stern pulpit.

**FIGURE 12-19.** The location of this panel isn't bad, but it will be shaded by the mainsail some of the time, and when furling sails, the crew must be careful not to step on it.

**FIGURE 12-20.** This fixed panel is well aft of the mainsail, which is good, but it looks like it will still be shaded much of the time. (Bruce Bingham photo)

**FIGURE 12-21.** BOC competitor Dan Byrne used four solar panels on adjustable ball-socket mounts. One was swept away in the Southern Ocean. (Herb McCormick photo)

**FIGURE 12-22.** A popular location is on top of the companionway hatch, though it's still vulnerable to being stepped on. A better choice is on top of the dodger, especially a hardtop dodger. (Bruce Bingham photo)

**FIGURE 12-23.** Aboard *Nike 11*, Richard Konkolski had a specially molded mount for his array of solar panels. (Gerard Pesty photo)

sion of the wires at the solar panel terminals, but the industry has made great strides in improving quality.

# INSTALLATION

Solar, wind, and water generators are no more difficult to install than a car stereo; only basic tools and attention to instructions are required. Frequently the most difficult aspect will be adapting mounting hardware to your boat. Some companies offer mounting kits, but in some situations, you may need to custom fabricate some of the hardware. Wiring should adhere to ABYC specifications.

## Installing Solar Panels

The orientation of the solar panel to the sun directly affects the amount of charge to the battery. Solar panels must be rotated to follow the path of the sun in order to deliver maximum charge. Leaving them flat on deck, as so many cruisers do, means about 35% less charging power.

As noted above, because each solar cell in a conventional panel is connected in series to the rest, a shadow across only a small part of the panel can reduce output of the array by a significant amount—80% or more. Therefore, it is necessary to locate the panels where rigging, sails, and lifelines aren't likely to cast their shadows across the panels. If mounting in an exposed area, some sort of detachable mount is a good idea for removal when the wind picks up. An exception, as noted earlier, is the less efficient Uni-Solar panel; if serious shading is unavoidable, it turns out to be a worthwhile trade-off.

Once you determine a suitable mounting site, it's time to wire the panel to the battery. The closer to the battery the better, because the longer the connecting wires, the greater the loss of current flowing through them. Use insulated wire of at least #18 AWG; the farther the distance, the thicker the wire.

If mounting on deck or on a hatch, make a template of the panel to transfer the holes for the mounting screws from the panel to the hatch. Drill holes and secure with stainless steel screws.

Remember to apply a bedding compound to the hole and threads of the screws to prevent water from creeping in, especially if the deck is cored. On many panels, the screws will be put in from inside the boat, coming up through the deck

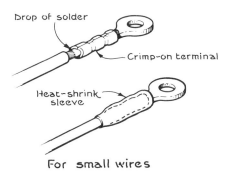

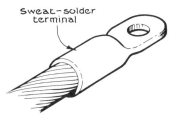

**FIGURE 12-24.** Terminal wires should be connected to the battery with crimp lugs, soldered for good connections, and protected with heat-shrink sleeves.

or hatch and into the holes in the frame of the panel's back. You will need an additional hole for the lead wires to pass through, taking the same precautions to make it waterproof.

Attach the red wire or the one marked with a "+" to the positive terminal on the battery; the other wire to the negative terminal. If the wires

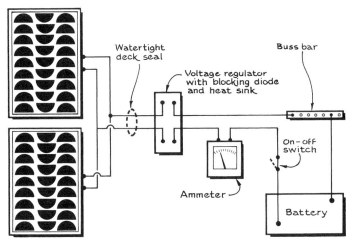

**FIGURE 12-25.** This schematic shows a typical solar panel electrical hookup to the battery, including voltage regulator and ammeter. With an on/off switch or a regulator, a blocking diode isn't necessary to prevent discharge of the battery at night.

aren't fitted with terminals, pick up some crimp lug eyes at your local chandlery or electrical supply shop. Crimp them on, and apply a drop of solder on each to ensure a good connection. Use a plastic heat-shrink sleeve to protect the joint (Figure 12-24).

Besides a blocking diode on the positive wire, some solar panel manufacturers also advise placing a fuse on the positive side to prevent damage to the panel in the event of shorts. Small in-line fuses are available at most chandleries or electronic stores. Figure 12-25 diagrams a typical installation.

About the only maintenance solar panels require is an occasional wash with a mild detergent and fresh water.

### Installing Wind and Water Generators

The electrical hookups of wind and water generators generally will follow those just given for solar panels. Permanently mounted wind generators can be fitted high up on the forward side of mizzen masts, at the masthead, or on a pipe/mast attached to the stern pulpit. The only other word of caution is that objects this size are subject to considerable stress from the wind, and so should be securely mounted with through-bolts. The vibration caused by many units is substantial and will loosen bolts and wear out bearings if not properly installed and inspected regularly.

It seems there are fewer ketches and yawls today, perhaps because the sloop is a more efficient rig, and the development of large electric winches and reliable furling gear make them feasible. Without the possibility of a mizzen mast mount, the wind generator is most sensibly mounted on a pole on the afterdeck or otherwise near the transom. Besides a strong base, there should be some sort of 90° side strut that anchors the pole to the pulpit or a 45° strut to the deck. For the sturdiest pole, run it through the deck to the hull.

Most water generators are designed to mount on the stern pulpit, and assuming the stern pulpit isn't about to fall off, this should be a sufficiently strong place for installation.

## FURTHER READING

*Boatowner's Illustrated Electrical Handbook.* 2nd ed. Charlie Wing. Camden, Maine: International Marine, 2006.

*Boatowner's Energy Planner: How to Make and Manage Electrical Energy on Board.* Nan and Kevin Jeffrey. Newport, Rhode Island: Seven Seas Press, 1991.

*The Solar Boat Book.* Pat Rand Rose. Berkeley, California: Ten Speed Press, 1983.

# THIRTEEN

# INSTRUMENTS AND THE ELECTRICAL SYSTEM

The first rule about marine electronics is that electricity and salt water don't mix. Once electrical wiring and appliances are wet, corrosion is swift and insidious.

The only way to avoid the hassle and frustration of failed electronics is not to have them. Considering that for 99.9% of human history electrical power was unharnessed (yet sailors voyaged round the world), it should be a worthwhile sacrifice for any of us to live at least a short while without it. Living simply better prepares one to cope with the exigencies of nature and the vagaries of man-made equipment.

Yet electrical conveniences have become so much a part of our daily lives, it is almost unthinkable to try doing without them. The size and scope of your electrical inventory is a controversial subject among cruising people. Purists burn oil lamps, toss the engine overboard, and eat out of cans until fresh meats and vegetables can be purchased. At the other end of the spectrum, large yachts cruise the world with air-conditioning, satellite navigation, and a deep freeze filled with steaks and frozen fish.

Electronics run afoul of my fundamental belief that as much of the boat's gear as possible should be repairable by the crew. Many electronic products are disposable, meaning that when they fail, it's cheaper to buy an entire new unit than repair the old one. And if repairs are your choice, you'll have to ship the unit back to the United States or point of origin. A lot of cruisers these days find themselves delayed in some port while awaiting the return of equipment from the manufacturer/repairer.

During my year's cruise of the East Coast and Bahamas (hardly a transoceanic slog through vicious winds and mountainous seas), practically every piece of electronic gear failed at least once—and it was all new! The equipment included VHF radio, autopilot, depth sounder, and log. The only thing that worked reliably was the Micrologic Explorer loran, which never winked, except for two months in the Bahamas, where loran coverage is poor and the displays are weird.

A good spare parts inventory and the ability to install them increases independence afloat. If an electrical item cannot be repaired, have a backup available, or you should be able to do without it for the duration of the cruise. Nowadays, handheld GPS units are so inexpensive that every boat carries two or three, though fixed-mount units are more user-friendly and many have more features. A shrinking number of cruisers still learn celestial navigation with a sextant, and there is no denying that it is a useful backup in case you lose your electronic means of position finding. I used to believe that taking off on a long passage without the knowledge or skill to navigate without electronics was plain dumb, but the reliability, ease of use, and low cost of GPS is undeniable.

Some "purists" like Lin and Larry Pardey believe that sailors who have such devices on board gradually develop unconscious dependencies on them, which reduces their ability or readiness to handle problems without the aid of electronics. While this may be true to a certain extent, it's not *wrong* to have electronics on your boat—it's more a function of your confidence in basic skills, how much you want to be in contact with the world, how much frustration you're willing to put up with when they fail, and how much money you're willing to spend. But you shouldn't overlook the advantages of such equipment, such as single-sideband (SSB) radio, which in the event of a medical emergency at sea may be your only means of communicating with a physician.

## NAVIGATION INSTRUMENTS

There is no doubt that a great deal of money can be spent on electronics. But like pocket calculators, television sets, and home computers, the price of sophisticated electronics has come down dramatically in recent years. This trend will continue. Several years ago, the cheapest and virtually only SatNav on the market was made by Magnavox and cost about $10,000. Today, you can buy a handheld GPS for $100. Where position-finding devices were once some of the most expensive instruments, today they sell for much less than radar, chart plotters, and even basic sailing instruments.

## Compass

The compass isn't really an electrical device in the conventional sense. But a good quality compass is the single most important piece of navigational equipment on a boat. Coastwise and even mid-ocean navigation is predicated on being able to tell what direction the boat is heading. The ancient Polynesians could navigate by the stars and sea alone. And Marvin Creamer, the New Jersey man who sailed around the world without instruments, developed a method of celestial navigation without instruments. Despite numerous articles explaining his techniques, it is doubtful that many people, most of whom have difficulty naming three constellations, will ever be able, or want, to learn them. At any rate, the rest of us remain dependent on the compass.

Don't skimp on the quality of compass you put on board. When buying a new or used boat, the compass that comes with it is often the least expensive "nice-looking" unit available. And for knocking about the bay, it probably does the job. But what a difference a good compass makes, with several 45° lubber lines, a large well-gimballed card, and a red nightlight.

The best compass, however, does little good if it isn't corrected. Procedures for completing a compass deviation card can be found in most navigation texts, including *Chapman*. The job is simple but does require some patience and time. The boat must be oriented along a number of headings whose true bearings are known from a chart or other instrument. Magnetic variation must be allowed for and the remaining error between the compass and the known bearing—deviation—recorded on the card for use in calculating future courses.

Locate the compass parallel to the centerline of the boat, yet easily read from both port and starboard helm positions. Be careful to mount it

**FIGURE 13-1.** The 5-inch (127 mm) Ritchie Globe-master SP-5C is probably the most popular compass for mounting on top of a steering pedestal. It has sapphire jewels and pivots, a brushed stainless steel mount, and reinforced fiberglass bowl. Price is around $500 (as of this writing). (Ritchie Navigation)

where it can't be damaged by an errant foot or sheet. Nor should it be near ferrous metals or electrical wiring. Wiring that, by necessity, must be run close to the compass should be twisted to minimize its effect (the positive and negative fields cancel each other). Typical mounts are on the cabin facing the cockpit and atop binnacles or wheel steering pedestals (Figure 13-1). The red nightlight wires are led to the bus bar and tied in with the navigation light circuit. When the running lights are turned on, the compass light comes on as well.

## Knotmeter and Log

A basic aid to dead reckoning (DR) is knowing how fast the boat is moving. The equation speed × time elapsed = distance traveled (e.g., 5 knots × 1 hour = 5 nautical miles) is fundamental. After you've sailed your boat awhile, you learn to estimate the speed of the boat fairly accurately even without a knotmeter. But to learn, you need some help, and a knotmeter is the instrument to use.

For a generation of cruisers, the patented Walker Log (Figure 13-2) was trailed behind the boat. By knowing the distance traveled and time elapsed between readings, average speed could be determined. The propeller sending unit was trailed over the transom on a long line, and it was very accurate. The only problems were that they became fouled with seaweed and sharks liked to eat them. Hiscock and others always advised carrying sev-

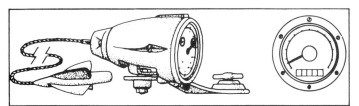

**FIGURE 13-2.** The Walker Log is a mechanical distance-measuring device hung over the stern and trailed behind the boat. By measuring distance and elapsed time, speed also can be determined. (Kathy Bray drawing)

eral spares. One of the reasons the trailing log is more accurate than sending units mounted on the hull is that turbulence from water passing around the hull can distort the readings. Taffrail logs are mechanical, meaning that the propeller at the end of the line turns a cable inside (just like bicycle speedometers), which turns dials in the display.

In contrast, electronic logs have processors that calculate distance traveled by first measuring speed, then multiplying it by time elapsed. The sensor, usually a paddlewheel (Figure 13-3), generates an electronic signal that is sent to the processor via a wire. Paddlewheels, too, of course, are subject to fouling. To clean inside the boat, unscrew the retaining ring, get the replacement dummy plug ready, hold your breath (remember, a 1½-inch/38 mm hole that is 2 feet/61 cm below the waterline admits 71 gallons/268.7 L of water per minute), and then yank the transducer out, immediately followed by slamming the dummy plug into place. If you have a heart attack during the operation, you'll go down with the boat—that's something your widow can tell the grandkids!

A few companies make sonic speed/log sensors that have no moving parts. Brookes & Gatehouse (www.bandg.com) makes two: The standard sonic sensor calculates speed by measuring the time it takes for pulses to travel through the water between one sensor positioned forward in the hull and a second sensor mounted aft. The B&G Ultrasonic Speed Sensor for Hercules and Hydra instrument systems uses echo sound to read beyond the turbulent boundary layer. It measures speeds from 0.1 knot to 60 knots and operates on 10 to 14 VDC on a frequency of 4.5 MHz. These are high-end systems, but getting rid of the paddlewheel is significant.

To install a sensor (paddlewheel or other type) in the hull, you have to cut a hole. Use a hole saw

**FIGURE 13-3.** This paddlewheel-type sensor (top) is very sensitive and gives accurate knotmeter readouts. But barnacles and other marine organisms can foul it easily, which is why the plug is sold with the unit. Most units come with a display, paddlewheel, and through-hull (bottom).

**FIGURE 13-4.** A hole saw attached to a power drill is used for cutting holes for depth sounder transducer and knotmeter sensors. The bit centers the hole saw.

for this purpose (Figure 13-4). Drilling from inside out usually chips the gelcoat on the outside, but not so much that it won't be covered by the flange of the sensor. If concerned about this, drill only until the pilot bit goes through the hull, then go outside and complete the hole.

Obviously, the size of the hole saw is dictated by the diameter of the sensor. The manufacturer generally will specify that dimension, something like 2⅜ inches (60 mm), just the sort of dimension you'll never need again. Hole saws are very useful, and most hardware stores sell seven-blade kits that are supposed to meet all requirements. Or you can buy a standard chuck and pilot bit and purchase the hole saws individually, according to the job at hand. When installing something through the hull, especially below the waterline, the hole must be cut to exact specifications to ensure a tight fit. A ¼ inch (6 mm) of slop around a knotmeter sensor is simply too much. Bedding compound may keep water out for a while, but what happens if you ground the boat or come hard off a wave? I want to know that everything below the water is well secured and watertight.

Use generous amounts of bedding compound, such as polysulfide, enough so that when you tighten down the backing plate, compound oozes out both inside and outside the hull. You can cut it away after it dries, so don't worry about how messy it looks.

Use a hole saw also to cut the hole in the bulkhead where the display will be mounted (even most square displays that mount flush on the bulkhead have round guts in back that protrude through the bulkhead). Run the wire between the two out of the way, such as behind bunks and cabinetry. Avoid pulling the wire tight because it could chafe on sharp edges. If there is any doubt about this, wrap tape around the wire where it might chafe, or better yet, slip plastic tubing over the wire. The ultimate protection is to run the entire wire through PVC conduit, but generally the wires for knotmeters are well-insulated and tough.

Knotmeters need calibrating (be suspicious of a unit that has no adjustment). Read the manual for instructions on entering the right menu. Calibration, or verification of the factory setting, is best done by running the boat over a measured course free of wind and current. Any known distance between two buoys or other land or sea

marks is suitable. For example, if the distance between two buoys is 1.2 miles, and the time elapsed during the run (with steady throttle) is 18 minutes (0.3 hour), the knotmeter should read 4 knots (1.2 nm/0.3 h = 4.0 kn). Keep running the boat at the same throttle while you figure the equation, so you can adjust the knotmeter while running at the speed used during the test. Or take note of the exact engine rpm used for the first run.

A GPS also gives a speed reading, but this is speed over ground (SOG), not through the water, which is what your knotmeter reads. If there is no current, the two should be nearly the same, but there are still subtle errors in the GPS system that are difficult to account for.

## Depth Sounder

You can do without depth sounders (Figure 13-5); traditionalists will tell you to use a lead line. Charge the hollow tip of the lead line with wax and you can even bring up a sample of the bottom—mud, coral, sand or gravel? It makes a difference in your anchoring strategy.

But why? Depth sounders can help prevent groundings by alerting the skipper to changing depths much faster than a lead line. Today there are sonar units that read ahead of the boat, giving even more advance warning of impending danger.

Navigation is a useful function of the depth sounder. Look on any chart at the contours of depth approaching a shoreline. Usually, the contours will read something like: 40 feet, 25 feet, 5 feet (12 m, 7.6 m, 1.5 m). Suppose you're feeling your way along a coast at night or in a fog. You know the shore is near. Turn on the depth

**FIGURE 13-5.** Depth sounders with digital displays seem more precise than analog displays. (Raymarine)

sounder and see what reading you get—41 feet (12.5 m), after a few minutes 23 feet (7 m). You can look at the chart and estimate your proximity to shore by comparing the depth on your sounder with the depth on the chart.

Wherever you mount the transducer, note how far beneath the surface it is and figure this into your readings. Most electronic depth sounders have a feature called "keel offset" so you don't have to add a certain number to that which the sounder gives you beneath its transducer. For example, if the transducer is 2 feet (61 cm) below the waterline, and the keel draws 4 feet (1.2 m), you can adjust the sounder to subtract 2 feet from its readings. Then, if you're in 6 feet of water, it will read 2 feet, which is the clearance between the bottom and the keel. Or, you can adjust the sounder to add 2 feet so that it reads actual water depth.

Transducers are available with two frequencies—50 kHz and 200 kHz. The lower-frequency transducer is best for depths greater than about 200 feet (61 m), say, for alerting you when coming on soundings from an offshore passage. For shallower waters, the 200 kHz frequency gives better resolution and a wider reading area. Some brands offer dual-frequency transducers so you can toggle back and forth between the two—that's ideal.

There's no real difference between installing a depth sounder transducer and a knotmeter sensor. Use the right size hole saw, use a good-quality bedding compound, and run your wires so they won't be damaged by water or chafe. A

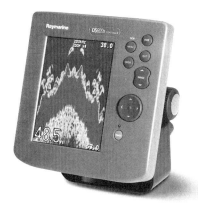

**FIGURE 13-7.** This Raymarine color fishfinder incorporates water temperature and speed, as well as bottom contour and fish, in one unit. (Raymarine)

fairing block (Figure 13-6) between the transducer and hull may be required to aim the transducer straight down to prevent erroneous readings. And never cut the wire between the transducer and instrument, as its length is part of the electronic design.

An inexpensive handheld depth sounder that basically looks like a flashlight (such as those made by NorCross, www.norcrossmarine.com) is useful when searching anchorages by dinghy.

Digital fishfinders (Figure 13-7) with LCD displays combine a lot of handy features in a small package, at not much more money than the single-feature sailboat depth sounder. Unfortunately, most are trunnion-mounted for powerboat consoles, though this doesn't mean you couldn't find a suitable place under the dodger on a cruising sailboat. Not only are bottom contours clearly visible, but many models also include water temperature and speed. And just because you're on a sailboat doesn't mean you're not interested in fish!

## GPS

Some years ago I received a call at *Cruising World* from a physician who had just completed a passage from Bermuda to Watch Hill, Rhode Island. His 31-foot (9.4 m) cutter had been badly damaged by gale-force winds and high, steep seas in the Gulf Stream. The outboard rudderstock had snapped, the companionway hatch busted open (the weather boards smashed and the hatch jammed open), the boat half filled with water, and all their electrics shorted out.

**FIGURE 13-6.** Depth sounder transducers must be mounted vertically, and because few hulls are flat-bottomed, hardwood fairing blocks must be fashioned to correctly position the transducer against the hull.

They had called the U.S. Coast Guard before losing power in their radio. An airplane flew over, dropped a large barrel with pumps and other gear astern, and left. Without a rudder, however, the crew was unable to maneuver back to pick up the package, so they continued on, using the sails to steer the boat. The *only* piece of navigational electronic gear that worked was the RDF, which they used to find their way into Watch Hill.

Why did the RDF work when all else had failed? Because their model used its own D batteries and therefore was not dependent on the ship's batteries. Also, it was located high on a shelf where water could not reach it.

While radio direction finders are near antiques, the handheld GPS has the same advantages of being battery powered and therefore immune to problems with the ship's electrical system. This doesn't mean you shouldn't have a fixed-mount or portable-mount GPS (Figure 13-8) as your primary navigation instrument; they have larger displays and keypads, and so are easier to use. But a handheld (Figure 13-9) backup is important.

GPS, as you probably know, stands for global positioning system and is run by the U.S. military. Satellites orbiting the Earth transmit signals that are picked up by the receiver on your boat. Signals from at least two and preferably more satellites are required to fix your position. Accuracy varies as the constellation of satellites changes, but it's generally within 33 feet (10 m). National security allows the military to arbitrarily degrade the signal, which greatly decreases accuracy. This fea-

FIGURE 13-9. Handheld GPS receivers are now available for as little as $100. Cartographic models, such as this Garmin eTrex Legend, run more. Carry at least one as a backup to your other position-finding instruments. (Garmin)

ture, called selective availability (SA), was turned off by President Clinton, but it could return at any time in the future. To correct for SA errors, something called Differential GPS (DGPS) was instituted in the 1990s, using ground beacons; the logic apparently was that only people in the United States would be able to receive these corrections, not terrorists in other countries. But when SA was turned off, consumer interest in the more expensive DGPS receiver stopped. In its place is another program called WAAS or wide area augmentation system. It is also a land-based system and is being developed mostly for aviation, though it works for marine, too. Accuracy with a WAAS receiver is around 10 feet (3 m).

Until some new navigation system is developed, GPS is the gold standard—highly accurate, highly reliable, and inexpensive. Just remember that it can go down, either due to equipment malfunction or because the government decides to turn it off. If and when either of these unlikely scenarios occur while you're at sea, you'll probably wish you'd learned celestial nav with a sextant after all.

## Loran-C

Loran, a largely coastal electronic nav system popular in the 1980s, is extremely accurate, utilizing pairs of pulsed radio signals from land-based transmitters to give the yacht's receiver a position fix. Accuracy is generally within an eighth of a mile (0.2 km), unless returning to a place it's already

FIGURE 13-8. An alternative to the handheld or fixed-mount GPS is the Garmin 276C portable model, which can be moved to different locations. (Garmin)

been (waypoint), in which case accuracy is much greater. Range is up to 700 miles (1,127 km) from transmitting stations during the day, and about 1,400 miles (2,254 km) at night.

Loran has been almost completely surpassed by GPS, but the government continues to maintain the loran system—at least for the time being. Fishermen, in particular, programmed pot and trap locations into their loran units so they could easily return to the same.

Most of the U.S. coastline and some of the European coastal waters are covered by Loran-C. Parts of the Caribbean are still uncovered, likewise the South Pacific and much of Asia. It seems ironic that sailors making transatlantic passages via the northern route report near continuous coverage between Great Britain and Canada, while just 50 miles (81 km) off the Florida coast, the signals turn fluky over the Bahamas.

Loran-C charts are overlaid by TD (time difference) lines, which can be referenced by the loran display. Loran units also can convert the Loran-C TD lines of position to latitude and longitude, which are printed on all charts and are more readily understood by the public. Lat/lon readouts, however, aren't as accurate as TDs.

If you're familiar with electronics, the manufacturer's instructions should be sufficient to guide you in installing the antenna and various components on your boat. These generally include the control unit, alternator capacitors to eliminate interference, the antenna, and a ground wire. Loran is often wired directly to the battery for maximum power and minimum interference. The battery is a natural noise filter. If wiring direct, be sure to fuse the positive lead, minimize the run, and use a large enough gauge wire to keep voltage drop to a minimum (try for less than 3%). Typical full operating load is several amps.

## *Electronic Chart Plotters*

Electronic charts, scanned from conventional NOAA and NGA (National Geospatial-Intelligence Agency, formerly the National Imagery and Mapping Agency) charts (http://nauticalcharts.noaa.gov), are available on cartridges that can be plugged into a dedicated chart plotter or a GPS/chart plotter combo (Figure 13-10). The decided advantage of the latter is that you can see your position flashing on the screen. Many units come with a base map, but for real accuracy, you have

**FIGURE 13-10.** Nearly all fixed-mount GPS units are now cartographic, blurring the line between chart plotters and GPS. Electronic charts are the current rage. With GPS plugged in, you can track your position across the screen. Shown here is a Garmin 172C. (Garmin)

to buy additional cartridges or CDs with a collection of regional maps. There are two basic types: raster and vector charts. Raster charts are like exact photocopies of real NOAA charts. Vector charts also begin with a digital scanned image, but data is stored in layers so that you don't always have to display everything on the screen. The principal sources of electronic charts are Garmin (www.garmin.com), also a maker of hardware; C-MAP (www.c-map.com), Navionics (www.navionics.com), and Lowrance (www.lowrance.com), another maker of hardware as well.

With multi-display panels at the nav station and a repeater at the helm, you can now view not only basic instrumentation like speed, depth, SOG (speed over ground), VMG (velocity made good), and crosstrack error, but also bring up a chart with your position marked, latitude and longitude of that position, or a radar image.

You'll note that electronic charts come with a disclaimer, some as idiotic as saying they're not meant for navigation. Of course the provider is worried about product liability, as well they should be, since sometimes egregious errors are made, like omitting a buoy marking a shoal. But by and large, they are quite good. Nevertheless, any discussion of electronic charts would be incomplete without the admonishment to carry paper charts as backups. I get the sense that more and more people are "cheating" on the paper, but hey, it's your life—and your crew's.

**FIGURE 13-11.** An alternative to buying a dedicated chart plotter is to use your laptop computer. (Patrick Childress photo)

## Computers

With the advent of the laptop computer (Figure 13-11), it's no surprise that more sailors are taking theirs to sea. With programs like The Cap'n (www.thecapn.com), and Visual Navigation Suite and Nobletec Admiral (www.nobletec.com), you can begin cruise planning at home, like identifying waypoints and entering them into your cruise plan. On board, you'll need a continuous power source and a safe, dry place to place the laptop. I've made numerous passages with a laptop wedged on the nav table, and the display showing the boat's position on the chart. Of course you can zoom in and out. These programs can display constantly updated data such as lat/lon, estimated time of arrival, course to steer, bearing, and much more.

## MARINE RADIOTELEPHONES

The two principal means of communication for boats at sea are VHF (very high frequency) and SSB radiotelephones. VHF radios are used by all types of commercial and recreational watercraft for ship-to-ship and ship-to-shore conversations. Their range is limited to line of sight and so they are used mostly for coastal cruising.

The jump to SSB is a major one—in terms of cost, installation, sophistication of circuitry, and operation. With the right equipment and atmospheric conditions, the range of an SSB radio is thousands of miles (Figure 13-12).

FCC (Federal Communications Commission) regulations require the use of VHF whenever its range is sufficient to establish communications; SSB therefore can be used only offshore or in the more remote areas of the world, but for the itinerant cruiser, it could prove invaluable. Figure 13-13 shows the spectrum of radio frequencies used on ships, from very low frequency omega to super high frequency radar.

While the levels of skill required to operate VHF and SSB vary greatly, there is a protocol involved in the proper use of each. Government publications detail these more specifically for VHF and SSB and are available to the user (see reading list at end of chapter).

## VHF

For calling the U.S. Coast Guard while cruising the coast, or talking to a fisherman or freighter passing by, the utility of a VHF radio is unsurpassed.

Today, $100 to $500 will buy a VHF (Figure 13-14) that picks up all of the available channels

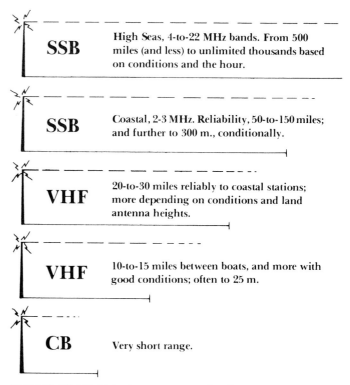

| | |
|---|---|
| **SSB** | High Seas, 4-to-22 MHz bands. From 500 miles (and less) to unlimited thousands based on conditions and the hour. |
| **SSB** | Coastal, 2-3 MHz. Reliability, 50-to-150 miles; and further to 300 m., conditionally. |
| **VHF** | 20-to-30 miles reliably to coastal stations; more depending on conditions and land antenna heights. |
| **VHF** | 10-to-15 miles between boats, and more with good conditions; often to 25 m. |
| **CB** | Very short range. |

**FIGURE 13-12.** This chart compares the distance capabilities of different radiotelephones.

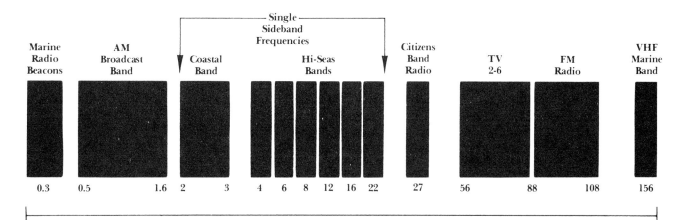

**FIGURE 13-13.** This chart shows the different radio frequencies assigned to various types of equipment. Frequencies are measured in megahertz. (Twentieth Century Publications, Inc.)

(Figure 13-15). (Old, nonsynthesized types required crystals for every channel.) VHF radios are almost always mounted inside the cabin, such as above the navigation station. Fixing the unit to the shelf is just a matter of drilling in a few screws through the bracket into the wood. Most models also may be flush mounted with a special kit. A waterproof second station can be mounted at the helm. Common features include scanning, dual watch (automatically toggle to listen between two designated channels), and NOAA weather broadcasts.

The antenna is the key to a good hookup. Because the range of VHF is line of sight, the higher the antenna, the farther the range. This means that a masthead antenna has a longer range than an antenna mounted on deck. Just how much is determined by the table in Figure 13-16.

For example, assume that the tip of a deck-mounted antenna is 12 feet (3.7 m) above sea level, and the height of the receiving antenna at a Coast Guard Station on shore is 50 feet (15.2 m) above sea level. From the table, the distance in nautical miles is 12.1 (22.4 km). A masthead antenna 44 feet (13.4 m) above sea level extends that range to 15.8 nm (29.2 km)—about 30% greater.

When reading about VHF radios, you usually see maximum distances of 25 or 35 miles (46.3 to 64.8 km). Several reasons exist for the discrepancies between these distances and the 12 to 15 miles just mentioned. First, a maximum range of 25 to 35 miles depends on good weather conditions, an excellent antenna installation, and no obstacles—such as an island—between the transmitter and receiver. Second, radio waves do tend to curve slightly around the Earth's surface.

The distance to the horizon is determined by this formula:

$$D = 1.144 \times \sqrt{H}$$

(where D is distance to the horizon in miles and H is the height of the observer above sea level in feet).

The formula is different for VHF radios, based on the knowledge of how much the wavelengths bend:

$$D = 1.4 \times \sqrt{H} \text{ (in feet)}$$

**FIGURE 13-14.** ICOM makes top-line marine electronic equipment, including this small, fully synthesized VHF transceiver. (ICOM)

## SELECTED VHF MARINE CHANNELS AND THEIR USES

| Channel Number | Frequency (MHz) Transmit | Frequency (MHz) Receive | Communications Purpose |
|---|---|---|---|
| 06 | 156.300 | 156.300 | Intership safety communications only. |
| 07A | 156.350 | 156.350 | Commercial intership and ship-to-coast; also channels 08*, 10, 18A, 19A, 79A, 90A, and others for specific geographic areas (* = intership only). |
| 09 | 156.450 | 156.450 | Commercial and noncommercial intership and ship-to-coast commercial docks, marinas, and some clubs; also used by recreational boaters as alternate calling channel. Also used at some locks and bridges. |
| 12 | 156.600 | 156.600 | Port Operations—traffic advisory—also USCG secondary working channel with non-USCG vessels. |
| 13 | 156.650 | 156.650 | Navigational—ship's bridge to ship's bridge (1 watt only). Available to all vessels and is required on passenger and commercial vessels (including many tugs), as well as all power-driven vessels more than 20 meters (65.6 ft.) in length. Used at some bridges. |
| 14 | 156.700 | 156.700 | Port Operations (intership and ship-to-coast). |
| 16 | 156.800 | 156.800 | Distress Safety and Calling (mandatory). All distress calls should be made on Channel 16. |
| 22A | 157.100 | 157.100 | Coast Guard Liaison and Maritime Safety Information Broadcasts; used for communications with USCG ship, coast, and aircraft stations after first establishing communications on Channel 16. |
| 24 | 157.250 | 161.850 | Public telephone (Marine Operator); also Channels 25, 27, 84, 85, 86, 88. |
| 26 | 157.300 | 161.900 | Public telephone (Marine Operator). |
| 28 | 157.400 | 162.000 | Public telephone (Marine Operator). |
| 65A | 156.275 | 156.275 | Port Operations (intership and ship-to-coast); also Channels 20A*, 66A, 73, 74, 77† (* = intership only; † = communications with pilots only). |
| 67 | 156.375 | 156.375 | Commercial intership all areas, plus noncommercial intership (Puget Sound and Strait of Juan de Fuca). In the Lower Mississippi River, use limited to navigational bridge-to-bridge navigational purposes (1 watt). |
| 68 | 156.425 | 156.425 | Noncommercial intership and ship-to-coast (marinas, yacht clubs, etc.) |
| 69 | 156.475 | 156.475 | Noncommercial intership and ship-to-coast. |
| 70 | 156.525 | 156.525 | Distress and safety calling, and general purpose calling; may only be used by vessels equipped with Digital Selective Calling (DSC). |
| 71 | 156.575 | 156.575 | Noncommercial intership and ship-to-coast. |
| 72 | 156.625 | 156.625 | Noncommerical intership only. |
| 78A | 156.925 | 156.925 | Noncommercial intership and ship-to-coast. |
| 79A | 156.975 | 156.975 | Commercial intership and ship-to-coast. Noncommercial intership on Great Lakes only. |
| 80A | 157.025 | 157.025 | Commercial intership and ship-to-coast. Noncommercial intership on Great Lakes only. |
| WX1 | | 162.550 | Weather broadcasts (receive only). |
| WX2 | | 162.400 | Weather broadcasts (receive only). |
| WX3 | | 162.475 | Weather broadcasts (receive only). |

**FIGURE 13-15.** FCC recommended VHF channels. *(Chapman Piloting)*

## DISTANCE TO OBJECT JUST VISIBLE ON HORIZON

| | | | | | | | *Height of Receiving Antenna in Feet* | | | | | | | | | | |
|---|---|---|---|---|---|---|---|---|---|---|---|---|---|---|---|---|---|
| | | **0** | **4** | **8** | **12** | **16** | **20** | **30** | **40** | **50** | **75** | **100** | **200** | **300** | **400** | **500** | **1000** | |
| | 4 | 2.3 | 4.6 | 5.6 | 6.3 | 6.9 | 7.4 | 8.6 | 9.6 | 10.4 | 12.3 | 13.8 | 18.6 | 22.2 | 25.3 | 28.0 | 38.7 | 4 |
| | 8 | 3.3 | 5.6 | 6.5 | 7.2 | 7.9 | 8.4 | 9.6 | 10.5 | 11.4 | 13.2 | 14.8 | 19.5 | 23.2 | 26.3 | 29.0 | 39.6 | 8 |
| | 12 | 4.0 | 6.3 | 7.2 | 8.0 | 8.6 | 9.1 | 10.3 | 11.3 | 12.1 | 13.9 | 15.5 | 20.2 | 23.9 | 27.0 | 29.7 | 40.3 | 12 |
| | 16 | 4.6 | 6.9 | 7.9 | 8.6 | 9.2 | 9.7 | 10.9 | 11.9 | 12.7 | 14.6 | 16.1 | 20.9 | 24.5 | 27.6 | 30.3 | 41.0 | 16 |
| | 20 | 5.1 | 7.4 | 8.4 | 9.1 | 9.7 | 10.3 | 11.4 | 12.4 | 13.3 | 15.1 | 16.6 | 21.4 | 25.1 | 28.1 | 30.9 | 41.5 | 20 |
| | 24 | 5.6 | 7.9 | 8.9 | 9.6 | 10.2 | 10.8 | 11.9 | 12.9 | 13.8 | 15.6 | 17.1 | 21.9 | 25.6 | 28.6 | 31.3 | 42.0 | 24 |
| | 28 | 6.1 | 8.4 | 9.3 | 10.1 | 10.7 | 11.2 | 12.4 | 13.4 | 14.2 | 16.0 | 17.6 | 22.3 | 26.0 | 29.1 | 31.8 | 42.5 | 28 |
| | 32 | 6.5 | 8.8 | 9.8 | 10.5 | 11.1 | 11.6 | 12.8 | 13.8 | 14.6 | 16.5 | 18.0 | 22.8 | 26.4 | 29.5 | 32.2 | 42.9 | 32 |
| | 36 | 6.9 | 9.2 | 10.2 | 10.9 | 11.5 | 12.0 | 13.2 | 14.2 | 15.0 | 16.9 | 18.4 | 23.2 | 26.8 | 29.9 | 32.6 | 43.3 | 36 |
| | 40 | 7.3 | 9.6 | 10.5 | 11.3 | 11.9 | 12.4 | 13.6 | 14.5 | 15.4 | 17.2 | 18.8 | 23.5 | 27.2 | 30.3 | 33.0 | 43.6 | 40 |
| | 44 | 7.6 | 9.9 | 10.9 | 11.6 | 12.2 | 12.8 | 13.9 | 14.9 | 15.8 | 17.6 | 19.1 | 23.9 | 27.5 | 30.6 | 33.3 | 44.0 | 44 |
| | 48 | 8.0 | 10.3 | 11.2 | 12.0 | 12.6 | 13.1 | 14.3 | 15.2 | 16.1 | 17.9 | 19.5 | 24.2 | 27.9 | 31.0 | 33.7 | 44.3 | 48 |
| | 52 | 8.3 | 10.6 | 11.5 | 12.3 | 12.9 | 13.4 | 14.6 | 15.6 | 16.4 | 18.3 | 19.8 | 24.6 | 28.2 | 31.3 | 34.0 | 44.7 | 52 |
| | 56 | 8.6 | 10.9 | 11.9 | 12.6 | 13.2 | 13.7 | 14.9 | 15.9 | 16.7 | 18.6 | 20.1 | 24.9 | 28.5 | 31.6 | 34.3 | 45.0 | 56 |
| | 60 | 8.9 | 11.2 | 12.2 | 12.9 | 13.5 | 14.1 | 15.2 | 16.2 | 17.0 | 18.9 | 20.4 | 25.2 | 28.8 | 31.9 | 34.6 | 45.3 | 60 |
| | 64 | 9.2 | 11.5 | 12.5 | 13.2 | 13.8 | 14.3 | 15.5 | 16.5 | 17.3 | 19.2 | 20.7 | 25.5 | 29.1 | 32.2 | 34.9 | 45.6 | 64 |

*Height of Transmitting Antenna in Feet* (left-axis label)

Note: *Values in table are in nautical miles.*

**FIGURE 13-16.** VHF range is line of sight; this table of distances to the horizon will help you determine your unit's range, depending on height of transmitter and receiver.

The difference in formulas is about 22%, and this increases our previous figures of 12.1 and 15.8 to 14.7[1] and 19.3.

The key to having a VHF that works at peak efficiency and reliability is the antenna hookup. Marine electronics dealers carry a variety of antennas. Usually, masthead antennas are 3 decibel (dB) gain and deck-mounted antennas 6 dB gain. The higher the gain, the longer the antenna, and the greater the range. However, the signal also becomes flatter, and this can cause receiving difficulties in rolly seas.

The distance from the antenna to the radio partly determines the size of cable needed—wire that's too thin, run over a long distance, loses

[1] To determine distance from the observer, or antenna, to the object sighted beyond the horizon, you also need to know the distance from the horizon to the tip of the receiving antenna. Distance from transmitter to receiver is:

$1.4 \times \sqrt{H}$ of transmitter + $1.4 \times \sqrt{H}$ of receiver.
Assume 12-foot transmitter, 50-foot receiver:

$1.4 \times \sqrt{12} + 1.4\sqrt{50} = 4.8 + 9.9 = 14.7$ nm

power. So, for 6 dB gain, deck-mounted antennas, about 20 feet (6 m) of ¼-inch (6 mm) cable is provided. It is too small however, for the 3 dB gain, masthead antenna, which preferably is ½-inch (12 mm) RG-8/U-type coaxial cable with a polyethylene core.

The masthead antenna should be securely mounted on the side of the mast with the bracket provided; the wire enters the mast through a hole, travels down to the base, where it exits the mast again and passes through the deck, through the cabin to the set. Rubber ferrules in the spar holes prevent cable abrasion. An alternative is to run the cable entirely inside the spar. The choice is essentially whether you want the connectors inside, out of the weather (but where any banging against the mast walls will be horrendous), or outside, where if a problem occurs—and it usually occurs at the connectors (Figure 13-17)—it is more readily accessible. Some weatherproofing with silicone and duct tape over the connectors certainly helps prevent corrosion.

I also carry a spare cable and a short, handheld antenna, available from RadioShack, for

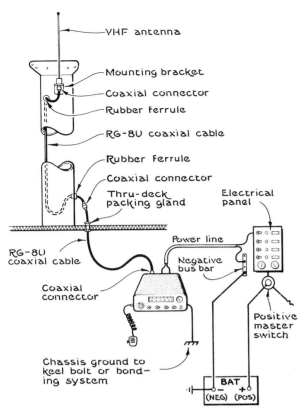

- VHF antenna
- Mounting bracket
- Coaxial connector
- Rubber ferrule
- RG-8U coaxial cable
- Rubber ferrule
- Coaxial connector
- Thru-deck packing gland
- Electrical panel
- Power line
- RG-8U coaxial cable
- Negative bus bar
- Coaxial connector
- Positive master switch
- Chassis ground to keel bolt or bonding system
- BAT
- (NEG) (POS)

**FIGURE 13-17.** Schematic of a proper VHF installation.

emergency use. You never know when the mast might come down or be struck by lightning, and it's comforting to have a backup.

Figure 13-18 shows several methods of securing the wires inside the mast (including the masthead light wire and any others), so they won't rattle. This noise drives me nuts. I haven't tried all of these solutions, but they seem as good as any. Kim Houghton of Rig-Rite (www.rigrite.com) in Warwick, Rhode Island, says his company retrofits spars with pop-riveted PVC pipe. They drill two holes, one to insert a coat hanger through to hold the PVC tight against the second hole. The PVC is drilled and pop-riveted, then the wire removed and a pop rivet put in the first hole to cover it. Yet another solution is to hoist a string of foam butterflies up inside the mast to compress the wiring against the mast wall.

A final note on installing the VHF radio: the closer the unit is to the battery, the shorter the power wires and therefore the less potential power loss. For runs up to about 12 feet (3.7 m), use #10 AWG wire with crimp lugs or eye terminals and plastic ties to hold them in place as you run them through the boat. The power wires can be led directly to the battery or to the main switch if the

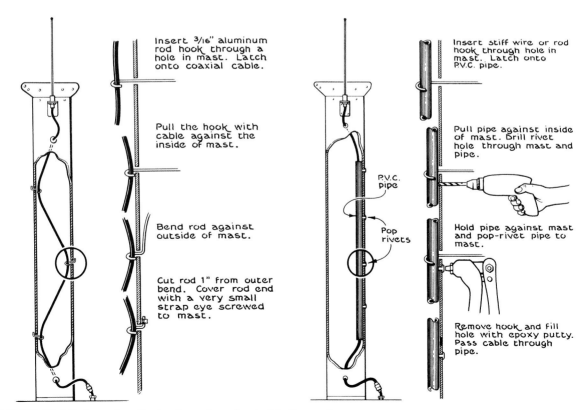

Insert 3/16" aluminum rod hook through a hole in mast. Latch onto coaxial cable.

Pull the hook with cable against the inside of mast.

Bend rod against outside of mast.

Cut rod 1" from outer bend. Cover rod end with a very small strap eye screwed to mast.

Insert stiff wire or rod hook through hole in mast. Latch onto P.V.C. pipe.

Pull pipe against inside of mast. Drill rivet hole through mast and pipe.

P.V.C. pipe

Pop rivets

Hold pipe against mast and pop-rivet pipe to mast.

Remove hook and fill hole with epoxy putty. Pass cable through pipe.

**FIGURE 13-18.** Several methods of securing wires inside the mast.

**FIGURE 13-19** The ICOM IC-M700 SSB (left) permits near worldwide audio communications, depending on time of day, weather, and operator proficiency. Ham radios (right) require amateur radio licenses to operate.

positive wire is fused and the gauge large enough for the distance run. You can wire to the distribution panel too, of course, which is common practice, but check to make sure you aren't losing too much power through a voltage drop caused by small-gauge wires.

### Single-Sideband (SSB) Radios

Beginning at around $1,500 you can buy a single-sideband radio (Figure 13-19) that will give you communications with at least part of the "other" world, whether the boat is in the middle of the Pacific or rounding Antarctica. However, purchasing SSB is not to be taken lightly—you don't simply identify the model that has an attractive case, pull it off the shelf, and screw it into your navigation station. Research SSB radios in yachting periodicals and technical bulletins from manufacturers, and consult with marine electronics technicians to learn about the features you need and the installation requirements of your boat.

Models range from 50 watts to 1,000 watts, but the largest are really intended for use only on large commercial ships. More power doesn't necessarily mean greater range or clarity. More important than power is the user's knowledge of frequencies, daily and seasonal effects, and his or her ability to tune the set properly. With the improved solid-state circuitry available today, a typical SSB for the cruising sailor might be rated at 150 watts and have the same range as the 1,000-watt sets.

SSB frequencies begin with the Middle Frequency (MF) coastal bands at 2 and 3 MHz. Frequencies from 4 MHz to 22 MHz are known as the High Frequency (HF) or High Seas bands. High-frequency transmissions result in ground waves that hug the Earth and are limited in range

to about 150 miles, depending upon conditions (Figure 13-20) and sky wave propagation (waves bounced off the ionosphere anywhere from 30 to 250 miles high). Under good conditions, you can get reception via sky waves up to about 5,000 miles. There is a Skip Zone between the ground waves and sky waves in which the SSB radio is ineffective. Typical frequency propagation for the different seasons is shown in Figure 13-21.

The effectiveness of SSB is very much dependent upon a good installation, and skilled technicians are required to do the job right. A ground plane must be established (Figure 13-22) that may involve adding ground screens beneath berths and tying together metal components (such as engine and tanks) inside the boat with woven copper straps. The antenna may be a whip type or use the backstay or, on ketches, the triatic stay, both of which must have insulators no closer than 4 feet (1.2 m) from the mastheads or deck. An antenna coupler electrically changes the antenna's

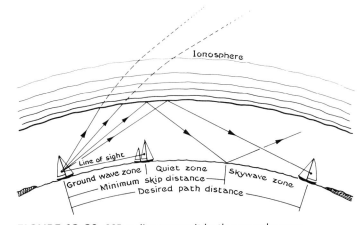

**FIGURE 13-20.** SSB radios transmit both ground waves and sky waves. Note the skip zones where there is little or no reception.

## TYPICAL FREQUENCY PROPAGATION SPRING AND SUMMER

| Frequency (kHz) | 4000 | | 8000 | | 12000 | | 16000 | |
|---|---|---|---|---|---|---|---|---|
| Propagation (Miles) | Min | Max | Min | Max | Min | Max | Min | Max |
| **Hours after sunset** | | | | | | | | |
| 1 | 50 | 250 | 200 | 1000 | 500 | 3500 | 750 | 6000 |
| 2 | 100 | 600 | 250 | 1500 | 500 | 3500 | 750 | 6000 |
| 3 | 100 | 600 | 250 | 2000 | 500 | 3500 | | |
| 4 | 100 | 800 | 250 | 2500 | | | | |
| 5 | 100 | 1000 | 250 | 2500 | | | | |
| 6 | 100 | 1500 | 400 | 3000 | | | | |
| 7 | 100 | 1500 | 500 | 3500 | | | | |
| 8 | 250 | 2000 | 750 | 4000 | | | | |
| 9 | 250 | 2500 | 750 | 4000 | | | | |
| 10 | 250 | 2500 | 750 | 4000 | | | | |
| 11 | 100 | 1000 | 500 | 2500 | | | | |
| **Hours after sunrise** | | | | | | | | |
| 1 | 100 | 500 | 400 | | | | | |
| 2 | 0 | 100 | 400 | 2000 | | | | |
| 3 | 0 | 100 | 250 | 1500 | | | | |
| 4 | 0 | 100 | 250 | 1500 | 500 | 1000 | | |
| 5 | 0 | 100 | 250 | 1500 | 500 | 1500 | | |
| 6 | 0 | 100 | 250 | 1500 | 500 | 2500 | 750 | 4000 |
| 7 | 0 | 100 | 250 | 1500 | 500 | 3500 | 750 | 4000 |
| 8 | 0 | 100 | 250 | 1500 | 500 | 3500 | 750 | 4000 |
| 9 | 0 | 100 | 250 | 1500 | 500 | 3500 | 750 | 4000 |
| 10 | 0 | 100 | 250 | 1500 | 500 | 3500 | 750 | 4000 |
| 11 | 0 | 100 | 150 | 500 | 500 | 3500 | 750 | 6000 |
| 12 | 0 | 200 | 150 | 500 | 500 | 3500 | 750 | 6000 |
| 13 | 50 | 250 | 150 | 750 | 500 | 3500 | 750 | 6000 |

## TYPICAL FREQUENCY PROPAGATION FALL AND WINTER

| Frequency (kHz) | 4000 | | 8000 | | 12000 | | 16000 | |
|---|---|---|---|---|---|---|---|---|
| Propagation (Miles) | Min | Max | Min | Max | Min | Max | Min | Max |
| **Hours after sunset** | | | | | | | | |
| 1 | 100 | 600 | 400 | 2000 | 500 | 3500 | 750 | 6000 |
| 2 | 100 | 800 | 400 | 2000 | 500 | 4000 | 750 | 6000 |
| 3 | 100 | 1000 | 400 | 2000 | 500 | 4000 | | |
| 4 | 100 | 1000 | 400 | 2500 | 500 | 4000 | | |
| 5 | 100 | 1000 | 400 | 3000 | 500 | 4000 | | |
| 6 | 100 | 1500 | 400 | 3500 | | | | |
| 7 | 250 | 2000 | 400 | 4000 | | | | |
| 8 | 250 | 2500 | 500 | 4000 | | | | |
| 9 | 500 | 3000 | 500 | 4000 | | | | |
| 10 | 500 | 4000 | 500 | 4000 | | | | |
| 11 | 500 | 3000 | 750 | 5000 | | | | |
| 12 | 250 | 2500 | 750 | 5000 | | | | |
| 13 | 250 | 1500 | 500 | 2500 | | | | |
| **Hours after sunrise** | | | | | | | | |
| 1 | 100 | 1000 | 400 | 2000 | | | | |
| 2 | 100 | 500 | 400 | 2000 | | | | |
| 3 | 0 | 100 | 400 | 2000 | 500 | 3500 | 750 | 4000 |
| 4 | 0 | 100 | 400 | 2000 | 500 | 3500 | 750 | 4000 |
| 5 | 0 | 100 | 250 | 1500 | 500 | 3500 | 750 | 4000 |
| 6 | 0 | 100 | 250 | 1500 | 500 | 3500 | 750 | 4000 |
| 7 | 0 | 100 | 250 | 1500 | 500 | 4000 | 750 | 5000 |
| 8 | 0 | 100 | 250 | 1500 | 500 | 4000 | 750 | 5000 |
| 9 | 0 | 100 | 250 | 1500 | 500 | 4000 | 750 | 6000 |
| 10 | 0 | 100 | 250 | 1000 | 500 | 3500 | 750 | 6000 |
| 11 | 0 | 250 | 250 | 1500 | 500 | 3500 | 750 | 6000 |

**FIGURE 13-21.** Typical frequency propagation for different seasons. (Twentieth Century Publications Inc.)

length to match the desired frequency. The coupler, plus the radio itself, must be properly located and installed.

While the time and money investment in SSB is considerable, SSBs have saved lives and expedited medical treatment. The majority of sailors might spend a lifetime at sea never needing SSB, but for those who have, it is difficult to imagine that they would go to sea again without it.

Many SSB radios today also offer ham capability, though to transmit on the latter's neighboring frequencies you need at least a General license. SSB radios also can be used to receive weather faxes and transmit laptop computer–generated e-mail messages to a shore-based Internet provider. The ICOM (www.icomamerica.com) IC-M802 was the first SSB to offer one-touch e-mail access, which means it can be set to memorize your HF e-mail access frequency, mode, and bandwidth settings. See below.

## E-MAIL

In the 21st century, the world does business by e-mail. And for many persons who want to go cruising, e-mail may be the only means of communication that makes it possible for them to get away. Wireless e-mail is a fast-developing technology, but the current choices can be summed up as SSB and satellite. A third choice popular with coastal cruisers, but not for the high seas, is PocketMail (www.pocketmail.com), which uses a small device that you write your message on, then take to a shoreside telephone for transmission.

If you already own an SSB and laptop computer, the least expensive wireless setup probably will be a service like SailMail (www.sailmail.com). This is a nonprofit group founded by West Coast sailors. With its software and a modem, you can send and receive brief e-mails via SailMail's various stations around the world. The rate of transmission is about 2,700 bps (bits per second). Members are asked to limit transmissions to 10 minutes per day. Cost of a new modem ranges upward from about $650, and cost to join SailMail is $250 per year.

Another SSB-based system is PinOakDigital (www.goals.com/sailscin/pinoak/podmain.htm). Again, you need an SSB and PC laptop, plus a modem and proprietary software. Because it operates on a private coast station, you have to become a member of its association. Hardware cost is something less than $2,000. Membership runs $275 and a typical 1 kilobyte e-mail costs about $1.

Globe Wireless (www.globewireless.com) specializes in providing communications for crews in commercial shipping. Both HF and satellite services are offered.

Inmarsat C (data only) and Mini-M (voice and data) are a step up from SSB (www.inmarsat.com). Each requires a hardware purchase of about $3,000 and $6,000 respectively. Standard C offers worldwide coverage but, at nearly a penny a character, it is too expensive for most people. Mini-M (Figure 13-23) is nearly worldwide, four times faster (about 2,400 bps) for data transfer than Standard C, and costs about $1.60 a minute. Voice

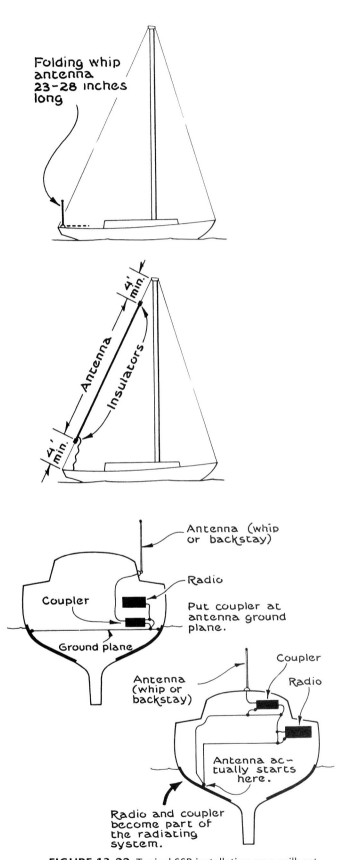

**FIGURE 13-22.** Typical SSB installation on a sailboat.

**FIGURE 13-23.** The KVH Tracphone provides voice and data transfer via the Inmarsat Mini-M network. Coverage is about 95% of the globe. (KVH)

is 4,800 bps. The unit is about the size of a laptop computer.

KVH's (www.kvh.com) eTrac mini-C/GPS is compatible with Inmarsat satellites and runs around $2,000 and a penny a character. There is no monthly fee.

The SkyMate (www.skymatewireless.com) 100 Communicator connects to your laptop and allows you to send and receive e-mails via Orbcomm satellites (Figure 13-24). Unlike the earlier Magellan GSC 100 (and other iterations), SkyMate doesn't make you wait for downloads. When send-

**FIGURE 13-24.** The SkyMate 100 Communicator attaches to a laptop and allows you to send brief e-mails economically. These go to a dispatch office, which then translates the messages into voice or fax for final transmission to your addressee. (SkyMate)

ing, the SkyMate systems translate your text message into a voice message, which is dispatched to your addressee by telephone or fax. Cost is about $800 plus a monthly service plan starting at less than $20.

Globalstar (www.globalstar.com) portable phones provide voice and data service for coastal regions of North, Central, and South America, up to about 200 miles offshore. Cost is about $550, plus $20 monthly service plan plus about $1 per minute of airtime.

Also for voice and data, Iridium (www.iridium. com) is a world satellite telephone service that like most competing systems has had financial ups and downs. It is presently (2006) operational. A phone costs about $1,500. The cost-per-minute of prepaid calling cards decreases the more minutes you buy: for example, 75 minutes for $130 or 500 minutes for $595.

Well, these are just some of the services available; no doubt the list will expand as more satellites are placed in service. While it's nice to be able to e-mail from the high seas, remember that you'll be spending more time in port, and that the growing number of Internet cafés around the world offer less expensive alternatives to carrying your own communication equipment on board.

## WEATHER AND TIME

Obtaining accurate, up-to-the-minute weather forecasts is important for anyone sailing even a few miles offshore. Similarly, the ocean navigator must know exact time (Greenwich Mean Time) if he is practicing celestial navigation. Both weather and time signals can be obtained with the right radio equipment—VHF picks up the NOAA weather broadcasts (WX1, 162.50 MHz; WX2, 162.400 MHz; WX3, 162.475 MHz), and SSB picks up time signals (WWV—Fort Collins, Colorado, 2.5, 5.0, 10.0, 15.0, and 20.0 MHz; WWVH—Kauai, Hawaii, 2.5, 5.0, 10.0, and 15.0 MHz (Figure 13-25). If you don't have VHF and SSB aboard, the least you should do is purchase a radio receiver, not only for NOAA weather broadcasts and WWV time signals, but also to pick up local weather and news in your area.

## EPIRB

EPIRB is an acronym for emergency position-indicating radio beacon. A typical model is about the size of a thermos bottle, and is used by sailors

**WWV (Ft. Collins, Colo.)**

*Frequencies—2.5, 5, 10, and 15 MHz*

| Times of Broadcast | Broadcast Area |
|---|---|
| 8 minutes past the hour | Storm information for |
| 9 minutes past the hour | western North Atlantic, including Gulf of Mexico and Caribbean Sea |
| 10 minutes past the hour | Storm information for |
| *11 minutes past the hour | North Pacific east of 140° W. |

**WWVH (Kauai, Hawaii)**

*Frequencies—2.5, 5, 10, and 15 MHz*

| Times of Broadcast | Broadcast Area |
|---|---|
| 48 minutes past the hour | Storm information for |
| 49 minutes past the hour | North Pacific; also |
| 50 minutes past the hour | the South Pacific to |
| *51 minutes past the hour | 25°S., 160°E–110°W. |

*An additional segment may be broadcast when there are unusually widespread storm conditions.

FIGURE 13-25. WWV and WWVH broadcast format for transmitting time signals.

to send emergency signals when the boat is in danger of sinking and radio communications have proven fruitless.

Class A (automatic on contact with water) and B (manual activation) EPIRBs transmit on 121.5 and 243 MHz. The signals' effective range is about 200 to 300 miles, hopefully enough for passing airplanes, satellites, and ships to detect. Commercial aircraft are required to monitor those frequencies only as cockpit time allows. And for a satellite to relay the signal to a ground station requires that both the EPIRB and ground station be in reach at the same time. With the development of 406 MHz EPIRBs, there really is no reason to carry either one of these. Further, NOAA will stop monitoring Class A and B signals in 2009.

The newer 406 MHz EPIRBs cost about $800 to $1,000 depending on the bracket. Category I brackets have hydrostatic releases. Category II brackets must be manually deployed. All EPIRB units activate on contact with the water, but a unit underwater can't transmit, hence the value of the hydrostatic release bracket. The satellites EPIRBs use can store the signal until they pass over a ground station. The ground station relays the information to NOAA, which in turn notifies the appropriate search and rescue authority, generally the Coast Guard in this country. This usually takes about an hour. Type 406 EPIRBs are programmed with personal codes for each set sold, so that assuming you were properly registered at the time of purchase, shore authorities will know who is in trouble, plus have a telephone number to call. (Your chances of rescue are greatly enhanced if you've filed a cruise plan with your designated emergency contact.) Standard EPIRBs locate your position to within about 2 nautical miles. For a few hundred dollars more, an EPIRB/GPS combination more closely pinpoints your location—to within 0.05 nautical mile—and relays it in only a matter of minutes, rather than the hour of non-GPS-equipped units.

Personal locator beacons (PLBs) are intended to be worn with other safety gear on each crew member. Unlike EPIRBs, however, they may not float, don't have strobe lights, and don't have as long battery life (12 hours versus 48 hours).

EPIRBs are safety gear you hope you'll never need, but ones you can't really afford to venture offshore without. Still, they are no substitute for quality life rafts and survival gear. An abandon-ship bag should always be at the ready, containing food, water, fishing tackle, mirrors, a means of desalination (solar still, or better, the Survivor-35 reverse osmosis watermaker—see Figure 5-30), and a handheld VHF radio to contact ships. The VHF is extremely important as life raft survivors nearly always report sighting dozens of ships they couldn't contact because flares were either used up or ineffective in attracting attention.

## RADAR

Cruisers spend a lot of time worrying whether commercial ships can see them. That's why you hang a radar reflector in the rigging. But how can you sleep after hearing stories about the watches on ships dozing off while little cruising boats get run down? Think how much better it would be if you could see them. Then it wouldn't matter so much whether they see you. The development of LCD radar in small, lightweight packages has brought the price down so that almost anyone can afford radar and find a place on the boat to mount it (Figure 13-26). Raymarine (www.raymarine.com) and Furuno (www.furuno.com) are leaders in the field, but also check out JRC (www.

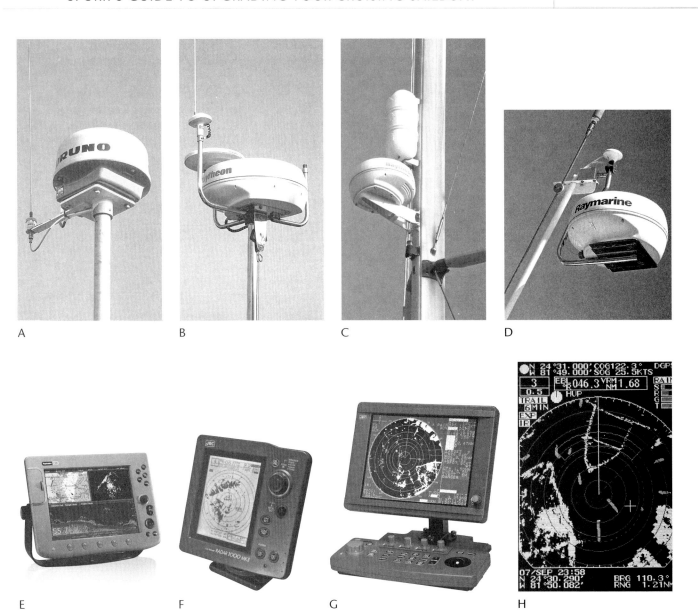

A  B  C  D

E  F  G  H

**FIGURE 13-26.** Radomes may be mounted in several locations: on a stern pole with fixed platform (A); on a stern pole with articulated mount (B) that can be adjusted to compensate for the boat's heel, so the radar doesn't scan the sky and water only; on the front of the main or mizzen mast (C); and on a gimballed fitting on the backstay (D). Raymarine's multifunction display can show not only radar but also electronic charts, fishfinder returns, and basic instrument data (E). A new generation of small and inexpensive LCD radars, such as the JRC 1000MKII with small black and white display (F), are now suitable for even small cruising boats. JRC's more expensive JMA 5106 Black Box Radar (G) has a 10.4-inch LCD screen and, with a 6 kW open array antenna, has a 72-nautical-mile range. It takes practice to read the screen for useful information (H), so you might benefit from a training program such as offered by Starpath School of Navigation (www.starpath.com). An acquaintance of mine lost his boat on a South Pacific reef when he failed to switch the range, thereby scanning the area beyond and over the reef. (Bruce Bingham photos: A, B, C, D; Raymarine: E; JRC: F, G)

jrcamerica.com). You might install the radome on top of a stern mast, which can double as a platform for GPS antenna and cockpit light, as well as an outboard motor hoist. Other possible sites are forward of the main or mizzen mast or gimballed on the backstay.

## HOW MUCH DO YOU REALLY NEED?

By now it should be clear that there is no end to the types and variety of electronic equipment available today. Boaters tend to be gearheads and enjoy playing with electronic instruments. And there is no question that electronics today are remarkable in their abilities. But radar and chart plotters aren't cheap, and like most anything else electrical on a boat, they are susceptible to abrupt failure. If you haven't the money or the inclination to deal with modern electronics, remember that my friend Danny Greene sailed more than 30,000 miles on a 26-foot boat (8 m) without even a VHF! He used celestial navigation with a sextant for position fixes and a transistor radio to home in on islands such as Bermuda. Like many other cruisers, he didn't let the lack of fancy gear prevent him from cruising. And then there is Jim Baldwin, who circumnavigated in a Triton, lamenting the hours spent stitching sails, who rationalized that he could be still working in a Detroit automobile factory earning money for a new

set. As means permit, you can add gear, but surprisingly little is absolutely required. More depends on your seamanship and good sense.

## ELECTRICAL BONDING

Once you have electricity on board, even if it's just an engine, battery, cabin lights, and VHF radio, the possibility exists of electrolytic corrosion to metal parts of the boat.

The ABYC is quite specific as to how bonding should be accomplished. ABYC's Standard E-11 applies to all DC systems under 50 volts.

The purpose of bonding, as described by ABYC, is to: (1) provide a low-resistance electrical path inside the hull between otherwise isolated metallic objects, especially those in common contact with seawater; (2) prevent the possibility of electrical potential on exposed metallic enclosures of electrical equipment; (3) provide a low-resistance path for excessively high voltages, such as when the boat is struck by lightning; and (4) minimize radio interference. Boats *without* permanently installed electrical systems do not need bonding.

The heart of the bonding system is a common bonding conductor, which is generally a length of bronze or copper metal at least ½ inch (12 mm) wide and no less than $\frac{1}{32}$ inch (0.8 mm) thick. It is laid inside the hull from stem to stern, and those metallic objects that are to be connected are done so by using #9 AWG wire or larger (Figure 13-27).

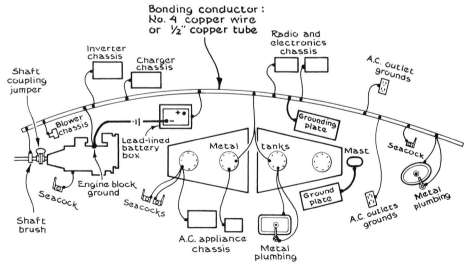

**FIGURE 13-27.** Metal objects inside the boat should be bonded according to ABYC recommendations to prevent corrosion and radio interference and to provide a low-resistance path for excessively high voltages, such as from lightning.

Items to be bonded include engines (use the engine negative terminal), metallic enclosures of electrical appliances, motors, generators and pump frames, fuel tanks, fuel deck fittings, and lead-lined battery trays.

It is not necessary to include in the bonding system electrically isolated through-hull fittings, if they are all of the same metal, or if they are protected by sacrificial anodes, as is common with propeller shafts.

On steel and aluminum hulls, the hull itself can serve as the common bonding conductor. In this instance, items to be bonded that are not in contact with the hull should be wired directly to the hull.

Not all authorities agree on the wisdom of bonding, however. It may be that each boat should be evaluated independently, based on the types of metals and electrical system circuitry, since in some instances bonding does minimize electrolytic corrosion, and in others it promotes it. There's a good discussion of the pros and cons in Charlie Wing's *Boatowner's Illustrated Electrical Handbook*.

## LIGHTNING GROUND PROTECTION

During a cruise to Green Bay one summer, *Adriana* was struck on the masthead by lightning. Though we didn't know it at the time, the reason we weren't hurt was because the boat was grounded. The shrouds were wired to a plate in the hull that gave a path for the lightning to follow to ground (earth). Nevertheless, the lights burned out, the diodes in the VHF were fried, the points in the engine ignition system were fused closed, and the battery casing was literally blown apart. Whether bonding these items to a common conductor tied in with the lightning ground would have prevented this damage, no one will ever know.

What I do know is that I never want to be struck again, and this presents a curious problem. Naval architect John Letcher told me that a grounded mast in fact increases the odds of your boat sustaining a lightning strike. Lightning doesn't actually "strike" the way it appears; rather a path from the atmosphere to ground must be present for the charge to pass through. Of course, an ungrounded mast also can be hit, and if it is, the damage will be much greater.

I have seen two boats hit by lightning that did not have grounded masts—one sank because the lightning exited the boat at the waterline, perforating the hull in a thousand tiny places. The other lost its mast when the lightning blew out the chainplates.

In any case, it's a sticky wicket—ground the mast and increase the odds of being struck, or go ungrounded and pray you're never struck. As terrifying as it was to be struck by lightning, I'd opt for the grounded system.

Our crew was saved from injury for two reasons. First, we were not touching the rigging or any part of the ground system or metal objects inside. And second, in the words of the ABYC Standard E-4, "A grounded conductor, or lightning protective mast, will generally deflect to itself direct hits which might otherwise fall within a cone-shaped space, the apex of which is the top of the conductor or lightning protective mast and the base is a circle at the surface of the water having a radius of approximately two times the height of the conductor." The probability of protection, ABYC reports, is 99% (Figure 13-28).

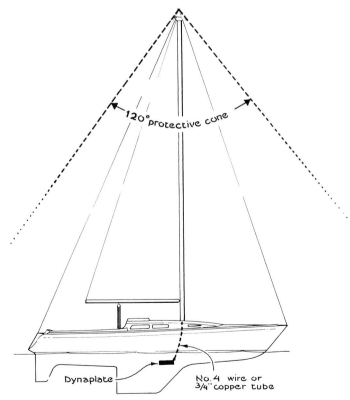

**FIGURE 13-28.** A lightning ground system routes electricity from the spar to a ground plate in the hull, and may be incorporated with the bonding system. When struck, the lightning rod or masthead deflects the lightning, creating a "cone of protection" underneath.

If your boat is not grounded, and you wish it to be, run #8 AWG wire from each shroud chainplate of an aluminum mast to a plate in the hull, such as a Dynaplate (www.marinco.com; Figure 13-29), of at least 1 square foot (0.09 m²).

But on deck-stepped spars without compression posts or bulkheads directly underneath, there's no way to run the ground wire straight down to the ground plate. Propellers, large metal rudders, or radio transmitter ground plates also can be used for grounds. However, it's not advisable to use the prop shaft or any other object that requires the lightning to make an abrupt turn—the system must be as vertical as possible. My Triton had a plate in the hull with a bolt protruding into the bilge to which the wires were connected. This is one reason not to use the engine as the ground, because the only electrical path to earth is horizontally via the propeller shaft.

Wood masts require a lightning rod at least 6 inches (152 mm) higher than the mast and connected to #8 AWG wire or larger run down the mast to the ground plate. All wires should run as vertically as possible and avoid sharp bends. Sailtracks also should be protected.

With wood and fiberglass hulls, the lightning ground system can be connected to any bonding system that exists to prevent surges of voltage through metal and electrical objects inside the boat. Steel boats can use the hull itself.

Lightweight carbon fiber masts are growing in popularity, and while they have many advantages, at present I don't know of a way to satisfactorily run a conductor down to ground. The problem is melting of the resin that sets the carbon. So you take your chances. Similarly, aramid rigging, though presently used mostly for runners on race boats, isn't a good conductor.

## SOME BASICS ABOUT 12-VOLT DC ELECTRICAL SYSTEMS

The boat's wiring system is all too often taken for granted, and it's not until you're tracing down a bad connection, trying to install a new piece of electrical equipment, or sniffing acrid smoke in the cabin that you begin to consider the merits of a well-planned and executed wiring system.

The two principal sets of standards for wiring on small sailboats are the ABYC *Standards and Technical Reports for Small Craft* (mentioned earlier) and the National Fire Protection Association's (NFPA) *National Electric Code*. Anyone considering major work with electrical systems would do well to read these documents.

Just because your boat's electrical system is only 12 volts (24 and 32 volts often appear as separate circuits on larger yachts) doesn't mean there isn't enough juice to pose a danger on board. Electrical fires are more common than one might suppose. Shoddy workmanship here, as anywhere else, soon tells. Because of this potential hazard, it is important to be able to pull off the cover of your electrical panel quickly, or better yet, quickly reach the main switch to shut off power.

If you are installing a new DC system from scratch, or modernizing an old one, be sure it is installed with the negative polarity grounded, which is now accepted practice and recommended by ABYC (Figure 13-30). Positive-ground electronic gear is difficult to come by.

DC wiring systems on boats are two-wire systems, with the hot or positive wire carrying power to lights and appliances and a separate, insulated wire returning to ground, generally the negative bus bar in the distribution panel, which in turn is connected to the common ground such as the engine block or ground plate bolted underwater outside the hull. If the boat is bonded, as described earlier, the bonding strip is not to be used as ground.

Most important to the average sailor is determining how to add electrical equipment. If there is room on the positive bus bar (distribution panel) and negative bus for a new circuit, this is preferable. This way, the new VHF or cabin fan will have its own circuit, fuse, or circuit breaker and switch. The possibility of overloading is, of course,

**FIGURE 13-29.** A Dynaplate makes an excellent ground for bonding or lightning protection. (Guest)

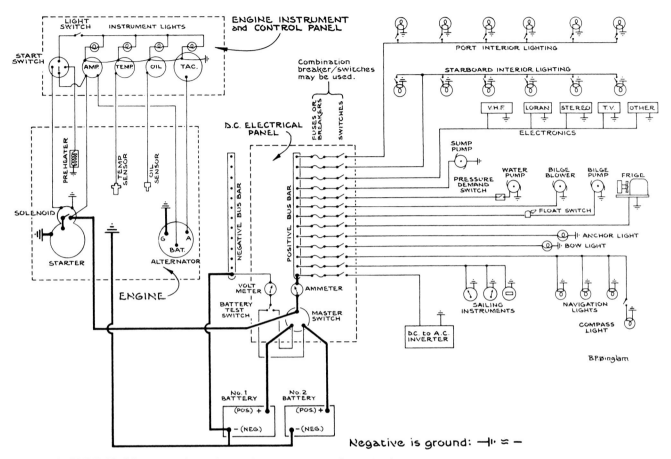

**FIGURE 13-30.** A typical DC electrical system on a single-engine boat.

reduced. Future troubleshooting will be vastly simplified if you follow the ABYC's recommended color-coding system when adding new equipment (Figure 13-31). If you can't handle buying all the different colors, at least buy tags ("cabin light," "bilge pump") that stick to the wires for future identification. Don't run wires in the bilge. Run them under the side decks, supported every 18 to 24 inches (457 mm to 610 mm). And near the compass, twist the positive and negative wires around each other over their entire length to minimize their influence.

If there is not room for a new, separate, circuit, the appliance can be added to an existing circuit. But care should be taken in selecting which one. For example, it would be unwise to use the same circuit for too many appliances that are likely to be used at the same time. If an electric bilge pump, spreader lights, and VHF radio are all on the same circuit, transmitting on VHF (especially at the 25-watt setting) while the other items also are in use could overload the system. What you need to do is add up the current draw of all

loads and make sure this number, say 7 amps, doesn't exceed the circuit breaker rating of, say, 5 amps. Common appliances could be grouped as follows:

- Cabin lights, fans, navigation station light
- Running lights, masthead tricolor, compass light, and other instrument lights, such as depth sounder
- VHF
- Electric pumps
- Autopilot
- Stereo, television

If the distribution panel cannot accommodate as many circuits as seems necessary, it might be a good idea to add a new bus with additional circuits. To determine whether you will be overloading a circuit, you need to know not only the total load (in amps) on the circuit, but also the wire size (gauge) and length of those wires. The table

## RECOMMENDED MARINE WIRING COLOR CODE DIRECT CURRENT SYSTEMS—UNDER 50 VOLTS

| Color | Item | Use |
|---|---|---|
| Yellow w/Red Stripe (YR) | Starting Circuit | Starting Switch to Solenoid |
| Brown/Yellow Stripe (BY) or Yellow (Y) | Bilge Blowers | Fuse or Switch to Blowers |
| Dark Gray (Gy) | Navigation Lights | Fuse or Switch to Lights |
| | Tachometer | Tachometer Sender to Gauge |
| Brown (Br) | Generator Armature | Generator Armature to Regulator |
| | Alternator Charge Light | Generator Terminal/Alternator |
| | | Auxiliary Terminal to Light and Regulator |
| | Pumps | Fuse or Switch to Pumps |
| Orange (O) | Accessory Feed | Ammeter to Alternator or Generator Output and Accessory Fuses or Switches |
| | | Distribution Panel to Accessory Switch |
| Purple (Pu) | Ignition | Ignition Switch to Coil and Electrical Instruments |
| | Instrument Feed | Distribution Panel to Electric Instruments |
| Dark Blue | Cabin and Instrument Lights | Fuse or Switch to Lights |
| Light Blue (Lt Bl) | Oil Pressure | Oil Pressure Sender to Gauge |
| Tan | Water Temperature | Water Temperature Sender to Gauge |
| Pink (Pk) | Fuel Gauge | Fuel Gauge Sender to Gauge |
| Green/Stripe (G/x) (except G/Y) | Tilt Down and /or Trim In | Tilt and/or Trim Circuits |
| Blue/Stripe (Bl/x) | Tilt Up and/or Trim Out | Tilt and/or Trim Circuits |

**FIGURE 13-31.** ABYC's recommended wiring color code for DC electrical systems under 50 volts.

in Figure 13-32, reprinted from ABYC's Standard E-11, will help.

The 10% voltage drops in the table of conductor sizes are acceptable for most equipment that isn't sensitive to noise interference or voltage drop (receivers and transmitters). Compare the wire size in this table with the sizes in Figure 13-33, which allow for only a 3% drop. The latter is preferable for appliances such as VHF, for which you might always want full power. For example, a circuit carrying 25 amps a distance of 15 feet (4.6 m) requires #14 AWG wire to keep the possible voltage drop at 10%; for a 3% drop, the size of wire increases to #8.

Each circuit should be protected by a fuse or trip-free circuit breaker, which is magnetically or thermally opened when an overload occurs. The circuit breaker is more convenient because it doesn't need replacement. Sometimes a piece of equipment, such as a stereo, will come with its own in-line fuse in the hot wire, and while this protects the stereo, it doesn't protect the other equipment on the same circuit.

### Battery Selector Switches and Isolators

Every cruising boat should carry more than one battery. A 30-foot (9.1 m) boat might have a 105-amp deep-cycle battery for lights and electronics, and an 80-amp or larger heavy-duty battery for starting the engine. Two deep-cycle batteries should also do the job. If the engine's battery is weak, turn the selector switch to "Both" to parallel the batteries for engine starting. For charging, switch to battery #1 for awhile, then to battery #2. And when the engine isn't running, alternate use of the two batteries each day to distribute the discharge evenly (Figure 13-34).

Consider a few variables before hooking up the switch: brand of alternator, internal or external regulator, and whether or not the alternator has isolating diodes built in.

285

## CONDUCTOR SIZES FOR 10% DROP IN VOLTAGE

| TOTAL CURRENT ON CIRCUIT IN AMPS | Length of Conductor from Source of Current to Device and Back to Source—Feet | | | | | | | | | | | | | | | | | | |
|---|---|---|---|---|---|---|---|---|---|---|---|---|---|---|---|---|---|---|---|
| | 10 | 15 | 20 | 25 | 30 | 40 | 50 | 60 | 70 | 80 | 90 | 100 | 110 | 120 | 130 | 140 | 150 | 160 | 170 |
| | 12 Volts—10% Drop Wire Sizes (gauge)—Based on Minimum CM Area | | | | | | | | | | | | | | | | | | |
| 5 | 18 | 18 | 18 | 18 | 18 | 16 | 16 | 14 | 14 | 14 | 12 | 12 | 12 | 12 | 12 | 10 | 10 | 10 | 10 |
| 10 | 18 | 18 | 16 | 16 | 14 | 14 | 12 | 12 | 10 | 10 | 10 | 10 | 8 | 8 | 8 | 8 | 8 | 8 | 6 |
| 15 | 18 | 16 | 14 | 14 | 12 | 12 | 10 | 10 | 8 | 8 | 8 | 8 | 8 | 6 | 6 | 6 | 6 | 6 | 6 |
| 20 | 16 | 14 | 14 | 12 | 12 | 10 | 10 | 8 | 8 | 8 | 6 | 6 | 6 | 6 | 6 | 6 | 4 | 4 | 4 |
| 25 | 16 | 14 | 12 | 12 | 10 | 10 | 8 | 8 | 6 | 6 | 6 | 6 | 6 | 4 | 4 | 4 | 4 | 4 | 2 |
| 30 | 14 | 12 | 12 | 10 | 10 | 8 | 8 | 6 | 6 | 6 | 6 | 4 | 4 | 4 | 4 | 2 | 2 | 2 | 2 |
| 40 | 14 | 12 | 10 | 10 | 8 | 8 | 6 | 6 | 6 | 4 | 4 | 4 | 2 | 2 | 2 | 2 | 2 | 2 | 2 |
| 50 | 12 | 10 | 10 | 8 | 8 | 6 | 6 | 4 | 4 | 4 | 2 | 2 | 2 | 2 | 2 | 1 | 1 | 1 | 1 |
| 60 | 12 | 10 | 8 | 8 | 6 | 6 | 4 | 4 | 2 | 2 | 2 | 2 | 2 | 1 | 1 | 1 | 0 | 0 | 0 |
| 70 | 10 | 8 | 8 | 6 | 6 | 6 | 4 | 2 | 2 | 2 | 2 | 1 | 1 | 1 | 0 | 0 | 0 | 2/0 | 2/0 |
| 80 | 10 | 8 | 8 | 6 | 6 | 4 | 4 | 2 | 2 | 2 | 1 | 1 | 0 | 0 | 0 | 2/0 | 2/0 | 2/0 | 2/0 |
| 90 | 10 | 8 | 6 | 6 | 6 | 4 | 2 | 2 | 2 | 1 | 1 | 0 | 0 | 0 | 2/0 | 2/0 | 2/0 | 3/0 | 3/0 |
| 100 | 10 | 8 | 6 | 6 | 4 | 4 | 2 | 2 | 1 | 1 | 0 | 0 | 0 | 2/0 | 2/0 | 2/0 | 3/0 | 3/0 | 3/0 |

**FIGURE 13-32.** This table indicates the size wires required to keep voltage drop to 10% or less. Loads (amps) and length of wires are shown.

It is more convenient if both batteries can be charged at the same time, and you'll be more secure knowing that one battery isn't discharging into the other. Guest (www.marinco.com) makes a battery isolator that can be installed in conjunction with a three-way switch. Without an isolator, when the switch is set for both batteries, there is the danger the more fully charged battery will discharge into the lesser-charged battery. An isolator isn't necessary if you charge battery #1 for a while as the engine runs, then switch to battery #2 for a while before shutting off the engine.

Battery life is extended if you carefully monitor the level of discharge (deep-cycle batteries shouldn't be taken below 50% discharge before charging) and the rate and amount of charge. Investment in quality electrical monitors makes this job easy. Also consider a smart three- or four-stage regulator to vary the rate of charge (see Chapter 12).

Chuck Hawley, West Marine's technical whiz, makes a strong case for isolating the house and engine start batteries or banks. In the company's catalog, a West Advisor titled "Creating a Reliable Battery System," Hawley recommends scrapping the traditional OFF—1—BOTH—2 switch for three off/on switches (Figure 13-35). This, combined with a device such as the West Marine Battery Combiner or Blue Sea Systems Automatic Combining Relay, saves you from discharging both batteries when the switch is inadvertently left in the BOTH position (common practice when trying to get maximum cranking power for starting the engine). What the Battery Combiner does is automatically sense the voltage of the two banks and when safely high (13.3 volts), it connects the two, so that both can be charged simultaneously by the same source, such as engine alternator or solar panel. When voltage drops below a set level, the Battery Combiner discon-

## CONDUCTORS SIZES FOR 3% DROP IN VOLTAGE

| | Length of Conductor from Source of Current to Device and Back to Source—Feet | | | | | | | | | | | | | | | | | | |
|---|---|---|---|---|---|---|---|---|---|---|---|---|---|---|---|---|---|---|---|
| TOTAL CURRENT ON CIRCUIT IN AMPS | 10 | 15 | 20 | 25 | 30 | 40 | 50 | 60 | 70 | 80 | 90 | 100 | 110 | 120 | 130 | 140 | 150 | 160 | 170 |
| *12 Volts—3% Drop Wire Sizes (gauge)—Based on Minimum CM Area* | | | | | | | | | | | | | | | | | | | |
| 5 | 18 | 16 | 14 | 12 | 12 | 10 | 10 | 10 | 8 | 8 | 8 | 6 | 6 | 6 | 6 | 6 | 6 | 6 | 6 |
| 10 | 14 | 12 | 10 | 10 | 10 | 8 | 6 | 6 | 6 | 6 | 4 | 4 | 4 | 4 | 2 | 2 | 2 | 2 | 2 |
| 15 | 12 | 10 | 10 | 8 | 8 | 6 | 6 | 6 | 4 | 4 | 2 | 2 | 2 | 2 | 2 | 1 | 1 | 1 | 1 |
| 20 | 10 | 10 | 8 | 6 | 6 | 6 | 4 | 4 | 2 | 2 | 2 | 2 | 1 | 1 | 1 | 0 | 0 | 0 | 2/0 |
| 25 | 10 | 8 | 6 | 6 | 6 | 4 | 4 | 2 | 2 | 2 | 1 | 1 | 0 | 0 | 0 | 2/0 | 2/0 | 2/0 | 3/0 |
| 30 | 10 | 8 | 6 | 6 | 4 | 4 | 2 | 2 | 1 | 1 | 0 | 0 | 0 | 2/0 | 2/0 | 3/0 | 3/0 | 3/0 | 3/0 |
| 40 | 8 | 6 | 6 | 4 | 4 | 2 | 2 | 1 | 0 | 0 | 2/0 | 2/0 | 3/0 | 3/0 | 3/0 | 4/0 | 4/0 | 4/0 | 4/0 |
| 50 | 6 | 6 | 4 | 4 | 2 | 2 | 1 | 0 | 2/0 | 2/0 | 3/0 | 3/0 | 4/0 | 4/0 | 4/0 | | | | |
| 60 | 6 | 4 | 4 | 2 | 2 | 1 | 0 | 2/0 | 3/0 | 3/0 | 4/0 | 4/0 | 4/0 | | | | | | |
| 70 | 6 | 4 | 2 | 2 | 1 | 0 | 2/0 | 3/0 | 3/0 | 4/0 | 4/0 | | | | | | | | |
| 80 | 6 | 4 | 2 | 2 | 1 | 0 | 3/0 | 3/0 | 4/0 | 4/0 | | | | | | | | | |
| 90 | 4 | 2 | 2 | 1 | 0 | 2/0 | 3/0 | 4/0 | 4/0 | | | | | | | | | | |
| 100 | 4 | 2 | 2 | 1 | 0 | 2/0 | 3/0 | 4/0 | | | | | | | | | | | |

FIGURE 13-33. This table indicates the size wires required to keep voltage drop to 3% or less. Loads (amps) and length of wires are shown.

nects them, so that one battery won't discharge into its weaker neighbor.

## INSTALLING SHORE POWER

Since most of us find ourselves alongside a dock from time to time, it's nice to have 110-volt AC power even for a short time. This is not to say the boat shouldn't be capable of generating its own DC or AC power underway, at anchor, or on the mooring. But it's generally easier and less expensive to use shore power when it's available.

I lived aboard in Newport Harbor for five years. During the summer the boat was on a mooring and, just as we have cruising, we relied on the ship's 12-volt electrical system, kerosene, solar panels, and diesel engine to supply our energy needs. During the winter, when we berthed at a marina slip, we used 110-volt shore power to run small space heaters and an electric blanket. A Tiny Tot fireplace supplemented the heat source. Friends continually asked, "Aren't you freezing?" To which I honestly replied, "No, the cabin is so small I can keep it at any temperature I want, certainly warmer than *your* house!"

The size of the extension cord from the AC outlet on the dock to the receptacle on your boat depends on the amount of juice you need. Most boats in the 30- to 40-foot (9.1 m to 12.2 m) range use 30-amp cable, though some opt for the larger 50-amp cable. Good-quality connectors, such as those made by Hubbell and Marinco, should be used on either end; cord kits with these three-prong connectors already attached are available from most chandleries or mail-order houses.

The male receptacle should be located somewhere on deck where it is relatively free from spray and other sources of moisture. A common location is on the side of the footwell, perhaps near the after end of the cockpit.

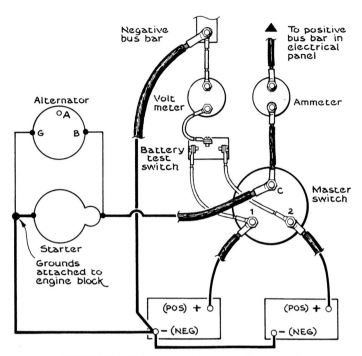

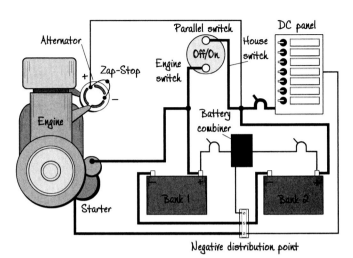

**FIGURE 13-35.** Using three off/on switches and a West Marine Battery Combiner or other voltage-controlled relay, both house and engine-start battery banks can be isolated to protect them from accidental discharge, but automatically connected for charging when voltage in each is high. (Fritz Seegers illustration)

**FIGURE 13-34.** A Guest three-way battery selector switch enables you to determine which battery you want to use for a given purpose—lighting and electronics or engine starting.

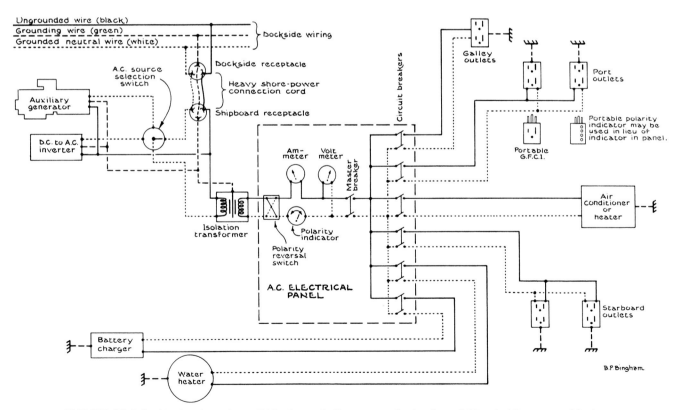

**FIGURE 13-36.** This drawing of an ABYC schematic illustrates a single-phase 120-volt AC system with shore-grounded neutral conductor and grounding conductor.

The boat's internal AC system of wires and outlets should be entirely separate from the DC system. However, you may wish to add a battery charger so that your AC shore power charges your DC battery when you're at the dock. In every case, you should also install a polarity indicator that will warn you if the polarity of the system has reversed itself. And it is important to install a main shore-power circuit breaker disconnect that will shut off all power coming into the boat with the throw of one switch. Each appliance or outlet should have its own branch circuit breaker as well.

Faults in an AC power system on board can be lethal, and for this reason, ground fault circuit interrupters (GFCI) are recommended. Hubbell makes a portable GFCI into which you plug appliances rather than directly into outlets. Pass and Seymour (www.passandseymour.com) and the Square D Company (www.squared.com) make GFCIs that are incorporated into the circuit breakers and trip open with a leak as little as 5 milliamps.

Figure 13-36 follows the ABYC recommended wiring installation of a shore-power system using 120 volts.

## FURTHER READING

*Boatowner's Illustrated Electrical Handbook.* 2nd ed. Charlie Wing. Camden, Maine: International Marine, 2006.

*Boatowner's Mechanical and Electrical Manual: How to Maintain, Repair, and Improve Your Boat's Essential Systems.* 3rd ed. Nigel Calder. Camden, Maine: International Marine, 2005.

*How to Use Your VHF Radio*—FCC Rules for Recreational Boaters; Part 83, Subpart CC; Superintendent of Documents, U.S. Government Printing Office; get at http://wireless.fcc.gov/rules/html (go to 80).

*Living on 12 Volts with Ample Power.* David Smead and Ruth Ishihara. Seattle: Robert Hale, 1998.

*Marine Electrical Practice.* 6th ed. rev. G. O. Watson. London; Boston: Butterworth, 1990.

*Marine Radiotelephone Users Handbook.* Radio Technical Commission for Marine Services. Washington, D.C.

*A Mariner's Guide to Radiofacsimile Weather Charts.* Dr. Joseph M. Bishop. Westborough, Massachusetts: Alden Electronics, 1988.

*Mariner's Guide to Single Sideband.* 6th ed. Frederick Graves. Mountlake Terrace, Washington: SEA, 2000.

*Metal Corrosion in Boats.* 2nd ed. Nigel Warren. Dobbs Ferry, New York: Sheridan House, 1998.

*Owner Repair of Radio Equipment.* Frank W. Glass. Los Gatos, California, 1979.

*Radar for Mariners.* David Burch. Camden, Maine: International Marine, 2005.

*Radio and Radar In Sail and Power Boats.* Kenneth Wilkes. Lymington, Hampshire, England: Nautical, 1980.

*The 12-Volt Doctor's Practical Handbook for the Boat's Electric System.* 5th ed. Weems and Plath, 1998; go to www.weems-plath.com.

*Your Boat's Electrical System.* 2nd rev. ed. Conrad Miller. Updated and enlarged by Elbert S. Maloney. New York: Hearst Marine Books, 1988.

# FOURTEEN

# BEATING THE HEAT AND COLD

No matter where you live or cruise, temperatures rise and fall enough to require most sailors to manipulate the temperature inside the cabin of their boat. Unless you live year-round in Tahiti, where the mean temperature, season to season, night to day, varies only about 20°F (about 7°C), heating and cooling devices, however simple, make life aboard more comfortable.

Exposure to extreme hot and cold temperatures might be adventurous, but at some point, it just ain't fun. In any case, the cruising sailor should equip and fit his or her boat, keeping the climates of the particular cruising areas in mind. A healthy, rested crew is less likely to make the stupid mistakes that often result from decisions made under fatigue (like running your boat up on a reef).

Depending on boat size, cruising area, and climate, heating and cooling systems may be sophisticated and expensive or simple and reasonably priced. Whatever the need, reasonable solutions are possible with a little effort and investment.

## AIR-CONDITIONING

One winter I went sailing with friends on a plush C&C Landfall 48 out of Port O'Connor, on the Texas Gulf Coast. One day it would be hot, and Jon Reeves, the skipper, would turn on the air-conditioning. The next day a Blue Norther would blast down from Oklahoma, and we'd run the heater every few hours to stay warm.

These operations were carried out by pushing buttons and flicking switches—as simple as keeping cool or warm at home. In reality, heating and air-conditioning on boats is probably more complicated than in houses, if only for the reason that cramped spaces make installation and maintenance more difficult.

Large marine air conditioners require 115-volt or 240-volt electrical power, obtained at the dock or from the yacht's auxiliary generator. No juice, no air-conditioning. Obviously, the first con-

sideration in adding air-conditioning is whether sufficient time will be spent at docks to make the expense worthwhile, and/or whether you have the space and money to invest in a diesel-fueled auxiliary generator. Using the main engine for this purpose, in my opinion, results in more wear and tear than it's worth to a very important and expensive piece of machinery. If the answer to either question is "no," then skip the rest of this section and start reading the Simpler Solutions section.

Marine Air Systems (www.marineair.com) and Cruisair (www.cruisair.com)—both now owned by Dometic—are just two of the many companies making air-conditioning systems for yachts, and most of their business is fitting out powerboats and larger sailing yachts, say, 45 feet (13.7 m) and up.

Some systems don't require hauling the boat for installation. Existing seacocks are tapped for the raw-water cooling intake and discharge hoses. Two sources of existing raw-water through-hulls are possible: the engine or genset intake or the head intake.

The above-mentioned systems work similarly to galley refrigerators; that is, seawater is used to cool (remove heat from) a refrigerant gas in a condenser and an evaporator/blower is used to get rid of the heat and provide cool air through the ducts and vents.

Before purchasing a system, consult the manufacturer for the number of Btu required to cool and heat your cabin space. Large yachts may require more than one unit or, at the least, a larger than normal condenser with several remote evaporator units. Figure 14-1 will help you determine the Btu capacity necessary to cool a given cabin space.

## HEATING

For about 15% extra cost, most air conditioners may be fitted with heating coils and pumps to provide reverse-cycle heat as well as air-conditioning.

However, the Cruisair people warn that heat pumps don't work very well in waters "much less than 38°F [3°C]." For winter liveaboards in northern regions, kerosene and diesel heaters are probably better choices.

Use the following formula for determining Btu: volume of cabin × climate factor = Btu.

Volume is the cubic feet of space to be heated. A climate factor of 10 is used for insulated boats or those in warm (Florida) climates; a factor of 20 is used for northern (New England) climates. As an example, the cabin of a 28-foot (8.5 m) boat might measure 8 feet by 8 feet by 6 feet (2.4 m by 2.4 m by 1.8 m) or 384 cubic feet (10.9 m³). Newport, Rhode Island, which is on an island surrounded by the relatively warm waters of Narragansett Bay, averages about 5 to 8° warmer than the nearby mainland. Here we can use a climate factor of 15: 384 × 15 = 5,760 Btu. This figure jibes fairly closely with the chart for air-conditioning: 8 feet by 8 feet = 64 square feet (5.9 m²); 5,000 Btu.

Notice that the figures for this cabin don't include the head or forward cabin. To heat those areas, while not as important, almost doubles the space and Btu. Convection or radiant-type heaters won't circulate air efficiently from one cabin to the next, so more than one outlet is necessary for an even distribution of heat. Ducted forced-air heaters do a much better job, and on a small boat, a small electric heater in the main cabin pushes enough air into the forward cabin to keep it moderately comfortable.

The best heating system for boats on the go, especially those not large enough to carry an auxiliary generator and those in near-freezing waters, are heaters using kerosene or diesel fuel. Wallas heaters (www.wallas.fi) are made in Finland and distributed in the United States by Scan Marine (www.scanmarineusa.com). These are very nice, quiet, kerosene-fueled cabin heaters that mount on a bulkhead or in a lazarette (Figure 14-2). A combination intake/outtake pipe must be run through the cabin roof. Outside air is sucked in, heated by a kerosene burner, and blown into the cabin via a fan.

Several ducts may be led to different cabins. The fan runs off 12 volts and, depending on model, draws between 0.4 and 3.9 amps. A gallon (3.8 L) of fuel lasts between 11 and 22 hours. Obviously, the larger the tank, the less often filling will be necessary. A 5-gallon (19 L) jerrican could be strapped into a seat locker. Or a larger perma-

## BTU REQUIRED TO COOL CABINS

| CAPACITY BTU/HR | Below-Deck Cabins | | Mid-Deck Cabins | | Above-Deck Cabins | |
|---|---|---|---|---|---|---|
| | Square Feet | Square Meters | Square Feet | Square Meters | Square Feet | Square Meters |
| 5,000 | 70 | 6.5 | 50 | 4.5 | 35 | 3.2 |
| 7,000 | 100 | 9.5 | 75 | 7.0 | 50 | 4.5 |
| 10,000 | 140 | 13.0 | 100 | 9.5 | 70 | 6.5 |
| 12,000 | 200 | 18.5 | 150 | 14.0 | 100 | 9.5 |
| 16,000 | 270 | 25.0 | 200 | 18.5 | 135 | 12.5 |
| 20,000 | 338 | 31.2 | 250 | 23.3 | 167 | 15.8 |
| 24,000 | 405 | 37.0 | 300 | 28.0 | 200 | 19.0 |
| 30,000 | 500 | 46.2 | 375 | 35.0 | 250 | 23.7 |
| 36,000 | 600 | 55.5 | 450 | 42.0 | 300 | 28.5 |
| 48,000 | 800 | 74.0 | 600 | 56.0 | 400 | 38.0 |

**FIGURE 14-1.** This table gives an approximate number of Btu necessary to heat different size cabins.

**FIGURE 14-2.** The Wallas kerosene bulkhead heater with fan. (Scan Marine)

nent fiberglass tank can be fabricated for installation in the cabin, under the cockpit or on deck.

Kerosene (called paraffin in Great Britain) is one of the most universally available fuels. If you've chosen it for cooking, you also may decide to use it for heating as well. More than likely you'll already have kerosene lighting on board, and the fewer fuels carried, the simpler your task of procuring fuel, stowing it, and keeping spare parts.

A permanent gravity-feed system like the one shown pictured in Figure 14-3 can be filled through the same sort of deck fill used for water and engine fuel—just be certain the fill is labeled correctly! A tank vent tube is necessary, and this may be routed through the deck or inside the cabin (refer back to Figure 5-7).

Nylon hose can be used to run kerosene from the gravity feed "header" tank to the stove and heater tanks, as can copper tubing and some types of PVC. Each tank should have a positive action valve, such as an in-line ball-valve. It's also handy to have a tap for filling lamps (use rigid tubing, not nylon); this is much less messy than pouring kerosene from a portable tank.

The tank end of the outlet pipe inside the fiberglass or stainless steel tank should *protrude up an inch* from the bottom so that sediment doesn't reach the stove and heater burners. Otherwise, install a filter in the system. Figure 14-4 diagrams a slightly more sophisticated system, not only with a

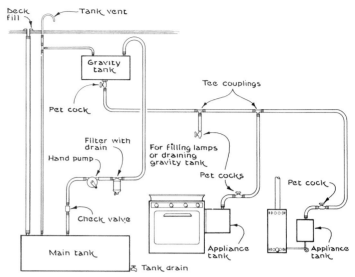

**FIGURE 14-4.** A slightly more sophisticated system has a large main tank located down low in the boat and a pump to move kerosene up to the header tank.

filter, but with a large main tank and pump to fill the day tank, which in turn feeds the stove and heater by gravity. A couple living aboard in a warm climate might expect to use about a gallon of kerosene each week for the stove/oven and cabin lamps. A 30-day supply could be contained in a 5-gallon gravity feed tank. Obviously a larger main tank, such as the one pictured in Figure 14-4, with a 20- to 30-gallon (76 L to 114 L) capacity, would give several months of fuel, although less in colder climates with a heater running.

Webasto Thermosystems (www.webasto.com) and Espar (www.espar.com) make heaters similar to the Wallas, which run off gasoline (avoid on boats), kerosene, and diesel. They look more like a canister vacuum cleaner and are quite compact (Figure 14-5). During my first winter in Newport, a neighbor on a Southern Cross 28 installed an Espar diesel heating system in his boat. Even when we were iced in, Charlie reported that he and his wife were quite comfortable. To save fuel, he didn't run the heater all day when they were at work, but he did run it in the evenings and on weekends. At night they turned it off, relying on their Airex-cored hull to retain the warmth a few hours and on their electric blanket when sleeping. Before getting up each morning, Charlie hopped out of bed to turn on the heater for 15 minutes, then back to bed until things warmed up. Espar heaters are made in Germany; parts and repairs may be expensive.

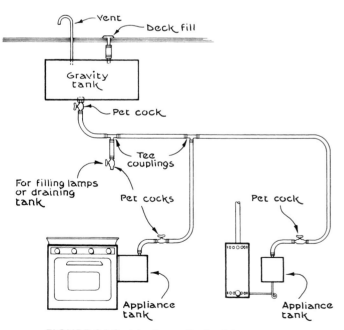

**FIGURE 14-3.** A basic gravity-feed, kerosene storage system.

**FIGURE 14-5.** An Espar diesel heater with fan; the company also makes gas and kerosene models. (Espar)

Like the Wallas, the Espar fan is 12-volt or 24-volt and ranges from 40 to 220 watts, depending on the model. Fuel consumption ranges from 20 hours per gallon for the smallest gasoline model to 6 hours per gallon for the largest diesel model.

These systems are highly efficient and not all that difficult to install, though a few days of planning and work are needed. However, routine duct work through bulkheads and vent pipes through the deck are not modifications to be taken lightly. How will they affect the hull and deck's supporting structure? Are adjacent surfaces exposed to dangerous levels of heat? Will deck fittings snag lines or trip people?

Drill the intake and/or exhaust pipe through the cabin roof with a hole saw. Seal the core mate-

rial—end-grain balsa or plywood—with epoxy or carve it out and fill with epoxy resin thickened with chopped strand (refer back to Figure 4-8). Run the wires to an extra circuit on the distribution panel (see Chapter 13).

Both Wallas and Espar heaters require no special insulation on the mounting surface, as do most solid-fuel heaters. Some typical installations for either type are shown in Figure 14-6.

## SIMPLER SOLUTIONS

There's a line in the theme song from the movie *Midnight Cowboy* that says, "Going where the weather suits my clothes." I've always taken this to recommend living in tropical climates where heaters and float coats just aren't necessary. This is the simplest way to beat the cold. Cruisers move with the seasons, but invariably everyone is sooner or later caught lagging. On a cruise down the Intracoastal Waterway, we dallied too long in New England and on Chesapeake Bay one year; by the time we reached Norfolk, Virginia, it was early November and snowing.

### Small Cabin Heaters

When cooking, the stove puts off a bit of heat, but this is a very inefficient way to warm the cabin, as well as expensive when compared with most other methods. The usual trick is to put a clay pot on top of the stove to radiate heat, but I've never found this practice very efficient or effective.

The next most primitive method is to rely on the kerosene cabin lamps. The conventional wick-type lamps and barnyard lanterns don't put out

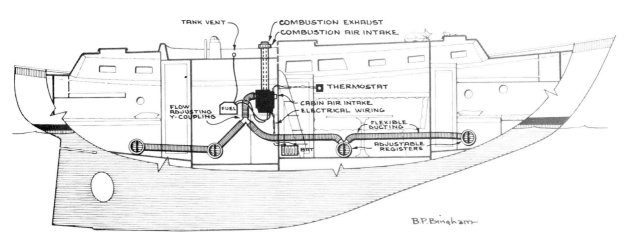

**FIGURE 14-6.** This drawing shows one possible installation of forced-air kerosene or diesel heaters.

much heat, but the Aladdin mantle kerosene lamps do (www.aladdinlamps.com). On summer nights in New England, which typically are cool, a bulkhead-mounted Aladdin lamp gives off sufficient heat to warm the cabin. When it is warmer, the Aladdin is sometimes too hot to use, and you may have to resort to 12-volt electric lights. Kerosene lamps and household-type kerosene heaters give off harmful fumes, so be sure to keep a hatch cracked to let in fresh air. In fact, I wouldn't use a kerosene heater unless it is vented through the deck. Remember, CO (carbon monoxide) is a by-product of combustion—colorless, odorless, and deadly; a CO detector/alarm is an excellent idea.

For a bit more heat than lamps and stoves, consider a floor or bulkhead-mounted cabin heater using solid or liquid fuel. Dickinson (www .dickinsonmarine.com) and Luke (www.peluke .com) manufacture small stoves that burn wood, coal, or charcoal briquettes. Dickinson's Newport solid fuel heater (Figure 14-7) is a light stainless steel unit weighing 12 pounds (5.4 kg). Luke makes heavier soapstone and tile fireplaces that are elegant—and expensive. As a permanent heat-

ing source, solid-fuel stoves aren't very practical because of the amount of fuel that must be stowed.

On the Vanguard, I had a Tiny Tot wood/coal stove (Figure 14-8) mounted under the bridge deck, against a bulkhead. The disadvantage of this location was that it wasn't centrally situated in the saloon, and the vent pipe exited under the canvas cockpit dodger, which then had to be dropped before building a fire. A coal bin under the cockpit was filled from the deck (Figure 14-9),

FIGURE 14-8. My Pearson Vanguard had a Tiny Tot coal/wood stove under the bridge deck. Notice the coal bin at bottom.

FIGURE 14-7. The Newport diesel heater by Dickinson is mounted on a bulkhead and can run on briquettes, wood, and coal. (Dickinson Marine)

FIGURE 14-9. A deck-loading coal bin in the Vanguard's cockpit.

ushering coal to a small hinged bin and accessible through a trapdoor next to the stove. It was a clever arrangement and did the trick in removing the chill from the air. Stoked full before bedtime, it burned most of the night. Heat from the smoke pipe was reflected by stainless steel plates on the cabin bulkhead, and smoke and fumes were exhausted through a Charlie Noble on deck (Figure 14-10).

You must be extremely careful with open flames on a boat. My daughter and I once went to sleep with an alcohol heater burning between our bunks. During the night, Adriana kicked off one of her blankets, and it fell on top of the heater. I began dreaming of fire, and awoke in the middle of the night unable to breathe and with the cabin full of smoke. Only quickly tossing the blanket and Adriana out into the cockpit saved us from certain suffocation.

A friend installed this Force 10 diesel heater in his hanging locker (Figure 14-11). A separate 10-

FIGURE 14-11. This Force 10 kerosene heater is rated at 6,000 to 9,000 Btu; the fuel tank is beneath, and on deck, there's a small vent with a 1-inch (25 mm) flue (inset).

FIGURE 14-10. The Tiny Tot's deck exhaust, popularly known as a Charlie Noble. Unfortunately, the dodger had to be retracted in order to make a fire.

gallon (38 L) fuel tank is sold as an option. But he had a small auxiliary diesel tank already installed for the stove/oven, which he tapped to supply fuel to his new heater. The burner is a modification of the standard Primus burner and works quite well, though it requires regular cleaning. And because there is no fan to spread the heat, he did need to supplement the Force 10 with an electric heater when the temperature dipped into the 20s. It is rated at 6,000 to 9,000 Btu and is vented through the cabin roof, so hatches may be kept closed.

Force 10 also makes a handsome LPG bulkhead-mounted cabin heater that burns 1 pound of fuel every 2.5 hours. On most boats cruising the high latitudes, it probably will be easier to carry the extra diesel fuel necessary for heating than propane in extra tanks.

A small 12-volt cabin fan helps circulate warm air throughout the boat. Most solid- and less expensive liquid-fuel heaters do not have fans to push air around, and this limits heating to the immediate area. If the heater doesn't have an internal fan, an external fan can be used for cooling in summer as well.

## Ventilation

Ventilating the cabin areas is vital to a dry, mildew-free living area that also is cool in hot weather—especially in the tropics. A closed boat soon develops condensation or retains humidity from breathing, cooking, lamps, and wet clothing. And nothing dries out dampness like the movement of air, which causes the water to evaporate. Therefore, good cross-flow of air should be planned from the forepeak to the farthest accessible end of the boat. Fresh air also is of value in minimizing the effects of seasickness when holed up below.

Vents typically found on boats are cowls, sometimes mounted on Dorade boxes (Figure 14-12) and mushrooms (Figure 14-13). Some may be

FIGURE 14-13. Mushroom vents can be screwed down tight from below, making them watertight.

FIGURE 14-12. A cowl vent mounted on a Dorade box (named after *Dorade,* a famous yacht designed by Olin Stephens). Because the top of this box is Plexiglas, you can see the pipe that carries air into the cabin below.

closed off entirely when water is coming over the deck, or a heavy rain finds its way through the vent. Those types that cannot be closed off (Figure 14-14) should either be modified or replaced with a closable model. Mushroom vents can be closed from the inside, which is an appreciated convenience. In fierce weather, cowl vents must be removed from the Dorade box, and a deck plate screwed on in its place.

A closable mushroom-type vent with a stainless steel cowling over it prevents rain from getting under the vent cap. (Give plastic cowlings a miss, as they break easily when stepped on.) The mushroom works in all but the worst conditions and does wonders in keeping air circulating below.

Nicro vents (www.marinco.com) with solar-powered fans also improve air circulation below; a tiny solar panel charges an internal battery, which keeps the fan turning even at night (Figure 14-15). They are very quiet.

**FIGURE 14-14.** The plastic vent mounted on this hatch has an internal baffle to keep spray and rain out, while allowing air to enter. But immersed in a large boarding wave, or with the boat upside down, there is no way to prevent water entering. It should be possible to make every vent watertight.

**FIGURE 14-15.** Nicro solar vents have small solar panels that turn fans inside to draw air down into the cabin. The Day&Night models have batteries to keep the fan turning when the sun is down.

Cowl vents probably move more air than any other type, but they also present special problems. For one, lines are easily snagged on them. And as mentioned, they cannot be closed from below without modification (Figure 14-16). Stainless steel cages (Figure 14-17) over the vent, bolted to the deck, are one solution to the line-snagging problem, and large PVC pipe, cut on one end at a diagonal and inserted into the vent, is another method of keeping out rain and spray. Shutters on the underside of the deck over the vent opening allow a degree of airflow control throughout the boat.

A primary source of ventilation, as well as access for persons, sails, and stoves, are hatches. Cast-aluminum hatches are stronger than extruded aluminum. But the main companionway hatch is often a weak link in the boat's armament against boarding seas. On many boats they are too large, and if you're considering buying a boat with a large hatch and no bridge deck, give extra thought to the purchase—remedying this problem could be more trouble than it's worth. Large hatches do make going below easier, and do admit more air, but this is no place for compromise.

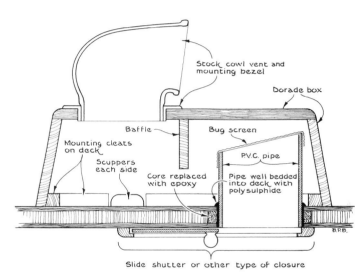

**FIGURE 14-16.** A standard Dorade-type vent with a PVC rain trap and sliding shutter to control airflow in the cabin.

**FIGURE 14-17.** Stainless steel pipe, formed over a tall-standing cowl vent, prevents lines from snagging the vent and tossing it overboard; however, the pipe does add weight and clutter.

### Opening Ports

Keeping the cabin cool in summer is easier and much less costly than heating it in winter. Good cross-ventilation is a starting point. It amazes me that more boats aren't equipped with opening ports to help accomplish this. A major reason is the cost-cutting measures of boatbuilders. When opening ports are installed, they often are of the cheap, plastic variety.

The Triton has two forward-facing opening portlights in the step in the coachroof, and these are of immense value when lying at anchor because the wind blows straight through them. Most coachroofs today are flat, and while they provide more headroom below, the distinct advantage of improved ventilation is lost.

Portlights aren't too expensive to purchase and install yourself. I'd opt for stainless steel from A&B Industries (www.abimarine.com), New Found Metals (www.newfoundmetals.com), or Hood Yacht Systems (www.hoodyachtsystems.com), or bronze ports, such as those available from Spartan Marine (www.spartanmarine.com) and New Found Metals. They're a bit more expensive, but much stronger and certainly better looking than plastic.

A new opening port can be installed where no present port exists, or if the opening port is larger than an existing fixed port, the old one can be removed and an opening one put in its place (Figure 14-18).

If the port doesn't come with a template to mark the size hole to be cut, make one out of cardboard. Use a pencil to mark the outline and then drill pilot holes large enough to accept a saber saw blade.

Small cutting errors of $\frac{1}{8}$ inch (3 mm) or so can be covered by the port flanges. Be sure to seal off any core material as described in Chapters 4 and 9. Use a good-quality bedding compound to prevent leaking around the port—surely the most common source of leaks. When the screws are tightened, the compound should ooze out everywhere. Don't worry, it can be cut away later. Rainhoods keep rain out when you want the port open for ventilation (Figure 14-19). You can form your own by heating thin sheets of Plexiglas with a torch. Simple wind scoops can be cut from Clorox bottles or any other plastic container that can be jammed into a port. The open end should face into the cabin; outside, on the forward side of the container, cut a large hole to funnel the wind.

Thought might also be given to fitting larger ports with storm shutters that can be quickly and easily fastened with machine screws (refer back to Figure 9-52).

Adding two- or four-way opening hatches also aids ventilation. The forward cabin hatch can be modified in this manner (refer back to Figure 9-17), or if there is sufficient room between the main hatch and mast, an extra hatch can be placed in the ceiling of the main cabin.

Several items can be fabricated from canvas that improve cabin coolness. None are very difficult to

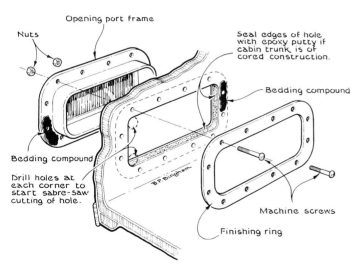

Opening port frame

Nuts

Seal edges of hole with epoxy putty if cabin trunk is of cored construction.

Bedding compound

Bedding compound

Drill holes at each corner to start sabre-saw cutting of hole.

Machine screws

Finishing ring

**FIGURE 14-18.** If you can substitute opening ports for fixed ports without dangerously increasing the size of the port, make a template of the new port, mark it on the cabin, and cut it out with a saber saw. Use a bedding compound to prevent leaks.

**FIGURE 14-19.** Port covers, like those made by Beckson (www.becksonmarine.com) and Sailing Specialties Inc. (www.ssicustomplastics.com), keep rain out when the port is open.

298

make, and each will improve your handiness with a needle and thread.

### Awnings

A cockpit awning keeps the cockpit and cabin cool (see the Full Deck Awning sidebar on page 190). We made one using white Dacron sailcloth, though UV-treated cloth will last longer. Measure the distance from the mast to the end of the boom or, if you're willing to be a little fancy, to the stern of the boat.

Everyone seems to have their favorite method of supporting awnings, and I've found PVC tubing to be ideal. It's lightweight, doesn't rust, is cheap, and bends to form a very attractive dome over the cockpit area. The lower sides keep more sun and rain out than flat awnings. Extending the awning to the mast might seem unnecessary, but shading the cabin top lowers temperatures down below. And when it rains, the extra length usually keeps the cockpit dry. While you're at it, you might consider a rainwater catchment system in your awning. (See also Figures 9-25 and 9-26.)

### Wind Scoops

Wind scoops funnel air into hatches quite efficiently, especially at anchor. Incidentally, one of the best ways to keep cool and avoid bugs is to stay away from shore as much as possible. In hot weather, it's always more comfortable at anchor than at a dock.

The familiar, brightly colored Windscoop (www.davisnet.com/marine) is well worth its modest price (Figure 14-20). However, if you'd like to make your own, there are easy patterns available. A four-sided pattern was made for me by Anne Correll, a costume maker. The advantage of her design is that it works without adjustment, even at the dock when the wind direction changes. Nylon spinnaker cloth can be used, but it probably won't last as long as a sturdier acrylic.

### Dodgers and Biminis

A cockpit dodger gives protection against wind and spray when it's cold, and shields two corners of the cockpit from the sun on hotter days.

Dodgers can be installed by professional canvasmakers, including the aluminum or stainless steel tubing (stainless steel is stronger), snap fasteners, and canvas work. Sailrite (www. sailrite.com) sells a dodger kit (canvas and frame are separate kits) that would make a good intro-

**FIGURE 14-20.** A Windscoop suspended over the forward hatch brings a generous breeze belowdecks and is much appreciated on a hot, still night. This arrangement makes a case for sleeping forward in the V-berth when in port or at anchor.

ductory project to canvasmaking—a worthwhile skill for the cruising man or woman (as well as a way to earn money as you go).

If the boat is fitted with boom gallows, or if you install another frame aft, the dodger may be extended aft over the cockpit to function as a bimini as well (Figure 14-21). In inclement weather, side curtains allow the cockpit to be used as a sort of bastardized porch, though they should probably be taken down when sailing as they impair visibility and won't hold up in higher winds.

In the tropics, a bimini minimizes exposure to the torrid sun and to unnecessary exposure from ultraviolet rays (Figure 14-22). Bright, hot sun not only ages your skin, but tires the crew more rapidly. In contrast to the sunbathing mania, people living in the equatorial regions generally wear more clothing than we do and avoid standing in the sun when possible.

Sunbrella (www.sunbrella.com) and Stamoid (www.stamoidmarine.com/gb) are popular canvas materials that are available in a wide variety of colors.

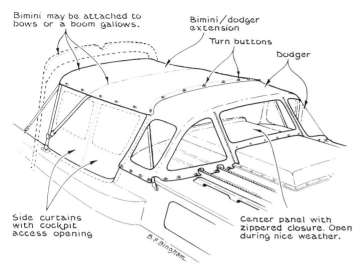

**FIGURE 14-21.** A cockpit dodger is good protection from forward-coming wind and water. If extended to the boom gallows, it also can function as a bimini.

**FIGURE 14-22.** Herb and Nancy Payson, aboard their Pacific Seacraft 34, can find shelter from the sun underneath a collapsible bimini.

Vinyl windows last longer if not repeatedly folded. The fact that most people seem to leave dodgers up all the time makes a good case for a fiberglass hardtop (refer back to Figure 9-57). Then you can also have a thicker, less wavy window material.

## Hull Color

As everyone knows, light colors are cooler than dark colors because they reflect rather than absorb the sun's rays. White decks, however, cause glare that can be hard on your eyes. Painting the

decks (Chapter 15) a light gray or green substantially reduces glare while making little difference to temperatures inside the cabin.

## Insulation

Heating or cooling the cabin is one thing, but keeping it that way is quite another. The answer is insulating the hull. Some of the newer fiberglass boats use Airex or Klegecell foam cores, which in effect add an insulating layer between the inner and outer layers of fiberglass. Condensation is virtually eliminated, and heat and cold are preserved long after the temperature has changed.

Styrofoam is one of the first materials people think of when the subject of insulation arises. There are three difficulties with it, however: it is rigid and does not conform well to the shape of the hull; it is brittle and must be covered with something to prevent it from chipping away; and if it ever burns, it gives off toxic fumes.

Urethane foam works well—2 inches (51 mm) of it would turn the hull into a thermos. However, it is expensive. People have tried all sorts of residential insulation in boats, including Ethafoam, a closed-cell polyethylene foam made by Dow Chemical (www.dow.com). It is rated at R-2.5, which is not as good an insulating factor as some other products, but definitely better than none at all. And, it is only ½ inch (12 mm) thick, so it is not difficult to work with. It comes in rolls 5 feet by 25 feet (1.5 m by 7.6 m) and reportedly has good compression resistance.

Check with the manufacturer about the right type of adhesive; contact cement, for example, will melt Styrofoam and doesn't allow you to move the foam around before it kicks.

To cover unsightly insulation, check out the wood ceiling described in Chapter 3 and also shown in Figure 14-23).

There is much to be said for insulation, but there is a downside, too. If the backing nuts and plates of through-deck fittings are covered, gaining access to them will require removing the insulation and possibly ruining your beautiful job. If water does enter through leaky through-deck bolts, closed-cell foam will not allow the water to migrate throughout the material. But if the glue hasn't bonded the foam to the hull absolutely everywhere, there could be room for water and condensation to collect.

We have all seen the horror of boats lined with indoor/outdoor carpeting. The idea is right, the material is wrong. I ripped out the mildewed

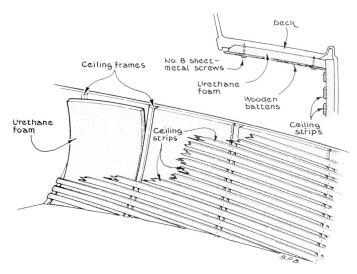

**FIGURE 14-23.** Urethane foam insulation can be glued to the hull with contact cement (make sure foam and glue are compatible) and covered with an attractive wood ceiling.

vinyl liner on the Vanguard and replaced it with a foam-backed, short-nap fabric designed for converting vans into playpens. It had a subtle ribbing, which I decided to align vertically. The foam had some insulating quality and in combination with the fabric served to minimize hull sweating and noise. Plus it was nice to the touch.

Howard Chapelle, the late marine historian of the Smithsonian Institute in Washington, D.C., once wrote, "exposed piping in a boat is a seamanlike feature." The same could be said for wiring, deck fittings, etc. The easier you can get to something, the quicker you can isolate the cause of a problem and fix it. On today's new boats you're supposed to be impressed if no part of the hull is visible. Be skeptical.

## Deck Prisms

Deck prisms and portlights (Figures 14-24 and 14-25) do a remarkable job of adding light below

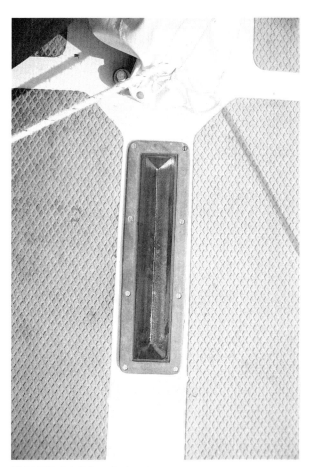

**FIGURE 14-24.** A deck prism.

**FIGURE 14-25.** A round glass portlight installed in a wood hatch lid brings light below.

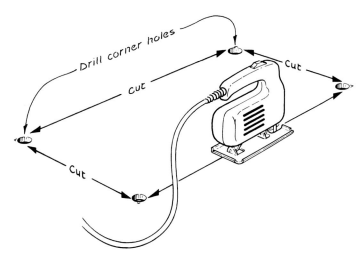

**FIGURE 14-26.** When cutting a hole in the deck for a prism or other fitting with square corners, drill pilot holes, large enough to insert the saber saw blade, in each corner.

without the obstruction typical of hatches. Bomar (www.pompanette.com/bomar) and Marine Skylights (www.boatdeckprism.com) both sell deck prisms that have wide mounting flanges to conceal the hideous look of rough-cut fiberglass and deck core. You can also make your own from Lexan, and if you don't want to see through, wet-sand the surfaces to make them translucent. Whenever cutting through the deck or cutting out a shape from inside a larger piece of material, first drill pilot holes *inside* the outline pattern (Figure 14-26), then insert the saber saw blade and make the cut.

Use a silicone or other bedding compound (don't use polysulfide with Lexan) and apply liberally between the flange and deck. If it oozes out when the flanges are bolted down tight, then you know you've used enough. Cut away the excess compound after it has hardened.

## FURTHER READING

*Air Conditioning: Home and Commercial.* 5th ed. Rex Miller, Mark Richard Miller, and Edwin P. Anderson. Indianapolis: Wiley, 2004.

*The Big Book of Boat Canvas.* Karen Lipe. Camden, Maine: International Marine, 1988.

*The Complete Canvasworker's Guide: How to Outfit Your Boat with Fabric.* 2nd ed. Jim Grant. Camden, Maine: International Marine, 1992.

*The Complete Live-Aboard Book.* Katy Burke. Newport, Rhode Island: Seven Seas Press, 1982.

# PAINTING AND VARNISHING

**B**oats of almost any material—fiberglass, wood, steel, aluminum, and even cardboard (those boats at your local Fool's Regatta)—benefit from protective coatings of paint. While rig and gear may represent more than half the cost of the vessel, the hull and deck comprise the boat in itself and ultimately are the most costly and difficult to replace or repair.

With the advent of the new linear polyurethane paints such as Awlgrip (www.awlgrip.com) and Interthane (www.yachtpaint.com), a new finish can be applied to the hull's surface by anyone willing to do the surface preparation and follow the manufacturer's instructions in applying the paint. In fact, some boatbuilders have dispensed with gelcoats altogether in favor of copolymer paints.

## PAINTING FIBERGLASS

Most production fiberglass boats are laid up in a mold that is first covered with a polyester resin gelcoat (the hard, shiny surface on the exterior of the hull). A gelcoat is usually about 18 to 22 mils (0.46 mm to 0.56 mm) thick, and it can be waxed and buffed to protect it from the sun's ultraviolet rays and to maintain an attractive high-gloss finish.

Gelcoats are susceptible to blistering, which can occur as the air inside expands and contracts, or if water migrates through the gelcoat to the void. (Although it doesn't appear so to the naked eye, gelcoat is slightly hygroscopic [porous] and will let fine amounts of water through, especially if there is a void on the inside.) Other causes for blistering include contamination by the sizing used to hold fibers together and poor bonding of the laminates. Tillotson-Pearson (once maker of J-Boats, Alden, and Freedom, now called Pearson Composites) pioneered the use of vinylester resin for at least the first lamination behind the gelcoat since this type of resin is less water permeable than polyester or epoxy.

Aside from blistering, gelcoats, especially dark colors, eventually chalk and fade. Therefore, at some point in the life of a fiberglass boat, refinishing the hull surface becomes necessary. Regelcoating is possible, though probably beyond the skills and equipment of most do-it-yourselfers because a top-quality job requires spray equipment and experience.

## PAINTING WOOD

Wood boats require repainting every several years, depending on the quality of the initial paint job, environment, working of the hull, and degree of abuse. The initial coatings may be repairable or coverable with a minimum of surface preparation for a period of years. But at some point, the hull will have to be taken down to bare wood again and fresh, fault-free coatings applied.

## PAINTING STEEL AND IRON

Steel and iron rust very quickly when exposed to salt water and oxygen and rely almost entirely on surface coatings for protection against corrosion. The Dutch have been building steel sailboats for more than a hundred years—many of them are still afloat—and with conscientious application and maintenance, the old paint systems got the job done. However, new developments in the chemistry of painting, such as shotblasting, zinc undercoats, and two-part linear polyurethane paints, have resulted in almost indefinite life spans for steel boats. Chlorinated rubber paints have also been used with some success.

## PAINTING ALUMINUM

Aluminum can be left uncoated without immediate concern for the integrity of the hull. Many of the so-called French "escape machines," made of

303

hard-chine bare aluminum, are simply the strongest, most maintenance-free hulls available. After all, there are literally thousands of masts and booms made of aluminum out there doing just fine—some with paint, some anodized, and some just bare aluminum. However, aluminum is subject to an oxidizing film when exposed to the oxygen in air or water. The result is minor pitting corrosion, which is arrested as the film covers the surface; clean the surface and the pitting begins anew. Painting eliminates any sort of corrosion or oxidizing film, gives a better appearance, and prevents the smudge from the film rubbing off on your clothes.

Even in this fast-paced, high-tech world, besieged by new wonder materials, there is still a place for good old-fashioned painting. And if you get right down to the chemistry of today's paints, you'll find them just as much a part of the space age.

## BOTTOM PAINTING

Traditional antifouling paints—those with a poison to kill fouling organisms—are made from two basic ingredients: (1) a binder or matrix that is durable enough to hold the biocide (antifoulant chemical) for the life of the paint, yet release it at a controllable rate over a period of time, and (2) a biocide that has sufficient toxicity to control fouling of the bottom (Figure 15-1). In formulating the paint, it is primarily the choice of a proper binder system and biocide that determines the quality of an antifouling paint.

There are three principal types of biocidal antifouling paints: (1) soluble matrix in which the binder literally dissolves over a period of time, releasing the biocide (usually cuprous oxide) as it goes; (2) diffusion-type, in which the biocide diffuses through the binder, killing organisms as it reaches the surface; and (3) copolymer, mostly with acrylic binders, that are united (copolymerized) by

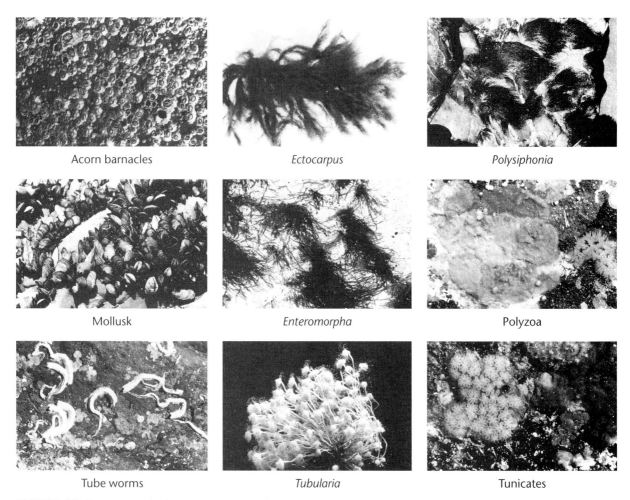

| Acorn barnacles | *Ectocarpus* | *Polysiphonia* |
| Mollusk | *Enteromorpha* | Polyzoa |
| Tube worms | *Tubularia* | Tunicates |

**FIGURE 15-1.** Common fouling organisms in salt water. (Interlux)

means of a chemical reaction in which the molecules of each ingredient are cross-linked.

Each type has its pros and cons (Figure 15-2). For years, tributyltin (TBT) paints were favored for many applications, especially in fresh water. Unfortunately, tin was found to be harmful to marine life such as shellfish, and in 1988 Congress outlawed it for most boats. That left cuprous oxide (copper) as the most effective biocide. To use cuprous oxide on metal hulls, however, durable barrier coats had to first be applied to prevent corrosion. The ban on tin sent paint companies scrambling to develop copper-based systems.

Today cuprous oxide also is coming under attack, especially in Europe, because it, too, is harmful to marine life. So paint companies now are researching and beginning to manufacture paints with the less toxic cuprous thiocyanate (mostly for aluminum outdrives now) and paints without any biocide. One example is Interlux's VC Performance Epoxy (www.yachtpaint.com),

which relies on Teflon to create a hard, smooth, slick surface that is difficult for organisms to attach themselves to. But such products tend to rely on the boat moving at high speeds (powerboats and some racing sailboats) and not kept for long periods at rest in the water—in other words, dry-sailed. Another interesting product is Interlux Veridian, a silicone-based paint that contains no biocide and tests very well. As of this writing, it is available only for outdrives, not hulls. But products like these will be available soon.

The effectiveness of any bottom paint depends on the type of use a boat receives, where it is sailed, and how much of the year it is in the water. For the weekend summer sailor who doesn't race, soluble matrix may be the most cost effective. Check the label for the percentage of copper, which ranges from about 30 to 65%. Generally speaking, the more biocide, the more effective the paint as an antifoulant, but not always; the binder system also is important.

| | Soluble Matrix Type | Diffusion Type | Copolymer Type |
|---|---|---|---|
| **Surface Condition (after prolonged use)** | Rough | Smooth | Smoothest |
| **Service Life** | 6 months to 2 years depending upon biocide level release rate. | Approximately 1 year. 2+ years possible. | Usually dependent upon film thickness. 4+ years possible. |
| **Cost** | Cheap to expensive. | Usually more expensive than soluble matrix type. | Most expensive. |
| **Color Range** | Limited to dull, dirty colors. | Very clean, even pastel shades possible. | Depends upons use of co-biocide. Color range can be clean to dirty, dull colors. |
| **Compatible Solvent** | Mineral spirits, aromatic solvents and ketones. Depends on modifying resin. | Ketones and/or aromatic solvent. | Hi *Flash* aromatic solvents and/or xylol. |
| **Current Binder Systems** | Rosin always present. Rosin may be modified with ester gum, vegetable oils, epoxy ester, vinyl, chlorinated rubber, etc. | Usually vinyl rosin or acrylic. | State of present art is arcylic, but may be other type in future. |
| **Market Popularity** | General use. Used on all substrates except aluminum. Has potential to set up galvanic cell on dissimilar metals. | Popular with sailboat racing enthusiasts. Recommended for freshwater as an anti-fouling paint. Safe to use on aluminum hulls. Wide range of colors possible. | Multi-seasonal paints. Excellent antifouling performance. Favorite of professional sailboat racers. Excellent film integrity. |

**FIGURE 15-2.** Characteristics of different antifouling paints. (Robert Wilkinson)

Much to-do has been made about several antifouling systems developed over the years that combine copper in an epoxy-modified, isophthalic-based unsaturated polyester resin. It may be sprayed into the hull mold at time of construction or applied later. It is about 12 to 15 mils thick and erodes slowly, so it may last the boat's lifetime. But in tests conducted by *Practical Sailor*, we found excessive amounts of slime developing.

Speaking of slime, this is an area that has received a lot of attention from paint manufacturers. Some have developed special slime inhibitors—Interlux adds Biolux to some of its products, and Pettit (www.pettitpaint.com) and Interlux add CIBA Irgarol to some, for example—that act more or less as sunblocks to prevent photosynthesis in the slime from occurring.

## Surface Preparation

As with most paint jobs, a good-looking, effective coating of antifouling paint depends to a large extent on surface preparation.

Some types of bottom paints aren't compatible with others (i.e., vinyls and non-vinyls), so it is wise to be sure what type of new paint you intend to apply to the old surface before you begin sanding. If the two paints aren't compatible, it may be necessary to take the surface coatings down to the bare hull or to use a tie coat that is compatible and bonds well to both the old and new paint. If they are compatible, cleaning and roughing up the surface may be all that's required.

If taking a hull down to the bare substrate, a power tool such as a random-orbit sander (Figure 15-3) is quicker than hand-sanding. Fit a foam pad between the disc and sandpaper (a standard and necessary practice) to prevent gouges if you use too much force. Apply only mild pressure; let the paper do the cutting. Home power drills fitted with foam pads can be used, but generally they aren't built to stand up to the constant nonstop, high-speed use necessary over large surface areas. Orbital and vibrating sanders may be used to clean and rough up old paint but are too slow in removing entire coatings. Belt sanders should never be used as they are capable of removing a great deal of material in a hurry, and it is very difficult to prevent cutting lines in the hull with them.

If using a buffer fitted with foam pad, avoid grit size coarser than about #100 to #120. Unless you are extremely conscientious with coarser grits, you run the risk, with a momentary lapse in

**FIGURE 15-3.** Random-orbit sanders are great for removing paint from hulls, as well as wood finishing, because the eccentric orbit of the head prevents cutting swirls.

concentration, of gouging the hull. Random-orbit sanders minimize the risk, so I use #80 grit with them, although care still is required.

If you're not taking the hull down to bare substrate, hand-sanding is a reasonable alternative. You'll be in no danger of damaging the hull, you'll have less obnoxious dust to breathe (in any case, always wear a dust mask), and, if you're in a pleasant country boatyard where the fruit trees are blossoming and the birds are singing, you won't have to listen to a whining motor.

I prefer wet-sanding below the waterline rather than using dry sandpaper.

Check with the yard first, as you may be required to capture runoff. This may be difficult, as is capturing dust from a sander. EPA rules intended to prevent harmful chemicals from entering the environment may make do-it-yourself bottom jobs a thing of the past. Ground tarps and curtains help capture particulate, but disposal remains a problem.

At least with wet-sanding there aren't any particles of paint in the air to breathe (the copper tastes sweet and suspiciously unhealthy in your mouth), the sandpaper doesn't clog as fast, and it seems that you get a smoother surface than with dry sandpaper. Fill a plastic bucket with fresh water, put 3M Wetordry sandpaper on a rubber block that conforms nicely to your hand and the hull, and use a sponge in your left hand to occasionally clean the hull where you've been sanding and to clean the sandpaper when it loads up. Both are dunked in the bucket every five or six strokes for cleaning. With the hull wet, it's sometimes difficult to see where you've sanded, so learn to use your fingertips to identify unsanded areas. When done, hose down the entire underbody and when dry, inspect both visually and by touch for areas you might have missed.

The bottom of the keel is often dented or gouged from those inevitable groundings, and if severe, I usually fill them up with Marine-Tex (www.marinetex.com) or epoxy resin mixed with microballoons. Same for the inevitable cracks between externally ballasted keels and the hull. Marine-Tex is a white two-part compound that trowels in nicely with a putty knife. When hardened—usually within a few hours—I sand with a grinder or, if the area is inaccessible, with a coarse file and then sandpaper. A sanding block *always* insures more even pressure on the surface and therefore a smoother, more uniform finish.

Also, take the opportunity at this time to inspect all through-hulls and transducers to make certain they are still well bedded. If you've had minor leaking around one, or if the compound seems to have worn away, either remove the through-hull and rebed (if the problem is serious) or sand all the paint from the surface around the fitting and squeeze in a good bedding compound such as polysulfide or Life Calk (www.boatlife. com). Smooth the compound around the fitting

and scrape off the excess. If it looks messy, wait until it's hardened to sand or cut smooth.

## Strippers

The most effective paint strippers contain methylene chloride; unfortunately, it is a known carcinogen. As a result, paint companies have developed a number of safer products, though most take much longer to work. Peel Away (www .peelaway.com) and West Marine Safety Strip (www.westmarine.com) are pastes you can trowel onto the boat's bottom and then cover with a special paper that comes with the product (Figure 15-4). This keeps the chemicals heated and active. After about 24 hours (wait too long and it starts to harden), you remove the paper, which carries with it much of the paste. Scrape off the remainder and rinse with a hose. Sounds simple, but it's fairly messy—bottoms always are. The good news is that these products will eat through multiple coats of old paint, so one application generally is all that's required. And the toxins are easily captured, making this a job you can do yourself.

While not as noxious as many other strippers, the chemicals in Peel Away and Marine Safety

**FIGURE 15-4.** Peel Away is a gel you trowel on to the boat's bottom, then cover with a plastic paper to keep the chemicals active overnight. While it takes 24 hours to work, Peel Away will eat through multiple coats of old bottom paint.

Strip (calcium hydroxide, magnesium hydroxide, aluminum silicate, di-basic esters, etc.) will still burn skin, so wear latex gloves when working with these products.

## Paint Application

Before painting, wipe down the hull with the paint manufacturer's recommended prewash solution, thinner, or solvent. If in doubt, an acetone-soaked cloth usually works fine. Not only does this clean the hull of dust and other impurities, but it also softens the old paint for better adhesion to the new coat.

Use masking tape (3M's Scotch Fine Line 218 works best) to mark the line between the bottom and boot (Figure 15-5). With the roll of tape in one hand, unroll it as the other hand presses the tape into place. Unroll about 2 feet at a time to help determine a straight line and to speed up the job. Be sure to run your finger along the edge to be painted to ensure good adhesion of the tape, thus preventing paint from getting underneath.

I usually paint bottoms with a roller, hitting hard-to-get-at places with a throwaway brush (they're hard to clean well enough for use topside later, and since you don't really care if a few bristles fall out, why waste the money on an expensive camel-hair brush?).

FIGURE 15-5. The type of masking tape you use for painting is critical, as ordinary tape left too long in the sun is very difficult to remove. For best results use one of 3M's specialty tapes and sight down the hull to apply as straight as possible (inset). A chart available in most chandleries shows how long you can leave on each product number. Good results can be had with 3M's Scotch Fine Line 218.

Soluble matrix paints may require just one coat if there's a base underneath of old paint; copolymer paints depend on film thickness to work effectively and so two coats are generally better than one. In fact, Interlux suggests two coats of Micron CSC, each a different color, so that when you next haul out, you can gauge the amount of paint left on the hull. Because hydrolysis and the speed of passing water are major factors in the release of some copolymer paints, you may find that some areas of the hull expose the undercoating, while other areas still show the top coat.

When done painting, remove the masking tape the same day, even while the paint is wet. Failure to do so will probably result in some of the tape sticking to the hull. While it can be removed with lighter fluid or alcohol, it's an unnecessary job.

Aluminum and steel bottoms require special protection. Common practice is to sandblast first. Washes, primers, and barrier coats will probably be required before actually applying the bottom paint. Different companies have different systems developed to be used together. Because of the corrosion problem, they are often reluctant to publish general guidelines, preferring instead to discuss the project with you personally. Stick with one company, always be sure to read manufacturer's instructions, and use the recommended products in the sequence and manner suggested.

Let the bottom dry for a day before taping off the boot stripe; this prevents the tape from peeling off the bottom paint when it's removed. Sand the boot stripe area. A hard antifouling paint keeps the boot cleaner than an enamel. If your cruising gear and stores have lowered the waterline, now's the time to raise the boot a few inches. If necessary, use a ruler to periodically measure the distance between the old waterline and the tape.

With the possible exception of the new copolymer bottom paints, most paints will necessitate hauling the boat at least once each year for sanding and painting. Again, frequency is determined by the quality of the paint job, effectiveness of the biocide in the waters being sailed, how much time is spent underway versus sitting at anchor in dirty harbors, etc.

For many cruising people, these haulouts and servicings are major expenses that must be planned with a degree of care and forethought. If you can't reach a suitable port with adequate haulout facilities, you may be faced with careening the boat or letting it dry on a tide so you can sand and paint before the tide comes back in. The easiest do-it-yourself method is probably drying out along a pier or wall (Figure 15-6). Check the tide tables for those days with the maximum rise and fall, but be certain there will be enough water to float you off when done—you could find yourself stranded for the next four weeks! And check that sanding bottom paint over the water is legal; this probably varies by country.

Inspect the bottom where you expect your keel to touch. Is it hard enough? If there are obstacles on the bottom, don a face mask and snorkel and clear the obstacles first. When you've determined the day, hour, and exact location, rig a sturdy fender board over two tough fenders and add a stout line to a masthead halyard for inclining the boat slightly toward the pier or wall. The line can be led to an anchor sunk into the adjacent land. Take up on the line with the mast winch as the boat settles. Have ready additional fenders, cushions, and whatever else seems necessary to shove in between the pier and boat as it may be difficult to predict exactly how the two will meet. As the water recedes, start scraping barnacles and sanding with wet or dry sandpaper (don't use power tools standing in the water!). You may not be able to do the absolute bottom of the keel effectively if the water doesn't completely expose the entire surface, but with a scraper and wet sandpaper, you can do a fair job. Be sure to allow time to paint the entire hull before the water rises again.

**FIGURE 15-6.** An economical haulout can be accomplished by positioning the boat next to a wall as the tide goes out, or by supporting the hull on both sides with timbers. This big ketch did the trick in a corner of Newport Harbor. (Steve Krous photo)

As long as you're working on the bottom, remember bare hulls covered with metal keels and centerboards and old paints incompatible with the new coating may require barrier or tie coats before you can successfully apply the new paint. Check with the manufacturer of your chosen paint to be sure, and use the product he recommends. Once you select a paint, you're best advised to use that company's entire product line for such things as surfacing compounds, solvents, and barrier coats as they are chemically designed as part of a unique system and may not work with other brands of paints.

## VARNISHES AND OILS

Keeping up with brightwork is a never-ending job, and, while most persons won't argue the attractiveness of satin-finish coamings, toe rails, and handrails, it can become burdensome for the cruiser on the go.

Non-liveaboards and liveaboards who stay more or less in one area will probably have a different attitude toward varnishing than the itinerant cruiser on a tight budget. When cruising poor, hostile, and/or less-developed countries, nothing says, "rich American yacht" quite so much as sparkling brightwork. Former *Cruising World* managing editor Betsy Hitz wrote an article titled, "Are Cruising Sailors Sitting Ducks?" after she and her companion were attacked in Bequia. "Even in an affluent nation like the U.S.," she wrote, "a yacht is erroneously thought to be a symbol of untold wealth, a toy of the idle rich. What must this same vessel represent to a man from Haiti, St. Vincent or Trinidad, whose annual income is less than the value of a winch?"

She then recounted the following conversation with a fellow cruiser moored nearby. "Richard Roderick, a sage Australian who is completing a seven-year circumnavigation with his family, learned long ago that the myth of the wealthy yachtsman creates a sometimes-dangerous image problem for cruising sailors. Lounging in a hammock strung between his masts, Richard would look up from his magazine at Jim and me varnishing our rails and polishing the hull in Bequia before our mishap.

"You got it all wrong, Mates," he'd sigh, shaking his head. "Those blokes in there are going to think you're bloody *millionaires*. You've got to poor it up. Let the varnish go. Look at that tight furl. Slop-it-up, Mates! Why that dinghy of yours hasn't even any *patches*. Look at that American flag—that's really asking for it. Might as well be flying a green dollar sign. When cruising, there's one thing you've got to learn about money: Never, but never, let anyone know you've got any."

This anecdote isn't intended to scare you, but Mr. Roderick isn't alone in his thinking. Many other cruisers have arrived at the same conclusion, and it's offered here as an incentive to people who already hate varnishing to paint it over! If you get a few scratches on a painted surface, just dab a bit of paint over the damaged area and it looks as good as new. When this happens to varnish, however, water discolors the wood underneath and the only way to restore the surface to its original state is to remove all the varnish, sand and possibly even bleach the wood, then start applying varnish all over again. I've owned several wood boats and though I love fashioning wood, I hate sanding it—it's no mystery to me why some people decide to paint varnished surfaces.

Where it's safe to look yachtie, or when you have the time and inclination to varnish, by all means do so. And, of course, there are usually dozens of places in a cabin that benefit from varnishing. There, safe from UV attack, varnish will last years.

## Surface Preparation

New wood requires only a light sanding—by hand or power sander, such as a vibrating type, that cuts with the grain—before varnishing. If it's porous, you might consider brushing on a filler coat, such as wood paste or clear acrylic, to fill up the grain and give your varnish the most mileage. Sand with the grain as much as possible and, if you must go across the grain to remove a spot, do so as lightly as possible because it will require more sanding with the grain to remove the cuts. Again, a sanding block assures a flat surface.

## Varnishing Tips

- Use paint and varnish remover with care, as it can eat through the gelcoat if dropped on deck.
- Bleaching wood to remove water discoloration is possible, but very tricky, and in my mind usually not worth the effort.
- Inside the cabin, vacuum as you sand to remove dust from the air.

- Avoid very coarse sandpaper because it is too difficult to remove the cut lines.
- Strain varnish with a nylon stocking to remove dirt and blobs—don't assume it comes out of the can free from contamination.
- Saturate the wet brush (a good-quality bristle one) thoroughly before applying varnish to prevent air bubbles.
- Use a piece of wire across the top of the can to "tap off" varnish, rather than using the lip of the can; again, air bubbles can result.
- Don't let the brush dry between uses as dried varnish will flake off the bristles and ruin your next coat.
- Use a brush cleaner compatible with your varnish after every use.
- Don't shake cans of varnish—yup, air bubbles again.
- Never apply varnish in full sun because it dries too quickly, and the finish will blister.
- Outside, use a varnish with a UV screen.
- Similarly, basements (in case you've brought home removable pieces of wood to work on) are often too damp for good varnishing. Use a dehumidifier if you must, and run a vacuum cleaner to keep dust out of the air.
- Sand in between coats to knock off bumps and pieces of dust. Use a tack cloth or cheesecloth to wipe the surface before applying the second coat.
- Use wood filler paste or clear acrylic filler before varnishing to fill the grain and minimize the number of coats required.
- Apply five coats of varnish as a minimum on surfaces exposed to moisture; six to eight coats are better. One or two annual coats on furniture is probably sufficient.
- Apply coats thinly on inclined surfaces, otherwise sag can occur.
- Store cans of varnish and paint upside down so scum forms on bottom of unused portion.
- Suspend your varnish brush on wire run through top of cleaner can so bristles aren't crushed.

Over the years I've observed on my boats that vertical varnished surfaces hold their film thickness much longer than horizontal surfaces. For this reason, if I were looking for brightwork to paint over, I'd attack the horizontal surfaces first.

## Teak Oils and Stains

Teak oils to me are just as much a nemesis as varnishing. Cleaning teak is a thankless task that leaves yellow hands, painful cuts, and discoloration of the topsides as it is washed off (though this is not so much a problem on dark-colored hulls). Most of these oils don't last very long, requiring reapplication about every three to four weeks. Otherwise you'll have to go through the first step of cleaning again. Some can be wiped or brushed on, but brushes seem to reach corners better and use less oil or stain. The trouble with vegetable oils has been that while they allow the wood to breathe, they often mildew and wear off. Synthetics, such as polyurethanes, don't allow the wood to breathe and keep moisture in.

Fortunately, the problem of maintaining teak has attracted considerable attention in recent years, and today there are a few products that will last up to a year, depending on surface preparation, number of coats, and geographic location. At *Practical Sailor* we tested dozens of teak treatments every year and the best included Sikkens Cetol Marine (www.yachtpaint.com) and Armada Wood Finishes (www.armadacoatings.com), both pigmented stains that may not thoroughly satisfy the varnish purist, but look pretty darn good to the rest of us (Figure 15-7). Smith

**FIGURE 15-7.** Pigmented stains such as Sikkens Cetol Marine last much longer than conventional teak oils, but some have an orange color. (Akzo Nobel/Interlux)

& Company's CPES (Clear Penetrating Epoxy System; www.smithandcompany.org) involves laying down a coat of epoxy on the bare wood, followed by varnish to protect the epoxy. The color is very rich and it lasts a long time, but like any hard coating, once water breaks through, it's basically all over as touch-ups don't look that great. Among two-part polyurethanes, Bristol Finish (www.bristolfinish.com) and Honey Teak (www.signaturefinish.com) perform well.

# TOPSIDE PAINTING

Running down to the nearest chandlery or paint store and purchasing a quart or two of a marine enamel, any old can of thinner or solvent, and a few brushes is not the most intelligent way to approach a painting project. When companies refer to various "systems" of paints they market, they're not kidding. The chemistry of formulating paints has developed so radically in recent years that it is important now to familiarize yourself with the types of paint available and their appropriate applications. Most of these paints—be they alkyd enamels or cross-linked polyurethanes—require prewashing the surface with cleaners, perhaps applying a primer or tie coat, and thinning the paint with a compatible solvent. The technique used in applying the paint makes a difference, too, as well as maintaining the pristine cleanliness of the surface to be painted.

## Surfacers

Surface nicks and dents should be filled before painting. They are most easily detected after the initial sanding of the hull or deck because they appear as bright spots, indentations that sandpaper cannot reach.

Clean the surface with the product recommended by the manufacturer of your paint and then fill in the spots with a surfacing putty. The smoother you apply it, the easier it will be to sand later on. There are several types: nitrocellulose lacquer, polyester two-part, acrylic lacquer, and modified vegetable oil types. For strength and durability, the two-part epoxies probably are best. When the putty has cured, sand to a smooth finish.

After the sanding residue has been removed with a tack cloth, and any grease, wax, and oil removed with a cheesecloth soaked with solvent (preferably the same type used with the paint), it may be advisable to coat the surface with a primer. One reason to do this is gelcoat porosity. Test for gelcoat porosity by brushing a small amount of any kind of paint on the surface. If the gelcoat is porous, tiny pinholes or craters of paint will be visible.

Surface primers vary considerably in both chemical and physical makeup. They can dry and/or cure by oxidation of a vegetable oil (alkyd types), by solvent evaporation (lacquer types), or by a chemical cross-linking (epoxy or polyurethane types). Each has its advantages and disadvantages. Lacquer types dry quickly, but shrink and consequently have little film buildup. These types have little solvent resistance and can be used only with spray-applied finishes or with brush-applied finishes that have weaker solvent systems than are required for lacquer.

Alkyd surface primers are used almost exclusively with alkyd finish enamels. Film buildup is very good as are brushing characteristics. Alkyds are the simplest system for most persons.

Two-part catalyzed epoxy or polyurethane primers are superior primers when used with the new two-part linear polyurethane enamels. They have excellent physical strength and solvent resistance. Hard primers such as these give better end results, but are difficult to sand. Soft primers are easier to sand because they have been loaded with more pigment. But they tend also to act like blotters when the finishing coat is applied. Porous surfacers also absorb moisture, and moisture is one of the worst enemies of a good paint job. Select a surfacer that is fairly hard (two-part epoxy), but not so hard that it can't be sanded reasonably well.

Above the water, two coats of surfacing primer generally should be used. Between coats, sand with #120 grit sandpaper. Wipe residue clean with cheesecloth and solvent. Again, be certain that the surfacing primer you have chosen is compatible with the paint you intend to use; if it isn't, you've got a real problem on your hands.

## Choosing a Paint

The oldest and best-known enamels are the alkyd types (Figure 15-8). These paints almost always contain mineral spirits as a solvent system. They are easy to apply and economical to use. But they do not possess the overall durability and gloss of some of the newer cross-linked polyurethanes.

From alkyd technology other types of enamels have been developed. For example, silicone resin is added to modify some alkyds to enhance gloss retention. While it may approach polyurethane paint in terms of gloss retention, it is not as resistant to abrasion. Oil-modified polyurethanes also are examples of modified alkyd technology and possess good drying properties and better abrasion resistance than standard alkyd types. Acrylic resins can be used as alkyd modifiers to improve "dust free" time and give whiter whites.

Alkyd enamels are compatible with most generic-type primers; however, read the manufacturer's literature carefully. (For example, when alkyd enamels are used over epoxy primers, special techniques should be used to ensure adhesion, such as the application of a tie-coat primer.)

Epoxy paints are very strong solvent- and chemical-resistant coatings, and they provide excellent binder resins for primers and sanding surfacers. As a class, they do have some shortcomings: They have a tendency to yellow quickly and lose gloss. They also require strong solvent systems and can be applied only over bare substrate or other well-cross-linked coating systems. Because of these characteristics, they seldom are used in the yacht finishing business as a top-coat enamel. But, because of their binder strength and water-resistant properties, they often are used as binders for high-quality primers and sanding surfacers.

Above the waterline, epoxy sanding surfacers almost always are recommended with two-part linear polyurethanes. The combination of a high-quality epoxy sanding surfacer and polyurethane enamel is an excellent paint system, the best all-around system currently available.

Two-part, cross-linked polyurethane enamels fall into two chemical classifications. There are aromatic and linear types. The aromatic polyurethanes have physical characteristics somewhat similar to epoxy resins inasmuch as they yellow and do not hold their gloss. Very good primers can be made from them, but they are not suitable for high-quality top-coat enamels. A big advantage of this type of primer, as opposed to an epoxy primer, is that the polyurethane generally will cure at lower temperatures.

Linear polyurethanes have excellent all-around properties, including gloss and color retention, in addition to resistance to scratch abrasion, solvents, and chemicals. Properly applied, these

## CHARACTERISTICS OF DIFFERENT TOPSIDE PAINTS

| Product Type | Ease of Application | How Paint Dries | Solvent Type | Cost | Durability | Toxicity |
|---|---|---|---|---|---|---|
| Old Line Alkyd Marine Enamel | Very good; can be brushed or sprayed | By solvent evaporation and oxidation of a vegetable oil | Usually mineral spirits; does not require strong solvent | Moderate | The standard from which other improvements are made | Low; mineral spirits solvent only |
| Silicone Alkyd | Same as alkyd | Same as alkyd | Same as alkyd | More expensive than alkyd | Gloss retention excellent; superior to other products of this type | Same as alkyd |
| Oil-Modified Polyurethane | Similar to alkyd, usually slightly better flow | Usually faster than alkyd, by oxidation of vegetable oil | Same as alkyd | More expensive than alkyd | Better abrasion resistance than alkyd | Same as alkyd |
| Acrylic-Modified Alkyd | Similar to alkyd | Similar to alkyd, usually slightly faster | Same as alkyd | More expensive than alkyd | Gloss retention and color usually slightly better than alkyd | Same as alkyd |
| Two-Part Polyurethane | Can be finicky; requires more attention to detail | By chemical cross-linking and solvent evaporation | Usually strong solvent: esters, ketones, and aromatics | Very expensive | Best | Very hazardous when sprayed; no problem when brush or roller used |
| Epoxy | Can be finicky; requires attention to detail | By chemical cross-linking and solvent evaporation | Same as urethanes | More expensive, than alkyds; not as expensive as polyurethanes | Excellent for primers and putties not used for finish coat | Has a hazard potential from solvent and epoxy constituents |
| Lacquers | Mostly used in putties | By solvent evaporation | Usually ketones and aromatic solvents | Moderate | Best feature is fast dry; has excessive shrinkage | Not usually a factor because of amounts used |

**FIGURE 15-8.** Characteristics of different topside paints. (Robert Wilkinson)

products represent the finest available air-cured paints for finishing above the waterline.

### Surface Preparation

Painting fiberglass usually is complicated by the fact that the gelcoat retains mold-release agents used in the production process to pop the hull and deck out of their molds. This wax must be removed; otherwise, it will cause the paint to form a soft waxy film, prevent the proper layout of the paint (crawling), and prevent the paint from ad-hering properly. Failure to remove this wax with the appropriate solvent wash compromises all paint applications that follow. The same applies to any waxes you've applied yourself over the years (Figure 15-9).

Examine the hull for surface imperfections and repair with surface putties and/or primers as mentioned earlier.

The grit size of the abrasive is important, though there are two schools of thought on this. Some persons specify using a fine paper of #220 grit or finer so as not to penetrate the "float" layer

**FIGURE 15-9.** Before painting, the topsides must be sanded smooth, whether the original surface is gelcoat or old paint.

on the surface, thereby exposing the porous layer beneath. This condition, as was mentioned earlier, requires the use of a primer to fill up the pores. On the other hand, fine-grit abrasives do not sufficiently rough up the surface, which is necessary for good adhesion of the paint. Sanding with coarser paper assures good adhesion. If porosity occurs, you'll wish you'd applied a primer or sanding surfacer.

As long as you're careful, you can use paper as coarse as #80 grit on gelcoats without causing problems. Again, I've found that I can use coarser grits with a random-orbit sander. Without a random-orbit sander, use #120 grit or #150 grit paper. Sand the gelcoat until all traces of gloss have been removed but not so much that the paint won't cover the sanding tracks.

If you're using a surface putty and/or primer, apply it at this time. If not, proceed directly with the finish coatings.

## Working with Two-Part Polyurethanes

Linear polyurethanes are distant cousins of the polyester resins used to build fiberglass sailboats. They harden, set, and cure by means of a chemical process called polymerization, in which long, skinny molecules cross-link to form a hard, impervious solid. These paints are prepared for polymerization by adding a catalyst (part A) to a base (part B).

The rate of polymerization is subject to temperature; the higher the temperature, the faster the cure. Allowing the paint to cure overnight is usually sufficient time between coats, and with linear polyurethanes, two coats are always required if applied by brush or roller. The full cure may not be completed for a number of days, and so it is wise to be gentle with the painted surface until it has finally cured.

Linear polyurethanes are relatively quick-drying. But don't confuse surface dryness with the curing process. Sanding too soon after the first coat has been applied could result in gumming up the sandpaper and botching the job.

Professional spray applications of linear polyurethanes almost always achieve better results, but the brushable versions of these paints can produce excellent results as well. Chances are, however, your second experience with these paints will produce better results than the first. So it never hurts to experiment with a dinghy, or at the very least, with a small area of the boat such under the transom.

Here are some tips to follow:

- Follow manufacturer's instructions to the letter.
- Dewax hull with specified solvent wash.
- Sand gelcoat with grit between #80 and #150 (Figure 15-10).
- Fill dents and nicks with specified surface filler putty (Figure 15-11).
- Sand putty with #80 grit or finer sandpaper (Figure 15-12).
- Apply two coats of surface primer, sanding with #120 grit paper in between (Figure 15-13).
- Sand surface primer with fine-grit paper until perfectly smooth, preferably with #340 grit wet paper or finer. Remove scum with freshwater rinse (Figure 15-14).
- The "ideal" day for painting is 75°F, no wind, relative humidity between 40 and 50%, and a work area out of the sun. Plan your day to start and finish on the shady side of the hull.
- Find the right mixing ratio of paint to thinner and experiment on a small area not readily noticeable. The right ratio will keep the paint wet so that overlaps flow together (Figure 15-15).

**FIGURE 15-10.** In this sequence of photos, courtesy Interlux, a boat is being prepared for painting with an Interlux polyurethane paint system. Here, the gelcoat is being sanded with an orbital sander.

**FIGURE 15-11.** A two-part surfacing putty is mixed and then applied over dings and gouges using a putty knife.

**FIGURE 15-12.** The surfacing putty is sanded smooth with an orbital sander.

**FIGURE 15-13.** A primer is used between the bare gelcoat and finish coatings to ensure good bonding.

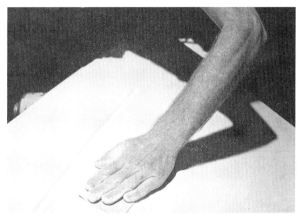

**FIGURE 15-14.** The dry primer is sanded by hand (a sanding block would be better). Afterward it is wiped clean with a tack rag.

- Only mix as much paint as needed to coat a continuous surface area, such as one side of the boat.
- You can premix batches, and refrigerate them to save time, improve flow, and minimize the amount of reducer required.
- Thin paint with specified solvent (in many ways, the proper use of solvents separates the professionals from the amateurs).
- One way to apply paint is to have a helper on hand. You can paint with a ⅛-inch nap (3 mm) polyurethane roller while your helper tips off the area with a fine-bristle brush (Figure 15-16).

**FIGURE 15-15.** Mixing the two-part polyurethane paint.

While the natural tendency is to stroke horizontally, as if the hull had wood planks, you can avoid much of the sagging common to linear polyurethane paints by stroking vertically from top to bottom. This way excess paint winds up on the masking tape at the boot, not on the hull.

The objective is to put enough paint on to level out, but not so much that it will sag (Figures 15-17 and 15-18). Surface tension varies with color. Dark colors sag more easily than light colors. White is easiest to work with.

**FIGURE 15-17.** Make sure while painting that sagging is not occurring from applying too much paint. Once the paint starts to cure, you can no longer go over it with a brush.

**FIGURE 15-16.** Two workers brush on the first finish coat, carefully thinning the paint as they go. Alternatively, the first can use a roller, while the second tips the paint with a high-quality brush. If using a foam brush, toss as soon as the tip loads up—they're cheap.

**FIGURE 15-18.** With the second and final coat applied, this once dingy-looking boat now looks brand-spanking-new.

- If painting decks, use a flattening agent to reduce gloss. Mixing in a nonskid compound also helps reduce gloss.

- For small touch-up jobs, use measuring spoons for accurate mixing of the two parts.

- Store brushes in paper towels after cleaning. Never hit the brush on wood to clean; use a pet comb to unclog bristles.

## Wood, Steel, and Aluminum Hulls

When the time comes to paint the topsides of a wood boat, the surface should be sanded smooth to bare wood or nearly so. Apply a wood preservative and allow to dry for a few days. Sand with #80 grit paper. On plywood hulls only, Interlux recommends next using a wood sealer. For a really smooth, fair hull, apply two coats of a sanding surfacer (lightly sand after the first coat), and allow each coat to dry overnight. Then apply finish coats of enamel, sanding lightly with #220 grit paper in between.

John Scarlett, author of *Wooden Boats*, prefers oil-based (alkyd) paints to epoxy and polyurethane types because they allow the wood underneath to breathe a bit. He writes, "Since boats have a nasty habit of damaging their paintwork, and any damage will let in moisture, it seems wise to use a finish which will let it out again."

Steel hulls, according to Interlux's specifications, should be sandblasted and then sprayed with the appropriate washes, primers, and barrier coats. Imperfections can be faired with microballoons, sanded, and wiped with solvent again.

Depending on finish paint type, wipe the surface with the correct reducing solvent, then apply the paint (see manufacturer's instructions for exact details), and wet sand with #320 grit paper in between. Some paints may require a primer coat as well.

Aluminum hulls also can be sandblasted, in which case a barrier coat is applied (Interlux's is a two-part epoxy). If it can't be sandblasted, disc sand. Per Interlux, it is important to end up with at least 6 mils (0.15 mm) of barrier coating even after sanding on all hull areas. No microballoons should be used after the top coat. If finishing with an enamel, use a primer first; if using a polyurethane, check with the manufacturer for exact instructions.

## Spars

It is common practice now to coat spars with two-part polyurethanes. The reason is that anodizing, which involves submersing the spar in a chemical bath and running an electrical current through it, produces toxic wastes that are expensive to dispose of according to EPA regulations. Different companies have different systems, so again, stick with the products recommended by the company you select.

The basic procedure for painting aluminum spars is to remove all fittings and sand with medium-grit emery cloth to remove oxidation and to form a light anchor pattern to help the paint adhere. Wipe down the spar with a zinc-chromate, self-etching vinyl butyral wash, then cover with two coats of paint. Allow the first coat to dry overnight, and sand with #320 grit dry or wet paper before applying the second coat.

## Decks

When the molded nonskid pattern on fiberglass decks wears smooth, you can glue on new nonskid pads such as Treadmaster (www.tiflex.co.uk/marine/marine.html) or the rubberized nonslip deck covering by Vetus (www.vetus.com). The alternative is to paint them with the hard, durable polyurethane paints mentioned for topsides. Surface preparation for decks is the same as for topsides. Specially formulated synthetic granules, such as Interlux's No Skid Compound, can be mixed in with the paint, or you can buy nonskid paint with the granules premixed.

Before painting, also take the time to repair gelcoat dings with one of the many kits available in chandleries.

On the 1975 C&C 33, I used a nonskid paint with the granules premixed. The instructions cautioned against working the paint too much, as the granules tend to load up in bunches. Despite great care with the roller, the granules did not lay down uniformly and I wasn't very happy with the result.

# FIBERGLASS RESTORERS

It's always tempting to find a simpler solution, and in the case of chalked topsides, some owners have turned to a new generation of acrylic film coatings generously called "fiberglass restorers." They go by the names of New Glass 2 (www.newglass2.com), Vertglas (www.lovettmarine.com),

Poli Glow (www.poliglowproducts.com), and others. These plastic films make a highly reflective surface with deeper, richer colors, just as it looks when wet—practically any liquid will do, the trick is one that stays attached to the hull.

Before applying a restorer you must clean the hull with an abrasive rubbing compound, then polish it. Reapplication after a year probably is necessary. Like varnish on wood, if you let the film deteriorate and flake off in spots, you'll have to remove the entire film before reapplication. Special removers may be required.

I view these products as temporary measures, merely putting off the day when you need to re-paint. And when you do finally decide to repaint, you'll work extra hard sanding away the remains of these films that have hidden like parasites in the tiny pores of your gelcoat.

## PAINTING THE BOAT'S NAME

BoatU.S. and West Marine each offer custom boat lettering for names and hailing ports. A wide variety of colors and fonts are offered, and the prices are reasonable. If you don't see what you want from such a service, your local sign maker often is able to create an imaginative design on the computer, which is then cut out of a sticky-sided vinyl sheet.

If you prefer to do the whole job yourself, the technique employed by decorators of vans and plastic sign painters is a comparatively inexpensive way to apply your boat's name on your transom or topsides.

1. Draw your boat's name full size on a piece of paper. Use rulers, French curves, and whatever other tools you find helpful in achieving the desired design. Here you can make mistakes, and they won't hurt. But what you see here is what you get on the boat.

2. Place the paper with your boat's name on the kitchen table with a cotton blanket beneath. Then, use a pounce wheel (which you can purchase for several dollars at an art supply store) or a common pin to perforate all the lines. When finished, lightly sand the backside of the paper to fully open the holes.

3. With acetone, Fantastik, or similar cleaner, clean the area on your boat that is to be painted.

4. Use masking tape to mark off the area to be painted. Leave a little more space than will be required by the name. Cover all areas outside the tape heavily and tightly with newspaper.

5. Purchase a quart of brushable or spray mask at an art supply store or auto body shop and apply to the exposed area. When dry, the mask is a thin film that is easy to cut away for your lettering. The rest peels off easily when the paint job is done.

6. Tape the boat's name over the mask in the correct location. Using a cloth and pounce powder, pat the cloth over the perforations so that the outline of your letters is shown on the mask. An alternative to pounce powder is the blue chalk powder used on carpenters' plumb lines; it's available at most hardware stores.

7. Using a razor blade or sharp knife, such as an X-Acto, lightly cut out your letters from the mask along the outline created by the pounce powder. A straightedge is helpful for straight lines.

8. Paint the exposed surface areas. Commendable results can be had with a brush or spray can. Dabbing with a stipple pad or wadded-up, fine-mesh cheesecloth will remove most of the brush marks. Good-quality enamel paints are suitable for lettering.

9. Allow the paint to dry for about 4 hours or longer, then remove all masking tape, mask, and newspaper. Masking tape that is left on the hull for several days can be hellish to remove. Do not wax the lettering for about one week.

Large, bold lettering, especially super-graphics, could discourage would-be thieves from pilfering your boat. But should your boat vanish anyway, the thin cut lines made by your knife when cutting away the mask could eventually help identify your boat.

If using a pounce wheel and powder seems like too much hassle, a simple alternative is to cover the back of the paper (which contains the boat's

FIGURE 15-19. An illustrator friend made a stencil for *Adriana*'s name, temporarily glued it to the transom, and used a spray can of enamel to paint the name.

FIGURE 15-20. *Viva*'s name was made up by a local sign maker, who designed it on a computer, then used an NC machine to cut the pattern out of a sheet of vinyl. To affix, tape the top edge of the sheet to the transom, then pull away the back covering over the adhesive, and press uniformly over the letters.

name) with charcoal chalk. Then tape the paper to the hull and trace the lettering with a pencil. Cut away the lettering along the outline as before.

This method allows you to demonstrate your creative talents, but with calculated safeguards. For most amateurs, freehand is just too risky and stick-on letters too blah. Even if you don't want a dreamy mood mural on the side of your boat, you can learn something from the fellows who decorate vans.

Richard Fritzler, a friend of mine who is a medical illustrator, showed me a simpler variation of this method. The boat's name was drawn on a piece of brown paper exactly the way we wanted to see it on the transom. We cut out each letter using a straightedge and X-Acto knife (make this part easy on yourself, buy a cheap set of French curves). Next we used spray mask to temporarily glue the brown paper stencil to *Adriana*'s transom. We then used a spray enamel paint to coat the areas cut away. Spray acrylics can be used

also. It is most important to spray the paint on thinly or else sagging inevitably occurs. You will probably have to go over the surface several times, but the whole process shouldn't take more than a few hours. The result is surprisingly professional looking. If you take your time in drawing the name, cutting it out, and applying the paint, there's no reason you can't do just as nice a job as in Figures 15-19 and 15-20.

## FURTHER READING

*Brightwork: The Art of Finishing Wood.* Rebecca J. Wittman. Camden, Maine: International Marine, 1990.

*The Brightwork Companion: Tried-and-True Methods and Strongly Held Opinions in Thirteen and One-Half Chapters.* Rebecca J. Wittman. Camden, Maine: International Marine, 2004.

*Complete Guide to Metal Boats.* 3rd ed. Bruce Roberts-Goodson. Camden, Maine: International Marine, 2005.

*Steel Away: A Guidebook to the World of Steel Sailboats.* LeCain W. Smith and Sheila Moir. Port Townsend, Washington: Windrose Productions, 1986.

*Wooden Boats: Restoration & Maintenance Manual.* John Scarlett. Newton Abbot, England; North Pomfret, Vermont: David and Charles, 1981 [1987].

# SIXTEEN

# DINGHIES

An undeniable objective—indeed the prime purpose of cruising—is exploring the unknown—at least what is unknown to us—and a sailboat is the perfect vehicle. It is able to go virtually anywhere there is water, it is largely self-sufficient, relatively inexpensive to operate, spiritually invigorating, and fun.

A keel boat is limited by its draft, usually to water at least 6 or so feet deep (1.8 m). Consequently, a tender or dinghy is essential cruising gear to get back and forth from shore and to investigate shoal waters. Choosing the right dinghy is not easy. You must consider how you intend to use it (row, motor, sail?), how much money you can spend ($400? $4,000?), and how you will carry it aboard the mother ship (davits, on deck, right side up, upside down, deflated?).

Here are some considerations:

- The dinghy should be capable of carrying most if not all the crew at one time to minimize the number of shore trips (long rowing trips are tiring, sometimes wet, and time consuming).
- It should be stable, tough, and repairable.
- It should be able to make headway in choppy water and high winds—without an outboard motor.
- It should be capable of being stowed safely on deck. Towing dinghies is dangerous and unseamanlike in rough weather, for it will surely swamp, possibly endangering the towing vessel as well.
- It should be fitted with hardware that allows it to be locked. Theft is all too common, even in the so-called civilized countries.

Like a sailboat, every dinghy is a compromise. One that rows well may be too large to stow on deck. One that planes with an outboard may be impossible to row. The more you know about your personal cruising style, the better prepared you are to buy or build the right dinghy. Are you a purist, eschewing motors, electronics, and cocktails before sunset? Or are you the sort who likes comfort, indulging in every convenience—electric winches on your 30-footer (9.1 m), stereo speakers implanted in the cockpit pillows, a Cuisinart for "blender sports"? Okay, that's harsh, but you get the gist. It probably has as much to do with the size of your boat, and the thickness of your wallet, as it does your philosophy.

## HARD VERSUS INFLATABLE

The first branch in the decision-making tree is whether to have a hard or soft dinghy. Inflatables are very popular because they are exceptionally stable, sexy, and fast when powered by even a modest outboard.

On the other side of the coin, inflatables don't row worth a damn (you have to feel sorry for the poor chap struggling against the breeze with those stubby plastic oars, especially when it's raining and his wife is sitting in the stern looking miserable!), don't tow worth a damn, don't stow worth a damn unless deflated (a pain), aren't terribly abrasion resistant (dock pilings and beaches), and are the favored targets of thieves.

Inflatables, to my mind, excel in two areas—speed and stability, especially when functioning as dive boats. In all other respects, I prefer a good hard dinghy, regardless of construction materials. It rows better, stows better, and lasts longer.

But there's a third option, the rigid inflatable boat (RIB) that during the 1990s became the most popular choice of tender amongst cruisers, at least of larger boats (Figure 16-1). While a few have aluminum hulls, most are fiberglass. Stability is achieved by a tubular, air-filled collar, same as a regular inflatable. The advantage of the RIB over others is that the V-shape of the hull makes it ride

**FIGURE 16-1.** The rigid inflatable boat (RIB) is now the most popular tender on larger cruising boats. Its V-shaped fiberglass bottom is durable and makes for a comfortable ride. (Bruce Bingham photo)

better and faster in a chop, plus it can take more punishment on a beach. Of course, it also means you can't stow the boat in as small a package as a 100% inflatable, although you can deflate the tubes and still stow the boat on deck.

## TYPES OF INFLATABLES

Among pure inflatables, there are three main types, each with its pros and cons. Generally speaking, those that are easiest and fastest to set up sacrifice something in the way of performance. Conversely, those that perform best are more of a pain to set up, so that you are tempted to leave them inflated as much as possible.

The roll-up, popularized by Avon (www .avonmarine.com), features a slatted wood or plastic board floor in which each board is connected to the next by a durable fabric. While it provides stiffness athwartship, it lacks stiffness fore and aft.

So-called sportboats have larger interlocking panels that provide equal stiffness athwartship and better stiffness fore and aft. But they must fit tightly to be effective.

The third type has a high-pressure floor that provides more stiffness than a floor with boards, is lightweight, and easy to deflate and stow. Like the roll-up and sportboat, high-pressure-floor boats usually have an inflatable tube under the floor running fore and aft to try to give a V-shape to the hull bottom.

For people with a minimum of space and a small budget, the British Tinker rigid-floor inflatable (www.tinker.co.uk) was billed as a yacht tender that could do double duty as a poor man's life raft. It could be ordered with a $CO_2$ inflation system and drogue, but the absence of buoyancy pouches made it less stable than a proper raft, and eventually the company felt obligated to discontinue this option. That's telling for anyone who thinks they can turn their inflatable into a bona fide life raft.

## PRODUCTION DINGHIES

There is no dearth of commercially produced dinghies from which to choose. The well-known Dyer dinghies (Figure 16-2), built by Anchorage (www.dyerboats.com), have been around since the Depression. Built in fiberglass now, the Dyer Dhow is available in various lengths, all with varnished mahogany seats, bronze oarlocks, and tough fabric-covered rubber gunwale guards.

Bruce Bingham's 10-foot (3 m) Trinka dinghy (Figure 16-3), built in Florida by Johannsen Boat Works (www.trinka.com), is as handsome as they come. Robert Perry's Periwinkle (www.perryboat .com) is no slouch either. If I owned *Ticonderoga* (the 72-foot ketch designed by L. Francis Herreshoff that some people, including me, think is the world's most beautiful yacht), I'd probably want a Whitehall skiff tender (www.whitehallrow .com)—something fine and lean, suitable for rowing m'lady about the anchorage.

Dozens of other production dinghies are available, ranging from graceful birds to ugly duck-

**FIGURE 16-2.** The Dyer Dhow, first built in wood, is a classic tender with varnished mahogany seats, bronze fittings, and a handsome rubrail.

lings, from glass-covered plywood to traditional planked construction, ABS plastic, and fiberglass. Examples that intrigue me are the folding Porta-Bote (www.porta-bote.com), Puddleduck from New England Skiff Builders (Figure 16-4) (www .by-the-sea.com/bakerboatworks/bbpuddle.html), and Lyle Hess' Fatty Knees (www.fattyknees.com). Prices tend to run high since the labor involved in construction is a significant factor. If you have the means, and if you can stow the dinghy on davits or on deck (infinitely preferable in a storm), then a production dinghy will serve just fine.

## BUILDING FROM PLANS

If there are a lot of production dinghy builders, there must be ten times as many building plans for amateurs available. Glen-L (www.glen-l.com) is a longstanding company that caters to home builders. In fact, you've probably seen some of its designs in *Popular Mechanics* over the years—duck boats, jonboats, bass boats, canoes, you name it. Clark Craft (www.clarkcraft.com), Bruce Roberts (www.bruce-roberts.com), and Jay Benford (www.benford.us) are other well-known plans factories.

The back pages of *WoodenBoat* magazine showcase many more excellent designs by people such as Joel White (www.brooklinboatyard.com) and Phil Bolger. The degree of difficulty in building these dinghies yourself varies widely. Traditional strip-planked construction, requiring the lofting of lines from the plans to the shop floor, will take a lot more skill and time than a plywood dinghy whose panels can be cut from full-size drawings. Be honest in evaluating your skills and the time available to build even an 8-foot (2.4 m) pram—it's always more than you think.

**FIGURE 16-3.** Bruce Bingham's Trinka is available in 8- and 10-foot lengths (2.4 m and 3 m) and sails surprisingly well for a small boat.

## NESTING DINGHIES

Small and midsize cruising boats often don't have the deck space necessary to carry an adequately sized one-piece hard dinghy. If we rule out towing and davits as acceptable all-weather means of carrying the dinghy, the only choice left is a nesting design. One part, being slightly shorter than the other, is carefully designed to fit inside the larger so that the total space required for on-deck stowage is just a bit more than half the total square-footage of the entire assembled dinghy.

**FIGURE 16-4.** The fiberglass Puddleduck was designed in 1951 by Robert Baker and is finished with oak, mahogany, and bronze. A Gunter rig with Sitka spruce spars can be hoisted quickly for exploring an anchorage.

Nesting dinghies are available commercially and for home construction in two, three, and four parts. For most people, a two-part design reduces the overall length enough to stow it abaft the mast and under the boom, which is all that's required of it (Figure 16-5). Because each part is in effect a separate boat, with its own "bow" and "transom," labor and materials escalate dramatically with each additional section.

To launch the dinghy, the larger part on top is lifted free and turned right side up. If it is too heavy to simply toss over the side with a painter attached, you can rig a bridle and use a halyard to lift the dinghy over the lifelines and drop it into the water. A halyard winch makes this a simple job. Once both parts are in the water, lower yourself into the larger and fasten the two together, usually with long machine bolts, washers, and nuts (Figure 16-6). To stow, just reverse the process. Remember, you need *two* painters!

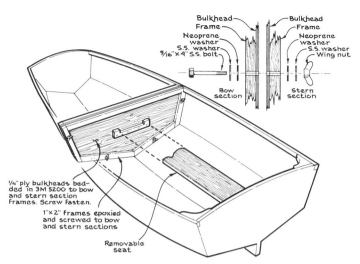

**FIGURE 16-6.** A simple method of quickly assembling nesting dinghies is the use of 6-inch (152 mm) bolts, washers, and wing nuts. The "bows" and "transoms" must be reinforced in these areas.

**FIGURE 16-5.** Our three-part Tryst design stowed under the boom of the Pearson Vanguard, and though it obscured visibility through the dodger window, we felt much safer knowing it was securely lashed on deck.

## STITCH-AND-TAPE CONSTRUCTION

Danny Greene (Offshore Design, P.O. Box 213, St. Georges, Bermuda GE BX) has expended a lot of energy in search of the perfect dinghy. He sells plans for several dinghy designs for amateur construction. As an itinerant cruiser, he's built them in backyards, in garages, and on beaches. Most have been nesting types, constructed of plywood using the stitch-and-tape method (a development of the stitch-and-glue method that was popular before the advent of fiberglass, in those dark ages when resorcinol was the superglue of yesteryear). The advantages are several: plywood is tough, cheap, and easy to work with; errors are fairly easy to disguise; and the average person can build a good, serviceable dinghy in a reasonable amount of time. The finished product won't look like a Herreshoff Columbia, but it will be a functional addition to your cruising gear that will reward you with years of good service.

Here's a summary of stitch-and-tape construction (Figure 16-7), based on Danny's three-part Tryst design I built some years ago. Scarf together two sheets of ¼-inch (6 mm), 4-foot by 8-foot (1.2 m by 2.4 m) exterior grade plywood (you can simply glass a narrow piece of plywood over the joint). From this, trace from the plan the lines of the various panels—bottom and sides—and cut out with a saber saw.

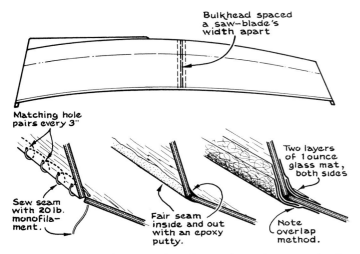

**FIGURE 16-7.** Stitch-and-tape plywood construction is ideal for the amateur who wants a rough, inexpensive dinghy without spending months of hard labor.

Set up the bulkheads (actually the bows and transoms) on a simple form to hold them in a vertical position, and temporarily screw the bottom panel to them. Bend the bottom, upside down, to give it some shape. Bend the topside panels around the sides of the bulkheads and temporarily hold them in place to the bottom and each other with Spanish windlasses.

There are four bulkheads for a three-part dinghy, fitted in pairs, one pair about 30% of the length aft from the bow, and the other pair about 80%. (This means the center section represents about 50% of the overall length.) Use wood spacers or nails to separate the pairs just enough so that when the boat is almost complete, you can saw the boat into thirds with a sabersaw.

At about 12-inch (305 mm) intervals, drill two holes in the bottom and sides, about ½ inch (12 mm) from the edge. Run copper wire through the two holes and twist it tight so the bottom and sides are held crudely in place. Once the shape is determined to be satisfactory, flip the boat right side up and fillet the seams (inside of the chines) with epoxy resin and a filler such as microballoons and Cab-O-Sil (refer back to Figure 2-9). The fillets cover the small pieces of wire showing on the inside. Once cured, this forms a temporary bond, which usually takes overnight.

Sand the fillet smooth and wet out two layers of fiberglass "tape" (actually the tape is just strips of chopped mat), making the second layer an inch or two wider than the first, and lay them over the seam. You can use polyester or epoxy resin, but

the latter is stronger and bonds better to wood. Since you'll use only a couple of gallons, the extra cost is nothing to worry about. After it has kicked, the structure is rigid and can be moved around without fear.

Flip the boat upside down again, snip off the twisted wire ends, plane the chine to a gentle radius, fill voids with epoxy putty, and cover with two layers of fiberglass tape.

Reinforce the gunwale with hardwood stock, about 1 inch by 2 inches (25 mm by 51 mm); glue it with epoxy; and fasten with screws. The boat can then be cut into thirds in the same manner that a magician cuts up his assistant in a box.

Use a grinder and electric sander to smooth all corners and rough patches of fiberglass. The boat can be left bare, or it can be painted; it's up to you. But the boat will be much stronger and more abrasion-resistant if you add a single covering of 6- or 10-ounce (200 g/m$^2$ or 330 g/m$^2$) fiberglass cloth. Unfortunately, this adds a lot of time and labor, and the weave also must be filled with fairing compound to give a smooth finished surface. A lot of sanding and fairing is required if you want a professional-looking job.

Screw some strakes to the bottom for directional stability while rowing and to function as sacrificial runners when dragging the boat over a rough beach.

Seats should be removable so they don't obstruct nesting one piece inside another. Danny's fore-and-aft seat in the center part works very well, leaving the bow and stern sections open for stores.

I finished the outside of *For Pete's Sake* with a two-part polyurethane paint, then screwed on a handsome rubber rub rail to protect the topsides of the big boat, as well as to absorb some of the force of the inevitable collisions with docks and pilings. A bronze towing eye and painter completed the job.

The three parts measured almost 16 feet (4.9 m) assembled (Figure 16-8), and though somewhat heavy (100-plus pounds/45 kg), it rowed with authority, carrying its way nicely. We left the third transom section home for our long cruise, since it towed too quickly, often passing us, and was that much more trouble to stow when brought on deck. Also, we found ourselves using the 6 hp Evinrude outboard much of the time, and it fit nicely on the transom of the second, center part. The bow and center sections measured about 12 feet (3.4 m), which is still much larger than the average dinghy carried on a 33-foot

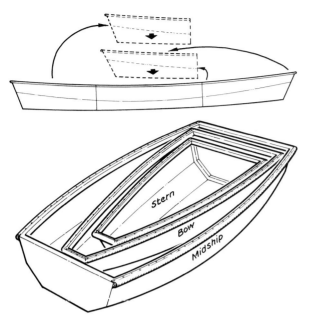

**FIGURE 16-8.** *For Pete's Sake* measured 16 feet (4.9 m) fully assembled. It rowed with authority and was eye-catching in any anchorage.

**FIGURE 16-9.** Without the smallest, third part, the transom stern of the middle section enabled us to motor with a 6 hp outboard at planing speeds. I wouldn't cruise without the capability of exploring reefs and shallow rivers quickly and comfortably.

(10 m) sailboat. I figure the whole job took me about 150 hours and cost $700.

In shallow-water cruising grounds such as the Florida Keys and Bahamas, we frequently were forced to anchor a long way from the shore, reefs, and other attractions we wished to visit. With the outboard (Figure 16-9), we were able to get the dinghy up on a plane and cover a few miles in a hurry—what a difference from rowing a 7-foot (2 m) pram, or even motoring a 7-foot pram with a 1.5 hp British Seagull outboard.

I felt pretty smug about my achievement, though no great skill had been required of me. *For Pete's Sake* enhanced our life aboard in many ways, and I would not have gone cruising without it.

## DINGHY STOWAGE

Offshore, dinghies cannot be towed behind the boat. Eventually, the strain on the painter will cause it to chafe and break. Similarly, stowing dinghies in davits hung over the stern invites disaster—one large wave washing over the transom could tear it away. And in a rolly anchorage, they are difficult to launch, especially by a single person. At the least, dinghies in davits should have strong canvas covers to keep them from filling with water.

Stowing dinghies on deck is safest, using through-bolted pad eyes with strong lashings over the upturned hull. On small boats, even a 7-foot dinghy is too large to stow on deck. And even if it can be wedged in somewhere, it could pose a danger to crew working on deck. Two-part nesting dinghies, described above, are the answer.

## FURTHER READING

*The Dinghy Book.* 2nd ed. Stan Grayson. Camden, Maine: International Marine, 1989.

# APPENDIX A

# Characteristics of Common Woods

## BASIC STRESSES FOR CLEAR LUMBER UNDER LONG-TIME SERVICE AT FULL DESIGN LOAD UNDER WET CONDITIONS

| Species | Extreme fiber in bending or tension parallel to grain | Maximum horizontal shear | Compression perpendicular to grain | Compression parallel to grain L/d = 11 or less | Modulus of elasticity in bending |
|---|---|---|---|---|---|
| 1 | 2 | 3 | 4 | 5 | 6 |
| | Psi | Psi | Psi | Psi | 1,000 psi |
| **SOFTWOODS** | | | | | |
| Bald cypress | 1,900 | 150 | 220 | 1,450 | 1,200 |
| Atlantic and northern white cedar | 1,100 | 100 | 130 | 750 | 800 |
| Douglas fir, coast type, medium-grain | 2,200 | 130 | 235 | 1,450 | 1,600 |
| Pine: | | | | | |
|     Eastern white, ponderosa, sugar, and western white | 1,300 | 120 | 185 | 1,000 | 1,000 |
|     Southern yellow | 2,200 | 160 | 235 | 1,450 | 1,600 |
| Spruce, red, white, and Sitka | 1,600 | 120 | 185 | 1,050 | 1,200 |
| **HARDWOODS** | | | | | |
| Ash, commercial white | 2,050 | 185 | 365 | 1,450 | 1,500 |
| Birch, sweet and yellow | 2,200 | 185 | 365 | 1,600 | 1,600 |
| Elm, American and slippery | 1,600 | 150 | 185 | 1,050 | 1,200 |
| Hickory, true and pecan | 2,800 | 205 | 440 | 2,000 | 1,800 |
| Mahogany | 2,200 | 175 | 450 | 1,500 | 1,300 |
| Maple, black and sugar | 2,200 | 185 | 365 | 1,600 | 1,600 |
| Oak | 2,050 | 185 | 365 | 1,350 | 1,500 |
| Teak | 2,750 | 200 | 600 | 1,900 | 1,600 |

## BASIC STRESSES FOR 1- AND 2-INCH NOMINAL CLEAR LUMBER UNDER LONG-TIME SERVICE AT FULL DESIGN LOAD UNDER DRY CONDITIONS

| Species | Extreme fiber in bending or tension parallel to grain | Maximum longitudinal shear | Compression perpendicular to grain | Compression parallel to grain | Modulus of elasticity in bending |
|---|---|---|---|---|---|
| 1 | 2 | 3 | 4 | 5 | 6 |
| | Psi | Psi | Psi | Psi | 1,000 psi |
| **SOFTWOODS** | | | | | |
| Cedar: | | | | | |
| Atlantic and northern white cedar | 1,400 | 115 | 195 | 1,050 | 900 |
| Douglas fir, coast type, medium-grain | 2,750 | 150 | 350 | 2,000 | 1,800 |
| Pine: | | | | | |
| Eastern white, ponderosa, sugar, and western white | 1,600 | 135 | 275 | 1,400 | 1,100 |
| Southern yellow | 2,750 | 180 | 350 | 2,000 | 1,800 |
| Spruce, red, white, and Sitka | 2,000 | 160 | 330 | 1,450 | 1,300 |
| **HARDWOOD** | | | | | |
| Ash, commercial white | 2,550 | 210 | 550 | 2,000 | 1,600 |
| Birch, sweet and yellow | 2,750 | 210 | 550 | 2,200 | 1,800 |
| Hickory, true and pecan | 3,500 | 235 | 660 | 2,750 | 2,000 |
| Mahogany | 2,750 | 200 | 675 | 2,050 | 1,400 |
| Maple, black and sugar | 2,750 | 210 | 550 | 2,200 | 1,800 |
| Oak | 2,550 | 210 | 550 | 1,850 | 1,600 |
| Teak | 3,450 | 230 | 900 | 2,600 | 1,800 |

# APPENDIX B

# Characteristics of Common Metals

## STAINLESS STEEL

Contrary to its name, stainless steel is not totally stainless. While there are many types of stainless steel, those of most interest to the sailor are alloys of iron, chromium and nickel. When chromium content exceeds 12%, corrosion resistance increases rapidly. Adding nickel, usually between 6 and 22%, improves resistance to acids.

Depending on the crystal structure of the alloy, stainless steels are grouped into three main types—*austentitic*, *ferritic*, and *martensitic*. There are many differences between them, but the most important for the majority of boatowners is that the marine grades used on boats are austenitic and are basically nonmagnetic. Ferritic and martensitic stainless steels are both magnetic, so it is often wise to test fasteners or gear with a magnet to determine that they are suitable for marine use.

Types 304 and 316 are the most widely used stainless steels for boats, with the latter preferred for its extra corrosion resistance obtained from small amounts of molybdenum. They may be used on deck exposed to the atmosphere, but should not be used underwater as they are subject to pitting corrosion. When they start to stain, you can wipe them down using dilute nitric acid, but rinse the deck first with water, then rinse again immediately after wiping down to prevent damage to other materials on the boat. Commercial cleaners also may be used.

Varieties of stainless steel such as Nitronic 50 (the steel Navtec uses for rod rigging and Universal uses for "Super Stainless" wire rigging—see Chapter 10) are stronger and less prone to tarnish than even Type 316. Nitronic 50 is quite expensive for many applications.

## COPPER, BRASS, AND BRONZE ALLOYS

Copper and nickel alloys are commonly used on boats for fittings, propeller shafts, and heavy gear castings. There are many variations, and only some are truly suitable for reliable service on the cruising boat.

Copper by itself is a soft metal with a long life span in the seawater environment. Though copper fasteners and sheathing on the bottom of wood sailing ships were once common, its use on boats today is largely limited to piping.

A copper and zinc alloy is called brass. Because it dezincifies in a marine environment (the zinc dissolves and leaves the copper soft and

These samples of rod were placed in warm salt water off North Carolina for 18 months with a rubber band around each. From left to right: Monel, 304 stainless steel, 316 stainless steel, and Nitronic 50 (a more corrosion-resistant form of stainless steel). The Monel was pitted everywhere except under the rubber band. The 304 and 316 sections were victims of crevice corrosion, while the Nitronic 50 was clean.

spongy), it should not be used for anything on deck—perhaps its best use is the ship's clock. Manganese bronze is actually a brass (60/40 copper to zinc) and therefore should not be used underwater, nor is it as wise a choice as some other metals above the water.

Bronze (zinc-free copper alloys using tin, aluminum, silicon, and nickel) is more corrosion resistant than brass. Gunmetal is an 88/12 alloy of copper and tin, though not as strong as aluminum bronze (90/10) and silicon bronze (96/4).

Copper-nickel alloys have been used to build boats that are reputedly free from bottom fouling due to organic growth. And although the alloys are quite strong, they are expensive. Monel, a proprietary name, is a copper-nickel alloy (70/30) and is both strong and corrosion resistant. It is frequently used for fuel tanks and propeller shafts.

Because copper alloys tarnish to a dirty green color in sea air, fittings and other finished objects are often plated with chromium. A good chrome job provides excellent protection against corrosion and tarnish, but it's not always easy to come by. The process involves several critical steps that must be done correctly to be effective. For instance, if the chrome layer exceeds 0.00001 inch, it may develop cracks. In his book, *Metal Corrosion in Boats*, Nigel Warren says that while regularly rubbing with an oily or waxed cloth will prolong its life, you usually have to buy on trust. Warren advises it isn't worth the risk.

## ALUMINUM

Some aluminum alloys are well suited for boats. They are light weight (about one-third the density of steel and copper), strong enough when engineered properly, and corrosion resistant. The corrosion resistance is the result of a white oxide film that develops on the bare metal when it is exposed to the oxygen in air or water. While not exactly pleasing in appearance, this film prevents aluminum from literally melting in seawater.

Aluminum can be cast (poured into a mold), wrought (forced into shape), rolled (pressed into plates), and extruded (pushed through a die to form a section such as a mast). Different alloys are used for each method of shaping aluminum. Aluminum is combined with magnesium, manganese, or silicon to produce marine-grade alloys.

If the white powder is removed from oxidized aluminum, the oxidization process begins again on the exposed surfaces. While this is not necessarily harmful, it is customary to anodize or paint aluminum for a smooth, corrosion-free surface. Anodizing is done by submerging the metal in a chemical bath and running an electrical charge through it. It is falling from favor, as the chemical bath is toxic and expensive to dispose of properly. Aluminum must be etched with a mild chemical wash (even vinegar works) before painting, but paint does last well on it. A chip in the paint won't cause the metal underneath to start rusting as with steel. On aluminum boats, bottom paints containing lead, mercury, or copper should never be used because the metals are galvanically incompatible (see Galvanic Series). Aluminum corrodes rapidly when in contact with more noble metals. Many spinnaker poles have cast aluminum jaws with stainless steel pistons—the result: galvanic action between these dissimilar metals causes pitting corrosion, which in short work makes the pistons impossible to open or close without mechanical advantage (hammers, Vise-Grips, screwdrivers). Larry Pardey has suggested that in these instances the piston surfaces be filed down so that the fit is actually sloppy.

If it is necessary to use stainless steel or bronze fastenings with aluminum, always insulate the fastener from direct contact with the aluminum. Use a bedding compound coating on the threads, under the head, and on the plastic tubing over the threads, or insert a plastic washer to prevent the fastener head from touching the surface (most appropriate when screwing through a thin layer of aluminum into wood or other material).

## STEEL AND IRON

Steel and iron are both manufactured from the same ore, but steel has less than 1.7% carbon added, iron has more. Both tend to rust rapidly in the marine environment, but their low price and high strength have encouraged boatbuilders to devise methods of protecting the metals to make them viable for boats.

The Dutch have been building boats in steel for over a century, while in North America steel has enjoyed, at best, a lukewarm reception among cruising people, despite possessing the ultimate protection against holing. Mild steel and Cor-Ten (with 0.5% copper and 0.6% chromium added) are both used for boatbuilding; the mill scale is removed by shotblasting, the surface is covered with

# GALVANIC SERIES OF METALS IN SEAWATER
## *METALS AND ALLOYS*

Anodic or Least Noble (Active)     Cathodic or Most Noble (Passive)

| Metals and Alloys | Range of Corrosion Potential (relative to silver/silver chloride half cell; volts) |
|---|---|
| Magnesium and Magnesium Alloys | –1.60 to –1.63 |
| Zinc | –0.98 to –1.03 |
| Galvanized Steel or Galvanized Wrought Iron | N/A |
| Aluminum Alloys | –0.76 to –1.00 |
| Cadmium | –0.70 to –0.73 |
| Mild Steel | –0.60 to –0.71 |
| Wrought Iron | –0.60 to –0.71 |
| Cast Iron | –0.60 to –0.71 |
| 13% Chromium Stainless Steel, Type 410 (active in still water) | –0.46 to –0.58 |
| 18-8 Stainless Steel, Type 304 (active in still water) | –0.46 to –0.58 |
| Ni-Resist | –0.46 to –0.58 |
| 18-8, 3% Mo Stainless Steel, Type 316 (active in still water) | –0.43 to –0.54 |
| 78% Ni/13.5% Cr/6% Fe (Inconel) (active in still water) | –0.35 to –0.46 |
| Aluminum Bronze (92% Cu/8% Al) | –0.31 to –0.42 |
| Naval Brass (60% Cu/39% Zn) | –0.30 to –0.40 |
| Yellow Brass (65% Cu/35% Zn) | –0.30 to –0.40 |
| Red Brass (85% Cu/15% Zn) | –0.30 to –0.40 |
| Muntz Metal (60% Cu/40% Zn) | –0.30 to –0.40 |
| Tin | –0.31 to –0.33 |
| Copper | –0.30 to –0.57 |
| 50-50 Lead/Tin Solder | –0.28 to –0.37 |
| Admiralty Brass (71% Cu/28% Zn/1% Sn) | –0.28 to –0.36 |
| Aluminum Brass (76% Cu/22% Zn/2% Al) | –0.28 to –0.36 |
| Manganese Bronze (58.5% Cu/39% Zn/1% Sn/1% Fe/0.3% Mn) | –0.27 to –0.34 |
| Silicon Bronze (96% Cu max./0.8% Fe/1.50% Zn/2.0% Si/0.75% Mn/1.60% Sn) | –0.26 to –0.29 |
| Bronze Composition G (88% Cu/2% Zn/10% Sn) | –0.24 to –0.31 |
| Bronze Composition M (88% Cu/3% Zn/6.5% Sn/1.5% Pb) | –0.24 to –0.31 |
| 13% Chromium Stainless Steel, Type 410 (passive) | –0.26 to –0.35 |
| 90% Cu/10% Ni | –0.21 to –0.28 |
| 75% Cu/20% Ni/5% Zn | –0.19 to –0.25 |
| Lead | –0.19 to –0.25 |
| 70% Cu/30% Ni | –0.18 to –0.23 |
| 78% Ni/13.5% Cr/6% Fe (Inconel) (passive) | –0.14 to –0.17 |
| Nickel 200 | –0.10 to –0.20 |
| 18-8 Stainless Steel, Type 304 (passive) | –0.05 to –0.10 |
| 70% Ni/30% Cu Monel 400, K-500 | –0.04 to –0.14 |
| 18-8, 3% Mo Stainless Steel, Type 316 (passive) | 0.00 to –0.10 |
| Titanium | –0.05 to +0.06 |
| Hastelloy C | –0.03 to +0.08 |
| Platinum | +0.19 to +0.25 |
| Graphite | +0.20 to +0.30 |

a self-etching primer, and a durable painting system is used as a finishing coating.

As with other metals, water passing over steel increases its corrosion rate. In still seawater, mild steel deteriorates at a rate of about 5 millimeters a year. Protected, it can virtually be brought to a halt.

Galvanizing is the most common method of protecting steel and iron gear. This process involves dipping the metal into molten zinc; it is much more effective than electroplating (usually done with cadmium), largely because of the greater thickness of the coating and the self-healing nature of zinc.

Before the development of stainless steels, galvanized wire rigging was common, but required periodic varnishing or wiping with linseed oil to prevent corrosion. There is still a place for galvanized steel on cruising boats, such as anchor chain and windlass housings, but for the most part it has been displaced on board by stainless steel, bronze, and aluminum.

# Good Old Boats

As a sailing magazine editor, perhaps the most common question I'm asked by readers is whether such and such a make is suitable for offshore work. Most people have difficulty making this determination for themselves, which must mean that the difference between a boat built for coastal sailing and one built for blue-water voyaging isn't obvious. With a little courage and a lot of luck, you can take just about any boat offshore, but to be safe and comfortable in big seas and high winds requires a boat of good design and solid construction.

In the following pages I discuss some of the production boats I consider qualified for crossing oceans. That doesn't mean they're ready to go right out of the box (most are older and left their boxes behind years ago), just that their basic design and structure are good foundations for fitting out for cruising. And certainly this list isn't all inclusive, so just because your favorite boat isn't here doesn't mean it won't make a good cruiser.

If you're curious as to the criteria I used to screen the hundreds of models, you might go back and review Chapter 1, but since this topic bears repeating, here's the short list:

- Sufficient displacement to carry the necessary water, fuel, and stores.
- Seaworthy bottom shape (i.e., not too flat).
- Well-stayed rig with easily balanced and shortened sail plan.
- Bulkheads tabbed to deck, not wedged into molded slot in headliner (this eliminates many boats!).
- Loads from externally ballasted keel well distributed by strong stringers, and floors bonded to the hull bottom, not just keel bolts passing through the hull bottom only.

- Strong rudder (find out what's inside) and stock.
- Interior furniture well bonded to hull.
- Hull-deck joint through-bolted, not screwed. Some newer boats have a structural adhesive such as Plexus in lieu of fasteners, and this, if applied properly, is very strong.

Other features, like strong stanchions and lifelines, handholds, sturdy cleats, big battery bank, and windlass can be retrofitted.

The joy of sailing begins with looking at boats. So enjoy, because once you make your pick, the real work begins.

## ALLIED BOAT COMPANY

Founded in 1962 in Catskill, New York, Allied built several classic designs back when "name" designers were used instead of the anonymous in-house designers of today. These included the Thomas Gilmer–designed Seawind 30 ketch (1962–1975), the first fiberglass boat to circumnavigate (1963–1969); the Luders 33 (1966), in which Robin Lee Graham finished his historic circumnavigation; the Seabreeze 35 (1964) by Frank MacLear and Bob Harris (sloop or yawl); and the Princess 36 (1972) and Mistress 39 (1971) by Art Edmonds. The Greenwich 24, which later became the Cape Dory 25, is narrow, tender, and not a good boat for cruising. The Chance 30-30 (1971) and XL-2 (1968) are racers.

Allied boats have basically sturdy construction with bulkheads tabbed to the deck. Many are full-keel designs with internal ballast. But I'd be leery of any boat built in the 1960s; nothing lasts forever, including fiberglass. After thirty-five to forty years, the deck core may be wet and separated from the fiberglass skins on either side. This is called delamination, and when widespread, it is too time consuming and therefore too expensive to be worth fixing on most production boats.

The electrical, plumbing, and mechanical systems on boats this old will also require upgrading—doable, but again, a lot of work. The interiors are plain but amenable to a decorator's touch. Paint, varnish, and new upholstery go a long way toward reviving any older boat.

When boat hunting, consider tankage: how much fuel and water can she carry? If not enough, where might you add tanks? (Refer back to Figure 5-1.)

And what about battery capacity? Today's cruiser wants more energy-hogging stuff—like an electric windlass, electronic chart plotter, television, maybe even electric winches—and that means 500 to 800 amp-hours in the house bank. Where will you fit three or four 4Ds?

Among the Allied fleet, it's hard not to admire the tough little Seawind, and its remake, the Seawind II; there's not a lot of room inside, but all the basics are there. And the ketch rig makes them easily balanced, especially with reefed or no main, jib, and mizzen. The Seabreeze is perhaps the prettiest, with the classic sheer and overhangs typical of the CCA rule. The Princess 36 is a stout cruiser but slow. Same for the Mistress, one of the earliest center-cockpit designs. For blue water, she'd be my choice.

## Seawind 30

| | |
|---|---|
| LOA | 30' 6" (9.3 m) |
| LWL | 24' 0" (7.3 m) |
| Beam | 9' 3" (2.8 m) |
| Draft | 4' 2" (1.3 m) |
| Displacement | 12,080 lbs. (5,477 kg) |
| Ballast | 4,200 lbs. (1,904 kg) |
| Sail area | 500 sq. ft./46.5 m² (ketch)<br>462 sq. ft./43 m² (sloop) |

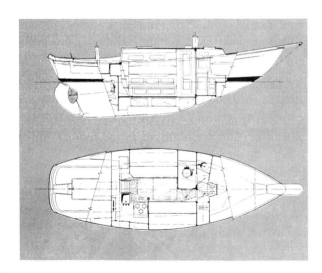

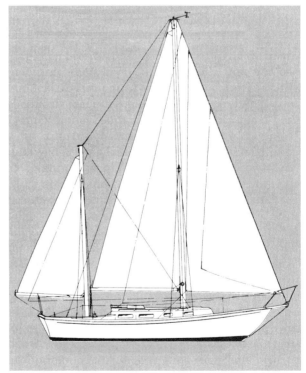

## Seabreeze 35

| | |
|---|---|
| LOA | 34' 6" (10.5 m) |
| LWL | 24' 0" (7.3 m) |
| Beam | 10' 3" (3.1 m) |
| Draft | 3' 10"/1.2 m (centerboard up) |
| Displacement | 13,000 lbs. (5,894 kg) |
| Ballast | 4,000 lbs. (1,814 kg) |
| Sail area | 550 sq. ft./51 m² (sloop) |
| | 575 sq. ft./53 m² (yawl) |

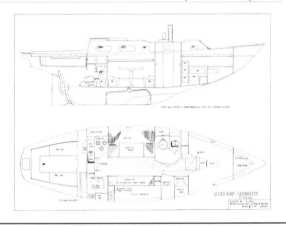

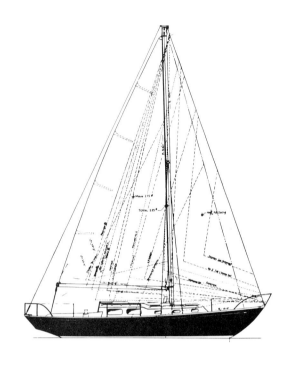

## Princess 36

| | |
|---|---|
| LOA | 36' 0" (11 m) |
| LWL | 27' 6" (8.4 m) |
| Beam | 11' 0" (3.4 m) |
| Draft | 4' 6" (1.4 m) |
| Displacement | 14,400 lbs. (6,529 kg) |
| Ballast | 5,000 lbs. (2,267 kg) |
| Sail area | 595 sq. ft./55 m² (sloop) |
| | 605 sq. ft./56 m² (ketch) |

## Mistress 39

| | |
|---|---|
| LOA | 38' 7" (11.8 m) |
| LWL | 29' 10" (9.1 m) |
| Beam | 12' 0" (3.7 m) |
| Draft | 4' 6" (1.4 m) |
| Displacement | 20,800 lbs. (9,431 kg) |
| Ballast | 5,600 lbs. (2,539 kg) |
| Sail area | 700 sq. ft./65 m² (ketch) |

# BRISTOL YACHTS

Cousins Clint and Everett Pearson founded Pearson Yachts in 1956. When they sold it to Grumman Allied Industries in 1964, Clint left and bought a small Rhode Island company called Sailstar. This evolved into Bristol Yachts, and the early boats were very similar to the Pearsons that Clint left behind. One was the lovely 22-foot 6-inch (6.9 m) Sea Sprite, designed by Carl Alberg, who'd done the Triton for Pearson Yachts, and later, the Cape Dorys for Andrew Vavolotis. By 1966 he offered the Bristol 27, 29, 32, 33, 35, and 39 by designers Alberg, Ted Hood, Halsey Herreshoff, and John Alden. The boats were structurally sound but—typical of that time—rather plain.

Around 1980 Clint Pearson decided to upscale his line, realizing you can make more money building a few big, expensive boats than dozens of small, cheap boats. Early models of this new era were the Bristol 35.5 and 45.5, followed by the 54.4 (1984), 60 (1987), and the 41.1, 47.7, 51.1, 65.5, and 72 (1988). The company was in and out of financial trouble for much of the 1980s and early 1990s, finally going down for the count in 1998.

Many of the Hood designs, like the 35.5 and 38.8, were offered with both fixed keels and keel/centerboard options, the public often favoring the latter for shoal-water cruising. Keel/cb boats, however, are more tender and hence not as good for offshore sailing. In fact, some skippers refuse to lower the board offshore for fear of damage coming off a wave.

All the boats of the 1980s and on were very well built, with lots of man-hours expended on detailed teak and mahogany interiors. Bulkheads were Brunzeel plywood, far superior to conventional plywood. Opening portlights improve ventilation.

Among the older designs, the Bristol 24 Corsair (1975) is one of the shippiest little boats ever built. The designer was Paul Coble, a master boatbuilder of the wooden boat era, and one of the first to professionalize the marine surveyor. The 32 (1966) is comparable to the Pearson Vanguard, though designed by Ted Hood rather than Philip Rhodes. Another classic Bristol is the 40, a Ted Hood design (1970). A development of the Bristol 39 (1966), the 40 has a long straight keel with attached rudder and beautiful overhangs.

## Bristol 24 Corsair

| | |
|---|---|
| LOA | 24' 7" (7.5 m) |
| LWL | 18' 1" (5.5 m) |
| Beam | 8' 0" (2.4 m) |
| Draft | 3' 5" (1 m) |
| Displacement | 5,920 lbs. (2,684 kg) |
| Ballast | 2,500 lbs. (762 kg) |
| Sail area | 296 sq. ft. (28 m²) |

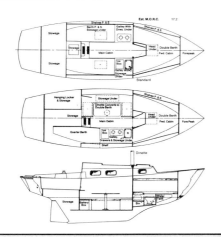

## Bristol 32

| | |
|---|---|
| LOA | 32' 1" (9.8 m) |
| LWL | 22' 0" (6.7 m) |
| Beam | 9' 5" (2.9 m) |
| Draft | 4' 7" (1.4 m) |
| Displacement | 10,800 lbs. (4,897 kg) |
| Ballast | 3,300 lbs. (1,496 kg) |
| Sail area | 505 sq. ft./47 m² (yawl) |

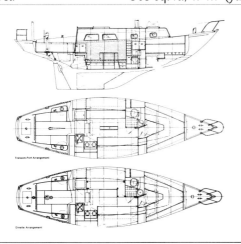

## Bristol 35.5

| | |
|---|---|
| LOA | 35' 6" (10.8 m) |
| LWL | 27' 6" (8.4 m) |
| Beam | 10' 10" (3.3 m) |
| Draft | 3' 9" to 5' 9" (1.1 m to 1.8 m) |
| Displacement | 15,000 lbs. (6,801 kg) |
| Ballast | 6,500 lbs. (2,947 kg) |
| Sail area | 589 sq. ft. (55 m²) |

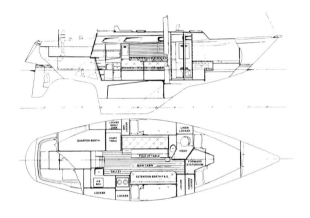

## Bristol 38.8

| | |
|---|---|
| LOA | 38' 3" (11.7 m) |
| LWL | 30' 7" (9.3 m) |
| Beam | 12' 1" (3.7 m) |
| Draft | 4' 6" to 10' 3" (1.4 m to 3.1 m) |
| Displacement | 19,150 lbs. (8,683 kg) |
| Ballast | 9,000 lbs. (4,081 kg) |
| Sail area | 766 sq. ft. (71 m²) |

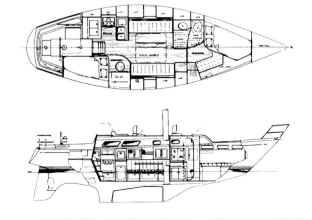

# CALIBER YACHTS

Brothers Michael and George McCreary founded this company in 1980. Based in Clearwater, Florida, Michael designs the boats and George handles the business end of things. Their first boat was the Caliber 28, followed by a succession of others, on up to the present Caliber 47 LRC. All of their boats are called LRC now, which stands for Long Range Cruiser.

Here's what I like about these boats: all bulkheads quadruple taped to the hull and deck, doubled elsewhere. When Robbie Robinson test sailed this boat for *Practical Sailor*, he called it "among the quietest boats we've sailed. In 5-foot Buzzard's Bay slop, the creaks and groans that can come with torquing and pounding in a seaway were absent." That's at least partly due to the taping mentioned above, in lieu of a huge fiberglass interior pan. The 33, at least, has a plywood deck core, rather than the usual balsa. Plywood core doesn't have to be removed in way of hardware, but it's heavier than balsa core, and god forbid it should ever get wet. (A new synthetic core called Core-Cell is now being used by a few builders in decks, and if it has the requisite stiffness and resistance to delamination, it will solve the age-old bugaboo of deck rot and delamination in fiberglass boats.)

I also like the appendages on most Calibers: a moderately large cruising fin with straight, horizontal run on the bottom, so the boat can stand up on its own when careened, and a skeg-mounted rudder. A well-built skeg (must have structural members, like steel, well secured into the hull) protects the rudder, adds directional stability, and helps prevent stalling.

The styling of the Calibers is somewhat unique. Robinson on the 33: "The sheerline, house crown, house edge, and cockpit coamings are, in designer McCreary's profile drawing and sail plan, dead straight. The real boat, however, is not as angular as the blueprint. Trim, accents, curved toe rails, stripes, and refraction all bend and soften those knife-edges; the boat has a 'sharp' look and (because most sailboats depend on fair curves for their appeal) the 33 is distinctive." Couldn't have said it any better myself.

This feature is interesting because fiberglass doesn't lend itself well to sharp edges, which is why so many boats have rounded corners. More than one builder and designer has lamented this as a loss: wooden boats can have sharp edges, giving them an elegant look not possible with boats poured from a drum into a mold. Caliber, for one, has made an admirable attempt to reclaim this classic look.

## Caliber 35

| LOA | 35' 9" (10.9 m) |
|---|---|
| LWL | 29' 10" (9.1 m) |
| Beam | 11' 4" (3.5 m) |
| Draft | 4' 6" (1.4 m) |
| Displacement | 13,100 lbs. (5,940 kg) |
| Ballast | 6,100 lbs. (2,766 kg) |
| Sail area | 563 sq. ft. (52 m²) |

## Caliber 38

| | |
|---|---|
| LOA | 38' 0" (11.6 m) |
| LWL | 32' 0" (9.8 m) |
| Beam | 12' 8" (3.8 m) |
| Draft | 4' 6" (1.4 m) |
| Displacement | 18,500 lbs. (8,388 kg) |
| Ballast | 9,500 lbs. (4,304 kg) |
| Sail area | N/A |

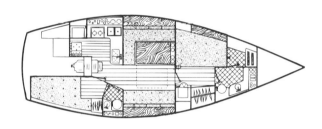

## Caliber 40

| | |
|---|---|
| LOA | 40' 11" (12.5 m) |
| LWL | 32' 6" (9.9 m) |
| Beam | 12' 8" (3.9 m) |
| Draft | 5' 0" (1.5 m) |
| Displacement | 21,600 lbs. (9,793 kg) |
| Ballast | 9,500 lbs. (4,307 kg) |
| Sail area | 739 sq. ft. (69 m$^2$) |

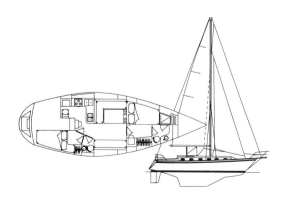

## Caliber 47*

| | |
|---|---|
| LOA | 51' 10" (15.8 m) |
| LWL | 36' 2" (11 m) |
| Beam | 13' 2" (4 m) |
| Draft | 5' 3" (1.6 m) |
| Displacement | 32,000 lbs. (14,509 kg) |
| Ballast | 14,000 lbs. (6,348 kg) |
| Sail area | 940 sq. ft. (87 m²) |

*Newer models of the 47 have slightly different specifications.

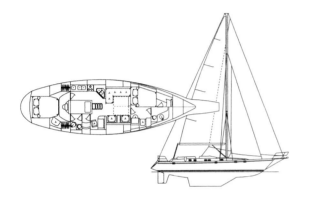

# CAPE DORY YACHTS

Andrew Vavolotis left Boston Whaler in 1962 to found Cape Dory Yachts. His first boats were sailing dinghies, followed by the Cape Dory 25, a resurrection of the Greenwich 24 originally built by the Allied Boat Company. As noted in that section, it's narrow and tender.

The boats that established the company were all designed by Carl Alberg: The Cape Dory 27, 28, 30, 31, 33, 36, 40, and 45. The 28 lacks the beauty of the others, and the 30 is smallish. Vavolotis told me once that with every new design he begged Alberg to give him more beam so he could add more interior. Alberg sternly replied that adding more than an inch or two simply wasn't right, and that if Vavolotis didn't like it, he could find another designer. That sort of interchange doesn't happen between builders and in-house designers on the company payroll, and I think that's too bad. Today's boat designs are driven by the marketing people, who react to the tire kickers at boat shows who ooh and aah at the interior, with no regard for sailing ability or seaworthiness.

Though dated by today's trends in yacht design, the Cape Dorys are excellent sea boats. Like other CCA-type boats, they heel easily to 15 to 20°, then bury their shoulders and become rock solid. The long overhangs immerse and sailing length is increased, adding speed. All have full keels with attached rudders, almost a thing of the past, but nevertheless good for cruising: internal ballast can't fall off, the boats can be careened against a seawall for maintenance, they track well (hold a course without a lot of hand steering), and the rudder and prop are protected.

While not fancy down below, there's a generous amount of teak that looks great varnished. As noted, they are not beamy boats, which is one reason why I prefer the larger models.

Cape Dory also built a few models of another line called Intrepid (35 and 40), but not many were built.

Cape Dory shut its doors in the late 1980s and Vavolotis moved to Maine where he opened a yard in Robinhood. Eventually he was able to reacquire the molds to the Cape Dory 36, which he resumed building as the Robinhood 36. I haven't seen one but if it's anything like the original, it would make a very good cruising boat.

## Cape Dory 33

| | |
|---|---|
| LOD | 33' ½" (10 m) |
| LWL | 24' 6" (7.5 m) |
| Beam | 10' 3" (3.1 m) |
| Draft | 4' 10" (1.5 m) |
| Displacement | 13,300 lbs. (6,032 kg) |
| Ballast | 5,500 lbs. (2,494 kg) |
| Sail area | 546 sq. ft. (51 m²) |

## Cape Dory 36

| | |
|---|---|
| LOD | 36' 1½" (11 m) |
| LWL | 27' 0" (8.2 m) |
| Beam | 10' 8" (3.2 m) |
| Draft | 5' 0" (1.5 m) |
| Displacement | 16,100 lbs. (7,300 kg) |
| Ballast | 6,050 lbs. (2,743 kg) |
| Sail area | 622 sq. ft. (58 m²) |

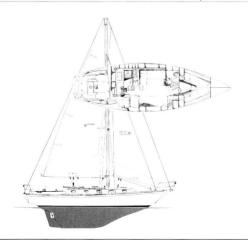

## Cape Dory 40

| | |
|---|---|
| LOD | 40' 2" (12.2 m) |
| LWL | 30' 0" (9.1 m) |
| Beam | 11' 8" (3.6 m) |
| Draft | 5' 8" (1.7 m) |
| Displacement | 19,500 lbs. (8,841 kg) |
| Ballast | 7,600 lbs. (3,446 kg) |
| Sail area | 776 sq. ft. (72 m²) |

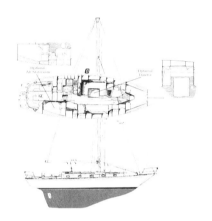

## Cape Dory 45

| | |
|---|---|
| LOD | 45' 3" (13.8 m) |
| LWL | 33' 6" (10.2 m) |
| Beam | 13' 0" (4 m) |
| Draft | 6' 3" (1.9 m) |
| Displacement | 24,000 lbs. (10,881 kg) |
| Ballast | 9,400 lbs. (4,262 kg) |
| Sail area | 936 sq. ft./87 m² (ketch) |
| | 882 sq. ft./82 m² (cutter) |

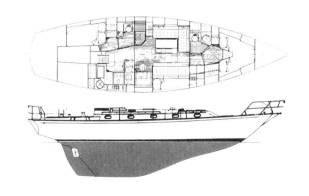

# FREEDOM YACHTS

No one in sailing has spent more time thinking outside the box than Garry Hoyt, a former ad and marketing exec turned yacht designer and inventor. Dismayed by what he perceived racing rules like the IOR (International Offshore Rule) were doing to yacht design, in the late 1970s he developed the Freedom 40—a cat ketch with unstayed spars and no engine. To draw attention, he challenged anyone to a race, putting up a purse of $5,000. There were no takers.

Commercial versions of the boat did have engines, but the unstayed spars found appeal in enough sailors to spawn an entire line of boats, ranging from 21 to 65 feet (6.4 m to 29.8 m). Hoyt designed some of them; later, Gary Mull, Ron Holland, and David Pedrick took turns. First built by TPI in Warren, Rhode Island, construction was later moved to an independent site on Narragansett Bay. The company is still in business, but mostly builds Legacy Down East–style express powerboats.

The Freedom line can be thought of as subdividing into the two generations alluded to above: the original cat ketches by Hoyt and the later "cat sloops" by other designers. Quality of construction is consistent throughout.

The original boats had sleeved sails that provided for smoother airflow around the mast, but were harder to reef and eventually discarded. Another innovation, found mostly on the Freedom 21, 25, and 32, is the Hoyt Gun Mount, which allows setting and dousing a spinnaker from the cockpit. Because the spinnaker is attached at both clews, you can actually sail the boat in circles without touching the sheets—I know, I've done it. This really takes the tension out of flying the kite, a real boon for downwind family sailing.

The underwater configuration of these small boats—fin keel and spade rudder—doesn't suggest blue water, but in fact several have made successful ocean passages. Among them, a 25 was sailed from California to Hawaii, and a 32 from Florida to Europe.

The 40 as originally configured has a large cockpit that holds too much water for offshore sailing, but the 44 improved on this and other aspects of the design, including a more efficient fin keel in place of the long, shallow keel of the 40. In the late 1990s, a Freedom 44 won the Bermunda One-Two. A 33 has regularly campaigned that race, too. In reaching conditions, the cat ketch rig excels. The 44 would be my choice for long-distance cruising, but for coastal, the 32 is a tidy package.

## Freedom 25

| | |
|---|---|
| LOA | 25' 0" (7.6 m) |
| LWL | 20' 0" (6.1 m) |
| Beam | 8' 5" (2.6 m) |
| Draft | 4' 5" (1.3 m) |
| Displacement | 3,800 lbs. (1,721 kg) |
| Ballast | 1,025 lbs. (464 kg) |
| Sail area | 260 sq. ft. (24 m²) |

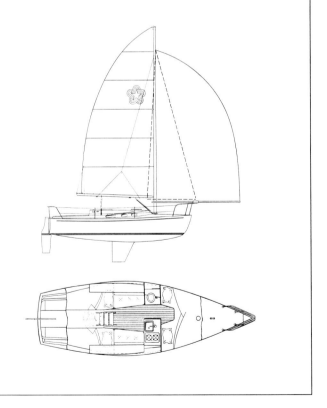

## Freedom 33

| | |
|---|---|
| LOA | 33' 0" (10.1 m) |
| LWL | 30' 0" (9.1 m) |
| Beam | 11' 0" (3.4 m) |
| Draft | 3' 6" to 6' 0" (1.1 m to 1.8 m) |
| Displacement | 12,000 lbs. (3,658 kg) |
| Ballast | 3,800 lbs. (1,723 kg) |
| Sail area | 516 sq. ft. (48 m²) |

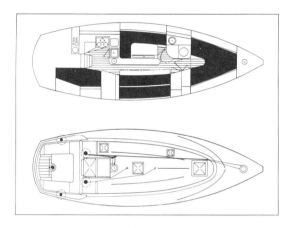

## Freedom 40

| | |
|---|---|
| LOA | 40' 0" (12.2 m) |
| LWL | 35' 0" (10.7 m) |
| Beam | 12' 0" (3.7 m) |
| Draft | 3' 4" to 6' 6" (1 m to 2 m) |
| Displacement | 20,000 lbs. (6,096 kg) |
| Ballast | 6,000 lbs. (1,829 kg) |
| Sail area | 784 sq. ft. (73 m²) |

## Freedom 44

| | |
|---|---|
| LOA | 44' 0" (13.4 m) |
| LWL | 39' 6" (12 m) |
| Beam | 12' 0" (3.7 m) |
| Draft | 6' 0" (1.8 m) |
| Displacement | 25, 000 lbs. (11,325 kg) |
| Ballast | N/A |
| Sail area | N/A |

## Hinterhoeller Yachts

Master builder George Hinterhoeller emigrated from Austria to Canada in 1952. First working in wood, he was shown how to laminate a fiberglass hull in a mold by a friend and was blown away. He went on to become one of the leading builders and innovators of fiberglass boats and their construction methods. He was a key player in C&C Yachts during the 1970s, but went back on his own in 1975. Among the boats he built that are of interest here are the Nonsuch line of catboats, and the Niagara sloops, all designed by Canadian Mark Ellis, with the exception of the Niagara 31, which was penned by German Frers.

The Nonsuch boats were the brainchild of Canadian sailor Gordon Fisher, who like Garry Hoyt, believed sailing could be made simpler. He commissioned Ellis to design a traditional catboat with modern underbody. Production eventually totaled 1,000 Nonsuch 22s, 26s, 30s, 324s, 33s, and 36s. These are coastal cruising boats, not intended for offshore. The reason is not construc-

tion, which is quite good and why I've included them in this book, but because of the lack of versatility of the sail plan. As a *Practical Sailor* review pointed out, "Whether it blows five knots or 25, the maximum amount of sail you can have is already up." That, of course, is also its virtue: no sail changes, and tacking requires just turning the wheel. No grinding winches.

The Niagara 31, 35, and 42 are good, solid cruising boats, especially the bigger two with their long, cruising fin keels. Generous beam provides good volume below. The 35 has a somewhat unusual accommodation plan with workbench and stowage in the forepeak and owner's stateroom and head aft.

Hinterhoeller was a leader in balsa sandwich construction, which makes for a lighter, stiffer hull than a solid, single skin hull, although this doesn't necessarily mean they are stronger. Abrasion resistance will be less simply because there is less structural glass, a factor to consider for people venturing to remote regions of the world. Also, cored hulls are more difficult to repair.

## Nonsuch 36

| | |
|---|---|
| LOA | 36' 0" (11 m) |
| LWL | 33' 9" (10.3 m) |
| Beam | 12' 8" (3.9 m) |
| Draft | 5' 6" (1.7 m) |
| Displacement | 17,000 lbs. (7,708 kg) |
| Ballast | N/A |
| Sail area | 742 sq. ft. (69 m²) |

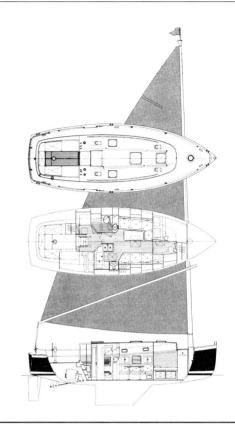

## Niagara 31

| | |
|---|---|
| LOA | 31' 3" (9.5 m) |
| LWL | 24' 3" (7.4 m) |
| Beam | 10' 3" (3.1 m) |
| Draft | 5' 0" (1.5 m) |
| Displacement | 8,500 lbs. (3,854 kg) |
| Ballast | 3,550 lbs. (1,610 kg) |
| Sail area | 492 sq. ft. (46 m²) |

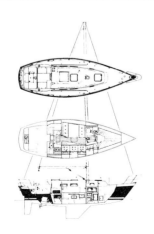

## Niagara 35

| | |
|---|---|
| LOA | 35' 1" (10.7 m) |
| LWL | 26' 8" (3.6 m) |
| Beam | 11' 5" (3.5 m) |
| Draft | 5' 2" (1.6 m) |
| Displacement | 14,000 lbs. (6,348 kg) |
| Ballast | 5,500 lbs. (2,494 kg) |
| Sail area | 598 sq. ft. (56 m²) |

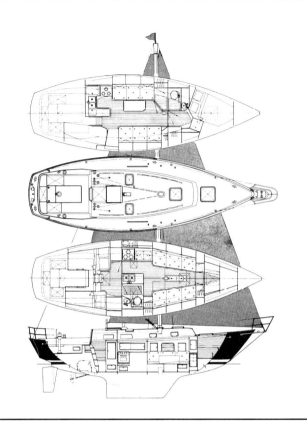

## Niagara 42

| | |
|---|---|
| LOA | 42' 2" (12.9 m) |
| LWL | 32' 6" (9.9 m) |
| Beam | 12' 9" (3.9 m) |
| Draft | 5' 8" (1.7 m) |
| Displacement | 19,800 lbs. (8,977 kg) |
| Ballast | 8,100 lbs. (2,469 kg) |
| Sail area | 850 sq. ft. (79 m²) |

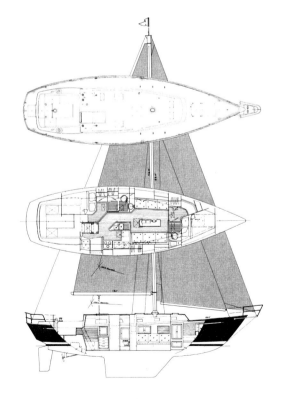

## PACIFIC SEACRAFT

Henry Mohrschladt and Mike Howarth quit their jobs in 1975, built a 25-footer to Henry's design, and exhibited it at that year's Newport Beach boat show. Mohrschladt had to sell his car to buy the cushions. Thirteen years later they were recognized by *Fortune* magazine as making one of America's top 100 products. Their line of cruising sailboats ranged from 20 to 44 feet (6 m to 13.4 m), and included the Dana 24 (1985), Pacific Seacraft 25 (1978), Orion 27 (1980), Mariah 31 (1979), Bruce Bingham's Flicka (1979) pocket cruiser, and a number of blue-water Bill Crealock designs—the 31 (1987), 34 (1984), 37 (1980), and 44 (1990).

The founding partners (who sold the company in 1988, took a month's rest, then started another company building sportfishermen) like to use a lot of fiberglass parts in their boats. This practice has advantages and disadvantages, to my mind at least. Advantages include more consistent quality than individually hand-fitted wood parts, great strength if properly designed and bonded to the hull or other structure, and resistance to rot. Disadvantages are that fiberglass pans are poor thermal and acoustic insulators (meaning they tend to be colder and noisier), they condense moisture inside, and they make it nearly impossible to make modifications to the interior. That said, Howarth is very proud of his tooling and is a firm believer in substituting fiberglass molded parts for wooden ones. In the Pacific Seacraft line, the cabin soles are fiberglass with wood floorboards. The berth foundations also are fiberglass, with teak trim. I prefer plywood, but do believe that the Pacific Seacraft boats, of the 1980s anyway, were well built. I haven't been aboard a boat built by the new owners.

A word about canoe sterns. While some devotees tout their so-called ability to part following seas (Robert Perry calls it the "Moses theory"), a round stern is really more of a styling element than anything else. Drawn well, they look nice, and Crealock has done a fine job with these boats. But there is a drawback, and that is the absence of an afterdeck. Of course, any boat with the cockpit pushed right to the stern has the same problem. And it is this: What little area there is outside the cockpit is cluttered with hardware such as cleats, chocks, and flagstaffs. Add bimini and dodger frames and getting in and around the cockpit becomes tricky, if not downright dangerous at times. I like to be able to walk past the cockpit to the stern on the side decks, *behind* seated passengers. On these boats, you have to step over them or onto the footwell and between them. That, and the fiberglass liners, are my only real gripes.

### Flicka 20

| | |
|---|---|
| LOA | 23' 7" (7.2 m) |
| LOD | 20' 0" (6.1 m) |
| LWL | 18' 2" (5.5 m) |
| Beam | 8' 0" (2.4 m) |
| Draft | 3' 3" (1 m) |
| Displacement | 5,500 lbs. (2,494 kg) |
| Ballast | 4,750 lbs. (1,448 kg) |
| Sail area | 250 sq. ft. (23 m²) |

349

## Dana 24

| | |
|---|---|
| LOA | 27' 3" (8.3 m) |
| LOD | 24' 0" (7.3 m) |
| LWL | 21' 5" (6.5 m) |
| Beam | 8' 7" (2.6 m) |
| Draft | 3' 10" (1.2 m) |
| Displacement | 8,000 lbs. (3,627 kg) |
| Ballast | 3,200 lbs. (1,451 kg) |
| Sail area | 358 sq. ft. (33 m²) |

## Pacific Seacraft 37

| | |
|---|---|
| LOA | 36' 11" (11.3 m) |
| LWL | 27' 9" (8.5 m) |
| Beam | 10' 10" (3.3 m) |
| Draft | 4' 5" to 5' 6" (1.3 m to 1.7 m) |
| Displacement | 16,000 lbs. (7,254 kg) |
| Ballast | 6,200 lbs. (2,811 kg) |
| Sail area | 619 sq. ft. (58 m²) |

## Pacific Seacraft 44

| | |
|---|---|
| LOA | 44' 1" (13.4 m) |
| LWL | 33' 7" (10.2 m) |
| Beam | 12' 8" (3.9 m) |
| Draft | 6' 3"/1.9 m (deep) |
| | 5' 3"/1.6 m (shoal) |
| Displacement | 27,500 lbs. (12,469 kg) |
| Ballast | 11,000 lbs. (4,987 kg) |
| Sail area | 971 sq. ft. (90 m²) |

# SABRE YACHTS

Canadian Roger Hewson was a building contractor before founding Sabre Yachts in South Casco, Maine, in 1969. He designed the first boat himself, the Sabre 28, and did a nice job of it. Construction was equally solid, with a solid fiberglass hull. Beginning with the Sabre 34 (1978), the hulls were balsa cored. The vast majority of decks by all companies are cored with balsa. A quality builder removes the balsa in the way of cleats and other deck hardware so that water will not leak down the bolt holes and cause rot, and the balsa does not crush when the bolts are tightened.

It's my opinion that Sabre Yachts and Tartan Yachts are the two best builders of fiberglass production boats in the United States. Both still build large wood interiors with components bonded directly to the hull, plus strong hull stiffening systems of stringers and floors.

While the Sabre 28 is small for a serious cruising boat, her larger sister ships are well qualified, despite the fin keels and rudders on partial skegs. The Sabre 34 (1977) and 36 (1984) are excellent values. For newer models check out the Sabre 362, 38, and 402, all designed by Jim Taylor. They look, and sail, great. The latter is still in production, along with a current model list that includes the 386, 426, and 452. Sabre uses up-to-date construction materials and techniques: SCRIMP resin infusion, vacuum bagging, PVC foam cores, generous backing plates on deck hardware, bulkheads tabbed to the deck, flush-mount through-hulls, through-bolted hull-deck joints, and its signature tool drawer.

## Sabre 28

| | |
|---|---|
| LOA | 28' 5" (8.7 m) |
| LWL | 22' 10" (7 m) |
| Beam | 9' 2" (2.8 m) |
| Draft | 4' 8"/1.4 m (standard) |
| | 3' 10"/1.2 m (shoal) |
| Displacement | 7,900 lbs. (3,582 kg) |
| Ballast | 3,100 lbs. (1,406 kg) |
| Sail area | 403 sq. ft. (35 m²) |

## Sabre 34

| | |
|---|---|
| LOA | 33' 8" (10.2 m) |
| LWL | 26' 3" (8 m) |
| Beam | 10' 6" (3.2 m) |
| Draft | 5' 6"/1.7 m (keel) |
| | 3' 11" to 7' 9"/1.2 m to 2.4 m (keel/centerboard) |
| Displacement | 11,400 lbs./5,169 kg (keel) |
| | 11,700 lbs./5,305 kg (keel/centerboard) |
| Ballast | 4,600 lbs./2,086 kg (keel) |
| | 4,900 lbs./2,222 kg (keel/centerboard) |
| Sail area | 507 sq. ft. (47 m²) |

## Sabre 36

| | |
|---|---|
| LOA | 36' 0" (11 m) |
| LWL | 29' 4" (8.9 m) |
| Beam | 11' 3" (3.4 m) |
| Draft | 6' 4"/1.9 m (keel) |
| | 4' 2" to 7' 8"/1.3 m to 2.3 m (keel/centerboard) |
| Displacement | 13,200 lbs./5,985 kg (keel) |
| | 13,500 lbs./6,121 kg (keel/centerboard) |
| Ballast | 5,400 lbs./2,448 kg (keel) |
| | 5,700 lbs./2,584 kg (keel/centerboard) |
| Sail area | 612 sq. ft. (56.9 m²) |

## Sabre 402

| | |
|---|---|
| LOA | 40' 2" (12.2 m) |
| LWL | 34' 0" (10.4 m) |
| Beam | 13' 4" (4.1 m) |
| Draft | 4' 11"/1.5 m (shoal) |
| | 6' 3"/1.9 m (deep) |
| Displacement | 18,500 lbs. (8,388 kg) |
| Ballast | 7,000 lbs. (3,174 kg) |
| Sail area | 822 sq. ft. (76 m²) |

# SHANNON YACHTS

Artist Walter Schulz and yacht broker David Walters founded Shannon Yachts in 1975. Their niche is semi-custom, blue-water cruisers. Semi-custom means the hulls are standard but owners can modify the interior plan and materials to a certain point. It's what Hinckley, Morris, and Alden do, too. Inevitably, these are high-quality, very expensive boats. Consequently, I've listed Shannon's older models, which once they get old enough might be affordable by people like you and me.

Walters left the company years ago to start Cambria, which he then sold to Cabo Rico. Schulz does his own design work, and being an artist, he's creative, as evidenced by his current model, the Shoalsailer 32, capable of sailing in just inches of water. Most of the time Schulz does very nice work, but I think there are instances where his lack of formal training in naval architecture shows, like a bit of weather helm on the 39.

In his 70s, yachting writer Monk Farnham sailed a Shannon 28 transatlantic, setting a record for the oldest person to do so. Other models besides the 28 (1978) include the 37 (1986), 38 (1976), 43 (1985), 50 (1981), and 51 (1984). Many were or still are available with pilothouse options.

There is no question Shannons are superbly constructed, with S glass and foam cores (Airex in the early days, Core-Cell later), longitudinal stringers, and bulkeads not only taped to the hull and deck, but drilled and stitched with fiberglass cords. The hull-deck joint is bolted on 5-inch (127 mm) centers. Ballast on most Shannons is internal, because that's where Schulz believes it belongs. Keel bolts in externally ballasted boats, he says, have a twenty-year life expectancy.

Schulz proudly claims that Shannon Yachts have entered every major port in the world, and they have as fine a blue-water record as any series of boats ever made by the same builder. That may be.

## Shannon 28

| | |
|---|---|
| LOA | 28' 2" (8.6 m) |
| LWL | 22' 11" (7 m) |
| Beam | 9' 6" (2.9 m) |
| Draft | 4' 3" (1.3 m) |
| Displacement | 9,300 lbs. (4,217 kg) |
| Ballast | 3,500 lbs. (1,587 kg) |
| Sail area | 470 sq. ft. (44 m$^2$) |

## Shannon 37

| | |
|---|---|
| LOA | 37' 9" (11.5 m) |
| LWL | 30' 10" (9.4 m) |
| Beam | 11' 6" (3.5 m) |
| Draft | 4' 3"/1.3 m (centerboard up) |
| | 5' 8"/1.7 m (keel) |
| Displacement | 17,500 lbs. (7,395 kg) |
| Ballast | 6,500 lbs. (2,947 kg) |
| Sail area | 751 sq. ft./70 m² (ketch) |
| | 703 sq. ft./65 m² (cutter) |

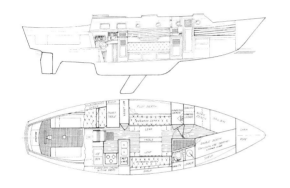

## Shannon 43

| | |
|---|---|
| LOA | 43' 10" (13.4 m) |
| LWL | 36' 7" (11.1 m) |
| Beam | 13' 0" (4 m) |
| Draft | 4' 9" to 8' 7"/1.4 m to 2.6 m (centerboard) |
| | 6' 6"/2 m (keel) |
| Displacement | 27,500 lbs. (12,458 kg) |
| Ballast | 10,500 lbs. (4,757 kg) |
| Sail area | 997 sq. ft./92.7 m² (ketch) |
| | 950 sq. ft./88.4 m² (cutter) |

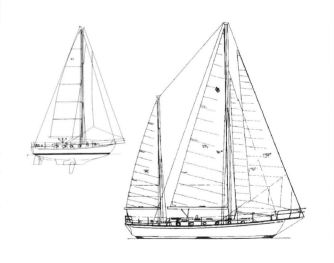

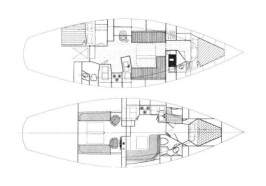

## Shannon 47

| | |
|---|---|
| LOA | 52' 7" (16 m) |
| LOD | 47' 6" (14.5 m) |
| LWL | 42' 7" (13 m) |
| Beam | 14' 3" (4.3 m) |
| Draft | 5' 7" to 9' 7"/1.7 m to 2.9 m (centerboard) |
| | 6' 6"/2 m (keel) |
| Displacement | 35,500 lbs. (16,082 kg) |
| Ballast | 13,500 lbs. (6,116 kg) |
| Sail area | 1,200 sq. ft./112 m² (cutter) |
| | 1,173 sq. ft./109 m² (ketch) |

# TARTAN YACHTS

The origins of this fine Midwest builder date to Ray McLeod Sr. and Gordon "Sandy" Douglass, who built daysailers like the Thistle and International 14 out of wood. In 1960 they partnered with Charlie Britton and built their first fiberglass auxiliary, the S&S-designed Tartan 27. It was an instant hit. In 1971, a fire forced Douglass & McLeod to sell their share to Britton. The second boat, a Ted Hood–designed yawl called the Black Watch (1966), made a circumnavigation, proving the pedigree of Tartan Yachts. Good boats that followed include the Tartan 26, 30, 34, 37, 41, 46, and 48.

Britton sold the company in 1983, and ownership has changed hands several times since, but quality only gets better. Where the old Tartans were all designed by S&S as dual-purpose racer/cruisers, today the Tartan line is decidedly more cruiser (which is why the company bought the C&C name to balance its offerings). Which is not to say that the new Tartans are pigs; to the contrary, they sail very well, but are loaded up with systems and wood interiors. In fact, Tartan joins Sabre as one of just a few U.S. production builders not using major fiberglass liners or pans for the sole and furniture foundations.

Among the older designs, the Tartan 34 is a classic but dated now. The slab-sided coamings make the cockpit rather uncomfortable. The second-generation Tartan 37 (1976–1988) is a great sailing boat and still handsome; the 41 was an IOR boat. I owned a stretch version called the 44 for a number of years and loved how she went to windward. Very powerful. Some old IOR boats can be had for a song and converted to cruising purposes, which is what I did. The Tartan Tock, with great aft cabin, was a bold design ahead of its time.

Tim Jackett is general manager and chief designer and continues in the S&S tradition. The Tartan 3500 (1991), 3800 (1993), and 4600 (1992) all would make good cruising boats. Obviously, the farther you're going, the bigger boats are better.

Construction is very good, with bulkheads tabbed to the deck, proper seacocks, rugged rigs, and so on. Today's boats are laminated entirely of epoxy resin, rather than the usual polyester.

## Tartan 3500

| | |
|---|---|
| LOA | 35' 3" (10.7 m) |
| LWL | 30' 0" (9.1 m) |
| Beam | 11' 9" (3.6 m) |
| Draft | 4' 10"/1.5 m (shoal) |
| | 6' 6"/2 m (deep) |
| Displacement | 11,400 lbs. (5,169 kg) |
| Ballast | 4,500 lbs. (2,040 kg) |
| Sail area | 615 sq. ft. (57 m²) |

## Tartan 37

| | |
|---|---|
| LOA | 37' 3" (11.4 m) |
| LWL | 28' 6" (8.7 m) |
| Beam | 11' 9" (3.6 m) |
| Draft | 4' 2"/1.3 m (centerboard up) |
| | 6' 7"/2 m (deep) |
| Displacement | 15,500 lbs. (7,028 kg) |
| Ballast | 7,200 lbs./3,264 kg (deep) |
| | 7,500 lbs./3,401 kg (centerboard) |
| Sail area | 625 sq. ft. (58 m²) |

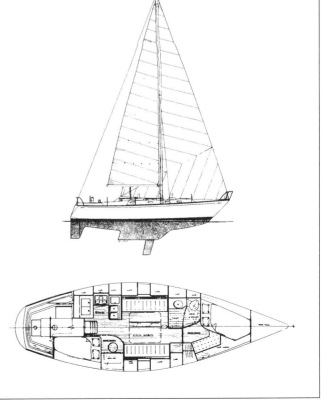

## Tartan 3800

| | |
|---|---|
| LOA | 38' 0" (11.6 m) |
| LWL | 31' 0" (9.4 m) |
| Beam | 12' 5" (3.8 m) |
| Draft | 5' 4"/1.6 m (shoal) |
| | 6' 10"/2.1 m (deep) |
| Displacement | 16,000 lbs. (7,254 kg) |
| Ballast | N/A |
| Sail area | 672 sq. ft. (62 m²) |

## Tartan 41

| | |
|---|---|
| LOA | 40' 8" (12.4 m) |
| LWL | 32' 5" (9.9 m) |
| Beam | 12' 3" (3.7 m) |
| Draft | 6' 4"/1.9 m (shoal) |
| | 7' 2"/2.2 m (deep) |
| Displacement | 17,850 lbs. (8,093 kg) |
| Ballast | 9,200 lbs. (2,804 kg) |
| Sail area | 725 sq. ft. (67 m²) |

# TAIWAN

The Republic of China became a major builder of sailboats and motoryachts after World War II, when servicemen stationed in Asia found they could have boats built there for a fraction of the cost in the United States. Wooden boats were built with quality teak lumber, and cheap labor rates allowed the Chinese carpenters to elaborate the interiors with beautiful carvings of dragons and poppy flowers. The switch to fiberglass really affected the hulls and decks only; the interiors continued to be constructed of all wood and remain so pretty much to this day.

As with all Asian-built boats, there may be problems with poor-grade metals, and surprises, like cockpit seats made of plywood with gelcoat brushed over. Always retain a surveyor before completing a purchase.

Robert Perry has designed as many cruising sailboats as just about anyone on the planet, and many of these were built in Taiwan in its heyday during the 1970s and '80s. There's still a strong boatbuilding industry there, but it's not as price competitive as it once was, thanks to a growing economy that raised labor rates. The CT 54 was the first of Perry's individual designs to be built, and it had a successful run for such a large boat. Built by Ta Chaio, it's a big, heavy ketch with what Perry calls a "piratey" sort of look. The boat is strong but certainly not high tech, nor would you expect it to be back when it was built. Production ran from 1975 to 1981. Displacement/length ratio is 302. This is a true world cruiser.

Ted Hood is a sailor of many talents: sailmaker, America's Cup winner, and yacht designer. The boats he has built are called Little Harbor this and that, and they've been built in several countries, but during the 1970s and '80s it was Taiwan. The Little Harbor 44 has a bold sheer and rakish bow, coupled to a slightly reversed transom. It has a style that will last a long time after its 1983 introduction. Both aft and center-cockpit arrangements were offered.

After the CT 54 was launched, John Edwards, the developer, commissioned Robert Perry to design the Hans Christian 34. Through a series of events, in which various people both in the United States and Taiwan attempted, and succeeded, in stealing the design, it was produced not only as the Hans Christian but also as the Polaris 36, EO 36, and Mao Ta 36—maybe more, who knows. The tooling was either passed around or splashed (copied). In any case, it's a stout little vessel with a canoe stern, bow platform, and cutter rig. As an example of stoutness, the deck is $\frac{5}{8}$-inch teak (16 mm) over a sandwich of $\frac{3}{8}$-inch (9.5 mm) fiberglass, $\frac{3}{4}$-inch (19 mm) core, and another layer of $\frac{3}{8}$-inch fiberglass!

We'll take a short break from Robert Perry to look at the Mason 43 (1978), a beautiful design from George Mason and imported to the United States by PAE. (Although PAE continues to import the Mason, these days it is selling a lot more Nordhavn passagemaking motoryachts than sailboats.) My former colleague George Day and his family circumnavigated aboard a Mason 43. In 1985 a different deck mold was tooled for the Mason 44. The boats are built by Ta Shing (perhaps the best yard in Taiwan) and have solid hulls, balsa-cored decks, and foam/fiberglass stringers. The hull-deck joint is through-bolted, screwed, and glassed over.

Stan Huntingford designed the Slocum 43 (1982) as an all-out blue-water cruiser. The hull is cored with Airex R60-80 foam, which isn't as stiff as balsa but has more resilience under impact. In fact, on the highly stressed crossbeam connections found on giant multihulls, it is used in place of Nomex because it acts as a type of shock absorber. The entire cabin sole can be removed for access to the engine, tanks, and bilges—an important feature not always addressed by designers and builders.

## CT 54

| | |
|---|---|
| LOA | 53' 7" (16.3 m) |
| LWL | 42' 6" (13 m) |
| Beam | 15' 1" (4.6 m) |
| Draft | 6' 6" (2 m) |
| Displacement | 57,000 lbs. (25,844 kg) |
| Ballast | 16,500 lbs. (7,481 kg) |
| Sail area | 1,245 sq. ft. (116 m²) |

## Hans Christian 34/36

| | HC 34 | HC36 |
|---|---|---|
| LOA | 33' 11" (10.3 m) | 35' 7" (10.8 m) |
| LWL | 29' 0" (8.8 m) | 30' 6" (9.3 m) |
| Beam | 10' 11" (3.3 m) | 11' 3" (3.4 m) |
| Draft | 5' 6" (1.7 m) | 5' 11" (1.8 m) |
| Displacement | 18,300 lbs. (8,297 kg) | 22,000 lbs. (9,975 kg) |
| Ballast | 7,000 lbs. (3,174 kg) | N/A |
| Sail area | 676 sq. ft. (63 m²) | 711 sq. ft. (66 m²) |

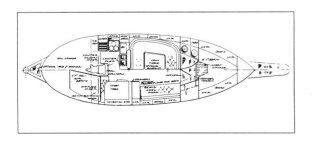

## *Mason 43*

| | |
|---|---|
| LOA | 43' 11" (13.7 m) |
| LWL | 31' 3" (9.5 m) |
| Beam | 12' 4" (3.8 m) |
| Draft | 5' 6"/1.7 m (shoal) |
| | 6' 3"/1.9 m (deep) |
| Displacement | 27,400 lbs. (12,423 kg) |
| Ballast | 8,400 lbs. (3,809 kg) |
| Sail area | 899 sq. ft./84 m² (cutter) |

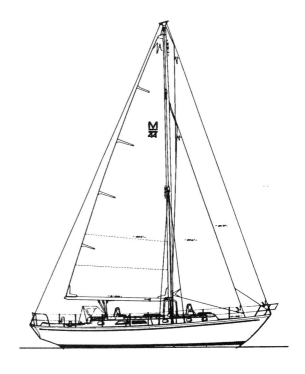

## *Slocum 43*

| | |
|---|---|
| LOA | 42' 6" (13 m) |
| LWL | 35' 10" (10.9 m) |
| Beam | 12' 11" (3.9 m) |
| Draft | 6' 4"/1.9 m (standard) |
| | 5' 6"/1.7 m (shoal) |
| Displacement | 28,104 lbs. (12,742 kg) |
| Ballast | 9,000 lbs. (4,081 kg) |
| Sail area | 808 sq. ft. (75 m²) |

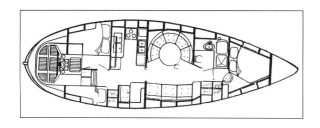

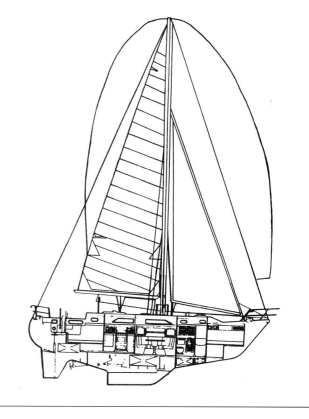

# TAIWAN II

The boats built in Taiwan generally originate in two ways: an enterprising Chinese boatbuilder (1) independently commissions a design, or (2) acquires a hull and deck mold, then builds and markets them. In Taipei you'll come across ads for boats sold direct from the yard. Few of these boats, however, seem to reach our shores. More likely, a U.S. or European marketing outfit commissions the design and then strikes a deal with a Taiwan builder to manufacture the boat. The marketer ships the boat to the United States, exhibits it at the boat shows, and runs advertisements in magazines. The boats discussed on these next pages are examples of each.

Robert Perry designed the Passport 40 (1984) for marketer Wendel Renken, a former furniture maker. Perry says Renken wanted "an extrapolation of the Islander Freeport 36," with head forward and a Pullman double berth aft of it. "It was," he said, "a classic case of a hull wrapped around an interior." Not that it's always a bad thing, but that's what often happens when marketers strongly influence the design. Comparing this, the first Passport, to Perry's landmark Valiant 40 is instructive. The canoe stern has been replaced by a more conventional transom stern, and the coach roof has more camber. There are other differences less visible: the Passport has asymmetrical waterlines, a wedge shape, and a flat bottom. Waterlines on the Valiant, Perry says, are symmetrical, and it has more deadrise. Both are nice to sail and cruise, each in its own way.

When Perry was screwed out of royalties for the Hans Christian 36 and knockoffs, he got revenge with the wildly successful Tayana 37 (1979), of which nearly 600 were built. This is a true double-ender with long, full keel and cutaway forefoot to reduce wetted surface area. It was offered as a cutter (Perry's preference) or ketch, and a few went out the door with the optional pilothouse. It's one of the best bargains in blue-water boats.

Our last selection wasn't built in Taiwan, but in Hong Kong, by one of the earliest yards to build yachts. The Cheoy Lee Clipper 42, designed by Bill Luders, is a graceful ketch with sweeping sheer, trailboards, and bowsprit. Jimmy Buffett cruised the Caribbean for a few years in its sister ship, the Clipper 47. Construction is good.

## Passport 40

| | |
|---|---|
| LOA | 39' 5" (12 m) |
| LWL | 33' 5" (10.2 m) |
| Beam | 12' 8" (3.9 m) |
| Draft | 5' 9"/1.8 m (standard) |
| | 5' 3"/1.6 m (shoal) |
| Displacement | 22,771 lbs. (10,324 kg) |
| Ballast | 8,500 lbs. (3,854 kg) |
| Sail area | 771 sq. ft. (72 m²) |

## Tayana 37

| | |
|---|---|
| LOA | 36' 8" (11.2 m) |
| LWL | 31' 10" (9.7 m) |
| Beam | 11' 6" (3.5 m) |
| Draft | 5' 8" (1.7 m) |
| Displacement | 24,000 lbs. (10,882 kg) |
| Ballast | 7,340 lbs. (3,328 kg) |
| Sail area | 864 sq. ft./80 m$^2$ (cutter) |
| | 768 sq. ft./71 m$^2$ (ketch) |

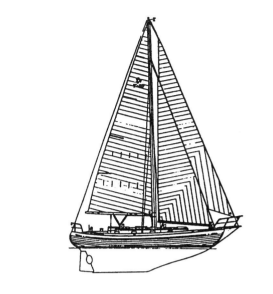

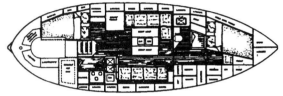

## Cheoy Lee Clipper 42

| | |
|---|---|
| LOA | 42' 5" (12.9 m) |
| LWL | 30' 0" (9.1 m) |
| Beam | 12' 1" (3.7 m) |
| Draft | N/A |
| Displacement | 23,500 lbs. (10,655 kg) |
| Ballast | 8,000 lbs. (3,627 kg) |
| Sail area | 928 sq. ft. (86 m$^2$) |

# SEMI-CUSTOM YACHTS

Up a notch from the best production builders, like Sabre, Tartan, and possibly Island Packet, are the semi-custom builders. What these builders do is design and make tooling (male plug, female mold) for a standard hull. Within the limitations of the hull, the builder might offer various deck configurations (standard and pilothouse option), as well as different interior layouts. The owner can select his or her favorite woods as alternatives to teak and mahogany; for example, bird's-eye maple table, cherry ceiling, and ash cabinetry. The systems will vary too, depending on whether the owners want a watermaker, auxiliary generator, electric windlass and winches, etc. The boats are, of course, expensive but ocean capable.

We start with the Alden 50, built in Portsmouth, Rhode Island, with stitched fabrics, balsa core, epoxy resin using wet pregs (fabrics wetted out with an impregnator before being laid in the mold), and vacuum bagging. As with many bigger boats, fixed-keel and keel/centerboard configurations are available. The smaller 44 and 46, termed by some as "a gentleman's offshore yacht," may be found on the used ("preowned"!) market and are good sailers.

For many years the Henry R. Hinckley Company in Southwest Harbor, Maine, has been regarded as the premier yacht builder in the United States. Its Bermuda 40, designed by the late Bill Tripp, enjoyed a thirty-year production run and is one of the most beautiful 40-footers ever drawn. Today, in boats like the Sou'wester 42, Hinckley uses a lot of S glass (better than E-glass), plus Kevlar in the outer skins and carbon in the inner skins. Major structures are SCRIMPed. Most spars are carbon fiber also. Hinckley makes many of its own parts, including fancy custom fittings such as stems.

Tom Morris, not far down the road from Hinckley, builds boats of equal quality, most designed by Chuck Payne. Back in the 1970s, his boats were small and all named after women: Frances 26, Leigh 30, Annie 30, and Justine 36 (1984). Now he builds only larger boats, most in the 40- and 50-foot range, and gives each the name Morris. Payne's styling is evident in each. (The Scheel keel noted below, named after its inventor, Henry Scheel, is a sort of half-bulb, half-wing shape.)

## Alden 50

| | |
|---|---|
| LOA | 50' 7" (15.4 m) |
| LWL | 37' 1" (11.3 m) |
| Beam | 13' 6" (4.1 m) |
| Draft | 5' 4" to 10' 1"/1.6 m to 3.1 m (keel/centerboard) 5' 6"/1.7 m (shoal) 7' 6"/2.3 m (deep) |
| Displacement | 32,000 lbs. (14,509 kg) |
| Ballast | 13,000 lbs. (5,894 kg) |
| Sail area | 1,022 sq. ft. (95 m²) |

## *Hinckley Bermuda 40*

| | |
|---|---|
| LOA | 40' 9" (12.4 m) |
| LWL | 28' 10" (8.8 m) |
| Beam | 11' 9" (3.6 m) |
| Draft | 4' 3" to 8' 9"/1.3 m to 2.7 m (keel/centerboard) |
| Displacement | 20,000 lbs. (9,068 kg) |
| Ballast | 6,500 lbs. (2,947 kg) |
| Sail area | 776 sq. ft. (72 m²) |

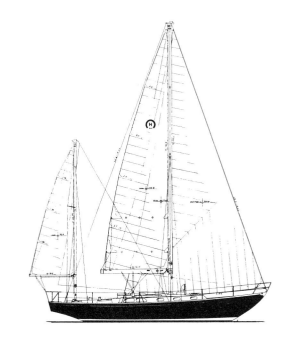

## *Hinckley Sou'wester 42*

| | |
|---|---|
| LOA | 42' 0" (12.8 m) |
| LWL | 31' 3" (9.5 m) |
| Beam | 12' 6" (3.8 m) |
| Draft | 5' 0" to 9' 1" (1.5 m to 2.8 m) |
| Displacement | 23,500 lbs. (10,655 kg) |
| Ballast | 9,000 lbs. (4,081 kg) |
| Sail area | 827 sq. ft. (77 m²) |

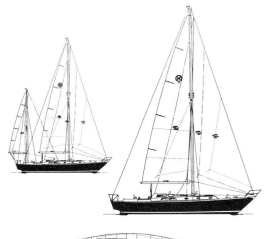

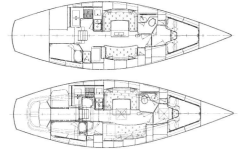

## Morris 36

| LOA | 36' 3" (11 m) |
|---|---|
| LWL | 29' 6" (9 m) |
| Beam | 11' 6" (3.5 m) |
| Draft | 4' 4"/1.3 m (Scheel keel) |
| | 5' 4"/1.6 m (deep) |
| Displacement | 15,500 lbs. (7,028 kg) |
| Ballast | 6,500 lbs. (2,947 kg) |
| Sail area | 8,657 sq. ft. (61 m²) |

# SCANDINAVIAN

The yacht builders in Sweden, Finland, and Norway are noted for good quality, as is much of Europe. One reason for this is that if you want to export to the United States, the world's largest economy, marketing and shipping costs make the manufacturing of high-end, expensive products more profitable than assembly-line-quality products.

Nautor of Finland is the builder of the Swan line of elegant cruiser/racers or racer/cruisers, depending on your perspective. Originally imported to the United States by builder Palmer Johnson, early boats were designed by S&S, including the original Swan 44 shown here (1972). Note its similarity to the S&S-designed Tartan 41. In 1990, the new Frers-designed 44 was launched. While still speedy, it has much more of a cruising interior than its predecessor. And gone is the trademark S&S wedge-shaped deckhouse.

Located in Pietarsaari, Finland, Baltic Yachts was founded in 1974 by defectors from Nautor. Early designs were by C&C, Doug Peterson, and Judel-Vrolijk. Like Nautor, its early boats were mostly standard, but over time they began catering to well-heeled customers who wanted things a little different. The hulls are mostly carbon pre-preg (i.e., pre-impregnated with resin by the manufacturer, then kept cold until it's time for the builder to laminate the hull; heat initiates the chemical reaction and cures it) and a lot of Nomex honeycomb core. This makes for a very light, stiff structure. The Baltic 52 bears the signature wedge-shaped deckhouse of the S&S Swans.

Nauticat is a Finnish builder of motorsailers. Most are big and rather clunky looking, but their heavy displacement makes for comfortable sea boats. The Nauticat 40, designed by S&S, is actually one of the more spritely models. Nauticats are built like tanks, with a lot of hardwood and solid glass—good quality, strong, but not very modern.

Sweden Yachts are built in Stenungsund, in Sweden, of course. Old pro Peter Norling is one of the designers, along with Jens Östmann, who takes Norlin's hulls to a complete yacht. The Sweden 370 and others in the line are intended as all-around good sailboats, tipping their hats little to striking performance or world-girdling cruising. Teak decks are laid without fasteners, which require bungs, which inevitably dry out and let water in. The risk of deck core rot, plus maintenance, plus weight has made teak decks fall out of favor, but they provide excellent traction, and when wet or oiled, they look great.

## Swan 44 x 2

| | 1972 | 1990 |
|---|---|---|
| LOA | 44' 1" (13.4 m) | 45' 11" (14 m) |
| LWL | 33' 11" (10.3 m) | 34' 8" (10.6 m) |
| Beam | 12' 7" (3.2 m) | 13' 9" (4.2 m) |
| Draft | 7' 5" (2.2 m) | 7' 2" (2.2 m) |
| Displacement | 28,000 lbs. (12,695 kg) | 24,300 lbs. (11,018 kg) |
| Ballast | 12,600 lbs. (5,713 kg) | 8,400 lbs. (3,809 kg) |
| Sail area | 920 sq. ft. (86 m$^2$) | 891 sq. ft. (83 m$^2$) |

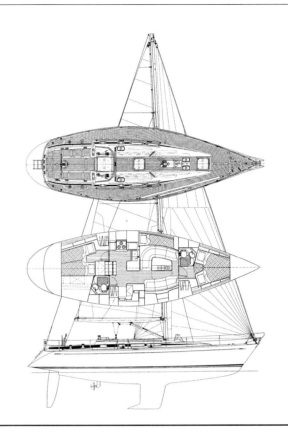

## Baltic 52

| | |
|---|---|
| LOA | 53' 5" (16.3 m) |
| LWL | 43' 2" (13.2 m) |
| Beam | 15' 5" (4.7 m) |
| Draft | 9' 11" (3 m) |
| Displacement | 31,967 lbs. (14,494 kg) |
| Ballast | 13,228 lbs. (5,998 kg) |
| Sail area | 1,228 sq. ft. (114 m$^2$) |

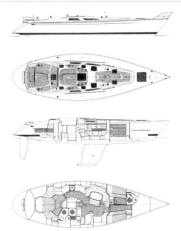

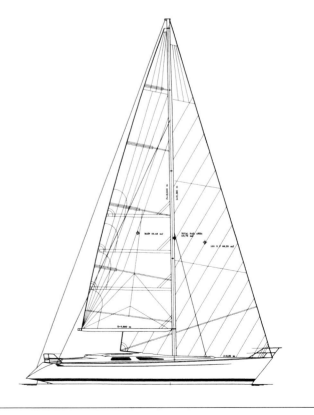

## Nauticat 40

| | |
|---|---|
| LOA | 39' 4" (12 m) |
| LWL | 32' 9" (10 m) |
| Beam | 13' 1" (4 m) |
| Displacement | 29,800 lbs. (13,512 kg) |
| Ballast | 8,800 lbs. (3,990 kg) |
| Sail area | 837 sq. ft./78 m² (ketch without bowsprit) |
| | 1,072 sq. ft./100 m² (ketch with bowsprit) |

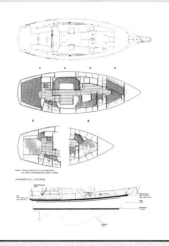

## Sweden 370

| | |
|---|---|
| LOA | 36' 7" (11.1 m) |
| LWL | 29' 6" (9 m) |
| Beam | 12' 0" (3.7 m) |
| Draft | 6' 9"/2.1 m (deep) |
| | 5' 7"/1.7 m (wing) |
| Displacement | 15,290 lbs. (6,932 kg) |
| Ballast | 6,050 lbs. (2,743 kg) |
| Sail area | 883 sq. ft. (82 m²) |

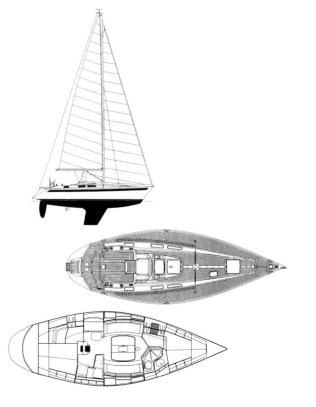

# CLASSICS I

Everyone has his and her list of favorite boats, and I have mine, too. They're all fiberglass, as that has been the dominating boatbuilding material since the 1950s. Of course, steel and aluminum deserve the cruiser's consideration, but they are almost exclusively custom. If there is ever a cruising sailboat hall of fame, the next 20 boats deserve admission.

Bill Crealock, designer of the larger Pacific Seacrafts, designed the Cabo Rico 38. It has been built in Costa Rica since 1977, a testament to its quality and popularity. A pilothouse is available though few have been sold. The interiors are mostly teak, but since the company now calls itself Cabo Rico Custom Yachts, I assume you can substitute other woods. Balsa, Airex, and Core-Cell are used by the company, but on the 38, in an interesting way. Instead of sandwiching the balsa core between two skins of fiberglass, it's bonded to the inside of what is essentially a single-skin hull and then covered with at thin layer of glass. Thus, it's used more for insulation than stiffness. Cabo Rico publishes its lamination schedule, which unfortunately is rather unusual in this business. If nothing else, it means it has nothing to hide.

Bill Tripp designed some really great boats before his untimely death in a 1971 car accident. (The Bill Tripp you hear about today is his son, also a yacht designer.) Among his best-known designs are the Block Island 40 and Hinckley Bermuda 40. He also did quite a few boats for Columbia Yachts, perhaps the largest production builder of fiberglass sailboats during the 1960s and 1970s. The Columbia 50 was for a time its flagship. It's a big, powerful sloop; authors and builders Steve and Linda Dashew completed their first circumnavigation in a Columbia 50. The quality isn't the same as many of the other boats in this section, having a lot of molded liners. But the basic structures were sound and, with some time and money invested in upgrades, one of these boats would be a hoot to sail.

Whereas many production builders today employ in-house designers, in the "old days" of fiberglass the companies hired name designers, and no one had more stars in its stable than Pearson Yachts. John Alden & Co. designed the Countess 44 with a flush deck forward and a large, distinctive cabin trunk. This boat has elements of a motorsailer, with a large deckhouse that looks out through the big windows. You'd definitely need to fit storm shutters for offshore. Though growing a little long in the tooth, there's no other boat quite like the Countess.

CSY was founded by a dentist who wanted to develop the perfect boat for the West Indies charter trade, and he came darn close. Only a few models were built: the 37 and 44 in 1977, and a 33 in 1979. Yachting writer Bill Robinson bought a 37 and cruised it extensively. But the center-cockpit CSY 44 was the mainstay of the fleet, some with a walk-through between the fore and aft cabins, others without this passageway. The company went out of business in the 1980s, ostensibly because the boats were built too well, at least for the price they could get.

## Cabo Rico 38

| | |
|---|---|
| LOA | 38' 0" (11.6 m) |
| LWL | 29' 3" (8.9 m) |
| Beam | 11' 6" (3.5 m) |
| Draft | 5' 0" (1.5 m) |
| Displacement | 21,000 lbs. (9,521 kg) |
| Ballast | 7,800 lbs. (3,537 kg) |
| Sail area | 817 sq. ft. (76 m²) |

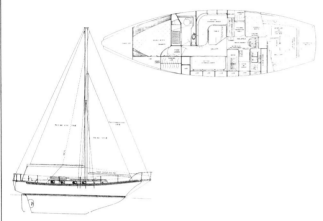

## Columbia 50

| | |
|---|---|
| LOA | 50' 0" (15.2 m) |
| LWL | 48' 11" (14.9 m) |
| Beam | 15' 4" (4.7 m) |
| Draft | 6' 7" (2 m) |
| Displacement | 34,000 lbs. (15,416 kg) |
| Ballast | 14,600 lbs. (6,620 kg) |
| Sail area | 977 sq. ft. (91 m²) |

## Countess 44

| | |
|---|---|
| LOA | 44' 6" (13.6 m) |
| LWL | 30' 6" (9.3 m) |
| Beam | 12' 0" (3.7 m) |
| Draft | 5' 4" (1.6 m) |
| Displacement | 28,000 lbs. (12,695 kg) |
| Ballast | 8,000 lbs. (3,627 kg) |
| Sail area | 856 sq. ft. (80 m$^2$) |

## CSY 44

| | |
|---|---|
| LOA | 44' 0" (13.4 m) |
| LWL | 36' 4" (11.1 m) |
| Beam | 13' 4" (4.1 m) |
| Draft | 6' 6"/2 m (standard) |
| | 4' 11"/1.5 m (shoal) |
| Displacement | 33,000 lbs./14,962 kg (standard keel) |
| | 31,000 lbs./14,055 kg (shoal keel) |
| Ballast | 12,000 lbs./5,441 kg (standard keel) |
| | 10,000 lbs./4,534 kg (shoal keel) |
| Sail area | 906 sq. ft. (84 m$^2$) |

# CLASSICS II

These five smaller boats come from both coasts of the United States, and one from Europe. Each has something unique about it, adding to its appeal.

Endeavour Yachts of Largo, Florida, like so many others, was formed by a couple of guys working at another company who wanted to go it on their own. In this case, the other company was several: Rob Valdez, younger brother of Dick Valdez who was a key figure at Columbia Yachts and Lancer Yachts, worked for Vince Lazzara at Gulfstar. There he met salesman John Brooks. To get them started on their own, Ted Irwin gave them the molds to the Irwin 32, which became the Endeavour 32. The year was 1974. The company changed directions several times, from run-of-the-mill production boats to hand-finished, high-end boats, and lastly to catamarans. The Endeavour 37 started life as the Creekmore 34, which the partners cut in half, added 3 feet (0.9 m) in the middle, and voilà!—the Endeavour 37. It's actually a decent sailing boat and well built. I sailed one for a week through the Abacos and enjoyed it—the boat's not fast, but the aft stateroom is unusual for a 37-footer (11.3 m). Great for privacy, but difficult to ventilate in the tropics.

The C. E. Ryder Corporation of Bristol, Rhode Island, built some very attractive boats in two lines—Southern Cross and Sea Sprite. The latter included a 23-foot Carl Alberg design that one intrepid young man sailed transatlantic. A Luders-designed Sea Sprite 34 also was built. But here we look at the Southern Cross 31, second smallest of the four in this line (the others were the Southern Cross 28, 35, and 39). It was designed by Thomas Gilmer of the U.S. Naval Academy in Annapolis, who also penned the Allied Seawind, first fiber-glass boat to circumnavigate. The Southern Cross 31 was available as a kit boat, so if looking at one, check the workmanship carefully. Some home builders do outstanding work, others range from so-so to disastrous. Also check the rudder cheeks; a friend of mine who owned one had to beef up his. Not a big boat, but capable and lovely.

Camper & Nicholson is a famous, old-time English builder and yard dating to 1824 when William Camper took over the lease of a yard in Gosport. Though the company now builds and re-fits mostly large yachts, in the 1960s and '70s it built some tough little cruisers, namely the Nicholson 31 and Nicholson 32, and later the Nicholson 35, of which 228 were sold in the mid-'80s. The Nicholsons have a reputation for being very fine sea boats.

## Endeavour 37

| LOA | 37' 5" (11.4 m) |
|---|---|
| LWL | 30' 0" (9.1 m) |
| Beam | 11' 7" (3.6 m) |
| Draft | 4' 6" (1.4 m) |
| Displacement | 21,000 lbs. (9,521 kg) |
| Ballast | 8,000 lbs. (2,438 kg) |
| Sail area | 580 sq. ft./54 m² (sloop) |
| | 640 sq. ft./60 m² (ketch) |

## Southern Cross 31

| LOA | 31' 0" (9.4 m) |
| --- | --- |
| LWL | 25' 0" (7.6 m) |
| Beam | 9' 6" (2.9 m) |
| Draft | 4' 7" (1.4 m) |
| Displacement | 13,600 lbs. (6,166 kg) |
| Ballast | 4,400 lbs. (1,995 kg) |
| Sail area | 447 sq. ft. (42 m²) |

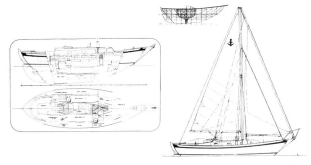

## Nicholson 35

| LOA | 35' 3" (10.7 m) |
| --- | --- |
| LWL | 26' 9" (8.2 m) |
| Beam | 10' 5" (3.2 m) |
| Draft | 5' 6" (1.7 m) |
| Displacement | 17,600 lbs. (8000 kg) |
| Ballast | N/A |
| Sail area | 757 sq. ft. (70 m²) |

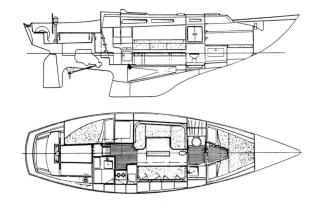

## CLASSICS III

The 40-foot (12.2 m) range is a nice size for a lot of couples, though certainly you can cross an ocean in a smaller boat, and certainly the trend in recent years has been toward even longer boats. Reliable roller furling headsails and mainsails, and electric winches, have radically changed cruising. But twenty to thirty years ago, when most of these boats were built, 40 feet was a pretty big boat for two people to handle.

Philip Rhodes (1895–1975) was one of the world's great yacht designers, and it has been said that no one drew a more lovely sheer line. The Vanguard and Rhodes 41 (1962) he did for Pearson Yachts are fine examples. Though he spent most of his career working in wood, he seemingly had no trouble or qualms about making the switch to fiberglass. Among his other notable designs in glass are the Rhodes Reliant with unusual offset companionway built by Cheoy Lee, and the Bounty II. His Rhodes 19 daysailer and Rhodes 22 trailer sailer are still in production decades after his death.

No cruising sailboat has earned cult status more than the Westsail 32. Founded by the husband and wife team of Snyder and Lynne Vick in 1971, this heavy double-ender was both factory finished and offered as a kit for owner completion. Ferenc Máté's classic book, *From a Bare Hull*, inspired a fair number of dreamers to try their hand at the shipwright's trade. Nicknamed the "Westsnail 32," the boat wasn't fast, but you knew it wouldn't fail you. The larger Westsail 42 was bought by television news anchor Walter Cronkite. The headline could have read: "The most trusted man in America buys the most trusted boat in America."

The Valiant 40 (1974) made Robert Perry a familiar name in cruising yacht design and led to the term "performance cruiser." Perry's background was racing, not cruising, so when he was commissioned to do this design, he gave it a divided but moderate underbody with cruising fin and skeg-mounted rudder. The canoe stern set it apart from the masses in terms of looks, and several circumnavigations, including a BOC round-the-world race by Dan Byrne, gave it credibility. Valiants are still built, now in Texas, and make fine offshore boats.

The Canadian-built Bayfield 40 was designed by Ted Gozzard and in production from 1984 to 1990. This is a very traditional boat with full keel and attached rudder, ketch rig, bowsprit, and trailboards. The accommodation plan shows the head forward and two double staterooms aft, where motion is least. That's great for sleeping at sea, but in port these cabins will get stuffy. I've always thought the sheer is a little off, especially the rise aft, but it's still a handsome boat and well built.

### Rhodes 41

| | |
|---|---|
| LOA | 41' 0" (12.5 m) |
| LWL | 28' 0" (8.5 m) |
| Beam | 10' 3" (3.1 m) |
| Draft | 5' 8" (1.7 m) |
| Displacement | 18,800 lbs. (8,524 kg) |
| Ballast | 8,075 lbs. (3,661 kg) |
| Sail area | 676 sq. ft./63 m² (sloop) |

## Westsail 32 and 42

|  | W32 | W42 |
|---|---|---|
| LOA | 32' 0" (9.8 m) | 42' 11" (13.1 m) |
| LWL | 27' 6" (8.4 m) | 33' 4" (10.2 m) |
| Beam | 11' 0" (3.4 m) | 13' 0" (3.9 m) |
| Draft | 5' 0" (1.5 m) | 5' 8" (1.7 m) |
| Displacement | 19,500 lbs. (8,841 kg) | 31,500 lbs. (14,282 kg) |
| Ballast | 7,000 lbs. (3,174 kg) | 11,000 lbs. (4,897 kg) |
| Sail area | 629 sq. ft. (58 m²) | 965 sq. ft. (90 m²) cutter |

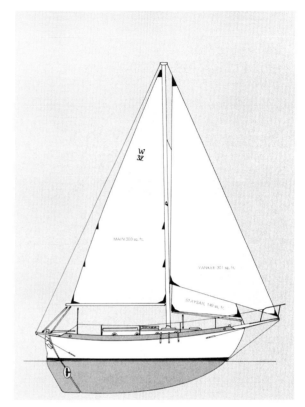

## Valiant 40

| LOA | 39' 10" (12.2 m) |
|---|---|
| LWL | 34' 0" (10.4 m) |
| Beam | 12' 4" (3.8 m) |
| Draft | 6' 0" (1.8 m) |
| Displacement | 22,500 lbs. (10,202 kg) |
| Ballast | 8,400 lbs. (3,809 kg) |
| Sail area | 840 sq. ft. (78 m²) |

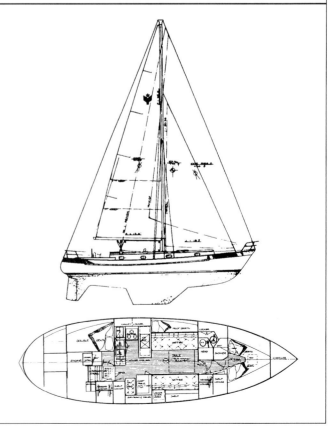

## Bayfield 40

| | |
|---|---|
| LOA | 45' 6" (13.9 m) |
| LOD | 40' 0" (12.2 m) |
| LWL | 30' 6" (9.3 m) |
| Beam | 12' 0" (3.7 m) |
| Draft | 5' 0" (1.5 m) |
| Displacement | 21,000 lbs. (9,521 kg) |
| Ballast | 8,200 lbs. (3,727 kg) |
| Sail area | 1,009 sq. ft. (94 m²) |

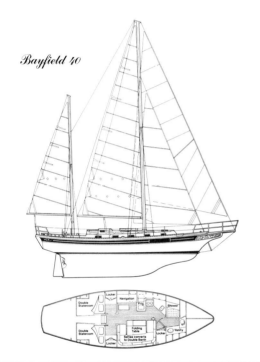

# CLASSICS IV

Well, here we are at the last four great boats.

Steve and Linda Dashew have made several circumnavigations and written numerous books about long-distance voyaging under sail. You can learn a lot on their website, www.setsail.com. Their first circumnavigation was on a Columbia 50, but since then they've built their own boats, in various countries. Early models were called Deerfoots. Some are in aluminum, some fiberglass. Steve has been instrumental in developing their distinctive design features. These include large roaches, low-aspect sail plans so the boats don't heel too much but have plenty of power; near-plumb bows; and hard dodgers or cuddies for the watch. I helped deliver a Sundeer 64 from Newport, Rhode Island, to Bermuda, and we averaged 10 knots under both sail and power. And, I might add, in great comfort. The Sundeers were built by TPI during the 1990s.

When most people think of J-Boats, they think of the hugely popular J/24 or one of the so-called sprit boats, like the J/80 that is set up to fly an asymmetrical spinnaker. But the company has produced a few cruising boats, too, though they are of relatively light displacement to keep them fast and responsive. A good example is the J/44, which won *Sailing World*'s Overall Boat of the Year Award in 1990. The boats were built by TPI using the SCRIMP resin infusion process.

Jensen Marine in Costa Mesa, California, was one of the leading builders of fiberglass boats during the region's heyday in the 1960s and 1970s. The Cal 40, designed by William Lapworth, was a hot racer and is still revered today for its basic, sturdy construction and speed. A larger cruising design by Lapworth was introduced in 1967, the Cal 46. Over the years, it was subtly changed and reissued as the Cal 2-46 and 3-46. When Jack Jensen retired from the company, he took off to the South Pacific in one of these. The layout is unique, with what you would almost call a living room with sofa bed, settees port and starboard, and a lot of floor space in between. Dual steering stations are a delight.

Ted Brewer just might have drawn more cruising sailboats than any man alive, and they are always sensible and attractive. He did the Whitby 42 in 1971. It's a big, serious, center-cockpit cruising ketch, well built by Whitby Boat Works in Ontario, Canada. The hull is balsa cored above the waterline, solid below, where the builder can add extra laminations without too much of a weight penalty. When the Whitby 42 ceased production Brewer modernized it for a new builder in Florida, which produced it as the Brewer 12.8 and later the Brewer 44. The boat is much the same except for the keel/centerboard configuration. Brewer's drawings are always a pleasure to study.

## Sundeer 64

| | |
|---|---|
| LOA | 64' 11" (19.8 m) |
| LWL | 64' 0" (19.5 m) |
| Beam | 15' 1" (4.6 m) |
| Draft | 6' 7" (2 m) |
| Displacement | 48,000 lbs. (21,763 kg) |
| Ballast | 14,200 lbs. (6,438 kg) |
| Sail area | 1,626 sq. ft./151 m$^2$ (cutter) |
| | 1,776 sq. ft./165 m$^2$ (ketch) |

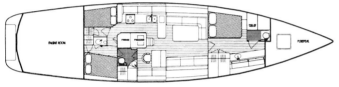

## J/44

| | |
|---|---|
| LOA | 44' 9" (13.6 m) |
| LWL | 39' 0" (11.9 m) |
| Beam | 13' 8" (4.2 m) |
| Draft | 8' 1"/2.5 m (deep) |
| | 6' 6"/2 m (shoal) |
| Displacement | 22,000 lbs. (9,975 kg) |
| Ballast | 9,000 lbs. (4,081 kg) |
| Sail area | 1,048 sq. ft. (97 m$^2$) |

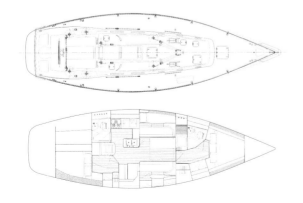

## Cal 46, 2-46,3-46

| | |
|---|---|
| LOA | 45' 6" (13.9 m) |
| LWL | 37' 6" (11.4 m) |
| Beam | 12' 6" (3.8 m) |
| Draft | 5' 0" (1.5 m) |
| Displacement | 30,000 lbs. (13,602 kg) |
| Ballast | 8,000 lbs. (2,438 kg) |
| Sail area | 784 sq. ft./73 m² (sloop) |
| | 864 sq. ft./80 m² (ketch) |

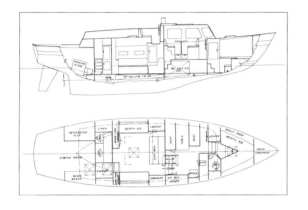

## Whitby 42 and Brewer 12.8

| | Whitby 42 | Brewer 12.8 |
|---|---|---|
| LOA | 42' 0" (12.2 m) | 42' 0" (12.8 m) |
| LWL | 32' 8" (10 m) | 33' 9" (10.3 m) |
| Beam | 13' 0" (4 m) | 13' 6" (4.1 m) |
| Draft | 5' 0" (1.5 m) | 4' 6" (1.4 m) |
| Displacement | 23,500 lbs. (10,655 kg) | 23,850 lbs. (10,814 kg) |
| Ballast | 8,500 lbs. (3,854 kg) | 9,000 lbs. (4,081 kg) |
| Sail area | 875 sq. ft. (81 m²) | 867 sq. ft. (81 m²) |

## Whitby 42 and Brewer 12.8 (cont.)

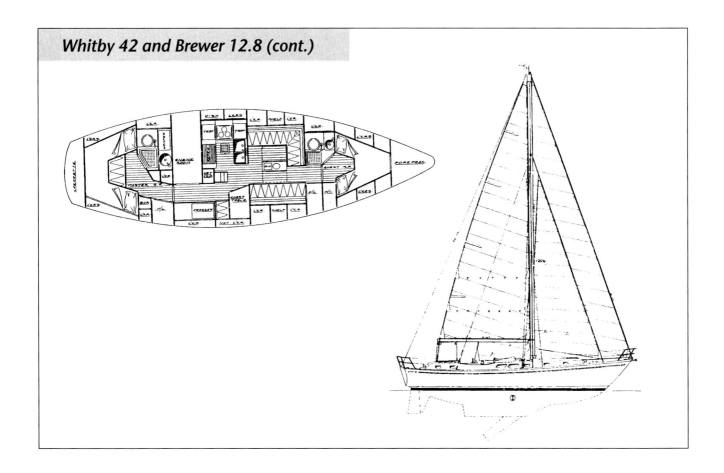

# Index

Numbers in **bold** refer to pages with illustrations